STUDIA POST-BIBLICA

VOLUMEN VICESIMUM OCTAVUM

STUDIA POST-BIBLICA

INSTITUTA A P. A. H. DE BOER

ADIUVANTIBUS

T. JANSMA ET J. SMIT SIBINGA

EDIDIT

J. C. H. LEBRAM

VOLUMEN VICESIMUM OCTAVUM

LEIDEN
E. J. BRILL
1977

THE PRINCIPLES
OF
SAMARITAN BIBLE EXEGESIS

BY

S. LOWY

LEIDEN
E. J. BRILL
1977

ISBN 90 04 04925 8

PRINTED IN BELGIUM

TO MY WIFE

בלב נבון תנוח חכמה
תנו לה מפרי ידיה
ויהללוה בשערים מעשיה

TABLE OF CONTENTS

PREFACE

Within recent years the important role played by Biblical interpretation in formation of various traditions has been widely recognized.

This work is an attempt to uncover and to illustrate one peculiar way in the interpretation of Scripture. Although I have long been concerned with the theme of Biblical Exegesis, it was only at the urging of Professor John Macdonald, the renowned Samaritan scholar, that I undertook to write a doctoral dissertation on this subject. To him I owe a debt of gratitude for introducing me to the field of Samaritan studies. It has also been my privilege to commence my work under his supervision. In particular, I am very grateful to him for putting his erudition and expertise in this complicated field of Samaritan research freely at my disposal, and for his constant encouragement.

The footnotes will indicate my indebtedness to many other authors who have laboured in this and cognate fields. Without their pioneering the way for future research, my own work would be very much poorer.

In preparing this study my purpose has not been so much to criticize and to analyse as to listen and to learn. Obviously, the system and the method of my work is necessarily different from that of my predecessors. It must be remembered that, even insofar as they have been interested in exegesis *per se*, their efforts represent but a first attempt, and in most cases they have had to rely on a single, and very often late and incorrect, manuscript. It has been not at all uncommon for some of them to have had to work from fragments only (cf. Bibliography : Drabkin, S. Kohn, Wreschner, etc.).

The progress of the present work has been much hindered by the inherent difficulties of the undertaking, especially the fact that only a very small part of the Samaritan literature relevant to the study of exegesis has as yet been published. It has thus been necessary to fall back on unpublished manuscripts. In certain cases, even published works have often required further elucidation, for which it has been essential to fall back on Mss.

To avoid the pitfalls involved in quoting inferior duplications of earlier exegesis, I have drawn heavily on the earliest sources. Thus, for the Arabic period, the two earliest and most authoritative works of the eleventh century are extensively and intensively investigated : the *Kitāb al-Ṭabbākh* by Abū'l Ḥasan al Ṣūri, and the *Kitāb al-Kāfi* by Yūsuf ibn

Salāmah (al-Askari). The *Ṭabbākh* and the *Kāfi* (as we refer to them throughout this work) are then clearly my most priomnent sources; but it is hoped that none of the later sources which could in any way throw light on the development of Samaritan exegesis or the application of its methods has been neglected. Some previously unpublished excerpts from these works were given in the Appendix of my thesis (SLTh.). Eventually, it became evident that the material was too vast for a single monograph and publication had to be limited to the bare minimum. Hence the frequent references to my thesis.

In cases however, where the exact wording of a certain text is essential to the theme, it appears in an abbreviated form in the footnotes. This apparently partial treatment of quotations has been found to be the most feasible method.

This book was written whilst I was at the University of Leeds. I should like to express my gratitude to the librarians and staff of the British Museum, London, and the John Rylands Library, Manchester, who have kindly assisted me for some years. I am also most grateful for being able to use the collection of Samaritan microfilms in the Department of Semitic Studies, Leeds University, collected by the previous Head of the Department, Professor John Bowman, now of Melbourne.

Among the many who have assisted me in numerous ways during the writing and editing of this book and to whom I am deeply indebted, I wish to single out in particular my friend and colleague Dr. B. S. J. Isserlin, Head of the Department of Semitic Studies at Leeds. He has supervised my thesis in its final stages. His careful re-reading of the entire work and his invaluable advice and suggestions for improvement are deeply appreciated.

I also have to thank my other colleagues at the Department for all the help and comradship in frequent discussions concerning various subjects related to my research. For their helpful advice in the fields of their special competence, I am especially under deep obligation to Drs M. J. L. Young, R. Y. Ebied and F. R. Farag. Among other friends who have helped me in various ways I wish to mention the Montague Burton Lecturers in this Department, with whom I had the privilege of exchanging fruitful ideas. I owe many valuable suggestions to Professors T. H. Gaster, N. W. Porteous and Geo Widengren.

I must state that with all the generous assistance which was always graciously supplied, they are in no way responsible for the deficiencies of this work.

I place on record my grateful thanks for the grants, to assist in the publication of this book, from funds channelled through the University of Leeds. I would like furthermore to thank the University for its own generous assistance.

Finally a few words of warm appreciation to my ever-devoted wife, who has laboured equally hard with me for years in the preparation of this book. Without her constant help in copying out and typing various drafts of this work, publication would have suffered further delays. In particular I would like to record gratefully her painstaking work on Samaritan texts. A token of my gratitude is indicated in the dedication.

Simeon LOWY

Department of Hebrew Studies
University of Witwatersrand
Johannesburg

ABBREVIATIONS

AJTh.	*American Journal of Theology.*
ALUOS	*Annual of Leeds University Oriental Society.*
A.V.	Authorized Version (of the Bible).
BA	*Biblical Archaeologist.*
Babyl.	Babylonian Talmud.
BASOR	*Bulletin American Schools of Oriental Research.*
B.C.E.	Before Common Era.
BJRL	*Bulletin of the John Rylands Library.*
B.M.	British Museum.
BO	*Bibliotheca Orientalis.*
BSOAS	*The Bulletin of the School of Oriental and African Studies.*
C.E.	Common Era.
cf.	confer (= compare).
Deut.	Deuteronomy (O.T.).
ed.	editor, etc.
e.g.	*exempli gratis* (= for example).
etc.	*et cetera.*
Ex.	Exodus (O.T.).
Gen.	Genesis (O.T.).
HB	*Hebraeische Bibliographie* (המזכיר).
Heb.	Hebrew.
HThR	*The Harvard Theological Review.*
HUCA	*Hebrew Union College Annual.*
ibid.	*ibidem.*
i.e.	*id est.*
IEJ	*Israel Exploration Journal.*
inf.	*infra* (= below).
JA	*Journal Asiatique.*
JAOS	*Journal of the American Oriental Society.*
JBL	*Journal of Biblical Literature.*
Jer.	(Jerushalmi) Paletinian Talmud.
JJS	*Journal of Jewish Studies.*
JQR	*The Jewish Quarterly Review.*
JR	*Journal of Religion.*
JRAS	*Journal of the Royal Asiatic Society.*
JRL	John Rylands Library.
JSS	*Journal of Semitic Studies.*
l.	line.
ll.	lines.
Lev.	Leviticus (O.T.).
loc. cit.	*loco citato.*
LXX	Septuagint.
MGWJ	*Monatsschrift für Geschichte und Wissenschaft des Judentums.*

Ms.	manuscript.
Mss.	manuscripts.
M.T.	Masoretic Text.
n.	note.
nn.	notes.
N.F.	*Neue Folge* (new series).
nos.	numbers.
N.S.	new series.
N.T.	New Testament.
NTS	*New Testament Studies.*
Num.	Numbers (O.T.).
op. cit.	*opere citato* (= in the work quoted).
O.T.	Old Testament
p.	page.
pp.	pages.
PAAJR	*Proceedings of the American Academy for Jewish Research.*
PEFQS	*Palestine Exploration Fund Quarterly Statement.*
PEQ	*The Palestine Exploration Quarterly.*
R.	Rabbah (e.g. Ex. R.).
RB	*Revue biblique.*
REJ	*Revue des études juives.*
RSR	*Recherches de science religieuse.*
Sam.	Samaritan.
SJT	*Scottish Journal of Theology.*
SLTh.	S. Lowy, *Thesis* (cf. Bibliography).
SLTh.A	*ibid.* Appendix.
S.P.	Samaritan Pentateuch.
S.T.	Samaritan Targum.
sup.	*supra* (= above).
TGUOS	*Transactions of Glasgow University Oriental Society.*
v.	verse.
VT	*Vetus Testamentum.*
vv.	verses.
ZAW	(*ZATW*), *Zeitschrift für die alttestamentliche Wissenschaft.*
ZDMG	*Zeitschrift der Deutschen Morgenländischen Gesellschaft.*
ZfHB	*Zeitschrift für hebraeische Bibliographie.*
ZNW	(*ZNTW*), *Zeitschrift für die neutestamentliche Wissenschaft.*
ZThK	*Zeitschrift für Theologie und Kirche.*

PART ONE

SAMARITAN STUDIES AND EXEGESIS

A. INTRODUCTION

Samaritan biblical exegesis — and even their hermeneutical principles — could not be entirely overlooked by those authors who have
constantly enriched our literature on the Samaritans. Since then most
of these works have been devoted to other aspects of the Samaritan
religion, such as theology, history, chronology and comparative studies,
no really penetrating attention has been paid to the elucidation of their
exegesis. Nonetheless, since the whole of Samaritan religion is based
on the Pentateuch (obviously the S.P.) and centres around it, it is
understandable that here and there some isolated references to its
exegesis should be found. Exegesis has not only been neglected, but
often accordingly misunderstood, and not seldom labelled as unoriginal,
betraying foreign influences etc.

The presumption that Samaritan exegesis is homogeneous and almost
unchanging in character, although it has indeed some truth in it, is
not entirely justified. A later literature often absorbs foreign colouring
which are still quite absent from earlier works. Unfortunately for us,
the surviving running commentaries on the Pentateuchal books are
invariably of late origin. In the present book a thoroughgoing attempt
is made to present Samaritan exegesis from the inside; and more particularly as it is reflected in the earlier Samaritan literary sources.

It is an undeniable fact that Samaritanism is one of the most conservative religions. For this very reason, scholars, when opening up new
fields in exegesis, have on the whole come very close to the truth, even
when they have necessarily utilised, in the main, very late sources.
Since, however, we are concerned with the theory underlying the
Samaritan hermeneutical principles, we must try to ascertain as far as
possible those elements of permanent value in the views proposed by
scholars concerning their ancient development.

Any investigation into the sources of the Samaritan midrash and
hermeneutical methods must take it for granted that only the second
province of exegesis falls within its purview. The fundamental work of
purely grammatical and semantic exploration, notwithstanding its
great significance, is totally outside the scope of this work.

Fortunately, we are now in a position to draw upon the results of researches mainly devoted to this fundamental province of Samaritan linguistics,[1] and our task has thus been greatly simplified. Many problems of Samaritan linguistics are, of course, still awaiting solution, and opinions differ as to what should be considered the right procedure in the interests of further progress.[2] Although by far the greater part of Samaritan exegesis follows the simple, and what seems to us the literal sense of scripture, we are concerned with its methods, not from the purely linguistic point of view, but only when they fall into a certain pattern of midrashic exposition.[3]

The line of demarcation between the two provinces is by no means rigid. The whole history of exegesis teaches us that interpretation is itself always a natural outgrowth of the texts it proposes to elucidate. Such an activity is at first naive and unmethodical; Scholars today often call the way it operates "organic thinking".[4] In effect very like the growth of an organism, the interpretation remains true to the nature and characteristics of the text, while slowly expanding and modifying and adapting its meaning via exegesis, in order to make it explicit and coherent. There is here an evolutionary process rather than any self-conscious innovation. Creativity here allies itself with conservatism, relying on intuitive traditions rather than on intentional and rational endeavours.[5]

Obviously, contextual links, idioms, metaphors and the like, may suggest new patterns, all depending on traditions and environmental influences. Again like an organism, exegesis may run wild, assuming fanciful shapes far removed from the original; and we have only to compare a sample of exegesis by the Samaritans with one by the Rabbis [6] to realize the marked differences in outlook and consequent development which differing traditions and environments make possible.

We may employ this term "organic thinking" for Samaritan exegesis only in a very relative sense with reference to other systems with their

---

[1] Ben-Ḥayyim, *Literary and Oral Traditions etc.*, *idem.* cf. articles in Bibliography: Murtonen, *Materials for a non-Massoretic Grammar*; Macuch, *Grammatik des samaritanischen Hebräisch.*

[2] cf. Ben-Ḥayyim, *Literary and Oral etc.*, IIIa, p. viii; *idem, Biblica* lii (1971), pp. 229-252; Murtonen, *op. cit.* III, pp. 22f.

[3] Part III, para (e) and (f).

[4] Kadushin, *Organic Thinking*, pp. 13f., *idem, The Rabbinic Mind, passim*; I. Heinemann, *Darkhei ha-Aggadah*, pp. 8f., 200f. (nn. 73ff.).

[5] Heinemann, *op. cit.* pp. 110f., 240f. (nn. 21-32 for further Bibliography).

[6] *idem, ibid.* pp. 163f., 257 (notes for cross-references).

rapid developments; for although it was indeed guided by rules (or 'exegetical principles')[7] the Samaritan system remained essentially static as compared with all others. Moreover, while in our other chapters we may simply gather the materials relevant to the midrashic approaches of the Samaritans and arrange them in such a way that they may speak for themselves, here we shall be obliged to broach a number of theories which must stand or fall by the confirmation they receive from available sources.

It is not the purpose of these introductory remarks to supply yet another historical sketch of the Samaritans or their religion or their literature. This task has been admirably fulfilled in many previous works.[8] Our concern here is to survey and assess the recent tendencies in Samaritan research which have a direct bearing on exegesis. Obviously, the issues which we are discussing in this chapter are not directly connected with hermeneutical methods and devices. Nevertheless, the theories proposed by generations of scholars in explanation of Samaritan origin and their probable links with those of other groups may serve to give a clearer understanding of the principles of Samaritan exegesis proper.

The origins of Samaritan exegesis are still a matter of dispute, and the problems will not be settled for some time yet by conflicting arguments; and if in future they are so solved, it will be on the firm basis of comparative and philological studies. We are neither inclined nor are we yet in a position to reach here any dogmatic conclusions. All we may hope to undertake is a much more humble task, that of trying to free ourselves from certain theories which now dominate the scholarly scene and often cause needless confusion because they are based on wrong premises. By our analysis we may reasonably expect that eventually Samaritan exegetical studies may be liberated from such preconceived patterns. While, of course, scholarly objectivity is a desideratum admired on all hands, we cannot well deny that Samaritan studies, which owe their development to the interest aroused at their beginnings

---

[7] cf. Part II, para (a) and (b), Part III para (g).

[8] There are whole books devoted to these subjects (cf. Bibliography: Montgomery, M. Gaster, Ben-Zevi etc.). Very useful notes are given on the Samaritan authors and their dates by Cowley, *The Sam. Liturgy*, II, pp. xviii-xxv (cf. also *ibid.*xliv-xlv); Ben-Ḥayyim, *Literary and Oral etc.* I. pp. כ״ט-נ׳; J. Macdonald, *The Theology of the Sam.* pp. 40-49 (cf. also Bibliography: Nutt, Miller etc.). For further literature cf. Ben-Ḥayyim, *op. cit.* I, p. כ״ט nn. 1-4.

by rival claims upheld by opposing religious groups, did in fact inherit some of these contentions and apologetic tinges in their later stages of development.[9] Even scholars who were themselves completely liberated from the apologetic approaches of previous generations often repeated the 'conclusions' reached by their predecessors even although these rested on very dubious grounds.

Only by a thorough and impartial reading of all Samaritan sources in their historical sequence can one appreciate the ideological background which motivates Samaritan exegesis. To be sure, the importance of treating all this material also as a homogenous unit has been largely accepted, for, after all, their efforts are directed to creating a continually renewed realisation of the "Pentateuchal Religion" and of its ideals as actualized in everyday life. This endeavour underlies their practices and their doctrines, and formulates their theology likewise, all of them forming a quite uniform pattern and all growing out from their exegesis. Yet their contact with their environment influences them in varying degrees and their outlook may even undergo perceptible change occasionally. This is the crux of our problem, to try to bring into true focus their major doctrines and practices as well as to reinvestigate the true extent of such environmental influences and how and where they are to be detected.

We are not here directly concerned with the Samaritan theological system as such [10] but a careful examination and penetrating analysis of their literature demonstrate that the awareness of this mental background governs nearly all aspects of their literal creativity. We must therefore deviate slightly from our narrow pursuit of exegetical devices proper, because it is essentially in regard to this region of ideological convictions that the most challenging views have been propounded. These discussions have a bearing in various ways on all regions of Samaritan research, and no doubt their re-opening will also contribute to the elucidation of the problems connected with the history of Samaritan exegesis.[11]

---

[9] Geiger, *Urschrift etc.*, pp. 10ff.; Montgomery, *The Sam.*, pp. 1-10.

[10] The greatest single attempt in this field is J. Macdonald's very extensive work, *op. cit.* (n. 8 *sup.*).

[11] In a similar way a recent work on the "concepts and beliefs" of the Rabbis (E.E. Urbach, *The Sages, etc.*) opened new avenues into the general understanding of the sources of Rabbinic hermeneutics (*ibid.* pp. 254ff.). The introductory chapter dealing with major trends of writers of the previous generation (*ibid.* pp. 1-14) puts this in clearer prospective.

B. 19TH CENTURY THEORIES

Various opinions have been expressed on the origins of the Samaritans, since the so-called 'Rediscovery of the Samaritans'.[12] The problems which have arisen from the study of the 'rediscovered' Samaritan Texts have been manifold, and, naturally, owing to the wideranging interest manifested by scholars, the attempted solutions have produced a voluminous literature. Features of the Samaritan religion apparently similar to those of other earlier sects have also been studied, and, inconclusive as the evidence seems to be, there have been some early attempts to trace connections between these sects. In particular, the rigorism so characteristic of the Samaritans makes such comparisons most attractive. Not infrequently, 'proofs' for exciting new theories have been claimed, although they amounted to no more than mere conjectures.

The most sensational stage of this speculative development came, however, only with the nineteenth century. The Samaritan Text and traditions were compared with the versions and traditions of other groups, for the purpose of establishing a comprehensive 'system' embracing the documentary sources of the Bible. The sectarian schisms were taken as the major causes of the developments leading to the later versions and consequently as the major sources of the separate traditions. This was the central idea which prompted most of the scholarly works of A. Geiger culminating in his *magnum opus*, the *Urschrift*.[13] According to this theory then (as the title of the book indicates), the Original and the Versions of the Bible are primarily dependent on the internal developments of Judaism.

Geiger took upon himself a double task in carrying out his plan: (1) to depict and interpret the development of Judaism from the Babylonian Exile to the end of the Talmudic period (2) to shed light on the history of the Text of the Bible, as a concomitant result of this process. This was a task involving two mutually dependent factors: the history of the Text was to be explained as an integral part of the history of the religion, and the latter was to be presented as evidenced testimonies of textual 'changes' and variants. The central concept in this ingeniously

---

[12] For a good summary, cf. Montgomery, *The Sam.*, pp. 1-12 and 46ff.

[13] The title of this book (Urschrift und Uebersetzungen der Bibel in ihrer Abhängigkeit von der inneren Entwickelung des Judentums) speaks for itself as to its tendentious nature. A convenient short presentation of Geiger's views on the sectarian schism is given by S. Poznanski, "Geschichte der Sekten und der Halacha" in *Abraham Geiger, Leben und Lebenswerk* (ed. L. Geiger, Berlin, 1910), pp. 352-387.

thought-out theory is clearly that there is a real possibility of reconstructing a single *Urtext* from which *all* the variants eventually branch down.[14] All 'changes' have thus to be explained as tendentious 'alterations' supporting differing points of view, determined by the developments of the several historical schisms.

The Masoretic Text on this view mirrors the developments which took place in Pharisaic Judaism and this version was crystallised only gradually. Its underlying texts in their minutest details were constantly influenced by the doctrinal and legal elaborations of the Talmudic Age. Each generation worked out new insights and viewpoints and the variant versions reflect the variant ideological backgrounds of each successive epoch.[15] This central hypothesis of Geiger's is painstakingly developed and clearly stated in his chapter dealing with the "reworking" carried out on the Biblical Text.[16] According to this theory, insomuch as the upholders of Scripture were not in slavish subjection to the 'dead letter', the pressing and ever-changing circumstances of the successive generations forced them to introduce *into the Text* their own ideological exigencies. Such too is the genesis of the 'expositions', either exegetical or doctrinal, which likewise crept into the versions of the Bible. Not only each verse but even each word was 'reworked' in this fashion.[17]

How reliable such considerations really are, one may judge for oneself from the perverse and hair-splitting arguments and 'proofs' supporting them. One example may suffice to demonstrate the arbitrary nature of such a 'reconstruction'. In illustration of the 'changes' resulting from the feud between the Jews and the Samaritans, Geiger quotes Genesis xxxiii, 18 ("and Jacob came in peace to Shechem"). According to his theory the words עיר שלם are later interpolations. And it is true that the LXX renders this verse "Came to Salem the city of Shechem".[18]

---

[14] Geiger, *Urschrift*, p. 423 "... doch höher muss uns gegenwärtig das Verlangen stehen, den Bibeltext in seiner kräftigen Ursprünglichkeit zu besitzen." cf. also *idem.* "Sadduzäer und Pharisäer", *Jüd. Zeitschr. für Wissenschaft und Leben* II (1863), pp. 11-54.

[15] *idem, Urschrift, etc.*, pp. 426f.

[16] *ibid.* part I, Ch. III ("Ueberarbeitung"), pp. 72ff.

[17] *ibid.* p. 74. "Wie sollte sie nun an anderen Ueberarbeitungen Anstoss nehmen können? Das religiös-nationale Bewusstsein hatte sich vollständig in den überlieferten heiligen Schatz eingelebt, es assimilierte ihn daher auch mit seinen Empfindungen und gestaltete ihn nach denselben um."

[18] καὶ ἦλθεν Ἰακὼβ εἰς Σαλὴμ πόλιν Σηκιμων....

However, this fact in itself does not justify the equation of this verse with Genesis xxxiv, 21.[19] Only by a great stretch of the imagination and indeed a violation of the text can one arrive at such a conclusion. As opposed to the many parallels between the LXX and the S.P., here both the S.P. and the S.T. are equivalent to the M.T. From the very sweeping conclusions of Geiger, it might be expected that here the S.P. would show a variant so as to outdo the LXX text. Furthermore, it is common knowledge that such and even more significant 'variants' occur in the LXX owing to misunderstanding or misreading of its unvocalised "Vorlage".

Geiger himself admits [20] that, except for certain texts kept (in his opinion in protest against the free-handling of texts in earlier times) in the Temple of Jerusalem (ספר העזרה) most of the copies, circulating freely and meant for popular use, were treated quite carelessly. Only very few of their 'emendations' gained the authority to penetrate into the Official Text, and thus a number of these 'corrections' crept into the various final versions. This is the reason for some 'inferior' readings (as compared to the M.T.). Some of them nevertheless appear in the LXX and the S.P. alike, despite the fact that there was apparently no connection between Egyptian Jewry (LXX) and the Samaritans. Geiger's hypothesis regarding the family relationships within the early Zadokite priesthood, which is supposed to have been the guardian of all the temples (in Jerusalem, Gerizim and Leontopolis) supplies the alleged reason for the exchange of Biblical versions. Evidently such a hypothesis hardly explains all the difficulties.[21]

The Samaritans retained the Pentateuch only and must have interpreted it throughout a period far earlier than our earliest Samaritan sources can reach, and stretching over many centuries. Without entering here into any speculations, we may presume that our knowledge of oral transmission in general can teach us something about the nature of the transmission and of the contents of the earliest layers of their exegetical endeavours. However, this subject is not sufficiently capable of clari-

---

[19] Geiger, *Urschrift etc.*, pp. 74ff. In the latter case the LXX agrees with the M.T. (οἱ ἄνθρωποι οὗτοι εἰρηνικοί εἰσιν).

[20] *Urschrift etc.*, pp. 97f.

[21] *ibid.* pp. 99f. "... allein zur Zeit als die Einen übersetzten (= LXX) und die Andern ihren Text sich feststellten (= S.P.), war derselbe in der Umgestaltung verbreitet, und erst später fingen die palestinenschen Juden an, durch sorgfältigere Kritik ihren Text seiner *ursprünglichen* Beschaffenheit conformer zu machen". cf. my article in *ALUOS* VI (1969) *passim*.

fication to enable us to reach firm conclusions concerning the origins and the true datings of their traditions. Even if we utilise to the full all the available and relevant external sources, it has to be admitted that, for the time being, we have to be content if we can understand tolerably well the specific hermeneutical problems, without venturing into any hypothesis regarding the ultimate genesis of the Samaritan Pentateuch itself.[22] As our working hypothesis, we may rest quite content, provisionally at least, to assume that, centuries before our earliest exegetical text came into being, there existed various versions side by side.[23] All the signs point to the assumption that the Samaritans totally relied on their distinctively sectarian Text for their exegesis, while other groups followed rather their own textual traditions.

At this point we may profitably look into Geiger's theory of an original 'ancient Halakhah', which he postulated as common at some time in very early antiquity to all the Jewish sects who inherited the Pentateuch. According to this theory, there were at that time hardly any outstanding distinctions in exegesis and practice between the various groups. Despite the great antagonism existing between the groups who held the rival sanctuaries, and despite the political, and later religious, strife between Gerizim and Jerusalem, no great pressures were exerted upon these groups causing them to differ radically either in their theology or in their Pentateuchal exegesis. Furthermore, according to this theory, it was comparatively easy for all these exegetes to overcome their 'slight' differences, since of the Davidic dynasty centred at Jerusalem, no specific mention is made in the Pentateuch. The 'minor' contextual changes (e.g. M.T. יבחר S.P. בחר) were thus developments which took place only later.[24] There was as yet no reason for any great differences in Biblical exegesis and practice to arise between the Jews and the Samaritans.[25]

This whole theory is built on a pragmatic reconstruction of the supposed political and social conditions. The political circumstances

---

[22] On the problem of the text of the S.P. and its origins there is a huge literature. cf. recently Purvis, *The Sam. Pentateuch etc.*, and the rich Bibliography on pp. 130-142. cf. however Ben-Ḥayyim's review in *Biblica* lii (1971), pp. 253-255.

[23] cf. my article *op. cit.* pp. 103ff., 138ff. (nn. 50ff.).

[24] Geiger, *Urschrift etc.*, pp. 74ff.

[25] *ibid.* cf. also *idem*, "Zur Theologie und Schrifterklärung der Sam.", *Nachgelassene Schriften*, III, p. 258. "Es kann nicht genügen die einzelnen Abweichungen zusammenzustellen; um ein Bild des innern samaritanischen Lebens zu gewinnen, muss Grund und Wurzel aufgewiesen werden, welche von der judäischen abweichende Gestaltung erzeugt hat."

during the Second Commonwealth led to the upper classes being represented by the Sadducees, whose struggle for power accordingly influenced
their methods of interpretation. The Samaritans, according to this theory,
who did not belong to the pure Jewish stock, had necessarily to join
forces with this struggle of the dominant group, in order to gain respect-
ability and thus become socially accepted amongst their brethren.
In so doing, they had also to accept and adopt the conservative exegetical
methods of the Sadducees. Only from this point of view (according
to Geiger) may we understand the Samaritans' divergence from the
'common' exegetical norms and gain a new insight into their dissenting
practices.[26] It was only after the Pharisees had become dominant that
they modified the 'ancient customs' through their newly developed
exegesis. This latter was essentially directed against the Sadducees, and
chiefly with a view to curbing the supreme power of their Priesthood.
The Samaritans, however, remained faithful to the 'ancient' conservative
exegesis and practice which they had inherited from the Sadducees.[27]
No doubt in certain respects Geiger's claims are justified. There are
numerous parallels, both in practice and in theory and much similarity.
Much that is known to us of the ancient Sadducees very often resembles
what we later find in Samaritan literature.[28] However, as stated before,
this general system of Geiger's unfortunately depends heavily on a constant recourse to a casuistry which is mostly unconvincing. The mere
fact that one has to 'discover' largely from the Pharisaic sources the
'Ancient Sadducean Halakhah' surely betrays very questionable eviden-
tial grounds. It has, moreover, to be taken into consideration, and this
was admitted by Geiger himself, that one must suppose this 'ancient
halakhah' to have been later suppressed by the Pharisees, and therefore
to be capable of reconstruction by hypothetical means only.[29]

Now we have to look into the claim that there once existed a single
common halakhah. Nobody would deny that the Rabbinic halakhah
was constantly evolving, but the causes of this evolution were undoubtedly mainly internal, rather than the direct products of sectarian strife.

---

[26] *ibid.* p. 260. cf. also *idem, Urschrift etc.*, pp. 56, 146, 172ff., 493.

[27] We cannot enter here into details. To take of the famous examples; the exegesis
of ממחרת השבת (*Lev.* xxiii), cf. Geiger, *Urschrift*, p. 137; *idem, Nachgelassene
Schriften* III, p. 260. cf. *inf.* n. 73.

[28] cf. my article in *JJS* IX (1953) pp. 131ff.

[29] Geiger, "Sadduzäer etc.", *Jüd. Zeitschr. für Wissenschaft und Leben* II (1863)
pp. 11ff.; *idem, Urschrift*, pp. 99ff.

It is of course true that the unremitting struggle of the Pharisees against
the sects forced the Rabbis to strengthen their own tradition by new
enactments framed to neutralise sectarian influences. We even find that
certain demonstrative actions were in fact avowedly introduced by the
Pharisees so as "to lend no support to the words of them that say"
the opposite, (e.g. *Ḥaggigah* II, 4; *Menaḥoth* X, 3).[30] However, these few
instances show a situation the exact opposite of that painted by Geiger;
only at a period when the strife was fierce and certain traditions and
exegesis ran definitely counter to the Pharisaic teachings, did the Pharisees react in this spirited manner.

The whole notion that the development of the Rabbinic halakhah
represents a series of deliberate changes, aimed solely to repress and
nullify the ancient customs of the Sadducees, becomes almost incredible,
if closely pursued. In illustration of this estimate a test may be carried
out on one of Geiger's own points, where he exemplifies the development
of the exegesis on *Exodus* xiii, 3-4.[31] The only original version, according
to him, is that of the LXX, "and leaven shall not be eaten for on this day
you go forth, etc.".[32] We are informed that both the 'ancient halakhah'
and the Samaritan text 'abandon' this original reading (M.T. ולא יאכל
חמץ היום אתם : S.P. ...חמץ היום ואתם), but that the 'later halakhah'
underlines it even more clearly, by taking it to meant that, on that occasion of the first Passover in Egypt, leaven was forbidden only on the
first day.

How on earth can such a theory claim to make good sense of the facts?
Is it not more satisfactory to suggest that each group instinctively
follows a scriptural and exegetical tradition? The LXX reading is itself
the product of an exegetical translation. The Pharisees, who inherit the
tradition of distinguishing between the 'Egyptian Passover' and the
'Passover of all Generations', read into their text (both 'ancient' and later
'new' halakhah) this very tradition.[33] The Samaritan Text is likewise
faithful to its own tradition, which does not distinguish the Passover
in Egypt from that of later generations. At any rate, this distinction has
no relevance to the practice and continuation of the tradition in the
group itself. The Rabbis, who eliminate such practices as 'eating it in

---

[30] cf. *sup.* n. 28.

[31] Geiger, *Urschrift etc.*, pp. 184f.

[32] Καὶ οὐ βρωθήσεται ζύμη ἐν γὰρ τῇ σήμερον κ.τ.λ.

[33] *Mekhilta* on *Ex.* xii, 7; *Pesaḥim* I, 5; *Babyl. T. ibid.* 96a; *Jer. ibid.* 36d-37a (cf.
Albeck, *Mishnah* II, p. 454).

haste' (Exodus xii, 11) etc. can well afford to read into the same context
even further differences between the 'Egyptian Passover' and that of
'All Other Generations'. Over and above all the other differences,
therefore, the Rabbis also hold that on the 'Passover in Egypt' leaven
was forbidden on the first day only.

On the other hand, the S.P. text includes the peg ואתם יצאים בחדש
האביב which mitigates the previous expression (היום) 'today'. In congruity
with the beginning of the verse [34] and other verses, it is understood that
each separate detail is an 'everlasting statute' referring to the Seven
Days of Pilgrimage,[35] during which leavened bread is naturally prohibited (Ex. xii, 15; ibid. 19; ibid. xiii, 6-7, etc.). More aptly than from any
other theme we can demonstrate the peculiarly Samaritan exegetical

---

[34] S.P. זכרו את היום הזה אשר יצאתם בו ממצרים cf. Ṭabbākh (on Ex. xii, 11)
f. 68b; (SLTh.A p. 110) and ibid. (on Ex. xii, 13) f. 65a; (SLTh.A p. 106).

[35] Kāfi, p. 316; (SLTh.A p. 38); Ṭabbākh ff.75a, 77b, 79a, 80b) (SLTh.A pp. 116,
118, 119 and 120 respectively). It is impossible to follow here Geiger's casuistic
arguments in all fields. We may just mention another case in connection with the
"second Passover" (Num. ix, 10) where we find only the slightest textual differences.
Actually the difference between the M.T. and the S.P. consists of a dot on the he of the
word רחקה, Geiger builds whole theories upon this variant (Urschrift etc., pp. 185f.),
since the Rabbinic midrash is intimately bound up with this single dot. But here
Geiger is is conspicuously silent about the S.P. (רחוקה), since it does not fit into
his system of 'ancient halakhah'. The Samaritans, despite their text, exclude from
participating in the Passover Sacrifice persons who were defiled (by any levitical
impurities = 'new halakhah'?). As a matter of fact the word רחוקה is employed
for various midrashim by the Samaritans. The Kāfi p. 221; (SLTh.A pp. 41f.) takes
this word as evidence that the Passover must be offered in the vicinity of Hargerizim,
otherwise this word would be redundant; obviously no superfluous words exist in
the Law. For this reason Samaritan tradition took it for granted if for any good
reason the passover could not be offered during the fixed time in the First Month
'it should be performed at the fixed time of the Second Month'. The Ṭabbākh uses
the expression במועדיו (Num. ix, 13 S.P.) to prove this point. But it goes even further,
by adducing this verse as an evidence for the "righteousness of the true (i.e. Sam.)
calendar." This argument (against Rabbinical postponements of the Feasts) goes
on the following lines: It would be unjust that a person should be punished ("shall
be cut off from his people"), if the "times" were doubtful, as it would be beyond
human power to carry out such an obligation. All the arguments of Wreschner
(Sam. Traditionen, p. 28: "Munagga aber, sowie der von ihm citierte Bibelglossator
wissen von diesen Textesabweichung nichts mehr und entlenen auch hier die Deduction
für ihr Gestetz den Karäern") are therefore totally invalidated. Unfortunately
Wreschner did not know the other parts of Munajja's work, where the polemics
against the Rabbis is more outspoken (Masa'il al-Khilāf Ia, p. 76), and there he
follows the line of the Ṭabbākh.

traditions from the theme of the Hebrew slavegirl. All the tortuous arguments of Geiger [36] are in reality entirely irrelevant here to the fruitful investigation of these traditions. Thus the hypothesis that או העבריה in *Deut*. xv, 12 is a later interpolation, has no support whatever in the text.[37] However, even if it be the case that we are dealing with a later interpolation, how can the 'ancient halakhah' be known to Tana'im if it is not in fact known to the ancient versions? The truth of the matter is that the development of the Rabbinic halakhah is based on exegetical harmonisations and has nothing in common with that of the Samaritans. The Samaritan tradition does not equate the "Hebrew slave" (*Exodus* xxi, 2-6; *Deuteronomy* xv, 12-19) simply with an Israelite, but extends this concept of "Hebrew" to all the descendents of Abraham (as e.g. Ishmaelites, Edomites, etc.),[38] while to the Israelite slave (*Lev*. xxv, 39-46) entirely different rules apply. Clearly, *Exodus* xxi, 7f. (upon which Geiger built his whole theory) has in Samaritan exegesis nothing to do with the preceding verses, and is taken as referring to the act of betrothal of an Israelite woman. From this very passage indeed, the Samaritan legal exegetes derive the major rules for marital duties.[39] Naturally, such a facile solution could only find place in the Samaritan exegesis. All the other systems, accepting the sanctity of the prophets, have to resort to the harmonisation of these passages, in consideration of *Jeremiah* xxxiv, 9.

In general, it may be asserted that we have no reliable means of getting behind our Biblical sources to discover a single *Urtext* and there are even fewer chances of discovering a common ancient halakhah.[40] If there were real similarities between some sectarian practices, these are rather to be attributed to common early exegetical traditions, before the branching-off of the existing variant Texts; and if this is so, then, together with these variant Texts, some exegetical traditions would also be transmitted. Geiger himself had his doubts on certain points, but he tried to gloss over such 'minor' exceptions as did not conform to his theory.[41]

---

[36] *Urschrift etc.*, pp. 187f.

[37] LXX: ἡ ʾΕβραία (the expression ὁ αδελφός may refer to both) and S.P. = M.T.

[38] *Kāfi* pp 258f. (SLTh.A pp. 55f). cf. now, Noja, *Il Kitāb al-Kāfi etc.*, pp. 125ff. (cf. *ibid*. n. 1 for further literature).

[39] *Kāfi* p. 199 (SLTh.A p. 22); *Tabbākh* f. 195b.

[40] cf. P.R. Weis, *"Ibn Ezra etc."*, *Melilah* I (1944), pp. 44f. cf. *ibid*. nn. 69-73 for the Karaites and nn. 74-76 for the Rabbis.

[41] One of these examples is the treatment of החוצה (*Deut*. xxv, 5) in connection

Even more complicated is the hypothesis of the existence of an 'ancient aggadah' which was supposedly common to all groups. The real evidence for the existence of an 'older' aggadah is even more elusive than that for the halakhah. There is in truth absolutely no evidence that the aggadic motifs of ancient times were exchanged for novel ones.[42]

Geiger is certainly right in maintaining that the ancient favourable attitude towards Enoch gradually became, with the years, progressively more hostile in the course of Rabbinic literature. We need not be afraid to admit that his refusal to understand *Ecclesiasticus* xliv, 16 in a pejorative sense is also justified. "An example of repentance to all generations" does not necessarily imply that Enoch was a sinner who repented only later in life, as Geiger rightly points out. In the light of all the other lavish praises of Enoch found in Ben Sirah, such a pedantic exegesis is definitely unwarranted. Nevertheless, from this very example we might deduce the total independence of the Samaritan exegetical tradition, for it is rightly sensed by Geiger that the true source of the hostile attitude of later Rabbinic literature towards the status and the piety of Enoch must be sought in polemical motives, arising from the employment of this figure and type by Christianity for Christological expositions. If we are to gain a deeper understanding of this change of attitude, we need to investigate briefly the origins of this polemics. The figure and type of Enoch were employed by early Christianity in proof of the superiority of 'faith' to 'works' (*Hebrews* xi, 5f).[43] Moreover the LXX rendering of the Hebrew words in *Genesis* v, 24 התהלך and לקח as 'well-pleasing' and 'to be translated' (or 'transferred) respectively,[44] was certainly

---

with Levirate marriage in the 'ancient halakhah". Despite Geiger's attempts to prove this point ("Zur Theologie etc." *Nachgelassene Schriften* III, p. 265; *Urschrift etc.*, p. 235) it is impossible to reconcile the discrepancies. The only common principle to all literalists (Sadducees, Samaritans and Karaites) is that they all agree that there is no contradiction in the Law. The positive command of Levirate marriage has no power to abolish the prohibition of marrying a brother's wife. Cf. my article in *ALUOS* VI (1969) pp. 111, 146 (n. 109), 163 (n. 230). One could quote many other casuistic arguments of Geiger on these lines (e.g. "But if mischief follow", *Ex.* xxi, 23, being connected with *Lev.* xxii, 28. cf. *Nachgelassene Schriften* III, pp. 263f.; *Urschrift*, pp. 436f. etc.).

[42] *Urschrift etc.*, pp. 197ff.

[43] χωρὶς δὲ πίστεως ἀδύνατον εὐαρεστῆσαι cf. also *ibid.* vii, 12. For the Samaritan both ideas, "the priesthood being changed" or the change of Law, would be equally objectionable. cf. *inf.* n. 46.

[44] εὐαρεστέω : μετατίθημι. cf. M. Black, "The Eschatology and the Similitudes of Enoch", *JTS* N.S. III (1952) pp. 1-10.

influential not only in this instance, but also in the regular preaching, directed as it was at the denial of the necessity for the performance of the Law.[45] Thus too, the fact that after the destruction of the Temple, the priestly office had lost almost all its practical and tangible significance in Rabbinic Law was also exploited by Christian apologists in proof of the change and abrogation of the Law. This same technical term ($\mu\epsilon\tau\alpha\tau\ell\theta\eta\mu\iota$) is employed in fact in *Hebrews* vii, 12 to prove that, just as the Aaronic priesthood had been changed (a Christian midrash on *Psalm* cx, 4), so too had the Law been changed. Although the Rabbis were clearly obliged to react fiercely to such attacks by corresponding counterattacks, such arguments against the priesthood hardly affected the Samaritan group, for in their tradition the priesthood with all its functions was demonstrably a viable and an "everlasting statute", and as such often employed in apologetics to illustrate their superiority [46] to other groups.

Returning now to the story of Enoch, it seems then that, in this instance too, the Samaritan tradition was unaffected. From the textual point of view, it is certain that in this passage the Samaritan Pentateuch has more in common with the Masoretic Text than with that of the LXX.[47] Unlike that of the Rabbis, their exegetical tradition in general was unaffected by such propaganda, although fo course they guarded at least as jealously as the Jews the literal observance of the Law.

Only the specifically Samaritan exegetical system can shed light on this distinctive feature. Marqah explains the expression התהלך, in view of the analogy with *Genesis* xvii, 1, as a synonym for worshipping God on Hargerizim.[48]

"Thus God wrote in His Scriptures concerning Enoch, *Enoch walked with God* (Genesis v. 22) — he knew the place of the True One, and hastened to it, just like Abraham...". The same tradition is also referred to in the *Asaṭir*.[49] There cannot have been much difficulty with the other

---

[45] cf. my article *JJS* xi (1960) pp. 6ff. (see specially nn. 37f., 58f.).

[46] The whole Samaritan literature is filled with this belief. *Kāfi* pp. 1-52 (part of it in SLTh.A pp. 103). cf. recently Noja, *II Kitāb al-Kāfi*, pp. 10-28; *Ṭabbākh* f. 3a-5a (SLTh.A pp. 81f.). cf. also Abdel Al, *A Comparative Study*, pp. 114f., 617f., 661f.

[47] cf. Geiger, "Die Lebensjahre etc", *Jüdische Zeitschrift für Wissenschaft und Leben* I (1862), p. 176.

[48] *Memar Marqah* (ed. Macdonald) I, p. 46 (= II, p. 74) חכם אתר ··ויתהלך
קשטה ורעט (= רהט) לידי כמה רעט אברהם (ברא' י"ז, א)

[49] II, 13-15 ואתהלך חנוך עם אלהים ובנה מדבח אדם סהבה cf. Gaster, *Asaṭir* (Hebr. Text p. 6, and translation *ibid.*), p. 202.

expression לקח either since the *Asaṭir* reports his burial at some length.[50] As stated above, it is not our intention to replace Geiger's hypothesis of an 'ancient aggadah' by any new ones. The only valid lesson, surely, arising from our investigation is found in the frank confession that we have very little trustworthy source-material with which to reconstruct any so-called pre-Rabbinic 'common' ancient exegetical tradition, and hence it is much more profitable to treat each exegetical tradition separately. Just because we can perceive certain distinctive scriptural traditions, we may seek to correlate them with similarly distinctive systems of exegesis arising from those variant readings.[51]

Nobody has, of course, ever denied that there may have existed in early antiquity a substantially homogeneous exegetical tradition, but a tradition exhibiting a number of divergent forms, each holding certain distinctive exegetical elements, each associated with its own text, and each of which may later, along with its distinctive text, have penetrated the various groups upholding *the same text*. Whether such distinctive elements go back to a common source in early antiquity, or whether they were independently introduced, owing to their having had to face similar scriptural difficulties, is a moot point. One cannot, moreover, entirely rule out some interdependence between the exegeses of the various groups.

One such example is the hermeneutical background of the 'Cushite woman', *Numbers* xii, 1.[52] Even more than the Jewish apologists, the Samaritans were eager to remove from Moses any possible slur by discarding all previous attempts at exegesis, and by placing on כשית a favourable construction.[53] On the other hand, one cannot altogether exclude the possibility of Jewish influence. Indeed, it has often been claimed [54] that the Samaritan Targum has been heavily influenced by Targum Onqelos. Thus יאירתה may well be a paraphrase of שפירתא (= ויאיתה) of Onqelos. Nevertheless, it seems that here we have to do with

---

[50] *ibid.* II, 32-41 (Gaster, Heb. Text pp. 8ff., translation pp. 206ff.). It is interesting to note that the Sam. Targum renders *Gen.* v, 24 וליתו הלה נסבו יתה מלאכיה. This, however, does not necessarily mean that he became an angel. The transformation of Enoch into Meṭṭaṭron of the Jewish mystical literature (cf. G.G. Scholem, *Jewish Gnosticism etc.*, pp. 9-13, 43ff.), is entirely irrelevant to Samaritan exegesis. (cf. Gaster, Asaṭir, pp. 107ff.).

[51] cf. my article *ALUOS* VI (1969) *passim.*

[52] Geiger, *Urschrift etc.*, p. 199.

[53] cf. Gaster, *Asatir*, p. 75.

[54] S. Kohn, *Sam. Studien*, pp. 14f. cf. also p. 96.

a different etymology [55] which may suggest an original Samaritan exegesis. This is taken for granted by Munajja,[56] who takes his analogy from *Dueteronomy* xxxii, 15, interpreting the word כשית (R.V. to become sleek) as "becoming nice" or "beautiful".[57] This impression of originality in exegesis in this case is also supported by Marqah.[58]

"Let us give thanks to the Merciful God who magnifies all his beloved at all times. Glory be to the great prophet Moses who said, *You waxed fat etc.* (Deuteronomy xxxii, 15)... He summarised this saying by the expression *You became nice* (כשית); everyone who sees something good praises it".

Although indeed we have no proof that these exegetical traditions are not derived from a common ancient origin in those groups who endeavoured in common to remove any slur from the personality of Moses, we have at least encouragement for the cautious approach which does not fall a victim to hasty conclusions drawn from 'parallels' and external resemblances.

There may thus have existed side by side different 'ancient traditions', some of them represented by Josephus (following Artapanos), some by Targumism, etc. which would for some time co-exist. The legend about Moses marrying the daughter of the Ethiopian King, for instance, may have appealed to some early exegetes, but have sounded blasphemous to others. Thus the latter may easily have found pegs in Scripture with the aid of which they endeavoured to go even so far as to make "the Ethiopian (כשית) change her skin".[59]

C. SUPERCRITICISM

Geiger's hypothesis on the resemblances in the matter of Laws between Samaritans and Karaites and his thesis that all these exegetical traditions go back to the Sadducees are often thought to be 'proved' by the fact that similar points are discussed (although rejected) by the early Rabbis. Some of these 'dissident' opinions are thus equated with

---

[55] Ben Ḥayyim, *Literary and Oral Trad. etc.* II, p. 296, ll. 290-292 (cf. notes *ibid.* for further literature).

[56] *Masā'il al-Khilāf*, Ib, p. 27. cf. previous n.

[57] כשית = S.T. אאשפירת

[58] *Memar Marqah* (ed. Macdonald) I, p. 90 (= II, p. 164). נודי לאלה רחמנה דמרבי לכל רחמיו בכל זבן ועדן ויתגלג נר״מ… כשית כל מן דעמה מאדם טב הוה משבח

[59] cf. Gaster, *Asaṭir*, p. 40.

the 'ancient halakhah'.[60] This whole method of trying to detect clues to earlier discussions of the ancient 'common' elements is built on artificial and often far-fetched 'reconstructions', dependent on what seems to the average student to be supercriticism. But was this the sole motive behind Geiger's work?

The admirers of Geiger have naturally seen in him the epitome of scholarship. By them his work is therefore described rather as a valid attempt at interpreting and underlining the various *exegetical* principles and their development in relation to the text than as a mere hypothesis to explain the origins of the sectarian schism.[61] This ideal picture is not altogether sound. It was not only a supercriticism which was at work in the mind of Geiger; His own son and biographer deemed it quite in keeping with his filial duty to stress constantly the theological background of these researches. There was always an intimate connection between Geiger's scholarly researches and his theological opinions, since they were meant to form the cornerstone whereon to build a modern approach to religion.[62]

The all-pervading determination of Geiger to build his reformatory theology on a strictly scientific basis naturally influenced his researches. The periodical *Wissenschaftliche Zeitschrift für Jüdische Theologie*, itself under Geiger's editorship,[63] reflected this only slightly veiled publicist slant. His publications were undoubtedly meant to further his aim to justify reform in the Jewish religion. Although ostensibly they were meant to express the objective results of scholarly research into the sources of Judaism, the all-pervading theological background could hardly be hidden.[64] Geiger was in fact quite critical of some of his contemporaries who, although they participated in these same scholarly activities, nevertheless did not share his theological bent. He considered himself the only one who did not stop at the examination of external phenomena, but who also arrived at and recorded the essence of the

---

[60] cf. S. Poznanski in *Abraham Geiger, Leben und Lebenswerk* (ed. L. Geiger, Berlin, 1910), pp. 358ff., 386f. (and notes *ibid.* for further bibliography).

[61] F. Perles in *Abraham Geiger, Leben etc.*, p. 319.

[62] Ludwig Geiger, *ibid.* pp. 215ff., 301-306.

[63] 1835 and following. I-IV (part I) Wiesbaden; IV (part II) - VI, Breslau.

[64] cf. Geiger's editorial "Das Judenthum unserer Zeit und die Bestrebungen in ihm", *Wissen, Zeitschr.* I, pp. 1-12; cf. also *idem. Nachgelassene Schriften* I, pp. 447ff. The significance of theological thinking and its relevance to historical research is evident in his other works. cf. "Einleitung in das Studium der jüdischen Theologie", *Nachgelassene Schriften* II, pp. 29ff. cf. also *ibid.* V. pp. 215, 330 etc.

matter and applied its results to practical theological use.[65] And although we are not here interested in his polemics against orthodoxy, we have to remember that, even when his arguments were firmly based on his researches into the sects, his bias must make us suspicious of the validity of his whole system.[66]

His *magnum opus*, the "*Urschrift*", is also permeated by such religious considerations, and quite obviously too. His interests were primarily directed towards them. Originally he intended to investigate the Karaites, who were then regarded as a 'reform' movement, objecting to the domination of Judaism by the 'catholic' fraction composed of the Rabbanites and the Talmudists, and he further intended to write a history of Karaism.[67] However, such a work would necessarily demand a preliminary investigation of the disputes between the Pharisees and the Sadducees. But the disputes between Pharisaism and Samaritanism had likewise to be taken into account, since these are an integral part of such a research; for the latter not only opposed the Rabbinic Oral Law, but denied altogether the validity of all other Scriptures but the Pentateuch. The most important task for us clearly is to test the value of his researches into the Samaritans. This task, however, may inevitably lead us to bring our test to bear on other fields as well. We may well find that, side by side with some most valuable observations, there are sweeping and unwarranted generalisations thrown out in the heat of

---

[65] "Jost, Zunz und Rappoport haben hier fruchtbar begonnen, Munk, Luzzatto und Dukes treflich mitgearbeitet, freilich meistens das Ausserliche beachtend, *während ich den inneren Kern immer mit zu verarbeiten und Resultate für die Reform daraus zu ziehen bemüht war*" (*Nachgelassene Schriften* II, p. 27).

[66] His polemics against orthodoxy are often supported by evidence taken from early Jewish sectarian movements. cf. "Festellung der jüdischen Kalenderberechnung, eine Geschichtbetrachtung". *Jüdische Zeitschrift für Wissenschaft und Leben* VI (1868), pp. 141-151.

[67] cf. his letter to Nöldeke (dated 28th August 1865), *Nachgelassene Schriften* V, p. 296. In the *Urschrift* the polemical tendency is entirely absent. However, in the light of his other publications (cf. previous nn.) the affinity of ideas and even the structural resemblance of his entire literary works is undeniable. It has to be admitted that there is hardly any explicit reference in the *Urschrift* to the contemporary controversial disputations concerning Jewish theology and practices. Nevertheless, the aim of the book is quite obvious. Geiger takes his stand on the side of "free research", in other words, that of the contemporary Protestant biblical scholarship (*Urschrift*, p. 14) and applies the same scale to the investigation of Jewish origins. Despite Geiger's justified criticisms of Z. Frankel (*ibid.* pp. 16f.) and Luzzatto (*ibid.* p. 18) some of his own postulates are heavily influenced by radical theological approach. (cf. *inf.* para (d)).

discussion which must either be firmly rejected or taken with a 'pinch of salt'. There is still therefore room for re-examining his general theories on tradition and historical development.[68] Needless to say, his major hypothesis on the sources of schism and their connections with the 'older halakhah' cannot be accepted without very serious modifications.[69]

D. Exegesis or Textual Emendations?

Our criticism of Geiger's system does not mean a rejection of all his findings. In many respects his merits are solid and his findings of permanent value. In the course of his investigation of Samaritan exegetical *details*, in which he compares their legal practices with those of the Jews, he has often hit the nail on the head.[70] Thus in his account of the Law of Sabbath [71] and its motivations, or in his description of the motivations and exegetical background of the prohibition against preparing food on the festivals [72] he has surpassed many contemporary scholars. On the other hand, in certain cases, and especially when the real differences between the Karaite and the Samaritan practices do not support his system he tends to turn a blind eye on certain outstanding discrepancies.[73]

---

[68] cf. Geiger, "Neuere Mitteilungen etc." *ZDMG* XVI (1862) p. 715.

[69] *ibid.* p. 716. It is particularly the interpretation of reasons which lie behind the legal differences between Jews and Samaritans which call for revaluation. (cf. "Die gesetzlichen Differenzen etc.", *ZDMG* XX (1866), pp. 527ff. = *Nachgelassene Schriften* III, pp. 283-321). The whole central idea of basing all differences on a hypothetical controversy between Judahist and Israelitic elements was never substantiated. The same applies to the role attributed to the Zadokite priesthood (cf. *sup.* n. 21).

[70] cf. "Die gesetzlichen Differenzen" (previous n.) and also *Nachgelassene Schriften* V. (Hebrew vol.) pp. 142-165.

[71] *ibid.* III, pp. 289f.; *idem.* "Sadduzäer und Pharisäer", *Jüd. Zeitschr.* II (1863) p. 53. cf. my article, *op. cit.* pp. 112f., 147f. (nn. 118-123).

[72] *Nachgelassene Schriften* III, pp. 290-293. cf. Hanover, *Das Festgesetz etc.*, pp. 6f., 19ff., 59 (n. 58). cf. also my article *op. cit.* pp. 112, 147 (nn. 116-117).

[73] Geiger tended to blur the differences between the Karaites and the Samaritans in connection with the fixing of the date of Pentacost (*Nachgelassene Schriften* III, pp. 294-296). One could expect in this respect a greater precision on the part of this scholar, since he was perfectly aware of the Samaritan polemics against the Karaites on the whole issue of calendaric calculations. It is also evident that this controversy is of an early origin. In fact Geiger's late source (the eighteenth century Pentateuch-Commentary of Meshalmah, completed by his nephew, Ibrāhim al-'Ayyah) carries on the polemics against Qirqisāni (*ibid.* pp. 293f.).

The real object of our discussion is not to assess the details of this system, but rather to examine again its central thesis, not only because it concerns Samaritan origins, but because its validity or otherwise concerns our understanding of exegesis in general.

Seeing that Scripture embodies a complete philosophy of life (in the firm belief of most exegetes), it is quite impossible to read it as a simple narrative, even in places where there are no ambiguities. Like the works of the great philosophers, then, the Biblical Word cannot be read for the first time with any sure and well-founded understanding. It is the unfailing practice of *all* exegetes to read and re-read the original text upon which they are commenting, since any part may contribute to the understanding of any other part. There are two approaches by which the 'proper' exegesis is always determined — firstly by the pragmatic mode of exposition, guided by a living tradition which is inherent in the mental make-up of each believer, and secondly, by the subjection of Scripture itself to a closer scrutiny with a view ot discovering its wealth of details; and here the 'ambiguous' parts are to be elucidated and interpreted by the parts more easily understood. Both ways are equally explored by all exegetes and all systems of exegesis. It is always wise, therefore, to explore both paths to these closely adjoining fields, because together they will lead us to a truer view of the ground which the expositor is cultivating. Since, however, both tradition and scripture are themselves subject to changes, either deliberate or fortuitous, each group, insofar as it diverges from others in these matters, deserves special treatment. A growing appreciation of style admittedly compelled the wellknown classical writers to re-write their compositions in many differing versions;[74] and if we cannot here enter into the almost irresolvable problems of the redaction of the Bible, we can at any rate begin our investigations with its so-called canonisation. At some stage or other (most probably around the second century B.C.E.), the *written* word became binding in the various groups. Obviously the 'true text' and its 'true exegesis' were the main bones of contention between the various sects and religious movements.[75]

Being mainly interested in the type of exegesis exemplified by the Samaritans, we have now to look into the more fundamental constituents

---

[74] F.L. Lucas, *Style* (Pan Books, London, 1964), pp. 9f. Concerning obscurity, cf. *ibid.* pp. 60ff., and on simile and metaphor, *ibid.* pp. 163ff.

[75] For a detailed discussion of this point, cf. my article *ALUOS* VI (1969), *passim.* (For further details cf. SLTh. pp. 668ff.)

of their system and, in particular, their literalism.[76] The most common feature of all kinds of literalist interpretations is that external matter, not explicitly mentioned in the Text, is introduced only very seldom. These literalist interpreters regard the Text as self-explanatory, self-contained and entirely independent of the inclinations, standpoints and motives of the exegete, and they therefore set themselves to interpret it as if it were axiomatic that no human agency is ever really indispensable to its proper (and only true) understanding.[77]

This approach, however, does not of itself facilitate the exposition of a 'deeper meaning', but this may be permitted if it does not palpably contradict the explicit sense. Midrash can indeed develop quite naively amongst literalists, if only they look out for details which are not explicitly present in the Text but may be 'suggested' by it. All systems of midrash (and so this term may be translated) are in fact a kind of 'searching' along the line of the minute and exhaustive exposition of details, a process often extending the original meaning, and even adding elements which 'aid' the 'perfect sense' of the text.[78]

Again this simple and literalist exegesis by its very nature remains static or develops only very slowly during many generations, since the changes in the semantic value of the Biblical language do not rapidly entail the loss of its original meanings. Unless such changes do take place, or unless some passages are misconstrued either through misunderstanding or through tradition or environment, or simply because they become unintelligible, the literal sense of the text may remain almost 'fossilised' for many successive generations. A living tradition in conjunction with a minimal elementary education among the masses may even prolong such a state of affairs.[79]

In a sense, the same is also the case with Rabbinic exegesis. We have to reckon with an unbroken and continuous process amongst the Pharisees which has its roots in the Biblical period.[80] It is hardly pos-

---

[76] cf. *inf.* Part III, para (a, 1).

[77] We cannot here enter into the problems of the slavishly literal translations of the S.T. Some of these readings seem to us nonsensical (cf. S. Kohn, *Sam. Studien*, pp. 35ff.). With the progress in research into the Aramaic of the Samaritans it becomes clearer that many of these previously abused mistranslations are in fact scribal corruptions and misunderstandings (cf. L. Goldberg, *Das samaritanische Pentateuchtargum, passim*, Ben Hayyim, *Literal and Oral Trad. etc.* I, pp. ס״ט ff.

[78] cf. on 'Analogy', 'harmonisation' etc., *inf.* Part III, para (g).

[79] cf. *inf.* Part II, nn. 125ff.

[80] Zunz, *Gottesdienstlichen Vorträge*, pp. 7ff., 230ff. Seligmann, "Voraussetzungen der Midrashexegese", *Congress Volume 1953*, (Suppl. *VT.* I) pp. 150-181.

sible even here to accept the notion that in Pharisaism there were constant and revolutionary changes. Geiger's claim [81] that each spiritual trend, and even each personality, imprinted its mark on the Scripture cannot reasonably be maintained. We cannot discover any sort of anarchy in their exegesis, such as would have been created by a 'free-for-all' policy. If changes did really come into their exegesis, this did not happen through any hypothetical constant revisions of the text, but rather through revisions of the exegesis itself. Daring as some of these hermeneutical devices were (especially in comparison with those of the Samaritans), we have so far no real proof that the Rabbis ever resorted to actual textual emendations.

The cause of the rapid development of Rabbinic midrashim must be sought in the firm belief that the Written Law was from the outset accompanied by an Oral Law. Actually, these are not two separate entities, but, according to the Rabbis, one indivisible unit. The Oral Law is enshrined by the Divine Legislator in the Written Law, but, unlike the latter, it has not been canonised, but is 'revealed' to all the generations to come through persevering and devout study, and finds its support in the very letters of Scripture.[82] It is an organism which grows spontaneously through the explaining away (rather than correcting or emending) of difficulties by constant harmonisations.[83]

The whole Rabbinic exegesis was progressively formulated in a system so as to obviate the general confusion which would ensue if each exegete were to 'invent' midrashim of his own fancy. Certain Hermeneutical Rules were devised which came to acquire the same sanctity as the Oral Law itself. Despite the manifold devices of midrash, which on the whole tended to atomise Scripture, their employment and outcome were regarded as constituting one homogeneous system.[84] The Rabbis did not find, or expect to find, any *real* contradiction between these two systems, the Written and the Oral Law. It was rather that essentially they believed that both the literal sense and the resultant midrash were equally true and equally valid; just as the two faces of the same coin more often complement than contradict each other, so in a similar way,

---

[81] *Urschrift*, p. 72.

[82] cf. my article, *op. cit.* pp. 101f., 134f. (nn. 26ff.). cf. recently E.E. Urbach, *The Sages*, pp. 254ff.

[83] M. Soloweitchik - S. Rubashoff, *The History of Bible Criticism*, (Hebrew, Berlin, 1925), pp. 12 (cf. n. b), 21f.

[84] Moore, *Judaism* I, p. 319.

midrash, with all its extravagant and fanciful details, was regarded as entirely compatible with the 'simple' and obvious sense. The two systems could co-exist side by side in the mind of the Rabbis as complementary halves which assisted each other in the full understanding of the whole Law.[85]

Even the extreme allegorists, who were consistently opposed by the other Jewish groups, certainly respected Scripture. The words of the Written Law, although in their view not meant to be understood according to their literal sense, served nevertheless as an envelope, and a necessary envelope, to cover the *real* and *true* sense of the Divine Word. Allegory always tended, naturally, to depreciate the force of the literal sense and to weaken the observance of the precepts. Thus in Christianity 'works', i.e. the actual carrying out of the precepts tended to lose their obligatory character, but, nevertheless, the Biblical Text remained no less hallowed.[86] It is of course true that the extreme sects such as the gnostics sadly misunderstood this freer approach, but this happened only under foreign influences.[87] In general, however, by the time of the birth of Christianity at least (and there is good reason to believe that this was the case generations before), the Biblical text was already firmly established. To be sure, there existed variant versions; but, as far as we can see, each group clung to its own traditional text, which embodied and guarded also its distinctive exegetical traditions.[88]

If we now consider the criticisms levelled against the system of Geiger by his contemporaries,[89] we move again into a realm of theological motives strangely mingled with scholarly objections.[90] On the one hand, it is wellknown that some Biblical critics (both his and our own contemporaries) have highly praised his particular critical approach,[91] and on

---

[85] cf. n. 82 *sup.*

[86] Soloweitchik-Rubashoff, *op. cit.* pp. 50ff. Urbach, *op. cit.* p. 262.

[87] Grant, *A Short History etc.*, p. 2.

[88] cf. my article *op. cit.* pp. 103f., 138f. (nn. 50ff.).

[89] Z.M. Pineles, *Darkah shel-Torah* (Vienna, 1861), pp. 168-201; J.L. Rapoport (שי״ר) in *Naḥlath Yehudah* (ed. Z. Bodek, Cracow, 1868); E. Baneth, "Ueber den Ursprung der Sadokäer und Bothosäer", *Magazin für die Wissenschaft des Judentums* IX. (1882), pp. 6-23.

[90] cf. however, my article *op. cit.* pp. 100, 134 (n. 25).

[91] This was rightly recognized by Nöldeke, cf. I. Löw in *Abraham Geiger, Leben etc.* (ed. L. Geiger), pp. 410f. The importance of Geiger's researches to all later investigations into the "origins" of the variant "Scriptures" was also emphasized by P. Kahle in his Introduction of the 2nd edition of the *Urschrift* (Frankfurt a/M., 1928).

the other, it is to be regretted that these critical voices, intent as they were on propagating their special theological opinions, often overplayed their attacks, and thereby caused even their well-founded and timely warnings to go often unheeded. Although we do not intend here to join the ranks of the defenders or Geiger's critics, it is only fair to point out that there are amongst these criticisms many justifiable claims which have not yet been seriously met.

The themes (out of many) discussed above, although not meant to demonstrate any new way of thinking, are nevertheless sufficiently thought-provoking to raise a fundamentally sound objection to any rigidly dogmatic approach. It is unquestionable that if one were to follow the oppositive course, one would be led into the kind of pitfalls indicated. As a matter of fact, this is exactly what did happen when a scholar who took this directly opposite line [92] worked out an inherently self-contradictory system. As the basis of this theory, the "normative' (i.e. Rabbinic) traditions were exhibited as the original ones, and all others as 'deviations' from this sole 'ancient' tradition. Understandably the effects of describing the Samaritan exegetical tradition in such terms were most astonishing, for here we were asked to believe that we cannot confidently rely on Samaritan tradition at all. The Samaritans were represented as constantly changing their outlook, practices, beliefs and exegesis, adopting bits and pieces of influence from every possible source. The artificiality of such a theory is self-evident, and it was only arrived at by frequent mishandling of the Samaritan sources themselves.[93]

A compromise between these two extremes is equally impossible, and would not advance our inquiry. We have, however, we trust, sufficient reason for believing in the real co-existence of several distinctive textual types and their accompanying and parallel exegetical traditions. This means that the Biblical textual types are intimately and inextricably bound up with their respective exegetical traditions. But we cannot here enter into the difficult problem of the origins of these textual arche-types.[94]

Although we freely admit to defeat in one field, in that we are unable, from the available Samaritan sources, to make a contribution to the

---

[92] Wreschner, *Sam. Traditionen*, p. vii, n. 4 and *passim*.

[93] cf. my article, *op. cit.* pp. 137 (n. 41), 142 (n. 84), 147 (n. 121), 149 (n. 127) and 161 (n. 217).

[94] cf. *sup.* n. 88.

solution of the vexed problem of the origins of the textual arche-types, we can nevertheless claim to have gained a clearer insight into the Samaritan traditions proper. But this we can say: those who have built so much on the supposition that exegeses of various kinds are conscious attempts to present the Biblical message in a form adapted to contemporary needs have never yet proved their point. The so-called 're-writing of the Bible' would only be possible as long as there were no firm traditions controlling new textual readings and emendatory innovations. Once a certain group had crystallised and gained a separate identity and existence, based on even the vaguest 'ideologies,' emendations of the Biblical text were almost impossible. The greater part of the ideological presuppositions which provoked a particular schism had been previously worked out from the groups' *own* Scriptures, which were already regarded as sacrosanct and canonised. The possible textual changes must have been severely limited by the accepted norms or traditions prevailing separately in each group.

E. PARALLELISM

Nobody can well deny that there exists parallelism in the matter of legal details between the various sectarian groups, and such resemblances are in fact largely dependent upon Scriptural exegesis. Now the problem arises as to how to explain this largely 'common' element. Since the idea of the 'ancient Sadducean tradition' gained ground, it has been commonly taken for granted that the source of all this 'identity' is the common Zadokite priesthood;[95] in other words, that the family relationships between the priesthood as found in Jerusalem, Shechem and Leontopolis may have facilitated a mutual exchange of ideas and influences. Thus the adherents of these respective sanctuaries, in accepting the authority of their local priests, may well have adopted the textual and exegetical features characteristic of the Zadokites.[96]

We cannot deal here with the complex history of the priesthood, which goes back far into Old Testament times.[97] But, as far as our evidence reveals, in Samaritan traditions the name of Zadok does not figure

---

[95] J. Bowman, "The Importance etc.", *ALUOS* I (1959) pp. 43-54.

[96] Gaster, *The Samaritans*, pp. 56f.; Bowman, "Is the Sam. Calendar the Old Zadokite one?" *PEQ* XCI (1959) pp. 23-37, cf. Rowley *Men of God* p. 264 n. 2.

[97] cf. A. Cody, *A History of O.T. Priesthood* (Analecta Biblica XXXV, Rome, 1969). pp. 88ff., 110ff.

prominently. Admitteldly, it occurs once in the list of High Priests,[98] but this Zadok is later by a century than the Biblical one. Although there are indeed divided opinions as to the reliability of Samaritan chronology,[99] an isolated name can hardly furnish adequate proof of a historical fact even if we may disregard the chronological problems involved.

In contrast with this line of thought, in Samaritan tradition the stress is manifestly on descent from Phinehas, and no criteria whatever are supplied for expressing a preference for one branch of the family over another. Having regard to that ingrained Samaritan conservatism which was so stoutly upheld by the priesthood,[100] some reminiscences of the Zadokite prominence would surely have survived if it had any basis in reality.

Speculations on such lines must therefore be treated with due reserve. Most unfounded of all, perhaps, is the theory [101] which endeavours to trace the supposed Zadokite elements back to the practices of the pre-Maccabean period. On such a hypothesis the Samaritan traditions are antecedent to the Pharisean Sadducean Schism. This argument rests on the further assumption that, since the Samaritans possess an "Oral Law", they must therefore share this ground with the common pre-Pharisean existence.[102] Looking, however, into the 'evidence' of

---

[98] Gaster, *Studies & Texts* I, p. 495 (= *JRAS* 1909, p. 413). cf. also Hebrew text *ibid.* III, p. 132 (= *JRAS* p. 409). cf. recently J. Macdonald, *Chronicle No. II*, pp. 216-219. In this Chronicle we find another Zadok who is not a priest but a 'prince' from the sons of Joseph (*ibid.* p. 167 = Hebrew text p. 78).

[99] Gaster admits some chronological confusions, but in general considers all chronicles as being based on the "Chain of Sam. High Priests" (*Studies and Texts* I, pp. 445ff. = *JRAS* pp. 393-420). cf. also Macdonald, *Chronicle No. II*, pp. 220ff. More sceptical was Vilmar, *Abulfathi Annales Sam.*, pp. xlix ff. The same line is also pursued by Ben-Zevi, "Principles of Sam. Chronology", *Sura* III (1957/8) pp. 5ff.

[100] cf. Part II, para (j).

[101] Gaster, *The Samaritans*, pp. 50ff.

[102] *ibid.* p. 51. The whole title of Gaster's other book, *The Samaritan Oral Law and Ancient Traditions* is misleading. The undeniable fact that the Samaritans were in possession of ancient oral tradition (*ibid.* pp. 17ff.) does not yet prove this was equated by them with 'Oral Law'. "... a sufficiently large literature exists among the Sam. to show the existence of an Oral and traditional practices" (*ibid.* p. 24). This and similar expressions are never properly analyzed and are based on confusing the terms 'tradition' and Oral Law. Later Gaster employs the term 'Unwritten Law' (pp. 55f.), but even this term cannot be freely equated with Samaritan traditions. It is evident that Gaster was mislead by the Hebrew terminology into which his translators rendered the Arabic texts. העתקה (cf. *ibid.* p. 59) is actually found in Medieval Hebrew literature as a synonym for Oral Law (דברי קבלה.), but this

this assertion, we discover that it rests on a late Medieval Samaritan legal collection called the *Hilukh*, which on this hypothesis is equated with the Rabbinic term of 'Halakhah', and thus means 'Oral Law'. Apart from the philological weakness of such an argument, this whole concept of a Divinely ordained Oral Law (having equal value with the Written one) is quite foreign to Samaritan thinking. With all their devotion to and admiration for their tradition, there is never any tendency to make of it a Divinely ordained vehicle, as is the case with the Rabbis.[103]

This whole idealistic picture, moreover, of a 'Popular Judaism' at the time of the Second Temple drawn in the light of Samaritan traditions,[104] enjoys little support in factual reality. Only if we accept the charge that Josephus has deliberately misled us concerning the divisions between the sects, can any such theory gain any foothold.

Notwithstanding some vague parallels, which do obviously exist, the 'evidence' adduced for such a common tradition is often self-contradictory. To point, for example, to the 'altar of incense' (in the cult of the fourth century B.C.E. Jewish colony of Elephantine) and compare it with the Samaritan 'altar of prayers'[105] is very far from proving any such thing. On the contrary, if we believe in such an entity, we have to posit that this type of 'Popular Judaism' of the Samaritans possessed a syncretistic character very similar to what which we know to have existed in Elephantine.[106] Besides, it has already been shown elsewhere

---

is due to the translator, who translated literally the Arabic term نقل (cf. Samuel ibn Tibbon פרוש המלות הזרות; s.v. עתק). The same value may be attached to the term משמע (سمعى). (For further discussion cf. SLTh pp. 826ff., 940 nn. 561ff.)·

[103] cf. Part II, para (h).

[104] Gaster, *Studies and Texts* II, p. 725-729. On the other hand his criticism of his predecessors, attributing to the Samaritans only foreign influences, is generally justified. These earlier scholars, who were largely dependent on the Sam. Liturgies, could easily find 'parallels' to most Sam. 'dogmas' in the cults of other religions (cf. *ibid.* p. 726).

[105] cf. *inf.* n. 107. Most unfortunate is the harmonizing tendency aiming at equating elements of Samaritanism with the Apocryphal literature. Apart from the impossible task of homogenizing the wide range of opinions expressed freely under the cloak of anonymity (and pseudepigrapha), chronologically they are many centuries earlier than the earliest Sam. sources. This is particularly obvious in the field of eschatology. cf. D.S. Russel, *The Method and Message of Jewish Apocalyptic* (London, 1964) and recently E.E. Urbach, *The Sages*, pp. 585ff.

[106] Despite the tempting identifications of some semi-pagan sanctuaries in Elephantine (ענתביתאל חרמביתאל) with Samaritan motifs (הרגריזים = ביתאל) there

that the Samaritan 'Altar of Prayers' had entirely different origins.[107]
Of even less value is any comparison of Marqah with the Kabbalah and
Simon Magnus.[108] Not only the implied great antiquity of the Kabbalah
but the very existence of mysticism amongst the Samaritans has yet to
be proved.[109]

F. DOES PARALLELISM PROVE IDENTITY?

While the judicious use of the comparative approach is certainly
fruitful in all its effects on critical studies, it may become positively
pernicious if it is employed without due discretion. The discovery of
the Dead Sea Scrolls at once raised manifold and widely ranging
problems, the solutions of which are often sought through comparative
studies; and in this work the Samaritans have also been taken into
account and their possible relationship to the Dead Sea Scrolls Sect
often put to the test.[110]

No doubt certain indications of parallelism may be discerned here and
there in the new material. Judging from our knowledge of such supposed
parallels, however, and despite all their apparent marks of resemblacne,
they by no means prove identity of matter, much less actual contact.
Furthermore, nothing substantial has so far been adduced which could
even remotely bridge the ideological dichotomy between these two
groups. Except for the so-called Zadokite priestly connections, the
flimsy grounds of which we have had occasion to discuss above,[111] no
real common ground can be discovered. There is no need here to amass
a great deal of corroborative evidence for this statement, fotı it is quite
sufficient to consider the contents of the Qumran Library to realise

---

is little factual ground in Sam. literature which would justify such sweeping identification. cf. A. Vincent, *La Religion des Judéo-Araméens d'Éléphantine* (Paris, 1937),
pp. 33ff.; E.G. Kraeling, "New Light on the Elephantine Colony", *BA*. XV (1952),
pp. 50-67. Nor does the term אשמביתאל have much in common with אשימה although
the accusation of the Samaritans of worshipping this idol goes back to biblical sources
(II *Kings*, xvii, 20). cf. Montgomery, *The Samaritans*, pp. 213 (n. 28) and 321.

[107] cf. my article *op. cit.* pp. 116, 151f. (nn. 141f.); Montgomery, *op. cit.* p. 44
(n. 60).

[108] Gaster, *Studies and Texts* II, p. 727.

[109] cf. my article, *op. cit.* pp, 99f., 109f., 132 (nn. 17-18), 142f. (nn. 89-101).

[110] Bowman, "Contact between Sam. Sects and Qumran?", *VT.* vii (1957),
pp. 184ff.; Massingberd-Ford, "Can we exclude Sam. influence from Qumran?",
Revue de Qumran VI (1967), pp. 109ff.

[111] cf. *sup.* nn. 95f.

the leading role of the Prophets of this sect. This fact alone would immediately rule out any ideological affinity with Samaritanism, the latter being, of course, totally opposed to all these 'false prophets'. All previous 'proofs' of affinity, based on the negative evidence that the Samaritan opposition to the authority of the Prophets is not attested in ancient external literature will not hold water. Their very opposition to Jerusalem, which may fairly be said to be their major distinctive doctrine, and which may well have been the prime cause of the creation of the Schism, would make their acceptance and use of the Prophets and Hagiographa totally impossible.[112] The Talmud itself does not throw in their faces the charge of their denial of the Prophets for the sole reason, surely, that there exist also other non-conformists who hold similar views.[113] There are indeed other Samaritan heretical practices and doctrines which are not explicitly mentioned by the Talmudic literature, nor in fact by any other external source. It is not without great significance that the rejection of Jerusalem is by the Talmud considered the most important dogma characterising the Samaritan schism. This is only logical since the Talmud's demand of the rejection of the claims of Gerizim and accepting those of Jerusalem implies the acceptance therwith of the whole Old Testament 'Canon'. This principle seems to underlie the Rabbinic stipulation for the acceptance of the Samaritans:[114] "When shall we take them back? — when they renounce Mount Gerizim and confess Jerusalem, etc.".

One cannot entirely exclude the possibility that, amongst the rigorous or almost puritanical sectarians within the non-conformists, as a whole, there existed some interchange of ideas.[115] There may thus have existed Samaritan non-conformists who may have entered into consultation with other 'reformist' groups. However, by this act they must have excluded themselves from the fold of their 'orthodox' clo-religionists who, even on the hostile testimony of the Talmud, 'adhered rigorously to their own traditions'.[116]

---

[112] This is evident from all Sam. Chronicles. cf. Vilmar, *Abulfathi Annales Sam.*, pp. 99f. and recently Macdonald, *Chronicle no. II*, Hebrew text, pp. 44f. (on Samuel), 75f. (on Elijah) etc.

[113] Marmorstein, "Judaism and Christianity etc." *HUCA* X (1935), p. 226, n. 13; cf. also my article *op. cit.* pp. 118, 153f. (nn. 161-166).

[114] *Massekheth Kuthim*, cf. Montgomery *op. cit.* p. 203.

[115] cf. my article *op. cit.* p. 138, n. 55.

[116] *Berakhoth* 47b (and parallels) כל מצוה שהחזיקו בה כותים הרבה מדקדקים בה יותר מישראל

Epiphanius (followed by others) counts the Essenes amongst the Samaritan sects.[117] This may be a genuine and trustworthy tradition, going back perhaps to the pre-Christian era; referring, however, to a *sect* within Samaritanism. It has already been suggested that this sect may have been one of those affiliated to the early Dositheans.[118] This brings us to a province which is quite outside the scope of our investigation, since nothing of the literature of these sects has come down to us. In our discussions of Samaritan principles we cannot include such sects as compromised with Essene and allied elements, thus obviously creating a syncretistic ideology, with the acceptance of the prophetic and other influences. The whole *Weltanschauung* of the 'normative' Samaritans would violently reject any such 'false' ideologies.

For us the paramount concern is exegesis, and in this field the contrast with other groups is most striking. Nothing could be further from the Samaritan mentality than the *Pesher* type of exegesis of Qumran;[119] figurative interpretations, even in aggadah, are extremely rare amongst the Samaritans. Real allegory creeps in occasionally but only when the Biblical background demands it.[120]

Accordingly, we may safely hold that the facile claim that the findings derived from the Dead Sea Scrolls support by their parallels some affinity with Samaritanism as well as with other groups, is harshly rebutted by the intrinsic character of this literature. No other exegetical tradition, in fact, shares the distinctive features of the *Pesher*.[121]

G. CONTEMPORARY HARMONISATIONS

Despite the cautious approach of most scholars, who have rightly emphasized the distinctively sectarian faetures of the Scrolls, there are still some who, led or misled by harmonizing tendencies, try to identify motives found in other movements with those found in the Qumran sect. The die-hard nineteenth-century heritage is even now almost as much with us as it was in the past days. The only new feature in this revival, called in modern terminology by such names as the 'general pre-Christian midrashic *genre*' the 'new synthesis of midrashic origins',

---

[117] Montgomery, *op. cit.* p. 253, n. 3.

[118] *ibid.* pp. 262ff.

[119] cf. *inf.* Part II, n. 152 (This is widely treated in SLTh pp. 688ff.).

[120] cf. *inf.* Part III, para (h, 2).

[121] F.F. Bruce, "The Dead Sea Habakkuk Scroll", *ALUOS* I (1959) pp. 5-7.

'comparative historical studies' etc.,[122] is that it now incorporates also the Jewish Targumim and some other hitherto neglected material. No doubt all this solid scholarly works brings its continuing contribution to a better and, may be, more critical estimate of the ancient exegesis, and its real value is all the more enhanced as it calls attention to previously unobserved parallelisms; at the same time, it perpetuates the danger inseparable from all harmonizers, in that it so often confuses parallelism with identity.

The inter-relation of the various midrashic traditions is not yet clear and needs to be worked out very thoroughly. Obviously we are not concerned here with reaching any final solutions. Nevertheless, we suggest, on the strength of the above-mentioned sharp distinctiveness of the Samaritan exegesis, that each and every exegetical tradition equally deserves special study, entirely independently of all harmonising tendencies. Not only is this task as fully important as any comparative study, but when such works, based on the evidence arising from the close examination of the productions of the groups themselves are finally compiled, at least the *data* will be at hand for delving into the field of the possibly intricate inter-relations with a far greater promise of success.

An interesting and significant development in recent work on exegesis is the employment of the Targumim for comparative studies, and it has been the Palestinian Targum in particular which has been singled out in this respect, because it contains much of a midrashic nature.[123] We cannot enter here into the problem of the exact dating of the midrashic element of the Targum, concerning which the debate is still going on.[124] Even if, however, we accept the now widely held opinion that this Palestinian Targum embodies "in the main material coming from pre-Christian times"[125] this in itself does not allow us to use it indiscriminately. It is even less probable that it actually embodies "the common" early midrashic *milieu*. We may learn at this point from the very cautious words of these scholars of the previous century who warned us not to rely too much on this and other familiar texts; even in regard to the

---

[122] Vermes, *Scripture and Tradition etc.*, pp. 1-10.

[123] *ibid.* p. 4.

[124] cf. A. Diez-Macho, "The Recently Discovered Palestinian Targum, its Antiquity...", Suppl. to *VT.* vii (1960), pp. 125ff. cf. however, Werberg Møller (*ibid.* pp. 333f.).

[125] Kahle, *The Cairo Geniza*, p. 208.

'normative' Tarqum Onqelos, which was constantly used by the Synagogue and received the official recognition of the Rabbis, it has been
shown that it was not free from variant versions.[126]

This warning should be even more seriously heeded when consideration is given to the Palestinian Targumim, which have been singled out
especially for their 'non-conformist' elements.[127] Such elements can have
survived only because, during the long oral and literary transmission
of these texts, they formed part of an entirely uncultivated field, and
hence were not 'supervised' by learned revisers. Thus, for example, the
recently published Targum 'Neofiti I' no less escaped grave errors due
to careless transcription, many of which go back to even earlier (now
lost) sources, which themselves similarly had such a 'vulgar' background.[128]

Fascinating and valuable though these Targumim are, only time
and much additional research will reveal their true provenance, and
their relations to other types of exegetical literature. We are interested
here only in their *direct* bearing on the problems of the origins of Samaritan exegesis, and accordingly we shall have to examine those "parallels"
which have been recently emphasised by scholars. Since, moreover,
these "parallels" have come to our notice by resuscitating the over-a-
century-old concept of a 'proto Tannaitic' common exegesis,[129] we shall
not here be in a position to separate the sources but must rather examine
some of the topics which may have even the remotest bearing on Samaritan exegesis, No words are too strong to warn the researcher against
the danger of a mere juxtaposition of the various commentaries, even
if this procedure yields apparent 'parallels'. Taken by itself, this is not
the way to solve questions of inter-dependence.

The midrashic background and the exegetical traditions are regularly
kept together in each particular group.[130] This is the reason why we

---

[126] S.D. Luzzatto, *Philoxenus* (אוהב גר Vienna, 1830), pp. xivff., 25ff. Obviously
the best version was not always the one which was widely accepted.

[127] cf. my article *op. cit.* pp. 99, 131 (n. 12). The intensive employment of this
Targum by Geigner (*Urschrift*), Excurs. II, pp. 451ff.) demonstrates that it contained
'non-conformist' elements.

[128] D. Reider, "On the Targum Yerusalmi I", *Tarbiz* xxxviii (1968) pp. 81-6.

[129] If these sources belong to variant traditions, comparison alone will not solve
the respective exegetical problems, nor prove interdependence. cf. M.R. Lehmann,
"IQ Genesis Apocryphon in the Light of the Targumim and Midrashim", *Revue
de Qumran* I (1958), pp. 249-263; cf. Vermes, *op. cit.* pp. 110f. n. 2.

[130] Vermes, *op. cit.* p. 124, n. 2.

find so much 'agreement' between the Books of Jubilees and the Genesis Apocryphon, namely that their ideological backgrounds show great affinity.[131] Some groups believed in 'inspired' exegesis, while others clung most firmly to the literal sense of Scripture. This was not merely or mainly a matter of taste, but more often depended on an ideological system from which, later, various "hermeneutical principles" developed, and always, in close adherence to the respective traditions of each group. This system again, often depended on a sense of spiritual affinity with aspects of Biblical thought and environment, and possibly with foreign influences; but, above all, on the whole educational background, which brings us back again to *tradition*.[132] No speculation can be indulged in here on a *terminus post quem* for Samaritan traditions. We have only to bear in mind that the fourth century C.E. will serve us very well as a *terminus ante quem*, from which we shall have to work our way back.[133]

To take a case in point, the claims that the exegetical traditions of Pseudo-Philo are early [134] may well be true. Such ancient writers (including Pseudo-Empedocles) may indeed express views which reflect on certain affinity with Samaritan views. Nevertheless, this affinity in itself does not justify any exaggerated claims for a common origin with Samaritan exegetical traditions. Just as in certain details some thoughts expressed by these writers coincide with Samaritan thoughts, so in the same way many other elements likewise coincide with Rabbinic and Christian views. Nevertheless, careful investigation here too shows that "parallels" do not prove identity.

From these arguments, derived as they are from external evidence, nothing certain may be deduced concerning the origins of the Samaritan text and exegesis; much less than has been supposed, do they possess any substantial weight at all. It is not at all impossible that at a time one or even two centuries B.C.E. the Samaritan textual and oral traditions assumed the form which we find extant only many centuries later.[135]

---

[131] *idem, ibid.* pp. 111 (on *Gen.* xii, 9), 113 (on v. 14), 113 (on v. 16) etc. cf. also *ibid.* pp. 122f.

[132] cf. my article *op. cit. passim.*

[133] The earliest *written* traditions can be dated to the early fourth century C.E. cf. Macdonald *Memar Marqah*, pp. xviif., xxxixf. *idem.* The Theology of the Sam. pp. 40ff.

[134] A. Spiro, "Sam. Tobiads etc.", *PAAJR* XX (1951), p. 281, n. 11.

[135] The dispute between Samaritans and Jews of Alexandria before Ptolemy Philometor was carried out "according to the Law of Moses" (Josephus, *Antiq.* xiii, iii, 4).

No external evidence in fact proves beyond doubt that the Samaritan schism, after its inception, did actually create a variety of Biblical texts and traditions, or that the Samaritan religion did actually undergo any major and drastic alterations. The mutual accusations by Jews and Samaritans from early antiquity of possessing falsified scriptures only serve to strengthen our general impression that at an early date there were in existence a number of distinctive scriptural versions, some of them characteristic of the Samaritans.[136]

We may therefore proceed to a detailed examination of some of the assumptions upon which these harmonisations have been based. If we examine the assumption that the earliest exegetical activities consist of explanatory textual glosses which by "amended readings" (קרי) are "to supplant the Written Word" (כתיב),[137] the evidence adduced by no means supports the conclusions drawn from it. If we take at random some examples of these variant readings from the Rabbis,[138] we ought to realise that we are here dealing with conscious preservations of ancient traditions. Often the 'reading' is an indication of an awareness of another tradition, and the stubborn insistence of the Rabbis on preserving their traditional text, despite the reading, surely disproves rather than proves

---

[136] Even the slanderous report of Josephus (*Antiq.* xi, viii, 7) that the sinners and criminals of Jerusalem found refuge among the Shechemites does not contradict our contention. These outcasts were only admitted because they could claim that they were "accused unjustly". This in itself shows that an ordinary sinner would not be admitted by the Samaritans. It is only logical to reconstruct the excuses of these outcasts, viz. they were persecuted because of their violation of the Pharisaic interpretation (or version) of the Scripture.

[137] Vermes, *op. cit.* pp. 228f. We cannot enter here into the hypothetical backgrounds of Biblical origins. At least from Samaritan sources there is no way to reconstruct any new points concerning 'higher criticism'. "The exegesis of the *primitive* Haggadah must coincide with that of the last redactors of the written Torah" (*ibid.* p. 127), and similar generalizations are not borne out by facts. The same applies to halakhic matters cf. e.g. the distinction made between פסח and חג המצות cf. recently Kippenberg, *Garizim etc.*, p. 230, nn. 172-173 (cf. *inf.* n. 257).

[138] cf. some examples of Kethibh (= K) and Qere (= Q) in *Genesis*: (K צביים) צבוים (*Gen.* xiv, 2; 8) Q = LXX and S.P.; ויושם (*Gen.* xxiv, 33) Q = S.P. (passive). The LXX has here the active (καὶ παρέθηκεν = K ויישם), however this is an entirely different tradition since the object is in the plural (αὐτοῖς ἄρτους φαγεῖν; M.T. = S.P. לפניו; גוים (*Gen.* xxv, 23) Q = S.P. and LXX. In this case the Rabbinic midrash follows the K. (גאים) cf. *Berakhoth* 57b, *Gen.* R. 63, 9 and parallels); the same applies in the case of תאמים (*ibid.* 24 = Q = LXX = S.P. but the Rabbinic midrash follows the K. (תומים); בגד (*Gen.* xxx, 11) K = S.P. = LXX (ἐν τύχῃ) while Q יעוש בא גד; (*Gen.* xxxvi, 5; 14 — K יעיש) Q = S.P. = LXX.

the initial assumption. In other words, there exist already clear and distinctive traditions both in Scripture and exegetical methods, and, furthermore, these two elements are closely inter-related. We do not deny that exegesis depends entirely on constant harmonisation, but we maintain that this is carried out "by particular religious circles for particular varying purposes".[139] The variety present in the fluid background is then the groundwork of the distinctive features on which each group prides itself.

We turn now to a famous aggadic exposition whose underlying scriptural versions are divided amongst themselves. It will, of course, be easily understood that it is not necessary to assume that even identical texts prompt the same "common" exegesis. In *Gen.* iv, 8, the Samaritan Pentateuch agrees with the LXX version in adding ("and Cain said unto Abel his brother") "let us go out".[140] Had there existed any common tradition, the Samaritan, whose official text included the words "let us go out", which is here the 'source' and the beginning of the midrashic conversation and dispute between the brothers,[141] the Samaritans could surely not have ignored such a challenge. What do we actually find in the Samaritan exegesis? Not only is there no trace of any theological dispute between the brothers [often supposed to form "the sources, based on the pre-masoretic reading, which they (i.e. these sources)

---

[139] cf. Vermes, *op. cit.* p. 229. Despite all similarities, the biblical exegesis of each group depended on their respective peculiar traditions. This is true not only concerning halakhic expositions but also in aggadah. Even the Qumran Sect, which in some respects resembles one group and in other respects another, was not experiencing any general chaos in the field of interpretation. The Sect clearly followed its distinct hermeneutical tradition (cf. my article, *op. cit.* pp. 120ff., 157ff., nn. 188ff.). It is wellknown that one of the devices upon which the *Pesher* is built is the 'atomizing of Scripture'. cf. Brownlee, "Biblical Interpretation etc." *BA.* XIV (1951) pp. 54ff. These devices were, nevertheless, distinct from those of the Rabbis. Often by exaggerated claims 'hermeneutical rules' as Gemaṭria and Notriqon were forcibly extracted from the Scrolls (cf. Yadin, "Three notes etc.", *IEJ* VI, 1956, pp. 158ff.). Even if we find the same "hermeneutical principles" as known from Rabbinic literature utilized by other Sects (cf. Ch. III *passim*) this in itself does not prove identity. It is undeniable that the Qumran sect used also some devices in common with the Rabbis (cf. N. Slomovic "Hermeneutical customs etc." *Revue de Qumran*, vii, 1969, pp. 162ff.). This in itself, however, does not entitle us to speak about "midrash pesher", or harmonizing Rabbinic exegesis with that of Qumran (cf. my article *op. cit.* pp. 159f., nn. 204ff).

[140] S.P.: נלכה השדה S.T.: נהלך לברה

[141] Vermes, "The Targumic version of *Gen.* iv, 3-16", *ALUOS* III (1963), pp. 83ff. (cf. specially pp. 100f.).

supplement with a long and significant haggadah"][142] but this midrashic element is conspicuously absent from Samaritan literature. Instead, we find that the Samaritans attribute the whole hatred between the brothers, not to any theological dispute, but to pure jealousy, caused by the favouritism of their parents. According to the *Asaṭir* Adam loved Abel, while Eve loved Cain.[143] The distinctively Samaritan exegesis is evident here, which bases the hatred on independent analogical devices, namely by comparing this story with the story of Jacob and Esau (*Gen.* xxv, 28) and that of Joseph and his brethren (*ibid.* xliv, 20).

It has moreover to be taken into account that the Rabbinic legends, going back also to ancient sources (cf. e.g. the Book of Jubilees) are also bent on looking for a mundane cause of the hatred, and do not attribute it to a theological dispute between the brothers. Amongst the reasons given, we find that the quarrel arises from jealousy because of a woman, or from the division of property.[144]

An attractive suggestion has been made that "the dispute between Cain and Abel may represent the controversy between Sadducees and Pharisees concerning the world to come".[145] But this theory is not tenable either. First of all, the motive of the "Day of Judgement" is put forward in Onqelos (verse 7),[146] which otherwise faithfully follows the Masoretic Text and has no trace of the aggadic dispute between the brothers; and secondly, Philo, (although following the LXX and similarly putting a

---

[142] *ibid.* p. 101. It is only natural that Onqelos follows the M.T. But even the other Targumim may have developed their exegesis upon the M.T. and the "let us go out" is only a midrashic (and not variant reading!) detail. It has to be borne in mind that the ambiguous text ("And Cain said to his brother. And it came to pass...") calls for an elucidation. It is only natural that amongst the answers given on the problem: "What did Cain say?", "let us go out", should take precedence, since the verse follows: "when they were in the field".

[143] *Asaṭir* I, 6ff. No significance is attached in Samaritan exegesis to the expression "let us go out" and no discussion between the brothers is ever mentioned. It seems that Samaritan exegetical traditions are following an independent line based on analogy, which has its roots in ancient times. The same analogy is employed by Marqah in a dfferent context. He compares the generations of Cain to those of the sons of Jacob, "I have chastized them by My Justice, but did not blot out their name" (*Memar* I, pp. 101f. = II, pp. 167f.).

[144] Ginzberg, *Legends of the Jews* I, p. 108; V. pp. 138f. (n. 17).

[145] Vermes, *ALUOS* III, p. 103. It is also most unlikely that the Pharisean controversy against the Sadducees should be based on a non-conformist textual variant.

[146] It is also remarkable that although the S.T. does not explicitly mention יום דינה the sense is very similar to that of Onqelos. cf. also Gaster, *Sam. Oral Law* I, p. 150.

theological dispute concerning divine justice into the mouths of the brothers)[147] is not at all suspect of polemicising against the Sadducees.

We are thus justified in concluding that it is far simpler to interpret the exegetical traditions in the light of their own individual character. The similarities, or even 'parallels', point rather to common problems and queries, which are solved by each group in accordance with its own tradition.

Although, as we have seen, the Jerusalem Targum occasionally represents non-normative views,[148] it is not necessary to postulate that it always represents "pre-masoretic *readings*". Even if the targumists were not aware of the *text* containing the words "Let us go out", this phrase could have been added, like all the other aggadic embellishments, as a result of the exegesis of this ambiguous passage. Again, as we have seen, all exegetes try to tackle the thorny problem of the hatred between the brethren. Had a common ancient aggadic motive existed, the Samaritans who supposedly preserved the so-called "pre-masoretic text", would surely have complied with such an exegetical tradition.

A further note may usefully here be added, though not too much reliance should be placed on this point. Some indication that the various exegetical traditions, which attempt elucidations of the text "let us go out", are really independent is the salient fact that none of the 'splinter-groups' have in this case any axe to grind; no polemical issue is here involved.[149] Nevertheless, there are clearly great differences of exegesis amongst those who possess the very same text.[150]

For such reasons as these, the legends concerning Abraham and "Ur (i.e. fire) of the Chaldees" are evidently aggadic expansions, such as would readily occur to all exegetes. One thus cannot speak of a common

---

[147] cf. Ginzberg, *ibid.* (n. 16). Philo's reconstruction of the dispute between the two brothers is very similar to that of the Rabbis, and deals also with Divine providence. But it is evidently dependent on the LXX rendering of v. 7 (probably understood as follows: הלא (אם היטבת שאת׳ לא היטבת לְפֶּתַח) חַטָּאת? רבץ! ואתה תמשל בו (= ἀποστρέφω cf. also *Gen.* III, 16) אליך תשובתו. From this it would be evident that the theological argument of the brothers originates not from the additional words of v. 6, but from the implications of v. 7.

[148] cf. *sup.* n. 127 and n. 142.

[149] cf. *sup.* nn. 145-147.

[150] The most striking difference is between the exegesis of Philo (= LXX) and that of the Samaritans (= S.P.). cf., however, Geiger, *Urschrift etc.*, pp. 249, followed by Gaster, *The Sam. Oral Law etc.* I, p. 44.

"strictly midrashic literary *genre*".[151] At least as regards the Samaritan midrashim, it seems beyond all doubt to be the case that the 'Birth-stories of all the Righteous' are mutually interwoven. Parallels to the legends surrounding the births of the heroes are accordingly freely borrowed from the legend of Moses and made to apply, not only to Abraham, but even to Noah.[152] Despite all the outward features shared in common with other groups (which are obviously midrashic answers to identical questions), the method prescribed by the interpretive tradition always gives to the Samaritan midrash its peculiar colouring. Although we are not here concerned with drawing comparisons between other groups, we may add that the same sort of difference of colouring is found on comparing the exegetical tradition of the Dead Sea Scroll Sect with that of the Rabbis.[153]

The same considerations apply equally to the legends surrounding the "binding of Isaac"; but the hermeneutical problem confronting all exegetes is created by the fact that Isaac appears in Scripture rather as an anti-hero. All the promises are in fact said to be bound up with Abraham and to redound to his honour (עקב אשר שמע אברהם) (*Gen.* xxvi, 3, 4, 5, 24 etc.). Nevertheless, the Samaritan exegete needs no extra-pentateuchal sources for building up his image of Isaac,[154] for the central point in the story of the binding of Isaac, *Gen.* xxii, 14, is already regarded by him as the proper source of such an image. The Samaritan Targum renders this verse as "in the Mount the Lord was seen";[155]

---

[151] The connections between the Rabbinic aggadah and the Book of Jubilees (Vermes, *Scripture & Tradition etc.*, p. 89, n. 1) is not more convincing than previous hypotheses, repudiated as being "chain of conjectures" (*ibid.* p. 91, n. 1).

[152] *Asaṭir* II, 15ff. (on Noah) and *ibid.* V, 16f. (on Abraham). Gaster's 'parallels' from the Apocryphal Literature (Asaṭir pp. 20ff.) are entirely irrelevant (cf. Ben-Ḥayyim, *Tarbiz* xiv (1943), pp. 104ff.).

[153] "Thy reward shall be exceedingly great" (*Gen.* xv, 1) is explained by the Rabbis as referring to the "world to come". The reason why the Genesis Apocryphon "appears not to be very preoccupied with after life" (Vermes, *Scripture etc.*, p. 121) depends rather on a different exegetical tradition (cf. also the same division of Tradition on *Gen.* iv, 8, *sup.* nn. 141ff.).

[154] Even for "the targumic belief that at the moment of sacrifice Isaac saw a divine, vision" there is absolutely no necessity to bring in the analogy to "the Servant of the Lord" (*Isaiah* liii). At any rate the artificial גזרה שוה of יראה (*Gen.* xxii, 14 = *Isaiah* liii, 11) has no support from any midrashic or Targumic source (cf. Vermes, *Scripture etc.*, p. 202, n. 1).

[155] ה׳ יראה דיתמר יומן בטורה ה׳ יחזי ינפש Actually the Targum does not translate יראה as Niph'al (= יֵרָאֶה) but as Qal (יִרְאֶה): in the former case the translation should

and in accordance with the constant tendency of the Targum to seek to eliminate any anthropomorphic expression,[156] this must not be allowed, of course, to be understood in the literal sense. Following a hint in early Samaritan exegesis, it has to be understood in the sense "God would manifest Himself by granting all requests made there".[157] It is indeed possible that this sense was already hinted at by the free translation of the LXX;[158] nevertheless it would not therefore be right to identify these two traditions.

The distinctiveness of the Samaritan exegesis becomes clear from the words of Marqah [159] ... "like Abraham when he came here (i.e. to Hargerizim) and was tested and had to bind Isaac, his son; he placed him on the altar and sought to do what he was commanded. God knew the sincerity of his heart and opened the *Garden* and sent him deliverance. He heard the blessing from the midst of heaven more than all (i.e. the Meritorious) who had gone before (him), *For I will surely bless you,* (Genesis xii, 17) ... do actions and walk like Isaac *when he saw his Lord*

---

have been יתחזי /יתנפש). The proper translation is "in the Mount the Lord will see". Nevertheless, we kept closer to the M.T. since this sense is also implied (cf. next note). It has been observed that the last word יראה is doubly translated (S. Kohn, *Sam. Studien*, p. 34). But it does not represent two Hebrew versions יראה and ירבה because ירבה should be translated as יסגי (or יסגה). It is more likely that the two words יחזי and ינפש are synonymous, originating from two separate translations of יראה. We find in fact the root נפש employed in a figurative sense, viz. "a man of wide views" (נבון) translated as נפוש. cf. Ben-Ḥayyim, *Literary and Oral Tred.* II, p. 528, n. 426).

[156] Although the Targum on this place eliminates the difficulty by translating "God will see", it is implied that Isaac was an exception who had the 'vision' (cf. nn. 159 and 162f.). Such devices are common to exegetes who try to eliminate the anthropomorphistic expression of "seeing God". In a similar vein was *Ex.* xxiv, 10, explained, "and they *feared* the God of Israel" ודחלו (=) מן אל' ישר' cf. also v. 11 (M.T. ויחזו, S.P. ויאחזו, S.T. ואחדו עם הא'). However, this easy way was not always possible (cf. *Ex.* xxxii, 20 and *ibid.* 23). Thus *Num.* xii, 8 was rendered the S.T. "and the radiance of the Lord shall be behold" ונעירות ה' יסתכל (=) נהירות).

[157] *Memar Marqah* (ed. Macdonald) I, p. 49 (= II, p. 78). This passage is late (judging from the language), but it represents the same type of (double) exegesis as the S.T. '(ברא השלישי עשר מקרתה דאברהם « שם המקום ההוא ה' יראה » י"ב י"ד) הודיע (=) « אשר יאמר היום » אן כל מדרש דידרש עליו (=) « בהר » לא ישוב מחסנה ריק (=) « ה' יראה »).

[158] ἐν τῷ ὄρει Κύριος ὤφθη On the relationship of ὁράω and the pass. ὤφθη cf. J.H. Moulton, *A Grammar of N.T. Greek* (3rd ed., Edinburgh 1908), pp. 110f. (cf. n. 160).

[159] *op. cit.* pp. 65f. (= II, p. 104).

and He multiplied his Blessing... He blessed him and went to Beersheba".
The Samaritan tradition thus derives from the 'seeing of Isaac" (although
it may have some vague parallels in other systems) a quite unique understanding. This fact can be fully realized only if we look more deeply
into the general Samaritan tradition; and in this tradition, Genesis
xxii, 2, already hints in the same direction. Admittedly, the understanding
of the expression "Land of Moriah" as "Land of Vision" is not exclusively Samaritan [160] but here there is more involved than the mere
translation of a proper placename, and more significant is the specifically
Samaritan exegesis which identifies "one of the mountains" (*ibid.*)
with Hargerizim.[161] If we now collate these details, we shall conclude
that the Samaritan exegetes see in Isaac the major hero of this legend,
since his vision is manifestly superior to that of Abraham.

This picture becomes clearer if we look at another Samaritan variant
reading: *Gen.* xxiv, 62, is understood by them as "and Isaac came (by
the way) of the desert (to) the well of living visions".[162] Although this
translation is substantially shared by the LXX, the general method
of Samaritan exegesis combining as it does these details into a whole,
is still unique, for it enables them to identify the well with the "Land of
Vision" to which he frequently went to worship.[163] We have deliberately

---

[160] S.P. המוראה S.T. חזיתה. This tradition is more explicitly stated by Marqah
(*op. cit.* I, p. 46; II, p. 74) ארעה מחזיה cf. also Ben-Ḥayyim, *Literary and Oral etc.*
II, p. 506, n. 131. That this was not an exclusive Sam. tradition can be verified from
Symmachus (τῆς ὀπτασίας) and Vulg. (visionis). A divergent tradition is that of the LXX
εἰς τὴν γῆν τὴν ὑψηλὴν = האמורי?). While the Syriac text (ܐܪܥܐ ܕܐܡܘܪܝܐ =
המרום?) may be identified with Jerusalem and the tradition of the M.T. cf. II Chronicles
III, 1. Obviously the divergent textual traditions point also to differences in exegesis
amongst the various groups.

[161] cf. *sup.* n. 157. The twelfth name of Hargerizim is "*One* of the Mountains"
(*Gen.* xxii, 2). Such harmonizations are frequent, thus "in *one* of your tribes" (*Deut.*
xii, 14) was similarly understood as the chosen tribe, i.e. Joseph. This was further
harmonized with *Gen.* xlviii, 22 (S.P. ואני נתתי לך שכם אחת). Shechem is this verse
(feminine) refers to the holy city. Here again one finds a similar reading in the LXX
(Σίκιμα). Nonetheless, the peculiar Sam. provenance of these harmonizations is
obvious (cf. also *inf.* n. 163).

[162] S.T. ויצחק אתי במדברה באר קעימה חזי (it may also be translated "well of
everlasting vision"). In this case there is also an affinity with the translation of the
LXX ('Ισαὰκ δὲ διεπορεύτο διὰ τῆς ἐρήμου κατὰ τὸ φρέαρ τῆς ὁράσεως). This fact only
adds weight to the antiquity of the Samaritan textual tradition, but, as said before,
does not betray common exegetical traditions. cf. next note.

[163] לשוח is translated by S.T. למצלאה. This interpretation is also shared by
others (LXX: ἀδολεσχῆσαι; Vulg. meditandum; cf. also *Berakhoth* 28a). It has to be

enlarged on these details because the various parallels attest the antiquity of these particular exegetical traditions. At the same time, it has again to be emphasized that these parallels as a whole in no way prove either influence or identity. Although indeed they share here and there in matters of detail some of the Samaritan traditions, none of the other traditions has ever connected this aggadic motive with Hargerizim.

At this point, it will not surprise us to learn that Salem (*Gen.* xiv, 18), identified by some traditions with Jerusalem [164] is by the Samaritan identified again with Hargarizim. But this is not the only distinguishing mark in their interpretation of this context. The ambiguous expression "and he gave him the tithe of everything" (*Gen.* xiv, 20) is understood by most traditions as having Abraham for the subject, that is, he gave the tithe to Melchizedek.[165] However, Samaritan tradition understands this expression to mean that the King of *Sodom* gave the tithe to Abraham.[166]

It is only to be expected, therefore, that, despite those slight textual differences which permanently divide the groups and their exegesis, in those cases (the great majority) where an almost identical text is the source of exegesis, we may well find great similarities of interpretation even amongst opposing groups, especially when doctrinal issues are not involved. Very little attention has been paid by those propogating of harmonising tendencies to the fact that, no less than their 'parallels', it is the fine points both of text and of exegesis, which essentially separate the groups, which are of primary and crucial importance.

As a matter of fact, the gulf dividing the various systems of exegesis is wider than could be observed from the standpoint of haphazard and often superficial comparisons. To take as an illustration the use of symbolism for the "centre of worship", this hardly exists amongst the Samaritans. Although other groups freely develop the symbol of

---

stressed that notwithstanding all these similarities in *details*, the major exegetical line of the Samaritans of identifying the "vision" with Hargerizim is unique. This is already a central point in the Samaritan "Ten Commandments (= *Num.* xi, 30)". This is the major source of all other harmonization; "near the *meadow of visions* opposite Schechem" (מול שכם מורא אלון אצל S.T. חזוה = חזבה מישר cf. also *Gen.* xii, 6 (S.P. מרא S.T. חזבה).

[164] cf. Vermes, *Scripture and Tradition etc.*, p. 119. The parting of the ways did not end with this identification, but it produced a whole chain reaction. cf. following nn.

[165] This is clearly indicated by the Genesis Apocryphon. cf. Vermes, *op. cit.* pp. 108f., 119f.

[166] cf. Part III, nn. 86f.

"Lebanon" in reference to the Temple at Jerusalem,[167] this finds no echo amongst the Samaritans. If the early followers of this tradition may have found a Pentateuchal peg in *Deut.* iii, 25 "that goodly mountain and the Lebanon", it is due to the other scriptures of the Prophets and Hagiographa that this expression becomes synonymous with "that goodly mountain of the Lebanon".[168] The Samaritan likewise takes the expression "the goodly mountain" as a reference to Hargerizim,[169] but owing to his rejection of all the scriptures except the Pentateuch, no symbolism based on the Lebanon is ever even suggested in the Samaritan literature. Nor is this difference fortuitous. The identification of this 'mountain' with the 'mountain of blessing' (cf. *Deut.* xi, 29) and other expressions in the Pentateuch, belongs to the cardinal tenets of Samaritan belief as based on their specific exegesis. The protracted polemical attacks of the Rabbis undoubtedly attest the antiquity of these specific forms of exegesis among the Samaritans.[170] It is not at all impossible that this polemic has its earlier form already in the Genesis Apocryphon.[171]

In contrast with such exegetical differences, there must have been more closely similar *neutral* traditions which could easily wander from one group to the other or may even go back to a common ancient targumic tradition wellknown in the whole of ancient Palestine. Place names, for example, are often translated by various traditions in the same way.[172] Nevertheless, such similarities or even "parallels" are much too commonplace to tempt us to attach to them more significance than they deserve.

---

[167] Vermes, *op. cit.* pp. 26ff.

[168] *ibid.* pp. 36f.

[169] *Memar Marqah* (ed. Macdonald) I, pp. 46ff.; II, pp. 73ff. cf. *sup.* n. 161.

[170] *Gen. R.* lxxxi, 3. ברικא טורא בהדא לצלאה טב ולא (a reference to the Samaritan interpretation of *Deut.* xi, 29, namely, that Hargerizim is the "Blessed Mountain". cf. also Jer. *'Abhodah Zarah*, V, 4; 44d, and another version in *Gen. R.* xxxii, 16 and parallels. As early as the end of the first century C.E. the Rabbis tried to deny that the Biblical Har Gerizim is near Shechem, cf. *Tosaphoth on Zebhaḥim* 113, s.v. לא cf. Geiger, *Urschrift*, p. 81. cf. n. 163 *sup.*

[171] Vermes, *op. cit.* p. 97, n. 2. There is absolutely no need to connect this with the Rabbinic midrash. Only by casuistic arguments may one harmonize all the sources. The Gen. Apoc. is not necessarily connected with the Pesher (or with the Qumran Sect in general!) and both are different from Rabbinic exegesis. cf. Vermes, *op. cit.* p. 35, nn. 3-5.

[172] e.g. Nile = Pishon or Gihon. cf. *Memar Marqah* (ed. Macdonald) I. p. 166; or, *Num.* xiii, 22 צען = S.T. טנס, LXX Τανις cf. Vermes, pp. 98f. (n. 4), 123 and cf.

By fastening our critical attention on one seemingly unimportant detail, we may perhaps be enabled to put our case into its proper perspective. It has been claimed that the story of Balaam may lead us back to the "scriptural origins of the Aggadah", or, in other words, that the primitive exegesis may "coincide with that of the last redactors" of Scripture.[173] We are not at all concerned here to discuss the validity of such claims, but rather to show that such speculations (valuable or otherwise) have absolutely no relevance to Samaritan exegesis. The touchstone of our claim for a distinctive Samaritan tradition is not to be sought so much in the detailed analysis of origins as in the general pattern emerging from Samaritan literature. As compared with the exegesis of other groups utilising Scripture like Micah vi, 5 and Nehemiah xiii, 2 that of the Samaritan, of course, relies on the Pentateuchal sources only. But in these sources alone there is quite enough material for creating a harmonised picture of Balaam.[174]

It is then perhaps not surprising that, as in the Talmudic literature [175] so also in that of the Samaritans, Balaam is depicted as the arch-villain. This, however, does not prevent either group from utilising his 'oracles' as prophecies of the future. The two contradictory portraits seem to cause little conflict in the minds of the ancient exegetes. Thus *Num.* xxiv, 5-6 (uttered at the command of God) might equally well by both groups, be reckoned amongst the most sacred possessions of the nation.[176] Similarly, *ibid.* verse 7, and others, are explained in messianic terms.[177]

BDB p. 858. Or, שעיר = גבלה = Gebal (S.T. *Gen.* xxxii, 4; xxxvi, 9; *Deut.* i, 2; ii, 1, 5; xxxiii, 2). cf. Gaster, *Asaṭir*, pp. 92f.; Vermes, *op. cit.* p. 118.

[173] Vermes, *ibid.* pp. 127f.

[174] The same result could be achieved by harmonizing *Num.* xii, with *ibid.* xxxi, 8, 6 and *Deut.* xxiii, 5-6.

[175] *Abhoth* vii, 2; *Soṭah* 10b; *Sanhedrin* 104a f. etc. cf. following notes.

[176] cf. *Memar Marqah* (ed. Macdonald) I, pp. 119f. (= II, p. 197). This midrash as well as those of the Rabbis or even those of their predecessors (cf. Vermes, *op. cit.* pp. 125ff. "The Scriptural origin of Haggadah" and *ibid.* pp. 157ff.) cannot be classified in accordance with categories borrowed from Source-critical, or documentary hypotheses. All midrash, at least in the form known to us, is built by its very nature upon harmonizations. This process, feeding on the eliminating of any discrepancies, would certainly blur even the most remote clues which might have pointed back to the sources of the pre-redacted Scriptural text. cf. my article *op. cit.* pp. 109f., 143f. (nn. 95ff.).

[177] On the curious history of various publications of the Sam. eschatological commentary on these verses, cf. Gaster, "Der Messias etc.", *ZDMG* lxiv (1910), pp. 446ff. cf. Vermes, *op. cit.* p. 159. Some of the other Samaritan legends on Balaam

One might go on and adduce similar 'parallels'. This however, will not bring us any nearer to our purpose. Disregarding this common ground, one point becomes clear: that, while Samaritan exegesis is built solely on the somewhat indiscriminate harmonisation of verses from the Pentateuch, the exegesis of the Rabbis, though depending on the same sort of system, employs also verses from other parts of the Bible;[178] and even if we assume, for instance, that Pseudo-Philo represents a tradition earlier than that of the two-above-mentioned groups, the possible difference in outlook need not be due to a radically different *milieu*. In any case, if that author could present a portrait of Balaam which reproduces even one of the so-called documentary sources,[179] there is no conceivable reason why the Targumim or the other early exegetical traditions could not do the same.

We must therefore hold to our originally propounded view that all the exegetical traditions are equally engaged in harmonisation; and once such harmonisations are known to be indiscriminately employed, surely all speculation regarding distinctive "ancient" sources is hopelessly wide of the mark. The now wellknown fact that all midrash is largely based on harmonisation makes all such speculation concerning its supposed dependence on "the documentary hypothesis" most unconvincing; and as regards the specifically Samaritan exegesis in particular, such speculation has no relevance whatsoever.

There is little doubt that the 'common' biblical exegesis always runs counter to the traditional Samaritan teachings whenever basic doctrinal issues are involved. To take as an example the curious story of Moses' returning to Egypt (*Ex.* iv, 24-26), it is evident that the differences between

---

are to be found in *Asaṭir*, Ch. X, 1-2 (ed. Gaster, pp. 284ff.). The Chronicles speak also about the Book of Balaam which caused the corruption of the Israelites in the period of Eli. cf. Vilmar, *Abulfathi Annales etc.*, p. 37, and recently Macdonald, *Sam. Chron. No. II*, pp. 110f. (Hebrew text, pp. 39f.).

[178] Taking only a few examples; the legend describing Balaam as an expert magician who could calculate the exact hour of God's wrath on Israel (*Berakhoth* 7a), or the comparison of Balaam's blessings to the curses of Ahiyah (*Ta'anith* 20a), are based on the employment of extra-Pentateuchal verses.

[179] cf. *sup.* n. 176. The whole argument is self-contradictory (cf. Vermes, *op. cit.* pp. 175-177). There is no sharp demarcation line in the *genre* of the various midrashim. Just as the Samaritans could develop a harmonized midrash without the aid of Scripture outside the Pentateuch, so could earlier midrashim (which are of the same character) project a harmonized portrait of Balaam. The resemblance to the P source is rather coincidental.

the various exegetical systems have become quite unbridgeable. It is of course true that the problems facing all the ancient exegetes are in all cases exacting;[180] nevertheless, the Samaritan exegete is at all times concerned with such specific solutions as are in keeping both with his own spiritual background and with his own version of the Pentateuch.

Whether or not the current theories regarding the so-called "common exegetical trends" have any real value or not, the Samaritans have no need of any such concept for their solutions. Thus, any sort of connection between the "blood of circumcision" and *Ex.* xxiv, 8, would be totally ruled out by the very nature of the Samaritan exegetical tradition. Despite the rigorous adherence of the Samaritans to this rite of circumcision (cf. *Gen.* xvii, 14, S.P.) the fact is that we hardly find in Samaritan literature any allusion to the redemptive power of blood. Such an *argumentum e silentio* has perhaps no great weight; but there are other clues which point to an entirely different textual and exegetical trend amongst the Samaritans. There is for instance a slightly variant reading in the Samaritan Pentateuch which shows that the principal hero of the narrative in their understanding, is neither Moses nor the infant but Zipporah.[181] Furthermore, there is an oral tradition implying a different reading,[182] which tends to explain away the whole notion of a *killing* of Moses or of the infant; it is understood that the verse refers to a *frightening* only. This change in the implied reading makes it also easier to understand the whole story as in fact dealing with an entirely different subject. The Samaritan exegetes understand that the theme of the passage is not circumcision, but the separation of Zipporah from Moses.[183] The Samaritans are not, of course, the only group who gloss

---

[180] cf. Vermes, *op. cit.* pp. 178ff.

[181] This is based on the variant spelling in *Ex.* iv, 26. M.T. ממנו S.P. ממנה.

[182] Although the spelling in both versions (M.T. = S.P.) is the same המיתו (*Ex.* iv, 24), the oral tradition preserved in Sam. reading (ל)המיתו? T.S. (למעצמאתה) understood this word differently. The root was not מות (as understood by all other versions) but המה meaning to disturb, frighten, to overwhelm etc. cf. Part II, nn. 82ff. and Part III, n. 78.

[183] At a point where one would expect Marqah to deal with this problem, (*Memar, op. cit.* I, p. 11; II, p. 14) there is no detailed exposition of this episode. It is disappointing to find this great Samaritan writer glossing over such an important issue (cf. נתן אפרשו and its implications in *Memar Marqah*, as discussed in Part II, n. 65). Despite Marqah's relative silence we may infer from his own words that he interpreted this passage in the same sense as it was found in later Samaritan exegesis. Even the *reading* of המיתו may be seen reflected in his words (*ibid.*) "and Moses'

over this episode.[184] Nevertheless, the silence and the glossing over of these points on the part of other may quite well (as we have seen) have their source in entirely different traditions.[185]

---

children turned back from close proximity (of Mount Sinai) as they were *afraid that night* of what they saw".

[184] cf. Vermes, *op. cit.* pp. 184-185.

[185] Since the investigation of the comparative exegesis of *Ex.* iv, 24-26 is outside the scope of the present work, we cannot indulge in the luxury of examining all the minute details of these verses, and the ways the various exegetes interpreted them (cf. Vermes, *op. cit.* pp. 178-192). Even so, it would be irresponsible to avoid at least some hints concerning the place which Samaritan exegesis occupies in the general picture of comparative interpretation. That there is an intimate connection between exegesis and theology is undeniable. But it is both misleading and self-contradictory to state in the same context that "in ancient Judaism systematic theology was unknown... and the development of doctrines and beliefs were effected within the framework of scriptural interpretation" and immediately to single out one type of exegesis as "of no great import to the faith and religious practice of Israel" and another as a "fundamental dogma" (*ibid.* p. 178). While modern critics may or may not agree to a certain theological classification which is based on a scale of priorities or preferences, the ancient exegete would not admit any such divisions (or dichotomy) into the "Word of God". It is similarly inaccurate to say that "the underlying Hebrew text (of the ancient versions of *Ex.* iv, 24f.) appears to be identical with the M.T." (*ibid.* p. 179). Apart from the fact that the S.P. was not taken into account (cf. *sup.* nn. 180-182), much more serious is the gratuitous glossing over of the variants of the LXX (cf. Vermes *op. cit.* p. 180, n. 1). It seems to us that we are confronted here with exegetical traditions based on variant scriptural readings. One could easily discern between exegetes following distinct lines as developed from their respective scriptural traditions. (cf. my article *op. cit. passim*). It would even be easy to 'reconstruct' the Hebrew background of the LXX (or proto-LXX), differing greatly from the M.T.:

(כ״ג) ... הנני הורג את בנך בכורך (כ״ד) ויהי בדרך במלון ויפגעהו ה' ויבקש המיתו (כ״ה) ... ותפגע לרגליו ותאמר חתם דם מולת בני (פגע = רות א' ט״ז)•

The centre of the story is the infant who was attacked because the "blood of the covenant of circumcision was not established". No implication of "sacrificial meaning" or "redemptive power of blood" should be read into this simple expression. The simple supplication (and later identical remark, v. 26) speaks of the neglected 'covenant' which was now finalized. It is absolutely unnecessary to suggest that this act has any connection with thoughts imported from the N.T. (ἡ καινή διαθήκη ἐν τῷ αἵματι μου *Luke* xxii, 20). The analogy of Vermes (*ibid.* p. 180) with *Luke* viii, 33 is likewise untenable. If the Armenian version is reliable, then the word ἔστη was not in its LXX *Vorlage* (perhaps [τοῦτο γάρ] ἐστιν το αἷμα κ.τ.λ. = (כי) הנה דם מולת בני)? But the Ethiopic version, on the other hand, is heavily loaded with N.T. ideology! Although the LXX (in common with other Targumim, cf. S.T. on *Gen.* v, 24, *sup.* n. 50; and Pseudo-Jonathan on *Gen.* xxxii, 29 etc.), changed the identity of the attacker to "the *Angel* of the Lord", later exegetes of this school (cf. Vermes, *op. cit.* p. 184) were still disturbed by this story and preferred to ignore it.

Such illustrations of the distinctively Samaritan exegetical tradition might be greatly multiplied. We cannot enter here into great detail or examine all the cases in which the Samaritans show quite clearly that,

---

This is a well known apologetical device of Hellenistic Jews, to gloss over difficulties (cf. SLTh. pp. 701ff.). The followers of the M.T. could not adopt such a system. No part of the Law could be ignored. The Targumim accordingly interpreted the passage in the vein of 'sin and punishment', in which the attack is aimed against Moses. Thus "the Angel" was transformed into the powers of evil: Pseudo-Jonathan (24) מלאך (26) מחבלא (25) Fragmentary Targum; מלאך חבלא (25, 26) מלאכא די״י מותא. This reminds us of the Talmudic equation of all evil agencies הוא השטן הוא יצה״ר הוא מלאך המ׳ (Babha Bathra 16a). Obviously there are in this tradition mitigating circumstances, to minimize the guilt of Moses. There is some similarity to this position in the Book of Jubilees (cf. Vermes op. cit. p. 185). It is, however, a very complicated problem to determine what type of textual version was followed in this work. Both the proto-Samaritan (or Palestinian) and the proto-Masoretic text could equally qualify as the source expounded by Jubilees. Long ago, however, it had been realized that all attempts to harmonize the traditions of Jubilees with those of any other known group would fail (Geiger, Urschrift etc., p. 480). While the book is written in a midrashic vein, it differs from later midrashim (cf. Bibliography B. Beer and Albeck). It is a tendentiously written book, mainly concerned with religious problems which were violated by Hellenistic influence (cf. H.H. Rowley, The Relevance of Apocalyptic, 2nd ed., 1949, pp. 84ff.). Jubilees portrays all the Patriarchs as paragons of piety, who kept the entire Law. Circumcision is greatly stressed (Jub. xv, 11f., 26) and those who are not circumcised belong to the realm of Belial (= Beliar, ibid. 33). Moses is described as praying that the spirit of Belial may not rule over Israel (ibid. I, 20). Therefore the whole idea that Moses might be guilty of neglecting the rite must have been anathema to the author of Jubilees. Actually apologetical omissions are quite frequent in the Book (e.g. Gen. xii, 10-20; ibid. xviii, 2-8; 16-33; ibid. xxx, 30-42 etc.) but they are not all of the same character. It is therefore necessary to point out that although the Samaritans have the highest regard for Moses, and are equally rigorous concerning circumcision (cf. recently Kippenberg, Gerizim etc., Register 1, s.v. "Beschneidung"), they still belong to an entirely different tradition. As we have seen, the latter explained away the whole episode as referring to the separation of Zipporah from Moses, nothing to do with circumcision. They resorted to the strangest exegetical devices, since for the Samaritans it would be unthinkable to ignore any detail of the Scripture, as was the case in the Book of Jubilees. What the author of Jubilees made of the omitted passage remains a mystery. Any exaggerated claims of affinity between Samaritanism and Jubilees (cf. Gaster, Asatir, pp. 109ff., 142) are totally unfounded (cf. sup. n. 152). Most probably the whole episode of Moses' encounter with Prince Mastema (= Beliar?) was only mentioned in Jubilees (xlviii, 2 without any reference to circumcision) because of the general dualistic tendencies of the Book (cf. x, 1-14; xi, 1-3, 11ff.; xii, 19f.; xvii, 16 - xviii, 12; xix, 28 and xlix, 2). We are here confronted with an entirely different exegetical tradition almost explicitly confessing determinism (cf. Jub. xv, 31f.). Now that actual fragments of this Book were discovered in Qumran (cf. R. de

at least in their case, the hypothesis of a "fundamental unity of exegetical tradition" is quite untenable.

We feel it to be our duty to emphasize most strongly that the foregoing examples are in no sense fortuitous exceptions. We may legitimately make the generalization that in most fields for which "a common exegetical trend", has been postulated, for the Samaritan traditions at least it provides no explanation. On the contrary, these Samaritan traditions run very largely in diametrical opposition to such common lines of exegesis. Obviously, in many cases where similar Biblical texts raise similar exegetical problems, the exegetes of the various groups tend also to find similar solutions. However, this fact in itself does not in any way prove or demand an identity of traditions.[186]

H. Genuine and quasi-Samaritanism

The need for an independent investigation of the Samaritan midrashic sources based on the earliest available Samaritan literature, has certainly become increasingly urgent in order that the results may be made available particularly to scholars working in cognate fields, who are unlikely to become specialists in these studies. Recently it became more and more usual and indeed fashionable for scholars who, for example, are primarily concerned with New Testament studies, to rely heavily on Samaritan background material. It is by no means our intention to belittle their efforts. It is, however, high time that such a thorough re-examination as we suggest should take place, so that fact may be clearly distinguished from fiction. Leaving aside for the moment all the alleged Christian influences upon the Samaritan exegesis, to which a special section has been devoted,[187] we have now to investigate the pos-

---

Vaux, "La grotte des manuscrits hébreux", *RB*. lvi, 1949, p. 597; C.C. Torrey, "A Hebrew Fragment of Jubilees", *JBL* lxxi, 1952, pp. 39ff.), the affinities and meanings of all these speculations about Belial and Mastemah became clearer. cf. A. Dupont-Sommer, *The Jewish Sect of Qumran and the Essenes* (transl. R.D. Barnett, London-N.Y., 1955), pp. 118-130.

[186] By the very nature of the narratives, especially of the Patriarchs, the exegetical midrashim of most groups were bound to have some resemblance to each other. If, for example, "all haggadic stories (of the ספר הישר) are intended as an answer to real exegetical questions" (Vermes, *op. cit.* p. 95), it is not surprising that earlier exegetes hit on similar solutions. As long as the textual traditions did not diverge, the similarity of exegesis neither proves identity nor mutual influence.

[187] cf. Part II para (1).

sible bearing which certain Samaritan ideas may have had on the origins of Christianity.

We have first of all to bear in mind that, although the extant Samaritan literature dates only from the fourth century C.E., all our postulated earlier Samaritan ideas must surely have left at least some echo in our existing Samaritan sources. We have no intention of entering upon any discussion with scholars about the origins of Christianity. All that we can hope to achieve is a re-examination, based on Samaritan literature, with a view to determining whether the claims made for certain 'proofs' derived from later Samaritan literature are really justified.

Some of these claims originate from the previous century.[188] At that time very little was known of the Samaritans, and often even that little was not properly applied.[189] Most distressing to us are the extreme and highly coloured pronouncements based upon figurative phrases taken from the Samaritan Liturgy, and which were initially meant by the liturgists to be purely poetical utterances, rather than confessions of faith. Furthermore, the actual publication of such sources also left much to be desired. To take, for example, the Liturgies as then published, we cannot do better than quote an expert from the early years of this present century as saying that the older publication "is very inaccurate both in text and translation".[190] We do not really need, therefore, to refute some of these untenable opinions;[191] it is enough to express our regret that even today some scholars still take some of these older opinions seriously. But we may well ignore such mere repetitions and proceed to look into some commonly made claims.

So far we have been dealing mainly with certain questions in such a way as to aid us in gaining a clearer view of the distinctively Samaritan exegetical principles, and especially in avoiding those harmonising methods which tend to blur their specific character. We have tried to

---

[188] cf. Bibliography, Heidenheim's articles in his *Virteljahrsschrift*. Most of his gross generalizations were later summarized in *idem*. "Über die Wichtigkeit etc.", *Vorhandlungen... Zürich 1887* (Leipzig, 1888), pp. 148ff.

[189] Heidenheim himself charges others with his own defect: "Some recent works are so full of forced and strained interpretation that they rather cause damage than being of any belp" (*Bibliotheca Samaritana* I, p. x). One example of Heidenheim's pet theories which mislead other scholars was his 'proofs' that Marqah had a different version of the S.P. (cf. *idem. Bibliotheca Samaritana III*, "Marqah's samarit. Pentateuchtexte", pp. xvf. and cf. my article *op. cit.* pp. 107 and 141 n. 75).

[190] Cowley, *The Sam. Liturgy* II, p. vii.

[191] cf. Heidenheim, *Bibl. Sam.* II, pp. xxviiiff.

show, and it is hoped with some success, that 'parallelism' in a few exegetical points is far from showing identity. The resultant confusion of the distinctive features of the ancient groups and the attribution to them of a common midrashic *milieu*, are not found to be justified by the existing Samaritan literature at any rate.

In the following lines we have to examine a rather different, though related, problem. It is frequently held that a few readings in the New Testament which bear some similarity to some in the Samaritan Pentateuch are actual quotations from Samaritan sources and so betray Samaritan influences.[192] We have dealt elsewhere with the thorny problem of the ancient Pentateuchal versions;[193] but it is worth noticing at this point that doubt has now been cast on certain payri which have hitherto been very commonly held to represent fragments from the Greek translation of the Samaritan Pentateuch ($\Sigma \alpha \mu \alpha \rho \epsilon \iota \tau \iota \kappa \acute{o} \nu$). It has now been conclusively shown that these fragments are actually nothing else than fragments of one of the revisions of the LXX.[194]

For such reasons as these, if we find certain expressions in the New Testament which are attested by the Samaritan Pentateuch only, this fact is in itself still no proof that we are here confronted with Samaritan influences. Unless such 'quotations' betray a distinctively Samaritan connotation, or unless such 'quotations' figure prominently in Samaritan exegesis, one has always to reckon with the real possibility of a "neutral" and popular Palestinian version of the topic in question. One further warning: we should add that, if *in the same context* there are found side by side quotations which are demonstrably not represented by the Samaritan Pentateuch but clearly mirror readings from other versions, then the whole claim for the supposed influence of Samaritanism defeats itself.

As has already been pointed out,[195] the greater number of such so-called Samaritanisms occur in the speech of Stephen (Acts VII). In this same speech, however, there are undoubtedly motives which are certainly

---

[192] Hammer, *Traktat vom Samaritanermessias.* cf. Kahle "Untersuchungen zur Geschichte etc.", *Opera Minora*, pp. 3-37. cf. also *idem. Cairo-Geniza* (1st ed. 1947), pp. 143-147 (in the 2nd ed. these remarks are absent!).

[193] cf. my article *op. cit.* pp. 103ff., 138f. (cf. especially nn. 57ff. for further bibliography).

[194] E. Tov, "Pap. Giessen 13, 19, 22, 26: A revision of the LXX", *RB*, lxxviii (1971), pp. 355-383.

[195] cf. *sup.* n. 192.

not from the Samaritan Pentateuch.[196] The most outstanding defect in the claim for the Samaritan provenance of Stephen's speech is the statement "Then sent Joseph and called his father to him and all his kindred, 75 souls" (*Acts* vii. 14 ἐν ψυχαῖς ἑβδομήκοντα πέντε). In this instance the Samaritan Pentateuch is in entire agreement with the Masoretic Text both consistently giving the number as *seventy* only.[197] And here it is curious to note that the sixteenth-century Azaria dei Rossi had already criticised Philo precisely on the score that he followed in this instance the reading of the LXX.[198] This most striking textual variant can at least serve to indicate that there are in this speech distinctively Hellenistic (LXX) elements which have no counterpart whatever in Samaritan tradition. However, even this description is itself not exact. It has been recently shown [199] from the finds of Qumran that this particular reading is not in fact exclusively Hellenistic, but has its followers in a popular Palestinian tradition;[200] but in any case not amongst the Samaritans. We have here in this instance a tradition which is stubbornly reflected both by the Samaritans and the Rabbis, most propably on the ground of their being heavily committed to their own respective Scriptural readings.[201]

The starting-point of these claims and discussions is that "Stephen was a Samaritan, according to the native tradition preserved by Abū'l-Fatḥ".[202] Whether or not Stephen's ethnic origins are in Samaritan

---

[196] Strangely enough, even readings occurring in Pseudo-Jonathan are to be found in this speech. cf. M. Wilcox, *The Samaritanism of Acts* (Oxford, 1965), pp. 26f. and 159.

[197] In this respect Samaritan tradition is the same as that of the Rabbis. We find only the number 70, never 75. cf. Strack-Billerbeck, *Kommentar etc.* II, pp. 671f. cf. next note.

[198] *Meor Enayim* (ed. Ben Yacob, Wilno, 1863), pp. 94, 103.

[199] F.F. Bruce, *Commentary on the Book of Acts* (London, 1954), p. 165.

[200] P.W. Skehan in *New Directions etc.* (ed. Freedman-Greenfield), p. 102.

[201] Recently a monograph has been devoted by the late A. Spiro to "Stephen's Samaritan Background" [T. Munk, *The Acts of the Apostles* (revised by W.F. Albright and C.S. Mann, Anchor Bible, N.Y., 1967), Appendix V, pp. 285-300]. This makes it more convenient to re-examine the claims made out for Samaritanisms. Naturally we will have to confine our discussions to the examples which are supposed to be supported by Samaritan sources. With all fairness to this late scholar it must be emphasized that the Appendix represents a condensation of much more extensive material. If in the future the whole material will be published, some of our points must be again reconsidered.

[202] *Abulfathi Annales etc.*, ed. Vilmar, p. 159.

stock is in truth irrelevant to our problems, for the mere fact that he preaches on behalf of Christian missionary ends indicates, of course, that he has previously espoused doctrines totally alien to the 'normative' Samaritans,[203] and thereby severed himself from their standpoint. But to return to the account of Abū'l-Fath,[204] the whole context centres around Dūsis, a Samaritan heretical sectarian of the fourth century C.E.; and moreover the whole account is confused and its reliability is more then doubtful. The celebrated Simon (Magus) is mentioned, who wants to destroy Christianity and asks for the help and collaboration of the Jewish philosopher, Philo of Alexandria; the latter, however, advises him to abandon his plan. It is indeed characteristic that Abū'l-Fath puts into the mouth of Philo a paraphrase of the New Testament words attributed to *Gamliel* (*Acts.* v, 39). This in itself surely betrays that the whole story must originate from secondary (Christian) sources (pseudepigrapha).

Abū'l-Fath continues: "Then this Simon returned to Beit 'Alin and died there and was buried in the valley opposite the house of the disciple who first bore witness to (and was martyred for) the Messiah, whose name was Seftān (Stephen)."[205] There is no mention here of the Samaritan affinities of Stephen; we have rather an account of sectarians who have left the Samaritan fold. If there were any truth in the hypothesis that Stephen's martyrdom was in some way connected with the Samaritan elements in his preaching [206] Abū'l-Fath's account would surely be entirely different.

We may now probe more closely the so-called Samaritanisms in Stephen's speech.[207] The tradition that Abraham's migration to Canaan was "after the death of his father" (*Acts.* vii, 4) is based on chronological calculations derived from the Samaritan Pentateuchal Text.[208] This is

---

[203] cf. *sup.* n. 199 and *inf.* nn. 240-243.

[204] *op. cit.* pp. 151ff.

[205] وعاد شمعون وجاء الى بيت علين ومات ودفن فى الوادى مقابل
بيت التلميذ الذى شهد للمسيح اولا واسمه سفطان

[206] Spiro, *op. cit.* (cf. n. 200), p. 298. "An irate mob thus presumably lynched Stephen not because of his Christianity but because he had carried on Samaritan propaganda in Jerusalem". For such a hypothesis there is no support whether in Christian or Samaritan sources.

[207] Spiro, *op. cit.* pp. 285.

[208] Terah was 70 years old (*Gen.* xi, 26) at the birth of Abraham. Abraham left Haran at the age of 75 (= 145). Now according to the M.T. "And the days of Terah

not, however, an exclusively Samaritan tradition, and, as has already been shown, the same tradition is known to Philo;[209] We cannot then rule out the possibility that Philo has before his eyes a Greek translation containing a variant similar to that which we now find only in the Samaritan Pentateuch.[210]

The next point to engage our attention is Stephen's extraordinary statement that the Patriarchs were buried at Shechem (*ibid.* v, 15, 16).[211] It has already been rightly remarked that there exists no such Samaritan tradition;[212] the only tradition in any way similar in Samaritan literature is that which relates that the grave of Joseph lies in the vicinity of Shechem, and in their chronicles even the performance of the burial of Joseph (*Joshua* xxiv, 32) is not given any emphasis.[213] We must conclude that there is some sort of confusion in Stephen's mind, shown either by his mentioning Abraham (*Gen.* xxiii, 16f.) instead of Jacob (*ibid.* xxxiii, 19), or by his quoting *Joshua* xxiv, 32 in a very loose and generalized way.[214]

Furthermore, in verse 32 Stephen quotes *Ex.* iii, 6, but with the variant "your fathers", which is indeed characteristic of the Samaritan Pentateuch (against the singular, "your father" of M.T. and LXX.).[215] In this case again, it has been previously shown [216] that the latter reading appears also in the Ethiopic and Coptic versions, which themselves originate from the LXX tradition. Moreover there is additional evidence that the former reading was also a part of popular tradition (although shared by the Samaritans). The notion that this quotation refers to different dieties (i.e. as if the God of Abraham were not identical with

---

were two hundred and five years" (*Gen.* xi, 32) while the S.P. gives him only 145 years.

[209] cf. Kahle, *Cairo Geniza* (1st ed.), pp. 143f. cf. also Bruce, *Commentary etc.* (*sup.* n. 199), p. 162, n. 1.

[210] Strack-Billerbeck, *Kommentar etc.* II, pp. 666f. cf. also previous n.

[211] Spiro, *op. cit.* (n. 200), p. 286. Stephen "transfers the cave of Machpela from Hebron (to Shechem)".

[212] Bowman, *Sam. Probleme*, p. 72; cf. however, Kippenberg, *Garizim etc.*, pp. 112f. (and literature quoted there, but all the arguments are not well founded. cf. Montgomery *The Sam.*, pp. 107f.).

[213] Juynboll, *Chronicon Samaritanum Liber Josuae*, pp. 294ff. cf. however, J. Macdonald, *Chronicle No. II*, p. 87 (Hebrew text, p. 18). Strangely the burial of Joseph is in an entirely different place than in the M.T.

[214] Bruce, *Commentary etc.* (*sup..* n. 199), p. 165.

[215] Spiro, *op. cit.* (n. 200), p. 295 (c).

[216] Kahle, *Cairo Geniza* (1st ed.), p. 144.

that of Isaac, etc.) has had to be eliminated; and we may thus confidently affirm that the connecting word in "*and* the God of Isaac",[217] which occurs in the LXX (but not in the M.T.) confers the same meaning on the verse as if it read more explicitly "God of your fathers", in the plural. And merely as a matter of interest, the Samaritans attack the Jews on account of this missing *Waw* in the M.T., but are silent on the word "fathers".[218]

In verse 37 in the middle of a narrative which is plainly derived from *Exodus*, we suddenly find a verse from *Deuteronomy* quoted.[219] This is a more serious argument in favour of a Samaritan origin, since in the Samaritan Pentateuch, after Exodus xx, 17, there is an addition (the Samaritan Tenth Commandment) evidently composed of verses identical with some of those in *Deuteronomy* xviii. Despite the fact that Stephen's quotation is closer to *Deuteronomy* xviii, 15 (which is not found in the S.P. in Exodus) than to *Deuteronomy* xviii, 18 (which is found in the S.P. in *Exodus*) this problem has not yet found its final solution.[220] It is perhaps only possible to suggest at present that the expectation of the future Prophet was so strong within all 'non-conformist' circles that they were in the habit of stringing together all manner of 'proof-texts' from whatever source, testifying to this belief.[221]

This last question is intimately associated with the figure of Moses, which dominates the greater part of Stephen's speech. It is especially the eschatological associations surrounding Moses which are alleged to have a specifically Samaritan background.[222] But there is no need to connect a simple emphasis on the role of Moses in Stephen's speech exclusively with Samaritan thought. Admittedly, Moses as the intercessor who stands between God and Israel is undoubtedly extolled in Samaritan literature.[223] This, however, is an entirely natural exegetical outcome (*Ex.* xxxii, 11f; *ibid.* xxxiv, 5ff; *Deut.* v, 5; *ibid.* 24 (= *Ex.* xx, 16f. S.P.); *Deut.* ix, 17f, 25f.);[224] and in fact there are similar features

---

[217] S.P. וֵאלֹהֵי יצחק LXX (= Acts) καὶ θεὼς Ἰσαὰκ
[218] cf. Part II, n. 265.
[219] Spiro, *op. cit.* p. 285 (d).
[220] Kahle, *Cairo Geniza* (1st ed.), pp. 144f.
[221] cf. Strack-Billerbeck, *Kommentar etc.* II, p. 363 (and cross-references *ibid.*).
[222] Spiro *op. cit.* (n. 200), p. 290. cf. Bowman, *Sam. Probleme*, p. 72.
[223] J. Macdonald, *The Theology etc.*, pp. 211f.
[224] cf., however, Macdonald, *ibid.*

in Rabbinic literature.[225] One might add that even eschatological speculations in connection with Moses and Aaron are not at all uncommon
amongst the Rabbis.[226] However, all this is beside the point. It should
rather be made abundantly clear that if Stephen equates the figure of
Moses with "the Righteous One" (v. 53, cf. also 55f.). such a type of
'intercessor' is neither Jewish nor Samaritan,[227] but purely Christian.
The whole speech leads to this summit as an integral part of Christian
teaching.[228]

Gratuitous speculations on the supposed "downgrading of Moses"
and the complementary "upgrading of Abraham" are patently devoid
of substance.[229] This whole picture of such a "reconstructed Samaritanism" supposed to have existed before the coming of Christianity,
has absolutely no support in any sources.[230] It might perhaps be thought
worthwhile to take up certain further points in these arguments for
Stephen's Samaritan background, were it not for the fact that most of
this material is based upon fancied Samaritan "allusions", *not* on explicit
quotations. All these arguments are thus of a purely conjectural nature,
and built largely on unfounded notions.[231] We may, therefore, dispense
with a refutation of their special points, since these are even less convincing than the so-called explicit Samaritan Pentateuchal quotations.
There are likewise many rash statements made in support of similar
attempts to force the whole background of Stephen's speech into an
artificial Samaritan framework. To take only the most obvious parallel,

---

[225] *Berakhoth* 32a, etc. cf. Ginzberg, *Legends* III, pp. 106-109, 474; *ibid.* VI, pp. 165
(n. 955), 195 (n. 73).

[226] Ginzberg, *Legends* III, p. 312, VI, p. 108, n. 613 and cross-references.

[227] cf. Part II, nn. 14f., 68ff. Recently some old ideas about gnostical connections
with Moses (ἑστώς cf. Heidenheim, *Bib. Sam.* II, pp. xxxi-xl) were revived, but these
do not carry much conviction either (Kippenberg, *Garizim*, pp. 306f.).

[228] F.F. Bruce, *The Epistle of John* (London, 1970), p. 49.

[229] Spiro, *op. cit.* (n. 200), pp. 289ff.

[230] The whole concept of Sam. suddenly changing their religious attitudes is
illfounded (cf. Spiro, *op. cit.* p. 293). "But the dominance of Moses reached great
heights among the Samaritans in the *centuries that followed Stephen*(?), for the longer
they lived under the Law, the deeper became their attachment to it, and the higher
Moses rose in their estimation". Such and similar statements (cf. *ibid.* p. 296) are
absolutely without any proof. On the contrary, we have seen that the religious attitudes
of the Samaritans changed very little during these centuries. cf. *sup.* nn. 135-136.

[231] Spiro, *op. cit.* p. 286 (i) (on *Acts* vii, 7), although there is some truth in the
statement that מקום is a "typical Sam. term for shrine", the same could be said about
הר (or ההר). Thus, juggling with "changed verses" is useless!

namely, Stephen's alleged opposition to the Temple (verses 47-50),[232] this may or may not be connected with the Samaritan controversy. It seems, on the face of it, more likely that such opposition to Temple-worship has closer affinities with the opinions of Jesus (cf. *Acts* vi, 14).[233] Again, no Samaritan would say "David found favour in the sight of God" (verse 46); this was of course a common Jewish belief, and both in Christianity and in the ideology of the Dead Sea Scrolls Sect the Davidic dynasty has great significance.[234] On probing deeper into such and similar 'parallels' it soon becomes clear that most of such similarities are much easier to explain otherwise than by constructing a forced Samaritan background. Both Qumranic and Jewish Christian elements have a probably more intimate and certainly more plausible, connection with these problems than any genuine Samaritan sources can possibly have.

Yet another point which argues even more strongly against the Samaritan provenance of Stephen's speech is his attitude to the Prophets. No Samaritan would or could say, "which of the prophets have not your fathers persecuted"? (verse 52). All the later prophets are regarded by the Samaritans as imposters;[235] for this very reason alone it would be ridiculous to put extra-Pentateuchal quotations into the mouth of a Samaritan (v. 42, 43, 49, 50). Even if we consider the suggestion that such extra-Pentateuchal quotations are pressed into the service of a genuine Samaritan bigotry,[236] this position could not possibly represent 'normative' Samaritan doctrine. Such utterances can come only from syncretistic sectarians who have previously accepted, amongst other elements, some of the Prophetic heritage,[237] while retaining also some of their basic Samaritan attitudes.

It is, moreover, very difficult to support the suggestion that the expression "Hebrews" denotes Samaritans in particular.[238] On the contrary,

---

[232] Spiro, *op. cit.* p. 288, cf. also Bowman, *Sam. Probleme*, pp. 72f.

[233] cf. Montgomery, *The Sam.*, pp. 70f. (cf. note there); nor can we rule out the probable influence of other rigorous groups who objected to the 'normative' temple service on different grounds. cf. my article *op. cit.* pp. 115, 150 (n. 135). cf. recently Y. Yadin, "The Temple Scroll", *BA.* XXX (1967), pp. 135ff. and *idem.* in *New Directions etc.* (ed. D.N. Freedman & J.C. Greenfield), pp. 156-166.

[234] cf. Millar Burrows, *More Light etc.*, p. 401.

[235] cf. Part II, nn. 48ff.

[236] Spiro, *op. cit.* (cf. n. 200), pp. 287ff. (j, l, m, n etc.).

[237] cf. n. 235 *sup.*

[238] Spiro, *op. cit.* pp. 292, 294.

the Samaritan traditions teach us that the term 'Hebrew' has a much wider meaning amongst the Samaritans themselves than amongst the Jews. The Samaritans in fact normally refer to themselves as Israelites, while the term 'Hebrew' includes all the descendants of Abraham (as, for example, Ishmaelites, Edomites, etc.).[239]

For the purpose of our investigation, we are not particularly concerned with the problem of Stephen's sectarian allegiances. It is no part of our task to label his allegiances as belonging to one sect or another.[240] The only thing that matters to us is that it is almost certain that Stephen's views do not represent any genuine and unadulterated Samaritan traditions. It has even been advocated that the expression "This land in which you are *now* living" (*Acts*. vii, 4), "shows that Stephen composed this tract for use among newcomers, that is, for the Diaspora synagogues in Jerusalem".[241] But how on earth could a Samaritan be accepted in these Synagogues? Would it not be more sensible to suggest (as the name *Stephen* already implies) that he himself belonged to such Hellenistic groups [242] as were represented by these Diaspora synagogues (*Acts*. vi, 9ff.). One cannot of course entirely exclude the possibility that such Jewish, Hellenistic and Samaritan non-conformists did share some common interests; this however could only happen after they had adopted a common syncretistic ideology which would automatically exclude them from the fellowship of the "normative" groups of their upbringing.[243] We may suitable conclude our discussion with a piece of advice to the scholar, which is based on the results of recent research on the Dead Sea Scrolls:[244] "And when confronted by the variant texts of the Pentateuch presupposed by *Acts* vii, he will not jump to conclusions that Luke (or Stephen) was under Samaritan influence. Instead one should infer only that the New Testament tradition knew a developed Palestinian text... whether the text was in Hebrew still, or now in Greek".

---

[239] *Kāfi*, pp. 258f. (SLTh.A pp. 55f.).

[240] Spiro, *op. cit.* pp. 286 (e), 295, 297.

[241] Bruce, *Commentary etc.* (*sup.* n. 198), pp. 156 (on *Acts* vi, 9), 157 (*ibid.* v. 13), 160f.

[242] cf. C.S. Mann in *Acts* (Anchor Bible, *sup.* n. 200), "The Organization etc.", pp. 276ff. *idem.* ibid. Appendix VI "Hellenists etc.", pp. 301ff., and more recently F.F. Bruce, *New Testament History* (London, 1969), pp. 206ff., 215ff.

[243] M. Black, *The Scrolls and Christian Origins*, pp. 54ff.

[244] Skehan in *New Directions etc.* (ed. D.N. Freedman & J.C. Greenfield), pp. 102f.

I. Authentic Samaritan Origins

Some light has, we hope, been shed on Samaritan origins even by the negative results emerging from the examination of previous theories. Many difficulties arising from mutually contradictory assumptions have been eliminated. Any help, whatever its source may be, in the clarification of early Samaritan origins is truly welcome, since the very earliest Samaritan sources do not antedate the fourth century C.E.

Our views on the probable origins of Samaritan exegesis are and must be intimately connected with our views on the origins of the Samaritan Pentateuch. The thorny problem of the alleged 'revisions' and 'corruptions' of this text has very closely, and fruitfully, engaged the interests of scholars since the early 19th century. Although often expressing somewhat exaggerated views, even these early studies [245] retain much of their value even in our own day. We cannot here enter into the details of the suggested datings, nor can we even devise guide-lines for such an investigation,[246] since this lies qiute outside the framework of our present task. Four purpose it is quite sufficient to observe that all the available Samaritan literature amply testifies that there was in the possession of this group a definite *textus receptus*, rigorously followed by all commentators.[247] The only problem we have to investigate centres round the question whether we may postulate that such a situation also existed centuries earlier.

From the rigorism (so typical of the Samaritan of all generations) and from their extreme conservatism,[248] one would naturally draw the conclusion that these characteristics go back to the very origins of the sect, that is, to the time of the schism and the beginning of their separate existence; and thus must mean, in face of the previously mentioned allegations [249] that the Samaritan Pentateuch underwent constant 'ten-

---

[245] Gesenius, *De Pentateuch Sam. origine*, pp. 59 (on the anti-anthropomorphic tendency of the S.P.) etc. Obviously we are not directly concerned with the "revisions" and the "reworking" of the S.P. since for our purpose these are irrelevant. The exegetes as far as they are known from the extant literature are all following the same version. Whether we may or may not call this common text "the Samaritan *textus receptus*", the fact remains that no trace of earlier, or different, readings of the S.P. can be found in all the works from the earliest to the latest exegetes.

[246] cf. S. Talmon, "Observations on the Sam. Pentateuch Version", *Tarbiz* XXII ,1951), pp. 124-128 and recently Purvis, *The Sam. Pentateuch*, pp. 69ff. (cf. *sup.* n. 22).

[247] cf. my article *op. cit. passim.* (cf. n. 245 *sup.*).

[248] cf. Part II, para (e).

[249] cf. *sup.* nn. 13ff., 189.

dentious changes', that its true nature must be ascertained from outside evidence. In view of the fact that, as has already been demonstrated, those who have regarded the Samaritans as 'reformers' have worked from a theologically biassed standpoint, we shall have to pursue a much more throughgoing investigation if we are to get at the truth of their more serious claims.

Before entering into the minutiae, it will not be out of place to make a critical scrutiny of this general theory. The very claim that a 'reformist' group can suddenly turn into a throughly conservative and traditionalist one is in itself surely almost incredible. Comparative studies of the history and sociology of religion, when describing the religious phenomenon generally described as 'transposition' into a sectarian movement, show beyond all doubt that by this process they do not as a rule change their basic characteristics.[250] If we speak here of the Samaritans as a 'sect', the term is not meant in a derogatory sense, but rather as a description of a separatist religious denomination, and usually a protest-movement reacting against the 'decadence' of the main body or of rival groups. This process normally culminates either in the protest-movement turning into a shismatic, but nevertheless traditional and deeply religious, organisation,[251] or, if the leaven continues to work within the sect itself, a further breaking-up into splinter-groups, or even in total disintegration. For this last event there is very little evidence; the occasionally emerging Samaritan splinter-groups are usually heavily loaded with new and syncretistic ideologies. These Samaritan heresies were as a matter of course excluded from the main body and consequently exerted no influence at all on the 'orthodox' Samaritan doctrines or practices.

Not only — we hold — did the 'orthodox' Samaritans not tamper with the text at random, but even in their exegesis one finds hardly any traces of 'reformist' tendencies. Unlike some other religions, in which 'modernisers' occasionally arrive at interpretations diametrically opposed to those of their predecessors,[252] the whole of Samaritan literature

---

[250] G. van der Leeuw, *Religion in Essence and Manifestation* (London, 1938), pp. 261ff., 610f.; J. Wach, *Sociology of Religion* (London, 1947), pp. 198ff., 302f.

[251] van der Leeuw, *op. cit.* pp. 611f.

[252] In our modern world such reformatory exegesis is almost commonplace. One extreme illustration may suffice. Islamic Tradition (ḥadith) based the prohibition against sculpture on the Koran (lix, 24). Since God is described as the Great Former (muṣawwir), humans are not allowed to copy His deeds. Modern exegetes derive from the same reference an opposite conclusion: it is a merit to follow His ways, thus sculpture (and art in general) is considered as being of great merit. cf. Baljon,

exhibits entirely differing tendencies, and its traditions remain virtually unchanged for many centuries.[253]

We attach great significance to these introductory notes, since even contemporary scholarly literature often depicts an entirely different situation. Among the curiosities of historical research, one has to count with the fact that certain theories, having once gained ground, may linger on even although they are in fact supported by no fresh evidence. Thus, for example, certain attractive harmonising pursuits present an irresistible challenge to the scholar and thereby assure themselves of longevity. This is the reason why early Rabbinic literature has been constantly used as a source of all sorts of harmonisations.[254] It has furthermore been found convenient to adopt the hypothesis of the 'ancient common halakhah' or of the Zadokite or Sadducean origins of all exegesis and hence to explain the later 'changes' as all originating from such a source.[255] Such a common source as the basis of the exegesis of all groups has undoubtedly suited the modern critical approach.

Without entering into any incriminations, we must point to another similar illustration of the hazards which face all new approaches. Any innovation which may distrub the 'accepted norms' is often frowned upon by the establishment of the existing 'schools'. Thus when an epoch-making new publication on the Samaritan linguistic traditions first appeared, it was greeted with sceptical tones even by the doyen of this specialist school.[256] Without entering into the details of its reception, it is noteworthy that the most hostile part of the criticism levelled against it has, ironically enough, found its own answer; the sarcastic question "but what shall we do with translations into Modern Hebrew?" has proved meanwhile to be totally without force. And now two very recent German scholars, although writing on entirely different subjects, constantly refer to this work, and in countless cases admit their indebteness to it.[257] The only moral we wish to draw from this and similar cases is

---

Modern Muslim Koran Interpretation, p. 119. Needless to say, the Samaritans did not change their attitude to the rigorous observance of "thou shalt not make unto thee a graven image". Their strict objection to images was not so much an Islamic influence as an original Israelite tradition. (For further Islamic influences cf. SLTh. pp. 807ff., 935ff.)

[253] cf. *sup.* nn. 247-248.
[254] cf. my article *op. cit.* pp. 98f., 126 (n. 3).
[255] On the survival of this system, cf. *ibid.* pp. 100, 134 (n. 25).
[256] cf. Kahle, The Cairo Geniza (2nd ed.), pp. 154f.
[257] cf. Macuch, *Grammatik*, pp. 567-568; Kippenberg, Garizim, *passim*. Ironically

that, no matter how deeprooted certain accepted opinions may be, they should never be blindly followed. Even the most 'logical' theory must be subjected to an occasional reassessment.

Now we propose to enter into some detailed comparisons in which the LXX figures prominently, but we do not intend to deal here with the possible exegetical relationships, for these are treated separately.[258] Our intention here is focussed with a view to testing the credibility of our own thesis that the Samaritan scriptural traditions are thoroughly conservative by their very nature. If, therefore, the Samaritan scriptural traditions show real affinities either with the M.T. of the LXX, or side with one against the other, we are in duty bound to re-examine these current theories regarding their mutual relationship. No matter how great the merits of these theories may be, they are neither to be treated as infallible, nor do they by their attractiveness exempt us from the duty of subjecting them to the same critical rules upon which they were originally framed. Unfortunately there is no reliable work which could serve as a conspectus of the results of the modern critical school in their bearing on the genesis of Samaritan exegesis.[259] For this reason alone, we must make some remarks on the subject, even if rather sketchy and random ones.

If we begin with a case in which more or less justice has been done to Samaritan traditions by the critics, we shall address ourselves to the problem of the treatment of the Tetragrammaton. It has indeed been

---

the latter writer polemicizes against Kahle concerning the definition of חג המצות (p. 208, n. 73). Obviously in this case Kahle was right and Kippenberg was mislead by the ambiguities of 18th century letters (*ibid.* p. 209 n.). Late commentaries express likewise some hesitation concerning this problem (cf. Hanover, *Das Festgesetz*, pp. ivf. = translation p. 38. cf. also p. 60, n. 67). Incidentally it may be noted that the author of this commentary is identical with the writer of the a.m. letters. The early literature, however, makes it abundantly clear that though the last day is the 'main pilgrimage', all other days of Passover are considered as days of pilgrimage. cf. *Kāfi*, pp. 214f., 223f.; (SLTh.A pp. 37f., 43).

[258] Part III, para (a 1, 3).

[259] From our point of view the most recent work by Kippenberg, *op. cit.* is of little help. While he gives a very useful summary of the contemporary state of research ("Der Stand der Forschung", pp. 1ff.), the author is too preoccupied with general problems and "religious history", leaving the problems of exegesis without special treatment. cf. "Aufgabe, Methode und Durchführung", pp. 27ff. More helpful is the other part of the book ("Traditionen etc.", pp. 175ff.), but even here the attention is focused, by the nature of the subject, on religious history and theology, and consequently the handling of specific exegetical problems is rather of secondary importance.

very illuminating to recognise that the Samaritans contributed something
to the elimination of the practice of pronouncing the Tetragrammaton
by reading its substitute 'The Name' (שמה).[260] But when this fact is made
to serve as a precedent for further general 'tendentious changes', it
behoves us to be much more wary. The suggestion that, because the
Samaritans had this natural dread of pronouncing the Tetragrammaton,
they tampered with their text by eliminating Divine names, has little
to support it. The evidence brought forward for such 'changes' is most
unconvincing.[261]

Again without entering into numerous details, we may take one
example to illustrate that, instead of being required to postulate arbitrary
changes, we are in fact confronted by genuine textual variants. These
variants may well be of the same antiquity as the S.P. itself, and thus
go back as far as the time of the emergence of distinctive Biblical texts.
The strangest of all postulates is that the Samaritans 'eliminated' the
word יה from *Ex.* xv, 2 by their reading זמרתי;[262] but in this instance the
LXX has likewise no mention of a Divine Name here, although its reading
is probably based on an entirely different textual tradition.[263]

The same remarks apply later in the chapter (*ibid.* v, 3), where it has
been alleged that the Samaritans, in order to eliminate anthropomor-

---

[260] Geiger, *Urschrift*, p. 262. cf. also Ben-Ḥayyim, *Eretz Israel* III (1954), pp. 147-
154; Macuch, *Grammatik etc.*, p. 53 (cf. however *ibid.* p. 15 and p. 103, n. 60).

[261] Geiger, *op. cit.* pp. 261-279. There is a logical fault in the harmonizing tendencies of these speculations. Evidently we are faced in this case with three distinct
oral traditions. The Rabbis pronounced the Tetragrammaton as אדני ("the Lord").
While the Hellenistic tradition is very similar to the latter (Κύριος) it is still not identical
with it. The difference between the last two traditions is mainly visible when the
Tetragrammaton is preceded by אדני, e.g. *Gen.* xv, 2, 8 Δέσποτα Κύριε; *Deut.* iii, 24
Κύριε θεέ; *ibid.* ix, 26 Κύριε βασιλεῦ τῶν θεῶν. It is very difficult to compare to any of
these three traditions that of Qumran (substitution by אל or Tetragrammaton spelled
in Palaeo-Hebrew characters — cf. early Greek Text with πιπι cf. O. Eissfeld,
"Ansetzung der Rollen nach paläographischen Kriterien", *Theologische Literatur-
zeitung*, lxxiv (1949), cols. 266-8; Kahle, *Die Hebräischen Handschriften aus der Höle*
(1951), pp. 63ff. and recently Siegel, "The Employment etc.", *HUCA* XLII (1971),
pp. 159-172.

[262] Geiger, *op. cit.* pp. 277f. von Gall, *Der hebräische Pent.*, ad loc. cites variant
וזמרתיה but this does not change the situation. cf. Ben-Ḥayyim, *Literary and Oral
Trad.* III a, p. 37.

[263] βουθὸς καὶ σκεπαστὴς ἐγένετό μοι εἰς σωτηρίαν. This indicates that against the
M.T. and the S.P. the Hebrew *Vorlage* could not be זמרת (perhaps ועזרתי? or
ומגיני?).

phism, changed the word איש of the M.T. Here again, the LXX shows
that the Samaritans were not the only ones who had here a different
scriptural tradition; but while the S.P. speaks of "the Hero *in* war",
the LXX, obviously depending on an equally ancient source, proposes
"abolishes wars".[264] A very similar feature characteristic of a distinctive
tradition may also be recognised by the consideration of another so-
called 'elimination of the Divine Name' in *Ex.* xvii, 16. Here the LXX
text agrees with the M.T., while the Samaritan tradition (as in *Ex.*
xv, 2) has nevertheless no trace of the word יה [265].

One could multiply examples but they all point in the same direction
in that they provide little or no evidence of any deliberate tampering
with the Text on the part of any group. Originally all texts may have
been closely related, especially prior to the schisms, which no doubt
came into being either through an accumulation of inadvertent changes,
or through a deliberate persistence and perseverance in adhering to a
'corrupt' text now traditionally reverenced by the group. Once, however,
such a schism has been created, the trend of textual transmission in
each group remains quite consistent; one might even say with truth
that, with the very growth and achievement of such consistency, the
gulfs dividing the various textual traditions grow ever deeper and
stronger.

The best examples to illustrate this consistency are found in those
celebrated cases in which the difference, or the 'alteration', consists in
a single letter; and the most common are those where the difference is
between a ד and a ר, which may easily be attributed to the graphic
resemblance of these two letters. In some of these cases one might reasonably attribute the adherence to the one or the other to a conscious theological bias.[266] However, in other cases there can be no doubt at all that
we have here genuine variants which grew out of the natural developments of the text. We are not at present concerned to distinguish between

---

[264] S.P. גבור במלחמה; LXX συτρίβων πολέμους. The underlying Hebrew of the
LXX may have been *similar* to S.P. (perhaps גביר מלחמות?). Macuch's conjecture
(*Grammatik etc.*, p. 492) that the ב of the S.P. was added for the sake of metre, is
not very convincing. cf. also *ibid.* p. 526 (on *Deut.* xxxii, 3).

[265] cf. *sup.* n. 263, cf. also Onqelos and Peshitta on *Ex.* vxii, 16.

[266] *Gen.* xlix, 7, M.T. ארור, S.P. אדיר. cf. Geiger, *Urschrift*, pp. 374; *Ex.* xxiii, 17
and xxxiv, 23, M.T. אדון, S.P. ארון. cf. Geiger, *op. cit.* pp. 337ff.; Lev. xviii, 21 and
xx, 2-5, M.T. להעביר, S.P. (here = LXX!) להעביד, cf. Geiger, *op. cit.* pp. 302f.
See also Macuch, *Grammatik*, p. 36 (on *Deut.* xxxiii, 25, M.T. דבאך S.P. רביך
and *ibid.* pp. 44ff.

those cases attributable to a different handling of the text by the scribes, and those arising from a misunderstanding of the respective text used by each group, in accordance with and favoured by their own exegetical traditions.[267]

It must be emphasised that it is not only the written word which keeps firmly its framework of tradition, but the exegesis too, as it emerges from the various texts, is strictly governed by the same tradition. Often too, oral traditions may be verified by the text when various groups happen to have the same version. Thus, for example, the Samaritan Targum may in a particular passage reflect an ancient tradition supported also by the translation of the LXX.[268] Similarly, the Samaritan midrashic expositions, based on a particular variant reading, may unexpectedly find support in a Hellenistic writer who bases his own midrash on a similar reading in one of the LXX-types of text.[269] Nevertheless, it is quite impossible to harmonise such cases in such a way that they form part of one 'common source'. It is equally impossible to maintain that we are here confronted with cases of deliberate changes. In some of these cases, as we have already seen,[270] although based on similar readings, the midrashic expositions branch out in different directions in conformity with the traditional peculiarities of the respective groups.

Obviously, some deliberate changes there must have been. Euphemistic expressions could not creep into the scriptural text inadvertently.[271]

---

[267] e.g. *Num.* xvi, 15, M.T. חמור S.P. חמוד (cf. LXX ἐπιθύμεμα); Deut. i, 22, M.T. ויחפרו, S.P. ויחפדו. The last example, however, is a *hapaxlegomenon* for the Samaritans, since it appears only once in the Pentateuch, cf. Part III, para (e, 3).

[268] cf. *Num.* xx, 19 במסילה נעלה. The Jewish Targumim renders it as "the main road" (Onqelos בארח כבישא, Pseudo Jonathan באסטרטיא דמלכא), while the S.T. as בכיפה נסק. There is no need to suggest that the S.T. had a different Hebrew background as בסלע נעלה (cf. Ben-Ḥayyim, Literary and Oral Trad. II, p. 537, l. 91). כיפה could also mean "mountain" and the S.T. may have preserved an ancient tradition reflected also by the LXX ὄρος (cf. however LXX on 2 *Samuel* xx, 12 τρίβος). Much more preliminary critical work is still needed for the elucidation of the S.T. before final conclusions may be reached in this field.

[269] The midrash on *Ex.* xii, 40, namely, that the Exodus took place after 430 years equally divided into 215 years in Canaan and 215 years in Egypt [cf. my article *op. cit.* pp. 108, 141f. (nn. 81ff.)] is also known to Josephus (Antiq. II, xv, 2). cf. Strack-Billerbeck, *Kommentar etc.* II, pp. 668ff.

[270] On *Gen.* iv, 8, cf. *sup.* nn. 140ff. On *Deut.* xxxii, 35 cf. my article *op. cit.* pp. 108, 142 (nn. 86f.).

[271] Geiger, *Urschrift*, p. 389 and recently Macuch, *Grammatik*, p. 217. cf. Part III, para (e, 2).

It is even less likely that those distinctively Samaritan variants, which have a real theological significance and have no counterpart or parallel in any other version, arose naturally from the common Pentateuchal sources.[272] Nevertheless, one should be careful in making sweeping generalisations on the nature of such 'tendentious' Samaritan textual variants,[273] since it becomes evident from their exegesis that not by any means *all* such peculiarly Samaritan readings are, or can be, the results of deliberate tampering with the text. From the whole development of Samaritan exegesis it becomes abundantly clear that midrashic and Scriptural traditions are always closely inter-related.[274] Insofar as there existed a revisionary tendency on the part of the guardians of the text, their revisions were not arbitrary changes, but rather the 'learned-scribal and authoritative' preferences of those guardians, and always dependent on early separatist traditions. At an early stage, when both text and tradition were in relatively fluid states, one type of textual reading would understandably be preferred to another. This preference, however, usually took place before the final crystallisaton of the sect and before its members reached agreement on a *textus receptus*. Sudden and revolutionary alterations would be totally out of keeping with the rigorism with which the Samaritans held to their traditions. As compared with the "revisions" of other groups,[275] the Samaritans' reworking of their text was the least revolutionary of all. Obviously no text is entirely exempt from emendation and 'slight' revisions must have slowly penetrated into the Samaritan text. Such alterations must have had some basis and justification in the general Samaritan outlook, and were thus easily absorbed into the general doctrinal framework of Scriptural exegesis, until even such altered forms themselves came to be regarded as part and parcel of the traditional 'truths'.

The crystallisation of each separate group in accordance with its peculiar exegesis must have taken effect along lines similar to those of the other groups. Apart from the distinctive characteristics of the various groups, therefore, the common ground was still so large that, even after the schisms had become complete, many similarities remained to tempt us of a later day to regard them as being interdependent.

---

[272] As for example the Samaritan tenth Commandment or the variants בחר (M.T. יבחר) etc. cf. recently Purvis, *The Sam. Pentateuch*, pp. 69ff.

[273] cf. Macuch, *Grammatik*, pp. 55ff.

[274] cf. Part II, para (i) and Part III, para (h, 2).

[275] The most extensive revisions were those of LXX types. cf. Würthwein, *The Text of the O.T.* (Oxford, 1957), pp. 46ff. cf. also my article *op. cit.* p. 147 (n. 117).

Admittedly, then, some exegetical traditions were as a matter of course inherited by all the groups along with their texts, which in the majority of places showed identical readings. Thus, for example, the rigorism of the Samaritans [276] invites us to compare them with other groups who share this or similar characteristics.[277]

We cannot here enter into such searching comparisons as would enable us adequately to delineate the characteristics of the Samaritan exegesis and its independent nature.[278] Notwithstanding all the outwardly close and superficially impressive 'parallels' between Samaritanism and other systems, the harmonising of Samaritan traits with those of any other group certainly leads to a blurring of the true facts. But even at this stage we may perhaps indicate [279] again some dividing-lines which firmly place the Samaritan traditions in a category of their own. Scholars who have not really succeeded in appreciating these traditions from the inside tend to give accounts of them which are both defective and superficial, because unsympathetic. We are not now trying to break new ground, but merely to confine ourselves to what should be obvious to the discerning student, for to him their outstanding features, illustrated by the entire Samaritan literature and emphasized by the differences between this literature and others, become immediately recognisable. The extent and significance of these differences must not of course be exaggerated, since only a balanced picture can make an objective assessment possible. Unfortunately, many previous attempts, by underestimating these very differences or by representing them as trivial, have failed to convince, since precisely owing to their excessive zeal for harmonisations there has emerged only a blurred and distorted picture.

Beyond doubt, the most objective assessment would be reached by refraining from labelling any specific exegetical tradition as belonging to any one particular group, and by looking rather for its roots. It is, however, unhappily impossible to find these roots unless their later developments are first carefully examined: hence the study of the actual and intrinsic developments, if possible by the separate analytical investigation of each tradition, should claim priority over comparative research. How much more, then, should such analytical investigation precede and hold in check all synthetic theories advocating some kind

---

[276] cf. Part III, para (e).

[277] cf. my article *op. cit. passim* and in *JJS* IX (1958), pp. 131-138.

[278] (An entire chapter has been devoted to this subject in SLTh. pp. 668ff.)

[279] cf. *sup.* nn. 33f., 48f., 143f. etc. cf. also n. 278.

of homogeneity amongst the *various* traditions! It has moreover been previously shown [280] that a not inconsiderable part of this whole problem is the product of a misleading terminology. The attempt to demarcate or label or pre-date a 'common' exegetical tradition often has its source either in avoidable or in subconscious confusions which could easily be dispelled by using clear and precise definitions. Terms like 'ancient halakhah' or 'pre-Christian midrashic *genre*' tend rather to confuse than to clarify problems.

It has already been pointed out [281] that, despite the Samaritans' strict adherence to their traditions, we must always avoid attributing to them the concept of "Oral Law", which is conspicuously absent from all their literature. There is here a fundamental divergence between two distinct types of belief in tradition, for, while the Rabbis elevate their Oral Law to the status of a Divine institution, which in many cases has the power to circumscribe the literal sense of the Scriptural Word and even to oppose it,[282] no such power is ever invested by the Samaritans in their own tradition. For the latter, an authentic tradition is exclusively one which can be tested by its thoroughly strict conformity with Scripture itself.[283]

This divergence is of a cardinal nature, and makes all claims for a 'Samaritan Oral Law' groundless; in fact, because of it, the Rabbis can safely allow themselves a much freer and more critical approach to the Written Law [284] than can the Samaritans. It is likewise much easier for the former to absorb novel ideas into their traditional corpus of teaching. The Rabbis, basing their hermeneutical rules as they do, on the Oral Law, and making them the major factor in their exegesis, display great boldness in incorporating their constantly developing applications into the body of the Oral Law itself and actually equating their purposes and values with the ancient oral and written traditions. Under this wide umbrella, which shelters both Laws, and under which Divine authority is claimed for both, it is only to be expected that the old and the new ideas should become rapidly and easily amalgamated.[285]

It is surely one of the paradoxes of history that it is the Pharisee

---

[280] cf. *sup.* para (e) and (g).

[281] cf. *sup.* n. 102, and Part II, para (h).

[282] cf. my article *ALUOS* VI (1969), p. 125 n. 2, and p. 157 n. 184.

[283] Part II, para (i).

[284] Urbach, *The Sages*, p. 258 and cf. also *inf.* Part II, nn. 98ff.

[285] Liberman, *Greek and Hellenism*, pp. 190f.; Urbach, *op. cit.* pp. 46f. and *passim.*

mainly who is accused of being enslaved by the 'dead letter', since even
the most cursory comparison between Rabbis and Samaritans makes it
abundantly clear that the former are far more prone to symbolical
exegesis [286] and far less to literalist exegesis than the latter. Although,
in general, the Rabbis are equally strongly opposed to pure allegorisation,
particularly in connection with legal matters, where such a method could
destroy their whole purpose and purport, and encourage the non-observance of the precepts, they cannot and do not wish to totally avoid
figurative interpretations. Even amongst the compilers of halakhah,
and even amongst those Tannaim who as a rule follow rigorously the
plain, literal sense of scripture, there occur some deviations, for traditional reasons, from their usual path, and some resorts to these figurative
interpretations.[287] If in halakhah these are only isolated cases, in Rabbinic aggadah the parable and the symbolical type of exegesis figure
quite prominently.[288]

Another matter of great significance for our problem is the concept
of 'unwritten law' amongst the Hellenists; this again is identical neither
with the Rabbinic Oral Law [289] nor with the concept of "tradition" as
understood amongst the Samaritans. It is therefore understandable that,
even in cases where exegeses of legal matters, stemming from various
sources, outwardly appear almost identical they cannot in fact be identified or equated with one another. It is quite sufficient to follow the
working-out of each case to realize that, despite all seeming similarities,
these legal expositions stem from different traditions. If we take one
example only, such as the precept of phylacteries, (*Deut.* vi, 8) the differences in treatment immediately become apparent. Philo clearly
does not know the Rabbinic practice and explains the Scripture allegorically.[290] One would naturally expect the Samaritans, renowned for
their extreme literalism,[291] to follow in this respect the literal sense, as
is done by the Rabbis, and to receive the precept as an obligation to
put on, literally, "signs" and "frontlets". However, these matters of
exegesis do not entirely depend on "logical" deductions, and the Samari-

---

[286] Liberman, *op. cit.* pp. 202f.

[287] Karl, "Biblical Exegesis etc.», *Kneset* II (1937), p. 418; Weiss, *Dor Dor etc.*,
I, p. 201 (cf. *ibid.* n. 1).

[288] Strack, *Introduction*, p. 97 (26, Mashal); Bacher, *Die jüdische Bibelexegese etc.*,
pp. 34f.

[289] Heinemann, "Die Lehre etc.", *HUCA* IV (1927), pp. 149-172 (cf. SLTh pp. 701ff.).

[290] Heinemann, *Philons... Bildung*, p. 167.

[291] cf. Part III para (a, 1).

tans in this case, together with other literalist sects, adopt the diametrically opposed course of explaining away these verses figuratively, as forming a general admonition to the keeping of the words of God. We are here confronted with ancient exegetical traditions, in which each group holds to its distinctive trend, and from which it does not depart.[292]

One may of course argue about the original meaning of this verse, for it is not at all clear whether it was meant to be carried out literally, or whether it was first framed in symbolical and metaphorical terms. All such arguments are, needless to say, quite immaterial to the case in question. Although to us the Samaritan understanding seems paradoxical and logically contrary to the general ethos of their exegetical norms of literalism, the power of tradition in such cases is far stronger than any rigid 'principle' or inflexible rule which we might expect them to follow consistently.

The case of the precept of the 'doorpost' signs (*Deut.* vi, 9 etc.) is even stranger. The Rabbis understand this command literally, that is, that a parchment scroll (containing *Deut.* vi, 4-9; *ibid.* xi, 13-21), folded in a specially prepared capsule, must be fixed upon the doorposts of homes and rooms.[293] Although Philo too knows the custom of putting inscriptions on doorposts,[294] many scholars believe that it probably has closer connections with Hellenistic or even ancient Egyptian practices than with the true traditions of the Pharisees. The literalist sects, as a rule, (and in fact the lowest, most boorish strata, the so-called 'Am ha-'Areṣ, among the Jews) do not observe any such precept.[295] If we find that amongst the Samaritans certain inscriptions, probably affixed to the entrances of synagogues, do exist,[296] this very sporadic custom is certainly not consistently practised. It reminds us of the Muslim

---

[292] cf. my article in *ALUOS* VI, pp. 103, 137 (n. 42).

[293] Besides the numerous scattered discussions on this subject, there is a whole collection devoted to *Mzuzah* in the Talmudic literature (cf. M. Higger, *Seven minor Treatises*, 1939).

[294] cf. *sup.* n. 290.

[295] Harkavi, *Zikhron le Rishonim*, p. 142, n. 12. There is a doubtful reference (*Kether Shem Tobh*, Venice, 1601, p. 640, para 754) to Karaites in Egypt inscribing the 'Shema' on stones. However, this may originate from confusing them with the Samaritans.

[296] Montgomery, *The Samaritans*, pp. 272ff. (and notes there); cf. also Bowman, "The Leeds Sam. Decalogue Inscription", Proceedings of *the Leeds Philosophical Society* VI (1951), pp. 567ff.

practice of putting verses from the Koran and related works on house entrances; but some of the Samaritan inscriptions are plainly of pre-Islamic provenance. It seems, therefore, that a limited early practice or custom of this kind existed, going back to antiquity. Surprisingly enough, this practice is not treated in Samaritan litreature as an explicit and binding precept to be carried out in the literal sense of Scripture.[297]

Apart from these and a few similar cases, where tradition probably requires a figurative exegesis to be employed, such expositions are in general almost absent from the entire Samaritan literature. As opposed to the Hellenistic system of allegorisation, the Samaritans take their stand on the other side, with their exegesis conceived in a severely literalist.[298] Even symbolical expositions, employed to explain in rational terms the reasons behind the precepts, devices so skilfully used by Josephus,[299] are totally absent from Samaritan literature.

It would be out of place to give here a full description of the exact nature of the Samaritan traditions.[300] Suffice it to say that their whole exegetical literature demonstrates that all these traditions are unquestioningly followed with very great consistency, and thus constitute a homogeneous structure of precepts and doctrines, upon which there is universal agreement amongst the Samaritans of all ages. Obviously, the emphasis may shift with changes in the environment and the social conditions; but books written many centuries apart reveal that the circumstances have caused very little significant change of outlook. Their tradition likewise emphasises certain attitudes which are not so emphasised in other traditions.[301] Their rigorism is of course a well-known characteristic; this however is not entirely peculiar to the Samari-

---

[297] Munajja, (*Masā'il al-Khilāf*, Ia, p. 30) explicitly treats this verse and the only exegesis he supplies is a figurative one, embroidered by allegorisations. The fact that this command is mentioned in the list of the 613 precepts (cf. Gaster, "Die 613 Gebote etc.", *Festschrift... jüd.-Theol. Seminars, Breslau* II, pp. 393ff. and pp. 35ff. of Hebrew part, positive command n. 184) does not alter the general picture. It must be borne in mind that in this list of precepts there are also some others which are not meant literally, e.g. on *Deut.* x, 12f. (*ibid.* positive command 186). The *Kāfi*, p. 46; (SLTh.A p. 9) takes this verse as an admonition towards spiritual "cleansing" of the heart. Abisha, in his *Commentary on the Liturgy* (p. 18), is even more explicit in this respect, but he virtually repeats what is said in the *Kāfi*.

[298] cf. Part III, para (h, 2).

[299] Heinemann, "The Method of Josephus etc.", *Zion* V (1940), p. 194.

[300] cf. Part II, para (g), (h) and (i).

[301] *ibid.* nn. 3f.

tans. To take, for example, the strict observance of ritual cleanliness and purification, so characteristic of Samaritan traditions, it has recently become fairly clear that the Dead Sea Scrolls Sect was probably even stricter in this respect.[302]

But our main concern is not in fact to indulge in comparisons or in placing Samaritan traditions in relation to others; the main problem which claims our interest here is the manner in which the transmission of these traditions is carried out. Despite the limitations imposed on us by the relatively late date of the literary evidence, there are good reasons for believing that during the many centuries prior to the appearance of these traditions in literary form they existed orally. Nor can we well exclude the possibility that certain marginal notes attached to scripture served as aids to this oral transmission, for we know of many cryptograms in the S.P. scrolls which chiefly reveal the names of the scribes who wrote them and their dates, and there are also some few cryptograms which supply traditional contextual notes.[303] No doubt in the case of the manuscripts of the Targums there must have been even more freedom for we know for certain that the Arabic translation is full of marginal glosses.[304] Bearing in mind the conservative nature of the Samaritans, it would not be rash to suggest that similar marginal notes may have already existed in their Aramaic Targum or even in their earlier Greek one. It must, however, be strongly emphasised that, even were we to deny the very existence of such marginal glosses or other written mnemonic signs, this would in no way diminish the claim for ancient traditions. The relatively simple traditions fo the Samaritans, being very close to the literal sense, could easily have been memorised, not only by learned individuals, but even by elementary schoolteachers and laymen in general. Even today modern Samaritan priests are renowned for their memories, since they can quote by heart not only scripture, but traditional material attached to it.

---

[302] cf. my article *op. cit.* pp. 193f., 149f. (nn. 127ff.) and recently Yadin in *New Directions* (ed. D.N. Freedman & J.C. Greenfield), pp. 159f., 165.

[303] cf. von Gall, *Der heb. Pentateuch etc.*, pp. xxxix (פלגה ארהותה etc.), lxvii. In all the Pentateuch Mss. including the Arabic translation, there are only such cryptograms (*ibid.* pp. lxxii, xcii), but no marginal glosses. cf. recently Macuch, *Grammatik*, pp. 11f.

[304] Juynboll, "Commentatio de versione etc.", *Orientalia* II (1846), pp. 115ff.; Kuenen, *Specimen etc., idem. Libri Exodi etc. passim*; Halkin, "The Scholia etc.", *JQR* N.S. xxxiv (1943/4), pp. 41ff.

It must, therefore, be clear that if we are to answer the many problems presented by Samaritan exegesis today in a really honest way, it is not sufficient to approach this problem only from a limited and selective point of view; all avenues of historical research as well as their results must be taken into account. But the greater part of the effort must be given to the cultivation of two hitherto greatly neglected fields. The first means an examination of the theories and ideologies which prompt the hermeneutics, invariably followed by the Samaritans. But of no lesser importance is the second field; and although logically we must put it in the second place, it contains, in truth, the very purpose of our research, for it means the study of the *methods* actually employed by the Samaritan exegetes.

Are we then permitted to speak of a "normative" Samaritan exegesis? In the mind of the Samaritan interpreter such a question never arises, for any doctrinal deviation from what is by tradition defined as the Word of God is likened to blasphemy.[305] The "truth" of the interpretation is, for the individual of course entirely dependent on his own subjective understanding, but it is nevertheless subordinated in its minutest details to the accepted traditional norms. There is in fact no set of abstract "hermeneutical rules", nor are there any other guidelines which the interpreter may follow in his private expositions. The only guidelines for the elucidation of scripture are the *traditions* upon which he and his co-religionists have been brought up.[306] The public recital of the law, the instruction of the children in the elements of religious knowledge, the work of the liturgists and indeed Samaritan literature in general, all alike take it for granted that the traditions, and these only, are to be followed generation after generation.[307] "It is written" is here the infallible maxim of the expositor, and at the same time the sole authority; in other words, the exposition of the written word must at all times be understood and interpreted as deemed right by the living tradition of the group.[308] As opposed to the concept of an exegetical inspiration (whether in the Alexandrian version or that of the *Pesher*) in accordance with which the exegete is the instrument of the Spirit of God who dictates to him the inspired interpretation, the Samaritans believe in the ultimate authority of the written word, which does not require any human or

---

[305] cf. Part II, para (a).
[306] *ibid.* para (j).
[307] *ibid.* para (d).
[308] *ibid.* para (i).

supernatural agencies in the task of discovering the truth. Even in the few cases requiring symbolical interpretations, insofar as these exist in Samaritan exegesis, they do not really depend on the taste of the exegete but are made clear to him through the unanimous testimony of ancestral tradition.[309] Even Marqah's 'mysteries of the Law' are not private revelations granted to his untrammelled thought but firmly established interpretations well-known to all his readers who are familiar with the Law and with the Lore of their tradition. Any novel observation is only the outcome of further inter-relating of data previously known from the literal and 'true' traditional understanding of the Torah.[310]

An attack of the kind directed in the New Testament against the Pharisees and the Scribes (*Mark* vii, 9) could hardly be levelled against the Samaritans. To their own minds, at any rate, no contradiction would ever arise between the written word and the tradition; and while we make full allowance for their emphasis on cultic precepts, these very precepts are inspired by the most deeply religious feelings. If we are permitted to employ a terminology borrowed from other religions, we may also be permitted to claim that their sole right to interpret the Pentateuch is the central *dogma* of Samaritan religion; and we may thus fairly equate their hermeneutical methodology with their basic doctrines.[311] Although we cannot take it for granted that the Samaritan religion has its dogmas as formulas embodied in the form of a stereotyped creeds, insofar as its doctrines are fixed, they are both the results of their Biblical exegesis and at the same time the guidelines for all further exegesis, for this is largely determined by the doctrines thus created. We may liken their hermeneutics to a loom perhaps, in which it is extremely difficult to discern between cause and effect.

The whole of Samaritan literature is inspired by the tireless endeavour to elucidate the Divine Word, and most of those records which contain midrashic elements are simply attempts to expound its meaning in the terms of their own thought-forms. Although by the Samaritan exegete himself (as by all others), these attempts are regarded as objective

---

[309] cf. Part III, para (a, 1).

[310] cf. my article *op. cit.* pp. 109f., 142f. (nn. 89ff.).

[311] The general ideological background of the Samaritans is therefore *ipso facto* the source of their 'hermeneutical principles'. For this very reason although the core of our investigation is concerned with actual exegetical devices (Part III), these would not be intelligible without the ideological background (Part II) which leads us often into the fields of theology and other cognate subjects.

reproductions of the Divine intention, we can nevertheless discover the way in which the Samaritan mind works and whereby he marks out his path to the desired end. To put it bluntly, we must point out the distinctive features of their methods and seek to discover the practical and mechanical devices they employ. Only thus can we demonstrate to the modern student that Samaritan exegesis does, after all, contain much of subjectiveness. Although their method of interpretation when it follows the explicit and literal meaning of the words may sometimes be correctly described as objective, as soon as this literalism broadens out anywhere into a structure based on the inherited tradition, its "objectivity" at once becomes suspect,[312] for the mere fact that this strong and unceasing power of tradition dominates the whole nature and development of their exegesis must inevitably induce a biassed and hence subjective approach.

---

[312] cf. n. 309 *sup.*

PART TWO

THE THEORIES UNDERLYING SAMARITAN EXEGESIS

A. THE AUTHORITY OF THE TORAH AND OF MOSES

Ancient biblical exegesis took it for granted that the books of the Torah constitute one literary unity. The theory of an internal connection between various chapters and books served as a hermeneutical device to explain, by comparison with and implication arising from the more explicit passages, the obscure and ambiguous details of others. The palpable justification for this system emerges from the cross-references in Scripture itself,[1] which provided the incentive to the commentators to be watchful for further, less ovbious, connections. Although this common element gave birth to a great variety of irreconcilable and distinctive exegetical systems one feature was retained by most of them in greater or lesser measure, nemely their insistence on proving the unity of the Torah by emphasizing the inner connection between its parts and by explaining away any seeming discrepancies which might be taken to be actual contradictions.

When Samaritan exegesis adopted the Mu'tazilite way of thought, it stipulated, in line with this ancient tradition, that even the ritual enactments of the Torah which could not have been inferred by rational deducation and which could not have been understood apart from a divine revelation, are nevertheless compatible with reason.[2] It may be at once asserted that there existed a closed circuit in which exegetical methods and theological deductions (or preconceived dogmas!) were constantly reacting on each other. This being the case, we may expect a fallacious exegesis to be motivated by adherence to theological dicta. Even in modern exegesis it may conceivably happen [3] that the exegete

---

[1] Thus e.g. the laconic expression "which knew not Joseph" (*Ex.* i, 8) refers back to the Joseph cycle in Genesis; and "Thus did your fathers" (*Num.* xxxii, 8) hints to earlier details (*ibid.* xiii-xiv). The Book of Deuteronomy is crammed with both halakhic and aggadic details which have relevance to the other books of the Pentateuch. *Memar Marqah*, Book IV, which is an expanded commentary on *Deut.* xxxii, abounds in such comparisons. Cf. also Heinemann, *Darkhei ha-Aggadah*, p. 56.

[2] Halkin, "The Relations of the Sam.", *Saadia Anniversary Vol.*, pp. 271ff.

[3] Barr, *The Semantics of Biblical Language*, p. 159.

takes one specific etymological sense as 'fundamental' (owing to its being congruous with his own ideas), while he explains away other possible senses as 'modifications' of it. More serious however are cases where theological concepts dominate the whole interpretation and no real attention is given to the etymological or semantic value of the words used. The Samaritans were by no means free from such paralogisms;[4] their conviction of the supreme authority of the Torah led them to limit the criteria directing their exegesis to theological concepts taken (at least according to Samaritan understanding) from the Torah itself. For this reason, they remained uninfluenced by Hellenistic modes of exegesis, in which there was a total freedom to expound verses in an arbitrary fashion by expansion, often even supplying details from outside sources or inventing them.[5]

It is therefore all the more important to look out for such distinctively Samaritan exegetical details as originate from this internal development. After all, the expositions of the Torah, in common with all ancient written records, are subject to the same types of problem as arise out of any text (containing elusive passages) mainly owing to its modes of transmission.[6] We know how tradition is responsible for spelling, for versions and variant readings, as well as for the 'canonization' of a particular text-type, all of which have great bearing upon the meaning and hence upon exegesis in general. On top of the possibility of a novel exegesis resulting from taking an etymology in the sense in which it is understood in another Semitic language (Aramaic or Arabic), there are other possibilities of distinctively Samaritan usages. Homonyms, synonyms and *hapax legomena* (the latter occurring with greater frequency among the Samaritans because they have no other Hebrew text than the Pentateuch) are especially prone to be subjected to distorted commentaries during the long history of transmission.[7] The responsibility for such divergences cannot be attributed merely to ignorance, lack of interest or learning. On the contrary, both doctrine and ritual, because of their cardinal importance, necessarily guard the transmitters from indifference to the sources. Differences in biblical exegesis cannot be invented by later generations, or devised on the spur of the moment as

---

[4] cf. *inf.* nn. 83-86.

[5] Heinemann, "Josephus' Method" *ZION* V (1940), p. 181.

[6] L. Bloomfield, *Language* (London, 1935), p. 294; cf. also *ibid.* pp. 518f. for further bibliography.

[7] Barr, *op. cit.* pp. 158f.

an afterthought to conceal ignorance or indifference to the text.[8] Commentary is as old as the very transmission of the text; and differences in exegesis between various sects (resulting in divergences in theory and practice) are in fact due to varying traditions.[9]

Just as the text is revered among the Samaritans to the point of prostrating themselves when the Scroll is exhibited,[10] so is tradition also revered. This is the meaning of the expression 'the Book of Life',[11] in that it upholds its devotees, and through its transmission perpetuates life and 'light'. Thus Marqah [12] in expounding Deuteronomy xxxiii, 4, lays the emphasis on this aspect: "... A holy Law inherited by the congregation of Jacob, generation after generation, not to be broken for ever ... He who was entrusted with such a treasure will be an everlasting guardian over it ... He (i.e. Moses) was the proclaimer without fault ...". The infallibility of the Torah is vouchsafed by the 'righteous' transmission.

The whole purpose of life, regarded as the creation and the giving of the Divine Light, if often used as a metaphor for the process of transmission, the guardian of the Divine Spirit functioning in mankind, and secured by the design of the Creator to be everlasting. The first thing created was this 'primal light' (*Gen.* i, 3) from which both material and spiritual enlightment draw their strength.[13] Although later Samaritan writers often give the impression that this is a pre-existant or primordial *logos-like* hypostasis,[14] the earlier literature does not bear out such an interpretation, and in conformity with Scripture even this all-powerful agency is described as created. We may put it in other words thus: the whole creation, its purpose and its permanence are conditioned by this Light, itself identified with Torah. This idea is fairly well developed already in the apocryphal literature.[15] Similarly in the Dead Sea Scroll Sect, where everything is determined by the contrast between Light and Darkness, such a 'primal light' is apparently regarded as conveying the

---

[8] cf. A. Spiro, "Samaritans, Tobiads, etc.", *PAAJR* XX (1951), pp. 291f., n. 30.

[9] See my article in *ALUOS* VI (1969), *passim*.

[10] Montgomery, *The Samaritans*, p. 234.

[11] Based on the theme "life" equalled to the observance of the Divine commandments in the Pentateuch (*Deut.* viii, 3; *ibid.* xxx, 20 etc.). cf. *inf.* nn. 13ff.

[12] *Memar Marqah*, ed. Macdonald, I, p. 121; II, p. 199.

[13] *ibid.* I, p. 50; II, p. 80f.

[14] J. Macdonald, *The Theology of the Sam.*, pp. 14; cf. n. 41 *inf.*

[15] The Law is the 'Light' and the 'Well' and the 'Shepherd' of the righteous. II *Baruch* lxxvii, 13-15 (cf. also *ibid.* lix, 2; II *Esdras* xiv, 20-21).

Divine Presence, but again without becoming a demi-God. Even here the main effect and function of the Light is to reveal the truth to men.[16] The same 'Light-Life' motive inhered also in the origins of Christianity, with the difference that here it was adapted to describe obedience not to the Law, but to the grace of God (manifest in the Messiah).[17]

At this point, we may assert that for the Samaritans "let there be light" (*Gen.* i, 3) was not merely a source for tropological interpretation, through which they merely added a secondary moral lesson to the original one by suggesting that it may also mean "may the faithful be mentally illuminated by God".[18] For them the concept of a 'primal light', appointed by the Creator to function perpetually in the world in accordance with the Divine purpose of activitating life by the illumination embodied in the Torah, was understood as the primary, and ultimately the only, meaning of Scripture. This is an extremely significant point for our understanding of Samaritan exegesis. No other explanation can be given for the contrast between the almost rationalistic opinions occasionally advocated by them, and, side by side with these, the most incredible literalness. The reason for such 'inconsistency' is their being in certain fields restricted by their theological dogmas, invariably strictly adhered to; which, however, did not prevent them from adopting philosophical opinions in the neighbouring fields where dogma was not in question. The 'original light' was one of the dogmas upon which the whole of Samaritan belief was based; and therefore, no matter how 'illogical' it might often appear, it could not be undermined by the influence of rationalistic ideas. On the contrary, all commentators had to adhere to such dogmas and to modify their novel philosophical outlook in order that it might be brought into harmony with the demands of the Torah as understood by the equally sacrosanct principle, which was tradition.

Even in comparison with Rabbinic literature, where the rich source of prophetic utterances about light (e.g. *Proverbs* vi, 23; *Isaiah* ix, 1; *ibid.* ii, 5 etc.) made the correlation of it with the Torah a commonplace,[19] the Samaritans were much more extreme in their procedure,

---

[16] Leanny, *The Rule of Qumran etc.*, pp. 41, 80 etc. Naturally in these circles one to has reckon with the influence of the Prophets (e.g. *Isaiah* xlii-xliii etc.). cf. *inf.* n. 19.

[17] Davis W.D., *Paul and Rabbinic Judaism* (London, 1955), pp. 148f.

[18] Macdonald, *The Theology of the Sam.*, pp. 91, 118ff.

[19] As e.g. in *Gen.R.* iii, 5, "R. Simon said five times is 'light' mentioned here, which parallel the five Books of Moses". Such comparisons are, however, rather

and they took the identification of the 'primal light' with Torah much
more literally. For this reason we are not entitled to reinterpret Samaritan dogma through modern terminology. No matter how absurd the
results appear to the European mind, we cannot explain them away
in order that they may be in harmony with rationalist thought.[20] From
Marqah onwards and down to modern Samaritan writers, this pattern
of keeping strictly to the literal sense of dogmatic utterances did not
change radically.[21] Marqah expresses his idea so vividly that one cannot
be misled as to his real intentions: "... thus our Lord has taught us that
we possess the light that illumines the world, written by God's finger
and descended from the Holy Habitation...". Later he adds regarding
Israel: "... they were honoured by a Book wholly of life, made perfect
with commandments, life-giving to those who keep them..."[22]. Neither
the 'light-darkness' theory of the Dead Sea Scroll Sect [23] nor the 'two
ways' of early Christianity [24] are in any way comparable with the strict
fundamentalism of the Samaritans. Although we cannot disregard the
basic similarities in the general tone of the admonitions, the Samaritan
type of exegesis stands out among all other systems, not only by the fact
of its utilizing no Scripture outside the Pentateuch, but much more by
its taking the Pentateuchal sources as an oracular teaching directed
by a single and traditionally obligatory sense, which does not allow of
any compromises or figurative modifications.

For this reason all former attempts to demonstrate the source-critical
approach, in which the parallel narratives concerning the creation of
the light were scrutinized in an endeavour to trace the course of the
Samaritan relationship with ancient Judea,[25] were doomed to failure,
because they missed the very point which the Samaritan exegetes tried
so strenuously to throw into relief. No terminology taken from Judaism,
and, much less, taken from Christianity, can be in any way usefully
employed without distorting the main dogmas of the Samaritans. The
same caveat applies to attempts made to explain the 'drop of light'

---

metaphorical comparisons which belong to the realm of parables. Cf. M. Guttmann,
Eine Untersuchung der mosaischen Gebote, p. 24.

[20] cf. Trotter, *A Critical Study etc.*, pp. 223f.

[21] cf. *sup.* n. 14 and *inf.* n. 41.

[22] *Memar Marqah* VI, 2; ed. Macdonald I, p. 134; II, pp. 218, 219. cf. n. 41 *inf.*

[23] cf. *sup.* n. 16.

[24] cf. *The Epistle of Barnabas*, Ch. XVIII-XX; *Didache*, Ch. I-III. cf. my article
JJS XI (1960), pp. 22f.

[25] Bin Gorion, *Sinai und Garizim*, pp. 22f. and 397f.

manifested (after passing through the generations) in Moses, in Islamic terms.[26] If Moses is described as "the Star of Creation whom God created from the six days", this does not mean that the Samaritans speculated about a pre-existant Moses or about any *logos*-theories,[27] but that from the 'primal light', which is the star (= light) of creation, originates the design which embraces the light of the prophets, and above all the star of Moses, which is the zenith of the divine design.

The only way to appreciate the gulf between various approaches lies through an insight into rhe respective exegeses upon which the dogmas rest. The best example is the central part of the priestly benediction: "the Lord makes His face shine upon thee..." (*Num.* vi, 25), which, if expounded, inevitably reveals what the exegete meant by this tradition. The Manual of Discipline has here a midrash (ii, 3): "may He enlighten your heart with understanding of life and may He bless you with eternal knowledge." Here, as in other midrashic sources, the 'radiation' is explained away as a metaphor.[28] As opposed to this general trend in various groups, Marqah's exposition is in harmony with his (and that of the general trend of Samaritan exegesis) dogmatic approach. He interprets the same verse by adding: "... He who keeps (the Divine Light = Torah) is kept (by it), and the divine will dwells upon him".[29] Although Marqah eliminates here the anthropomorphism by substituting 'will' for "face" nevertheless there is no attempt to allegorize the radiation motive in the benediction; and the sense indicates that the 'shining' or 'radiation' is a tangible one, although naturally invisible when it refers to the 'primal light',[30] the perpetual presence of which is a concrete existence equivalent to the will of God acting perpetually in the world.

One might even go a step further and suggest that the Samaritan doctrine of 'light', although construed literally, was invested with the same characteristics as the 'divine spirit' of Philo or 'the Holy Spirit' of

---

[26] Macdonald, *The Theology of the Sam.*, pp. 38.

[27] cf. Montgomery, *The Samaritans*, pp. 228f.

[28] Kahle, *The Cairo Geniza*, pp. 98f.

[29] מן נטר אתנטר ורצונה ישרי עליו *Memar Marqah*, ed. Macdonald, I, p. 65; II, p. 103. This addition makes sense only if the benediction was understood as referring to an *actual* light. There are similar midrashim in Rabbinic literature (*Ex. R.* xxxvi, 3, *Soṭah* 21a and parallels). These are, however, based on verses like *Proverbs* xx, 27, which in itself is evidence that the lights (both that of God and of man) are meant figuratively.

[30] *Memar Marqah, op. cit.* I, p. 132 = II p. 214.

the Rabbis, which prompts the Prophet to prophecy.[31] This becomes plausible from Marqah's employment of the 'spirit'-terminology of the Pentateuch, which one might expect to be expounded and elaborated, or at least emphasized as is the case with Scripture itself. However, this is not the case. In connection with the elaborated exposition of Deuteronomy xxxi, 30, Marqah quotes [32] the verses about the seventy elders who were inspired by the spirit of Moses: "... and I will take [33] of the spirit which is upon thee, and I will put it upon them", but there is no comment here on the nature of this 'spirit'. Instead, it is taken for granted that it must be nothing else but the 'light'. This is made clear from the eulogies that follow: "where is there anyone like Moses ... who was strengthened with much wisdom from the *light* of the Divine One". From such deliberate belittling of the 'spirit'-terminology and the attempt to explain it away as if it were identical with 'light', one may justly conclude that the Samaritans were aware of the significance attached to the 'spirit' by other religions, and that they followed their own traditions despite the tempting 'proof-texts'.

It is to be regretted that Marqah does not treat the biblical narrative dealing with the birth of Moses. However, his line of thought may be inferred from his description of the Torah:[34]

> It was established from creation; it was made in the *light*; it was made known from the mouth of its Composer. A prophet received it, who was full of *this glory*. From his very birth he was revealed as the saviour of the congregation of the Hebrew.[35] The glory was revealed for his sake to magnify him, the angels assembled by reason of his *perfection*, as when the wonders were brought together before him. Glory came to strengthen him as when the *Good* came and vested him with the crown. Holiness appeared and anointed his body, Faith came and set out laws for him.

---

[31] Wolfson, *Philo* II, p. 30 (and cf. *ibid.* nn. 43-45).

[32] *Memar Marqah* IV, 1, ed. Macdonald I, p. 84; II, p. 134. There is another midrash (I, p. 135; II, p. 221) where again 'spirit' is turned into 'light', 'illumination' etc.

[33] Marqah uses the expression וְאַשֵׁזוֹב (and I will deliver, or save) reflecting the S.P. וְהִצַּלְתִּי from נצל. [Such is also the interpretation of the *Ṭabbākh* (f. 158b): Moses being the source of prophecy, the radiation of 'light' was flowing from him towards the others, without his own prophecy being diminished.] The root אצל is not known to the Sam.; *Gen.* xxvii, 36 was also understood in this sense.

[34] *Memar Marqah* VI, 2, ed. Macdonald I, p. 134; II, p. 219.

[35] cf. Baneth, *Des Samaritaners Marqah an die 22 Buchstaben etc.*, pp. 46f. Although his text was slightly different, he understood perfectly the manifold sense of the references to Moses (cf. *ibid.* n. 83).

Marqah's implicit midrash becomes clear only if we look for his proof-text. He is drawing an analogy between the two expressions כי טוב thus inferring identity. Just as in the story of creation it was stated that "God saw the light, *that it was good*" (*Gen.* i, 4), which meant that it was pre-destined to become the source of perfection, so the expression concerning Moses "that he was good" (*Ex.* ii, 2) has the same connotation. We may therefore take Marqah's word quite literally. As, in their infancy-stories, ancient writers were convinced that the birth of figures prominent in the history of salvation was signalized by a miraculous sign, and marvellous events such as light-phenomena [36] and the appearance of angels, etc. so did Marqah imagine the birth of Moses. Truth to tell, there is not really much difference between this description and the later expression of the Asaṭir — "the star of Israel"[37] — which is also meant literally, i.e. that a heavenly light signalized the birth of the saviour.

The Urim and the Thummin are also understood as the "light of perfection" guiding by a prophetic illumination the high-priest in the sanctuary.[38] This illumination, which permeates the whole Samaritan theology, was regarded as resulting from the merit of Moses. The Ṭabbākh puts this quite bluntly:[39]

> Through him (Moses) did the tribe (of Levi) reach its perfection, and he made it *lustrous*, in accordance with his saying 'thy Thummin (understood as from תמם = perfection) and thy Urim (אור = luminiferous) are with thy goodly one' (*Deut.* xxxiii, 8) to wit, he ranked you in justice according to the (supreme) status which is the exclusive (degree) of the servants of the Holy Sanctuary.

In reality there is very little difference between all these theological speculations of many centuries. They all rest on the very same exegetical principle. The same motif is met at every turn, since this assumption that the Divine action permeates all existence through the agency of "the light", is the foundation stone of Samaritan dogma. Hence we

---

[36] Vermes, *Scripture and Tradition etc.*, pp. 90ff.

[37] *Asaṭir* VIII, 6, ed. Ben-Hayyim, *Tarbiz* XIV-XV (1943-4), pp. 18f., 42f. (For further details cf. SLTh. pp. 788ff.)

[38] The Sam. Targum understood this expression (*Ex.* xxvii, 30; *Lev.* viii, 8) as שלמיך ואוריך (*Deut.* xxxiii, 8) as תומיך ואוריך; or ית נאיריה (= נהיריה) וית שלמיה cf. the expression אורתום in the Dead Sea Scrolls (*Hymns of Thanksgiving* IV, 6, 23; xviii, 29).

[39] f. 204a. الذى به كمل السبط وبهاه حسب قوله تميك واوريك لائيش حسيدك
اعنى مرتبك على الانصاف فى المنازل فيها يختص بخدم المشكان الشريف

cannot be surprised that the hymns on the birth of Moses written centuries later, although more explicit, nevertheless keep strictly to the same line of thought. Taking for example the hymns of the fourteenth-century Abdallah b. Solomon,[40] we find his exposition is not essentially different from Marqah's. The millennium of separation in time wholly changed the mode of expression but not the substance. Abdallah describes the sun as if it were to say: "My light is subdued by his (Moses's) light. Before me the light was prepared (reserved) for him." One has only to be familiar with Marqah's exposition, relying on analogical words, in order to discover that the same midrash is also followed by Abdallah.[41]

The significance of the "light"-motif is not limited to details only but it is a general principle upon which the Divine origin of Scripture and its transmission are alike based. Although tradition did not develop among the Samaritans into an independent discipline like the 'Oral Law' in Judaism, it was nevertheless viewed as having been vouchsafed by the same 'light' or Divine Providence which guaranteed the reliability of Scripture itself.

A direct result of these dogmas is the belief in the indefectibility and perfection of the Law (and tradition), which cannot possibly tolerate any contradictions or discrepancies, whether in the text or in interpretation. One cannot imagine that exegetical principles based on conflicting verses (as for example the fourth principle of Hillel or the thirteenth of R. Ishmael)[42] could ever have been conceivable amongst the Samaritans. Naturally, in Rabbinic literature too there existed a theoretical principle that there are no contradictions either in the Scripture or in its tradition. In practice however, there were often found 'apparently' contradictory passages which were interpreted in such a manner that they should not conflict. This practice became a rule of exegesis for the Rabbis, demanding a *conscious* harmonization by which the conflicting utterances are either made to apply to different matters or are explained in such a manner that they may appear to be in agreement with each

---

[40] cf. Cowley, *Liturgy* I, p. xcvi.

[41] *ibid.* II, p. 749 וקדם בעל ממשלת היום (בראשית א׳, ט״ז) ואמר נורי אתכבש מן נורו וקדמי אתעתד לו הנור ודן מימרה אקרו מאז אמר « יהי אור » (בראשית א׳, א׳) אלהים אמסרו טפה « וירא (שם, שם, ד׳) אותו כי טוב » (נ״ש; שמות ב׳ ב׳) ולזבן מולדו אסתירו.

[42] A. Schwarz, "Die Hauptergebnisse etc.", *Scripta Univers... Hierosolymitanarum etc.* I, pp. 10f., idem. *Die hermeneutische Antinomie etc. passim.* Weiss, *Dor Dor etc.* I, p. 9, n.

other, or the one is given preference over the other.[43] There is no lack
of examples in Talmudic aggadic sources, where 'apparent' contradictions are artificially multiplied in order to drive home some homiletical
moral.[44] All such hermeneutical devices were inadmissible in Samaritan
exegesis because of the reverence for the soundness of the texts and the
traditions, which both originate in the 'light'; and, this being so, no
contradiction whatsoever, even 'apparent', may be detected in them.

Without entering here into the delicate problem whether the talmudic
ruling that "a biblical prohibition can be liable to limitation by another
command"[45] is in itself a contradiction or not, according to the Samaritan standards at any rate such a ruling would be impossible. As we shall
see, this was also the opinion of the Karaites, who by applying literalist
methods of exegesis likewise ruled out any possibility of conflict between
one precept and the other.[46] However, the Samaritans were even more
extreme than the other literalists since for them the mere allegation of
any discrepancy in the Divine Word would be abhorrent. It is thus
possible to affirm that the Samaritans represent the most rigoristic position in this respect, a fact which in itself makes all allegations of adopting
foreign influences, such as for instance Islamic ones, utterly ridiculous.
In Islam the discrepancies in the Koran, both in matters of ritual and
in metaphysical questions, were never denied even by their most eminent
apologists; it was even admitted that the Prophet altered his rulings
from day to day.[47]

The extreme sanctification of the Torah as the only Word of God
serves as an excuse on the part of the Samaritans for rejecting any
other scriptures.[48] It is not altogether impossible that Marqah's warnings
against 'external' influences are already directed against the influences
of those Hebrew scriptures outside the Pentateuch.[49] A more philosoph-

---

[43] Rosenblatt, *The Interpretation of the Bible in the Mishnah*, p. 30. cf. also Bardo-
witcz, *Die Abfassungszeit der Baraita etc.*, p. 63.

[44] Heinemann, *Darkhei ha-Aggadah*, p. 58.

[45] עשה דוחה לא תעשה cf. M. Guttmann, *Eine Untersuchung etc.*, p. 38. cf. my
article, *ALUOS* VI (1969), pp. 111f.; 145ff. (nn. 106f.).

[46] Poznanski, *The Karaite Literary Opponents etc.*, p. 26; Ankori, *Karaites in
Byzantium*, pp. 400ff.

[47] D.S. Margoliouth, *The Early Development of Mohamedanism*, pp. 45-50.

[48] In the later Chronicles, *Ex.* xxiii, 1 is quoted as a warning against 'false' prophets.
cf. Adler-Seligsohn, "Une nouvelle chronique Sam.", *REJ* XLIV (1902), p. 213. The
Hillukh (p. 232) adduces as evidence *Deut.* xii, 1f. But the usual 'proof-texts' are
Deut. iv, 2; *ibid.* xii, 32 (*Hillukh*, p. 233).

[49] *Memar Marqah*, ed. Macdonald I, p. 36 = II, pp. 222f.; I, p. 145 = II, p. 239.

ical approach appears only in the Ṭabbākh, where a distinction is made between prophets and the apostle.[50] But even in this case, the leading arguments for the only 'apostleship', which is reserved for Moses, are based on Pentateuchal proof-texts which ascribe the same uniqueness to Moses as had already been ascribed by Marqah.[51] Only the twelfth-century Munajja uses other biblical stories, like the capture of the Ark of God by the Philistine (I Samuel iv, f.), and seeks to ridicule them as subverting the 'true' faith.[52]

After all this, it must be obvious that any possibility of the abrogation of the Law or any part of it, which was the major issue of controversy on the part of Christianity and Islam alike against the Jews, was firmly and irrevocably rejected by the Samaritans. The Islamic environment in particular, by allowing for alteration even of their own Scripture,[53] made the fierce combating of all such ideas on the part of the Samaritans absolutely imperative. Although the Samaritans could avail themselves of the polemics against abrogation of the Law employed by their Jewish (both Rabbanite and Karaite) predecessors in this field,[54] yet the tenets and principles upon which these battles are fought by the

---

[50] In the chapter of the degrees of prophecy (ff. 156a-159a) there are two characteristics mentioned, prophetical inspiration together with heralding of the (true) faith, with which two only Moses was gifted. واما الرساله فهي تحمل الوحى وادا الامانه وقد يجتمع هاتين الرتبتان والذى اختص به السيد الرسول ... (f. 157a). There is later another chapter on the 'qualifications of the apostle' in which additional attributes are mentioned. These are, however, mostly polemical ones, to eliminate the claims for 'apostleship' by others. cf. Halkin, "Relations of Sam. to Saadia", *Saadia Anniversary Vol.*, p. 313.

[51] cf. n. 49 *sup.*

[52] *Masā'il al-Khilāf* Ib, pp. 116f.

[53] According to Koran (e.g. XIII, 39, "God abolisheth and establisheth what He pleaseth and from Him is the source of the Book") and the commentators Divine revelation can be altered by the Will of God. cf. D.S. Margoliouth, *The Early Development of Mohamedanism*, p. 10. Altogether, the precepts of the Koran, often contradicting each other (*ibid.* pp. 77f.), can be interpreted only by the principle of respective mutual abrogation (*ibid.* p. 48). According to a tradition (حديث) the Prophet himself admitted his fallibility. cf. Guillaume, *The Traditions of Islam*, pp. 154f.

[54] cf. Halkin, "Relations of Sam. to Saadia etc.", *Saadia Anniversary Vol.*, pp. 323ff It goes without saying that Karaites were equally engaged in these polemics Qirqisāni's detailed treatment (*Kitāb al-Anwār etc* IV, 52-55; ed Nemoy II, pp 440-453) shows more affinities to Sam thinking

Samaritans depend on their ancient tradition, itself based upon biblical exegesis.[55]

The extreme glorification of Moses by the Samaritans,[56] while firmly based on Scripture,[57] was fortified by the intimate identification of his figure with the infallible Law. Marqah constantly paraphrases Deuteronomy xxxiv, 10, "there has not risen any like Moses and never will arise".[58] This assertion is an echo of ancient traditions, singling out Moses as the only prophet who was entrusted with things seen and unseen or, in other words, with the mysteries of both worlds. These innermost secrets were known only to the prophet who received the Law from the hand of God and transcribed it faithfully. The references to Moses in Scripture are not the words of Moses himself, but what "the Lord wrote of him". This tradition was the cornerstone of Samaritan belief throughout all generations, and the polemics against the Jews were invariably based on the assumption that no other authority whether of prophets or sages, whether in written or in oral form, may be placed alongside or supersed this all-embracing unique revelation.[59] However much the other ancient sects revered Moses,[60] the Samaritans outdid them all by their turning this reverence into an Article of Faith almost as firm as their belief in God and his revelation. This was, after all, only natural, if we seriously take into account their rejection of all those extra-Pentateuchal books which were freely accepted as all alike parts of Scripture by all other ancient sects. Against Rabbinic Judaism they also raised other claims, for instance, that of belittling this exalted stature of Moses by asserting that the patriarchs or the Messiah are even greater

---

[55] Halkin, *ibid* pp 324f, nn 291-296

[56] de Sacy, *Mémoire etc.*, pp. 7ff.; Kohn, *De Pentateucho Sam. etc.*, p. 20.

[57] *Ex* xiv, 31; *ibid* xix, 9; *Deut* xxxiv, 10 The last verse was rendered by the Sam. Targum נביא בישראל כמשה (חורי =) ולא יקום עורי cf next note

[58] *Memar Marqah*, ed Macdonald I, p 93 (= II, pp 151f); I, p 105 (= II, p 175); I, p 128 (= II, p 209); I, p 142 (= II, p 223); I, p 145 (= II, pp. 239f.).

[59] Vilmar, *Abulfathi annales Sam.*, pp. 99f. (based upon *Deut*. xxxiv, 10 and *ibid*. iv, 2 (= *ibid*. xiii, 1).

[60] On the Essenes, cf. Josephus, *The Wars of the Jews* II, viii, 9; Philo, *Apology for the Jews* I. On the Dead Sea Scrolls Sect, cf. Leaney, *The Rule of Qumram etc.*, pp. 188f Cf. also Wieder, *The Judean Scrolls etc.*, pp. 70ff. cf. also my article *ALUOS* VI (1969), pp. 118 and 154 (n. 165). It seems that even among Jewish-Christians there was a certain glorification of Moses. Cf. Schoeps, *Theologie und Geschichte etc.*, p. 110. Cf. C.K. Barret, *The Gospel according to St. John* (London, 1960), p. 225 (on *John* v, 45).

than Moses.[61] The heat of their polemics was therefore turned chiefly on the Rabbis; but undoubtedly it was turned even on those sects who, although they too went to extraordinary lengths to glorify Moses, nevertheless accepted the sanctity of the prophets. The exalted eminence of Moses cannot in itself therefore serve as the *Shiboleth* by which one could adduce evidence of possible inter-relations between the Samaritans and other sects.[62] The uniqueness of the Samaritans rests upon their peculiarly harmonistic exegesis, by which they pressed all the available 'pegs' from the Pentateuch into the service of a preconceived dogmatism, in order to establish the immaculate and infallible character of Moses, who should thus stand out as the *only* harbinger ever commissioned to bestow the divine revelation on mankind.

Thus any unsavoury expression applied to Moses had to be mitigated by the Samaritan exegete in order to remove the offence. It was not at all easy to circumvent the literal meaning of some uncomplimentary expressions, but the dogmatic discrepencies had to be eliminated. Samaritan interpretation went always hand in hand with apologetics. Often when they polemicised against a 'wrong' meaning of 'mistranslation' of Scripture upheld by thier opponents, where nothing more was involved than supplying the 'correct' meaning, their tone is calm, but it becomes passionate where a dogmatic point is at issue.[63] The honour of Moses therefore had to be defended even by a forced re-interpretation of the Scripture. Some examples of such exercises are already found in the Samaritan Targum. Thus "the Lord was wroth with me" (*Deut.* iii, 26) is rendered by the Samaritan Targum, ואתעזר ה' בעותי. The reason is obvious: since it is not possible that God should be angry with Moses, the verse is paraphrased to mean "the Lord passed by my entreaty".[64] It has to be admitted that the Targum is not consistent

---

[61] Ginzberg, *The Legends etc.* VI, pp. 141f. (n. 836); cf. Heinemann, *Darkhei ha-Aggadah*, p. 98. In earlier times, and especially among Hellenistic Jews, the situation was almost the same as among the early sects (cf. previous note). Both Philo and Josephus agree concerning Moses' superiority to all other pious and righteous ones. Cf. Ginzberg, *op. cit.* II, pp. 423f.; VI, pp. 90f. (n. 490) and p. 166 (n. 961); Wolfson, *Philo* I, pp. 450f.

[62] cf. J. Bowman, "The Exegesis etc.", *Oudtestamentische Studien* IX (1950), pp. 225, 257; Massingberd-Ford, "Can we exclude, etc.", *Revue de Qumran* VI (1967), p. 115.

[63] Halkin, "The Relation etc.", *Saadia Anniversary Vol.*, pp. 291f. cf. also *idem.* "The Scholia etc.", *JQR* N.S. XXXIV (1943/4), pp. 291f.

[64] Kohn, *Samaritanische Studien*, p. 79, cf. *ibid.* for further examples.

in this respect. However, Marqah carries this system much further, by applying it also to passages not mentioned by the Targum. The verse "and the anger of the Lord was kindled against Moses" (*Ex.* iv, 14) must indeed have been very embarrassing to Samaritan feeling. Marqah reinterprets this whole passage; and far from laying any blame on Moses for refusing to accept his mission, he praises him. He goes even further by putting these commendations into the mouth of God:

> ... the Lord said to him, 'blest is the hearer who is worthy to hear all this from his Lord! Let your heart be strong, my prophet, for I will manifest to you the sign which you are to perform before the congregation...'

Although these commendations are repeated by Marqah himself, the crucial verse which puts the blame on Moses is avoided. Marqah paraphrases this verse as follows:

> ... the Lord spoke to him with mighty power and the world was filled with dread of Him... Were it not for may favour towards you from the beginning, my anger *would have* reached you... [65]

After all, even amongst the Rabbis opinions were divided as to whether there is any rebuke of Moses implied here.[66] It is the way the text is forcibly explained away which is extraordinary, since in every other respect the Samaritans are of course reputed for their literalism. Such and other similar false exegesis, employed for the glorification of Moses in cases where Scripture is offensive when taken in its literal sense, would strictly speaking be irreconcilable with their own doctrine, thus showing that the Samaritans during the Roman period were already committed to a fixed dogma. Although such dogmas were largely based upon Scripture, they were so rigid that they could not be put in doubt by a single discordant verse; and since scriptural emendations were at least by that time out of the question, the traditional literalist exegesis had to give way to a more recondite system.

There is no need whatever to look for external sources for the formula-

---

[65] *Memar Marqah*, ed. Macdonald I, pp. 9f.; II, pp. 10f. He uses for this purpose a technical term נתן אפרשו the exact meaning of which is not clear, but the context indicates: "let us set out (the whole) section (and not dwell on single expressions). cf. *inf.* n. 86. In the exposition of the 'curses', some passages (III, para. 5ff.) are introduced by the term נתן אפרשו. Most probably Marqah intended to gloss over the details in these cases. The only probable explanation for this exercise is that there existed an unresolved doubt in Marqah's mind as to in which cases does a 'curse' mean a total rejection and in which case is repentance still possible. Cf. *inf.* section (e).

[66] *Zebhaḥim*, 102a, cf. also *Shabbath*, 97a.

tion of the Samaritan concept of Moses. Neither the language [67] nor the motives [68] are Christian in origin, let alone Muslim.[69] Marqah makes it quite clear that Moses is not invested with any divine or semi-divine characteristics. He limits the power delegated to Moses exclusively to matters of this world: "... for you are my second in the *lower* world".[70] Despite all the pre-eminence of Moses above all the prophets, it is only the perfectness of his prophethood and his apostleship which truly matters:

> ... were it not for your prophethood I would not have revealed myself, and my words would not have been heard as long as the world lasts. I revealed myself to *former good men through an angel*, not by revelations of my *own mighty self*. Behold, I reveal *myself* and make my voice to be heard by you...[71]

In later literature there is a more systematic presentation, based on various verses and showing that all other revelations are by way of media (e.g. dreams, visions), and that only Moses merited a genuine divine "mouth-to-mouth" revelation (Num. xii, 6-8).[72] However, the sources of this dogma are already implicit in Marqah :

> "No prophet like Moses has arisen or ever will arise.[73] He was exalted above the whole human race and he attained to be joined by the angels — as it was said to him, 'and there I will meet with thee' (*Exod.* xxv, 22) [74].

Contrary to any superficial impression, Marqah is far from asserting here that Moses' prophecy was commuted through the medium of angels. They are mentioned here only because the biblical verse upon

---

[67] cf. *sup.* Part I, n. 227 and text there.

[68] Marqah's expression: "He who believes in Moses believes in his Lord" is a simple midrash on *Ex.* xiv, 31, and does not imply any soterical powers on the part of Moses (cf. J. Macdonald, *Theology etc.*, p. 150). Furthermore, faith alone has no saving power in Sam. religion. Cf. my article in *ALUOS* VI (1969), pp. 110, 143 (nn. 95, 101). This problem will be dealt with in para (g) *inf.*

[69] cf. Thomson, *The Samaritans*, p. 192.

[70] *Memar Marqah*, ed. Macdonald I, p. 10 = II, p. 12: ‏דאתהו תניני בעלמה דלרע‎. This is a midrash to explain away the expressions ‏אלהים‎ in *Ex.* iv, 16 and *ibid.* vii, 1, which are paraphrased (at the end of the paragraph) by Marqah as having authority only upon the "lower world". cf. *Tanḥuma*, ed. Buber, Vaera para 9.

[71] *Memar Marqah* I, p. 21 = II, p. 32. cf. also *ibid.* I, p. 5 = II, p. 4; cf. the midrash on "Moses Moses" which has the same connotation.

[72] The most systematic prestation is that of Abraham Qabaṣi, *Sir al-qalb*, pp. 64f.

[73] *Memar Marqah*, ed. Macdonald I, p. 111 = II, p. 186. cf. Editor's n. *ibid.* II, n. 269 and *sup.* nn. 57-58.

[74] ‏ואמטה עד אזדמן במלאכיה הך דאמיר לה ואזדמן לך‎

which the midrash is built deals with the cherubim, which according to Samaritan thinking symbolize the angels (cf. *Gen.* iii, 24). Indeed, the 'mercy-seat' in the sanctuary was regarded as the dwelling-place of the angels. For this reason, only the high-priest was allowed to enter there once a year. Nonetheless the revelation to Moses "from between the two cherubim" could not have been through angels, otherwise Marqah would have contradicted himself, since in the same context (a few lines later) he says: "where is there a prophet like Moses whom God addressed mouth-to-mouth?" Here again, Marqah rather reproduces an ancient tradition which might be as old as the Samaritan Pentateuch. Marqah's words "and there I will meet with thee" indicate that this is an exclusive prerogative of Moses, this verse having thus the same connotation as *Num.* xxii, 8. No other person can ever attain this privilege of 'meeting with God' or conversing with Him 'mouth-to-mouth'. This creed is evident from the Samaritan Pentateuch, which has a harmonized text rendering always "I will meet *thee*", in the singular, even in places where the Massoretic text has "with *yuo*", in the plural (*Ex.* xxix, 42; *Num.* xvii, 19).[75] Curiously enough, these variants are supported by the Septuagint.[76]

Another of these ancient traditions may be discerned in Memar Marqah.[77] In praising the letter Phi (= mouth), Moses tells her that although she was not distinguished by beginning a section of the Law yet her merit is greater than all:

---

[75] This is also the reason for the variant ונדרשתי in the Sam. Pentateuch *Ex.* xxix, 43 (M.T. ונועדתי); since "meeting God" could not apply to all the people of Israel. cf. next n.

[76] Geiger, *Nachgelassene Schriften* V, pp. 165f.

[77] I, p. 143 = II, p. 235. Unfortunately, the faulty text caused the Arabic translators to misunderstand this passage. It should read: מן אהן מקומה אתודעת מיתוביתיך אקרי (דאקריך) מרך מיסתיך פ' כל אהן איקרה רבה דבה אתוקרתי Although normally we are not in favour of textual emendations, here the context demands such a slight correction, without which the theme becomes unintelligible. The parallel passages, concerning the other letters, make it also clear that in all of them the sense is the same: 'Why are you claiming more distinctions, are the former ones not sufficient for you?' cf. letter 'ט (I, p. 138 = II, p. 226): מיסתיך אהן איקרה רבה דאתעבד ליך; or, letter 'נ (I, p. 140 = II, p. 229): מיסתיך נ' במד הוה ליך Although different in vocabulary the same sense occurs in connection with letter 'ס (I, p. 142 = II, p. 223): כיתיך דעבדתי עם שרה ... ליתיך or, in letter 'צ (I, p. 144 = II, p. 237) ליך נמי סגי מן הדה or צריכה לרב מן הדה or letter 'ק (I, p. 145 = II, p. 239): ליך אה ק' רב מכן This usage of מיסתיך is also attested by the Talmud, e.g. מיסתיך דקא חזית Giṭṭin 56b (cf. also Babha Bathra 126a, Berakoth 55a etc.).

"with him I speak mouth to mouth (*Num.* xii 8), from this place your status and
the glory by which your Lord glorifies you was made known. Sufficient for you,
o Phi (= mouth), all this glory with which I was glorified."

The letter Phi is comforted by the knowledge of the glory which she
symbolizes, namely the unique distinction of Moses who alone attained
the direct "mouth-to-mouth" (= *Phi*) revelation.

No wonder in later literature Moses is entitled the 'crown of the
prophets'[78] or the 'seal of the prophets', reminiscent of the Islamic title
for their prophet. Here again, despite the tempting resemblance, there
is no reason to assume that, in the interests of elevating the status of
Moses, the Samaritans were prepared to accept external influences to the
neglect of their own doctrine.[79] All such expressions, including even
'prophet of *all* worlds' (a midrash on *Ex.* xix, 9), are nothing else than
"the extent of the Samaritan Israelites' view of the prophet's mission and
commission".[80]

We shall not be far wide of the mark, either in attempting to show that
the legend concerning the birth of Moses, and the all-embracing position
granted to his personality as compared with all others since the Creation,[81] are based upon earlier tradition.

One classical example which nevertheless merits our enquiry here
is the exegesis of the obscure passage in *Ex.* iv, 24-26 which has perplexed
commentators from very ancient times.[82] The Septuagint already renders
this text in an apologetic way by adding that it was "the angel of the
Lord" (and not the Lord himself) who sought to kill Moses. The Samaritans were not so much troubled by this point.[83] For them the whole
story of Moses' neglecting to carry out the rite of circumcision on his
son was untenable and unacceptable. They had to reinterpret this story
in a casuistic manner, alleging that the purport of it concerns Moses'
separation from his wife. There are some divergences between the

---

[78] غِرّة e.g. in *Exodus Commentary* (attributed to Ghazal al-Duweik), p. 93. This
is, however, a midrash on "Moses Moses" (*Ex.* iii, 4) following Marqah (cf. *sup.* n. 71).

[79] cf. J. Macdonald, *Theology etc.*, p. 148 (cf. *ibid.* n. 1).

[80] *ibid.* p. 208.

[81] *Exodus Commentary* (cf. *sup.* n. 78) pp. 41ff., 81ff. From the rich list of authorities
mentioned it is obvious that he tried to utilize any Sam. material he could lay hands on.

[82] cf. *sup.* Part I, nn. 179ff. and text there.

[83] The Sam. Targum does not mention "angel" here, but the Targum is not consistent in this respect (cf. *Gen.* xviii, 33 etc.). On the other hand, the translation of
Abu-Saʿīd (سلاك الله) may be due to the influence of Saadia.

Aramaic Targum and the later Arabic translation of Abu-Saʿīd, but on the main principle there is general agreement throughout the whole Samaritan literature. We cannot here enter into the details of these Samaritan acrobatics, upon which much has been written.[84] We are mainly concerned with the development of this interpretation. It seems that it was based at least on some scriptural pegs. From the Targum on verse 24 (ובעו למעצמאתה) it is apparent that in their oral traditions they read the Hebrew word המיתו not as if it meant "death" (מות), but as if it originated from the root המה, thus giving the sense "and sought to *disturb* him". Secondly, the Samaritan Pentateuch has a slight textual variant: instead of ממנו of the Masoretic Text in verse 26, the Samaritan Pentateuch reads ממנה "and he left her". This raises the question : how was the passage understood in ancient times? The variant itself suggests that at least this verse was already considered in ancient times as referring to the separation of Moses from his wife. This, however, gives a new slant to the whole passage, and from here the way is wide open to the interpretation of the whole story as referring rather to this separation [85] than to the circumcision of the infant, which had to be explained away anyhow, for dogmatic reasons.

It is very unfortunate for us that Marqah treats this passage with great evasiveness,[86] and we cannot reconstruct his interpretation in

---

[84] Geiger, "Neuere Mittheilungen etc.", *ZDMG* XX (1866), pp. 165-170; Kohn, *Samaritanische Studien*, pp. 76-79; Kahle, *Die arabische Bibelübersetzungen*, pp. 23-26; Halkin, "Relation of Sam. to Saadia Gaon", *Saadia Anniversary Vol.*, pp. 287-291.

[85] There is still an appreciable difference between the Sam. Targum and the Arabic translation of Abu-Saʿīd in verse 25 ונסבת צפורה נהר וקעימת עם בטול בנואה/ فاخذت صفوره ضايقة فقطعت رذيلة تبننها. However, the meaning of the Targum as suggested by Kohn (*op. cit.* p. 79); "And Zipporah took a light and made a covenant by the foreskin of her son" does not make any sense. Furthermore, בנואה can not mean 'her son' since this is rendered by the Targum as ברה It is not entirely impossible that the two translations are closer to each other than is apparent from a first glance. The Targum may mean: "and Zipporah took a light" (i.e. *understood* the cause of the disturbance). This may be close to the meaning of the Arabic translation, although the interpretation of צור was derived from different roots — in the Targum from צהר, and in the Arabic translation from צרר. (Cf. Kohn, *ibid.*) "and she cut off (or, left off, as קעמת in *Gen.* xxix, 35; xxx, 9) the vice of her conceiving" (i.e. she decided to stop her marital relations with Moses. This is a Midrash built on שלוחיה *Ex.* xviii, 2, which was understood as synonymous with וירף ממנה). Cf. R. Joshua *Mekhiltha, ad. loc.* (ed. J.H. Weiss, Vienna, 1865, p. 66); Yalquṭ Shimoni I, para 268.

[86] *Memar Marqah*, ed. Macdonald I, p. 11 (= II, p. 14). As in a previous case (cf. *sup.* n. 65), Marqah uses the term נתן אפרשו in order to gloss over the details of the controversial passage.

detail. However, one thing is certain, that Marqah bases his interpretation on the same scriptural 'peg' as the Targum. This is evident from his summary of the story: "and Moses' children turned back (= וירף ממנה) ... as they were afraid (= המיתו from the root המה) that night of what they saw". It is very possible that in the time of Marqah there were still variant opinions on the interpretation of this passage, which led him to hesitate whether or not to commit himself to any of them. While these variant exegetical opinions concerning details may have co-existed for quite a long period, it seems almost certain that on the matter of principle they all agreed that one can not attribute any sin to the Prophet, least of all one involving the death penalty. The Samaritan dogma which was prepared to go to any lengths in glorifying Moses and in absolving him from any unsavoury attribute could never allow the stigma of disobedience to be attached to his figure.

It is, therefore, plain anachronism to assert that the Samaritans adopted the Muslim principle of the Prophet's immunity from sin (عصمة).[87] Long before Islam the Samaritans led the way in this respect, and their glorification of Moses went far beyond anything known in other religions.

This extreme reverence for Moses does not depend on some mysterious type of Messianic speculation or logos-like hypostatical dignity attached to him, but is mainly assignable to his position as the great and *only* Law-giver. The Ṭabbākh makes this point clear [88] by asserting that the purpose underlying the command to the Israelites in Egypt, on the night prior to their leaving Egypt, "and none of you shall go out of the door of his house until morning" (*Ex.* xii, 22) was to uphold the authority of Moses. The purpose of it was to attest the words of the Messenger, because he was directly commissioned by God, and whatever he brought forth must become a Law "which cannot be abrogated".

To understand this statement one has to look into the midrashic background of the story. After the 'plague of darkness' Moses said to Pharaoh "I will see thy face again no more" (*Ex.* x, 29). However, God in his foreknowledge knew that he would be called back, and therefore did not allow Moses to leave the royal palace.[89] It was only after

---

[87] cf. Halkin, *op. cit.* p. 290f. (n. 98).

[88] f. 70a (SLTh.A p. 111).

[89] The scriptural peg upon which this midrash is based is the absence of any mention after *Ex.* x, 29 (despite the long additions in the Sam. Pentateuch following *ibid.* xi, 3) that Moses left Pharaoh. On the contrary, the Sam. Pentateuch states

announcing the last plague to Pharaoh that Moses "went out from Pharaoh in hot anger" (*Ex.* xi, 8). He could never again return to Paraoh, lest his previous words should be broken. This being the case, it would be improper for the elders or for any of the Israelites to be present with the Egyptians after the Prophet had left in anger. The commandment "none of you shall go out" became an injunction to protect the dignity of Moses and to show to all future generations that his words have the power of Law.

This exaggerated force attached to the words of Moses is only another aspect of the supreme dignity of the Law for the Samaritan faith, a dignity unparalleled in any other religion. All other designations of Moses which may occasionally suggest some resemblance to what has been said in other religions about their own founders, are only verbal modifications of this basic concept.[90]

B. THE TORAH THE WORD OF GOD, WRITTEN BY GOD

The belief in the divine origin of the Torah was taken literally by the Samaritans. "The great book received by the great prophet from the right hand of the great king" is a recurring motif in the whole of Samaritan literature.[91] Marqah [92] makes it quite clear that he identifies the sanctity of the Torah with that of the two tablets of the ten commandments, in that they both not only have equal status but also originate directly from the finger and mouth of God. "It was written by the finger of God and descended from heaven on two stone tablets. It was from the mouth of its composer; a prophet received it; ..."[93]

Here as in other places, however, it looks as if two different concepts have been combined into one by Marqah. In some places it looks as though he advocates the doctrine that the Torah was actually written "by the finger of God";[94] while in other places one receives the impres-

---

(*ibid.* 4): "And Moses spoke to Pharaoh" which indicates also that he was still in his presence.

[90] cf. n. 87 *sup.* The foreign phraseology does not change the principles.

[91] אהנו כתבה רבה דקבלה נביה רבה מן ימינה דמלכה רבה Cowley, *Sam. Liturgy* I, p. 49 (letter א) cf. *ibid.* pp. 51, 53, 55, 56, 59, 145 etc. cf. *sup.* n. 58 and text there.

[92] *Memar Marqah,* ed. Macdonald I, p. 134 (= II, p. 219).

[93] For the continuation cf. *sup.* nn. 34-36 and text there.

[94] יהב לך כתבה מכלל בחיין כתבה באצבעה ואושטה מן ימינה לנביא מהימן
Memar Marqah, ed. Macdonald, I, p. 145 (= II, p. 239).

sion that it was written by Moses upon God's command.[95] Although
Marqah does not offer an explicit solution to this discrepancy, there
is no need to assume that there was a conflict in his mind. Any attempt,
however, to reconstruct Marqah's entire way of thought would be too
speculative; instead we may obtain a clearer idea of it from the words
of Abū-l Ḥasan-al-Ṣūrī. He is very careful to reproduce ancient traditions and, in spite of his rationalistic bent, does not deviate from the
traditional path when dogmatic questions are involved. In his chapter
dealing with the attitude of men to the Islamic idea of the "Uncreatedness
of the word of God"[96] he disposes briefly of this problem, by showing
in a rationalistic manner the absurdity of this claim.[97] Although he
adopts a Mu'tazilite argument for proving that the Torah was created,
the major part of the chapter is a defence of the traditional Samaritan
dogma on the "word of God". In this respect, therefore, Abū-l Ḥasan's
arguments no longer follow the rationalistic trend, but are all based on
scriptural exegesis; such a defence is naturally in accordance with the
traditional Samaritan system.

From the beginning of Abū-l Ḥasan's argument,[98] it becomes obvious
that there could not have been a tradition that Marqah even remotely
considered that Moses could have been responsible for committing the
Torah, which he had received orally from God, to writing, since this is
a point which Abū-l Ḥasan vehemently opposes. If the Torah could
have been revealed gradually and then written down in that order,
one would expect a strict chronological order in its sequence; however
the opposite is the case. He bases his main arguments on various
scriptures, the first of these being the story of the manna; at the beginning of the story it is stated that it took place "on the fifteenth day
of the second month after their departing out of the land of Egypt"
(*Ex.* xvi, 1) and then it states, although it was still the first year of their
being in the desert that "the children of Israel did eat manna forty
years" (*ibid.* 35). If the allegation of progressive revelations were true,
then the latter verse should have been after the death of Moses, at the end
of the Pentateuch. There are many other examples revealing the same
truth.[99]

---

[95] כתב ארהותה על מימר ה׳ *ibid.* I, p. 128 (= II, p. 209).

[96] *Ṭabbākh*, f. 167b-176a.

[97] cf. Halkin, "The Relations etc.", *Saadia Anniversary Vol.*, pp. 307-8 (nn. 198-201).

[98] ff. 168b, f.

[99] The other example is that of the law of "water of separation" (מינדה.), the
detailed explanation of which appears only in *Num.* xix, whereas it should have

It is interesting to note that the Rabbis also held to the principle that there is no chronological sequence in the Torah;[100] however, this was never utilized by them as an argument for the divine *writing* of the Law, or for its being revealed in one single instance.[101] Abū-l Ḥasan, on the other hand, takes the traditional Samaritan dogmatic approach that this is a proof that "the messenger was given a perfect and clear book".[102] Furthermore, the exact details of the stories of creation, the tower of Babel, the flood, and the stories of the Patriarchs, are all cited as evidence that the Torah was given by God in the form of a book. It could not have been given in an oral tradition, because then it could have been easily expanded or abridged, which would be quite impossible as regards the Torah.[103] Abū-l Ḥasan claims that there is even biblical evidence for God's writing of the law, "... and I will give thee the tablets of stone *and the Law* and the commandments *which I have written* ...". (*Ex.* xxiv, 12). "I have written" is in the past tense, and according to Abū-l Ḥasan it is a reference to the time before creation. Here a semi-rational reasoning carries this point even further, thus: since the purpose of man's creation was his obedience to God — just as He has prepared all his physical needs for him — so did God *write the Law* for his sake before he was created. In general, however, all the arguments are based on the Samaritan fundamentalist approach which claims that this *Book*, containing the whole Pentateuch from creation to the song of Moses, to the blessing of Moses and even to his death, was revealed on Sinai, written by the finger of God, through the medium of the twentytwo

---

immediately followed the death of the sons of Aaron (*Lev.* x). According to the *Ṭabbākh* (f. 169b) there are so many other examples that it would be impossible to enumerate them.

[100] *Pesaḥim*, 6b. cf. also Rashi on *Gen.* vi, 3; *ibid.* xviii, 3; *Ex.* iv, 20.

[101] cf. *Giṭṭin*, 60a (תורה מגילות מגילות נתנה). In passing it should be noted that in the Talmud one finds expressions that certain passages in the Pentateuch were said by Moses of his own accord. cf. the opinion of Abayye, *Megillah* 31b, (on *Deut.* xviii) והללו בלשון יחיד אמורות ומשה מפי עצמו אמרן. On the other hand there are diametrically opposing statements (cf. *Sanhedrin* 69a). How much of these expressions are results of polemics, is a vexed question. cf. Joël, *Blicke in die Religionsgeschichte etc.* II, pp. 175ff.

[102] ff. 169b, f.

[103] منقول من الاخبار f. 170a. It is very possible that this low opinion concerning 'oral tradition' was expressed only for apologetical reasons, to strengthen the doctrine of the Divine origin of every little detail in the scripture. In general the *Ṭabbākh* regards tradition very highly.

letters, on the cloud with fire.[104] Abū-l Ḥasan considers that the verse: "... when Moses had made an end of writing the words of the Law in a book *until they were finished,*" (*Deut.* xxxi, 24) proves his point, since the copying out of the divine book by Moses was *finished* in such a miraculous way. This was not unlike his words predicting the miracles before their actual occurrence.[105] Such reasoning abandons altogether any rational arguments, and substitutes in their place extreme super-natural dogma. According to such a theory — although Abū-l Ḥasan does not say this explicitly — there are no problems even about verses which indicate that Moses asked God about the details of certain laws,[106] since everything can be explained away as part of that miracle. This is the meaning, according to Abū-l Ḥasan of the expression "That it may be for a witness" (*Deut.* xxxi, 26), since after the occurrence of all these events they opened the Torah in which all was stated, which by its very truth serves as a witness.

Abū-l Ḥasan insists that the Torah is to be attributed to God not only in the broad sense that a Law book is attributed to a certain sultan, although it has in actual fact been written by men on his staff, on his orders. He quotes the liturgies [107] to demonstrate that the 'giving' of the Torah to Moses by God was meant literally. This transfer took place during Moses' first ascent of Mount Sinai, where he stayed for forty days. The scriptural evidence is the following saying of God: "And I will give thee the tablets of stone and the Law and the command-ments *which I have written...*" (*Ex.* xxiv, 12). Later it is stated (*ibid.* xxxi, 18) "And he gave unto Moses, when he had made an end of com-muning with him upon Mount Sinai...", which indicates that Moses received all that he had been promised from God. Since it would be impossible for God to promise him two things (the tablets and the Law) and then only give him one (the tablets only as stated in scripture), and since the tablets were only explicitly mentioned on account of their being broken, it must be assumed that Moses took the Law away with him. This was the purpose of his erecting 'the tent of meeting', "that everyone which sought the Lord went out..." (*Ex.* xxxiii, 7) for it was where the Torah was kept.

---

[104] *ibid.* f. 171a.

[105] *ibid.* f. 171b.

[106] cf. *Lev.* xxiv, 12; *Num.* ix, 8; *ibid.* xv, 34; *ibid.* xxvii, 5; *ibid.* xxxvi, 5. cf. Kroch-mal, *More Neboche Ha-seman,* p. 163.

[107] *ibid.* f. 172b. cf. *sup.* n. 91.

It is not improbable that Marqah's opinions resembled Abū-l Ḥasan's here, and we need not necessarily conclude that there are any contradictions in his opinions; for while it is possible that no detailed theological concept was ever formulated by him, in general one can assume that he thought along the same lines, i.e. the divine writing was given to Moses and was faithfully copied out by him, this copy becoming the prototype which was carefully preserved by tradition.

Although there are some vague expressions in the pseudepigraphical literature about Laws written by God's own hand, no parallel to such an extreme literalist opinion about the origin of the Torah, as we have seen among the Samaritans, can be found among them. The only possible exception to this conclusion is to be found amongst the Dead Sea Scroll Sect, where it is implied that the whole of the Law was written on tablets like the two tablets mentioned (*Ex.* xxxii, 16).[108] We do not, however, know what conclusions were drawn by this sect from such a statement Judging from their treatment of the scriptural text, which often reproduced a perplexing mixture of different traditions, it seems in all likelihood that they accepted many variant texts as equally sacred.[109] This fact alone does not allow us to view their treatment of the text with great reverence. In complete contrast to this approach the Samaritans drew their extreme conclusion that every word and letter, as it is found in their own version, is of divine origin without the slightest change or permutation, and hence every detail is sacred.[110]

Comparison with the medieval sects shows even more clearly how the Samaritans' literal belief in the divine origin of the Torah was distinct from the rest. The Karaites, as represented by Qirqisāni, were content to interpret *Deut.* xxxi, 9 as meaning that Moses was 'the compiler' of the Torah.[111] They too believed that the entire Pentateuch, from Genesis to the end of Deuteronomy, including the story of Moses' death, was written by Moses himself, but they have no doctrine of a divinely written original. Indeed, despite their literal exegesis, the

---

[108] *Manual of Discipline*, pl. X-XI; cf. Th. H. Gaster, *The Scriptures of the Dead Sea Sect*, p. 199 (n. 9).

[109] cf. my article in *ALUOS* VI (1969), pp. 105, 121f., 140 (n. 64), 158ff. (nn. 193-209).

[110] Gaster, *Eschatology*, p. 29. cf. now J.D. Purvis, *The Samaritan Pentateuch and the Origin of the Sam. Sect* (Cambridge, Mass, 1968), pp. 58f. Purvis's comparison of the Sam. inconsistencies in matter of spelling to this of the Dead Sea Scrolls Sect is far-fetched (cf. n. 109) and his criticism of Ben Ḥayyim is not justified.

[111] H. Hirschfeld, *Qirqisāni Studies*, pp. 23, 43 (proposition n. 1).

Karaites were more open to rationalistic influences than were the Samaritans. This may be the cause for their admitting that: "In many sentences there occurs a word which is a mere *Lapsus*, not being required at all", or that certain verses "contain repetitions which might have been omitted."[112] The Samaritans, on the other hand, would never have dared to use such expressions about the divine text.

We may assert that Samaritan exegesis went furthest in upholding the doctrine of the infallible inspiration of Scripture, extending this infallibiliy to every aspect and detail of the divine word. Consequently, doctrines and practices based on such an infallible scripture could not be subject to any change.[113] Indeed, the motif of 'Perfection', although originating from Scripture (*Deut.* xxxii, 4),[114] was treated in the most literal manner when applied to Moses. The list of expressions which were used to denote the Torah,[115] also indicates that there was nothing against which its sanctity and perfection could be compared.

Judaism, when developing its concept of the Torah, regarded it also as being created before the world.[116] Philo even went to the extreme of postulating a pre-existance of the Torah, almost identical with the Platonic pre-existance of the 'Ideas'.[117] However, despite all the strict legalistic tendencies of Judaism, elevating the Law above all other aspects of doctrine and theology,[118] its exponents could never match the inflexible stand taken by the Samaritans in this field. Thus despite all their harmonizations, the Rabbis had to admit that verses may sometimes contradict one another.[119] The Samaritans, on the other hand, would never admit the remotest possibility of such contradictory verses existing even for didactic purposes or to derive a moral or a new teaching from 'apparent difficulties'.

We have seen how similar the opinions expressed by Marqah on the origin of the Torah, are to those of the Ṭabbākh, although they were

---

[112] *ibid.* pp. 37, 57 (proposition 21).

[113] Smart, *The Interpretation of Scripture*, p. 183.

[114] *Memar Marqah* (ed. Macdonald), I, p. 97 = II, pp. 140f. cf. Editor's n. 41.

[115] cf. Vilmar, *Abulfathi annales Sam.*, p. xcviii.

[116] Schechter, *Some aspects of Rab. Theology*, p. 128; Moore, *Judaism* I, p. 526; Bonsirven, *Le Judaisme Palestinien* I, pp. 250f.

[117] Wolfson, *Philo* I, p. 183. The Sam. who rejected the Islamic doctrine of 'Eternity of the Word of God' (sup. nn. 96ff.) would have rejected Philo's ideas on the same ground.

[118] Moore, *op. cit.* I, p. 263; Bonsirven, *op. cit.* I, p. 248.

[119] cf. *sup.* nn. 42-45 and text there.

separated by many centuries. It is therefore not surprising that the same subject repeated by the Hillukh (written approximately three centuries after the Ṭabbākh) hardly contains any new elements.[120] Of course, this is not the only field in which Samaritan writers, parted by many centuries and in some cases even by a millennium, agree on a traditional matter, and we may say in fact that this is the usual state of affairs, as can be amply shown by examples in almost every other field.

It would, therefore, be erroneous to suggest that the Samaritan Pentateuch which, as we know, by its very nature consists of a text amplified by harmonizations, was constantly being altered by the Samaritans.[121] Not only did their concept of the 'Perfect Law', which could in no sense whatsoever be deficient, prohibit any emmendations, but it even prevented tampering with its minutest details. So the allegations that Marqah used a different text from that of later generations, were either based on faulty texts or misunderstandings.[122] Although we cannot enter into the complicated problems of the origins of the Samaritan Pentateuch here, one can safely assume that it goes back to pre-Christian times and that in its essentials the text today is the same as it was then.[123] In general, all the Samaritan writers known to us quote accurately from the Pentateuch, and it is very seldom that one finds any deviations from their 'Textus Receptus', and only in very rare cases misquotations. These, however, are in the majority of cases due to the carelessness of writers who quoted orally or by heart, and their memories most probably failed them.[124]

It would not be too far-fetched to suggest that the doctrines about the perfection or the Torah mentioned above, were in fact instrumental

---

[120] *Hillukh*, pp. 239-249. The evidence from *Deut.* iv, 9; and *ibid.* x, 21 ("the things which thine eyes saw") as a reference to Divine writing by the 22 Ancient Hebrew letters was already implied by Abū-l Ḥasan (cf. *sup.* n. 105). The same applies about the evidence from "blot me out of thy book" (*Ex.* xxxii, 32) as a proof that it is identical with God's original of the Torah, since already Marqah considers all details about Moses being written by God (cf. *sup.* n. 59 and text there). The only novel element is the 'proof' that Pentecost is also called "the Giving of the Law", to which the Jews also agree, that the Law was "given" (not only dictated) by God . (cf., however, Abūl-Ḥasan's interpretation of *Ex.* xxx, 18, *sup.*).

[121] cf. Abdel-Al, *A Comparative Study, etc.*, p. 23.

[122] cf. my article in *ALUOS* VI (1969), pp. 107f., 141 (n. 75f.).

[123] Albright, *From Stone Age, etc.*, p. 345; cf. also my article *op. cit.* pp. 105f., 139f. (nn. 57f.). cf. now Purvis, *op. cit.* (n. 110), pp. 50f., 86 (and *ibid.* n. 151).

[124] Ben-Ḥayyim, *Literary and Oral Tradition etc.* I, pp. 254 (n. 5), 255 (n. 8), 257 (n. 11) and 268 (n. 4).

in shaping the principles for its exegesis. For the extreme legalistic approach to the text, in conjunction with the constant and mutual relationship between a 'perfect' text and a 'perfect' tradition, could well have cultivated a mode of interpretation which adheres to the literal sense of the words. From the earliest times the Samaritans could easily claim that by being loyal to the letter of the text, they were also the guardians of the sense, in that they were continually preserving the original intention of the divine legislator. Just as the Pharisean Jew relying on the 'Oral Law', and the Alexandrian Hellenistic Jew believing in his inspirations, which prompted him to allegorize, based their exegesis upon their respective texts — which according to the best of their belief contained all the 'hints' or 'pegs' necessary for the advancement of their respective traditions — so also the Samaritans affected by their 'perfect' text, in that their individual tendencies towards a more figurative and revolutionary interpretation of scripture were seriously limited and curbed by it.[125] In the conflict between the Torah and external influences like those of philosophy, science, and modernization due to changes in the mode of life,[126] the letter of the Law and the rigoristic simplicity of its meaning always gained the upper hand. In contrast to the other systems of exegesis, the Samaritans believed that "the Torah speaks mainly in a human language".[127] This is applied not only to the straightforward laws but also to matters of prophecy or eschatology, where one is likewise expected to understand the words in a literal sense. Thus, for example, the introduction to 'the blessing of the tribes' (*Deut.* xxxiii) although directed against infidels, is set out in a clear and unambiguous form in order "that the infidel should not take its expressions and misinterpret it in the wrong way..."[128]

In general, it could be said that the Samaritans believed that the text which they had inherited demanded a verbal explanation, following the sense that was understood from a literal or simple interpretation of the words. Nevertheless, it would be going too far to state that they themselves believed that every detail could be understood from the

---

[125] cf. my article *op. cit.*, *passim*.

[126] cf. *inf.* para (f).

[127] cf. Heinemann, *Darkhei Ha-Aggadah*, pp. 12, 96ff., 183.

[128] *Ṭabbākh*, f. 201b. جعلها تعالى مقدمه الايه حتى لا يبقى للمحالف طريق الى ان يتناول فى الفاظها ما لا يليق بها الكلام فى معرفة الحدود الداله على حقايق المعلومات

literal meaning or the words. In the Ṭabbākh, Abū-l Ḥasan is forced
to admit that the reare four possible methods of interpretation. In a
long-winded chapted fealing with the philosophical definitions of words,
entitled "A chapter on the science of definition, indicating the truthful-
ness of cognition",[129] he investigates the possible approaches to the
interpretation of words. It is to be regretted that these long philosophical
and psychological definitions cannot be reproduced here as they have
no direct bearing on biblical exegesis proper. However, we are concerned
with his definition of the four types of sense. These are: 1) Factual,
2) Figurative, 3) (what suggests) a general meaning, 4) (a text which)
lends itself to explanation or (explaining it in a figurative way).[130]
Unfortunately, the fact that Abū-l Ḥasan does not enter into the actual
definition of exegetical forms here, makes our task very difficult when we
try to discover in what circumstances one of the four forms of interpretation could be applied. However, the general drift of his words seems
to be, that in the majority of cases the factual or literal interpretation
is to be followed, the only exception being when the text indicates that
either a figurative, or a general meaning, or an 'explaining away' —
whether for theological or other reasons — is intended. Elsewhere,
however, he appears more explicit. In his chapter devoted to refuting
the philosophers' attacks against the Torah, he explains himself more
fully and uses examples which makes his definitions clearer.[131] Even
here, however, there is no clear indication as to which way to follow,
but he does divide the semantic field into two major categories. The
problem discussed is, how can the expression 'saying ' be used in the
case of something which is hidden in the heart, especially in connection
with *Gen.* xxvii, 41? The explanation which follows states that the
language is subordinate to the sense, which can be divided into two,
one being the factual (literal sense) and the other being the figurative.
He defines the factual sense as being the explicit meaning, using trans-

---

[129] ff. 176a-185b. For the general philosophical ideas, cf. (SLTh. pp. 852f.).

[130] محتمل التأويل 1) حقيقه 2, مجاز 3) محوى 4,

[131] ff. 103a f. اعلم ان اللفظ مسخر المعني وفيه مجاز وحقيقه فالحقيقه ما
يستفاد معناه بظاهر الفاظه وفي مواضعة اللغه والمجاز المعبد عنه بخلاف ما
وضع له في اللغه وكل مجاز له حقيقه والذي اشار اليه مورده الشبهه محتمل
التأويل فكلما كان محتملا للتاؤتل لا يجوز ان يتخد دلاله ولا سيما في الامور
الشريعيه

parent language, while the figurative is the exact opposite, with the
evasiveness of the language giving rise to many possible interpretations.
Each figurative meaning, however, has its factual basis and he disposes
of the arguments of those who try to find discrepancies in the biblical
text by stating that anything which lends itself to various interpretations (تأويل) cannot be used as reliable evidence in matters of law and
belief. This principle is reaffirmed in a different context when the problem
arises as to whether the 'priestly benediction' may be recited at a time
when there is no King. He gives the answer that the verse (*Gen.* xlviii,
20) where the sense allegedly indicates that the blessing is only valid in the
presence of a king like Joseph, cannot be taken as a proof. "If any contradiction exists in the scripture, part of which is explicit while the other
part is doubtful, it is imperative that the explicit part should decide
the case. The opaque scripture cannot serve either as evidence against
a prophecy or for a prohibition or for a legal permission."[132] It is
impossible to deduce from all these examples in what circumstances,
if ever, one is permitted to use a figurative interpretation. Indeed, the
cases mentioned by Abū-l Ḥasan only indicate that the Islamic principle
of (تأويل i.e. deeper and inner interpretation) cannot be used as an
important method to eliminate doubt in cases where it would contradict
more explicit rules or opinions.[133] This, however, is only a general
principle of exegesis that, whenever one is in doubt about the exact
meaning of a passage, one must utilize a more explicit part of the scripture
in order to elucidate the 'dark' saying. In fact this is the general principle
which is behind all types of exegesis, whether Rabbinical midrash, or
Samaritan, or even other sectarian commentaries which all in common
employ analogy in order to understand passages that are doubtful,
from those which are clear.[134]

   Although we did not find any clear ruling, it is certain that the
general tendency was to be extremely literalistic whenever possible.
This approach is also based upon the traditional interpretations of earlier
generations, where we have already found that Marqah frequently

---

[132] f. 193b. الجواب اعلم ادام الله تاييدك ان النصوص اذا تعارضت
فكان منهم محكم ومتشابه ان يرد المتشابه الى المحكم ولا يجوز ان يستدل
بالنص المتشابه على نبوة نبى ولا تحرتم ولا على اباحه

[133] cf. Halkin, "The Relation of the Sam. to Saadia Gaon", *Saadia Anniversary
Vol.*, p. 286, nn. 82-3.

[134] cf. my article in *ALUOS* VI (1969), pp. 125f. (n. 2).

attempts to impose a literal meaning even in cases where another type of interpretation would appear more logical. Thus we find that in his interpretation of the song of Moses, regardless of the fact that the language is poetical and readily lends itself to figurative interpretation, he always attempts to give the literal meaning, especially if by using this method he can make it appear more miraculous. It must be admitted, however, that these passages are suspect because of their confused language, and it is very doubtful whether they can be genuinely attributed to Marqah. All the same, they show a pattern of early Samaritan exegesis and the following are just two examples of this. The first is taken from the eighth miracle concerning the Red Sea.[135] "The sea was changed into a dry state (*Ex.* xiv, 21). He made the sea into dry land, as though there had not been any water flowing over it since the day it was created, so that Israel would not be smitten while passing through it." This is evidently a midrash on the words "dry Land", which shows to what extremes they went in their literalistic interpretation. We find a similar exposition in the second example, taken from the thirteenth miracle from there, which says:[136] "Its voice (of the Water) was heard from all directions at the time when the water was flowing so that even the nations heard it. By this the great prophet Moses was recognized in his prophethood ...". This is again a literalistic midrash on *Ex.* xv, 14, which gives the impression that it was not a rumour that the nations heard, but the actual sound of the waters of the Red Sea dividing.

Such inferences from explicit sayings to more obscure ones are very common in Samaritan exegesis, and are even applied in matters of capital punishment. Thus we find for example that the laws for intentional murder are deduced from those dealing with unintentional murder by inference from the verses in *Num.* xxxv, 9 and what follows, and *Deut.* xix, 4, with the restult that the Kāfi[137] puts forward three conditions which show that murder was intentional: 1) enmity, 2) hatred, and 3) seeking the harm (of the victim). It is obvious that the first condition is taken from *Deut.* xix, 4, while the second and the third are from *Num.* xxxv, 23. Naturally, the Kāfi is not satisfied with a literal exposition, but also includes cases which are not mentioned explicitly, as for example the case of killing by poison found further on in the same chapter. Here again the literal interpretation is applied, but its scope is greatly

---

[135] *Memar Marqah*, ed. Macdonald, I, p. 34 (= II, p. 51).
[136] *ibid.*
[137] p. 273.

extended, for it is very possible that *Ex.* xxi, 14 was used as the source, i.e. "to slay him by guile" although it is not explicitly quoted, since this law could be taken to include any murder which involves crafty plotting, such as poisoning.

A further exposition of this type is to be found in the case of an injured person who does not die.[138] "If he rise again and walk about upon his staff then shall he that smote him be quit." (*ibid.* 19) as opposed to the case in which a master smites his slave where it is explicitly stated: "Notwithstanding, if he continue a day or two, he shall not be punished." (*ibid.* 21). Since the former case of a free man being injured appears ambiguous, they once again resort to comparison with the more explicit case, namely the injury of the slave, and arrive at the conclusion that there must be a difference between the killing of a free person and that of a slave, and consequently if the slave is given two days in which to die, the free person must have more; (one opinion is seven days — five more than the slave, according to the number of the books of the Pentateuch!; another is at least a lunar month, according to the days of mourning; while yet another opinion is more literalistic in only lifting the death penalty if the victim "walked about"). This literal interpretation was doubtless also the source of a previous ruling, namely if a person survived the injuries for some days and then died without being able to walk outside. Here the analogy to the slave is not practicable, since, although he might live longer than the days already specified, he could nevertheless have died as a direct result of his injuries. Here the Kāfi rules that the verdict will depend upon medical evidence as to whether the person died from his injuries or from another cause.

There is no limit to such literalistic exposition in which the obscure details are explained by various types of analogy with more explicit verses. However, in most of these cases the interpretation does not deviate from the literal sense of scripture. It is in the field of civil law that one most frequently finds such elucidations, as it entails an abundance of details and parallel sources which make comparative deductions almost unavoidable.[139]

Another important principle of the Samaritans, arising from their belief in the literal and verbal inspiration of the text, is their insistence

---

[138] pp. 276f.

[139] The same pattern is followed in the laws of "Deposits", pp. 288f. (cf. Abdel-Al, *A Comparative Study etc.*, pp. 604; 713); the laws of "Borrowing", pp. 290f. (Abdel-Al, *ibid.* pp. 608; 715); on the laws of "Usury", pp. 294f. (Abdel-Al, *ibid.* pp. 609, 716), etc.

on all its details being absolutely necessary. There are no redundant words or superfluous letters, and even the minutest parts of scripture are all sacred and must have a special reason for being there. According to this principle, the expression "or be in a journey afar off" (*Num.* ix, 10) is used by the Kāfi as evidence that the passover sacrifice can only be offered at the 'Chosen Place'. The argument is as follows: if this were not the case and sacrifices could be offered at any of the Samaritan villages, then this clause would be superfluous, as there is hardly a place in Palestine from which one could not have easily reached a Samaritan settlement, since they were scattered over the whole land.[140]

No effort was spared in emphasizing that the literal text must be meticulously followed. Although we will have to deal separately with the general arguments employed by the Samaritans in their staunch defence of the infallibility of their text over all the other versions known to them,[141] at this juncture we are only concerned with those arguments which they supported by exegetical proofs, in order to demonstrate the validity of their version alone. Regarding the famous text: "and on the seventh day God finished his work" (*Gen.* ii, 2), the Samaritan text (in agreement with the LXX and the Peshitta) has the variant: "on the sixth day".[142] The Ṭabbākh, after quoting the argument used by the Jews in defence of their text — that God knows the exact definition of "day" and He did not therefore have to stop his work before the exact beginning of the "seventh day"[143] — points out a logical flaw in this argument.[144] They have to admit that the word "day" is not decisively confined to one specific meaning, since it can mean either a full day or 'day-light time' as in *Gen.* i, 5. According to the argument which has

---

[140] p. 221 (cf. SLTh.A pp. 41f.).

[141] *inf.* para (c).

[142] The Rabbis were also aware of this variant, and explained it (*Megillah* 9a) as a deliberate paraphrasing on the part of the 'Elders' who translated the text. This is one of the 'changes' upon which all the translators agreed 'miraculously', although they were separated into solitary chambers and therefore could not communicate with each other.

[143] Such is the opinion of R. Simeon b. Yoḥai (*Gen.* Rabba, para x, 10). However, the Rabbis did not expect outsiders to follow this argument and hence the legend on the origins of the LXX (cf. previous note).

[144] f. 191b. اعلم ايدك الله ان كل نص يحتمل التأويل لا يجب ان يتحدد دليلا وان اليوم فى العبرانى يفيد سبعة اقسام يوم يفيد زمان الضو حسب قوله ויקרא אלהים לאור יום القسم الثانى ...

already been frequently cited, such an ambiguous expression cannot serve as a 'proof text' and therefore the Jews' text and exegesis cannot be correct.

The Kāfi, being less polemical in tone, does not usually mention either the version or the exegesis of their opponents in similar cases. However it does defend the 'right' version by exegetical devices, taken from the strictly literal sense of scripture. One example may serve to illustrate such implicit defence of their version. On the verse "Ye shall not eat of anything that dieth of itself etc." (נבלה Deut. xiv, 21), the Samaritan version, which differs only by one letter from the Massoretic text (M.T. מכר; S.P. מכרה), gives it a different sense in: "Thou mayest give it unto the stranger ... that he may eat it; or he may sell it to a foreigner." The Kāfi maintains [145] that this reading is the only possible one, since an Israelite is forbidden to sell the carcase (which is considered as causing Levitical defilement) and this meaning is, moreover, implied in the end of the verse : "for thou art an holy people unto the Lord." One could naturally quote many such cases of literalistic rigidity in exegesis, which occur even more frequently in places where there are no textual differences.[146]

It would be wrong to conclude that the Samaritans only took the trouble to indulge in such detailed and exacting exegesis, which kept meticulously close to the text, when halakhic issues were involved. We can take any instance where no obvious halakhic deductions can be drawn, or where no major doctrinal issues are involved, and still find the same line followed. One example of this is the exegesis of the Ṭabbākh on the order in which Joseph made his brethren sit : "The firstborn according to his birthright and youngest according to his youth." (Gen. xliii, 33).[147] Here no less than three different expositions are quoted but all of them are in strict accordance with their traditional literalism.

When we inquire further into the principles behind the literalistic philosophy in which linguistic and thought structures create an inseparable magic circle, we are led closer towards the definition of the relationship between this literalism and the belief in 'verbal inspiration'. Indeed, there is no doubt that the views held by the Samaritans on the nature of 'the Divine Word' are directly responsible for their rigid

---

[145] pp. 315ff. cf. the Rabbinic opinions on this matter (Pesaḥim 22b).
[146] cf. n. 139 sup.
[147] f. 50a f. (cf. SLTh.A pp. 92f.).

approach to its exegesis. In contrast to some modern scholars who try to distinguish between 'verbal inspiration' and 'inerrancy',[148] for the Samaritans at least such fine distinctions did not exist. Their belief in the sanctity of each and every detail of the Scriptures, all of them being infused with divine purpose and meaning, not only raised the text above possible error but at the same time created the belief in 'inerrancy', both in its transmission and in its exegesis. There was no place afforded to any human element in its treatment, and the possibility of interference with the text by the introduction of 'external' details into its commentary was equally denied. It was firmly believed that the exegete is guided by a self-explanatory and an unmistakable sense of the Word.

Only by comparison with other systems may we gain a real understanding of the distinctive features of the principles underlying the Samaritan exegesis. The extreme opposite to their system was that of Rabbinic Judaism, which proudly asserted the validity of manifold interpretation of the biblical text, all levels of which were considered true. Despite the fact that all the deductions which were derived from the various layers of scripture were mutually incompatible, they could nevertheless all be considered as being: "the words of the living God."[149] Although we cannot deny that there existed some faint awareness among the Rabbis of the 'plain' sense of scripture, it is not easy to discern between straightforward exegesis and mere employment of scripture as a mnemotechnical aid, or as a 'peg' upon which to hang rabbinical sayings.[150]

The Dead Sea Scroll Sect, although holding to a strictly literalistic exegesis in matters of religious law, followed a free figurative exposition in other fields where they applied the system of *pesher*.[151] Presumably one of the hermeneutical principles upon which the whole system of *pesher* was built, is the assigning of more than one meaning to the words of scripture.[152] Although, due to the lack of written sources, we have

---

[148] cf. Smart, *The Interpretation etc.*, pp. 194-5.

[149] The most outspoken expressions are: (on *Jeremiah* xxiii, 29) "as the sledge-hammer (when shattered by the harder rock) is divided into many shivers so the words of the Torah differ in Commentaries" (*Sanhedrin* 34a); or (on *Song of Songs* V, 11) "mounds of (halakhoth may be expounded) on every tip (of the letters of the Torah), (*Erubhin* 21b; *Menaḥoth* 29b). cf. my article in *ALUOS* VI (1969), pp. 101, 135f. (nn. 32-33).

[150] Weiss, *Dor Dor etc.* I, pp. 150, 194.

[151] cf. my article in *ALUOS* VI (1969), pp. 122, 159f. (nn. 203-209).

[152] Brownlee, "Biblical Interpretation etc.", *BA* XIV (1951), p. 74 (cf. also *ibid.* p. 61).

no means of comparing the exegetical methods of other Jewish sects of the pre-Christian era, it seems fair to assume that by that time at least, the Samaritans (perhaps with the exception of the Sadducees) were already the most extreme literalists. The system most diametrically opposed to theirs was that followed by the Christian church, which up to modern times has accepted that exegesis should be built on the principle of multiple meaning in the scriptural text.[153]

Comparison with the medieval type of literalism as displayed by the Karaites also shows that the Samaritans went much further than they did in following their own extremist traditions. Qirqisāni's exegetical principles modify absolute literalism, because if one were to follow such a rigid system in every case "this would lay the biblical word open to misconceptions."[154] Hence, in such cases where they considered the literal concept impossible, they employed allegorical methods instead. Although the same type of philosophical enlightenment which prompted the Karaites to allegorize also had its impact on the Samaritans, they nevertheless refrained from making sweeping generalizations regarding allegorical interpretations. The Samaritans included the Karaites in their usual criticism of Judaism, namely that they had falsified the sacred text,[155] and in particular that they had deviated from the literal observance of certain precepts, especially those which were ordained in the Pentateuch to be "everlasting Statutes".[156] Their inclusion of the Karaites in this criticism must have been justified by the fact that they, in holding to the sanctity of the Prophets and the Hagiographa, were becoming more and more accustomed to figurative explanations arising from the subject matter of these latter texts, which by their nature alone prompted allegorizations. The fact that the Prophets and the Hagiographa abound in expressions which can only be interpreted allegorically was acknowledged even by they Rabbis. Their opposition to allegorization was therefore not absolute but directed only against over-indulgence in this type of interpretation and its employment in fields where it endangered the plain sense in matters of law and doctrine.[157]

---

[153] Even the School of Antioch, although repudiating allegory, by employing typology admitted nevertheless the multiple meaning of the Biblical word. cf. A. Vidler, *The Modernist Movement in the Roman Church* (Cambridge, 1934), pp. 217ff.

[154] Hirschfeld, *Qirqisāni Studies*, p. 24.

[155] cf. *inf.* para (c).

[156] Munajja, *Masā'il al-Khilāf* II, p. 124. cf. also my article *op. cit.* pp. 114, 119, 149 (n. 131), 155 (n. 172).

[157] cf. *sup.* nn. 150-151.

It is strange that the Talmud, although it often attacks the Sadducees for their literalism and even pokes fun at their sluggish understanding of scripture,[158] does not throw the charge of literalism in the face of the Samaritans. However, we cannot derive any conclusions from this silence. It is possible that this attitude towards the Sadducees originates from the Pharisean belief that Tradition and Oral Law are equally binding upon all Jews, and the Sadducees were therefore heretics who transgressed the 'Ancestral Traditions'. Often, indeed, the charge of hypocrisy was added to these Rabbinical polemics, indicating that the Sadducees were worldly people and pleasure seekers and their ideology nothing more than a pretext for their ungodliness.[159] The Samaritans, on the other hand, were considered sincere people, so much so in fact that the Talmud itself testifies that "They are very strict in their observances, even more so than Israel".[160] These same sources, however, also indicate that the Samaritans 'are ignorant of the subtle points (and details) of the ritual laws". These references undoubtedly contain veiled abuse of their ignorance of the 'real' interpretation of the Law, implying that these rituals so meticulously observed by the Samaritans are only based on their 'ignorant' literalistic exegesis.

The Samaritan Targum, which is amongst the earliest written records, does not always give a clear picture as to the extent to which literalism was practised by the Samaritans. The Rabbinical Targumim, namely the Greek of Aquila and the Aramaic of Onqelos, are also to a greater extent literalistic. The fact that the Samaritan Targum slavishly follows the Samaritan Pentateuch to the point of occasionally rendering an unintelligible Aramaic text,[161] does not signify that the Targum took literalism to greater lengths than later Samaritan writers. In general it may be stated that not all details which appear as meaningless tautologies, are in reality of this nature. Often what is unintelligible in the Samaritan Pentateuch is explained by the midrash implicit in the Targum. Thus for example, *Gen.* xxi, 23 with its Samaritan variant is totally unintelligible (M.T. ולנכדי; S.P. ולנגדי).[162] The Targum in rendering ולניני by

---

[158] *Sukkah* 48b.

[159] *Aboth de Rabbi Nathan* I, ch. 5; II, ch. 10 (ed. Schechter, p. 26).

[160] *Berakhoth* 47b; *Giṭṭin* 10a; *Qiddushin* 76a; *Ḥullin* 4a.

[161] Kohn, *Samaritanische Studien*, pp. 36f.

[162] The change from כ to ג must be very early; in the palaeo-Hebrew script of the Dead Sea Scrolls (especially the Leviticus fragment, 2Q5) the two letters are still very close. In Sam. script they are more distinct. cf now J.D. Purvis, *The Sam. Pentateuch etc.* (Cambridge, Mass., 1968), Tables III and VI respectively.

ולמולדי makes the meaning clear; for since the latter expression includes all descendents, the former cannot mean "grandson", since both words are *hapax legomena* for the Samaritans in that they appear only once in the Pentateuch, they must therefore have understood the verse as follows: "... that thou wilt not deal falsely with me, nor with my off-spring, nor with those that stand before me — but according to the kindness. ..."

It is not easy to deal in detail with the Targum, since many of the direct renderings are still unintelligible to us. However, they undoubtedly originate in an exegesis which depended on a different usage of Hebrew by the Samaritans, or are due to textual difficulties.[163] Unfortunately it is precisely because of the word-for-word rendering of the Targum, and its literalism, that so many of these expositions remain a complete mystery.

Marqah's expositions are much clearer, since he takes the same midrashic elements and reproduces them in a wider context. In following his exegesis, however, one is struck by his persistent attempt to keep close to the literal meaning; for even in the case of the exposition of *Deut.* xxxii, which was understood as an oracular prophecy and by its very nature would use figurative expressions, his aim is to follow the literal sense. For example, verse 13 was understood by Marqah as a reference to past events but it was to be taken literally.[164] Consequently he connected it with a story about the Hebrew children in Egypt when Pharaoh had decreed: "Every son that is born, ye shall cast into the river" (*Ex.* i, 22). The Israelite women therefore gave birth to their children in the wilderness in order to circumvent Pharaoh's decree. In the event of sons being born, they were left in the wilderness (cf. *Deut.* xxxii, 10), where they were miraculously fed. Hence the expression "He made him to suck honey out of the rock and oil out of the flinty rock" could be taken literally. Naturally, such legends built on similar literalistic elements were also to be found in Rabbinic literature.[165]

At this juncture the question arises as to what occurs in cases similar to this, where the literal meaning is totally unacceptable. If one considers,

---

[163] cf. Kohn, *op. cit.* pp. 62f.

[164] *Memar Marqah* (ed. Macdonald) I, pp. 103f. (= II, p. 172). The origin of the midrash is *Deut.* xxxii, 10 יאמצהו בארץ מדבר (S.P.).

[165] Ginzberg, *Legends* II, pp. 257f.; III, p. 33; V, p. 344 (n. 25); VI, p. 12 (n. 61).

for instance, the verses which speak of God "executing judgment" upon
the Egyptian Gods (*Ex.* xii, 12; *Num.* xxxiii, 4), they imply in their
strictly literal sense that these Gods were real powers. Obviously no
theologian could allow such a 'misunderstanding', i.e. that scripture
itself testifies to the reality of idols, to be admitted. Furthermore, such a
'misinterpretation' would openly contradict other verses explicitly
denying the existence of any other powers besides God. Marqah disposes
of this difficulty[166] by implying that their destruction was not due to
their possessing any celestial vigour, but rather because their worshippers
became corrupted and defiled through them. By means of this device
Marqah was able to retain the literal meaning of the verse and at the
same time to give a rational reason for "executing judgment" upon the
idols. It appears that in Marqah's mind the prohibition against the
Asherah (*Ex.* xxxiv, 13; *Deut.* vii, 5; *ibid.* xii, 3; *ibid.* xvi, 21) and against
Molech (*Lev.* xviii, 21; *ibid.* xx, 1-5) were fused together as one concept,
namely that children were used as sacrifices to certain trees. He therefore
states that God "slew unclean firstborn and defiling[167] Gods". The
firstborn and the Gods are interrelated in Marqah's exegesis since the
former were intended as victims for the latter. For this reason alone,
and not because God was jealous of them or considered them as rivals,
the source of the corruption and the defilement had to be totally uprooted;
so God "destroyed *trees* planted upon uncleanness".[168] Finally he reveals
the background on which his reasoning is based when he says : "He
slew firstborn who were offered to the demons."[169] Here Marqah is
using another analogy in interweaving *Deut.* xxxii, 17 into the complex
of his anti-idolatory preaching, with the probable intention of giving a
further rationalistic bent to these implied criticisms of this superstition.
He intended to show how all these corrupting practices are built upon
non-existent or 'imaginary devils' which can only demand sacrifices
but are otherwise powerless, and can in no way aid their worshippers.

---

[166] *Memar Marqah* (*idem.*) I, pp. 23f. (= II, p. 36).

[167] מסאבין אלהין מסיבין = מסאבין Arabic translation طميّة

[168] « סבה על מנצבין דהוו אילניה » « סבה » here undoubtedly stands for סאבה
cf. Targum on *Gen.* xxxiv, 5. The Arabic translation on Marqah paraphrases סבה as
الحيض (= נדה?). This is also the meaning of the addition in Ms. K. which reads:
שבשבהתה דהות נציבה על סובתה (= שבשהתה?) "corrupting (idols or trees)
planted upon uncleanness".

[169] קטל בוכרין דהוו מקרבין לשידין

In another instance [170] where he is dealing with the sinfulness of man, Marqah makes it clear that his homilies on Deut. xxxii, 17 are intended in such a way, when he says that the "perfect tree" planted by God (*Gen.* ii, 9)[171] is meant as the antidote against the corrupting and defiling sinfulness (Asherah?) causing death. Later Marqah makes it clear [172] that these 'demons' to which people sacrifice are absolutely powerless, in interpreting the second part of *Deut.* xxxii, 17 as meaning "gods who knew them not." This interpretation is obvious from Marqah's description of these gods, who "keep them in suspense, (just as their worshippers) arrive there, (so do) they return (without benefit). This evil (fate of the worshippers) of having no one to turn to, neither a redeemer nor a helper, was occasioned by themselves."[173] Marqah goes even further in asserting that the origin of their apostasy is not founded upon realities but upon forsaking God, thereby only causing themselves distress, since their idols have no power even to know them, let alone to assist them.

Undoubtedly there is much in Marqah's exposition which cannot be qualified as the literal meaning of the text according to modern standards. However, this does not alter the fact that the whole purpose of such homiletic exercises was, at least to the Samaritan mind, directed to keeping as close as possible to the literal meaning. The 'additional' material is culled by analogists from other parts of scripture, after they have been harmonized, in order to create one unit in which all the verses used for background and for exegesis are interrelated, and combined in order to enhance the simple meaning. It is therefore interesting to compare how the same problem is dealt with by commentators centuries later.

The Ṭabbākh, which is even more rationalistically inclined than Marqah, takes it for granted that there is no sense in "executing judgement" upon idols for their own sake, for by that time and considering the environment in which the Ṭabbākh was written, such an act against dumb and unreal creatures would appear ridiculous. Abū-l Ḥasan, nevertheless preserves the literal meaning of these biblical expressions. In order, however to justify such an act, he invents (or reproduces a tradition about) details not mentioned in scripture. According to the

---

[170] *Memar Marqah* IV, 5; (ed. Macdonald) I, pp. 91ff. (= II, pp. 149ff.).

[171] *ibid.* I, p. 92 (= II, p. 150).

[172] *ibid.* I, p. 94 (= II, pp. 153f.).

[173] אשדה (=) אשתדה) לון לתמן ימטון ומתמן יעזרון דאה עובד ביש עבדו בקנומון‏
לא דבוק ולא פרוק ולא סעוד‏

Ṭabbākh,[174] after the plague of the firstborn the Egyptians ran into their sanctuaries to pray to their idols for help. For this reason there was a need to "execute judgement" on the idols themselves, as a result of which their sanctuaires became abandoned and desolate. Abū-l Ḥasan connects this with the obligation of pilgrimage and of making offerings in the 'chosen place', which is expected to the exact opposite of what happened to the Egyptians and their sanctuaries. This is again related to the commandment to uproot the places of idol worship (*Deut.* xii, 2), which is immediately followed by the command "Ye shall not do so unto the Lord your God" (*ibid.* 4). Abū-l Ḥasan takes this verse (which cannot possibly mean that an Israelite is forbidden to destroy his own sanctuaries) as a reference to positive action; i.e. frequenting the place of worship. Although we find here again a departure from the literal sense, it is done with the intention of preserving the dignity of Scripture. In the case of 'Smiting the Gods' the apology is not far removed from that of Marqah, while the connection with the 'chosen place' and the pilgrimage is intended to glorify one of the central tenets of Samaritan observance.[175] In order to obtain an idea of the significance of the worship on Hargerizim, it is sufficient to cite one example: the verse "And thou shalt turn in the morning and go unto thy tents" (*Deut.* xvi, 7) was taken literally as a positive command for the observance of the festival on the Mount. The verse was understood to imply that during the days of the festival, the pilgrims are forbidden to dwell in their villages or towns but should encamp in tents near the 'House of God'. "The reason for this is that they shall concentrate solely on the worship of God and that nothing shall distract them from Him."[176]

Subsequent chapters will substantiate the points which are at present only mentioned in passing. For our present concern is the direct connection between a literalistic type of exegesis and the principle of the divinely inspired biblical word. So far we have seen that the Samaritans' understanding of verbal inspiration was that any text can have only one simple meaning. One wonders therefore about serious cases of deviation from this rule, which even to the ingenuous Samaritans could hardly have passed unnoticed. The most puzzling of these are homiletic interpretations based on single letters (taking a word as an acrostic) or the use of letters for their numerical value. Marqah in particular is very fond of

---

[174] f. 79a; (cf. SLTh.A p. 119).

[175] The whole *raison d'être* of Sam. separate existence is built on this principle.

[176] *Ṭabbākh*, f. 86b; (cf. SLTh.A p. 126).

such plays upon letters but it has been employed throughout Samaritan history to modern times to a greater or lesser degree.[177] Just one example from Marqah will be sufficient to demonstrate that the actual theory of 'multiple meaning' of scripture was not intended in this innocent play on letters. When Marqah interprets the meaning of "God of Faithfulness" (*Deut.* xxxii, 4),[178] he takes each letter as an acrostic to signify that this 'faithfulness' includes not only His attributes but also every relevant aspects of His manifestations in the world, through His revealed Will (א divinity; מ prophethood; ו creation; נ priesthood; ה Scripture). It seems quite obvious that this is only the result of a very rigid belief in 'literal inspiration', according to which, on top of the verbal sense, each letter was imbued by its Creator with an additional deeper sense which, if exposed by 'wisdom', clarifies the understanding of the verbal exposition.

One can of course find cases where their exegesis is far removed from the literal sense, and is built on similar lines to numerous Rabbinic midrashim. For instance the verse : "A wandering Aramean was my father" (*Deut.* xxvi, 5) is interpreted by the Kāfi [179] as referring to Laban (i.e. "The Aramean") who almost caused "My father" (i.e. Jacob) "to perish". There is no need to assume Jewish influence in such cases, nor is it certain whether such additions came from very ancient common traditions. The context of this expression and its proximity to the precept of tithing (*ibid.* 12f.) could easily have led the exegete to the conclusion that one must find an illustration of this precept from the lives of the Patriarchs. The example of Abraham (Gen. xiv, 20) could not serve this purpose, since there is no mention of him having any dealings with an Aramean. The analogy with Jacob, however, (*ibid.* xxviii, 22) admirably served this purpose. Nevertheless, as we have seen in earlier examples when analogy was employed to elucidate 'ambiguous' passages, the verses that were utilized were mutually harmonized. It seems reasonable to assume that such elucidations through harmonizations were not considered — at least by the Samaritans — as opposed to the

---

[177] The *Kāfi* illustrates his discussion on the Priesthood (pp. 5f.) with such acrostics of the word כהן cf. Abdel-Al, *A Comparative Study etc.*, pp. 617ff., 661f. For other instances in the *Kāfi* cf. N. Cohn, *Die Zarâath Gesetze etc.*, p. 14. cf. *inf*. Part III, para (g, 7).

[178] *Nemar Marqah* (ed. Macdonald) I, p. 90 (= II, p. 146).

[179] pp. 28f. (cf. SLTh.A p. 1). For the Rabbinic parallels cf. *Sifri, ad loc.*; *Rashi, ad loc.* and *The Passover Haggadah*.

literal meaning, but rather as the only possible sense. Because they had
such a *naïve* approach, they found no difficulty in adopting similar far-
fetched exegesis and therefore discovered no need to develop a theory
of 'multiple meanings' of scripture.

When they were using their system of harmonization through analogy,
the Samaritans also applied the rule that every passage must be preserved
in its original context. It is therefore safe to assume that in most cases
they did not allow analogies to get out of hand, since this might divorce
from their original context either of the sources compared. This rule
can also be found to apply in both the fields of Samaritan Halakhah
and Agadah.[180] It is sufficient, for our present purpose at least, to illustrate this method by taking one of their cardinal precepts. The verse:
"Let no man go out of his place on the seventh day" (*Ex.* xvi, 29) is ambiguous. Through analogy one could infer that it is absolutely forbidden
to move on the Sabbath (some Karaites and even some Samaritans
actually understood it this way). On the other hand it is equally possible
to infer by means of other analogies that only "going out of one's place"
is forbidden; that doing hard labour in the house itself may be permitted.
The Kāfi deals with this problem in several places, but at one point it
states [181] quite emphatically that this verse cannot be taken out of its
context. Since it was said in connection with the manna, it was meant
as a prohibition against going out as customary on working days to
gather manna. Similarly it should be applied to any work involving the
preparation of food or to earning a living.

Nothing would be further from the truth than to pretend that the
Samaritans' obsession with a concept of 'verbal inspiration' invariably
guided their exegetes into following the 'literal' sense only. Even before
describing the exceptional cases where the Samaritans themselves were
aware that only a figurative sense could have been implied in the text,
it must be pointed out that even their intended literalism would not
always be passed as literalism according to modern standards. We have
seens on previous cases that what the Samaritan exegete would term the
literal sense is not necessarily the plain meaning. Furthermore, the
uncritical Samaritan mind could not be expected to develop a consistent semantic theory of an absolute value. Therefore if we claim that
in general they are rigid literalists, this definition must be severely
qualified. Although one can truthfully say that the Samaritans sought

---

[180] cf. *inf.* Part III, para (b, 1).
[181] *Kāfi*, pp. 328f.; (cf. SLTh.A pp. 69f.).

for the "meaning intended by the author" this search was nevertheless pursued in accordance with their own preconceived and uncritical way of thinking. Secondly, even if they could have been aware of the concept of 'historical sense', it would not have meant for them that a critical examination of the probable historical setting of the expounded text must be undertaken, but rather that they should adhere to their own tradition. Indeed, for most ancient and medieval exponents, the dictates of their own tradition would be the only possible basis for a reconstruction of what they would term as the historical setting. In other words, the literalism of the Samaritans can only be defined in negative terms, namely that it arises out of their conscious rejection of exegetical devices which tend to obliterate the reality of the words of revelation by a mist of symbols, allegories and shadowy enigmas. Admittedly we do not find any explicit mention of such clear cut policies in Samaritan literature. However, such an assessment can be reasonably drawn from the afore-mentioned considerations.

It is therefore surprising when one finds generalizations implying that the Samaritans "have given large play to allegorizing" or that "their exegesis is frequently rational and spiritual."[182] Even taking into consideration that such assessments are usually arrived at by way of comparison with other groups, they are still highly exaggerated. One has to bear in mind that despite the favourable verdict on Samaritan exegesis as compared to that of the Rabbis, this in itself, even if it could be substantiated, does not necessarily prove that the former are superior to the latter in being less literalistic. In fact the stigma of 'literalism' applied in a perjorative sense against Judaism [183] was maintained only because it was contrasted to 'spiritual' exegesis by theologians who were convinced that the glorification of 'spirit' could only be achieved at the expense of the 'letter'. Another factor which may have contributed to the false notion that the Samaritans tended to 'spiritualize' their religion is the 'simple' — that is, only in comparison with the Rabbinic — appearance of their halakhah. Although this comparison is valid, the underlying motives have been misunderstood. It is true that ever increasing insistence of the Rabbis on the minutest details of the ritual finds no echo in Samaritan circles, but this cannot be explained on the grounds that the latter opposed ritual or tended to spiritualize

---

[182] Montgomery, *The Samaritans*, pp. 44f.

[183] Farrar, *History of Interpretation*, pp. xix and xx; Grant, *Letter and Spirit*, 91-92; cf. however Smart, *The Interpretation of Scripture*, pp. 14f., 76.

their rites.[184] The opposite is rather the case, that precisely because of their scrupulous literalism they could not develop any theory of Oral Law being in any way independent of the literal interpretation of the written, let alone as being something superior ot it. The Samaritans, who were the most extreme of all the literalists, would certainly agree with the Dead Sea Scroll sects' description of their opponents' brand of Torah as "smooth things",[185] since according to their opinion it consisted of a lenient type of exegesis designed to whittle down the Torah and make it easy to observe.[186] Indeed, most of their polemics are based on such results of Rabbinic exegesis which seemed to them, as well as to the Karaites, to be the relaxing of considerable portions of the severe ruling of the Written Law. It looks as if the intensive polemics against the Rabbanites in the Ṭabbākh and in the Masā'il al-Khilāf are only reiterating earlier Karaite polemics on the same theme.[187]

Deviations from the strict literal exegesis depend upon the exegete's own need to explain away certain details which cannot be expounded according to their 'plain' meaning. Naturally such considerations as to what is to be regarded as self-explanatory according to its "plain' meaning and what requires a figurative explanation, depend very much upon the subjectivity of the exegete. Hence, the more sophisticated the expounder the more details he will find difficult, and in order to 'explain' them he will employ more and more metaphorical devices. On the other hand, men with a primitive and fundamentalist way of thinking have no need of such methods, since the very rationalistic difficulties which lead to apologetical metaphors are not present for them.[188] It seems, however, upon examining the exegetical literature of various groups, that the individual exegete was not given total freedom in making such decisions, but was rather guided — or even vigorously directed — by accepted norms, depending upon the respective traditions of the group.[189] Samaritan literature in particular offers very little evidence for the existence of arbitrary commentaries in which contradictory opinions are introduced side by side. Taking into consideration

---

[184] cf. my article *op. cit.*, pp. 110, 143 (n. 96).

[185] *The Thanksgiving Scroll* IV, 11, 10-11.

[186] Brownlee, "Biblical Interpretation etc.", *BA* XIV (1951), p. 59; Wieder, *Judean Scrolls and Karaism*, p. 135.

[187] cf. Halkin, *PAAJR* VIII, pp. 13ff.

[188] Heinemann, *Altjüdische Allegoristik*, pp. 10f. and on 'real allegories' *ibid.* pp. 34f.

[189] cf. my article, *op. cit.*, *passim.*

the relatively long history of this literature, and seeing at the same time the large degree of homogeneity in exposition, the practice of following strictly traditional lines becomes even more evident.

Obviously there are features common to all the groups, and while the degree of departure from the literal to the figurative sense is varied according to the respective traditions of each group, the actual principles upon which these departures are allowed to occur can be traced back to similar apologetical reasons. Thus in Rabbinic literature there was an attempt to deviate from the 'plain' sense whenever by this device they could 1) protect the honour of Israel and her Righteous, 2) defend the purity of their concept of the deity, or 3) advocate the concept of biblical morals.[190] While these principles cannot be mechanically transferred to Samaritan exegesis, there are nevertheless many resemblances. Furthermore, there are other common features which are even more universal, the most oustanding example of which is the existence of scriptures which by their very nature indicate that they were intended as oracular sources or prophecies, coined in an enigmatic language, and which in all groups had to be interpreted figuratively.[191] A particular usage of prophecies, as for example *Gen.* xlix, 1, for elaborate eschatological expositions is found among the Samaritans as well as among other groups.[192] They do not, however, confine the purpose of prophetical scripture to the subject of 'afterlife' and matters akin to it. While it is partially true that relatively little (according to the literal sense alone, almost nothing) is said on eschatological subjects in the Pentateuch, this in itself would not induce the Samaritan exegetes to violate the sense of their sacred text.[193] Indeed, only if one tries to force hypothetical or non-existant midrashim on their exegetes, in an attempt to harmonize the relatively late Samaritan sources with Philo and other ancient sources, does the Samaritan exegete acquire such a strange and forceful license.[194] In general, however, while the 'afterlife' has a very important place in these 'figurative' interpretations,[195] other subjects are most certainly covered

---

[190] Heinemann, *Darkhei ha-Aggadah*, pp. 154f.

[191] cf. my article *op. cit.* pp. 130f. (n. 9), 142 (n. 87), 159f. (nn. 204-207).

[192] Merx, *Der Messias oder Ta'eb etc.*, p. 18 (and cf. notes for parallels in other groups); on *Deut.* iv, 25 — *ibid.* p. 59; on *Deut.* xxx, 1 — *ibid.* p. 60; on *Deut.* xxxiv, 1f. — *ibid.* pp. 63-65. On *Gen.* xv, 17 — Gaster, *Eschatology*, pp. 237f.

[193] cf. Gaster, *op. cit.* pp. 129ff.

[194] cf. *ibid.* pp. 29, 34.

[195] As for example the expression "gathered unto his people" (*Num.* xx, 24; 26; *ibid.* xxvii, 13) as referring to the soul. Gaster, *ibid.* pp. 134f.

in such interpretations. For example, as in the case of the Rabbanites such interpretation is employed for emphasizing religious morals, as is clearly showh in *Gen.* ii, 14, being understood as "and the Lord God took Adam and placed him in the garden of Eden to serve Him and to keep (His commands)".[196] Similarly one cannot assume that all exegesis pertaining to eschatology must necessarily be fanciful. Although the "wine of Sodom" and the "grapes of Gomorrah" are taken to refer to sins, the rest of the verse is explained as closely to the 'plain' sense as could be expected in the exegesis of such a poetical oracle.[197]

The truth of the matter is, that although many passages of the Pentateuch were understood by all the groups as being 'oracular' prophecies, which by their very nature demanded a figurative exegesis, the exact ruling as to which verses should be included in this category still depended upon the tradition of each group. It is not always easy to distinguish which tradition is a real allegory and which is the result of an exaggerated sense of literalism. For example, the expression of Marqah "Gihon (or Pishon) the tributary of Eden", which is taken as a reference to the Nile,[198] although it appears to convey some deep allegorical meaning, is in reality nothing more than the extreme result of the most literalistic explanation of *Gen.* ii, 13. However, the literalistic origins are not always so obvious. One wonders what the relationship is between *Ex.* iii, 14: "I will be who I will be" and Marqahs' exposition[199] in which he says : "Who set up the garden and wrote about the recompense of Sodom". Only if we accept that Marqah took the expression : "I will be who I will be" literally, that is as meaning 'who was and will be', can we presume that in addition to the idea of reward and punishment, it also refers to the Ever-lasting, "who set up the Garden (= Creation) and the One who punishes Sodom (= the Day of Revenge = the End of Days)".[200]

Another common feature is the avoidance of anthropomorphic expression for God. This feature is well illustrated in the Targumim.[201]

---

[196] *ibid.* p. 136. This reference is taken from the Hillukh, but it was already implied by Marqah (cf. *sup.* n. 171 and text there).

[197] Gaster, *ibid.* pp. 162f.

[198] *Memar Marqah*, ed. Macdonald, I, p. 7 (= II, p. 7); I, p. 12.

[199] *ibid.* I, p. 8 (= II, p. 8).

[200] cf. *inf.* n. 207.

[201] S. Kohn, *Samaritanische Studien*, p. 8, n. 10. A. Berliner, *Targum Onkelos* II, pp. 102ff., 222-224; T. Fritsch, *The Anti-Anthropomorphisms of the Greek Pentateuch* (Princeton, 1943), *passim*.

The Samaritan Targum does not show much consistancy in this respect but nevertheless many examples can be brought from it to prove that such attempts at avoiding anthropomorphisms [202] belong to an early Samaritan tradition.[203] In this respect, then, the Samaritans felt no need to accept the principle of 'deeper interpretation' from the Muslim ta'wīl, let alone from Saadya Gaon.[204] Although Mu'tazilite influence, most probably derived from Karaite sources,[205] helped them in systematizing their anti-anthropomorphic tendencies, the roots of this practice go back to tradition. The Ṭabbākh, in its refutation of the attacks of the 'infidels' who accused Scripture of anthropomorphism,[206] sets forward proofs taken from Scripture itself, namely that all such accusations are false, since all the attributes of God are clearly stated in Scripture in a manner that leaves one in no doubt about anthropomorphism. The following examples are quoted, i.e. for Eternity, Ex. iii, 14;[207] for Unity, Deut. vi, 4; for God not being limited in space, ibid. iv, 39; and for Him not having a figure or likeness, ibid. 12. A similar argument, though in a shorter form, is presented in the chapter which explains the Schema' (Deut. vi, 4).[208] The very same problem is tackled by Munajja,[209] who gathers together all the verses which if understood in their literal sense would imply anthropomorphism, and he clearly lays down the general rule, already mentioned by the Ṭabbākh, that in all cases where the literal meaning opposes the logical truth, a figurative exegesis is necessary. He briefly presents the same argument with almost identical verses (e.g. Ex. xix, 9; ibid. xxxiv, 5; etc.).[210] At this juncture, however, it becomes obvious (from his attack on the anthropomorphisms of the

---

[202] e.g. the word פני is translated רחותי (= favour) in Ex. xxxiii, 14; Deut. xxxi, 17-18; but in Ex. xxxiii, 23 קדמי, Deut. xxxii, 20 פני. It is interesting to note that the Ṭabbākh (f. 222b), in one of the few cases where a translation is given, renders the last verse احفى رضواني. Thus also Saadia.

[203] Another curiosity is the paraphrasing of יד by "place". Kohn, op. cit. pp. 74f. On the other hand Marqah, Memar I, p. 126 (= II, 205) identifies כפי in Ex. xxxiii, 22f. with the "cloud". On the various figurative usages of רגל cf. Kohn, op. cit. pp. 68f.

[204] cf. Halkin, "The Relation of the Sam. etc.", Saadia Anniversary Vol., pp. 285-6.

[205] ibid. pp. 271ff.

[206] ff. 92a-94b (for text and translation cf. SLTh.A pp. 132-134).

[207] This proof is the same as that of Marqah (sup. nn. 199-200), which proves the pre-Islamic origin of these traditions.

[208] ff. 135b-138b; cf. Abdel-Al, A Comparative Study etc., pp. 468f.; 653f.

[209] Masā'il al-Khilāf, Ib, pp. 90-94.

[210] ibid. pp. 42f.

Rabbis) that he took his material from the Karaites.[211] As we have seen earlier, license to employ figurative interpretation when the literal sense opposes the truth, is used both by the Ṭabbākh and the Masā'il al-Khilāf very sparingly. As opposed to the Rabbanites and Karaite Mu'tazilites, who adopted ta'wīl quite frequently, the Samaritans limited figurative usage to cases where their traditional biblical exegesis had a precedent for it. This is evident from their strict literalistic treatment of the concept of 'Torah written by God' or Moses copying it out *in toto* including the story of his own death.[212]

In diametrical contrast to the limitations imposed by tradition on figurative exegesis, when it could have contradicted earlier established dogmas, in the instance of such beliefs being jeopardized by the literal sense, the Samaritans had no qualms whatsoever about employing the most extravagant figurative interpretations. Again, as in many other groups when the honour of the Righteous had to be protected, if the literal sense had occasioned this defamation, it had to be explained away.[213]

It is true that one figurative interpretation gained a foothold upon Samaritan ground, it could not be limited to major dogmatic issues. Thus occasionally one finds the most fanciful and midrashic type of exegesis which totally excluded the literal sense for no apparent reason. Often misunderstandings, biblical discrepancies and theological discussions played a part in creating such figurative interpretations, but not every istance of their rejection of the literal sense can be justified on such grounds.[214]

When one examines their halakhic interpretations, it becomes even more obvious that it was tradition more than any other factor which determined the mode of exegesis of a given text. In this field the arbitrary and spontaneous elements must have been even more restricted, since in deviating from the literal sense the Samaritans would have been laying

---

[211] *Masa'il al-Khilāf* Ib, pp. 42f.

[212] cf. *sup.* nn. 91ff.

[213] On the ambiguous passage of *Ex.* iv, 24-26, cf. *sup.* nn. 83ff. Similar is the case of the "Kushite woman", *Num.* xii, 1-2, cf. *sup.* Part I, n. 52 etc. Concerning the last case, S. Kohn (*Sam. Studien*, pp. 14-15) tries to make out a case for Rabbanite influence. After all, Onkelos and the S.T. could have both relied on ancient apologetical sources. On the other hand this type of explaining away any slur cast upon the personality of Moses is typical to Sam. exegesis.

[214] cf. e.g. Ben-Ḥayyim, *Literary and Oral Tradition etc.* II, p. 573, n. 122; p. 597, nn. 132-134; p. 598, n. 136 etc.

themselves open to the same accusations that they themselves used against the Jews.[215]

The most celebrated figurative interpretation is that of "brethren" (*Deut.* xxv, 5f.) in regard to the case of Levirate marriage. The Talmud already attests that the Samaritans interpreted this passage figuratively and the practices of other literalistic sects were similar here.[216] There is no difference in exegesis amongst the Samaritans on this matter, and throughout, from the Kāfi [217] to the Hillukh,[218] they exhibit the very same ancient traditions. However, from this chapter on the Levirate marriage we learn that there existed other figurative interpretations of the word 'Brother', extended into various fields.[219] Although the antiquity of these cases is not attested by outside sources, it seems safe to assume that they stem from the same ancient tradition as their explaining away of 'brother' in the instance of the Levirate marriage.

Another well known example in the figurative explanation of "signs upon the hands and frontlets between the eyes", which from ancient times divided the literalists from Rabbinic Judaism. As opposed to the Rabbinic practice of 'Phylacteries', the Samaritans explained these verses figuratively.[220]

The interplay between Scripture and Tradition will occupy our attention later.[221] Here we have simple endeavoured to show how tradition was the major factor in determining the usage of figurative explanations. Those cases where the Samaritans totally abandoned literalism were in fact comparatively few, and they serve rather to underline the general rule, namely, that Scripture should be interpreted in accordance with its obvious sense.

C. The True Version

The Samaritans firmly believed that their text was the only authentic version of Scripture. Their entire literature is full of apologetics for their

---

[215] cf. *sup.* n. 59 and text there.

[216] cf. Geiger, *Nachgelassene Schriften*, vol. V (Hebr.), pp. 159ff.

[217] pp. 267-271. (For text and translation cf. SLTh.A pp. 63-69.)

[218] pp. 215f.

[219] For "brethren" among the Nazirites cf. *Kāfi* p. 229 (SLTh.A p. 47) cf. also N. Cohn, *Die Zaraat etc.*, pp. iii, iv, n. (d). On the extension of 'Broderhood' to Christians and Muslims, cf. *sup.* n. 48, and text there.

[220] cf. e.g. *Tabbākh* quoted in n. 208 *sup.*

[221] cf. *inf.* para (g).

sacred text and they missed no opportunity of defending it. They had good reason for defending it, as the Bible, since the earliest times, had been constantly reviled as a baseless fabrication. We have substantial proof of such attacks, as the ancient Jewish sources are full of apologetics for the Bible against these vilifications.[222] All believers did this with equal zeal. In particular, they had to defend the miraculous elements in their Scriptures, as these were the most vulnerable to attack from the pagans. Often their defence of Scripture is thinly veiled, as for instance in the reference to Josephus's personal recollection of having seen the pillar of salt into which Lot's wife was turned.[223]

Marqah was probably upholding Scripture when he wrote, "The true One concealed it until Moses appeared."[224] He perhaps meant that, as God chose to reveal the Torah only to the Israelites, the other nations could not possibly know anything worthwhile about it. Furthermore, God's Scripture could be transmitted only by his chosen people, in direct succession to Moses; and thus, if other nations happened to gain possession of it, they were bound to corrupt and misinterpret the text, because they were not in possession of the genuine tradition.

The same theme recurs throughout Samaritan literature. They continually assert that they alone have carried out the command in *Deut.* iv, 2; *ibid.* xiii, 1, "not to add to and not do diminish" the words of Scripture. They themselves ware able to do this because they possessed the true tradition which had been transmitted from Moses to the elders, who in turn handed it on to the successive generations of elders.[225] Naturally enough, the Samaritans held that they were the only true Israelites to uphold this tradition faithfully. This conviction of their being the true guardians of the Law overrides all the charges of tempering with the text that are ever levelled against them. They were even more incensed at the mere suggestion that any portion of the Law could be abrogated.[226] For these reasons, they actually resorted to the extreme expedient of reinterpreting their name 'Samaritans', asserting that it

---

[222] Bergmann, *Jüdische Apologetik etc.*, p. 58.

[223] B. Heller, "Grundzüge der Aggada des F. Josephus", *MGWJ* LXXX (1936), p. 239.

[224] *Memar Marqah*, ed. Macdonald, I, p. 136 (= II, p. 222). It is doubtful whether this opinion was shared by all Samaritans, since according to the *Asaṭir*, there were already scriptures in existence before the coming of Moses.

[225] Vilmar, *Abulfathi annales Sam.*, pp. 100f.

[226] Halkin, "The Relation of the Sam. etc.", *Saadia Anniversary Vol.*, p. 324. cf. *inf.* n. 252.

originates from the root שמר i.e. that they are the exclusive Guardians of the Law.[227]

They were in even greater need of apologetic writings in defence of their texts because they were under attack from the Jews themselves, right from the beginning of their separate history. There is no need here to dwell on the enmity between the two groups as it is common knowledge; suffice it to mention the Jews' ancient practice of attributing to the Samaritans all the unworthy actions related in the stories of the Patriarchs, and especially those connected with Shechem. For instance, in the pseudepigrapha they write that it is hardly surprising that the Samaritans act as they do, since they had persecuted Abraham and tried to violate Sarah.[228]

The accusation that the Samaritans were strangers or of mixed race [229] aggravated Jewish polemics against their religious observances and their version of Scripture. It is a facile assumption that a people of mixed race must necessarily have foreign elements both in their Scripture and in their religious beliefs. Talmudic Judaism continued its polemics on the same lines, stressing in particular the falsification of the text.[230] This attitude is not surprising since some modern scholars think the same, alleging that the Samaritans were constantly emending their text even to the extent of accommodating new ideas.[231] Admittedly the Samaritan Pentateuch is full of alternative readings to the Masoretic Text.[232]

The reason why the Samaritans have been accused of tampering with their text rests on the fact that it has many additions which are unique to their version, and its orthography is also markedly different from that of the Masoretic Text. However, the recent finds of scriptural passages among the Dead Sea Scrolls do not support this accusation, for among these texts is the prototype of the Samaritan text, and it is seen to exhibit scholarly revisions, evidently from very ancient times.[233]

Various opinions are held on the reliability of the Samaritan tradition. The Talmud, despite its great hostility, testifies that precepts maintained by the Samaritans were more rigourously carried out by them than by

---

[227] Montgomery, *The Samaritans*, p. 318f.

[228] The Testament of Levi, VI, 8-9.

[229] Appel, *Quaestiones de rebus Sam.*, p. 11. cf. *ibid.* nn. 1, 2, for further bibliography.

[230] Brül, *Zur Geschichte etc.*, pp. 32f.

[231] cf. my article *ALUOS* VI (1969), pp. 106, 140 (nn. 68f.).

[232] Peterman, *Versuch einer heb. Formen Lehre etc.*, pp. 219-326.

[233] Cross, "The History of the Biblical Text etc.", *HThR* LVII (1964), p. 297.

the Jews. In the same context [234] the Rabbis discuss the possibility of the
Samaritans' abiding by certain precepts not mentioned in the Pentateuch. This would indicate that the Rabbis themselves did not consider
their tradition unstable. Among modern scholars opinions range from
one extreme to the other.[235] The true picture appears to be that their
tradition was in fact reliable, and that the orthographical divergencies
are due rather to variations in spelling than to actual differences in traditions. It seems that the Samaritan scribes allowed themselves great
freedom in spelling, their main concern being for the reading and the
sense.[236]

The purpose of our enquiry is not however directed towards the estimation of the validity of the respective texts: we will merely touch on the
main grounds of contention. Even those few scholars who consider that
Deut. xxvii, 4 has been altered by the Jews [237] have to admit that not all
variant readings can be thus accounted for. On the other hand, scholars
who assert that the tenth Commandment in the Samaritan text is a
forgery (because of its length, literal parallelism with other verses, and
lack of support in the other versions) [238] cannot use such evidence for
other variant readings. In any case, these 'falsifications', if such they were,
must originate from a period many centuries prior to the beginning
of Samaritan exegesis, and this fact naturally takes the problem outside
our present enquiry.

Judging from our present Samaritan sources, from the time of the
Targum and Marqah down to modern Samaritan writers, both in their
biblical quotations and their allusions to them in their commentaries,
all the evidence points to the Samaritans' possessing one common
version [239] — apart from the differences in orthography that we have
already mentioned. Accusations that their quotations are not accurate
and complete [240] are based on quotations from liturgical and poetical
writings, which themselves are not in reality intended as anything other
than paraphrases. In general, their quotations are correct and point

---

[234] *Ḥullin*, 4a (and parallels).

[235] Ben-Ḥayyim, *Literary and Oral Tradition etc.*, p. 'ז.

[236] *ibid.* pp. כ״ד; ג״ח; *idem.*, "Deut. xxxiii in Sam. Hebrew", *Leshonenu* XV (1947/8),
pp. 76f.; cf. *sup.* n. 110.

[237] E. Meyer, *Die Israeliten und ihre Nachbarstamme* (Halle, 1906), pp. 534-47;
C.C. Torrey, *Ezra Studies* (Chicago, 1910), p. 329.

[238] Kahle, *The Cairo Geniza*, p. 145.

[239] cf. my article *ALUOS* VI (1969), pp. 107f., 141 (nn. 75f.).

[240] Miller, *The Sam. Molad Mosheh*, pp. 234f.

unquestionably to a common text available to all; and in the few places where there are inaccuracies these can be attributed to quoting from memory (so confusing two different texts) or to scribal errors.[241]

Spurred on by their unshakable conviction that theirs was the only true version, they incessantly engaged in active polemics against all other groups possessing different versions, and in particular against the Jews. The latter were their main target, owing to the proximity of their geographical position and to the fact of their broadly common beliefs, practices and text being so similar to their own, and particularly owing to the Jews' own attacks on them, in which they were bitterly accused of falsifying the sacred text. The well-known dispute over the centre of worship, i.e. Jerusalem versus Hargerizim, based on their respective texts, need not be entered into here.[242] The Talmudic attacks on the Samaritan falsification of the text were centred on this very point, alleging that they had interpolated additional proofs of the sanctity of Hargerizim, even where they were demonstrably superfluous.[243]

Many centuries before the time of the Massoretes we have records of the meticulous care with which the Pharisean scribes preserved their text. Typical of these testimonies is this one of Josephus:[244] "During so many ages as have elapsed, no one has been so bold as to add anything to the words of Scripture or to take anything therefrom." This attitude is similarly upheld in the Talmud, when R. Ishmael warns R. Meir (whose profession was copying out the Scriptures) that his work is for Heaven and even the minutest mistake is comparable to bringing destruction upon the whole world.[245] We could quote many more examples of the reverence with which the Jews treated their text, but as this is a subject which has been dealt with fully elsewhere,[246] there is no need to do so here.

Despite this impressive evidence, scholars do not, however, accept these testimonies at their face value but, as a result of a detailed comparison of the M.T. with the LXX and the S.P., have concluded on the contrary that, in early times at least, the scribes took great liberties in their

---

[241] cf. *sup.* n. 124.
[242] Halkin, "Sam. Polemics etc.", *PAAJR* VIII (1935/6), pp. 31-35.
[243] Hamburger, *Real-Encyclopädie etc.* II, p. 1071.
[244] *Against Apion* I, 8.
[245] *Erubhin*, 13a, *Soṭah*, 20a.
[246] I. Harris, "The History and Development etc.", *JQR* I (1889), pp. 128f.

treatment of the text.[247] Recently, moreover, after the discoveries of the Dead Sea Scrolls, a new theory has been developed from the evidence therein presented, that the various groups used localized texts from which the prototypes of the later versions originate.[248] It may now be said with a high degree of certainty that the several groups, e.g. the Hellenist of Alexandria, with their prototype of the LXX, the Pharisees with their Proto-Massoretic version and again the Samaritans with their protype, all closely adhered to their respective texts.[249]

The ancient and medieval mentality considered that variations between the other groups' texts and their own were quite simply due to falsification of the true text which they alone possessed. Typical of the medieval Jewish attitude is the thirteenth century Tanḥum Jerushalmi, who, centuries before Christian scholars rediscovered the Samaritans, developed a whole theory of the Hebrew script by which he sought to explain the distinction between the Samaritans and the Jews. He pointed out tha the Jewish script, Ashuri, (supposedly derived from מאושר or מיושר) represented the correct script because it was reserved for sacred purposes, while the Samaritan script (עברי) (supposedly derived from עבר meaning transitory) was only used for secular documents. According to his theory, the Jews, when they felt compelled to give the Torah to the Kuthim, deliberately transcribed it in the secular script in order to divorce them from the body of orthodox Jewry.[250] The same sentiments are expressed, two generations later by another Jew who knew the Samaritans well, when he testifies that, having examined their Torah he could hardly find a chapter that they had not falsified.[251]

The Ṭabbākh, anxious to refute the aspersions cast on the Samaritans' pure Israelite descent, actually utilizes Jewish allegations [252] in order to prove how false such a charge is. Thus the curses calling for subsequent destruction of the land (*Deut.* xxix, 21) were taken by the Jews to refer only to Shechem and the Samaritans. Abū-l Ḥasan however

---

[247] Geiger, *Urschrift etc.*, pp. 8-19; 231-259. cf. Harris, *op. cit.* p. 131 (and *ibid.* n. 2 for further literature).

[248] Cross, *op. cit.* pp. 286ff.

[249] cf. my article in *ALUOS* VI (1969), pp. 105ff.

[250] Bacher, *Aus dem Wörterbuche Tanchum Jeruschalmi's*, p. 19. cf. Arabic text

وله الزمو بكتابة ال תורה לכותים كتبوها لهم بذلك الخط وخرجو (*ibid.* p. 22)

عنه ليله يصير بيننا وبينهم خلطه ومشاركة في خط واحد — — —

[251] Estori Pharehi, *Caftor wa-Pherach*, ff. 11b.

[252] ff. 55b f. (SLTh.A pp. 98f.). cf. Halkin, *op. cit.* pp. 26-27.

raises the objection that Scripture itself testifies that this punishment
was meted out to them because they had transgressed God's commandments and broken his covenant (*ibid.* 23f.). Yet in *Deut.* xxxiii, 4, "Moses
commanded us a Law, and inheritance for the assembly of Jacob",
it is clearly implied that the only people who could transgress God's
commandments were the Israelites, and therefore, if the destruction of
the land referred to Shechem and the Samaritans, these must necessarily
be Israelites. This device of turning the Jews' weapons against themselves, and disproving their allegations by means of their own words,
was especially favoured by Munajja.[253] In his attack on the Jewish text,
practice and, in particular, Oral Law, which they claim must be authentic because they are held by the largest group, he utilizes the contradictions found in the Oral Law itself to prove that it is unreliable. His
attack is based on Karaite sources, which drew from the Talmud itself
evidence showing that the Jews' claim for the antiquity of their calendaric system (the most significant part of oral tradition) is contradicted
by Talmudic literature itself.[254] The Samaritan's minority complex
shows itself in the utilization of Scripture to prove that the question of
right or wrong does not at all depend on numbers. Munajja [255] sees in
the story of Joseph (*Gen.* xxxvii) proof that the one brother only, and
not all eleven, was right, and therefore by analogy all the Jewish oral
tradition is worthless, despite its being the tradition of the majority.

Samaritan chroniclers naturally attempt to present their own version
in the most favourable light, putting forward an unbroken chain of
authorities right back to Moses. They constantly refer to the times of
Samuel and Saul, when, they assert, the only difference between them
and the Jews was in the place of worship.[256] Even in the time of David
there was, they insist, only one Torah with no variations whatsoever,
and in the Samaritan script, identical with the "Torah which is in our
hands up to this day."[257]
Surprisingly, in the light of all this, they still compare the Jewish
version with their own as additional evidence of the validity of their
own tradition. Thus in the course of establishing the correct locality

---

[253] *Masā'il al-Khilāf*, Ia, pp. 62f.

[254] *ibid.* pp. 68-88 (cf. SLTh pp. 880ff., 935).

[255] *Masā'il al-Khilāf*, Ib, pp. 117-122.

[256] cf. recently J. Macdonald, *The Sam. Chronicle No. II* (Beihefte *ZATW* 107,
1969), p. 49.

[257] *ibid.* p. 55: כי הכל יקרו בספרי התורה מקרא אחד ואותיות אחת ככל התורה
אשר בידנו עד היום הזה

of the centre of worship from the stories of the Patriarchs, as for example that of the sacrifice of Isaac (*Gen.* xxii, 3) or the dream of Jacob (*ibid.* xxviii), the Kāfi adds the remark "in this case the Jewish version is like ours."[258]

One of their most pointed arguments for the validity of their version is their employment of the well-known fact that the 'cursed' Ezra added letters to the alphabet (to the original 22 he added a further 5, i.e. the final letters) when he changed the acient script of Scripture into the square characters (Ashuri).[259] They argued that, once he had embarked on falsifications, others naturally followed, and whole passages might have been rewritten in favour of Judaism. The Hillukh even goes so far as to imply that *Ex.* xxxii, 33, "Whosoever hath sinned against me, him I will blot out of my book" refers specifically to this alteration of the script, and that on account of this crime, the Jews were blotted out of God's book for ever.[260]

The Talmud is well aware of the change of script from the ancient Hebrew to the Ashuri and likewise ascribes it to Erza, who brought it with him from Babylonia.[261] We are not concerned with the historical truth of the Samaritan and Talmudic statements in this regard, it is sufficient to say that modern scholars have placed the change of script and the development of the Samaritan characters from the ancient Hebrew in the Maccabean period.[262]

The Samaritan attacks on the Jews on the grounds of falsification of the text naturally included the Karaites. Munajja maintains that the latter possessed the same script, pronunciation and language, a fact which inevitably led them to accept a similarly false text.[263] In spite of the Samaritans' contempt for the Massoretic text they still refer to it, even in cases where the differences are crucial. The most striking example of this is the proof-text for their doctrines of an after-life and an eschatology (*Deut.* xxxii, 35), which, according to their chroniclers, were already

---

[258] *Kāfi*, p. 206f. (SLTh.A p. 31f.).

[259] Vilmar, *Abulfathi annales Sam.*, p. 74. cf. *sup.* nn. 54-55.

[260] *Hillukh*, p. 34.

[261] A midrash on משנה (*Deut.* xvii, 18) עתידה להשתנות *Tos. Sanhedrin* IV, 7 (ed. Zuckermandel, p. 422); *Siphri Deut.*, para 160; *Jer. Megillah* I, 11; 71b and c, *Sanhedrin*, 21b (cf. *Zebhaḥim*, 62b).

[262] A Spiro, "Samaritans, Tobiads, etc.", *PAAJR* XX (1951), pp. 286f., nn. 22-24; cf. now J.D. Purvis, *The Sam. Pentateuch and the Origin of the Sam. Sect.* (Cambridge, Mass., 1968), pp. 18-52; 85 (n. 150).

[263] cf. *sup.* n. 156.

hotly disputed at the time of the translation of the Septuagint.[264] From this it emerges that the Samaritans were aware that they possessed at least in some cases the same reading as the Septuagint. In later writings their polemics are more fanatical and they even go so far as to accuse the Jews of Polytheism, on the grounds that the Masoretic text (in their view), by missing out a *waw* in *Ex.* iii, 15, implies the existence of more than one God.[265]

Their relative silence on the falsity of Christian and Muhammedan texts is particularly surprising in the light of their intensive attacks on the Jewish Scriptures. Typical of the Christian accusations against the Jews in general is that they are corrupters of the Word of God and have misinterpreted the words of Moses.[266] In particular the Christians opposed the Jewish doctrine of being the chosen people. All these charges of falsely claiming election, of misinterpretation of the Law of Moses and of a listeralist adherence to the letter of the law, "which killeth", would apply even more to the Samaritans.[267] There is a remote possibility that they suffered from a guilt complex — dating from the Byzantine period when, under duress, many, including prominent leaders, were forcibly converted to Christianity [268] — which made them forbear from detailed comparisons with Christianity.

The problem becomes much more intricate when one examines their Halakhah, which displays a favourable attitude both to Christians and Moslems. According to the Kāfi (in the chapter on Usury)[269] the expression "unto *thy brother* thou shalt not lend upon usury" (*Deut.* xxiii, 20), supported by analogy with *Deut.* ii, 8, refers to the sons of Esau (i.e. Christians) and, by a further analogy to the sons of Ishmael (i.e. Moslems). There are many other examples of a similar favourable attitude

---

[264] Vilmar, *Abulfathi annales Sam.*, pp. 97f., 233; cf. my article *op. cit.* pp. 108, 142 (n. 86).

[265] *Exodus Commentary* (attributed to Ghazal al-Duweik), pp. 114f.

[266] Güdemann, "Spirit and letter in Judaism and Christianity", *JQR* IV (1892), pp. 351f.

[267] cf. *inf.* Part III, para (a, 1).

[268] Avi-Yona, *Eretz Israel* IV (1956), p. 132.

[269] *Kāfi*, pp. 294f. cf. Abdel-Al, *A Comparative Study etc.*, pp. 609ff., 716ff. On the diametrically opposite Rabbinic ruling, cf. Maimonides, *Mishneh Torah*, Book XIII, Part III (Creditor and Debtor), Ch. V, para 1 (cf. also *RABhaD's* objection and supercommentaries, *ibid.*). For further favourable laws concerning Christians and Mohamedans, derived from the expansionist exegesis of "Hebrew", cf. *sup.* Part I, nn. 37ff.

in the Samaritan Halakhah. Nevertheless, this in itself does not throw enough light on the initial problem of the Samaritans' silence.

A possibile explanation of this silence on the falsity of the Christian text may well be that the enormous gulf between their respective dogmas and practices gave no point to any discussion on textual differences.

The problem is no less obscure in reference to the Moslem charges of textual corruptions. The followers of Islam held that the "Moslems have replaced the children of Israel who originally were preferred by God" (Koran XLV, 15), and so attacked the Jewish doctrine of divine election; and it is a well-known fact that the Koran distorts biblical stories. The Moslems resorted to the stratagem of reconstructing an hypothetical original version of the Bible, which the Jews and Christians were supposed to have corrupted, when they dealt with the obvious discrepancies between the biblical text and the Koranic stories. Similar methods were used for explaining away differences in dietary laws and other religious observances.[270] In the Ṭabbākh's elaborate discussion of the Islamic doctrine of 'abrogation of previous revelations', it is evident that the author felt no necessity for entering into the niceties of textual differences.[271]

The fact that modern Moslem exegetes find themselves in an embarrassing situation as regards abrogation, and are attempting to explain it away,[272] underlines the ease with which arguments can be found against it. Obviously the Samaritans, in laying such a heavy charge as the complete falsity of the Koran and Mohammed's prophethood, felt no need to mention the relatively insignificant charges liad against their text.[273] The favourable attitude found in the Samaritan halakhic rulings, mentioned above,[274] has little bearing on the defence of their sacred text.

The Samaritan attitude towards the supreme validity of their text is best reflected in the chapter of the Ṭabbākh in refutation of the

---

[270] D.S. Margoliouth, *The Early Development etc.*, pp. 233f.; Geiger, *Was hat Mohammed etc.*, pp. 135-137; Goldziher, "Über mohammedanische Polemik etc.", *ZDMG* XXXII (1878), pp. 372f.; M. Zucker, "Religious polemics etc.", *A Kaminka Festschrift* (Wien, 1937), pp. 31-48.

[271] f. 150a-151b; cf. Halkin, "The Relation of the Sam. etc.", *Saadia Anniversary Vol.*, pp. 321f.

[272] Baljon, *Modern Muslim, etc.*, pp. 48f.; al-Fārūqī, "Towards a New Methodology", *Islamic Studies* I (1962), pp. 42f.

[273] cf. my article, *ALUOS* VI (1969), pp. 104 and 134f. (n. 56).

[274] cf. n. 269 *sup.*

doctrine of the eternity of the Word of God as held by one of the Moslem sects.[275] Abū-l Ḥasan disposes of this doctrine by showing that it is totally illogical. His major argument is directed along the lines that, although the Torah was indeed created, it is in the full literal sense the Word of God. Moses was only instrumental in copying out God's *Book*; the authenticity of all its minutest details rests on the inherent guarantee of an unbroken chain of infallible tradition. In contrast to the Jews, who were rivals to this claim and therefore had to be argued against on textual grounds, the Christians and Moslems held (according to the Samaritans) no such valid claim to an unbroken chain of tradition stretching back to Moses; detailed polemics on such subjects could therefore be dispensed with in their case.

D. The Educational Background of the Samaritans

Unlike Judaism, with its Synagogue usually performing the dual function of 'house of prayer' and 'academy', the Samaritan tradition affords no evidence of the existence of any such institution. Perhaps this is a main contributory factor in the noticeably differing approach to biblical exegesis adopted by the two parties. Judaism, through its academies, concentrated on its 'Oral Law', which eventually led to casuistic expositions of the *pilpul*. The references of European scholars to this type of 'school-man' are by no means complimentary.[276] Their criticism is based on the assumption that an undue attention to external observances inevitably detracts from the inner spiritual values. However, both among the Jews and among the Samaritans this emphasis on observances and the keeping of the Law was held as a reflection and a symbol of the inner essence of religion. Both the exposition and the observance of the Law were regarded as the fulfilment of the Divine Will.

Apart from talmudic literature, we have Philo's testimony to this dual function of the Synagogue. He speaks of the Law being interpreted to the people in the Synagogue on the Sabbath day.[277] From Philo's testimony, however, we can observe the basic difference between the Hellenistic and the Rabbinic uses of the synagogue. The former confined its use to the Sabbath and holidays alone, while the latter required attendance several times daily. Perhaps this latter use is the reason for a

---

[275] ff. 167b-176a; cf. *sup.* nn. 96-107, and respective texts there.
[276] Farrar, *History of Interpretation*, p. 10.
[277] Wolfson, *Philo* I, pp. 80, 96.

division, in some groups, between the house of worship and the house of study. The Samaritans also regarded their Synagogues merely as places of worship. Indeed, their literature [278] goes so far as to say that a man should not frequent the place of worship except at specified times, namely Sabbath and holidays.

The main similarity between the different groups was that some part of their service was still devoted to the exposition of the Law to the people. This is the reason why groups who in no way accepted the Rabbinical hermeneutic rules, or devices of a like nature, still produced homiletic expositions, paradoxes and exaggerations which have evidently originated in preaching and rhetorical requirements.[279] Among the Samaritans, Marqah is the most outstanding representative of such homiletic trends, notwithstanding his literalistic outlook.

The Pharisees were not alone in their insistence on upholding institutions of permanent study. That great differences existed between these groups is borne out by the fact that the Dead Sea Scroll Sect maintained continuous study by day and by night, in watches.[280] There is no evidence at all of a similar practice among the Samaritans.

Since the possibilities of study are determined by the extent of literacy present among the general public, our next concern must be to investigate the prevalence of writing in ancient Israel. One opinion is that, apart from families of professional scribes, writing became widespread only under Hellenistic influences. On the other hand, the evidence of the Elephantine Papyri points to a different estimate, namely, that as early as the fifth century B.C. literacy was not confined to a narrow elite. These papyri, however, could of course have been written by professional scribes, and this is substantiated by the close relationships between the writers, such as father and son.[281]

The rewriting of biblical history about the beginning of the Common Era (e.g. the Book of Jubilees and Pseudo-Philo) has given rise to the theory that literacy and learning came relatively late, for otherwise the scribes would not have been able to rewrite history with impunity.[282] To our purpose, however, this discussion has little relevance, as our

---

[278] *Kāfi*, pp. 102ff. (cf. text and translation, SLTh.A pp. 16f.).

[279] Heinemann, *Darkhei ha-Aggadah*, p. 12.

[280] *Manual of Discipline* VI, 6f.

[281] Driver, *Semitic Writing*, pp. 88ff., 122-123.

[282] A. Spiro, "Samaritans, Tobiads, etc.", *PAAJR* XX (1951), pp. 284ff. (cf. n. 30, pp. 291f.).

inquiry is into the Samaritans' exegesis, the earliest sources of which go back as far as the fourth century of the Common Era, when the situation was entirely changed.

Among the Pharisees, schools — including elementary ones for children — were maintained at least before Christian times.[283] Similarly, the Samaritan Targum — translating שוטר by 'scribe' in common with LXX — shows that scribes and teachers were employed in early times. This tradition of learning is abundantly substantiated by Marqah's expositions.[284] The liturgists in the Defter, from the Roman period, also use the metaphors of 'school' and 'teacher', which show that they were a familiar sight.[285]

The Ṭabbākh in its extensive commentary on the Shema' (Deut. vi, 5f.)[286] interprets the words of verse 8 (ibid.) "between thine eyes" (which the Jews interpreted as phylacteries), as enjoining that Hebrew writing should be taught, because it was the language in which the Commandments were written and was thus essential for their comprehension.[287] The problem was, who was to be comprised in this commandment? It was a regular feature of the orient that men normally held the dominant position while women were relegated to the shadows. This attitude is reflected in the Ṭabbākh [288] where, in interpreting the Passover sacrifice, the author discusses why a male sacrifice was demanded (Ex. xii, 5), and states that it was decreed of set purpose, in order to emphasize man's superiority over woman. In general, however, the Samaritans — in contrast to the Rabbinic Law exempting women from certain observances — do not make any distinction between the sexes in reference to their common obligation to carry out the Law. Were there any age-limits applied to the obligation to learn the Hebrew language? As the Samaritans were notorious for their rigid enforcement of the Law even upon babies (e.g. fasting on the Day of Atonement etc.), it seems likely that they demanded a similar strictness in the field of education. Yet in contrast to other groups who imposed various age-limits for the carrying out of religious responsibilities, in some cases

---

[283] Baron, Social and Religious History of the Jews II, pp. 274ff.

[284] For more details on the translation of שוטר as ספרה (S.T.) or γραμματεύς (LXX), cf. my article ALUOS VI (1969), pp. 119, 156 (n. 178).

[285] Brown, A Critical Edition etc., pp. 240f.

[286] cf. n. 208 sup.

[287] Abdel-Al, A Comparative Study etc., pp. 344, 346.

[288] f. 60b (cf. SLTh.A p. 102).

the upper age-limit being twenty,[289] no such considerations are found in early Samaritan literature. Only in later literature [290] do we find an injunction, based on *Deut.* xxxi, 13, to all boys over the age of ten to attend services at the Synagogue, and women are alike included. This would indicate that they had all had enough previous instruction to enable them to follow the service. The *Malef*, the literary pattern of which is the familiar one of question and answer, and can, therefore, be called a catechism, was probably specially devised for the simple instruction of children in the religious traditions.[291]

There is nothing extraordinary in the fact that a literalistic sect should devote so much attention to the religious education of their young. Indeed, we find that a similarly literalistic group, the Falashas, likewise devoted much energy to their religious instruction, for in almost every village they established schools, and whenever they encountered European Jews their main concern was to recruit more teachers and obtain books.[292]

Exaggerated claims have been made for the Samaritans' width of learning, and even that they possessed a Massorah of their own Pentateuch.[293] In spite of all their assiduous attention to children's education, there is nowhere any evidence for the existence of academies or institutions for the further education of adults. As regards the problem of *Qetafim*, that is, abbreviated versions of Scripture to be recited during services, some far-fetched theories have gained currency that these were supplied to the congregation to serve as pointers to, or reminders of points of Law, as they would then know what was being passed over. There is no evidence whatsoever to show that the majority of adult Samaritans were educated enough to follow such exercises.[294]

From the Samaritan chroniclers an idealistic picture of Baba Rabba's reform emerges.[295] The conclusion too often drawn from this exag-

---

[289] *Niddah* V, 9; Albeck, *Das Buch der Jubiläen etc.*, pp. 14f. cf. T.H. Gaster, *The Scripture of the Dead Sea Sect*, p. 285.

[290] Abisha's *Commentary on the Liturgy*, p. 38.

[291] cf. Baguley, *A Critical Edition... Malef etc.*, pp. i-vii.

[292] Aescoly, *Sepher ha-Falashim*, p. 20.

[293] Gaster, *Sam. Oral Law* I, p. 103.

[294] Boys, *A Critical Edition etc.*, pp. cxxi, cxxxviii, cf. Bowman, "Sam. Studies", *BJRL* XL (1958), pp. 315-327.

[295] Vilmar, *Abulfathi annales etc.*, pp. 129f.; Neubauer, "Chronique sam. etc.", *JA* .1869), p. 440; Adler and Seligson, *Une nouvelle chronique sam.*, pp. 51f. The reliability of the Baba Rabba stories is doubtful. The stories of the political success of this hero are legends which caused embarrassment to Abū-l Fatḥ, (*ibid.* p. 139) who claims

gerated picture, is that he established academies of learning. This view is based on the report that he "decreed the recitation of the Law". This, however, does not establish anything other than simple teaching of the Law according to its literal meaning, and certainly does not imply the existence of centres of higher learning. From the testimony of Samaritan writers of recent centuries, it is clear that their teachers were ignorant of the correct reading, and that occasionally even the actual transmission of the text was faulty.[296] In modern times, when an accurate census of Samaritan literacy was conducted, it was found that the illiteracy level was very high (42% among the men and 89% among the women).[297] Actually, in comparison with their neighbours their level of literacy was very good, but from our point of view it was only just sufficient to maintain an elementary cultural level.

We have now to consider what were the principles underlying the Samaritans' concept of education. Was their main priority theory, i.e. learning for its own sake, or practice, with the learning merely as a means to an end? In Rabbinic Judaism the emphasis was finally on practice.[298] Even those who preferred study were bound to admit that this was only because "study leads to doing".[299] Even in the isolated circle of Philo, where philosophy was their main concern, one can still find approximations to this approach.[300] This qualified emphasis on practice among the Rabbis, however, in no way diminished the prestige of learning, as expressed in their favourite maxim: "Turn it and turn it again (i.e. the Torah), for everything is in it."[301]

As opposed to this attitude the Samaritans, typified by Marqah's reproduction of an ancient maxim in the name of 'the grandson of Eden' (= Joshua), "In proportion to the action, is the reward,"[302] stress the absolute superiority of deeds.

Since the Samaritans did not concede a high place to learning for its own sake, it is not surprising that they did not foster a lofty regard for

---

that he cannot accept responsibility for their validity, cf. also Widengren, "Tradition of Literature etc.", *NVMEN* X (1963), p. 82.

[296] Ben-Hayyim, *Literary and Oral Tradition etc.* I, pp. 142f.

[297] Ben-Zevi, *Sepher ha-Shomronim*, p. 152.

[298] *Abhoth* I, 17.

[299] *Kiddushin* 40b; cf. Büchler, *Types of Jewish-Palestinian Piety etc.*, pp. 84f.

[300] Wolfson, *Philo* II, pp. 261f.

[301] *Abhoth* V, 22; cf. *ibid.* 23 another opinion of Ben He-He is, "According to the suffering (or effort) qo is the reward", cf. next note.

[302] *Memar Marqah* cf. Macdonald, I, p. 89 (= II, 145). וכן אמר בן בן עדן לפם די עבידתה הוא אגרה cf. Liberman, *Greek in Jewish Palestine*, p. 123, n. 111.

'Oral Law', which requires a life-time of devoted study. Unlike that of
the Rabbis, who proudly admitted the existence of many laws only
remotely connected with Scripture,[303] the Samaritans' attitude did not
allow of such possibilities. Similarly, whole chapters of Mishna, embracing purely academic laws which could have no practical application but
which were studied by the Rabbis with a view to gaining a reward for
learning,[304] could have no point whatsoever in the eyes of the Samaritans. Again, the whole system of Midrashic interpretations, so beloved
of the Rabbis and based on the assumption that individual parts of
words could be interpreted independently and entirely without regard
for the literal sense of the context,[305] held even less appeal for the Samaritans. As for the Rabbinic practice of special casuistic exercises, intended
to sharpen the pupil's mind,[306] this again was quite inconceivable to
the Samaritan mind. To exemplify the tremendous gulf between the two
approaches it may be helpful to quote Resh Laqish's [307] saying, "There
are many scriptures which could well be burned; however, they are the
actual body of the Torah." Such an admission, together with the
Midrashim that were built on it, would be utter sacrilege to the
Samaritans.

Surprisingly enough, the Karaites, who were themselves also extreme
literalists, nevertheless adopted the reverential attitude to learning evinced
by the Talmudists. They established academies modelled upon Rabbanite ideals and institutions;[308] but the Samaritans albeit greatly influenced by them in many respects remained unmoved by this example.

Intensive study tends always to foster mysticism, which is normally
the direct result of a belief in the manifold meanings of the biblical text.
We have already seen that such study made little appeal to the Samaritans.[309] Their whole system of education, together with their literalism,
succeeded in making them immune to such speculations.

In contradistinction to the Dead Sea Scroll Sect who, although they
likewise confined themselves to the literal interpretation of the Law,
allowed themselves greater freedom of interpretation in the pesher

---

[303] cf. my article *ALUOS* VI (1969), pp. 98, 128 (n. 6).

[304] *inf.* Part III, para (h. 3).

[305] Heinemann, *Darkhei ha-Aggadah*, pp. 103f.

[306] Weiss, *Dor Dor ve-Dorshav* III, p. 21.

[307] *Ḥullin*, 70b. אמר ר״ל הרבה מקראות שראויין להשרף והן הן גופי תורה

[308] Ankori, *Karaites in Byzantium*, pp. 249ff. (cf. especially nn. 100-103).

[309] cf. *sup.* para (b).

type of Aggadic themes,[310] the Samaritans applied their literalism far more consistently. If thoroughly investigated, the mysticism attributed to Marqah in recent publications proves to be nothing else than straightforward biblical exegesis, that is, simply midrash.[311] The same applies to many expressions of 'mysteries' and 'arcana' appearing in the Samaritan liturgies.[312]

As to Gnosticism, even in the Dead Sea Scrolls — which are indeed more mystically inclined — the experts themselves have been unwilling to commit themselves to a definite opinion.[313] If it is so difficult to find among the Dead Sea Scroll Sect any positive evidence for this element, it is even more impossible that the Samaritans, with their rudimentary type of education, should have been capable of developing such a way of thinking.

E. The Devotional Aspect of Samaritan Exegesis

For a clear understanding of Samaritan exegesis, it is necessary to assess carefully the depth of their religious devotion, since this is the main factor in determining their whole theological outlook, which in turn directs and influences their exegesis from every standpoint. Having considered their extreme fanaticism in advocating their theories in regard to the Law, the verbal inspiration of Scripture and the glorification of Moses, we must now deal with the question how these theories were in reality put into practice. Similarly, we must investigate the many defamatory accusations levelled against them. Instances of these are that they worshipped the image of a dove,[314] and that they worshipped an idol called Ashimah.[315] Insofar as these accusations have any real basis, they must unquestionably stem from the period when there was a universal belief in national gods who might combat one another. However, with the establishment of the second Hebrew Commonwealth, and as the Samaritans, in common with the Judahites, were gradually

---

[310] cf. my article *ALUOS* VI (1969), pp. 121f., 158f. (nn. 195f.).

[311] *op. cit.* pp. 109f., 142f. (nn. 90f.).

[312] cf. S. Brown, *A Critical Edition*, p. 270.

[313] Scholem, *Gnosticism etc.*, p. 3f.

[314] Montgomery, *The Samaritans*, p. 320. cf. also Jeremias, "Die Passahfeier etc.", *ZATW* Beiheft 59, pp. 59-60 and notes.

[315] Montgomery, *op. cit.* p. 213, n. 28. cf. also M. Noth, *Die israelitischen Personennamen in Rahmen der gemein semitischen Namengebung* (Beiträge zur Wissenschaft vom Alten und Neuen Testament, Dritte Folge, Heft 10, Stuttgart, 1928), pp. 123-126.

dominated by the ideals expressed in the Pentateuch, they too liberated themselves from these pagan conceptions.[316] The striking testimony to their strict adherence to their precepts given by the Rabbis, affords the best possible proof of their consistent practice of their religion as against all contrary accusations.[317] Since such testimonies were not called forth by a generous attitude to the Samaritans, but rather persisted in spite of the generally hostile relationship between the two factions, they must have had a firm historical basis. The common belief, expressed by the other nations, that the Jews hated outsiders, was based on their attributing the Jews' separatism to anti-social tendencies, and on their failure to understand the Jews' real motive in adhering to their religious code.[318] The Samaritans' exclusiveness was actually far more marked, and their outward attitude to foreigners was clearly expressed in the dictum, "Touch me not". The fact that they in particular were notorious for this separatist outlook only serves to show how rigidly they observed their Laws. It is irrelevant to our purpose that these very laws were carried out not by all the Samaritans but by a religious elite. Among the Jews too, when Pharisaism became dominant, there were still a great number of uneducated boors who did not trouble to learn or practice the Law.[319]

The same particularism which arose from the need felt after the persucations of Antiochus Epiphanes and the consequent dangers of assimilation (which were counteracted in the case of the Pharisees by "putting a fence around the Torah"), had its effect also among the Samaritans. In both cases, seeing that the historical background was the same, the dangers of Hellenization justified the great emphasis laid on ritual.[320] The constant pressures brought to bear upon the Samaritans, from the hegemony of the Greeks down to that of the Arabs, urging them to abandon their specific culture, coupled with the very fact of their unpredictable survival, also testify to their intense religious devotion. Apart from the Samaritan chronicles, full as they are of heroic martyrdoms and valiant and stubborn resistance to forced conversion,

---

[316] E. Kaufman, *The History of the Israelite Religion* VII, pp. 21f., 31f. etc.

[317] Tosephta, *Pesahim* I, 15 (ed. Zuckermandel, p. 156) and parallels.

[318] Tcherikover, *Hellenistic Civilization and the Jews*, pp. 368, 532 (nn. 98-99).

[319] Büchler, *Der galiläische Am-ha-Ares etc.*, pp. 65f., 212. Although the locality and the fixed period of these boors was rightly disputed (cf. Alon, *Studies* I, pp. 158ff.) their existence is undeniable.

[320] C.G. Montefiore, *The Origin and Growth of Religion... of the Ancient Hebrews* (Hibbert Lectures, 1892), pp. 435f.; cf. Davies, *Paul and Rabbinic Judaism*, pp. 61f.

external sources testify also to their unremitting rebellion. Their situation forcibly reminds us of the fate of another literalist group, the Falashas, who from the uncomplimentary descriptions given of them by the Abyssinian chroniclers as trouble-makers, emerge as a sect stubbornly defending their faith against overwhelming odds.[321]

No observance of mere ritual could of itself sustain a people against such fierce oppression. It was faith which kept alive both their observance and their resistance to external pressures. Although we cannot enter here into a precise definition of the nature of this faith,[322] one fact is certain, that they had enough pentateuchal support for a naive doctrine both of the faithfulness of God towards man and of the steadfast belief of man in God. Just as such a belief is inseparable from the main body of this Samaritan pentateuchal religion, so also are other inner cleavages inconceivable to the Samaritans. Both the ritual and the moral Laws found in the Pentateuch were regarded as equally sacred [323] and hence it is pointless to attempt to sunder these two concepts in the Samaritan religion. It is equally futile to speak of epochs of 'ritualizing' or 'moralizing' among the Samaritans, as such concepts were totally alien to them. Nor can the religious leadership be artificially divided into the orders of priests and laymen. The Samaritans' lack of compilations of regulative norms (like the Oral Law among the Jews) cannot be attributed to any absence of lay leadership among them.[324] Likewise, the much overestimated religious reformation of Baba Rabba, which allegedly places the status of layman above that of priest,[325] cannot be substantiated from any other Samaritan sources. On the contrary, later literature gives no support whatever to the supposed subordination of the priests to the laymen. The usage already embodied in the Targum of translating "judges and officers" (*Deut.* xvi, 18) as "judges and scribes", on the clear understanding that "judges" refers to high priests, runs through all Samaritan tradition, thus indicating the order of importance by the serial order of the words as revealed by God.[326] All theories that attribute to Marqah a desire to replace a priestly religion by a speculative type of religion, based on 'wisdom',[327] are without any foundation.

---

[321] Aescoly, *Sepher Ha-Falashim*, p. 146.

[322] cf. Barr, *The Semantics of Biblical Language*, pp. 161f.

[323] cf. Montefiore, *Some elements etc.*, pp. 24f.

[324] cf. Abdel-Al, *A Comparative Study etc.*, p. 44. cf. *inf.* para (j).

[325] cf. *sup.* nn. 295f. and text there and *inf.* para (k).

[326] cf. *sup.* nn. 284-5.

[327] cf. my article *op. cit.* pp. 109f. (nn. 93ff.).

With regard to the Samaritans' staunch conviction of the self-sufficiency of their own religion, we shall let the sources speak for themselves. Most typical is Marqah's constant assertion: "How could our souls be in need of anyone else, when all are in need of us?"[328] He is referring here to the Torah which the whole world could presumably learn from them. It is only because they have transgressed the Torah that the glory which was originally exclusive to the possessros of the Torah has gone from them; but if they repent it will return.

On this basis is the whole Samaritan theodicy built. In Marqah's exposition of "For all his ways are judgment" (*Deut.* xxxii, 4),[329] he plays on the word KI,[330] making it refer to the beginning and the end of the world. As the beginning of the world was justice, so also will the end of the world be justice. This justice is completely identified with the idea of the divine election and the preservation of the Torah. If divine justice is not seen to operate in the world, this is entirely due to human failure and lack of knowledge.

We should not make the assumption from this that Marqah's main emphasis was on knowledge, for elsewhere [331] he explicitly states that "the reward is meted out according to the action". Of outstanding interest here is Marqah's parable of human kidness : if among men one is expected to repay a fellow-being's kindness, how much more should one repay God's perpetual loving-kindness! This teaching elucidates for us the pessimistic mood of his preaching, which stems from his theodicy, ascribing all misfortunes past and future to human shortcomings rather than God's vengeance.[332] Of special relevance is Marqah's belief that God has exempted Israel from the government of the stars for the sake of the Torah, while other nations are under their sway :[333]

---

[328] *Memar Marqah* (ed. Macdonald) I, pp. 136f. (= II, pp. 223f.).

[329] *Memar Marqah* (ed. Macdonald) I, p. 88 (= II, p. 142).

[330] "As the first KI (*Deut.* xxxii, 3) is the beginning of the world, so the second (*ibid.* 4) is the road to the next world." Later, however, Marqah employs a similar midrash in order to show that Moses knew all the 'secrets' of the world when he says: "He said KI KOL (*ibid.*) — KI the beginning and KOL the end".

[331] *ibid.* I, pp. 132f. (= II, 217), cf. Baneth, *Des Sam. Marqah an die 22 Buchstaben etc.*, p. 39, n. 59 (cf. *sup.* n. 302).

[332] *Memar Marqah* (ed. Macdonald) I, pp. 106f. (= II, p. 178). Here the "Ten Judgements" of the Day of Vengeance (extracted from *Deut.* xxxii, 21ff.) are illustrated by verses from the Curses (*Lev.* xxvi, 14ff.; *Deut.* xxviii) in order to show that all retribution is the direct result of human wickedness.

[333] *ibid.* I, p. 106 (= II, pp. 176f.). Similar opinions were also expressed they Rabbis (*Shabbath* 156a), although amongst them there existed also other opinions (*ibid.* and *Mo'ed Qaṭan* 28a).

He fixed the bounds (*Deut.* xxxii, 8), a statement which He connects with His statement, *according to the numbers of the sons of Israel. And your descendants shall be as the stars of heaven* (*Gen.* xxii, 17), twelve above (= zodiacs) and twelve below (= tribes of Israel). When He said, *As the stars of heaven*, they did not need to be governed ever, but all the peoples of the world are without law or commandment; therefore they are guided by the stars. The law is in your hand, O Isreal.

This very element of divine justice, which was a factor in the Samaritan religion from the earliest times, contributed to its easy assimilation of the Mu'tazilite philosophy. In the *Ṭabbākh*,[334] *Deut.* xxxii, 40 is explained as an Oath taken by God upon his everlasting righteousness, which naturally embraces this world. He swore this in order to teach his people the truth of the divine justice, to shield them from sinning. In the case of Munajja the Mu'tazilite influence is even more pronounced, in that the devotes a whole chapter [335] to 'divine justice'. Following on his discussion of divine attributes, conducted entirely in a Mu'tazilite spirit, he elaborates on them by stating "He is the Provider, who created the world out of His goodness and loving-kindness." In interpreting אש דת (*Deut.* xxxiii, 2), the *Ṭabbākh*,[336] renders it as "a religion of fire"; namely that the Torah is comparable to fire. Just as fire purifies matter from defilement, so does the Torah save the body from retribution through the observance of its commandments. Just as fire illuminates, so does the Torah enlighten and guide men. It is of special significance that דת was understood by Abū-l Ḥasan as the traditional Law. This belief in the power of the Torah to preserve one from blemishes is expounded in the *Ṭabbākh* in another place:[337]

> ... It occurs in two ways, one by the way of divine revelation, indicated by Scripture, and the second, by the arguments of Tradition. The latter is superior, since everything is verified through it. Therefore it is imperative to know the conditions and proofs of the Tradition, to distinguish the true one from the faulty one. Such are the arguments of the Tradition, transmitted by (our) congregation, which was never corrupted.

---

[334] f. 228a, f.

[335] *Masā'il al Khilāf* Ib, p. 77.

[336] f. 202b.

[337] f. 151b. f. ... يحصل من طريقين منه ما يحصل من السمع با يدل عليه

نصه ومنه ما يعلم من جهة النقل وهو ابهر في الاستدلال لان به تصح
الجمله وجب لاجل ذلك معرفة النقل وشروط صحته ليتميز النقل الصحيح
من السقيم بيان ذلك النقل وهو الموخود عن جماعه لا يجوز عليهم تواطوا
ولا لشاعر ...

From this we can see that the peculiarly Samaritan exclusiveness dominates all their religious outlook. The fact that tradition actually was esteemed by them more highly than Scripture betokens their unconditional reliance on their 'unbroken chain' of tradition. This dual principle of Scripture and Tradition and of their interdependence keeps the believer in the right path, which is the 'true' will of God. This walking in the right path was given a double meaning, i.e. that of man's walking in the right path and that of God's making man's way blessed. This notion is frequently expressed in literature [338] and firmly based on Scripture (i.e. *Gen.* xxiv, 40; *ibid.* xxviii, 15). In a prayer of Abraham Qabaṣi [339] it is quite pointedly expressed: "Know that on your right and on your left scribes record your deed; it is sealed up in God's storehouse for the Day of Vengeance and Recompense". There is no variation in regard to this attitude between Marqah and Qabaṣi, although they are divided by a full millenium.

A good example of the Samaritans' attitude of religious exclusiveness based on the Torah can be found in their preparatory prayer preceding the washing of hands for divine worship. This prayer [340] implies that the water symbolizes the Torah and that, just as water cleanses the body, so also the Torah cleanses the soul. The essence of the prayer is the suppliant's plea to become one of the 'keepers' of the Law.

This exclusiveness of the Samaritans was not based on nationalist or racialist prejudices, but even conceded the possibility of any person embracing their religion. *Deut.* xxxii, 43, is interpreted by the *Ṭabbākh* [341] as meaning that, when the nations see the rewards of the Israelites on the 'Day of Judgment', they will envy them their lot. The latter half of the verse is interpreted in various ways, one of them being: "anyone who seeks their nearness by being a proselyte and is buried in their soil, will benefit". Although there is no historical evidence for any widespread missionary activities on the part of the Samaritans, nevertheless, if the occasion arose, they would in fact warmly welcome any convert to their religion.[342] Again, although the biblical word גר is interpreted

---

[338] *Sir al-Qalb*, p. 46.

[339] Cowley, *The Sam. Liturgy* I, p. 233. cf. J. Macdonald, *The Theology of the Sam.*, p. 384.

[340] *Kāfi*, pp. 49f. (Text and translation, cf. SLTh.A p. 12.)

[341] f. 229a. cf. J. Macdonald, *op. cit.* p. 272.

[342] cf. Halkin, "The Relation etc.", *Saadia Anniversary Vol.*, p. 272 (n. 9 and literature quoted there).

by them in several ways, such as 'stranger' or 'sojourner', it is frequently taken to mean 'proselyte'. Marqah's [343] exposition of *Deut.* xxvii, 19. affirms that there are seven commandments regarding kind treatment of the sojourner. He says: "Notice how He puts the sojourner first and again mentions the orphan and the widow". It is inconceivable that a heathen sojourner should be given preferential treatment over the widow and the orphan from their own fold. In his later treatment of the sojourner he thus makes it quite clear that he is a proselyte, for in his further exposition of this question he says: "*You shall not wrong (Lev.* xix, 33, cf. *Ex.* xxii, 21) in speech or in action, lest the sojourner grieve for what he has left behind or abhor what he has come to." These sentiments about the proselyte are outlined more explicitly in later literature [344] but the line of though is the same as that of Marqah.

Perhaps the reason that there is not much evidence for proselytes can be explained by the fact that, outwardly at any rate, the Samaritan religion looked austere and stern, and therefore was unattractive to potential adherents. Needless to say, the Samaritans themselves did not regard their religion as unduly austere, nor their obligations to God as impossible to fulfil. Marqah [345] stoutly denies that God demands that one should do anything which is quite beyond one's capacity. He emphasizes that the doing of good and justice rewards the believer in two ways, namely that he reaps the fruit of his labour and that he concurrently becomes a righteous man. He concludes by saying: "You are not expected to do something that is not in your power to do, but God demands from you (only) what is in your ability (to do) and that you do not love evil. Were it beyond your power, God would not demand it from you." Although such sentiments are, to be sure, expressed in the Koran (II, 286),[346] there is no reason for supposing that the later Samaritans

---

[343] *Memar Marqah* (ed. Macdonald) I, p. 73 (= II, p. 118). In the Talmud also (*Babha Bathra* 59b) the biblical warnings against the ill-treatment of the proselyte are enumerated (36 times, or 46 times according to other opinions).

[344] *Ṭabbākh* f. 73b, and 74a (cf. SLTh.A p. 114 and 115 respectively).

[345] *Memar Marqah* I, p. 77 (= II, p. 125). Marqah introduces this theme by saying "Make your deed to be fixed to righteousness and you will be magnified with two good things; the reward of your labour (= deeds = merit) and the reward of the Righteous, and what you desire will come about for you". Also, from the admonitions with which he concludes his words, it is obvious that he did not refer here to one who "could not attain to love of God". cf. J. Macdonald, *The Theology of the Sam.*, p. 339.

[346] Islamic exegetes often understood the maxim as an excuse for non-observance of the religious obligations if observation would cause hardship. The Rabbinic rule: "We most not impose a *restriction* (גזרה) on the public which the majority can not

were in any way influenced by Islam, seeing that they had their own pre-Islamic traditions to rely upon. Furthermore, this maxim did not lead the Samaritans to relaxation of their rigid religious self-discipline, as was the case in Islam. For the scope of this maxim among the former was strictly confined to the encouragement of the devout, in holding before them the accessibility of God.

No specific statements are made to explain such an interdependence. However, the problem posed by a feasible interpretation of "to observe (לעשות) the Sabbath", (*Ex.* xxxi, 16) is tackled by the *Ṭabbākh* [347] in the following manner: Since a man cannot 'make the Sabbath', nor can he perform a continuous special act throughout it, the meaning must be that he must observe the time-limits (both its commencement and its termination). The line of argument is that man cannot 'make' the Sabbath, since such an operation is carried out by the constellations, and the precept must therefore mean to 'observe', since God never demands the impossible from man. The same argument is brought forward when the *Ṭabbākh* deals with the intricate problem of the calendar, which may conceivably give rise to inaccuracies in religious observances. Abū-l Ḥasan generalizes on each of the commandments:[348]

> ... That it should be within the ability of the adherent to carry it out; otherwise it contradicts the divine wisdom and justice, since it is one of the principles that there should not be punishment without sin. A person cannot be commanded to do what is beyond his capability to carry out. Therefore it is impossible that God should command and then prevent the execution of his command at the proper time, and in consequence condemn the offender by capital punishment. If there were no possibility of knowing the exact time, this would create agnosticism...

Not only did God not command man to do the impossible, but he also

---

endure" (*Babha Qama* 79b; *Babha Meṣia* 60b), has absolutely no relevance to this Islamic tradition. cf. J. Katch, *Judaism and the Koran* (N.Y., 1962), p. 188. The Rabbis and the Samaritans alike took it for granted that the observance of the Law depended entirely on the free will of the individual.

[347] f. 32b (SLTh.A p. 88).

[348] *ibid.* f. 188b. ... ان يكون مقدورا للمكلف والا ودا الى ما تقتضيه

الحكمه والعدل لان من قضايا العدل ان لا يعذب من غير جرم ولا يكلف

ما لا يطاق فاذا كان ذلك كذلك فلا يحسن منه تعالى بان يامر بتكليف

ويعدق فعله بزمان ويقضى على الاخلال به باراقة الدم فلا طريق الى

معرفة ذلك الزمان حتى يكون مظنون ...

showed his consideration for human difficulties in the compassionate way in which he ordained his Law. Thus we find in the precepts of Passover that domestic animals (*Deut.* xiv, 4f.) and not game were required for the sacrifice, since the latter was food only for kings and princes, and almost beyond the means of the people in general. God would not impose a burden which was impossible for man to bear.[349]

This belief of theirs in God's benevolence towards them made the Samaritans go so far as to imply that God helped them even in the observance of His commands. Maybe this is the meaning implicit in Marqah's statement about God's exemption of Israel from the government of the Zodiac, in relation to which the Torah operates as a counteracting force.[350] This again implies that, not only has God cancelled all the powers of determinism in the world, but he has even given his people positive grace to aide them in the very observance of the Torah. This fundamental concept is further developed in subsequent exegesis when *Deut.* xxxiii, 26 "who rideth upon the heaven for *thy* help", is interpreted in a similar way. The *Ṭabbākh*[351] offers two interpretations of this verse. The first is historical, referring it to the pillar of cloud which overshadowed and protected Israel in their journey through the desert. The second is even more interesting, in that it makes it refer to God's changing their adversity into prosperity,[352] in order that they might become the 'chosen' ones who should obey him. Munajja's approach to this theme is very similar.[353] However, he appears to admit the influence of the zodiac on the world, with the reservation that God helps his people within this astrological system. Later exegetes[354] combine the verse in question with *Gen.* ii, 15 to illustrate both spiritual aid coming from God to man and man's obligation to serve God.

Although the belief in man's absolute free-will may be found among other religious groups,[355] the Samaritans went so far as to postulate a

---

[349] *ibid.* f. 61a (cf. SLTh.A pp. 102f.).

[350] *sup.* n. 333.

[351] f. 211b.

[352] وقيل انه اقلب لهم النحوس سعودا It seems that this is identical with Marqah's opinion of God excluding Israel from the domain of the stars (*sup.* n. 333). Abū-l Ḥasan's words should have been translated literally, viz. "God changed their *ill luck* luck into a *good omen*".

[353] *Masā'il al-Khilāf* Ib, p. 170.

[354] Abisha's *Commentary on Liturgy*, p. 5.

[355] Free will was the norm of early Judaism, as expressed by Ben Sirah (*Ecclesiasticus* xv, 20; cf. M.H. Segal, *Sepher Ben-Sira ha-Shalem*, p. 38). The only exceptions

divine aid active in the furtherance of man's right choice. This explains their constant preoccupation with the problem of their ill-fate, since it clearly jeopardized their firm belief in God's benevolence. Scholars [356] have recognized for a long time that this is the motive underlying those constant admonitions in which they bitterly blame themselves and their own sins for precipitating all their calamities. Their exaggerated guilt-complex even attributed the sufferings of the 'Chosen men, the Sons of the Righteous' to the sins of their fellow-believers.[357]

These fierce self-accusations were not totally unfounded, for each generation must have had its share of sinners and nonconformists who could be charged with the collective guilt of the community. Their literature testifies to the presence of such groups, of which we shall mention only the most obvious cases. Thus the *Ṭabbākh*,[358] when it treats of the Laws of the Sabbath, speaks of those who do not preserve the sanctity of the Sabbath. It is consequently stated [359] that all the curses specified both in *Leviticus* (xxvi) and in *Deuteronomy* (xxviii) have been meted out during the long period of the Panutha (divine disfavour) as a direct result of this type of sin. Similarly the *Kāfi*,[360] in connection with the obligation of attending the Synagogue, inveighs against villagers who are lax in this matter and, as a result of it, bring themselves into the domain of evil and hence will not accept any admonition or chastisement. Because of their unrepentant attitude, he writes them off as excluding themselves from the congregation of the law of Moses. Most probably in such instances of invincible laxity in religious observance, these offenders ended up by total assimilation to their Muslim nieghbours, culminating in a formal conversion.

We must now examine the Samaritan attitude to sinners and to their opportunities for repentance. Among the various religious groups conflicting opinions existed on this problem, ranging from the extreme attitude of denying the gross offender an opportunity for repentance to that of elevating the renegade to a higher position than that of the

---

were the Sadducees and the Dead Sea Scroll Sect. cf. Driver, *Judaean Scrolls*, p. 560). The Talmud knows also about divine help towards the strengthening of those who go on the right way (*Aboth* IV, 2; *Shabbath* 32a; *ibid.* 104a etc.).

[356] Gaster, *The Samaritans*, p. 19.

[357] Cowley, "Description of Four Sam. Mss. etc.", *PEFQS*, 1904, pp. 74 and 75f. (cf. Cowley, *The Sam. Liturgy* I, pp. 13 and 14 respectively).

[358] f. 34a (SLTh.A p. 89).

[359] *ibid.* f. 35-36b (SLTh.A pp. 91-92), cf. *sup.* n. 332.

[360] p. 101.

righteous man who has never sinned. Jesus' attitude to sinners brought upon him the scornful title of 'friend of sinners', but he only consorted with them in order to persuade them to abandon their sin.[361] This does not mean that pharisaic Judaism was opposed to the repentance of sinners, for, on the contrary, there was an opinion that the repentant are higher in rank than the righteous: "In the place where the repentant stand, the perfectly righteous do no stand."[362] It seems, then, that the Rabbis were torn between two conflicting ideas, one that it is a duty to elevate the sincerely repentant man, and the other that an over-indulgent attitude to the sinner must undermine the seriousness of sin. Philo,[363] unlike the Rabbis, puts the repentant only one stage below the perfectly righteous.

The other extreme is found among the Essenes, who, according to Josephus,[364] in the case of heinous sins excommunicated the renegades, an act which frequently resulted in their dying of starvation. It seems that the Dead Sea Scroll sect held a similar attitude to sinners.

Maybe the Samaritans were in a similar dilemma to that of the Rabbis. On the one hand, we have Marqah's severe sentences against the sinner and, on the other, the fact that if, as we have seen, the proselytism of heathens was possible, then surely an erring one of their own number could hardly be debarred from regaining the divine grace. Marqah is in line with the pentateuchal tradition of the 'two ways', according to which he who offends against the Law is accursed and considered as rejected: moreover, he brings this dictum to its logical conclusion by saying, "He who is accursed is rejected. He is never accepted."[365] His midrash [366] on the Samaritan version of *Deut.* xxvii, 26 (adding *all* to the sentence) argues that the curse attached to the one who does not confirm *all* the words of the law by his action is attached also to the one who transgresses even parts of it:

> He who alters a statute of it enters into the curse. He who breaks a fence enters into the curse. He who is warned by a priest of my words and disobeys enters into the curse. He who is directed by a judge and rebels enters into the curse. He who makes himself an anemy to God enters into the curse in this world and will suffer very severe retribution in the next.

---

[361] Montefiore, *Some elements etc.*, pp. 56f.
[362] *Berakoth* 34b.
[363] Wolfson, *Philo* II, p. 258 (nn. 126, 127).
[364] *Wars* II, VIII, 8. cf. *Manual of Discipline*, viii, 20 - ix, 2.
[365] *Memar Marqah* (ed. Macdonald) I, p. 68 (= II, p. 108).
[366] *ibid.* I, p. 77 (= II, pp. 124f.).

He emphasizes both before and after this passage that this expression "Law" does not refer to this one specific passage (*Deut*. xxvii, 9-26) only, but rather to the entire pentateuch. It is nevertheless inconceivable that Marqah should have thus denied the possibility of repentance if one considers his numerous exhortations to repentance and his benevolent attitude to the proselyte, whose aspirations he could surely not have considered empty and vain. Although we have to admit a certain degree of inconsistency on the part of Marqah, just as we have seen it in the case of the Rabbis, yet there must have been some definite line that they followed in dealing with repentants. This becomes clear from the *Ṭabbākh* [367] when it treats one of the problems involved in the passover offering. According to *Ex*. xii, 48, the proselyte is allowed to participate, and the reason given for this is that Israel should be reminded of the pressing need for repentance. If then the proselyte, who when a heathen and an unbeliever was denied any dealings with the Israelites, can now perform the supreme sacred act of participating in the sacrifice, how much more is the lapsed bel*i*ever, who has after all a preferential status, acceptable after repentance.

The relative position assigned to practice as against doctrine has often been seriously misunderstood, in the sense that scholars, being very often chiefly familiar with the liturgical writings, where doctrine naturally occupies a more important place, have come to the conclusion that doctrine played the greater part in Samaritan religion. This misunderstanding has been partly grounded in the prejudices derived from a comparison with Rabbinic Judaism, which has been characterized as a religion in which practice was important and doctrine was almost non-existent.[368] Hence, as opposed to the alleged Rabbinic 'orthopraxy', the Samaritans appeared in contrast to stand for doctrinal orthodoxy. However, even this attitude towards Judaism was mistaken, since there doctrine played a much greater part than was generally assumed. According to Massekheth Kuthim,[369] the Samaritans are accepted if they renounce their belief in Hargerizim and accept the belief in Jerusalem and in the resurrection of the dead. Similarly, Jewish

---

[367] f. 71b. (For text and translation cf. SLTh.A p. 113.)

[368] cf. Davis, *Paul and Rab. Judaism*, p. 73 (and sources mentioned in n. 6). The whole illustration from the career of Elisha b. Abuyah is wrong. In so far as Aḥer is mentioned and accepted, he is regarded as a halakhist whose decision is binding. cf. Weiss, *Dor Dor etc*. II, p. 126 (and n. 1 *ibid*.).

[369] Montgomery, *The Samaritans*, p. 203.

Christians, as they appear in the pseudo-Clementines, are regarded by early Judaism as apostates, in spite of their Judaizing religious observances.[370] All this proves beyond doubt that doctrine was treated as of equal standing with practice in Judaism. Similarly, the opinion, often expressed, that, as compared with Judaism, the Samaritans emphasized doctrine, is built on false premises.[371] In both groups the two factors played an equal part in expressing religious convictions and were regarded as inter-dependent. This whole misconception plainly arises from the attempt to introduce the Christian conflict of "faith versus works" into religions where such a dichotomy never existed.

Marqah [372] himself puts this very inderdependence of doctrine and practice into sharp relief when he says, in apologising for the letter צ (symbolizing מצוה, commandment) not being at the beginning of a biblical section:

> The reading is not efficacious, the prayer is not acceptable, unless it comes from a heart full of repentance. If we read and do not practice what we have read, what is the point of such reading? If we pray with a heart adulterated with something other than God, the prayer is not accepted and the petition is not answered. We walk after self-desire, not after the desire of our Lord. In idolatry every day we are involved, and the words of truth we deny.

In another place,[373] he puts it even more blunty, asserting that a person who knows the truth, but does not practice it, is worse than Pharaoh.

Although one could hardly expect to find a strict line of demarcation between theology and ritual in the writings of the Byzantine period, such a division — if it existed — must have been entirely subconscious. Even so, when theology was systematized among the Samaritans under the influence of the Mu'tazilite philosophy, reaching them through the channels of Karaite writing, there was in fact hardly any new development in the matter of laying more emphasis on doctrine. The only difference was that a more rationalistic trend of thought was developed. However, this rationalistic philosophy, which religious polemics demanded, was itself severely curbed and limited by earlier doctrines.[374]

---

[370] Marmorstein, "Judaism and Christianity etc.", *HUCA* X (1935), p. 230.

[371] Bowman, "Sam. Studies", *BJRL* XL (1958), p. 309; Abdel-Al, *A Comparative Study etc.*, pp. 30f.; Trotter, *A Critical Study etc.*, p. 343. Naturally, once the whole theory is proved to be non-existent, there is no need to refute the conclusions derived from it about the Sam. "Gnosticism".

[372] *Memar Marqah* (ed. Macdonald) I, p. 144 (= II, p. 237).

[373] *ibid.* I, p. 71 (= II, pp. 114f.).

[374] cf. *inf.* para (f) (cf. also SLTh. pp. 899f.).

Nevertheless, the later literature of the Islamic period, despite its philosophical bent, did not attempt to harmonize the contradiction between the constant admonition to repentence and the belief in the total rejection of the 'sinner'. Maybe the problem was deliberately left open in order to save the common people (who might occasionally fall into 'sin') from total despair. This and other problems of Samaritan religious psychology will be dealt with separately.[375] In general it may be stated that later generations accepted the lead of Marqah in this respect too, who, despite his total condemnation of the 'wicked', concludes his sermon with a note of hope:[376]

> ... Apply your mind to learn from these (wicked). If you behave like them you will perish like them. Close up this school (of thought) and do not open it, for the serpent and the Belial are contained in it. Open rather the gate of goodness and enter into it safely.

The gate of repentance is wide open, not only for the individual, but for the whole people, in order that they may repent and revert by it to their original status. Although Marqah constantly brings up serious self-accusations (because all misfortunes, including the entrance of the 'divine disfavour', were caused by man), he nevertheless also expresses the hope that repentance is possible.[377] When the people do this, they will revert to their original status and God will make good his oath and keep his covenant.

F. The Extent of Samaritan Rationalism

The contemptuous attitude towards Samaritan learning, adopted by the Rabbis, has to be taken with a grain of salt, since it arises from a comparison between their own intricate hermeneutical principles of exegesis and the Samaritans' relatively simple and literalistic treatment of Scripture. The Rabbis themselves, however, despite their sophisticated methods, were from the standpoint of rationalism equally naive. Although modern scholars now feel entirely justified in deprecating the usage of linguistic material in order to extract abstruse, notional and philo-sophical concepts of biblical theology therefrom,[378] up to recent times this method has been the only one employed by exegetes. For example,

---

[375] cf. *inf.* para (g).
[376] *Memar Marqah* (ed. Macdonald) I, pp. 101f. (= II, pp. 167f.).
[377] *ibid.* I, p. 107 (= II, pp. 179f.).
[378] Barr, *Biblical Semantics*, pp. 4f.

no real attempts was made by the Samaritans themselves to reconcile the attributes of God as received from scriptural data with such abstract ideas as were adopted from the Greeks. The naive biblical attributes and the abstract philosophical speculations were interwoven without ever being logically integrated into one consistent whole.[379]

Organic thinking, which is a marked characteristic both of the Rabbinic[380] and the Samaritan exegesis, does not subordinate the sensuous and pictorial approaches to the purely intellectual. This is, of course, a common feature of all oriental thinking, that it grasps images rather than abstract concepts. This popular and imaginative thinking concentrates on visual details rather than on building a philosophical system. This does not mean to say that there were no philosophical influences whatsoever. Although there were very few who had any direct contact with the Greek philosophical literature, nevertheless, intelligent people were largely guided by the ideas contained in it.[381] As was later the case in Islam,[382] these philosophical influences, just because they came *after* the formulation of the basic tenets of the religion, could not radically change its dogmas.

Especially in the field of exegesis, there was little Greek influence, as the traditional method of simple analogies was preferred to the Greek system of dialectics. Marqah's work abounds in such primitive analogies as could not pass the scrutiny of any rational thinking. To take, for example, his analogical comparison of the Blessing of Moses with the Blessing of Jacob:[383] one finds items more suited to the pulpit than to philosophical thinking. Marqah admits a self-contradiction into his work that no philosopher would allow, when he implies in one place that prayer is efficacious only on Hargerizim, while in other places he clearly intimates that there is no geographical limit to the reception of prayer.[384]

Marqah is only following in such cases what he believes are the true messages of Scripture, without trying at all to reconcile the discrepancies. Recognizable aspects of the essence and function of the Deity (known in theological terms as Immanence and Transcendence) are never rationally defined.[385]

---

[379] J. Macdonald, *The Theology of the Sam.*, p. 87.

[380] Heinemann, *Darkhei ha-Aggadah*, p. 15.

[381] Macdonald, *op. cit.* pp. 30f., 127f.

[382] Margoliouth, *The Early Development of Mohomedanism*, pp. 205f.

[383] *Memar Marqah* (ed. Macdonald) I, p. 120 (= II, pp. 198f.), cf. *sup.* n. 379.

[384] cf. J. Macdonald, *The Theology of the Sam.*, p. 332.

[385] *ibid.* p. 67, cf. *sup.* nn. 73-76.

On the other hand, naivety, as we find it manifested in primitive exegetical devices, is in itself not necessarily an argument against their essential reationalism. Such plays on words and letters as are employed by Marqah should not appear especially ridiculous to us, since they are also found among other groups, as for example the early Christians. Among the Rabbis too, there is no real discrimination between straightforward exegesis and naive plays on words and letters.[386]

The much disputed problem of the Samaritan creed [387] likewise rests on a false premise. Although Christian and Islamic influences at length made the Samaritans aware of the necessity of formulating their own tenets of faith, so that they might resemble the creeds of other religions, there is no positive evidence that this awareness existed in ancient times. For Marqah, as for Judaism, every article of religious belief and practice would have been of equal significance. He may have emphasized, in speaking of his beliefs, those which were easy to comprehend. Thus, for example, if he does not mention on such occasions the belief in the Day of Vengeance and Recompense, this does not imply that this particular belief is of later development.[388] The importance of this same belief is well attested in his book, where indeed it occupies so prominent a place. Later,[389] naturally, constant intercourse with Muslims led to a more keenly felt need to include, in the 'cardinal dogmas', this additional tenet because of eschatological significance. Most of these misconceptions are due to the faulty interpretation of Samaritan theology in terms of categories borrowed from alien ways of thought. As we have seen in earlier cases, when we dealt with biblical exegesis in general,[390] most scholars have been unduly misled by attaching too much significance

---

[386] cf. my articles in *JJS* XI (1960), p. 18 (nn. 124-125) and in *ALUOS* VI (1969) pp. 135f. (nn. 32-33).

[387] cf. Bowman, "Sam. Studies", *BJRL* XL (1958), pp. 309f. (based on Montgomery, *The Sam.*, p. 207; Vilmar, *Abulfathi etc.*, pp. xxxiv f.).

[388] The Day of Vengeance is the theme of *Memar Marqah* IV, para 12, but the whole of the Book is filled with ideas connected with it. Thus the most important admonitions concerning 'repentance' (*ibid.* para 6) as well as the belief in other 'tenets' of the 'creed' (*ibid.* para 7) are based on the fear of the Day of Vengeance. cf. J. Macdonald, *The Theology of the Sam.*, p. 51 and Montgomery, *op. cit.* p. 207.

[389] cf. n. 387 *sup.* and Miller, *The Sam. Molad Mosheh*, pp. 236f. (cf. *ibid.* n. 26). In passing, it may be noted that even in this late composition there is no unity. On pp. 192f. there are only four fundaments (عقائد = dogmas) mentioned. Here also the belief in the day of Vengenace is lacking (cf. *inf.* n. 429).

[390] cf. *sup.* Part I, para (b, c, e, and g).

to the supposed agreement between the various systems, thus ignoring their distinctive features. In regard to the Samaritans, this approach is even more misguided since their individuality is so much more marked.[391]

Although their individuality, much less their 'rationalism', cannot be reduced by a deductive process to a perfectly coherent system, this does not mean that their thought was altogether incoherent. On the contrary, it has both method and unity, that is, it relies on naively harmonized concepts resulting from the analogical exegesis of their proof-texts in the Pentateuch. This also explains the limited extent of its development, thanks to a living tradition which kept it tenaciously on the same course.

The following example will serve to illustrate how dangerous it is to apply to the Samaritans terminology borrowed from another religion; "It will be seen that the theological anthropology of the Samaritans was limited in its scope; the question of Freedom of the Will never seems to have emerged, nor any of the questions connected with Original Sin."[392] As regards the question of 'free will', we have seen time and again that beyond doubt the Samaritans upheld the total freedom of the individual. The Samaritans here occupied the same position as was held by Judaism, where, to be sure, the exact demarcation between free will and divine providence was very indistinct, although in fact they laid equally great stress on either side, without worrying about the seeming inconsistences. All such problems have been raised by interrelating Samaritan beliefs with Christian theological concepts arising from the partial determinism occasioned by Original Sin and its antidote, divine grace. Samaritanism, like Judaism believing in the Torah as the only Source of Grace and denying any form of determinism, had no share in the above-mentioned theological development. If Marqah,[393] refers

---

[391] cf. *inf.* para (h), "The Sam. Midrash".

[392] Thomson, *The Samaritans*, p. 187. As compared with Montgomery (*The Samaritans*, p. 224), this is certainly a retrogression, due to confusion of Samaritan beliefs with Christian theological concepts. The Pharisees held a medial position between the extreme determinism of the Essenes and the total denial of Divine providence of the Sadducees (Josephus, *Wars* II, viii, 14; *Antiq.* XIII, v, 9) This is admirably expressed by the saying: "All is foreseen, but freedom of choice is given" (*Abhoth* III, 16). On the reconciliation between the Divine 'foresight' and human free will, cf. Hamburger, *Real-Encyclopädie etc.* II, pp. 102-106 (s.v. Bestimmung). The Sam. position is very close to that of the Rabbis (J. Macdonald, *The Theology of the Sam.*, pp. 231, 278f.).

[393] cf. Trotter, *A Critical Study etc.*, pp. 153ff. Marqah's remarks on the death of Moses (*Memar* I, p. 118 = II, p. 195) are in full accord with Rabbinic ideas as expressed

to the sin of Adam and its repercussions, such a reference should not be equated with the theory of 'original sin', since Marqah's exposition follows throughout the line of pre-Christian exegesis. Naturally, too, the whole Christian controversy with Pelagianism has no relevance whatever here.

Although, as we have seen,[394] the question of how to deal with sin continually occupied their minds, there was a deliberate avoidance of dogmatism on the subject. The problem of sin and reward and punishment, as well as that of the evil befalling the Righteous, remained unsolved. Even to a philosophically trained mind like that of Philo,[395] the recurring problem of the suffering of the Righteous presented grave contradictions. He offers three alternative solutions which are hardly mutually compatible : (1) The righteous man who suffers cannot be entirely perfect; (2) The wicked man's prosperity cannot be 'the good' in the absolute sense; (3) The sufferings of the Righteous are salutary trials. Similarly, Josephus deftly evades this issue only by explaining away divine retribution to suit the taste of his Greek readers. In the light of all this, how could one fairly expect a systematic approach from the primitive mind of the Samaritans? One can therefore only describe the Samaritans' theology as "a well-formulated and integrated system of beliefs",[396] in contrast with that of the Rabbis, wherein contradictory views were largely allowed to exist side by side. Of course, under Mu'tazilite influence, as we have seen above,[397] there was a marked tendency towards rational thinking mainly owing to polemical needs, but even so many of these problems remained unsolved. When the

---

in *Siphre Deut.*, para 305. cf. S. Rappaport, *Agada und Exegese etc.*, p. 127; S.A. Loewenstamm, "The Death of Moses", *Tarbiz* XXVII (1958), pp. 148ff. In Marqah as well as in the whole Sam. literature there are no elements reminiscent of the Christian dogma of Original Sin (as the salvation by 'Grace' because of man's total moral inability implied determinism etc.). cf. J. Macdonald, *The Theology of the Sam.*, pp. 215ff. Trotter's statement (*op. cit.* pp. 194f.) that 'Abdullah [b. Solomon] would appear to support a doctrine of pre-destination, even in a full Calvinistic sense" is based on the misunderstanding of the sources (Cowley, *The Sam. Liturgy*, pp. 324, 336) which are in no way different from the usual Sam. doctrines.

[394] cf. *sup.* para (e).

[395] Wolfson, *Philo* II, pp. 291f.; for Josephus, cf. Heinemann, "The method of Josephus etc.", *Zion* V (1940), p. 192.

[396] J. Macdonald, *The Theology of the Sam.*, p. 453. For the reasons for the homogeneity of Sam. doctrines and practices cf. *inf.* para (k).

[397] cf. nn. 47ff.

Samaritans were under Karaite influence, they adopted the terminology (shared by Rabbanites as well) which was customarily employed in defence of the doctrine of free-will.[398] The *Ṭabbākh* [399] interprets *Deut.* xxxii, 4, thus: "sinners have free will, and are potentially able to act according to their wish without any compulsion."

As with Rabbinic literature, where the exact demarcation between personal immortality, the coming of the Messianic Age, and the Resurrection of the Dead, was never clearly drawn,[400] the Samaritans also left wide ambiguities in their treatment of these interrelated subjects. Any attempt at dating the origins of Samaritan eschatology from the available literature is extremely precarious, as similar attempts in regard to other groups have proved.[401]

As they felt no external need to systematize their eschatological speculations, these remained vague. Such an external need was felt by the Muslims, who were forced by the vast number of martyrs falling in the Holy War to insist that there would be no delay between their death and entry into paradise. In this manner the two concepts of resurrection and paradise had to be satisfactorily interrelated.[402] Although this happy solution had no influence on the Samaritans, certain Muslim concepts, incorporated in the Mu'tazilite philosophy, brought a number of points into sharp relief for them. Still, under these influences, their eschatological outlook did not become more 'rational' than it had been in the Byzantine Era.

The far-reaching antithesis of abstract versus concrete thought as

---

[398] H. Hirschfeld, *Qirqisāni Studies*, p. 19. As in the case of Jewish sects the Islamic terminology did not alter the basic tenet of religious doctrines. In any case, the problem of 'free will' was deeply rooted both amongst the Sam. and the Jews before its emergence in Islam, where it was influenced by political considerations (cf. D.S. Margoliouth, *The Early Development of Mohamedanism*, p. 212; Guillaume, *The Traditions of Islam*, pp. 171f.).

[399] f. 217b.

[400] cf. my article *JJS* XI (1960), p. 8 (n. 50); Moore, *Judaism* II, p. 378; Bonsirven, *Le judaïsme Palestinien* I, pp. 307f.; Strack-Billerbeck, *Kommentar etc.* IV, pp. 799f.

[401] As we have seen (cf. *sup.* nn. 387f.), the fact that Marqah does not mention the Day of Vengeance amongst the principles of belief (considered by scholars as his 'creed'), does not prove that it is of later origin. The attempt to date the Dead Sea Scroll type of eschatological thought to the First Christian Century (Driver, *Judean Scrolls*, pp. 561f.) only because earlier "the major if not the only questions perplexing the loyal Jew were political" is likewise untenable. cf. Bamberger, "The Dating of Aggadic Materials", *JBL*, LXVIII (1949), pp. 115ff. cf. *inf.* nn. 406f.

[402] D.S. Margoliouth, *op. cit.* p. 202.

between Athens and Jerusalem is pertinent to our approach to Samaritan exegesis, which followed Jerusalem in this respect. Although in modern times such generalizations are in disfavour,[403] this one is still representative of earlier Hebraic thinking and of Samaritan thought in particular. One of the manifestations of such 'concrete' thought is the prevalent emphasis on action, as expressed by verbs rather than by abstract nouns, especially in the sphere of portraying God's attributes. Often the Samaritans pursued the same method as the Rabbis who, although they unquestionably believed in God's incorporeality, nevertheless employed frankly anthropomorphic expressions for exegetical purposes and moral exhortations.[404] This may partially account for the inconsistency shown in their attempted treatment of anthropomorphism,[405] and therefore does not in itself prove that their approach was unreasoning (mentally immature). In fact, it merely underlines the utter impossibility of measuring the extent of their rationality in this field.

Attempts have been made to predate certain Samaritan literature as for example, the *Asaṭir*, by drawing comparisons with the pseudepigraphical literature, and thus inferring that the 'sober' and simple approach of the former, as opposed to the latter's mythological thinking,

---

[403] Barr, *The Semantics of Biblical Language*, pp. 11f.; 84. cf. *ibid.* n. 2. Although it is true that linguistic structure is more important than the consideration as to whether verbal or nominal forms are used, yet the assumption that the static nature of Greek intellectualization prefers the use of abstract nouns as against the Hebrew type of actualization with its stress on activity and preference for verbs, is quite correct. (Snaith, *Distinctive Ideas of the O.T.*, p. 174). The objection raised from the Song of Songs, "where one might expect to find a typical Hebrew feeling for the subject of love, the noun is more frequent than the verb" is misleading. Presuming that by the noun 'love' an abstract idea is meant, this may be attributed to the uniqueness of the Book which is in any case thought to be under Greek influence (cf. H. Graetz, *Schir ha-Schirim* (= oder der salomonische Hohelied, übersetzt und kritisch erläutert, 1871); cf. also Kuenen, *JQR* IV (1892), p. 595. Secondly, this Book is at variance by its language from the other parts of the Hebrew Bible, and by its ideas in contrast to them. cf. M. Jastrow, *The Song of Songs* (Philadelphia, 1921), pp. 175 (n. 10), 178 (n. 1), 190 (n. 18), 219 (n. 10) etc. Furthermore, the term *Ahavah* (II, 7; III, 5; VII, 7) is rightly translated by some commentators, not as an *abstract* "love", but rather as a *concrete* endearment of the 'beloved' (cf. שאהבה נפשי). In general, however, the verb is far more frequent than the noun, especially when the theological concept of 'love' is involved.

[404] M. Guttmann, *Die Darstellung etc.*, p. 36; M. Guttmann, *Eine Untersuchung...* *Geltungsumfang etc.*, pp. 35f. Heinemann, *Darkhei ha-Aggadah*, p. 85.

[405] J. Macdonald, *The Theology of the Sam.*, pp. 68f.

implies its greater antiquity.[406] Such comparisons, especially in the case
of writings originating in different groups, have no value. Such a procedure of restricting certain ideas to a fixed period of time, ragardless of the
diversities and differences between the various groups at that time, must
be doomed to failure.[407] If Philo, a single individual with a thorough
philosophical training, displays self-contradictions in his work,[408] how
can one rightly expect the Samaritans, a whole group and embodying
a culture of many centuries, to be more rational? This does not mean,
on the other hand, that one should expect among non-philosophical
exegetes, such as the Samaritans or the Rabbis, constant self-contradictions or a system entirely devoid of any self-consistency. To take the
case of the Rabbis, who were admittedly familiar with Greek systems
of logic and who even acknowledged the presence of "wisdom among
the Gentiles", one still finds that they regarded their own wisdom,
derived as it was from the Torah, as greatly superior. Even in practical
matters and in matters of common sense, they considered themselves
more proficient.[409] Again, although the Greek philosophers tended to

---

[406] Gaster, *Asatir*, p. 108 (and *passim.*). The numerous parallels between the
Asaṭir and the Palestinian Targum (*ibid.* p. 84) invalidates such exaggerated claims.

[407] cf. n. 401 *sup.* Much has been written on the study of the historical development of 'exegetical traditions'. Even granting that originally they all go back to the
same source (which in itself is very doubtful), once split up into various groups in
far different epochs, the study of such development must be restricted to a specific
group. After all, even the same 'traditions' may have meant different things to different
people. cf. J. Heinemann's review of G. Vermes, "Scripture and Tradition", *Tarbiz*
XXXV (1965), pp. 84-94. The comparison of a great variety of sources may greatly
enrich comparative studies, however, for the history of transmission their value is
minimal unless great care is taken to distinguish their sectarian provenance and their
dating (cf. Bowker, *The Targums etc.*, p. 27, n. 1 and *ibid.* p. 232).

[408] Siegfried, *Philo von Alex. als Ausleger des A.T.*, pp. 162, 166f.; Heinemann,
Darkhei ha-Aggadah, pp. 59, 244 (n. 35); cf. Wolfson, (*Philo I*, p. 114) who sets out
to prove that despite Philo's eclectic approach "he built up a system of philosophy
which is consistent, coherent, and free of contradictions, all of it being based upon
certain fundamental principles." Despite Wolfson's great philosophical acumen in
trying to reconcile contradictions, very often his arguments are forced and hair-
splitting. cf. I, pp. 129-131 on the precepts as to which is to be accepted literally and
which to interpret allegorically; *ibid.* p. 202 and 275ff. on God called an *idea*, cf.
also pp. 282-288; on whether stars have souls, I, pp. 364f. (nn. 36-38); on the Logos, I,
p. 375 (n. 77); on evil Angels, pp. 381f.; on free will pp. 442f, 452ff. (cf. also pp. 455f.);
II, 91 on knowing God cf. *ibid.* pp. 155f. etc.

[409] *Bekhoroth* 8b; *Lamentation* R to I, i s.v. רבתי cf. Barr, *Old and New in
Interpretation*, pp. 54f.

transcendentalize their God or gods, this cannot be attributed to their 'rationality' alone, but rather to their whole mode of thinking and cogniz- ing. Similarly, one cannot attribute the Jews' preference for an immanent God to their scorn of rationality. It is more true to say that it was the natural product of their culture, based on the Law.[410] Despite their belief in an immanent God the Samaritans, no less than the Jews, staunchly upheld the belief in the incorporeality of God. Thus the liturgist Amram Dara of Byzantine times, in describing God as "without substance" and as "He whom nothing resembles" (Lit. p. 27), was only following the traditional belief of his people. There are no grounds at all for assum- ing any influence of the Arian heresy [411] on his thinking.

It is often suggested that a contradiction may be detected in the Samaritan writings in the matter of primordial light; that, while Marqah clearly believes in it, a millenium later its existence is denied. Marqah's opinion is as follows:[412]

> ... Observe these things and realize that they are evidences, testifying of Him that He is one in His essence. When He brought light into being, it was manifest to the whole world. He ordered it in His greatness and the light of the sun was produced from it, and also that of the moon and all the stars.

Here, as in other places, it is evident that one cannot speak at all of 'primordial light' in the strict sense, since, although it preceded all the rest of creation, it was nevertheless created. It is safe to assume that for this very reason, there was no conflict whatsoever in the minds of the Samaritans throughout the stages of their history. It is more than likely that the numerous problems encountered by the Muslims when they tried to expound *creatio ex nihilo* [413] did not engage the Samaritans' attention, since they took it for granted that this was the actual meaning of the pentateuchal creation-story, which they invariably took literally. All such 'dogmas' as were derived from the exegesis of Scripture domi- nated their outlook to the exclusion of all other possibilities.

---

[410] cf. Davies, *Paul and Rab. Judaism*, pp. 11, 164ff. (and cf. notes *ibid.*).

[411] cf. J. Macdonald, *The Theology of the Sam.*, pp. 65ff. (cf. SLTh. pp. 790f. and p. 932). There is similarly no shred of evidence that "the fourteenth century Samaritan writers have difficulty in reconciling Moses of the Pentateuch, with the assessment and interpretation of him, against the overtones of Christian environment." cf. Trotter, *A Critical Study etc.*, p. 227 (and *ibid.* p. 27 for Arianism).

[412] *Memar Marqah* (ed. Macdonald), I, p. 131 (= II, p. 214). cf. J. Macdonald, *The Theology of the Sam.*, pp. 119ff.

[413] D.S. Margoliouth, *The Early Development etc.*, pp. 220f.

To cite only one similar case (which occupied our attention earlier), there is the dogma of the literal transmission of the Ten Commandments to Moses, in which the anthropormorphic expression "His finger" and "with His hand" are preserved, in spite of their usual horror of humanizing God.

One should not be expected to judge Marqah by the yardstick of established philosophical standpoints, not even those of his own epoch; after all, we cannot arbitrarily reconstruct a twofold personality, now philosopher and now doctrinaire.[414] All his writings in fact testify to his having a homogeneous approach, which, although not thoroughly philosophical, is nevertheless quite coherent.

To complicate our judgment on Marqah even further, we need to realize that some parts of his alleged writings (especially those which are a mixture of Hebrew and Aramaic) may well be, or contain, interpolations.[415]

---

[414] cf. J. Macdonald, *Theology*, p. 140. It is extremely difficult to reconstruct a comprehensive picture of Marqah's psychology. It is more logical to assume that his whole concept is built upon doctrinal elements, thus as in other cases, his adherence to the strict boundaries of tradition severely limits his rationalism. One could only *guess* that here also Scripture is the background of his speculations: although the division of body and soul is quite clear (צעורה דגויתה ויסודה דנפשה), when it comes to the parts of the soul there is no clear-cut division in Marqah's mind. Most probably on the basis of the scriptural background it was impossible to assign definite functions to the various faculties of the soul. On the one hand it is 'soul' (both נפש and נשמה) which is the life-sustaining principle (*Gen.* ii, 7), but elsewhere (*Gen.* VI, 17; vii, 15, 22) the same vitalizing function is assigned to the 'spirit' (רוח which may refer also to animals). Nonetheless, it is the 'spirit' which is constantly associated with God (*Gen.* xli, 38; *Ex.* xxxi, 3; *ibid.* xxxviii, 31). The same 'spirit' is also associated with wisdom (*Ex.* xxviii, 3; *Deut.* xxxiv, 9) and with prophecy (*Num.* xi, *passim.*). Yet 'spirit' could not have been singled out as the sole faculty for the intelligence, because of its association with the general vitalizing power. In one instance only does Marqah clearly distinguish between 'soul' and 'spirit', when he says (I, p. 18 = II, pp. 26f.) that human beings are governed by soul ans spirit, while animals by soul alone. This, however, is a polemical answer to oppose the Egyptian belief about animals possessing (divine) 'spirit'. This is a midrash on תועבה *Ex.* viii, 22 understood (upon analogy with *Gen.* xliii, 32, and *ibid.* xlvi, 34) as 'idol'. Only to oppose the Egyptian deification of animals, does Marqah draw such a drastic demarcation line (cf. Trotter, *A Critical Study etc.*, p. 152). Normally neither Marqah nor later Sam. writers have any definite description of the exact functions of the parts of the soul. They conform with the harmonized concept inherited from Scripture. This situation may be partially responsible for the prominent employment of the 'light' metaphor in Sam. literature for 'spiritual' topics. cf. *inf.* n. 418.

[415] Especially passages containing philosophical terminology are suspect of being

Even during the period when Mu'tazilite influence was at its height, the rationalistic trend did not gain the upper hand over Scripture and tradition. The best instance of this point is the *Ṭabbākh*'s treatment of the problem of angels.[416] On rationalistic principles, the biblical references to angels could easily have been explained away as referring to natural causes. However, this is not the case. Abū-l Ḥasan rationalizes only insofar as his literalistic exegesis permits; he asserts quite bluntly of the Samaritan literalistic belief in Angels that: "it has been established by the proof of reason and of what has been transmitted by tradition."

Similarly, most of the 'inconsistencies' which we readily find in Samaritan exegesis can be attributed, not so much to incoherent thinking as rather to devotion to the scriptural word.[417] So, even in the extreme case of Ben Manir who is notorious for his absorption of foreign ideas, one should not always jump to the conclusion that everything that at first appears alien is in reality so. With all due allowance for rationalistic thinking, the core of his expositions is still severely confined to the traditional way of exegesis.[418] It seems fitting therefore to conclude with the

---

interpolations. For instance: "All the names of God are attributive שמות שותפו except the name Lord (Tetragrammaton) which does not contain any attribute (שותף)". *Memar Marqah* (ed. Macdonald), I, p. 43f. (= II, p. 69). It seems that we have here a reflection of the Medieval philosophical term اسم مشترك or its Hebrew translation שם משותף. As for the subject matter, cf. Maimonides, *Guide for the Perplexed*, I, Ch. 61.

[416] f. 123b-127a. قد ثبت بدليل العقل والسمع. Needless to say, the part of tradition (i.e. literalist and analogical exegesis of Scripture) outweighs that of pure rationalist reasoning.

[417] cf. *sup*. nn. 166-175 (and text there), 179, 202 etc.

[418] cf. Cowley, *Liturgy*, I, p. 179. The expression referring to Moses as קטף כל נשמה is nothing more than a synonym of דמע כל בשר and it is impossible to derive any psychological conclusion from it. The suggestion "that Ben-Manir agrees with Zohar" (cf. Trotter, *A Critical Study etc.*, pp. 147f.) shows great misunderstanding of the Zoharic psychology, with its stress on the connection of נר"ן with the Sephiroth. cf. Scholem, *Major trends in Jewish Mysticism*, pp. 240ff. If elsewhere Ben Manir uses נפש and רוח (Cowley, *Liturgy*, I, pp. 178 and 184 respectively) this alone, together with נשמה in connection with Moses, does not as yet indicate that "he was aware of the graduated distinctions of the soul made by the writer of the Zohar". These distinctions (a heritage of Greek philosophy) with the above terminology and the same graduated order, were used already by Saadia (*Kitāb al-Amānāt etc.* ed. Laudauer, Leiden 1880, p. 195) and employed by other medieval Jewish philosophers. cf. S. Horovitz, *Die Psychologie der jüdischen Religionsphilosophie des Mittelalters von Saadia bis Maimuni* (Breslau 1898-1912), II, p. 115, III, p. 174,

comment of one of the earlier pioneers in this field,[419] who found that, basically, Samaritan theology is virtually the same as that of the Pentateuch, most of its details being derived from exegesis.

G. The Religious Psychology of the Samaritans and its Relationship to Exegesis

We are not primarily concerned here with any opinions on psychology proper, nor with the relationship of body and soul, except in cases when they have some relevance to biblical exegesis. Similarly, platonic dualism, as opposed to the so-called Israelite parallelism, has no bearing at all on our research into exegesis.[420] What are more significant are rather the dispositions which limit or affect inward activity, and which in consequence have their impact on all outward activity, and by their appearance in visible form give a particular colouring to biblical exegesis. Thus, for example, the problems of the individual, his psychological make-up and his subjective experience concern us [421] only insofar as we can derive from them a general picture of the Samaritan religious and psychological background, on which evidently the whole of Samaritan life is built.

That there is a direct relationship between religious psychology and the progressive development of dogmas was already realized by scholars more than a century ago.[422] The fundamental dualism of evil inclination versus good inclination is to be found in the extant literature

---

IV, p. 224f. We cannot enter here into the problem of *Zelem* mentioned by Ben Manir (Cowley, *Liturgy*, II, 650 צלמיה לבש והנור). At any rate, the connections with Maimonides (*Guide for the Perplexed*, I, Ch. I), with εἰκών of the LXX, the same expression in the *Epistle to the Hebrews* (X, 1) etc. (Trotter, *op. cit.* pp. 132f.), to say the least, is unconvincing. The association of Maimonides' *Zelem* (originating from Aristotle's μόρφη) with the *Hebrews* (where εἰκών is the opposite to σκιά) is most arbitrary. It is far easier to solve these problems of Sam. psychology (cf. n. 414 *sup.*) by looking for their midrashic bacground in the Pentateuch.

[419] de Sacy, "Mémoire sur l'état actuel etc.", *Annuales des voyages et de la géographie*, XIX (1812), pp. 50f.

[420] cf. *sup.* nn. 414 and 418.

[421] Since the epoch making book of W. James (*The Varieties of Religious Experience*, 1902), this subject has been extensively investigated, and an enormous literature grew out of it under the name of "Psychology of Religion". For a short treatment of this subject with special reference to Judaism, cf. M.Z. Sole, *Psychologia shel ha-Dat* (Hebrew), Jerusalem 1944.

[422] cf. H. Faber, *Das Wesen der Religionspsychologie und ihre Bedeutung für die Dogmatik* (Tübingen 1913), p. 5 (for English scholars) and p. 7 (French).

of all periods, and naturally finds its confirmation in biblical texts, all the extensive literature on the so-called 'two ways' having a direct bearing on this problem. We can at once see how the same biblical verses are utilized by various groups.[423]

Admittedly, one cannot find in the Pentateuch explicit psychological explanations, just as one cannot find ethical principles enunciated in a form which befits a scientific system. However, from the material which has been transmitted there, in the form of fact, narrative and sermon, one can at least see that there emerges a distinctive psychological outlook, which one could learn as exactly as one could learn from Scripture a religious and moral outlook.[424] No doubt the Samaritan mentality knew how to harmonize its proof-texts effectively in order to build a certain system, which in one aspect we may call a religious psychology. Thus Marqah, in his explanation of the four seasons with reference to the four elements, plays on the analogy of this number 'four' with the four divisions of the soul.[425] Then he continues:

> He has created four divisions in you (too), so that you may exist and be developed in power. These four are desire and idea and conscience and reason, hidden deep within you. He who created them knows their true state. Each one of them has a powerful controlling force in your body.

It is immaterial whether these four divisions are based on purely midrashic sources or whether they are further developments of speculations having their true source in Greek psychology, which indeed analyses the soul into four divisions. The important point for us is that Marqah is aware of the significance of these psychological data on the religious development of the individual.

How far one can justifiably link such speculations with Scripture is a moot point. There already exists a whole literature on the psychological problems considered in the Hebrew Bible.[426] There are even attempts to

---

[423] cf. e.g. Driver, *Judaean Scrolls etc.*, pp. 550f.

[424] F. Delitzsch, *System der biblischen Psychologie* (2nd ed. 1861), p. 14.

[425] *Memar Marqah* (ed. Macdonald), I, pp. 131f. (= II, p. 214). It has already been pointed out by Baneth (*Des Samaritaners Marqah etc.*, p. 24, n. 18) that it is difficult to determine what are the exact functions of these four parts of the soul controlling the body (cf. also *sup.* n. 414); יצר ועניו ורז וחשבה originate from *Gen.* vi, 5 where יצר מחשבות is translated by the Targum as רז עניו. Actually the 'four' are two identical pairs of concepts (Hebrew and Aramaic respectively). It would be futile to investigate further the exact functions of these powers, since it is stated that they are 'hidden', their true nature being known only to the Creator.

[426] cf. G. Traue, *Die neueren Methoden der Religionspsychologie* (Gütersloh 1922), pp. 8f.

show the antiquity of such religious questioning. However, for us these problems are not so very important, since formulated discussions were in any case outweighed in the Samaritan mentality by the demand for action; and on this account we may again return to Marqah, who penetratingly examines the constant interaction between the senses, the intellect and religious behaviour. Having described this inter-relation in detail [427], he then depicts the heart as saying to the intellect: "and the five (senses) are dependent on you. Wherever you appear, we depart". Of course, a very important postulate lies behind these words, namely, that the intellect and the will should always rule the emotional and the sensual part of the man, a well-known motive in biblical exhortation. It is therefore not at all surprising to learn that, later, when the Mu'ta-zilite influence makes itself felt among the Samaritans, the outstanding representative of this school of thought, Munajja, is felt to have had a predecessor in Marqah in preaching the ruling function of the intel-lect.[428] According to this standpoint, man is the zenith of God's creation just because of his intellect, and because man has been endowed with the power and the ability to carry out the dictates of his intellectual selfhood, dictates which by their nature must issue in obedience, the seeking of wisdom and so forth. Later writers made the whole privilege of divine election subservient to this principle:[429] "He chose you from among other peoples, and He marked you out by four fundamental beliefs (= dogmas) from the rest of the world, through which you can return to God. They are : (1) the Sender, (2) the Messenger, (3) the Mission, and (4) the House of the Mission." Moreover, we shall not be perturbed to find, as we have already mentioned, that these "fundamen-tals" do not entirely tally with what has elsewhere been described as "the Samaritan Creed", since here the writer is interested only in its intellectual and psychological aspects, and hence one could hardly expect complete consistency.

For our purpose, it is extremely important to see the social implica-tions of this psychological awareness. The demand for a common bond among co-religionists has a dual effect on their religious development: it asserts itself both in exegesis and in practice. The latter effect is well

---

[427] *Memar Marqah* (ed. Macdonald), I, p. 69 (= II, p. 109). It seems that such expressions are expositions of verses like "and that ye go not about after your own heart and your own eye..." (*Num.* xv, 39).

[428] *Masā'il al-Khilāf*, Ib, pp. 109 and 140.

[429] Miller, *The Sam. Molad Mosheh*, pp. 192f. (cf. n. 389 *sup.* and text there).

illustrated by the fact that one of the ordinances on the Passover, according to the *Ṭabbākh*,[430] is that the people should be together at the eating
of the sacrifice, and that they should not scatter, each to his own house.
The reason given in support is that this will create a strong bond between
them, and that such ordinances are meant to promote a communal
feeling in religious matters. Of much greater significance, however, is
the demand for a common bond as it finds expression in the general
belief in an unbroken communal life, which embodies the religious tradition and itself provides the guiding light for exegesis. In another place,
the *Ṭabbākh* [431] in expounding the whole revelation and prophecy of
Moses to the six hundred thousand Israelites and the implied commission to the true bearers of tradition, which guarantees the true transmission, is at pains to show their total dependence on this common
bond. The same exposition pays great attention to the verses on reward
and punishment which both stress and guarantee the communal life
and the purity of tradition; and long passages are quoted in this connection to exemplify that the whole concept of a covenant is bound up with
it. This would imply, then, that, despite individual deviations, their
whole existence and, in their own belief, even their perpetual existence,
depends on this communal concept of a tradition based on the Covenant.

Although in modern biblical studies, it has been freely acknowledged
that one should never be led to infer the psychological uniqueness of
a particular ethnic group by overstressing the etymological relations of
words,[432] nevertheless, with regard to exegetical patterns in any ethnic
group, nobody could deny that such factors did have a great bearing
both on their exegesis and on the development of specific cultic concepts.
Although the biblical style can to a considerable extent be preserved
in any translation, nevertheless one should realize that stylistic peculiarities, especially among a close-knit group, are very often greatly indebted
to ethno-psychological factors. The most important problem facing us
in our inquiry is to discover these important elements of language, and
of semantics in particular, and their relationships to the manners of
expression and the patterns of thinking distinctive of the Samaritan
mentality. Typical of this type of thinking is the description in the
Kāfi [433] of the Pilgrimage and of the whole dependence of 'Israel' on the

---

[430] f. 69b (SLTh.A, p. 111).

[431] ff. 146b-149a. All this is in line with Marqah's preaching (cf. n. 377 *sup.*).

[432] Barr, *Semantics of Bib. Language*, p. 118.

[433] pp. 219ff. (SLTh.A, pp. 40f.).

land of Joseph. Clearly, the points there mentioned concerning the Passover Sacrifice, the cult of Pilgrimage, the Blessing, the seeing and coming into contact with the High Priest, the bringing there of the tithe, etc. are all enjoined in the Torah (*Deut.* xii, etc.). While these points are straightforward deductions from the biblical verses, they nevertheless bring an altered psychological colouring to the whole exegesis.

The same psychological factor which stressed so much the common bond, the Covenant and the doctrine of election, is also manifest in their Laws and regulations. For example, the *Kāfi* [434] in two places deals with problems which are in fact solved by an appeal to this feeling of superiority. The question arises as to whether Samaritans are allowed to wear expensive clothing and jewelry, a practice which was most probably opposed by certain strict Samaritans with a strong ascetic bent. The reply is in substance based on this ideology of election, i.e. Israel, being the 'peculiar' and elect People of God, the chosen ones, could not properly be forbidden to wear the choicest of garments. Evidence is also found in the wealth which the Israelites possessed during the erection of the Tabernacles in the desert, which proves that they possessed all manner of precious materials. The other problem of a similar nature is whether carpets made up from wool are allowed to be used. Here the same leading idea is seized upon, namely, that the whole of practical wisdom, and all social organisations, including political and military systems, were borrowed from Israel, other nations learning from them. Then the argument follows that it is absurd to consider banning things which were originally borrowed from the Israelites and merely copied by others. Such expressions of aloofness and feelings of being exalted in wisdom and morals above all other peoples, were an integral part of their rigid and separatist religious life. This was based, apart from psychological reasons, on their whole approach towards biblical exegesis, from which they derived support for their separatism. The *Kāfi* [435] stresses this need for keeping away, especially on the Sabbath Day or whenever alien influences may be felt, from places where non-Samaritans dwell, and even for not walking in their streets. In addition to the general reason for fearing foreign influences or being contaminated by levitical defilement, there was an original psychological reason which they understood to be based on Scripture. 'The dwelling separately', according to them, is a biblical enactment, which, although not explicitly expressed, is nevertheless

---

[434] pp. 191 and 201 (SLTh.A, pp. 22 and 29 respectively).
[435] p. 203. cf. Abdel-Al, *A Comparative Study etc.*, pp. 588f., 707.

mentioned in the Bible (*Num.* xxiii, 9; *Deut.* xxxiii, 28). It is by no means easy to determine whether or not such feelings were itensified by a minority-complex similar to that which plainly existed among the Karaites;[436] but it is certain that this aloofness, this constant effort to forge a psychological instrument to reinforce their sense of unity and this demand for the creation of a common bond has an inestimable influence on their religious development and exegesis.

Whether further investigations whould show their religion in general to be an expression of their whole social entity, is debatable. In any case, such investigation should be left to the experts in the field of the anthropology and sociology of religion.[437] But for us at least, the Samaritans as a unit are only of interest (seeing that we are chiefly concerned with their exegesis) only from the period after their acceptance of the Pentateuch. Even if their Scripture had originally various layers, it was totally harmonized by them. No clue is left to the stages of their eventual development in the course of their acceptance as Scripture.

An additional limitation to the investigation of their religious psychology is the strange one-sidedness of their religious experience. All personal problems and their psychological effects are of only secondary importance for the Samaritans. As we have seen, the Samaritan religion, like Judaism, saw in every religious observance a communion with God in and through everyday actions; and therefore purely subjective constructions, such as soteriology or other theological concerns, were again of only secondary importance. The latter emerged only when the need was felt, for apologetical reasons, to combat foreign influences, and to prove by methods borrowed from foreign theology and philosophy that there is no contradiction between logic and their own beliefs. Their descriptions of religious experience, to which clues were already to be found in the Bible,[438] are therefore concentrated around the matter of divine worship. There is, as with Judaism, a magic circle, one in which the love of God and the fear of God are interrelated, and in which either awakes the other, and at the same time also supports the other. No

---

[436] Ankori, *Karaites in Byzantium*, p. 54 n. 73.

[437] We are not concerned with the controversy about the role of society and social conditions in the creation of religion (cf. W. Wundt, *Völkerspsychologie, Mytos und Religion*, 3 vols., 1905-1909; M. Weber, *Gesammelte Aufsätze zur Religionssoziologie*, Tübingen 1920, I, p. 240 etc.). For a good summary of the various systems, cf. J. Wach, *Sociology of Religion* (London 1947), pp. 4ff. and notes there for further bibliography. cf. *inf.* para (1).

[438] Traue, *op. cit.* p. 11.

conflict was ever caused in the Samaritan mind by this joint principle of the love and the fear of God being the centre of their religion. The *Ṭabbākh* goes so far [439] as to divide people into eight different classes; what we are interested in here, however, is his definition of the good person as the one who knows, and who acts according to his knowledge. This approach is not at all surprising, for, as we have seen,[440] the whole creation and even the heavenly powers were regarded as being rightly employed only when directed towards this one aim of worshipping God. Here one must add that such views on supernatural aid in no way limited the responsibility of the individual or his possession of free- will.

Now this circle of the love and fear of God depends first of all on belief. Although this concept of 'belief' is never given the status of a superior stepping-stone on the way towards salvation, it is taken for granted on the basis of numerous scriptural warrants that belief issuing in 'faith' is the ultimate motive behind all doctrine and practice. With the Mu'tazilite influence this principle is brought into sharp relief, and just as easily assimilated by the Samaritans as it was by the Jews.[441] The *Kāfi* and the *Ṭabbākh* alike [442] call the Samaritans either "the people of faith" or "the people of justice and monotheism", either description signifying that when this increased awareness of 'belief" and faith became operative, there was enough support in earlier traditional expositions to lend weight to it and to lead it to be accepted as a matter of course.

In earlier literature, although this vocabulary of 'belief' and 'faith' is not so much in evidence, it is yet implied by the constant use of the term 'the truth'; and as in the Dead Sea Scrolls Sect [443] so also in Marqah we find this term being frequently employed, and that he is wholly convinced that, as with God so also with the Righteous, perfection is a matter both of deed and of the establishment of truth, i.e. belief. A similar concept of belief as leading to faith is advocated by Philo,[444] for whom those who believe in revealed truth stand on a higher level than those who have arrived at their religious standpoint by reason

---

[439] ff. 163b-164a.

[440] cf. *sup.* nn. 331, 337, 338 etc.

[441] cf. *sup.* para (f).

[442] The *Kāfi* uses the expression اهل المله (cf. Abdel-Al, *op. cit.* p. 688), while the *Ṭabbākh* اهل العدل والتوحيد cf. 59a (cf. SLTh.A, p. 101).

[443] Wieder, *The Judean Scrolls and Karaism*, p. 148.

[444] Wolfson, *Philo*, II, pp. 216f., 261f.

alone. In his view, they stand the ultimate test of truth, and their faith is always evidenced by the type of conduct in which this truth is put into effect in daily life. Although one cannot discover any historical link between Philo and Marqah, this concept of faith, held by both in common, in which faith is in fact always being translated into truth, is typical of ancient thinking. It has not yet anything in it of the later Christian type of 'faith', with its soteriological undertones. This new Christian concept is based on the belief (supported by some verses in the Hebrew Bible) that not 'works' but 'faith' are ordained by God to justify and bring salvation to mankind.[445]

Obviously there is no lack of biblical verses in which the need for faith is emphasized. However, no attempt was made by the Samaritans to weave these verses [446] into a coherent system which would elaborate the meaning of 'belief', although Marqah's sermons on belief in God and on Moses are often built on such verses.

The truth as the ground of belief in God is bound up with believing also in God's righteousness, and with eliminating any notion of predestination from this belief in Him, and with putting all the blame for evil on man himself. The emphasis on this strong tendency amongst the Samaritans is already manifest in the Samaritan Pentateuch, in the addition of certain verses (*Ex.* vii, 18f.; 19f.; viii, 19f.; ix, 5, 19; x, 2; xi, 4) designed to prove that God did not cause Pharaoh to sin but that, on the contrary, he was in fact warned and was in possession of free-will.

---

[445] This is the major treatise in the preaching to the Gentiles, and the whole *Epistle to the Romans* is centred around this idea (cf. also *Galatians* iii; Gilbert, *The First Interpreters etc.*, p. 49). cf. *sup.* n. 322.

[446] Unlike Christianity (cf. previous n.) even the example of Abraham, whose belief in God was pointed out as righteousness (*Gen.* xv, 6), is not emphasized. Marqah mentions this in passing, while expounding *Ex.* xv, 2 "this is my God" (I, pp. 42f. = II, 66f.). As in Judaism (cf. *Shabbath*, 97a) it was not felt necessary to dwell philosophically on 'belief'. The same applies to belief in Moses (*Ex.* iv, 3; *ibid.* xix, 9). Although later these two became the first items of the so-called "Samaritan Creed", originally they were understood as being synonymous with the observance of the Torah. As in the case of Philo (cf. n. 444 *sup.*) the speculative side of 'faith' was overshadowed by its practical application, since the revealed 'truth' of Scripture prescribes the belief in God. The freedom of choice of the individual and the whole people, even in matters of faith, was nonetheless not minimized. How could it be otherwise in the face of *Num.* xx, 12? The trustfulness of God (*Deut.* vii, 6 הנאמן; *ibid.* xxxii, 4 אמונה) remained likewise undeveloped philosophically for the very same reasons, nonetheless it was always considered as being at the roots of both observance and doctrine (cf. *inf.* nn. 455ff.).

Marqah likewise plays on this same motif;[447] and elsewhere too he repeats this idea [448] that all punishments (even those of Paraoh) can be justified, "and He dealt with every one of these according to what they had first done". In later literature [449] the full import of this apologetical purpose in explaining away the apparent harshness of Pharaoh's fate is made quite evident. It is stated that the expression "God hardened the heart of Pharaoh" (*Ex.* ix, 12 etc.) should be understood figuratively. The meaning is said to be that Pharaoh was thus encouraged not to become a coward, but that he gained the false notion that it did not behove a King to go back on his word.

According to the *Ṭabbākh*,[450] even the faith of the Israelites when they were still in Egypt was tested. This explains the placing of the sign on the doorpost by the sprinkling of blood. It is meant to demonstrate to Israel that there should not be among them anyone whose trust in in God is not firm enough to remove his fear of the Egyptians: neither their earlier disappointment, nor even their fear that they are not to be delivered should discourage this open defiance of the Egyptians. Similarly, the functions both of prophecy and of priesthood especially, are also connected, according to the *Ṭabbākh*, with the establishment of belief. The priests' main duties are two: firstly, to serve in the name of God, and secondly, to foster belief in the hearts of the people.[451]

A very weighty principle with respect to this concept of belief is that it lies at the very root of the problem of reward and punishment. It is indeed already a Pentateuchal postulate [452] that reward and punishment, good an evil, are all of man's own making. This particular aspect of belief is closely bound up with belief in revelation, and it also serves as the centre of that magic circle of the love of God and the fear of God, which both alike rest on the same principle. According to Marqah אהיה אשר אהיה *Ex.* iii, 14 is bound up with the interpretation of אני אני הוא *Deut.* xxxii, 39. From this analogy it becomes evident that God is manifest through His providence both in Creation and in the "Day

---

[447] *Memar Marqah* (ed. Macdonald), I, p. 34 (= II, pp. 52f.). cf. *idem, The Theology of the Sam.*, p. 258.

[448] *Memar Marqah*, I, p. 90 (= II, pp. 146f.).

[449] *Exodus Commentary* (attributed to Ghazal al-Duweik), p. 151.

[450] f. 64b (SLTh.A, p. 106).

[451] f. 34a f. (SLTh.A, p. 81). This idea is often repeated in the *Ṭabbākh* (ff. 185b f.; 186b f.).

[452] The portion ראו למדתי (*Deut.* iv, 5 - vi, 25) which includes the Ten Commandments and repeated references to Divine Providence is of great significance, both for exegesis and liturgy.

of Vengeance and Recompense".[453] This again implies the same circle
of belief, compacted of the elements of love and fear, which prevails
throughout the whole of history. It may now be asserted that Marqah's
system, Torah-centred as it is, although not strictly methodical, does
analyse problems on their own merits, and then endeavours to harmonize
the results of scriptural exegesis with the results of the semi-rationalist
speculation current in his own culture. There is here no perfect self-
consistency, but there is logic, at least as far as the biblical exegesis
allows. Marqah, very similarly to the Rabbis, makes no attempt to
explain the motives of Divine Providence, nor to ask exactly how it
operates, in contrast to Philo and Josephus, who can freely deviate
from Scripture in their own speculative ways.[454]

The philosophical implications of suffering and theodicy did not occupy
the Samaritan mind of the Byzantine period. Unquestionably, however,
the psychological task of justifying the deeds of God was understood
from Scripture to constitute part of that 'belief' which should be
accepted without demur. Marqah's lengthy and involved exegesis of
"The Day of Vengeance" and of other problems of reward and punishment based on *Deut.* xxxii, takes it very much for granted [455] that all
God's actions are grounded in his faithfulness and righteousness, in
which a person must naturally believe.

The choice of 'life', at the parting of 'the two ways', through love,
obedience and cleavage to God, or, in other words, through the Torah
as the source of 'life' and length of days, is in fact a biblical belief based
on *Deut.* xxxi, 19-20, which is often reproduced in the liturgy in the form:
"Life from everlasting life is the great Scripture".[456] It looks as if, in
common with that of the Rabbis, this doctrine of the hallowing of life
through the commandments is not only intended for the strengthening
of belief itself, but as if Law, as the source of life, is *ipso facto* also
'natural law'. Therefore it has not only a relative value but rather an
absolute one. It is a universal law inherent both in man and God.[457]

---

[453] *Memar Marqah*, I, p. 98 (= II, pp. 161f.). cf. *sup.* n. 330. The general concept
that all reward and punishment depends on one's own efforts is frequently employed
by Marqah (cf. *sup.* nn. 302, 331).

[454] cf. my article ALUOS VI (1969), pp. 117, 153 (nn. 153ff.); Heineman, "The
Method of Josephus etc.", ZION V (1940), pp. 185, 199.

[455] *Memar Marqah*, I, pp. 109f. (= II, pp. 182f.). (cf. *sup.* n. 445).

[456] Cowley, *Liturgy*, I, p. 50 חייה דמן חיי עולם כתבה רבה Needless to say,
this saying has no relevance to *John* v, 39. (cf. Trotter, *op. cit.* p. 315).

[457] The Rabbis went even further, imposing the observance of the Law even on
its Giver. cf. Joël, *Blicke in die Religionsgeschichte etc.*, II, pp. 172ff.

Such a belief in the universality and the primordial background of Scripture lends their psychological development an entirely new colouring; for the natural phenomena, just as much as the supernatural, are instruments for carrying out the Divine Providence as prefigured in the Law. In the later literature, Munajja expresses this even more explicitly, and in bluntly rationalist terms saying that in fact everything is a testimony to the wisdom of God.[458] So too, as the luminaries (*Gen.* i, 14) were given for a sign of the power, wisdom and providence of God in the world, so the whole Creation proves the same, a truth which further fertilizes the psychological approach to religion. All things, even the hidden things, are the outcome of this divine providence.

The *Kāfi* explains,[459] in the case of a person being sold into slavery or becoming impoverished, that this is only the result of his having been ungrateful to God. Similarly, it may well be a punishment for not having had enough faith to carry out the commandment of opening his hand (*Deut.* xv, 11). This again proves that everything in the world is ordered in accordance with the Divine plan. There is even a moral attached, namely that no person shall say, on misfortunes befalling him, that 'they are mere chance'. The *Kāfi* goes even further [460] in stating that, if a person does not openly acknowledge God's benevolence, by his being mean, or by his not displaying the blessings of God according to his ability, then he is punished. In accordance with this psychological approach, a person is bound to display God's blessings in public by his actions, and he should not be greatly concerned about the jealousy or the greed of others, because God has these things under control and will Himself requite the jealous and the greedy. Altogether, this whole approach takes its stand on a Law which is all but equated with a natural cause and an effective organ of providence. As we shall see later, this reasoning and its assumed truth were so deeply ingrained in Samaritan psychology that they offered them in evidence as having the force

---

[458] *Masā'il al-Khilāf*, Ib, p. 103. A century earlier Abū-l Ḥasan al Ṣūri expressed similar sentiments (Cowley, *Liturgy*, I, p. 71) which are reminiscent of *Psalms* XIX. But in the light of the aforesaid argument in favour of the independent nature of Samaritan religious psychology, there is no need to conclude that Abū-l Ḥasan was influenced by the Psalms. (cf. also Macdonald, *The Theology of the Sam.*, p. 76).

[459] p. 266 (SLTh.A, p. 60). The same explanation is given concerning a person who has the ability but does not lend money to the needy, p. 296f. (cf. Abdel-Al, *op. cit.* pp. 611, 717).

[460] p. 191 (SLTh.A, p. 22).

of a *reductio ad absurdum*, i.e. the whole of existence would be meaning-less if we could not take it for granted that divine providence is at work in the world. If such were the case, then the lot of animals would be better than that of the Righteous.[461]

In the light of the aforesaid, the concept of the 'fear of God', for which one could find a whole armoury of biblical support,[462] becomes almost self-explanatory; and it is even easier to integrate this element into Samaritan religious psychology. Although 'fear' and 'love' often occur as aspects of an indivisible whole, the former carries far greater weight with the average person. It is held [463] that the fear of God is primarily intended for the benefit of human beings, in order that they should keep the commandments and for this merit be properly rewarded. This is the reason for the *Kāfi* [464] attaching so much importance to the hearing of, and the listening to, the commandments. In the Samaritan mentality, as indeed in the Bible, hearing is identified with listening, with heeding and thus with obedience. Among the prayers, and in particular the one for the washing of the ears, there is a special recitation, since the ears are the only organs of hearing. This whole psychological system of fear and love and obedience and service depends on them, hence we can readily understand how the ears are singled out as the major channel of man's inner religious life. One could go on and quote almost any part of their exegesis to show that the whole is governed by this approach to the fear of God, which is there, if not explicitly, then implicitly and between the lines, on almost every page.

It is undeniable that there are sporadic cases, actually mentioned in their literature, of those who do not possess this 'fear'. In the *Kāfi* [465]

---

[461] *Hillukh*, pp. 281f. This idea was taken from Munajja and applied to this problem (cf. n. 473 *inf.*).

[462] The main "proof-text" often quoted is *Deut.* x, 12-13, where 'love' and fear are amalgamated. Although the Samaritans did not have the rich admonitions of *Proverbs* or verses like *Psalms* XIX, 10, they learnt the same sentiments by dramatizing the narratives in which "the fear of the Lord" appeared. e.g. Adam (*Gen.* iii, 10), Abraham (*ibid.* xx, 21), Jacob (*ibid.* xxviii, 17), Joseph (*ibid.* xliv, 18), the Israelite midwives (*Ex.* i, 17), Moses (*ibid.* iii, 6).

[463] Qabaṣi, *Sir al-qalb*, pp. 142-144. After an elaborate explanation of the various types of 'fear', and explaining the reasons behind 'the fear of the Lord', there is a long list (pp. 144-147) on 14 biblical proofs. (cf. previous note. However, it should be noted that the case of Moses is considered by Qabaṣi "a fear of one creature from the other", because the verse is apologetically explained as referring to an Angel).

[464] p. 48 (SLTh.A, p. 11).

[465] p. 194f. (SLTh.A, p. 24).

there is a case of a woman of easy virtue who, owing to her connexions with leading persons from amongst their dominant non-Samaritan neighbours, evaded punishment and perhaps even rebuke. However, the mention of such cases is very rare and is rather the exception which proves the rule; i.e. that, in general, the Samaritan mentality entirely espoused these psychological motifs taken from scripture.

One might assume that since the Samaritans did not have the book of Psalms, where more than elsewhere expressions of a fervid love for God appear as a religious and psychological phenomenon, this theme was not in fact stressed by them. There are, however, enough proof-texts for such a love, especially in the book of Deuteronomy, (vi, 5; xi, 1; xiii, 4; xix, 9 etc.) to make us retract this view. Phrases of religious devotion, which normally finds its expression in psalms, were replaced among the Samaritans by interpretations of expressions of "rejoicing" (*Lev.* xxiii, 40; *Deut.* xxii, 18; *ibid.* xv, 15; etc.) in the sense of "rejoicing in His love". Even negative expressions, from which the positive counter-part might be understood, were pressed into the service of 'love'; thus for example, *Deut.* xxviii, 47 was interpreted as an implicit command to worship the Lord 'with joyfulness and with gladness of heart', which surely are identical with love and religious devotion.[466] Marqah already had this theme very much on his mind when he linked sincerity of heart with fear and love and walking in God's way, and finally spoke as if all these sentiments were almost synonymous.[467] In later literature [468] the theme of love is greatly amplified by setting forth the various types of love, (1) from above to below, i.e. from God to Man, (2) from Man to God, (3) between man and man. All three types are richly illustrated from Scripture or from quotations from earlier writers, including Abū-l Ḥasan. It goes without saying that the divine love for man is not at all an unconditional matter, but is rather conditioned by man's righteous-ness; and here we have the link with fear. Both the love and the fear of God are closely identified with the observance of the Torah, which ensures an ethically merited reward. There is here no possibility of any arbitrary behaviour on the part of God.[469]

---

[466] Abisha's *Commentary on the Liturgy*, pp. 27f.

[467] *Memar Marqah* (ed. Macdonald), I, p. 141 (= II, p. 231).

[468] Qabaṣi, *Sir al-qalb*, pp. 147-152.

[469] In contrast with some Islamic thinkers who thought that God's love resembles human affection in some respects (cf. D.S. Margoliouth, *The Early Development etc.*, pp. 175f.), the Samaritans strictly adhered to the absolute justice of God.

The often repeated allegation that the Samaritans failed to develop the concept of God as 'Father' has little to do with the doctrine of love.[470] In the first place, this whole allegation is scarcely in accordance with the facts, since the divine Fatherhood could not be convincingly denied when there is in fact an explicit verse on this very matter (*Deut.* xxxii, 6) which is duly explained by Marqah.[471] But in the second place, what one can safely say about this concept of the Fatherhood of God is that it is certainly not emphasized, since the relationship between God and Man is securely based on the Torah and its Righteousness. The concept of a Loving Father is not brought into relief; Samaritan psychology understands that love is to be expressed by walking in His ways. Although these ways are often fraught with trials and dangers, they should be followed in love. This following, then, is the mark of love when it is done in devotion. Thus Marqa says [472]

> The way of Enoch is the way of the True One; in it Abraham was led; in it Isaac walked and was magnified; and likewise Jacob. Thus the great prophet Moses said, having knowledge of the truth, *for all his ways are justice* (*Deut.* xxxii, 4). O men, believe in this and learn in this knowledge. How great is this statement which the great prophet Moses made.

'The way', so often emphasized, embraces all the demands which Scripture makes on the individual. Those who earn God's commendation have followed in this way in spite of many a trial. The significance of the trial is stressed by Munajja,[473] using as his basis *Deut.* xiii, 4 and *Exod.* xvii, 4. He maintains that, despite the truth and justice of God's ways

---

[470] Montgomery (*The Samaritans*, p. 213) describes this as an influence of Sadducean theology. However, all our sources show that the Samaritans are much closer to "the more intense personal religion of the Pharisees". Unfortunately Montgomery's remarks were uncritically accepted, and even expanded, by later scholars. In so far as our problem is concerned with the Fatherhood of God, there can be no question that from the point of view of 'Love of God' this was upheld both from man towards God and *vice versa* (Deut. vii, 13; *ibid.* xxiii, 6 etc.). cf. also J. Macdonald, *The Theology of the Sam.*, pp. 66, 93.

[471] *Memar Marqah*, I, p. 43 (= II, p. 68); I, pp. 96f. (= II, p. 159).

[472] I, pp. 88f. (= II, pp. 143f.). The origin of the Midrash is *Gen.* v, 24 "And Enoch *walked with God*: and he was not; for God took him". This was understood as the martyrdom of Enoch, for his walking in the "path of God". On this analogy, the "path" of the meritorious, who have always prepared to sacrifice their lives for the love of God, was described as filled with trials.

[473] *Masā'il al-Khilāf*, Ib, pp. 80-85. All this is based on argument from *reductio ad absurdum*; were there an arbitrary fate, human beings would be in a worse position than animals (who have no intelligence and free will), cf. n. 461 *sup.* and text there.

and the reality of Divine providence, the trial is essential both for the verification of our beliefs and for the strengthening of our observance. The same sort of reasoning applies to the Commandments as well as to the Law and the Prophets, and all of which would be of no avail unless reinforced by Divine retribution. Besides, it is morally impossible to attribute to God such flagrant injustice as the infliction of tribulations for no clear reason, when we know (*Exod.* xxxiv, 6) of his manifold loving kindnesses. Like Marqah, Munajja also relies on verses such as : "For all his ways are justice", this one proving that it is inconceivable that God should not have ordained his scheme of reward and punishment according to the scales of perfect justice. That this one was so often and so intensively drawn upon in later literature [474], shows how popular this theme was for many centuries. Trials are ascribed to all the Patriarchs, beginning with Adam, down to Moses, some of them undergoing as many as ten trials!

Much more prevalent, however, than this consideration of trials, punishment for sins and the guilt-consciousness, was the positive side of the Samaritan religious psychology expressed in terms in conformity with those of the Rabbis,[475] who found that very many scriptural texts testified to the Covenant, and thus took it for granted that the Covenant made by God with Israel on Sinai was to continue to be binding throughout all generations and even milleniums, without any special act of renewal. So too, verses referring to the Covenant as it affected circumcision and the Sabbath were invariably understood by the Samaritans in the same way.[476] This "perpetual covenant" is closely bound up with the idea of holiness; and, in the case of the Sabbath for instance (*Exod.* xxxi, 16), whose observance throughout the generations virtually ensures the keeping of this Covenant on the part of God, is understood to be identified with the demand for holiness itself. The *Ṭabbākh* [477] is quite explicit on this point, assembling five attributes of the Sabbath, or, more precisely, four in addition to that which pertains to the Sabbath by its nature, namely Covenant, Sign, Holiness and Blessing. All these expressions are taken from scriptural sources. But, from a further scrutiny

---

[474] Qabaṣi (*Sir al-qalb*, pp. 91-131) is very fond of this subject and multiplies details of trials.

[475] Büchler, *Studies in Sin and Atonement*, pp 10f. For Marqah's views cf. *sup.* n. 377 and text there.

[476] J. Macdonald, *The Theology of the Sam.*, p. 298.

[477] ff. 26a f. (SLTh.A, p. 82f.).

of the *Ṭabbākh*, it becomes evident that this Blessing and this Covenant in relation to Holiness have in reality reference to divine providence. The author, by an example taken from a verse dealing with the observance of the pilgrimages, shows distinctly that this concept of 'Covenant' is not limited to the Sabbath alone, at which point it is explicitly mentioned, but includes all the commandments of the Law. Although this conclusion is not explicitly stated, it becomes obvious from the whole discussion. Often, however, other arguments are offered, unconnected with the 'Covenant'. The *Kāfi* deals in two places with the expression "to observe the Sabbath" (*Exod.* xxxi, 16), in the same manner as the *Ṭabbākh*, although here the notion of 'holiness' rather than the 'Covenant' is the centre of attention. The interpretations given of this verse are virtually the same as those found in the *Ṭabbākh*. 'Holiness' requires that the Sabbath should be devoted to study and prayer with a view to the edification of the soul, and as remedies for its contamination during the six days of labour. This is reiterated in another place by adding the explanation that 'holiness' is achieved by the separation of the devout person from profane things, whether of speech or of action or even of thought.[478]

The Commandments were thus not understood as a burden but rather as a privilege and a means of sanctification. In their religious psychology, the element of 'rejoicing in the heart' was by far the strongest, although, of course, the observance of commandments was more particularly connected with reward and punishment. The *Ṭabbākh*,[479] in explaining the Passover Offering, expounds the expression in *Exod.* xii, 3 : "Take unto you" as meaning that if one takes one's lamb for sacrifice, it is for one's own spiritual benefit, for one's own good, alluding here to the rewards received for fulfilling the Commandments. Similar Midrashim can also be found in Rabbinic literature, where the "Rejoicing in the Miṣwah" became one of the indispensible foundations of religious psychology.

Naturally, to these concepts of Holiness and Covenant, one must also add the election of Israel to the office of "a nation of priests". The aspiration of achieving sanctification, through the fact of belonging to this superior order, inevitably fired the Samaritan imagination with the

---

[478] *Kāfi*, pp. 84f. and 106 (cf. SLTh.A, pp. 14 and 18 respectively).

[479] f. 58b (SLTh.A, p. 101). cf. *Rashi* on *Gen.* xii, 1, s.v. לך לך. For many other midrashim not only from Talmudic literature but also from Philo etc., cf. Heinemann, *Darkhei ha-Aggadah*, p. 97.

awareness of a participation in the divine providence in the world. This explains why the *Ṭabbākh* [480] assigns such a prominent place to the Laws of Passover. These Laws are the first to appear in the Torah as promulgated by Moses, because in and through them one may realize the greatness of the divine grace towards Israel. In the elevation of a whole people to the office of priests, by allowing them all to participate in these offerings, the superior status of Israel is demonstrated. Furthermore, these laws are declared to be connected with the expression "an everlasting statute", whereby the perpetual status of its observants is guaranteed. This is also the motive behind Abū-l Ḥasan's exercise of multiplying the laws concerning Passover to the huge figure of sixty, thus magnifying the importance of the original precepts, through the keeping of which the maximum reward is earned by the people of Israel.

The positive side to the Samaritan religion, seen so clearly in this "rejoicing in the Commandments of God", also presents us with an entirely different picture, and one which the prevalent guilt-consciousness could never effectively obliterate. Probably this is one of the main reasons why, not only in Judaism but equally among the Samaritans, the demand for perfection and moral integrity was never so exaggerated as to lead to a division of men into black and white, or to their division into the totally guilty and the totally guiltless. Maybe here is an additional reason why we cannot in these two groups trace the exact boundary between the possibility of final penitence and that of final impenitence. [481] Integrity (תמים, תם), the biblical examples of which are mainly those of Noah, Abraham and Jacob, thus implies, not only sincerity and genuineness, but also uprightness both in thought and deed, all of which are manifestly dependent on one's relationship to God. Clearly God himself sets the true standard through the medium of the Law, which at the same time determines this mutual relationship and in accordance with which man receives reward and punishment. Integrity, in short, means for both these groups a sincere effort to walk in utter devotion and undeflected obedience in the way of God.

Despite the rigoristic demands imposed by the pursuit of perfection, for the purpose of ensuring a general adherence to the religious pattern expected, and of encouraging the people not to despair, there was understandably a need for a constant mending of ways and for repentance.

---

[480] f. 58a (SLTh.A, p. 100). Concerning the significance of the number 60, cf. *inf.* Part III para (g. 7).

[481] cf. *sup.* para (e). cf. also n. 468 and text there.

Although this need must create a plain contradiction from the psychological point of view, there was a real necessity to leave a passage open, and not to be unduly harsh, so that if a person lapsed or fell into a moral snare, or was forced by circumstances to compromise, he should not immediately feel rejected. Possibly this was the reason why the possibility of repentance was not confined to any particular case of sin or to any circumstance. In one instance it seems unquestionable that we may detect a deliberate tendency to remain ambiguous concerning the possibilities of repentance. Thus when Marqah explains the significance of the letter Samekh (symbolizing forgiveness סלח), he deliberately avoids committing himself to any one view. The whole chapter, and the emphasis therein, put on this letter above all other letters, carries the underlying suggestion that the gate of repentance is never tightly closed. It is significant that in this place he gives a negative definition of what is meant by 'perfection', and especially by perfection of conduct, which is so important in Samaritan religious psychology. He says perfection of conduct means *not* committing any evil deeds as, for example, murder, idolatry and adultery.[482] It seems that these cardinal sins are singled out quite deliberately in order to minimise the feeling of despair on the part of the potential penitent, and to show that as long as a person does not transgress these ultimate limits, there is still a chance for him to be readmitted.

From an investigation of the pentateuchal 'proof-texts' from which such a demand for repentance and return could be derived, it is also evident that a certain unresolvable tension exists: on the one hand, repentance is described as easy ,and (*Deut.* xxx, 1-10; cf. *ibid.* 11-14) the impression given that, even in the case of the most grievous sins, one still has a chance to repent; on the other hand, from the chapters on the 'Curses', one is led to assume that, even for the least grievous sins, one may be totally rejected. A fundamental and deeprooted optimism,

---

[482] *Memar Marqah* (ed. Macdonald), I, p. 141 (= II, p. 231). In Talmudic literature (*Sanhedrin* 74a) the same three cardinal sins are singled out but for a different purpose. If one is under duress he should rather transgress all other commandments in order to save his life (the Rabbis understood "he shall live by them" *Lev.* xviii, 5 as indicating also the opposite 'that he shall not die by carrying them out'). However, in the case of the three cardinal sins one should rather suffer martyrdom than transgress them. This however has no bearing on the problem of repentance, of which, because of the tension between the need for condemnation of the transgressor and the encouragement of repentance, no categorical definitions were possible (cf. however, *Yoma* viii, 8-9, and Büchler, *op. cit. passim*).

although often disturbed by a guilt-consciousness and expressions of despair, shows nevertheless the sensibility of Samaritan religious psychology. Marqah himself is strongly in favour of such preaching, for in one place he says,[483] "Greatness belongs to God, who is indulgent towards the sinners and bears with them in his mercy so that they may repent."

The often remarked ambiguity belonging to the possibility of repentance is most probably not entirely unintentional, and it seems that there must even have been some awareness of the inherent difficulty. Otherwise, it is very difficult to resolve certain paradoxes. One of the paradoxical expressions of Marqah [484] is extremely interesting, because it is both strict and lenient at one and the same time. He says :

> O priests, give heed to this great honour and do not forsake your status. The whole congregation of Israel, if they err, may be accepted. Thus the True One said "*You shall return*" (*Deut.* xxx, 2). (*Then the Lord*)... *will return*. But the priests are not reaccepted if they are defiled. A defiled one cannot return (to become) holy. Fire will consume him, a punishment for his defilement.

Precisely because of the severity shown towards the priests, it is imperative to notice his leniency towards Israel, in that, if they err, they may repent and be accepted. As for the later literature, we find that it is pervaded throughout by the idea of the possibility of repentance. The Thirteen Attributes of God which occur in Scripture (*Ex.* xxxiv, 6-7) are all interpreted to show how God's purpose is directed mainly to the problem of how to bestow mercy and secure the acceptance of the sinner.[485] The *Ṭabbākh* likewise earnestly encourages repentance, leaving, however, the question as to what degree of gravity renders a sin pardonable, or otherwise, quite open. In his interpretation of *Deut.* xxxii, which deals mainly with the rewards and punishments of the Day of Vengeance,[486] on verse 4, when speaking of the righteousness and perfection of God, he says : "He shows mercy to those who deserve it, long-suffering towards those whom his wisdom deems worthy of it, acquits and forgives the perfect penitent who has repudiated the evils which he has committed." Although there are indeed several degrees of

---

[483] *Memar*, I, p. 87 (= II, p. 140). מגלגלון ברחמיו means the same as מגלגל עם in Talmudic literature (cf. *Kethuboth* 67b; 111a). Maybe there is also some connection with נתגלגלו רחמיו and similar expressions in Rabbinic literature (cf. *Tanḥuma* Wayyiggash, para 4, etc. cf. Targum *Onqelos* on *Gen.* xliii, 30).

[484] *Memar Marqah*, I, p. 58 (= II, p. 91).

[485] Thus for example Qabaṣi (*Sir al-qalb*, pp. 65ff.) followed by others.

[486] ff. 139a-140a.

Divine mercy, it depends entirely on the judgment of God as to who is to be deemed capable of repentance or deserving of mercy or long-suffering. There is no attempt whatever to show that there is a standardized measuring-rod. In other words, it seems that, as with so many other psychological questions to which there is no clear-cut or wholly rational answer, this too is left to the will of God, although this in itself is not always, and cannot be, known to human beings.

Munajja, in treating the same verses as the *Ṭabbākh*, lays even greater stress on the opposing extremes, namely, God's mercy and his "consuming fire" (*Deut.* iv, 24).[487] Munajja's treatment demonstrates even more plainly how these opposing manifestations of the divine attitude are entirely at God's own discretion and within his control. Later, however, a slight quirk is given to the discussion, in that the quality of Mercy is emphasized more than the quality of wrath. According to this emphasis, repentance absolves all things, though of course on certain conditions, namely that the sinner truly repents and has truly humbled himself. Moreover, it is not certain even here whether the teaching on leniency is carried in this instance a stage further towards an even greater emphasis on Mercy. It might be claimed that it is meant only as an an admonition, uttered in the hope of encouraging sinners to repent.

From the exposition of legal matter such as in the *Kāfi*,[488] it is evident that, in cases where capital punishment is to be inflicted, there is no mercy. It is even explicitly said that in these cases, even if the sinner pleads before the Judge, or again, in cases where a person has cursed his parents, the Judge is not allowed to heed the pleas of the parents. In another place too,[489] the *Kāfi* is more rigid than is normally the case in Samaritan literature. Here the topic of discussion is purification, where it is stated that certain serious defilements can only be cleansed by fire, whereas moral sins and spiritual defilements cannot even be cleansed by fire. The latter judgment applies to sexual offences, obscene language, etc., from which there is no cleansing. As a matter of fact,

---

[487] *Masā'il al-Khilāf*, Ib, p. 86. God's preference of mercy is also the opinion of the Rabbis (*Rosh Hashanah*, 17b. cf. also *Yoma*, 37b; 86a). The expression "consuming fire" (*Deut.* iv, 24) often quoted in the *Liturgy* (cf. e.g. I, pp. 50, 60 etc.), has to be understood in this context. No other theories can be built on this quotation except these which we find in the Samaritan Traditional midrash. cf. Trotter, *A Critical Study etc.*, pp. 338 and 347 (respectively).

[488] pp. 274f. It is only stated that after the sentence was carried out "the One who knows the hidden things may pardon him".

[489] pp. 157ff. (cf. Abdel-Al, *A Comparative Study etc.*, pp. 525f., 687f.).

the *Kāfi* even quotes an earlier authority,[490] as saying that in cases of such deep defilement: "The great sea does not cleanse him". But here again, it is wellnigh impossible to draw a demarcation-line between defilements and sins. This in any case shows that, even in the case of lesser offences, the way to repentance is not always too smooth. Maybe, as in many other cases,[491] the *Kāfi's* presentation here is more legalistic than that of other authorities, which is easily explained by its outline being strictly limited to halakhic matter, hardly leaving any space for matters of pure doctrine or theology. There is, however, no need to assume any real contradiction with the rest of Samaritan literature. It is rather a matter of emphasis. The *Kāfi*, mainly concerned with ritual, has to adopt a more rigid stand point, in order that the religious and psychological outlook of the people shall not be threatened by the danger of self-indulgence, thus promoting laxity. Others, who were themselves interested in doctrine and in the religious devotion of the Samaritans [492] directed their writings to this same end; consequently, there arose an urgent need not to over-emphasize — at least in the admonitions to repentance — those rigid aspects which might discourage potential penitents.

H. The Samaritan Midrash

Our next concern is to examine those qualities in the Samaritan midrash which distinguish it from those of the other midrashic schools. By determining these distinctive qualities, we can define the degree of its originality, subsequently compare it with similar expositions in other groups and thus discover the influences it has most probably undergone. As we have already seen,[493] the concept of a fundamental exegesis for the composition of midrashim, common to, and underlying, all groups at

---

[490] *ibid.* p. 158 (Abdel-Al, *ibid.*). This ancient writer الشيخ ابو عوض في مدينه يبا is not known from elsewhere. It is also a moot point whether a book ("fair city") is meant or is it the place of this Abū Awaḍ? However from his Aramaic style (ימה רבה לא מדכי לה) it is quite reasonable to assume that he belongs to the Aramaic period (circa 4-11 cent.).

[491] cf. nn. 464, 478 *sup.* and text there. These are not the only cases when sanctity is translated in the *Kāfi* into terms of ritual. Ch. XXIX of the *Kāfi* dealing with forbidden foods (pp. 315ff.) has in its title في تشريف النفوس. It is interesting to note that the subject of repentance itself is not explicitly treated, but rather taken for granted.

[492] cf. *sup.* nn. 338, 468 etc. and the whole paragraph (e) on "the Religious Devotion of the Sam.".

[493] cf. *sup.* Part I, para (b, e, f, and i).

a definite period, is unrealistic, since the various groups, in any limited period, would have differing aims, needs, and even doctrines. The true character of Samaritan midrash can therefore only be determined by a comparison of the interpretations of similar texts by Samaritan writers of different epochs.

To take only one instance, it is noteworthy that, although Philo [494] has his predecessors who had interpreted Scripture philosophically, he alone is responsible for consistently developing the Hellenistic system of allegorical interpretation. Despite the fact that he utilizes both oral and written sources, and despite his broad affinity with his predecessors, the major characteristics of this method are forged by him. Needless to say, then, his method owes even less to other midrashic schools.

In evaluating all midrashic methods one must take into consideration the actual traditions of the respective groups. Although it is no doubt true that, in certain groups, the final word lay with the "verdict of the majority", one must not ignore the fact that one is dealing here, not so much with legislators, as with exegetes, preachers and transmitters of tradition. Even in the case of the Dead Sea Scroll Sect [495] where "the many" decided disputed matters by their votes, too much weight has been allowed to the supposedly spontaneous and occasional elements in such decision-making, and too little attention has been paid to the important part played by tradition. Even among the Rabbis, where individual or contradictory opinions could co-exist [496] and there was the ruling that the ultimate decision lay with the majority, the choice was a restricted one, a choice among the various existing traditions, rather than among arbitrary sentiments. Among the Samaritans, of course, such a provision was needless, since their simple type of exegesis did not, and could not, give rise to so many contradictory opinions; and, as we shall see later, there was a centralized control over such matters. The Samaritans had no equivalent to the long transitional process between creativity and 'commenting', manifested in the activities of the prophets and later the scribes.[497] For them, there was only 'commenting' and the detailed and minute application of their Torah, given to them in an almost finalized condition prior to their existence as a separate group.

---

[494] Siegfried, *Philo von Alex. als Ausleger des A.T.*, p. 26.

[495] cf. my article in *ALUOS* VI (1969), pp. 121f.; 158f. (nn. 199f.).

[496] Jer. *Sanhedrin* IV, 2; 22a (and parallels) cf. Rawidowicz "On Interpretation", *PAAJR* xxvi (1957), p. 95.

[497] *idem. ibid.* pp. 89f.

There is a basic similarity in the development of midrashic pursuits between the Rabbis and the Samaritans, for they both alike rely on exegetical devices based on simple logical analogies. These analogies, as, for example, inferences from minor to major premises or vice-versa, passed through many stages of development. Although the logicality of some of the more advanced stages may legitimately be questioned,[498] there can be no doubt that the general principles upon which they are built are sound.

Among the Rabbis this practice develop through associative psychology into a comprehensive system, which in turn led to a great amplification of the basic principle of utilizing various types of analogies.[499] From their application in exegesis the need arose to formulate the method in a general philosophy. The basic principle, the groundwork of this whole philosophy of exegesis, can already be found in its essence in Scripture, where a particular instance gives rise to a generalization, and, conversely, a generalization demands rules for its detailed application. At any rate, it appears certain that a traditional exegesis and practice predated hermeneutical principles by centuries.

The simple type of exegesis employed by the Samaritans did not necessitate such an elaborate development of hermeneutical principles. It is a recurrent feature among unsophisticated peoples, practising 'organic thinking', that they always take it for granted that a text needs expounding. This outlook is commonly displayed in commentaries on ancient documents other than the Bible. Even among the Rabbis, for whom hermeneutical principles are of such high importance, these principles do not in fact in themselves give us a full insight into their outlook.[500] In our research into the Samaritans our concern is not with conjectural hermeneutical principles, which in any case may never have been consciously present to their minds, but rather with an assessment of their way of thinking and of the elements which govern it.

The Halakhah is very instructive in this respect, both in view of its adverse criticism by European scholars [501] and in view of its binding nature, which compels its exponent to rigidly adhere to traditional

---

[498] A. Schwartz, "Die Hauptergebnisse etc.", *Scripta Universitatis... Hierosolymitanarum etc.*, I, pp., 4f. There are some exaggerations in details about the rationalistic elements of these hermeneutic principles, but in their original form they are certainly based on logical deductions.

[499] *ibid.* pp. 16f.

[500] Heinemann, *Darkhei ha-Aggadah*, p. 96.

[501] cf. e.g. Farrar, *History of Interpretation*, p. 84.

practices. The Aggadic midrash is better understood in comparison with the halakhic one originating from the same environment, than in comparison with the aggadic midrashim of other groups. The explanation of this lies in the fact that the midrashim were much too closely tied to the written word to be guided by any fanciful inventions of the mind. Returning to the Samaritans, upon investigation we find that even the midrashim which seem entirely unrelated to Scripture prove to originate from the exegesis of biblical concepts and themes. As we have remarked above, Marqah's apparently 'free' midrash, if properly looked into, invariably reveals its exegetical elements. This is even more apparent in the later writings of the Islamic era which reveal, in their constant quotations from Scripture, their origin in straightforward exegesis. The *Kāfi* time and again refers his readers to his commentary on the Pentateuch, unfortunately lost to us.[502] It seems that underlying all the Samaritan midrashim, there was a foundation in a simple running commentary on Scripture. Their belief in the antiquity of their exegetical traditions, which is the source of their Midrashim, is neatly expressed by a late writer, who nevertheless voices much earlier sentiments, when he says : "(Moses) author of the Diwan, both the Law and the interpretation and the clear faith."[503]

The following view, however, is altogether too sweeping and can only be accepted with some modifications : "The exegesis of the Samaritans, strange as it may appear, is thus almost identical with that followed by the Jews in their endeavour to find the Oral Law in the Written, and to adjust the practices that have grown up in the course of time to the Word of the Law."[504] The Samaritans cannot be said to possess such a reverence for Oral Law that they can give it an independent status. The case is rather that, in the Samaritan mind, oral tradition is integrated so completely into exegesis that it is totally identified with it, all possibility of its having an independent existence and development being thus excluded. Marqah's mode of expression makes it abundantly clear that he assumes that his readers will have a sound knowledge of Scripture and its traditional exegesis. In fact his most complex and 'mysterious' midrashim are nothing else than combinations of exegetical details.[505]

---

[502] pp. 215, 223, 229 etc. (cf. SLTh.A, pp. 37, 43, 47 respectively). One could say that Marqah was already relying for his midrashic expositions on exegesis which was well known to his readers. cf. *inf.* n. 505.

[503] Miller, *Molad Mosheh*, pp. 188f.

[504] Gaster, *Eschatology*, p. 36.

[505] cf. my article, *op. cit.*, pp. 107-110; 141f. (nn. 76-85); 142ff. (nn. 89-101).

The deeply felt need of the Sadducees, who formed the earliest literalistic sect and were radically opposed to Oral Law in any form, to codify their practices (and maybe their doctrines),[506] did not make itself felt among the Samaritans. Perhaps the close bond between traditional exegesis and the text made such codification superfluous. This does not mean to say that the Samaritans did not deduce certain regulations from their exegesis of the text. We have already seen how they based the intercalation of the solar and the lunar year on their exegesis of the biblical narrative, not on the legal section of the Pentateuch. This was also common practice among the Rabbis, who utilized narrative sections for legal purposes.[507] Needless to say, all the pre-sinaitic customs mentioned in the Pentateuch were freely used by the Rabbis, as they were by other groups, for deriving additional religious regulations.[508]

In other words, Samaritan midrash embodies all the elements that are common to midrash in other groups. The midrashic system may be considered under two major categories,[509] one being 'creative description' and the other 'creative interpretation'. The former is historiographical and employs organic thinking, by posing questions not posed in Scripture and answering them in practical terms. In this way many kindred details may be subjoined to the biblical narratives. 'Creative interpretation', on the other hand, may be designated as an organic type of philology, in which each and every detail of Scripture is scrutinized with a view to bringing out new aspects of teaching. This method may be employed for the derivation of permutations and combinations of details, either through analogy or deduction.

It is possible that the constant preference shown for the 'question-and-answer method' by the Samaritan writers, is largely due to its being the method most suited to midrashic writing, for it is clearly serviceable for clarifying doubts and obscurities which could not be unmistakably understood from a general statement of the rule or from a running commentary. The contrast between their own treatment of midrash and a more straightforward exegesis is clearly observable in the *Kāfi*, which is constructed in the form of question-and-answer; while for a straigthforward exegesis the reader is referred to the author's exegetical work on the Pentateuch.[510]

---

[506] *ibid.* p. 130 (n. 7).

[507] M. Guttmann, *Eine Untersuchung... Geltungsumfang etc.*, p. 2, n. 1.

[508] *idem.*, *Die Anlehnung*, p. 22.

[509] cf. n. 500 *sup.*

[510] cf. *sup.* n. 502.

There is little room for doubt that this organic thinking, so characteristic of them, which was persistently striving to answer questions on
form and to clarify doubts, was not associated with the written word
only, but must also have given rise to some oral traditions.[511] However,
even the oral traditions, replete with fanciful details such as the exact
dates for certain events, have for their ultimate inspiration certain
biblical phrases. One example of these from the *Asaṭir* [512] is the account
of the sin of the Israelites in Shittim (*Num.* xxv, 1-9). Many details are
added, including the exact date and hour of this happening, which
resulted, according to the *Asaṭir*, from Balaam's advice to Balak. Balaam
knew that God hates defilement; he accordingly advised Balak to make
his people "commit whoredom". As in Rabbinic literature, the theme
is derived by analogy from another verse (*Num.* xxxi, 16) : "Behold,
these caused the children of Israel, through the counsel of Balaam, to
committ trespass against the Lord." The biblical starting-point is not
always so easy to discern. Often biblical and non-biblical sources are so
interwoven as to create a piece of syncretism in which the biblical element
can no longer be recognised.[513]

Even the earlier midrashim, as the following example from Marqah

---

[511] Ben-Hayyim, "Sepher Asaṭir", *Tarbiz* xiv and xv (1943 and 1944), pp. 1ff.

[512] *ibid.* pp. 19f., 46. It is possible that the coming of the prostitutes on the Sabbath
is a further development of the midrash: "Balaam knew that the God of Israel hates
defilement", he chose therefore the Sabbath which is normally associated with sanctification in order that the sacrilege should be magnified. This might be also the reason
for choosing the third hour (about 9 o'clock, a.m.) which is normally the time for
divine worship. Even the description of the tribes participating in the sacrilege is not
arbitrary: "And the heads of the congregation stayed before the Tent of Meeting
on the south" (cf. *Num.* iii, 29 on the Kohathites = Moses and Aaron, presumably
the Elders stood around them). "And the camping place of Reuben was *there*".
(cf. *Num.* ii, 10). However, "the standard of the camp of Reuben" included also the
tribes of Simeon and Gad, therefore they were all on the south, all in one line, Reuben
"on the western (side), Simeon in the middle, and Gad on the eastern side". These
tribes were singled out because, after the plague following the sin with the Moabite
girls, they are counted first (*Num.* xxvi, cf. *ibid.* ii, where "the standard of the camp
of Judah is first!). Furthermore, it is not impossible that the maxim אורי לרשע ואוי
לשכנו so frequent among the Rabbis (cf. *Num. Rabbah* XVIII, para 4; Rashi on
Num. iii, 29 etc.), was also known among the Samaritans. Zimri (who is singled out
also in *Memar Marqah* as the arch-villain) was "a prince of a father's house among
the Simeonites" (*Num.* xxv, 14) and similarly some of the Reubenites joined the
rebellion against Moses (*ibid.* xvi, 1), thus the generalization on the whole "standard
of the camp of Reuben" was only natural.

[513] cf. Gaster, *Asaṭir*, p. 18.

will show, appear, at least on a first glance, to be mere figments of the imagination. Here [514] a conversation takes place between Pharaoh and Moses, in which Pharaoh suggests that the Israelites should sacrifice in Egypt. Moses und Aaron answer :

> You say that there are two gods in the universe, one in heaven and another on earth: but we say that there is only one God, the sole *possessor of heaven and earth* (*Gen.* xiv, 19). You say that spirits are shared among the dumb (animals) and the speaking (man), but we speak of soul and spirit, referring the soul to the body and the spirit to the speaking (man). The control of living human beings is both by soul and spirit. The control of the dumb (animals) is performed sufficiently by soul. You say the eating of flesh is not permissible. We want to slaughter and sacrifice cattle. You worship animal forms but we sacrifice animal flesh to our God. There is a considerable difference between us.

Upon a closer examination it becomes evident that this is a midrash based on *Ex.* vii, 22: ("Lo, shall we sacrifice the abomination of the Egyptians before their eyes, and will they not stone us?")

Hence, Scripture is everywhere the guiding factor in determining their midrash. The reader is even guided by cantilation marks so that there can be no doubt about the correct meaning of the words. From the correct reading of the text the midrash and Halakhah would be taken, and therefore it is essential that the reader should always provide the correct reading, since the Halakhah forms the basis of their religion.[515]

That the Samaritans practised a simple form of midrash can be seen from the fact that one can almost invariably guess the eventual form of the midrash from the plain reading of Scripture. This is in marked contrast to the complicated system employed by the Rabbis, in which even the minutest details could be pressed into service. The spirit of the Rabbinic midrash tended to differentiate between 'decrees of Scripture' connoting ritual commandments not normally explainable by rational means, and rational or ethical commandments.[516] While the former had to be accepted unquestioned, the latter could be modified, in the way either of amplification or restriction, by the demands of reason. In this regard, minute details, supplied by Scripture, were invaluable. Often

---

[514] *Memar Marqah* (ed. Macdonald), I, p. 18 (= II, pp. 28f.). The midrash is based on תועבה, in analogy with *Gen.* xliii, 32; xlvi, 34, understood both as 'abomination' and as 'idol'. The same double translation occurs already in the Versions (cf. LXX, Onqelos, Vulgate, Peshitta and Rashi on *Ex.* viii, 22. cf. also *Zohar* III (Phinehas) f. 250b).

[515] Ben-Hayyim, *Literary and Oral Trad. etc.*, II, p. 292 (cf. ibid. n. 16).

[516] M. Guttmann, *Eine Untersuchung... Geltungsumfang etc.*, p. 20.

the 'plene' or the defective spelling, even of a single word, could here be of great significance.[517] This approach to the text is admirably illustrated in the etymological translation of Scripture by Akylas, who himself followed Rabbi Akiba's method of exegesis, in translating every syllable and every letter. This is shown not only by his translating the *nota accusativa* את by σύν, but by the whole of his hermeneutics.[518]

In contrast to all this, the Samaritan Midrash, even at its most abstruse form, does not posit any such intricate deductions, but is based rather on a fairly simple welding together of biblical motives and analogies. One might take, for example, the perplexing midrash in the *Asaṭir*,[519]

---

[517] Krochmal, *More Nebhoche ha-Zeman*, p. 171.

[518] Field, *Hexapla*, pp. xvi-xxvii.

[519] Ben-Hayyim, "Sepher Asaṭir", *op. cit.* pp. 13, 29. The sentence דו שפך אל עלמה
דלית אשתה קרבה ליד הרגריזים ... must be wholly a reference to Hargerizim and not to Mount Ebal. The general sense seems to be as follows: Why did Enoch (or Adam?) command that the place should become a cemetery? "Because it is the *highest* place upon (על = אל) the world and above it is the Gate of Heaven (cf. *Gen.* xxviii, 17) and no fire can reach the *vicinity* of Hargerizim etc." שפך as many other expressions are used by the Sam. to express highness, height, and heaven, שפך must be identified with שוביך and שוביכה cf. Sam. T. on *Gen.* i, 17; *ibid.* xi, 4, 5 and 8. cf. S. Kohn, *Sam. Studien*, p. 106. (The only objection one may raise against Kohn's opinions, is that the Heb. שובך itself is also possibly derived from similar roots meaning 'towering', 'lofty', etc. (cf. *Soṭah* 42b). If there is any connection to the Arabic etymology it is not to شباك but rather to سبك / سكر cf. Hebrew רקע, רקיע, רקיע (Hiph'il). This compares favourably with פלוק, פלוך (and some versions of Targum פלקולילה *Gen.* xi, 8). cf. Kohn, *op. cit.* p. 31. (Again his etymological connections are doubtful. Instead of فلك 'roundness' the connections are rather with فلكى 'celestial' or even with فلقى / فليق 'sublime', 'wonderful', etc.). The next example of equating sky with height is שחיק. Sam. Targum renders גבוהים *Gen.* vii, 19 as שחיקיה (most probably originating as a midrash from שחקים *Deut.* xxxiii, 26, which is a *hapax legomenon* for the Sam.). cf. Kohn, *op. cit.* pp. 84-87. In this case also, despite that all of Kohn's lengthy discussion is still valid, etymologically his predecessors (*exelsus, sublimis* شاهق) were closer to the truth. שחק here has nothing to do with 'crushing' or 'destroying' but it is a literal translation of גבוה (cf. further in the midrash). It is interesting to note that in their Hebrew, recent Sam. translators often employ שחוק in the sense of 'high', 'lofty', etc. The same applies even to שמים used for translating 'high', 'roof', 'overshadowing' etc. (cf. later Marqah). Further research in matters of semantics must be left to experts in this field. The midrashic background of the Asaṭir seems to be a play on the expression עולם (גבעת = גבהת) עולם (cf. *Gen.* xlix, 26; *Deut.* xxxiii, 15) which is one of the synonyms of Hargerizim. A similar play on *Habakkuk* III, 6 is to be found in the *Zadokite Fragments*, pl. I, l. 15 (גבהות עולם). Such must be also a midrash by Marqah (*Memar* I, p. 64 = II, p. 101) : "There was no mountain *elevated* (שממ) cf. Arabic root سا or سموا / سماوي ;ساوي ;سام

stating that the mountain of Ebal was so named because the people mourned [עיבל = אבל] Enoch there, and thereafter it became the recognized burial-place: "The reason for this was that fire cannot reach within two thousand cubits of the surroundings of Hargerizim, since it is called 'an asylum for fleers', [to the?] 'Rock of Salvation'." Although at first glance this appears to be an entirely free midrash, bereft of any biblical foundation whatsoever, upon closer scrutiny one can uncover its biblical sources with a high degree of certainty. The midrash was originally prompted by the need to explain away the fact that Joseph and other 'Righteous' of the Samaritans were buried on 'the mountain of curses', and not in the cave of Machpelah in Hebron. The fanciful etymological identification of Ebal with mourning is employed to remove the sting of the association of 'curses'. The proximity of Hargerizim to this mountain is, of course, common knowledge, and the fact of this proximity leads to several biblical motives being forged into a chain, in order to build this Midrash. Thus, in the narrative of the killing of the people of Shechem by Simeon and Levi (*Gen.* xxxiv) it is implied that they found asylum in Bethel (where was the altar to God, *Gen.* xxxv, 7; cf. *ibid.* 14 and *Gen.* xxviii, 18. cf. also *Ex.* xxi, 14). Again, the 'city of refuge' (*Num.* xxxv, 11) is identified with the cities of the Levites which extended their limits by two thousand cubits in all directions (*ibid.* 5). Further supporting evidence for the saving power of Hargerizim is found in its identification with the abode of "the Rock of Salvation" (*Deut.* xxxii, 15).[520]

---

etc.) above the waters of the Flood except this one (Hargerizim), while all (other) mountains were submerged". If we do not translate it in this way the midrash becomes self-contradictory, because it is further stated... דמי מבולה לא מטה בה ולא אבד בה נפש לטמאתה. Marqah was probably not aware of the Rabbinic polemical midrash (cf. Kohn, *ibid.*). The same tradition is also the root of the homiletics concerning the eleventh name of Hargerizim (*Memar Marqah*, I, p. 48 = II, p. 78): "*The Everlasting Hill* (or rather: The Loftiest place on Earth?) *the head of ancient mountains* (*Deut.* xxxiii, 15) (ranges) above all mountains in holiness and glory". Although this passage is suspect because of its language, even if it were a later interpolation its content is in full accord with Marqah's genuine writings, and taken for granted by the earliest writers in the Arabic language (*Ṭabbākh*, ff. 207b-208a; *Kāfi*, p. 219; cf. SLTh.A, p. 40). Through the chain of these midrashic motives it becomes self-explanatory why עיבל (= אבל) was in the neighbourhood of Hargerizim and not *on* it.

520. The Sanctuary (worship and pilgrimage) was considered an antidote to the 'curses' which prevent salvation (cf. *Deut.* xxviii, 29, 31; and cf. *Ṭabbākh* and *Kāfi* in previous note). From Marqah's interpretation (*Memar*, I, p. 93 = II, p. 152 on

This intricate form of midrash is typical of the *Asaṭir*, not so much because it is essentially based on difficult exegetical principles, as rather because it draws from different and often mutually contradictory midrashic sources, conflating them in an obscurely 'mystical' style and without any clear indication of their scriptural bases. An additional example from the *Asaṭir* will illustrate this intricate style even more strikingly. Here we cannot deal with the comparative problem of the sons of Mizraim (*Gen.* x, 13-14) who were supposed to have been exterminated during their wars with Nimrod.[521] Owing to the inherent difficulties of exegesis in this passage, various groups arrived at broadly similar conclusions. However, the *Asaṭir* provides it with fresh complications. It gives an account of the seven wars of the 'wicked' (most probably the whole family of Ham, who is considered as accursed), based on the seven names of the sons of Mizraim.[522] These names, with their strange forms and all appearing in the plural, give rise to the notion that they were embroiled both in external enmity against Nimrod and in internal enmity among themselves, which alike caused their ultimate destruction. The latter notion gives rise to the further inference from the verse that the eighth son of Mizraim had to forsake the territory of of Egypt and conquer for himself new territories. This inference is understood to be the secret of their present survival and finds support in the verse : "whence went forth the Pelishtim" (= the Philistines) (*ibid.* 14). These speculations are not framed in a vacuum, but are adduced to explain why the Philistines (sons of Mizraim) are living in the land bestowed on the Canaanites. According to the Samaritan Pentateuch, "the border of the Canaanites was from the river of Mizraim to the great river of Euphrates" (*ibid.* 19). This is the true reason behind

---

וי_נבלו צור ישועתו, *Deut.* xxxii, 15) it seems that it was translated by the Sam. as "The Rock of his salvation will disgrace him". Despite the general attitude of God ("The Rock... perfect", *Deut.* xxxii, 4; cf. *ibid.* xxxiii, 29) manifested in 'salvation', here (*Deut.* xxxii, 15) because of their ungratefulness in forsaking Him, "He made known that... He recompenses every doer according to his deed, and He reveals the truth (of His justice) in that event!".

[521] cf. Gaster, *Asaṭir*, p. 20.

[522] Ben-Hayyim, "Sepher Asaṭir", *Tarbiz* XIV and XV (1943 and 1945), pp. 15, 34f. (cf. *ibid.* p. 33. Nimrod the ruler of the Sons of Ham built Babylon). This may explain why here the Euphrates is called "the river of Cush" (Nimrod, son of Cush). (cf. later in the *Asaṭir*, *op. cit.* pp. 16, 36): Terah went out to the land of Canaan after Nimrod's death to establish his "Kingdom", which coincided with boundaries mentioned in verse 19, S.P. (*Asaṭir. op. cit.* pp. 17, 40).

the *Asaṭir*'s report that "the Philistines ruled from Egypt to the river of Cush" (= Nimrod); and for the same reason it is understood that the Philistines had conquered this region and seized it from the over-lordship of Nimrod.

The complications do not end here. It appears that several traditions have been interwoven. First of all there is the tradition of the disappearance of the sons of Mizraim. This contradicts the fact that the Egyptians continued to exist later and to figure prominently in Scripture; and, of course, the Copts (descendents of the old stock) existed at the time when the *Asaṭir* was written. There must have existed a parallel tradition based on the continued existence of the Egyptians, a tradition which would go far to explain these difficulties. The Samaritan text itself shows a variant reading on the sons of Ham (*ibid.* 6, M.T. וּפוּט S.P. (פּוּט), which may have given rise to the interpretation that Put was synonymous with Mizraim. This alternative interpretation is further strengthened by the fact that the descendants of Put are never referred to, unlike the descendants of all the other sons of Ham mentioned in Scripture. If, on the other hand, Put is identified with Mizraim, there is no need to give a list of his descendants. This is the background for the following midrash of the *Asaṭir*: "and they appointed a leader from their midst, the firstborn of Lehadim (= Ludim) whose name was Giṭaṭ (for גיפט derived from פּוּט?), and after whose name the Copts (גיבטאי = גיפטאי) are called.[523]

These abstruse examples have been deliberately chosen in order to illustrate that even in this type the midrash does not lack a certain biblical basis. In the field of halakhah, however, this fact is so evident that we hardly need to amass examples. This does not mean to say that Halakhic midrash is not occasionally based on far-fetched analogies. To cite only one instance from the *Kāfi*,[524] where the treatment is not so mystical as that of the *Asaṭir*, we may consider the laws of purification. Here we are presented with three stages of purification, corresponding to the three

---

[523] It has to be admitted that not all problems of this abscure passage can be satisfactorily solved. The translations of both Ben-Hayyim and Gaster (*Asaṭir*, p. 240) are not free of difficulties. It is also possible that the text itself is corrupt. The major points, however, are clear and they are based on genuine scriptural difficulties. The midrash comes to explain the fate of the seven sons of Mizraim, who, as opposed to the Philistines, are wrapped in a shroud of mystery. The Sam. Text מצרים פּוּט furnished a peg upon which to hang the midrash גיפטאי = גפט = פּוּט, who in turn are identified with the remnants of the sons of Mizraim (i.e. the Egyptians).

[524] pp. 43f. (SLTh.A, p. 7f.).

degrees of defilement : a slight degree of defilement demands only the washing of the body; a more serious one, the laundering of the clothes in addition; and the most serious one, total immersion in water in addition to the other rites. Although the reasons determining which degree of defilement a particular act belongs to are not very obvious, they can nevertheless be referred to 'proof-texts'. From the halakhic midrash one may gather that this unfailing reliance on Scripture is a general principle. Even abstruse aggadic midrash will likewise be found to originate from similar exegetical derivations which themselves rely on such 'proof-texts'.

The question now arises as to how the Samaritans regarded their 'proof-texts'. Attitudes towards proof-texts varied between the one extreme, adopted by the heretical groups, of regarding certain parts of the Scripture as false, and the other, diametrically opposite, extreme, of regarding the entire Scripture, in all its minute detail as so sacred that any phrase might serve as a 'proof-text' of equal importance with any other phrase.[525]

The attitude, for example, of the Dead Sea Scrolls Sect is illustrated by the fact that a commentator may quote a verse in one form and then offer an interpretation which presupposes a different reading of the text. Presumably, their religious devotion and their critical faculty were not completely reconciled.[526] This situation most probably gave rise to their established practice of assembling verses on one topic which was central to their religious dogmas, in order to dismiss the contradictions arising from the variant texts and from the inconsistent exegesis that such variant readings occasioned.[527]

In a similar way, Philo too uses one verse : "God is not as man" (*Num.* xxiii, 19), as a proof-text in refutation of other verses where an anthropomorphic expression occurs which in his view should be taken figuratively, since, if taken literally, it "contradicts the truth".[528] Naturally, once the door is open to such a selective approach it may

---

[525] On the one extreme are some Christian Sects (cf. Schoeps, *Theologie und Geschichte, p. 168.* There were also some Jewish heretics with similar opinions (Marmorstein, *HUCA* X (1935), pp. 226f.) but, in general, Jewish sects tended to the opposite extreme. The Rabbis were famous for their exposition of every detail in scripture. cf. e.g. *sup.* nn. 515-518, and *inf.* text and n. 529f.

[526] M. Burrows, *More Light on the D.S.S.,* p. 163.

[527] *ibid.* p. 400, 409; Driver, *The Judean Scrolls,* p. 527. This is most probably the explanation of the cryptic signs on the margin of biblical texts from Qumran.

[528] Wolfson, *Philo,* I, p. 116.

lead to a more recklessly figurative exegesis, even culminating in fanciful allegories.

The Rabbis, on the other hand, although they admittedly employed complicated hermeneutical principles, nevertheless felt compelled to allow for the interplay between the various sources. Even where, in the Mishnah, for purposes of codification the midrashic background is generally omitted, the Talmud supplies it and shows that it all firmly based on biblical midrash.[529] The latter is not allowed to be selective in its interpretation, but has to consider all the sources relevant to the matter in hand. Hence, it is fair to assert that whether the Midrash is the source of all Halakhah and Aggadhah, or whether tradition preceeds Midrash, which itself finds support for tradition in Scripture,[530] the overall position of the Rabbis will be the same, namely that they have to consider all biblical sources as equally important.

The Samaritan approach to 'proof-texts' was very closely akin to that of the Rabbis. Their literalistic approach however demanded, even more than in the case of the Rabbis, that the midrash should be in full harmony with each and every discoverable detail yielded by Scripture. All verses relevant to the problem discussed had to be interpreted in conformity with their literal sense. The rationale, therefore, behind some of their intricate midrashim is due, not so much to abstruse hermeneutical principles, as rather to the need to justify every seeming discrepancy which should arise when related passages were subjected to comparison. One example which it will be worthwhile to quote is Marqah's treatment [531] of the theological question as to whether God can be provoked, or, in this context, be put to the proof. The question itself is never asked in so many words, but rather implied and expounded in a whole chain of proof-texts, which by their very interplay are supposed to answer this question. The implied answer is that it is not in God's nature to be provoked, but that any alleged 'provocation' is merely an inevitable consequence of the character of the Israelites themselves, who, by their constant deviations from His will, bring upon themselves divine retribution, which in biblical language is expressed as 'provoking' or 'testing God'.

They have provoked me (*Deut.* xxxii, 21) — an evil offence and a testimony to evil (it is like) God's statement: *They have put me to the proof ten times* (*Num.*

---

[529] Weiss, *Dor Dor etc.*, III, p. 4.

[330] cf. my article in *ALUOS* VI (1969), pp. 124f. (n. 1).

[531] *Memar Marqah* (ed. Macdonald), I, pp. 100f. (= II, pp. 166f.).

xiv, 22); *How long... refuse?* (*Ex.* xiv, 28); *How long... despise me?* (*Num.* xiv, 11); *How long shall this wicked generation...?* (*Num.* xiv, 27).

As against three (evils) three (utterances) were said, and each one of them is more severe than the preceding one: (1) *How long... refuse? ...* reference to those leaving Egypt. Ishmael was there to teach them hardness.[532] (2) *How long will these people despise me?* — i.e. the children who despised (me) and learnt from Esau.[533] (3) *How long shall this wicked congregation...?* — a provocative gathering came here: *Let us chosse a captain and go back to Egypt* (*Num.* xiv, 4).

When at the (Red) Sea, they were (already) divided into three divisions. Each class made a statement and the great prophet made a reply corresponding to each statement.

The first division [534] said: "*Let us... go back to Egypt* (*Num.* xiv, 4) *and let us serve the Egyptians... for it would have been better for us... than to die in the wilderness*" (*Ex.* xiv, 12). The great prophet Moses said: "*You shall see them again no more for ever*" (*Ex.* xiv, 13).[535]

The second division said: "Let us flee from the Egyptians into the desert." The great prophet Moses said to them: "*stand firm and see the salvation of the Lord, which he will work for you today*" (*ibid.*).[536]

The third division said: "Let us arise and fight against the Egyptians". The great prophet Moses said to them : "*The Lord will fight for you and you have only to be still*" (*Ex.* xiv, 14).[537]

By creating a dialogue, based on the simple words of Scripture, Marqah thus demonstrates by the interplay of the verses the righteousness of God, and, moreover, how this type of wickedness was inherent in the

---

[532] A midrash on רבי קשת (*Gen.* xxi, 20, M.T. רבה) "he taught them archery" (ילפנון קשותה). His being in Egypt is inferred from his having an Egyptian wife (*ibid.* 21).

[533] A further midrash based rather on the analogy of ideas than on actual words: they learnt to despise God from Esau who did the same when he "despised his birthright" (*Gen.* xxv, 34).

[534] Now the order is reverted, the most severe division (those who wanted to return and serve the Egyptians) are now the "first". According to the Samaritan text those who preferred slavery (*Ex.* xiv, 12) are identified with those who "harkened not unto Moses" (*Ex.* vi, 9) right at the beginning of his mission. (cf. also *Ex.* v, 21).

[535] A play on "go back" נעזר and "again" תעזרון (תוסיפון S.T. תוזפון) to emphasize that not only their evil design to "serve" the Egyptians has failed, but that they will never see them again.

[536] This is the division which despise God (cf. *sup.* n. 533) therefore they do not believe in Him, neither have any selfrespect to defend themselves.

[537] This division is the lesser of all evils, since they at least are ready to put up a fight (cf. *sup.* n. 532). A similar division is also found in Talmudic literature (J. *Ta'anith*, II, 5: 65d).

Israelites even when they were in Egypt. By this device he skilfully answers the theological problem.

It would be no exaggeration to claim that for them, strictly speaking, the 'proof-text' has no place, as they regard every detail of Scripture as having equal value and validity.

The 'selected verses' (Qaṭaf), forming the kernel of the Samaritan services since ancient times,[538] are not 'proof-texts' in a strict sense. Although it has been discovered that such 'snippets' from the Law have assumed three distinct forms, each designated for a specific liturgical purpose, these are still far from resembling Biblical *Testimonia*, or compendiums of biblical texts exemplifying the doctrinal principles of a group. All three forms have this feature in common, that they provide an aid to the mastery of certain themes or motives which can be read in a short time and without the essential purport of Scripture suffering serious loss by being thus wrenched form its context.

Even when dealing with halakhah, and with one of their basic tenets, the definition of the locality of Hargerizim, the Samaritans still reveal the same tendency. Although the number ten has a quite special significance and, in conformity with this, Samaritan tradition upholds a definition based on ten verses,[539] these verses are nevertheless selected from different parts of the Pentateuch. Four of them are taken from the narratives of Abraham, two from those of Jacob, and four from the sayings of Moses. They are all harmonized and given equal weight.

We should not therefore be perturbed to find that in certain Messianic expositions the 'important proof-texts,'[540] such as Deuteronomy xviii, 18, is in fact missing. In the same context we find the Samaritans employing different verses in support of their doctrine, and any such verse (e.g. *Gen.* xv or *Num.* xxiv) would of course have in their eyes a value equal to that of any other pertaining to the same theme. An example of this is their use of *Gen.* xlix, 1 & 2, which is taken to refer to prophecies both of the period of 'Divine disfavour' and of the period of the Second Kingdom, i.e. the Messianic era.[541] The first verse, containing the verb אסף, is interpreted as indicating the former period, while the other verse, with the verb קבץ, as indicating the latter. Here it is not chiefly a question

---

[538] Cowley, "The Sam. Liturgy and Reading of the Law", *JQR* VII (1894), pp. 121-140; *idem. Sam. Liturgy*, II, p. xxi. J. Macdonald, "Comprehensive and Thematic Reading etc.", *JJS* X (1959), pp. 67-74. cf. *sup.* n. 294 and text there.

[539] *Ṭabbākh*, ff. 115b f.

[540] cf. Merx, *Der Messias oder Ta'eb etc.*, p. 35.

[541] *ibid.* p. 55.

of a 'proof-text', but rather that the second verse, with the verb קבץ, can be utilized for verbal analogy with *Deut.* xxx, 4, "Will the Lord *gather* (יקבצך) thee". Here as in other cases it is the interplay of midrashic elements which is of prime importance.

The opposite extreme to the practice of selecting 'proof-texts' is perhaps this tendency to amass all possible sources which, by their interaction, forge the doctrine. Just as no need is felt for a 'creed', the words of which are fixed beyond alteration, so their doctrines are in general independent of verbal formulations, since they consist of self-explanatory harmonized texts. Often, by merely supplying the biblical sources of such homilies, it becomes clear that these verses by their interaction forge the doctrine in question. Marqah, in expounding the cardinal doctrine of the Torah's all-embracing authority, instead of exemplifying, by scriptural proofs, its light as conveyed to the world and the nations, which is his major thesis, concentrates rather on its miraculous origins:[542]

> ... Its origins have been heard from heaven with ten great mighty wonders — fire (*Deut.* v, 13), lights (*Ex.* xx, 15), darkness (*Deut.* v, 20), cloud (*Ex.* xix, 16), thunder (*Ex.* xx, 15), lightning (*Ex.* xix, 16), the sound of the trumpet (*Ex.* xx, 15), mighty quaking (either *Ex.* xix, 18; or *ibid.* xx, 15), great stillness (*Deut.* v, 27f. also in S.P. before *Ex.* xx, 19), the assembly of the angelic ranks (לקראת האלהים *Ex.* xix, 17), a mighty, incalculable affair.

It has already been pointed out that Marqah is very fond of such midrashim based on numbers.[543] In general, the number ten is specially favoured. This is shown in many places, as for example in his depiction of Moses averting the wrath of the Lord, which was ten times manifested and ten times averted by Moses.[544] It is not always easy to pinpoint the exact biblical references in such compilations. We have seen this in the case of the ten miracles which were performed on the sea itself during the night of the crossing of the Red Sea.[545] Often it would have been possible for the exegete to find more than ten. Occasionally the so-called 'proof-texts' are deliberately multiplied to make them up to the round figure of ten. Marqah's use of 'ten' which pertain to the Sabbath' is a good illustration of this. They are : "the covenant, holiness, blessing, rest, warning, observance of it, life, death, cessation from work

---

[542] *Memar Marqah* (ed. Macdonald), I, p. 134 (= II, p. 218).
[543] Rettig, *Memar Marqa*, p. 23.
[544] *Memar Marqah* (ed. Macdonald), I, p. 148 (= II, p. 245).
[545] *ibid.* I, p. 36 (= II, p. 55).

and prayer."[546] Here it would surely be very easy to find biblical warrants
for these ten and then to produce many more supprting expressions.
In fact some of thse single items could well be expanded, as is shown in
his later treatment of prayer, where he presents four types of prayer
(those of the Patriarchs and of Moses).

Although the Samaritans show a preference for round numbers, this
does not lead them into the forced type of midrashim found among
the Rabbis, where a traditional number is artificially extracted from
Scripture.[547] The only exceptions to this generalization may be found,
perhaps, in the *Asaṭir*,[548] where one finds statements like : "Thus said
the founders of the faith ,(that) all all the affairs of the Righteous are
linked to (numbers) seven and eight." Although this certainly demonstrates that here the tradition favourable to the numbers seven and eight
is the basis of their midrash, it is still entirely possible, as in other cases
in the *Asaṭir*, that the tradition itself grew out of earlier scriptural interpretation.

Qabaṣi, whose avowed purpose is to guide men in "the way", in order
to prove his major thesis similarly produces ten 'proof-texts'.[549] He
however introduces his biblical proofs in the course of showing how
'the way' can be learned from the Patriarchs, and then from what Moses
learned from his father-in-law, a treatment which brings the number
up to at least twelve.

When the same Qabaṣi [550] is describing the long succession of the
'Meritorious' who underwent 'trials' from God, the fifth in line is
Abraham, who underwent ten trials; and so we find in Rabbinic litera-
ture also. However, the actual term 'trial' only occurs once in the biblical

---

[546] *Memar Marqah* (ed. Macdonald), I, p. 86 (= II, p. 138). cf. editor's n. 28.
There are many more examples of Marqah's use of the number Ten. cf. the Ten
Judgements, *sup*. n. 332; "The ten things that bear witness on God's might (day,
night, four seasons and four elements)", cf. SLTh. pp. 892f. Naturally, other
numbers are also employed as e.g. the warnings against the oppression of the sojourner
(7), the orphan (7) and the widow (6), altogether twenty warnings. cf. *sup*. n. 343,
and *inf*. nn. 636-638.

[547] M. Guttmann, *Eine Untersuchung über den Geltungsumfang etc.*, pp. 25f.

[548] Ben-Hayyim, "Sepher Asaṭir", *Tarbiz* xiv-xv (1943-1944), pp. 20, 47. cf.
sup. nn. 511f.

[549] *Sir al-qalb*, pp. 43-46. Even the ten verses taken from the words of Moses
one could criticize: in one of them (*Deut*. xiii, 5) instead of דרך there os only תלכון
If we use verses for 'proof-text' where there is the expression 'to walk' one could
add many more, e.g. *Lev*. xviii, 4; *ibid*. xxvi, 3; *Deut*. xiii, 6 etc.

[550] *ibid*. pp. 95-108. cf. *Abhoth* V, 3; *Abhoth de Rabbi Nathan* (ed. Schechter),
pp. 94-95.

text itself (*Gen.* xxii, 1), and such examples as are offered to represent 'trials' can be made to fit any desired number. He also uses other special numbers, as for example twenty, in his treatment of the murmurings of the Israelites in the desert, where, although he cites biblical sources to make-up this number, these could easily have been made up to another and greater number.[551]

In common with other and later writers, Qabaṣi is inclined to use certain artificial devices as well, in order to arrive at a certain midrash based on numbers. To take only one example,[552] there is his midrash on the twenty-two thousand angels ministering to Moses, which he clarifies by asserting that each letter of the alphabet is served by a thousand angels. It goes without saying that when he refers to the earthly sanctuary where the twenty-two thousand Levites minister (*Num.* iii, 39), we cannot but realise the artificiality of this whole midrash.

Yet another late writer shows the same attachment to numbers, as one can see, for instance, from the way that he makes Moses order the appearance of darkness three times.[553] It is for him a simple matter of collecting together three verses in each of which darkness is associated with the narrative of Moses. An even more artificial approach is exhibited when the same writer, owing to Moses' being eighty when he prophesied, makes the number of miracles wrought by Moses into eighty also.[554]

In the halakhah such plays on numbers are naturally not so prevalent. If they do occur, it is mainly for the purpose of explaining numbers already present in the Bible, and showing why that particular number is given. One example will suffice, that of *Ex.* xxi, 27, where the penalty for a man who steals an ox or a sheep, and kills it or sells it, is: "he shall pay five oxen for an ox and four sheep for a sheep." The explanation given is very naive,[555] in that it relies on the fact that 'ox' has been mentioned five times in the Scripture and 'sheep' four times. Surprisingly, he gives two different versions of these 'proof-texts', thus showing the artificiality of the whole exercise. Indeed, in comparison with the moral explanation given by the Rabbis in this instance, this type of Samaritan exegesis strikes us as very childish.

---

[551] *Sir al-qalb*, pp. 132b.

[552] *ibid.* pp. 27f.

[553] Miller, *The Sam. Molad Mosheh*, pp. 120-121.

[554] *ibid.* pp. 312-313.

[555] *Kāfi*, pp. 283-286. In Part III we will see more of this type of primitive explanations of biblical number. As for the Rabbis, cf. *Babha Qamma* 71b; *ibid.* 79b; Maimonides, *Guide for the Perplexed*, III, ch. 41.

I. Samaritan 'Oral Law'

Judging from our general picture of Samaritan midrashic literature, we may affirm that oral tradition is not a very prominent contributory factor. As we have seen, there is no 'hallowed' doctrine independent of Scripture, guiding the exponent to selected 'proof-texts' upon which to rely, but, on the contrary, almost the whole of the Scripture is utilized for midrashic expositions in the interest of creating the norms both for practice and doctrine. Even the 'formal' midrashim, based on the exposition of numbers, are entirely subordinated to the need for adding force and weight to the 'opinions' arrived at by harmonizations of Scripture. Nevertheless, it would be wrong to deny flatly the existence of certain traditions which appear to have been transmitted orally for many generations, even such as are in no way connected with Scripture. The problem of the genuineness of such oral traditions is a thorny one, to be sure, for it is a general feature of religious development that, with changing circumstances, even established religious opinions find themselves in need of being modified. Although the more conservative religions commonly present these modifications in the garb of 'Tradition' or 'Oral Law' in order to persuade themselves that they are keeping to the paths of their forefathers,[556] often enough this thin disguise does not entirely hide the elements of foreing influences.[557]

We may then ask if in fact there were any alien influences that induced the Samaritans to develop the idea of oral tradition, or was it developed by them independently? We have seen time and again the hazard involved in drawing far-reaching conclusions from the juxtaposition of 'corresponding ' traditions taken from various groups. On this very ground we had to abandon the nineteenth-century theory (still claiming some supporters in the present) as to the common origin of all 'traditions' in an 'ancient exegesis', going back to pre-Christian times, and presumably identical with that of the Sadduceans.[558] While the proper instructive value of comparisons with other groups is not denied, the primary

---

[556] Farrar, *History of Interpretation*, p 11 (cf. next n.).

[557] *ibid.* p. 452f. On the whole problem of the interplay between 'tradition' and innovation, cf. J.L. Blau "Tradition and Innovation", *Essays... in honour of S.W. Baron*, pp. 97f.

[558] cf. my article *ALUOS* VI (1969), pp. 100, 102f., 134 (nn. 24-5) and 137 (nn. 39-40). Recently a similar attempt was made to date the Dead Sea Scrolls by comparison to hypothetical developments in Pharisaic halakhah, cf. Driver, *The Judaean Scrolls*, p. 88.

task of our investigation is concerned with the inner development of Samaritan exegesis itself, since (as we have so often seen) despite all similarities, traditions vary from group to group.

In Pharisaic Judaism itself the concept of 'Ancestral Laws' had very probably several meanings, but common to all was the understanding that it connoted, as a supplement to the 'Law' derived from Scripture, the 'customs' and 'regulations' handed down by tradition.[559] Such a general awareness of the value of tradition may very well have been shared also by the Samaritans of the earliest periods. It would, however, be pointless to draw analogies here, when a variety of interpretations divided the Pharisees even amongst themselves.[560] The evidence suggests that the apocalyptic group stood very much further apart, since they, with their written 'revelationary' books (again supplementary to the Bible) stood in diametric opposition to all groups believing in an 'oral Tradition', by their own presupposition that the only authoritative Book was Scripture.[561] The possibility of effective relations with the Sadducees in this field is even more remote, since these latter denied the value of tradition altogether.[562]

On the question of a Samaritan 'Oral Law' there are radically opposed views, ranging from outright denial of its very existence to gross exaggeration of its scope.[563] It seems that both extreme views should be severely

---

[559] cf. *ALUOS* VI (1969), p. 125, n. 2. Opinions are divided on the problem whether Philo's 'unwritten laws' are identical with the Rabbinic 'oral Law' (Krochmal, *More Neboche Ha-seman*, p. 168; Wolfson, *Philo*, I, pp. 190f.; II, pp. 181f. cf. also *sup.* Part I, nn. 4, 5, 150 and 283), or whether it is a different concept. (Heinemann, *Philons... Bildung*, pp. 10, 124ff., 540; cf. also my article, *op. cit.* pp. 117, 153, nn. 151, 153, 156-160). The latter opinion is however supported by the totally Hellenistic outlook of Philo and his ignorance of Rabbinic halakhah (Heinemann, *op. cit.* p. 282, n. 2).

[560] Hellenistic Jews did not regard the "unwritten law" (ἄγραφος νόμος) as authoritatively as was the case with the Rabbis' total submission to their 'Oral Law' תורה שבעל פה). cf. previous note and Heinemann, "Die Lehre vom ungeschriebenen Gesetz etc.", *HUCA* IV (1927), pp. 149ff.

[561] Widengren, "Tradition and Literature etc.", *NVMEN* X (1963), pp. 53 (and *ibid.* n. 19 for further literature), 57-60.

[562] Josephus, *Antiq.* XII, x, 6; *ibid.* XVIII, I, 4.

[563] "The Samaritans never developed any Oral Law, and held that the written Torah provided all necessary rules of life". Abdel-Al, *A Comparative Study etc.*, p. 48 "... On the other hand there were many practices possible for the Samaritan in his everyday life without the interference of the Law, while for the Jew every step in life was blueprinted by the halakhah of Mishnah and Talmud"... *ibid.* p. 49. As opposed to this, Gaster, *Eschatology etc.*, p. 24 : "Scholars were satisfied with merely

curtailed. While it is true that, *vis-a-vis* the Rabbinic Oral Law, its Samaritan counterpart is a very meagre affair, nevertheless it has sufficient vitality to serve as a fertilizing agent to all Samaritan practices and beliefs, and to invigorate all facets of life. On the other hand, any unbridled claims for a sacrosanct 'Oral Law' must certainly be curbed by the Samaritans' own concept of a 'perfect' Law, a concept which implies that the one and only source of authority is Scripture, and that, consequently, all 'oral law' must necessarily be closely bound up with it, or even be regarded as being deduced from it.

At any rate, there are among them no inflated claims to huge masses of oral traditions committed to memory, as is the case with other groups.[564] Accordingly, the sanctity of Scripture creates amongst the Samaritans no such qualms as to prevent them from writing other books. Unlike other groups,[565] they do not develop any dogma that oral tradition must invariably be transmitted exclusively by word of mouth, thus reserving to Scripture the sole right to be committed to writing. Neither Marqah nor any other writer, from Byzantine times onward, feels himself called upon to apologize for recording tradition or liturgies in written form. On the contrary, it is a common feature of Samaritan chronicles to lament the destruction by their enemies of their ancient books, of which only a small fraction have survived.[566] It is in fact very possible that the Samaritans pursued the practice of the Gloss, as it was known to them, from Roman Legal Codes (and later adapted to the Biblical Gloss by the Church). The Samaritans may have utilized the margins of Scripture, its Targums or its translations, for appending glosses to the text in order to preserve their tradition, which would otherwise have been entirely at the mercy of fallible human memory. It is hard to assess

---

copying meagre and brief references in the correspondence, and yet, as will be seen, a sufficiently large literature exists among the Samaritans to show the existence of an Oral Law and traditional practices...", cf. the careful words of J. Macdonald, *The Theology of the Sam.*, p. 290.

[564] This and similar comparative problems need further alucidation, cf. SLTh., p. 837 and nn. there.

[565] *ibid.* p. 822, nn. 186f.

[566] Montgomery, *op. cit.* pp. 92ff. On the ancient Samaritans writings in Greek, cf. K.F.A. Lincke, *Samaria und seine Propheten* (Tübingen-Leipzig 1903), pp. 133f.; Montgomery, *The Samaritans*, p. 284 and recently J.D. Purvis, *The Samaritan Pentateuch and the Origin of the Sam. Sect.* (Cambridge, Mass. 1968), p. 13, n. 21. cf. A. Spiro, "Samaritans Tobiads, etc.", *PAAJR* XX (1951-, pp. 280ff. and especially 287f. n. 24, who denies the existence of such literature. However, for our problems this is irrelevent, since in any case these fragments have no bearings on exegesis.

the extent of such glosses, but there can be no real doubt about their existence. As a matter of fact, it has already been noted by scholars that such marginal glosses were employed in the service of exegesis and polemics.[567] There is a hypothesis that there existed extensive marginal notes, serving to enumerate the precepts of the Law or even to classify them into groups of positive decrees and prohibitions.[568] Although admittedly there is no documentary evidence for such a systematic exercise from ancient times, the emergence of Samaritan Halakhic literature in the eleventh century must surely have been greatly indebted to such glosses, which would aid the writers to reach a greater systematization.

In some such way we may gain a clearer picture of the development of Samaritan literature from the early practice of random and unsystematic glosses. Although occasionally we meet with expressions implying that tradition takes precedence over the written revelation,[569] this does not necessarily mean that it has to be preserved strictly orally. Just as in the Scrolls, meant for public reading, a way is found to indicate the writer and the date of writing by using a cryptogram,[570] so too, in books intended for study and private use, one may add mnemonic remarks on the margin as an aid to the student. Nor is it impossible that such notes were added to by various hands, as in the case of Glosses. Such desultory private notes, which would increase in number as well as in size with the passing generations, may also have run some risk of incorporating foreign elements of a 'heretical' nature. Since the Samaritans were never entirely free from alien influences, absorbed by hearsay and in smaller measure by the reading of their neighbours' books, there arose the need for a constant watch over and criticism of these glosses, lest they should get out of hand.[571]

If we are in any way justified in speaking of a 'Samaritan Oral Law', we are so justified only with the following reservations : we may call all the extra-scriptural material — by the Samaritans themselves called

---

[567] Wreschner, *Sam. Traditionen*, p. 19 (cf. also *inf.* n. 571).

[568] Gaster, "Die 613 Gebote etc.", *Festschrift Breslau Seminar II*, pp. 402f. On the Sam. enumeration of precepts cf. Haran, "The Song of precepts etc.", *The Israel Academy of Sciences and Humanities, Proceedings*, V (1974), pp. 174ff.

[569] cf. *sup.* nn. 103, 337 and text there.

[570] Montgomery, *The Samaritans*, p. 228, n. 39; von Gall, *Der Hebräische Pent. der Sam.*, pp. I-lxxxvii.

[571] Ben-Ḥayyim, "Sepher Asaṭir", *op. cit.* p. 2. (cf. *ibid.* n. 4 for glosses on the Arabic translation of the Pentateuch).

'tradition' — Oral Law, even though this term was not known to them, since none of this material was ever codified in canonical form. On the other hand, the outstanding fact that we cannot discover any lawlessness in this voluminous material is a clear proof that its form was not left to the individual fancy or to the momentary caprice of the exegete. From all available sources it becomes evident that its remarkable cohesion stood even the supreme test of time; and the monolithic character of the Samaritan religion is beyond doubt greatly indebted to this Oral Law, which shows very great consistency throughout its long history. And as regards the Samaritan Halakhah — which after all is the back-bone of the Samaritan religious organism — it can justify its claim to a coherent system which we may call 'Oral Law'. To take as an example the regulations regarding the water used for purification, a subject on which the Scripture is totally silent, these alone, so systematically treated,[572] show the meticulous care taken in preserving all minutiae of their Oral Law. Here too it is made clear that the rules for purification comprise both scriptural decrees and traditions,[573] the latter sometimes indeed having greater weight than the former.

The discussion of the domestic duties of the wife towards her husband is another case which illustrates the partial superiority of Tradition (and common sense). Here too there are scriptural 'pegs' on which the Kāfi supports its evidence.[574] However, the strength of tradition and common sense is such that "it does not require any proof". Established traditions must of course exert a decisive influence on exegesis, since no scripture can be interpreted against a tradition. One example of such restriction of exegesis is apparent in the prohibition of the consumption of intoxicating drinks upon Hargerizim. From *Deut.* xiv, 26 it would seem that pilgrims are in fact allowed to partake of wine; this verse is however explained away as referring only to the journey, in order that its exegesis should not clash with their Oral Law.[575]

Nonetheless, it would be wrong to rashly assume that there exists a dichotomy between their Oral Law and Scripture. As in the last-mentioned case, the scriptural word is not at at all cancelled. It may only

---

[572] Kāfi pp. 33ff. (SLTh. A pp. 3ff.).

[573] *ibid.* pp. 45f. (SLTh.A, pp. 9f.). As for the power of tradition, cf. *ibid.* p. 49 (SLTh.A, p. 12). cf. also n. 569 *sup.*

[574] p. 195 (SLTh.A, p. 25).

[575] *Kāfi*, p. 226 (SLTh.A, p. 45). cf. also my article in *ALUOS* VI (1969), pp. 115, 150 (n. 134).

be slightly modified, since in any case no command or prohibition is
here involved. For this reason only may it be restricted in its exegesis.
Not only is there no possibility whatever of abrogation, but the Samaritans categorically deny any contradictions, either as between various
scriptures, or as between Scripture and tradition, or as between the
various exegetical analogies derived from scriptures. This becomes clear
from their explanations of the laws of levirate marriage, which in their
teaching do not refer to the blood-brother of the deceased, but to a more
distant relative.[576] *Lev.* xviii, 4 is here cited to prove that both "statutes"
(i.e. Scripture) and "Judgements" (i.e. its exegesis by analogies etc.) are
of permanent validity, and their binding force thus perpetual. In other
words, "these should be observed, and handed down in tradition from
generation to generation". There is absolutely no licence to deviate
from them, since every-one is in duty bound "to accept the teaching of
the elders, the wise and learned..."

We have seen on previous occasions the great significance attached
to these traditions,[577] which in some sense justify the term Oral Law.
The *Ṭabbākh* specifically puts tradition on an equal footing with Scripture by employing the similes based on the Song of Moses ("doctrine" =
Scripture; "speech" = tradition),[578] so indicating that in certain respects
tradition has even some little advantage, at least temporally, over Scripture. Naturally this does not mean that tradition may overrule a scriptural utterance, or establish for itself a sacrosanct status which may
jeopardize the authority of Scripture. After all, one of the conditions of
the validity and trustworthiness of tradition is that "it should not be
contrary to Scripture (and to common sense)".[579] This dictum is even
more clearly affirmed in connection with a dispute over a case of consanguinity, in which contrary opinions seek support from Scripture,

---

[576] *Kāfi*, p. 271 (SLTh.A, p. 64), cf. my article *op. cit.* pp. 111, 146 (nn. 108-109),
163 (n. 230).

[577] *Ṭabbākh*, ff. 151b-156a (cf. *sup.* n. 337).

[578] *ibid.* f. 153b. جه الجامعه الخطبه في السلام عليه الرسول ذكر وقد ...
النقل والسمع وهو قوله عليه السلام יערף כמטר לקחי ותאזל כטל אמירתי
وما مثله علته السلام بكلامها اعلام الامه ان الحاجه داعيه الى النقل
كالحاجه الى السمع ...

This is even more clearly explained in f. 216b.

[579] *Ṭabbākh*, f. 152a (cf. n. 588 *inf.*).

tradition and analogy. *Abū-l Ḥasan* [580] opposes the extreme employment of analogy (in the name of tradition) as this would render all blood-relations of the one partner in marriage forbidden to those of the other partner. Such a view would entail the prohibition of two brothers marrying two sisters, and thus cause only distress and perplexity. Such an extreme practice "would have made tradition invalid, because it is not possible that the nation should transmit a tradition from the messengers of God which contradicts His Law."

The question now poses itself, how is it possible that a literalist exegesis like that of the Samaritans, which moreover imposes such severe curtailments upon the function of tradition, gives nevertheless such a high status to tradition? It has been noticed [581] that precisely in those places in the Pentateuch (*Ex.* xxv, 8, 40; xxvi, 30; xxvii, 8; *Num.* viii, 4) where the lack of details is most remarkable, is it stated that "God showed Moses". Whether it was the intention of the authors of Scripture to indicate that such items of information as were not mentioned explicitly were shown to Moses in a vision, or whether this notion was simply taken for granted by the exegetes, it opened a door to the concept of Oral Law. In just such cases as these where Scripture was evidently silent on matters of detail, the exegete was expected to rely upon Tradition, and thus all ambiguous and unelaborated points of the Law were subject to traditional elucidations. While the Samaritans did not speak of "Sinaitic Oral Revelation" as did the Rabbis,[582] the fact that their many Traditions have parallels in the Oral Law shows that, along with the written text, they had to admit exegetical details taken from an ancient common origin. This is obvious from their descriptions of ritual observances, which are greatly elaborated by non-Scriptural data, such as the laws of slaughtering, levitical purity, marriage [583] etc. The remarkable homogeneity of the Samaritan tradition, which despite its long history displays little alteration, novelty or innovation, likewise strengthens our impression that this self-consistency stems from a traditional system going back to remote antiquity. Admitteldly, there

---

[580] *ibid.* f. 45a. وكان يودى الي فساد استعمال الناقله فلا يجوز ان ينقـل

القوم عن رسول الله ما يخالف شريعته

[581] U. Cassuto, *A Commentary on the Book of Exodus* (Hebrew, Jerusalem, 1951), p. 222.

[582] Cf. next note.

[583] Abdel-Al, *A Comparative Study etc.*, pp. 155, 190, 280 respectively.

are differences in different ages in the treatment of the themes of this tradition, as regards length,[584] form, interest, and emphasis; but one can find hardly any serious contradictions or discrepancies among Samaritan scholars, separated, it may be, by many centuries.

In this connection it is highly significant that even the most cherished principle of Samaritan religion and the one which persistently forms the bone of contention with other groups, the Sanctity of Hargerizim, depends, apart from some hints in Scripture, very largely on the strength of oral law: "God would not have told Moses to command the people to offer sacrifices and to bring tithes etc. unless He had *told* them where to bring them".[585] All those rubrics regarding the celebration of the pilgrimages, so clearly defined,[586] yet without scriptural foundation, must of course be entirely dependent on oral tradition. One may even go further and maintain that, even in the transmission of their written heritage, the oral factor is of paramount importance, inasmuch as their reading tradition, which chiefly gives the sense and thus influences the written form, shapes the exegesis on which both practices and doctrines are based.[587]

There is no surer way of understanding the significance of the Oral tradition than to reflect on the Samaritans' own estimate of their Scripture. This is regarded — as we have seen on previous occasions — as a final and divinely authorized revelation to which nothing can at any time be added, and yet it is destined to serve as a perpetual guide and inspiration for all generations to come. Since its sanctity and perfection demand that it shall neither contain ambiguous passages nor be conducive to misunderstanding, its intelligibility must have been complete from its very revelation. Whatever in tradition is not stated explicitly in writing must have been conveyed to men from the *same Authority* by oral channels. Thus we may understand the age-old principles of tradition as being by their nature directly associated with and inseparable from the written word. Upon these principles four strict conditions are

---

[584] Taking for example the rules about the water to be used for purification, despite the long treatment of the *Kāfi* (cf. *sup.* nn. 572f.) and the very much abbreviated one of the *Ṭabbākh* (f. 55a, SLTh.A, pp. 97f.), they are essentially the same.

[585] Vilmar, *Abulfathi annales Sam.*, pp. 94f., cf. *Kāfi*, pp. 31, 219 (= SLTh.A, pp. 2, 40), *Ṭabbakh* f. 79b (SLTh.A, p. 120) etc.

[586] *Kāfi*, p. 223 (= SLTh.A, p. 43).

[587] cf. *sup.* n. 110.

superimposed [588] with the object of ensuring the genuineness of any tradition: (1) It must be transmitted by a great multitude who were actual contemporaries of Moses, receiving this tradition directly from him, (2) The transmitters must form a direct, unbroken and successive dynasty, whose members possess an indisputable familiarity with this tradition, (3) It must meet with the unanimous agreement of the transmitters, (4) It must not be contradicted by the plain meaning of the (Written) Law.

The usual concept of 'Oral Law', as possessing a great measure of freedom and independence from the written word, and even, in certain cases, of superiority to it, cannot be applied to Samaritan tradition. One does not find in Samaritan tradition any attempt at reshaping or even reassessing the Biblical themes. Admittedly, there are new elements in the tradition which originate from exegesis. However, these elements are not expressly invented and then pressed into service in order to make Scripture better adapted to the outlook of later generations. Unlike allegories, which are mainly devised to bridge the gap between antiquated documents and progressive views, Samaritan traditional exegesis is built upon organic thinking, which always develops naturally out of the concepts inherent in the expounded texts. On very much the same lines as that of the Rabbis,[589] this exegesis is securely built on theological tenets and an organic thinking which attempt to harmonize the several teachings of Scripture in order to sort out the alleged 'discrepancies'. The Samaritan tradition, however, never claims for itself the privileges which the Pharisaic Oral Law always commands; and therefore its subordination to Scripture is complete, and there is no possibility at all of an Oral Law being at variance with Scripture.[590]

How much in the way of a common origin may we assume for these oral traditions of the various groups? It is an undeniable fact that some of the traditions of one group, not excluding their minute details, have

---

[588] *Ṭabbākh*, p. 152a وشروط صحته اربعه الاول منها يجب ان يكون ماخوذا
عن جماعة كثيره العدد ينتهون الى رسول الله عاصروه واخذوا عنه الشرط
الثانى يكون الناقله له الخلف منهم ليعدوه ويحصل لهم العلم به ضروريا
الشرط الثالث يجمعون على الموافقه عليه الشرط الرابع لا يفسد من جهة
العقل ولا من جهة السمع

[589] Heinemann, *Darkhei ha-Aggadah*, pp. 163f.
[590] cf. *sup.* nn. 45, 504-505 and text there.

close 'parallels' in the traditions or Oral Law of other groups, a fact
which on a first approach certainly points to a common origin in early
antiquity.[591] In particular, those rigoristic practices associated with the
laws of Sabbath and other observances, on which many 'sectarian'
groups prided themselves as being signs of piety, received zealous support
even in early Pharisaism prior to the absolute dominance of the School
of Hillel.[592] Nevertheless, sweeping generalizations in this respect may
be very misleading, since one has to reckon with the fact that in early
pre-Rabbinic times and prior to the stern control of the academies,
several varieties of opinion might have co-existed within the proto-
Pharisaic groups; and in point of fact, local Palestinian rigoristic views
(very similar to those of the early sects) were prevalent among the Rabbis
down to late Tannaitic times. The lenient views of the House of Hillel,
which eventually became the only 'normative' forces on which the whole
Pharisaic system, including its hermeneutical principles, took its stand,
were based on an entirely different tradition. For these reasons one
cannot speak of direct influences on either side. For instance, where one
finds closely similar rites, as in the laws of Sabbath,[593] one may be faced
with parallel developments in which each one of the particular traditions
is instrumental in shaping the norms in line with the principles followed
by the group.

Although there are indeed occasionally some striking similarities,
these should not be exaggerated. If we find, for example, that the Samaritan calendar, with its Ṣimmuth sixty days before Passover and the
Feast of Booths, paralleled in the Jewish calendar by two minor holidays
(15th of Shebhaṭ and 15th of Abh respectively), this in itself by no means
proves dependence.[594] Although it has been advocated that the characteristics of both calendars, namely the Samaritan and the Jewish, betray
uniform general principles, modified only in matters of detail,[595] this
is not borne out by facts. The divergencies are too great and far outweigh
the few and random similarities; and moreover they evince rather a
change in the underlying traditional and exegetical principles than mere
differences in detail.[596] Furthermore, we have seen on previous occasions

---

[591] cf. my article in *JJS* IX (1958), pp. 131-137.

[592] M. Guttmann, *Eine Untersuchung über den Geltungsumfang etc.*, pp. 39f.

[593] cf. my article *ALUOS* VI (1969), pp. 111-113, 145-148 (nn. 105-124, especially
the first and the last note).

[594] Abdel-Al, *A Comparative Study etc.*, pp. 313ff.

[595] P.R. Weiss, "Abū'l-Hasan's Discourse etc.", *BJRL* XXX (1946), pp. 145ff.

[596] cf. n. 594 *sup*.

that, even in the Pharisaic fold itself, there existed traditions which did not conform with the views of the 'normative' majority.[597] Although Samaritan practices may on occasion resemble those of certain of such other groups, the explanation of this fact is to be sought, not so much in an ancient common source, as in similar exegetical devices used in common by the relevant groups. To take the instance of Marqah's enumeration of the three cardinal sins (murder, idolatry and adultery), which appears to be taken from the Rabbis,[598] this already occurs in the Book of Jubilees (Ch. VII) which assuredly cannot be attributed to the 'normative' type of Pharisaism. Thus while certain oral material may of course go back to a 'common origin' which may itself in part have been transmitted from ancient times together with the written text, by various groups accustomed to expounding the same (or a similar) text in an exegesis not distantly removed from the original oral one, no similarities can in any sense betray mutual borrowings. It has always to be borne in mind that each group unfailingly uses its 'oral tradition' in such a way as to justify its own doctrinal standpoint, to strengthen its own position, and to defeat that held by any other.[599]

Despite our contention that Samaritan 'Oral Law' is not in general the product of wholesale borrowing from the Rabbis, but on the contrary an independent development of similar exegetical motives at work on similar problems, one cannot turn a blind eye on certain cases of outright plagiarism. One may even find in Samaritan literature whole sections taken from non-Pentateuchal Scripture,[600] without the writer's disclosing, of course, that they were taken from the 'Scriptures of the Infidels'. Such 'anonymous' borrowing mays be detected more especially in traditions which were transmitted by oral means. However, no generalizations can be made at this state of research, and each individual tradition will be judged on its own merits.

J. TRADITION VERSUS SCRIPTURE

In the course of our previous discussions we have acquired ample evidence that in the Samaritan religion there is no tension whatsoever between tradition and Scripture. It seems unquestionable that neither

---

[597] cf. my article *op. cit.* pp. 99, 131 (n. 12).

[598] cf. *sup.* n. 482.

[599] cf. Gaster, *Eschatology*, pp. 32f.

[600] Ben-Hayyim, *The literary & Oral Trad. etc.*, I, p. ק״ב.

of these two major components of their religious foundation was ever held to be entirely independent of the other; just as the authenticity of Scripture depended entirely upon its faithful transmission within the living tradition, so did the whole content of this living tradition (oral, ceremonial, and exegetical) derive its binding authority from Scripture. This interdependence is viewed not as a matter of general consonance in respect of the fundamental rules of doctrine only, but is in fact constantly viewed as a regulative force in making specific decisions. Thus in the case of the rules of "washing",[601] derived partly from (scriptural) laws and partly from 'tradition', the traditional customs themselves are referred to scriptural details taken from the narratives of the Patriarchs, (*Gen.* xviii, 4; *ibid.* xliii, 31 etc.). Here one may find the explanation for the close harmony which exists between the two sources of their religion, viz. that, although tradition precedes the (scriptural) decrees, it does not assume an independent authority; and not only does it not surpass in importance the written word, but it is at all times dependent on it, deriving its compulsive force from constantly renewed harmonizations with scriptural elements. This is also the reason why often it is not at all easy to determine which elements of the tenets originate from 'tradition' and which from Scripture. Such is also the background of the regulations concerning ablutions before prayers, or before setting oneself to read in the Law.[602] Although these likewise are regarded as originating partly from tradition and partly from Scripture, some (like those to do with washing the hands and feet) which are usually considered 'traditional' are nevertheless fortified by a 'decree' (*Ex.* xxx, 21) providing for the harsh punishment of those who profane those rites, and thus underlining their solemnity.

One is often puzzled by this relationship of the oral tradition to the written word, since the boundaries are not clearly defined and it is hard to find where biblical law ends and where oral tradition begins; one often gets the impression that the two territories are much more closely allied than has commonly been thought. Even a few examples may serve to illustrate this close interdependence. To take, then, one of the laws of the Passover Sacrifice: it is enjoined without any scriptural support

---

[601] *Kāfi*, p. 45 (SLTh.A, p. 9).

[602] *ibid.* p. 47 (SLTh.A, p. 10). There are also other cases there is no clear cut demarcation line between the 'tradition' and the 'scriptural' law, like in the case of prayers (*Kāfi*, p. 54) etc. In the last case it is stated that matter pertaining to a certain fixed time are considered a (scriptural) decree. However this rule cannot be worked out consistently.

that the blood of the victim is to be collected in a vessel.[603] This seems
to be an oral traditions from which the logical inference has been deduced
that this regulation is essential if the law is to be properly complied
with, because if blood is spilt on the ground it congeals. It is interesting
to note that the Rabbis have a similar oral tradition of "receiving the
blood in a vessel" (in order to sprinkle it on the altar).[604] Despite the
tempting assumption that both groups derive this oral tradition from
a common "ancient halakhah", an assumption which might indeed be
plausibly justified on the grounds that, at least from the Samaritan side,
no biblical verses are offered in support of this 'tradition' and that the
reason propounded is rather a later rationalization of an unexplained
custom, there is actually very little evidence to bear out such a claim.
The Talmudic injunction has an entirely different purpose, namely to
connect the Sacrifice with the historical existence of the altar and the
Sanctuary, while for the Samaritans it purports to be "an ordinance for
ever" (*Ex.* xii, 14, 17) and implies for them, the obligation of its perpetual observance irrespective of any dependence on the Sanctuary or
sprinkling of the blood upon the altar. Furthermore, by a deeper insight
into Scripture one may come to realise that such a 'tradition' may
well have originated from exegesis. This consideration is particularly
relevent to our present investigation because it fortifies our contention
regarding the total mutual interdependence of tradition and Scripture.
The tradition of gathering the blood of the Passover Offering in a vessel,
in order, as is claimed, "to carry out the commandment" properly,
is undoubtedly a reference to the sprinkling of the blood upon the
doorposts (*Ex.* xii, 22). Now, this text was by an analogical process
compared with references to other sacrifices where it is explicitly stated
that the blood is to be gathered in a vessel (e.g. *Ex.* xxiv, 6, 8 etc.). It
seems that, in this case at least, the 'traditions' arise from straightforward biblical exegesis.

Another example is the fixed time-limit (of a whole solar calendar-
year) for the Naziriteship.[605] Although it is here stated (as in many
other cases) that this regulation is based on three recognized principles,
namely, on tradition, logical inference and the Law, the burden of

---

[603] This is the fourteenth of the sixty special regulations of the Passover offering.
Ṭabbākh, f. 62b (SLTh.A, p. 104). cf. *inf.* nn. 610-611.

[604] *Pesaḥim* V, 2 and 6; Babyl, *ibid.* 64a f. We cannot enter here into the intricate
problem of how this tradition was connected to scripture. cf. *Tosaphoth* on *Pesaḥim*
64b, s.v. אתיא זריקה etc.

[605] *Kāfi*, p. 238 (SLTh.A, pp. 53f.). In this case there is no Rabbinic parallel.

evidence really rests on exegesis, often of the most bizarre types of Gemaṭria. From this, and from other examples,[606] it becomes obvious that exegesis occupies a very prominent place in Samaritan 'tradition'.

We may infer from the treatment of Scripture itself how 'tradition' is in fact treated: as in the case of Scripture, it is postulated that its Divine origin precludes any possibility of discrepancy in the text, let alone contradiction, so that, if each tradition shares the same Divine authority, it too must be free from any conflict with Scripture or with other traditions. Any apparent or at first sight 'real' contradiction has to be harmonized for the sake of strengthening the doctrines of the group. Often 'traditional' exegesis originates from such efforts towards harmonization. In Rabbinic literature similarly this eagerness to reconcile contradictory verses is a common feature [607] and it certainly contributes a new ethos to the development of the Oral Law. We have seen on many occasions that this is also the practice of the Samaritans, comprising the harmonizing both of contradictory scriptures and of Scripture with tradition. Marqah is particularly fond of such exercises.[608] Naturally such harmonizations normally result in verbal compromises. It has to be stressed, however, that these compromises do not amount to leniency or lighthearted treatment of 'tradition'.

One of the outstanding examples of such compromises in 'traditional' law is the dowry of the widows, which was fixed at half that of the virgins.[609] It has always to be remembered that the whole institution

---

[606] The Samaritan practice of purification by fire is also based on 'tradition' (*Kāfi*, p. 156, cf. Abdel-Al, *A Comparative Study etc.*, pp. 522f., 687f), which however is based upon *Num.* xxxi, 23, although no scriptural basis is adduced in this connection. Similarly the diagnosis of certain cases of leprosy in the *Ṭabbākh* [cf. P.R. Weis, "Abū'l-Ḥasan... on ... Leprosy etc.", *BJRL* XXXII (1950/51), p. 132], introduced without scriptural support as 'tradition' are derived from exegesis.

[607] Rosenblatt, *The Interpretation etc.*, p. 2, n. 7.

[608] cf. *sup.* nn. 531ff. A classical example of such harmonization is his treatment of Asher who, despite being of the children of the 'handmaids' and receiving the curse upon Mount Ebal, was nevertheless blessed by Moses (*Deut.* xxxiii, 24). In the same context he also harmonizes the contradictions about the role of the proselyte in the Blessing of Hargerizim (*Memar Marqah*, ed. Macdonald, I, pp. 61f. = II, pp. 95f.). Unfortunately, because of the length of this midrash, detailed exposition must be postponed.

[609] *Kāfi*, pp. 225f. (cf. Abdel-Al, *op. cit.* pp. 601, 711). It seems, however, that the exact 'minimum' amount was not fixed (as in the case of the Rabbis, cf. *Mekhilta*, *ad. loc.*; *Kethubhoth*, I, 4; V, 1; *Bab.* 10a, 38a; etc.) but left to the discretion of the celebrant in each generation.

of dowry as an indispensible part of the marriage ceremony, without which the latter is not valid, is in essence a traditional requirement. Nonetheless, here again there is a scriptural warrant in *Ex.* xxii, 16-17, which although it does not deal directly with marriage, lends itself to being used by the traditional exegete as an analogy by which to establish the 'traditional' practice in this case too. The same verses which speak of the "dowry of the virgins" suggest that there existed also a dowry of similar type. In other words, even such "compromises" in the traditional lore still depend upon exegesis and upon biblical warrants being found for them.

In the view of the loose method of recording traditions in pre-11th century Samaritanism, prior to the great legislative activities in the Arabic language and when these traditions mainly depended (save for some sporadic and random marginal notes on the biblical texts) upon oral transmission, the real possibility of consequent lapses of memory, and thus of modifications, must be taken into account. Especially in fields where there was as yet no established practice, or where this could not be carried out because it depended on the presence of the Sanctuary, the oral transmission might well have failed owing to faulty memory. Ordinary matters of precedure, frequently practised, were guarded with the utmost care by the priesthood and the learned lay-leaders, whose utterances were heeded by the people as the very words of the Law. Even in such instances, however, there could have been some forgetfulness, especially following on a state of emergency and during persecutions. In later times when their traditions had all been committed to writing, such persecutions still caused great confusion. To take one example only, when they were prevented for forty years from celebrating the Passover Offering upon Hargerizim, and were forced to perform it in their homes,[610] some details of the cultus could certainly have been confused. In this case we are fortunate in having direct evidence [611] that certain details of the prescribed ordinances (including the ceremony of the blood, mentioned earlier) were indeed in later times missed out, and most probably as a result of the forty years' cessation of public sacrifice upon the Mount itself.

Notwithstanding such few lapses, the general picture which emerges

---

[610] cf. Jeremias, "Die Passahfeier etc.", *ZATW, Beiheft 59*, p. 83.

[611] *ibid.* p. 87, n. 1. Jeremias attributes the lapse to the fact that the passover coincided with the Muslim festival, however it seems more likely that the omission was caused by forgetfulness of traditions. cf. *sup.* nn. 603f.

from a comparison of their practices, as gathered from the extra-Samaritan literature of early times and the later Samaritan codices compiled many centuries later, shows that such occasional modifications are rather the exception, while in general these Samaritan practices seem to be stable, even static, and exempt from any great changes.[612] The explanation for this situation surely turns largely on the 'fossilization' of the Samaritans' religion in consequence of the authoritarian vigilance of their leaders;[613] but it is certainly not permissible to minimize the all-pervasive influence of their 'tradition' itself, which by its own characteristics worked powerfully for self-preservation. The fact that all oral tradition was so closely linked with Scripture saved its transmitters from unresolvable confusion and irretrievable forgetfulness.

One may even assert that the content and form of Samaritan midrashim are greatly influenced by this close proximity of text to tradition. Although both the Rabbinic and the Samaritan traditions depend largely upon an exegesis based on 'organic thinking' rather than on strictly rational deductions, the latter regularly remains much closer to the literal sense of the Scripture than the former. Evidently the major reason for this situation is the Samaritans' consciously strict adherence to this literal sense, while the Rabbis feel free to consciously deviate from literalness whenever the 'Oral Law' and its developments prompt it. However, even in the Rabbinic Midrashim, the interpretation of the Scripture is kept within the general framework of its original literal meaning and the outline demanded by the Biblical text is faithfully preserved. Even when analogies or other hermeneutical devices are applied to the whole subject, they are grounded quite squarely in logical premises. It is only when it comes to details and to the analysis of the text into its elements, and then mainly when pressing these elements into service as 'supports' for the 'Oral Law, that highly sophisticated symbolical devices, allusions and intimations are used.[614]

As opposed to this practice, the Samaritan 'oral tradition' is not sufficiently removed from Scripture to allow such a free treatment even in the matter of details. Although the employment of the type of exegesis known as 'organic thinking' is not of course ruled out by the Samaritans, nevertheless, this is employed sparingly, and even the

---

[612] cf. *inf.* para (k).

[613] The *Kāfi* has a whole chapter on the Priesthood (pp. 5-27) dealing mainly with this subject.

[614] M. Guttmann, *Die Anlehnung etc.*, p. 32.

exposition of details is closely bound up with the general sense of the context in which they appear.

This may be illustrated by the exegesis of *Lev.* x, 9-11. According to the Rabbis, this prohibition of the drinking of wine by the Priests includes not only priests while ministering, but any lay-teacher while rendering legal or ritual decision ("and that ye may put a difference...") or while teaching ("that ye may teach..."). Hence the details of verses 10-11 are understood as intimations embracing all the various aspects of 'Oral Law'.[615] In Samaritan tradition there is no such outright extension of this text as to find in it intimations of external matters, but rather the details are employed to clarify the principle of the prohibition itself. The *Kāfi* [616], adding here a traditional restriction on the priests by indicating that "when ye go into" may in fact mean "before or after coming to the Sanctuary", remains nevertheless strictly within the limits of the literal sense of the verse. Even in the *Tabbākh*,[617] where the expression "and that ye may put a difference between the holy, etc." is extended to include the prohibition of the partaking of intoxicating drinks by any person who is bidden to observe any 'holiness' and to a much greater degree than is done by the Rabbis, the exposition still remains strictly within the limits of the biblical sense.

There is to be sure no lack of examples in many other fields to show this independent character of Samaritan tradition and exegesis. The mere fact that the results reached are so often different from those of the Rabbis, proves that in each group the innate vitality is a greater directive force for its own tradition than any supposed "common ancient heritage". Very often the same biblical sources if diligently expanded in accordance with different 'traditions' result in diametrically opposite practices.[618]

---

[615] Siphra Shemini (*ad. loc.*, ed. Weiss, f. 46b); cf. *Kerithoth* 13b.

[616] p. 230 (SLTh.A, p. 48). [The prohibition of wine on the Sabbath is taken for granted by the *Kāfi*, cf. pp. 336f.; SLTh.A, pp. 74f.]

[617] f. 31b; (SLTh.A, p. 87). [cf. my article in *ALUOS* VI (1969), pp. 112f., 114f.; 147f. (n. 121), 150 (n. 134).] In another place (f. 192a) the *Tabbākh* employs the biblical expression "put difference" as one of the aids to determine the concept of 'a day' as regards to impurity. However, this is still within the limits of the general sense which determines the ministerial functions of the priests.

[618] The law of the 'Hebrew slave' (*Kāfi*, pp. 308f.; SLTh.A, p. 55f.), the Law of the Sabbath rest, and especially the prohibition of using fire (*ibid.* pp. 332f.; SLThA, pp. 71f.) and many others, while emphasizing the same scriptural sources as used by the Rabbis, result in different practices from that of the Rabbis.

For the aforised reason one has to be extremely wary on discovering
'parallels' between Samaritan observances and those of the Rabbis, of
jumping to hasty conclusions of 'interdependence'. The special genius
of the exegetical methods of either group will not permit the blind acceptance of a 'tradition' based on principles alien to the group. It goes
without saying that the unguarded allegation that the Samaritans were
wide open to all kinds of external influences [619] is not borne out by the
sources. Even in the very few cases where the Talmudic sources and the
Church Fathers agree in their assessment of the Samaritans, one may
still ponder whether this is not rather a matter of sweeping generalization. With regard, for example, to the case of the alleged denial of the
resurrection by the Samaritans, only a careful re-examination of the
midrashic sources is competent to determine whether acceptance of hits
doctrine in their later literature (since Byzantine times) is in reality an
innovation, or whether on the other hand the external sources alleging
the Samaritans' total denial of the afterlife are guilty of gross exaggeration arising from the fact that the Samaritans did not accept their *own*
doctrine of resurrection.[620]

Obviously, there exists the further possibility that the Samaritans
safeguard themselves when adopting extraneous and alien influences by
constantly seeking for these novel elements some firm support in the
biblical text.[621] Had this been the case, the inner conflict within their own
literature would of course yield some clear clues to such a procedure.
However, neither the internal comparison of their own traditions,
stretching over a long period of many centuries nor the comparison
of this relatively homogeneous body of material with external sources
touching upon Samaritan traditions serves to substantiate any such
supposition.

Not only in matters of practice and doctrine is this strong bond
between Scripture and Tradition maintained, but also in Aggadic
subjects. What seems at first glance a legend borrowed from outside
sources may not seldom be traced back to the Samaritans' original
midrashic expositions securely built on Scripture.

We may take as an illustration one of those legends about the Israelite
children in Egypt which seem at the outset to be borrowed from Rabbinic

---

[619] Wreschner, *Sam. Traditionen*, pp. VIIff.

[620] Merx, *Der Messias etc.*, p. 44.

[621] cf. n. 619 *sup.* and J. Macdonald, *The Theology of the Sam.*, p. 449.

sources.[622] Although in Marqah [623] it is based upon the same verse (*Deut.* xxxii, 13), as in the Rabbis, its midrashic elements are nevertheless entirely independent of the Rabbinic sources. It may even be asserted that the particular form of the Samaritan text of the Pentateuch lends support to the version of the legend as it is reproduced by Marqah. The legend is built on the Egyptian decree ordering the killing of the Israelite boys and the saving of the girls (*Ex.* i, 16; 22),[624] upon which Marqah greatly elaborates thus:

> The pregnant women were like wild beasts (Midrash on *Ex.* i, 19). When the time for their delivery came, they went far away into the desert... They examined the child born and if it was a daughter they entered with her (into the city), but if it was a son they wrapped him in a coarse garment and left him in the desert — as Hagar did: for she said, '*Let me not look upon the death of the child*' (*Gen.* xxi, 16). The Merciful King sent the angels to suckle him *with honey from the hard stone and oil from the flinty rock* (*Deut.* xxxii, 13). And they (i.e. the angels) surrounded him, as He said, '*He strengthened* [625] *him... He encircled him, He cared for him*' (*Deut.* xxxii, 10) until he grew and was weaned. He educated [626] him in His goodness and he came to the house of his parents.

From the continuation of the Midrash as it is woven by Marqah upon harmonization,[627] it becomes quite obvious that his particular system is entirely original, and that this supposed parallel with the Talmudic legends is in fact of a coincidental nature, or derived independently by similar techniques from the same Scripture.

Often it is thought that expressions denoting 'universalism'[628] cannot originate with Marqah and must therefore be of foreign influence. Such

---

[622] cf. *Soṭah* 11b., where this legend is greatly expanded with the help of non-Pentateuchal verses of which the Samaritans could not avail themselves.

[623] *Memar Marqah* (ed. Macdonald), I, pp. 103f. (= II, p. 172).

[624] The Samaritan text suggests that the decree was aimed at the Hebrews only (הילד לעברים *Ex.* i, 22) and hence the miracle of saving these infants from death is even more logical.

[625] Samaritan Pentateuch יאמיצהו = encouraged him. cf. also other changes in the same verse. It is quite common in Samaritan literature to transfer to Angels functions attributed to God.

[626] A paraphrase of ויבננהו (*Deut.* xxxii, 10).

[627] Marqah compares this Divine favour to the Manna, on which it was stated that it tasted "like wafers made in *honey*" (*Ex.* xvi, 31) and "like cakes baked with *oil*", *Num.* xi, 8. Similarly Marqah's exhortations against the *hardness* of their heart (*Deut.* xv, 7) and *stiff-neckedness* (*ibid.* x, 16), playing on the *motif* of Rock = hardness, stiffness, is typical to his general midrashic system.

[628] "It is good for us to purify our heart and know the truth... and then teach *all nations*. Thus our Lord has taught us that we possess light that *illuminates the world*...", *Memar Marqah* (ed. Macdonald), I, p. 134 (= II, p. 218). cf. *sup.* n. 328.

expressions, however, are always closely related to the privilege of possessing the Torah. This shows that they are midrash, built on the acknowledged wisdom and understanding of the Israelites "in the sight of the
peoples" (*Deut.* iv, 5-8). This being the case, the need does not arise to
postulate any influence from the prophets, and accordingly 'parallels'
to other external literary sources must be quite accidental.

The overzealous hunt for 'parallels' in Rabbinic sources to the
midrashim cited by Marqah has been rightly criticized.[629] After all, we
have to bear in mind that similar traditions may very well originate
from the common lore of the country, shared by Jews and Samaritans
alike.

K. SAMARITAN CONSERVATISM

The rigid exclusiveness of the Samaritans was dependent upon a
priestly type of legalism which was jealously guarded by their leadership
with the primary object of the meticulous fulfilment of the Law. Only
through this constant supervision by the priestly hierarchy, responsible
for the transmission both of their written Law and of their tradition,
could their age-old exegesis remain in its fully stable condition, without
being endangered by major upheavals or being subjected to the far-
reaching effects of external influences.

While other sects, like the Essenes and the Dead Sea Scroll Sect,
were also based on a similarly rigoristic priestly organization, this was
not the only factor in their sectarian background. It seems undeniable
that a certain syncretistic tendency in these other sects welded together
trends of diverse origin. Along with this rigoristic priestly trend went
another and in part opposing 'prophetic' trend, which exerted a strong
influence upon these sects, kindling in them a deep interest in 'prophe-
sying'.[630] The outcome of this amalgamation of trends was that, although
in the matter of halakhah the rigoristic approach was strictly kept,[631]
in the matters of doctrine and aggadah their prophetic type of exegesis,
the *Pesher*, exerted a reformistic and progressive type of theological
influence, leading to constantly developing eschatological speculations.[632]
It is not entirely impossible that the Dead Sea Scroll sect's later extension

---

[629] Hildesheimer, *Marqah's Buch der Wunder etc.*, pp. 7 and 15.

[630] M. Black, *The Scrolls etc.*, p. 118. cf. my article in *ALUOS* VI (1969), pp. 98ff.,
121ff., 158f. (nn. 193f.).

[631] cf. my article *op. cit.* nn. 207-208.

[632] Bruce, *Biblical Exegesis in the Qumran Texts*, pp. 7, 11f.

of the application of this practice of the Pesher to the legal sphere introduced, concurrently, conflicting legal interpretations, thus creating
splinter-groups with their own idiosyncrasies and contributing towards
the final disintegration of this and other sects.[633]

Similar dangers again were very much a preoccupation of early Christianity, when expressions like "Seek and ye shall find" (*Matthew* vii, 7)
were commonly understood by enthusiastic sectarian and heretical
exegetes as a general licence to apply free interpretations, in order to
extract all kinds of gnostic ideas from the Bible. Tertullian,[634] fully aware
of these dangerous tendencies by which the very existence of the Church
was threatened, found himself forced to counteract them by limiting
the scope of exegetical freedom.

In early Judaism itself, prior to the sectarian strifes, the control of
'tradition' and the interpretation of the Law were entirely in the hands
of the priest.[635] In later times and under Greek domination, when the
institution of the Sanhedrin came into being, this central authority,
which itself in its early years experienced a considerable priestly influence,[636] progressively took over these responsibilities. The struggle for
power between the priesthood and the ever more influential lay-leaders
ended as we know eventually with the almost complete victory of the
latter. Nevertheless, the establishment of this central authority, despite
its being headed by the Patriarch, prevented the anarchy which befel
othere religions as a result of the decline of their priesthood.

In Alexandria, where the Jewish community consistently followed
traditions dating back to a time when the priesthood was the sole custodian of the interpretation of the Law, the priests continued to function
in that capacity until after the time of Philo.[637] It is entirely feasible to

---

[633] cf. my article *op. cit.* pp. 122, 160 (nn. 208-9).

[634] *Praescriptione Haereticorum*, VIII f.

[635] Krochmal, *More Neboche Ha-seman*, pp. 164-5; Seeligmann, "Voraussetzungen
der Midraschexegese", *Congress Vol.*, 1953 (Supplements VT I), p. 177; Gerhardsson,
Memory and Manuscript, p. 86, n. 5.

[636] Krochmal, *op. cit.* pp. 186-7; Geiger, *Urschrift etc.*, p. 116. cf. previous note.

[637] Wolfson, *Philo*, I, p. 144, II, pp. 341f.; cf. Heinemann, *Philons... Bildung*,
pp. 181f. Heinemann's attempt to show that Philo's identification of the 'Judges'
with the priests denotes Greek influence, and that "judgment" (*Deut.* xvii, 8), did not
include the rendering of halakhic decisions, is unconvincing. This was done (against
his own general system) to bring Philo nearer to Rabbinic halakhah. The same applies
to Belkin (*Philo and the Oral Law*, pp. 190f.) who tries to harmonize Philo's description
of the Sanhedrin with the Rabbinic tradition about its president (The Patriarch) and
his deputy. The whole unrealistic description of Philo goes back to an ancient tradition when the Sanhedrin was ruled by the Priesthood.

affirm that the disappearance of this interpretative authority of the priesthood brought with it the disintegration of this Alexandrian type of Hellenistic Judaism, which in all likelihood was partly assimilated to other Hellenistic philosophical groups and partly absorbed into the fold of Rabbinic Judaism.

Amongst the Rabbis, where opposing exegetical traditions could legitimately coexist, there was nevertheless a tendency to coordinate the variant tangible results of these intellectual pursuits into a certain pattern of 'orthopraxis'. Whatever religious powers were already provided by the Rabbis as alternatives to those of the lapsed priestly leadership, were vested with the utmost binding authority.[638] This authority, fortified by Rabbinical enactments, subsequently established the so-called "Jewish Self-government" during the Middle Ages,[639] and without doubt eventually preserved Judaism from disintegration into numerous sects.

The Karaites show an entirely different approach by having neither a priestly authority nor any other authoritative institution which might replace it. Although they continued with the traditions of the priesthood, this was deprived of any effective controlling power (as was the case with the Rabbanites). Even their most outstanding leaders and reformers were quite unable to fill the vacuum created by the lack of a centralized authority possessing an undisputed control over the modes of exegesis. Such a deficiency must always cause a state of anarchy in the realm of legislation. At certain periods there were hardly any two Karaites practising the same customs or able to agree on any one mode of Biblical exegesis.[640] But even amongst the Karaites, the above-mentioned 'progressive' force, which ensured the constant reinterpretation of Scripture in various manners, had to give way to another of their chief sectarian characteristics, namely to their inveterate conservatism. So they instinctively rid themselves of their early disruptive tendencies

---

[638] Albeck, *Introduction to the Mishnah*, p. 61 (cf. for further literature, *ibid.* nn. 33, 34).

[639] S. Assaf, *Bate ha-Din ve-Sidrehem aḥare ḥatimat ha-Talmud* (Hebrew, Jerusalem 1923), pp. 11f.; 25ff.; 51f. L. Finkelstein, *Jewish Self-government in the Middle Ages* (NY. 1924), pp. 20f., 111f., 148f., 150f.

[640] Gottlober, *Bikkoret etc.*, p. 76. It is still not without doubt whether Karaites just followed Anan in his call "Search the Scripture", or whether they were also in possession of earlier tradition. (cf. Wieder, *Judean Scrolls etc.*, pp. 53f., 62f. and cf. *sup.* nn. 630-633). At any rate, the freedom of the individual exegete multiplied the differences of opinions.

which had led them to totally disregard any central authority. By this step they followed the Rabbanites in setting up deliberately a sternly autocratic 'self-governemnt'. This was in fact put into the hands of the Courts, which by the power of excommunication wielded enormous disciplinary powers.[641] Only through this self-imposed change of attitude and policy was it possible to prevent the total disintegration of the Sect.

If we now compare the absolute priestly authority amongst the Samaritans, possessed as it was of all its autocratic and legalistic characteristics, with the leadership of other groups, we shall understand how their extreme conservatism caused, and was bound to cause, the almost total immovability of their religion. This total authority, with its mandate for the sole and absolute guardianship of the law, its 'traditions' and exegesis, prevented any multiplicity of views from arising amongst the faithful. On examining Samaritan sources we are often struck by the fact that there are hardly any differences of outlook even amongst authors separated by many centuries. Maybe it was this very situation which encouraged later Samaritan authors to incorporate in their own work whole sections from the writings of their predecessors without any acknowledgement,[642] since they may well have felt that anyhow all of them virtually reproduced the very *same* tradition. As opposed to the Rabbis with their 'Oral Law' and their pride in its 'novellae',[643] emphasizing as they did that, despite the essential changelessness of the tradition, there was a constant fund of novel ideas, the Samaritans were no less pround of the static and rigid character of their own tradi- tion. They may even have considered this static character and this inflexible changelessness as further evidence for the validity of their religion.

It has, moreover, to be pointed out that the fact that lay religious leaders coexisted with the priesthood and in such a way that the former were often in a position to outshine the latter by their intellectual superiority, did not at all diminish the status of the priesthood.[644] As

---

[641] Benjamin Nahawendi, *Masa'ath Benyamin*, f. 2a; Hadassi, *Eshkol ha-Kofer* (Alphabetha 371), p. 147a.

[642] Gaster, *Eschatology*, p. 67.

[643] *Ḥaggigah* 3a. א״א לביה״מ בלא חידוש

[644] It is also very doubtful whether the lay leadership has any direct connection with "producing authoritative compilations, which are put on the same level as the Bible". (cf. *sup.* n. 324 and text there). Such opinions were based on those of Geiger (cf. *sup.* Part I, para (b, c and d) about the Israelite-priestly group as against Pharisaic- Judahistic one. The fallacy of such sweeping generalizations is evident from Philo

long as the order of the priesthood upheld its prerogatives by adhering to the established manner of fulfilling its manifold functions, the lay-leaders (including those who surpassed by their learning their priestly colleagues) were regarded only as auxiliaries to the unchallenged priestly leadership.

Despite our lengthy discussion, which we have pursued (in Part I) in an endeavour to substantiate this presentation from Samaritan sources, we cannot refrain at this time from adding a chiding note to discourage certain widely circulated theories as to the Zadokite character of the Samaritan priesthood. It is true that the Tolidah [645] mentions a certain Zadok in the long course of its priestly genealogy; this, however, in itself certainly does not prove the point at issue.[646] It is even less convincing to argue that the function of the priesthood in the field of education and in rendering legal decisions resembles in any way that of "keeping the covenant" "according to the sons of Zadok", as it appears in the *Zadokite fragments*.[647] One fails to find in Samaritan literature any echo of a 'mystery cult' or a priestly 'esoteric' teaching.[648] The truth is that Samaritan priestly rigorism is based on their own tradition, emanating from their own Pentateuchal exegesis.

The source for the accepted precedence of the priestly authority over that of the lay-leaders is found in *Deut.* xvi, 18, translated and understood as "judges and scribes", and indicating by its very sequence that the priestly "judges" precede in significance also the lay "scribes" or teachers.[649]

---

and the practice of the Alexandrians (*sup.* n. 637), who otherwise follow the Pharisaic line. On the role of the lay leader, cf. *inf.* nn. 665f.

[645] Ed. Neubauer, *JA* (1869), p. 400 (צדיק); ed. Bowman, p. 13a (צדוק).

[646] cf. Bowman, "Ezekiel and the Zadokite Priesthood", *TGUOS* XVI (1955/6), p. 6.

[647] cf. Abdel-Al, *A Comparative Study etc.*, pp. 45 (and n. 1 *ibid.*); 53 etc.

[648] cf. *sup.* nn. 630-32 and text there. Similarly, all speculations on the pre-Exilic and post-Exilic priesthood (Bowman, *op. cit.* p. 9, Abdel-Al, *op. cit.* p. 125) or the comparisons with Pharisaism on the problem of the manifold functions of the priest-hood (*ibid.* p. 128), do not hold water [cf. my article, *ALUOS* VI (1969), pp. 119f., 155f. (nn. 175-183)].

[649] cf. my article *op. cit.* n. 180. It is significant that in the Samaritan Pentateuch the text of *Deut.* xxi, 2 reads (M.T. זקניך ושופטיך) זקניך ושוטריך ויצאו the order of which caused various interpretation amongst the Rabbis, cf. *Soṭah* IX, 1 (the anonymous mishnah as opposed to R. Judah). The order here is also logical, because only the 'wise and scribes" (S. Targ. חכימיך וספריך) perform the task to "go out", while for the priest only the superior task is preserved ("and the priests the sons of

This is a tradition running through the whole of Samaritan literature. Marqah already takes it for granted when he arranges the speeches of Moses before his death in a corresponding order. He speaks first to the Leaders of the Priests, to Joshua and the Levites ("You will direct the Judgements for Jacob and the Laws for Israel").[650] Only later does he speak to the "Princes of the Tribes", the lay "judges" and the lay "teachers". It seems that this arrangement, in putting the priests before the layleaders and the High Priest before the King (= Joshua), represents an ancient tradition (based on the exegesis of *Num.* xxvii, 21) and one which is indeed explicitly mentioned in the Samaritan 'Book of Joshua'.[651]

The supreme power of the High Priests finds its justification in the understanding that "the Judge" in *Deut.* xvii, 9 and 12 is a reference to him,[652] and hence the final verdict in all religious and juridical matters must necessarily be within his sole competence. The authority of the High Priest, however, is not guaranteed by any supernatural or prophetic faculties possessed by the temporary incumbent of this office, but rather

---

Levi shall come near... according to their word shall every controversy and every stroke be", *ibid.* 5).

[650] *Memar Marqah* (ed. Macdonald), I, pp. 121f. (= II, pp. 149f.) אתון תשכילון דיניה ליעקב ותורותיה לישראל which is said to the Levites, is a paraphrase of *Deut.* xxxiii, 10. The whole order is an implicit midrash based on the exegesis of *Deut.* xxix, 9: ראשיכם = leaders, i.e. The Priest, the King (Joshua) and the Levites; זקניכם = the Princes: שבטיכם = lay judges (דיניה); שוטריכם (cf. Targum וספריכון) = lay teachers. A similar order may be the skeleton upon which the IIIrd Book of the *Memar* is built (with the addition of blessing and curses in connection with the priestly prerogative).

[651] Juynboll, *Chronicon Sam... Liber Josuae*, p. 25 (of the Arabic text). We cannot enter here into the priestly prerogative of the Blessing but Marqah's hypothetical question concerning this matter (Memar, I, p. 85f.; II, p. 136) putting an opposing opinion in the mouth of the questioner, was in the long run meant to settle this problem. Although from the words of Moses one could understand that the supreme blessedness belongs to Joseph (*Deut.* xxxiii, 13f.) the *pronouncing* of the Blessing, which is an exclusive priestly function (*ibid.* xxi, 5), is of a higher degree.

[652] Gaster, *The Samaritans*, pp. 56f.; the positive commandment, n. 211 of the Samaritans (built upon *Deut.* xvii, 11) is also a reference to be obedient to the rulings emerging from the High Priest. In Rabbinic literature (Siphre *Deut. ad. loc., Sanhedrin* 86b f.; Maimonides, *Sepher ha-Miṣwoth*, Positive com. 174) this command is transferred to strengthen the authority of the Sanhedrin. In the *Kāfi* (p. 278) it is explicitly stated that "the judge" must be respected and anyone who opposes him is under penalty of death (based upon *Lev.* xxiv, 16; *Ex.* xxii, 27, God in sense of Judge, and *Deut.* xvii, 12).

by the direct chain formed by his lineage and succession and by his function as custodian of the 'truth' of the Torah. Thus the High Priest is in no way expected to cultivate such prophetic gifts as may lead him to utter new revelations. On the contrary, his authority is established precisely for the purpose of preserving the traditions in their original form. As opposed to the 'illuminational' and 'progressive' interpretations of the Zadokite priesthood, for the Samaritans the rulings of the High Priest must by their nature be pressed into the service of an extreme conservatism. Since his office and his personality are intended to represent for them the 'true' tradition, which he inherently possesses by his direct lineage and his spiritual inheritance, he is expected to be in full and intact possession of all the learning transmitted to him through his ancestors and his immediate predecessors.

We do indeed hear of a 'mystery' adhering to the personality of the High Priest; such a concept, however, always has reference to his special learning in a field in which the knowledge of the layman or even of the ordinary priest could not safely be trusted.[653] It is possible that for polemical reasons this 'mystery' is in some degree emphasized, yet it never becomes an attribute in virtue of which the High Priest can introduce innovations by claiming to have acquired special 'mystical faculties'.

This point again becomes clear from the polemics of Munajja [654] against the Karaites, who opposed the binding force of tradition. By referring to *Deut.* xvii, 8-13, he tries to prove that in matters like calendar-calculations one should ascribe (by analogy) the same authority to 'the priest' as was given to him by the Law in the matter of leprosy (Lev. xiii). In all such cases it is clear that this type of 'mystery' surrounding the High Priest only helps to strengthen the control of the priesthood as exercised in the enforcement of the traditions, and this control in itself again becomes a factor contributing to the continuing fossilization of Samaritan religion.

"The convenant of an everlasting priesthood" (*Num.* xxv, 13) is understood as a guaranty for the perpetual Divine Favour towards the

---

[653] cf. J. Macdonald, *The Theology of the Sam.*, p. 311.

[654] *Masā'il al-Khilāf*, Ia, pp. 15f. As opposed to this the Karaites claimed יען כי הסתרת המצוות אין בכתובים כ״א בילדים and therefore only explicit sources and their logical (analogical) study is admissible (Hadasi, *Eshkol ha-Kofer*, Alpha Betha, 175; f. 71c.). The mystery of the calendaric calculations depends upon the tradition that these details were handed down only by oral means from Phinehas, who received it from Moses and adapted it to the geographical conditions of Hargerizim (*Tolidah*, beginning, cf. *Ṭabbākh*, ff. 82a f. (SLTh.A, pp. 122-125).

people through the authority of the High Priesthood. It entails three 'good tidings':[655] (1) an everlasting dynasty (from Phinehas), (2) an existence for the people as long as the priesthood is preserved in its purity, (3) Divine forgiveness and atonement ratified in obedience to the High Priest, which in their turn are the pledges of the future existence of the people. Each one of these 'tidings' forges a link in a magic chain wherein each one activates the others. However, practical power is in the hands of High Priest, to whom are entrusted the authority and responsibility for upholding the whole religious system.

Thus the High Priest personifies the priestly office in its manifold aspects. According to Samaritan exegesis of *Deut.* xxxiii, 10, its activities include the following:[656] "They are the source of legislation and judgement through which the truth is clearly established. They are responsible for the final verdict concerning what is forbidden and what is permissible, what is (ritually) unclean or clean ...". From the verse that follows (*ibid.* 11) it is understood that this is a solemn warning to those who disobey the priests.[657] In all these discussions it is regularly taken for granted that amongst the priests themselves there could not be any disagreement. The authoritative position of the High Priest prevents any possible disagreement within the ranks of the priesthood.

It is instructive to note that, despite the differences in approach between the *Kāfi* and the *Ṭabbākh*, both introduce their work with a chapter on the priesthood (although in the *Ṭabbākh* the heading is misleading, being styled "on prophecy"). The *Kāfi* states quite bluntly

---

[655] *Ṭabbākh*, ff. 4b-5a (SLTh.A, p. 82); this idea is already hinted at by Marqah (*Memar*, I, p. 140 = II, p. 229) בסרה לה ולישראל the third condition is however different in Marqah: it is built on *Deut.* xxxiii, 11 (Sam. Pent.) indicating that by obedience to Levi (= Priesthood) the people will overcome all its enemies. cf. also *Memar Marqah*, I, p. 145 = II, pp. 238f. on letter ק' cf. *inf.* 657.

[656] *Ṭabbākh*, f. 205a. واليهم تنتهى الاحكام وتبان الحقايق فيها وعنهم توخذ الفتاوى والحرام والحلال والطا والطهر حسب قوله

יורו משפטיך ליעקב cf. previous note. A similar opinion is also expressed in the *Kāfi* (pp. 17f.) in the sense that all 'tradition' originates from them. But the *Kāfi* makes it clear that matters like the calendar calculations are dependent upon the High Priest (cf. Abdel-Al, *op. cit.* p. 666).

[657] *Ṭabbākh*, f. 205b. The verse is divided into two parts: מחץ מתני קמיו ומשנאיו is compared to one who partakes of poison (for one who opposes the priesthood knows the consequences). מי יקימנו is a further warning to the people from opposing them (تحذير الامه من معاندته). It is possible that this was also the meaning of Marqah's exposition (cf. *sup.* n. 655).

that the reason for this is that it serves as evidence for the authenticity of the Samaritan religion, since their priesthood itself testifies to the unbroken chain of their whole tradition, a chain which does not exist among the Jews (including Rabbanites and Karaites).[658] Since the *Kāfi* is on the whole less polemical than the *Ṭabbākh* and yet both are distinctly polemical, we may assume that these were broadly similar polemical tendencies in the general background. There are also other similarities, especially in connexion with the priesthood, between the two works,[659] which strongly suggest that both are dependent on earlier sources. The *Kāfi* claims quite bluntly that he depends both on the voluminous work of the ancient priests [660] and on other sources, including the theological discussions of his own contemporaries. The *Ṭabbākh* does not reveal his sources; but from all reasonable comparisons we may assume that they are the very same as those used by the *Kāfi*. The preoccupation of both works with the priesthood may point to these same priestly sources of their material, and satisfactorily account for their total submission to the authority of the priesthood, a feature which is also evident from their treatment of this and other subjects.

It seems very likely that 'the Sheikh', so often quoted in the *Kāfi*, is none other than the High Priest.[661] In some other places also this figure quite explicitly designates the role of the High Priest. Thus, for example, when certain Samaritans introduce a custom opposed to the accepted norm — although they can certainly find biblical warrant in support of their practice, it is energetically terminated by the contemporary High Priest.[662]

To the student of Samaritan literature it comes as an unpleasant surprise to realise how very easily a single source may mislead generations of scholars into accepting it as valid, even though it stands in patent contradiction to all other known sources. We refer here to the fantastic overstatements of the Samaritan Chronicles regarding the role of Baba Rabbah, and especially regarding his alleged limitation of the priestly

---

[658] p. 4. اليهود طايفت عند معدوم هوا ما وذلك cf. N. Cohn, *Die Zarâath Gesetze*, p. 5.

[659] cf. Abdel-Al, *op. cit.* p. 117 and on other suggestions of the sources, *ibid.* pp. 90 and 105f. (cf. *sup.* n. 451).

[660] N. Cohn, *op. cit.* pp. 4f. (= *Kāfi*, pp. 2f.). Here we have also quite explicitly another reason for beginning the Book with the priesthood, i.e. because of its cardinal importance etc.

[661] cf. Abdel Al, *op. cit.* pp. 90ff.

[662] *Kāfi*, p. 77 (SLTh.A, p. 13).

leadership in favour of the lay leadership.[663] Had such a radical 'reform' really taken place in the fourth century, it would have been wholly impossible for the literature of the eleventh century (as we have seen) to advocate the very opposite course. Furthermore, why should Baba, himself a priest, seek to subvert the cherished traditions of his own priestly order? Strangely enough, the 'evidence' sometimes adduced for this 'reform' is the occasional functioning of lay-leaders alongside the priests, or in their absence.[664] Clearly, the existence of lay-leaders, teachers as well as exegetes, in no way detracts from the superior role of the priesthood.

The whole argument of the Chronicles and their upholders is based on wrong premises, inasmuch as it takes it for granted that prior to Baba *all* leaders must necessarily have been priests. It is entirely superfluous to go to the trouble of refuting such preconceptions, since from all the verses employed by the Samaritans in their exegesis in favour of the exaltation of the priesthood, it is always evident that the presence of the lay-leaders beside the priests is invariably taken for granted by all sources, as a truth of even biblical origin. All the preachings of Marqah (a contemporary of Baba) are based on this acknowledged principle,[665] a position adhered to also in the literature of the later Islamic period. From the Samaritan Targum [666] again it is obvious that the "elders" are identified with the 'wise' and the 'learned', not of priestly descent, a fact which in itself reflects the consistent biblical tradition on the lay "elders". Marqah [667] says the very same thing:

---

[663] Montgomery, *The Samaritans*, p. 102f. (cf. *ibid.* n. 73, for the sources).

[664] cf. Abdel-Al, *op. cit.* p. 51 and note there.

[665] cf. *sup.* nn. 649, 650 and 651. The attempt to show that Marqah supported by his midrash the reforms of Baba [Ben-Ḥayyim, "On the Study etc.", *Tarbiz* X (1938/9), pp. 87f.] is built upon total misunderstanding. Marqah had no intention in this midrash to prove that "the faithful" were appointed to render ritual decisions and to judge. מלי קשטה means *prophecy*. The whole midrash (cf. ed. Macdonald, I, p. 84 = II, p. 136) is based on the repetition of "giving the law to the priests" in *Deut.* xxxi, 1 and 25. The implicit question is, how is this possible if he *said* it only later (*ibid.* 24 and 30)? The answer is hinted in עד תמם that these were prophets (74 perfect, i.e. Eleazer, Phinehas, Eldad, Medad and the 70 elders) who knew it by prophecy. Some lines earlier Marqah says מהימנין אנון גבריה דאתבחרו ואנון שבעין גבר מסהבי עמה. which shows that these 'faithful' and their *prophecy* is the core of the Midrash. If anything, Marqah tries to elevate the priests to this originally higher degree of prophecy.

[666] זקניכם *Deut.* xxix, 10 is rendered by the Targum as חכימיכון and so also other similar expressions (cf. the curious translation of *Gen.* xxxvii, 3). cf. *sup.* n. 594.

[667] *Memar Marqah* (ed. Macdonald), I, p. 98 = II, p. 162.

Your elders and they will tell you (*Deut.* xxxii, 7) the decrees, the statutes, judgments and all the laws and what is too wonderful for you. They will direct you to Him; then you will be called illuminated and *wise*, and will teach those who come after you.

The same verse is explained in the same way by the *Ṭabbākh*.[668] Even the *Kāfi*, although it is indeed bent on extending the priestly influence, would beyond doubt accept whole-heartedly the function of the lay-leaders. It even goes against its customary thesis in putting a 'wise' person on an equality with a 'fully fledged priest'.[669] Naturally, this is quite compatible with its thoroughgoing priestly sympathies and standpoints, since such was *always* the traditional Samaritan approach.

There was, however, through the hegemony of the priestly leadership, a constant control over the lay-leaders which prevented any relaxation of the rigorism for which the Samaritans were notorious throughout their history. Even in later times, in the seventeenth century when the Aaronite priesthood died out,[670] the Levitical 'priesthood' which succeeded it followed its tradition in all respects. It may in truth be said that this was the secret of the survival of the Samaritan religion; for, by adhering firmly to this priestly tradition with all its rigid laws, this religion was enabled to keep its original form throughout its long movement through history.

The priestly conservatism manifested itself in a constant supervision over the people's religious life and thought, in order to ensure that there should be no lapses from the rigorous tradition. It maintained a legalistic approach in the endeavour to make it possible for all to follow the perfect way of the Torah. In some respects one may find a certain parallelism in the 'perfectionism' sought after by the Dead Sea Scroll Sect.[671] No doubt, as in the case of this Sect,[672] the Samaritans too looked upon all divergent interpretations of the Scripture by their opponents as grave distortions of the truth, especially if they detected any deviation from the 'orthodox' practice and doctrine to which they were accustomed through their own interpretation. This they at once

---

[668] f. 208a   يريد اهل العلم العارفين يخبرون بما يفعله تعالى

[669] pp. 337f. (SLTh.A, p. 75).

[670] cf. Montgomery, *The Samaritans*, p. 139 (and *ibid.* n. 52); Cowley, "Description of Four Sam. Mss.", *PEFQS* 1904, p. 73.

[671] Leaney, *The Rule of Qumran*, p. 125.

[672] Wieder, *The Judean Scrolls and Karaism*, p. 135.

branded as a deliberate 'tampering' with the Law, as a lax exegesis making observance easier at the expense of the 'truth'.

But here too the analogy ends. As opposed to the Dead Sea Scroll Sect, the Samaritans do not show evidence of any esoterically revealed ascetical practices founded on illuminations on the part of the leader or on constantly emerging revelations by which the whole community will have to abide in the interest of their perfection. The Samaritans firmly believe in a 'perfect Law', which does not in any way depend on mystical asceticism. From Philo's [673] description of the Therapeutae (another Essene-type of ascetic group) it is manifest that it is necessary for them to "allegorise the ancestral philosophy" if they are to find asceticism stressed in Scripture. In contradistinction to all such devices, the Samaritans are doggedly faithful to the literal sense of their Scripture and tradition. If there exists any direct kinship between the ancient Rehabites or Kenites and the ascetic movements of later times,[674] the Samaritans stand clearly outside this sphere of influence, since their rigorism lacks all the marks of a self-inflicted catharsis. All they ever strive for is the meticulous observance of the Law in accordance with its literal sense.

Again, when we come to compare Samaritan rigorism in the Middle Ages with that of the Karaites, the same distinction is to be made. As we have seen,[675] the sources of Karaism go back in fact to ascetical sectarianism. Moreover, the 'progressive uncovering of the Law' and the accusation of leniency against those who do not accept the results of this type of exegesis [676] belong to the same line of thought, in which Samaritanism has no share. Although (as we shall see later) many of the literalist sectarian practices were very similar (which also made the constantly recurring attacks of the Karaites upon the Rabbanites [677] a convenient source for Samaritan polemics) yet the origins of these seeming 'parallels' are entirely different. In the case of the Karaites one often finds the most bizarre exegetical methods employed in order to find biblical support for a certain practice.[678] Nevertheless, despite

---

[673] *Vita Contemplativa* 28-9; cf. Grant, *Letter & Spirit*, pp. 32f.

[674] cf. Schoeps, *Theologie und Geschichte etc.*, pp. 252f.; Black, *Scrolls etc.*, p. 15;

[675] cf. *sup.* nn. 54f. cf. next note.

[676] Wieder, *Judean Scrolls etc.*, pp. 67f., 136f.

[677] Pinsker, *Lickute Kadmoniot*, II, pp. 27ff. For another list of the most common Karaite "stricter practices" as compared to Rabbanite norm, cf. Gottlober, *Bikkoreth etc.*, pp. 10f.

[678] Gottlober, *Bikkoret*, p. 29; Ankori, *Karaites in Byzantium*, p. 17.

all the differences in exegesis and in the principles upon which it is based, since very often these principles themselves betray their origin in the ancient rigoristic sectarian practices, we are justified in using these practices (but not their exegetical background) for the sake of comparison.

One of the common sectarian austerities is the obligation of the observance of the Law by infants. Qirqisāni reports [679] that Benjamin al-Nahāwandi made all the Laws obligatory upon children as soon as they began to speak. The Rabbis, on the other hand, postponed the age of legal responsibility until puberty.[680] In this respect the Samaritans show the most thoroughgoing approach. Munajja dedicates a whole chapter to this subject.[681] He states explicitly that, irrespective of the understanding of the children, the observances are obligatory upon them, since the Law is not directed to them but to their custodians. It is the duty of those who do understand to compel their children to fulfil the minutest details of the Law.

We may here, by way of further illustration, single out the harsh demand that children fast on the Day of Atonement irrespective of their age, which is often a source of controversy with other sects and a favourite polemical theme. The entire Samaritan literature is unanimous on this rule, and even later compilations [682] stress this same precept in all its strictness and mention also other restrictions quite unknown to the Rabbis.[683]

Another common sectarian tendency, also going back to antiquity, is the extension of the death penalty to sections of Law not explicitly mentioned in Scripture. This can readily be seen in the Book of Jubilees and may even be the case in the Zadokite Fragments.[684] The Karaites, who obviously could not put the principle of capital punishment into

---

[679] *Kitāb al-Anwār etc.*, I, 14, 1 end (ed. Nemoy, I, p. 55) = *idem. HUCA* VII (1930), p. 387.

[680] *Mekhilta*, Mishpaṭim IV, 12 [ed. Friedmann f. 80a, cf. Editor's n.] cf. also *Abhoth* V, 21; *Sanhedrin* VIII, 1; *Niddah* VI, 11.

[681] Wreschner, *Samaritanische Traditionen*, p. xxv.

[682] *Hillukh*, pp. 163f. (cf. also Wreschner, *op. cit.* p. xxviii). The same rule applies to people who are ill. Additional restriction mentioned in *Hillukh*: not to smell anything, not to leave the Synagogue and not to stop the prayer day and night.

[683] *Yoma* 82a. In earlier times there were some rigoristic opinions also amongst the Palestinian Rabbis. cf. Shamai in *Tosephta Yoma* V, 2 (ed. Zuckermandel, p. 189; cf. variant readings, the present text is = Babyl. 77b!). cf. Derenbourg, *Essai d'Histoire etc.*, p. 100.

[684] cf. however Rabin, *The Zadokite Documents* (on IX, 1, n. 8), p. 44.

practical effect, had to be satisfied with imposing the ban of excommunication on offenders.[685] In Samaritan literature no attention was paid to the impracticability of the death-penalty, and all their books dealing with the Laws refer to this penalty as if it were actually practised. Rabbinic literature follows the same practice (including a constant reference to guilt-offerings etc.), although capital punishment was abolished before the destruction of the Second Temple (Abhodah-Zarah 8,b). Both these latter groups merely maintained the traditional method of expounding the Law in this respect; and thus, whenever a cardinal sin was dealt with, its appropriate penalty was also assigned, although this was not meant to be carried out. For the purposes of our enquiry, the question is whether the Samaritans further extended the death penalty to cases not explicitly mentioned in the Pentateuch, or whether they dissented from this sectarian severity. We have seen in previous discussions that mercy in all such cases is entirely ruled out.[686] But even more characteristic is the drawing of a generalization from the Laws of the Sabbath in such a way that anyone who does any kind of work whatever falls under the death penalty. Here [687] too we may find the true reason for this overzealousness, since it is mainly exercised on behalf of moral ends, to warn the potential offender that, if he commits any such sin secretly, God will assuredly take vengeance on him. Moreover, in this case too, we see their extreme sectarian rigorism, since such offences are extended far beyond what is explicitly mentioned in the Scripture. We have only to remind ourselves of the Biblical prohibition of kindling fire on the Sabbath; this is extended by Samaritan (and other sectarian) exegesis to fire which has been burning since Friday. This rigorism is not relaxed even in the later compilations. Thus for example the *Hillukh* [688] connects the 'profanation' of the Sabbath which

---

[685] Nemoy, *Karaite Anthology*, pp. 14f., 323f.; cf. Ben-Sasson, "The First of the Karaites etc.", *Zion* XV (1952), pp. 52f.

[686] cf. *sup*. n. 488. Although in this case (*Kāfi*, p. 275), it is mentioned in connection with one who curses or smites his parents (*Ex*. xxi, 17; *Lev*. xx, 9) that if he is a young child he is only punished and chastised, and only if he grows up he is to be executed, this is not meant to rule more leniently than the Torah. Even in the case of the "stubborn and rebellious son" (*Deut*. xxi, 18) they might have interpreted it in such a way: "they chasten him" while he is still a child, "will not hearken unto them" when grown up. Munajja, although advocating a strict observance of the laws for children (*sup*. n. 681), excludes them from cases where "diminished responsibilities" renders them unfit, as for example in cases of testimony, marriage, etc.

[687] *Ṭabbākh*, f. 29b f. (SLTh.A, pp. 85f.).

[688] p. 80, cf. also *sup*. n. 435.

is punishable by death (*Ex.* xxxi, 14) with mixing on this day with Gentiles and conversing with them in profane speech.

These cases amply show that the rigour of the Samaritans emanates essentially from their extreme conservatism, which compels them to be utterly faithful to their traditions, as regulated by the Law and its exegesis. It may in truth be added that, although Samaritan literature nowhere supplies any explicit and detailed description of their ideological aims, 'piety' is the watchword of the Sect. This may fairly be culled from their own self-designations in the Chronicles and their Epistles to Europe, wherein they specifically call themselves "the keepers", "the keepers in truth", or even "the Pious".[689] These terms do not imply an aspiration to reach an ideal moral perfection by ascetical practices directed to the chastening of the soul, as is the case with some monastic movements, but only to reach the type of perfection derived from and expected by the Law. Possibly the Samaritans did not entirely escape certain tendencies to overdo their devotional zeal by occasional ascetical outbursts, as was certainly the case with the *Ḥasid* among the Pharisees. However, the centre of gravity in both groups [690] did not consist in striving after an abstract ideal of moral asceticism, but in the meticulous performance of all the realizable requirements of the Law according to the strictest demands of the tradition. As we have seen, this is already the opinion of Marqah who states : "you are not expected to do something that is not in your power to do".[691] What is demanded, according to Marqah, is the love of God and not of evil, a phrase which is clearly an epitome of Scripture itself.

Now, we look at their strict rulings and it becomes evident that at least to Samaritan ways of thinking, these are all regarded as the 'true' meanings of the explicit Divine commandments. This is obvious from their exegesis on the "sanctification"[692] and "profanation"[693] of the Sabbath, including, as it does, practices regarded as relevant by "tradition". Such is also the background to the prohibition of the consumption of intoxicating beverages on Holy-days.[694] In all these standards of

---

[689] Vilmar, *Abulfathi annales Sam. etc.*, p. 102 (الحسيديم ومعناها الصلحا‎);
Montgomery, *The Sam.*, p. 318; J. Macdonald, *The Theology of the Sam.*, p. 25 etc.
חסידים, השמרים על האמת, שמרים.

[690] cf. *sup.* para (e).
[691] cf. *sup.* n. 345.
[692] cf. *sup.* nn. 477-8.
[693] cf. *sup.* n. 688.
[694] *Kāfi*, p. 107 (SLTh.A, p. 18).

'sanctity' or 'piety' there is no single practice or precept which could be termed 'voluntary' or 'optional', much less an addition to the demands of the law. Of course, we may hear on rare occasions that the optimal standard of perfectionism fails to meet with due compliance;[695] but it is precisely the fear of the possible contamination of the 'righteous' which hardens the original inflexibility of the group even more.

The same line is pursued in the Laws governing the other festivals. To take Passover as an instance, distinguished by the performance of the Paschal offering, all its details have to be rigidly observed. The slightest negligence invalidates the whole sacrifice. Although performed with the full awareness of the Samaritans of being the only group to practise any type of blood-sacrifice, this distinctive feature also goes back to ancient times, and is determined by their traditional exegesis. Thus we know that what is left over from the victim until the morning must be burnt by fire (*Ex.* xii, 10). If, however, the portions of the sacrifice are left over by *negligence* 'the sages' demand another sacrifice in the Second Month (cf. *Num.* ix, 10f.).[696] Certainly this ruling is not stated explicitly in Scripture, but is again taken from the tradition which takes it for granted that offerings should be performed with the greatest of care and that any negligence renders them unworthy. Such and similar restrictions nowhere mentioned in Scripture pervade their whole legislative literature, even those of later times.[697]

On certain other Laws of Passover which were observed also by the Jews, as for example the prohibition of leavened bread, there were even more rigid restrictive rules among the Samaritans. One example is the Rabbinic rule that the possession by a Jew of leaven which happens to be (even temporarily) in the keeping of a non-Jew during the festival, is not to be considered an offence (against the command of *Ex.* xiii, 7).[698] The Samaritan exegesis of this verse forbids this.[699] The sale of leaven during Passover to non-Jews was hotly debated also by the

---

[695] cf. *sup.* nn. 358-9.

[696] *Ṭabbākh*, f. 68a (SLTh.A, p. 109).

[697] Thus the *Hillukh* (p. 112) polemicises against the Jews who did not demand the compulsion for children to partake in the Passover offering. In line with the general Samaritan insistence about children being forced to fulfil all command (cf. *sup.* nn. 681-3), it brings a whole array of evidence in this respect.

[698] cf. *Pesaḥim*, II, 2.

[699] *Ṭabbākh*, f. 85b (SLTh.A, pp. 125f.).

Karaites, but chiefly regarded as an illegitimate evasion based on a legal fiction.[700]

Another long list of rigoristic injunctions has to do with the realm of ritual cleanliness. Here, not only were these laws preserved by the Samaritans, whereas the Rabbis had totally abolished them, together with other rules appertaining to the Temple or to the Land of Israel, but their provisions were much stricter than those of the Rabbinic rules of the same kind. The logic underlying the Samaritans' preservation of these laws is the same logic which calls forth their rigorism in respect of their provisions. Just as it is for them impossible to abrogate those laws which are termed "everlasting statutes", so it is imperative to adhere to all their restrictive practices in all their details. In such cases too even the later codes [701] still emphasize the same rigid approach as is manifested in earlier times.

We cannot of course enumerate here even a fraction of these rigoristic practices, but the few examples cited fully prove that they are all maintained in their strict form, owing to the unremitting effort of the Samaritans to remain faithful to the very letter of the Law, with all the rigours demanded by it. Even those regulations which seem to have almost no biblical source [702] turn out on examination to be derivations by analogy or extensions of Scriptural warrants.

The only field where one may pardonably suspect certain 'ascetical' tendencies is that occupied by the Nazirite. Although such an approach to this subject would be quite natural, inasmuch as this biblical character is in fact assumed to be the prototype for all other persons desirous of practising self-denial and abstinence, the truth of the matter is that even in this field there is no trace of any *real* asceticism. The stress is rather on the legalistic approach towards supreme 'holiness' than on the realization of any abstract moral ideal. This concept underlies the

---

[700] Qirqisāni, *Kitāb al-Anwār etc.*, I, 3, 30 (ed. Nemoy, I, p. 24) = *idem, HUCA* VII (1930), p. 334.

[701] *Hillukh*, p. 228.

[702] For example the law that a Samaritan is not allowed to walk alone on a journey if the distance from his abode exceeds three days walk (*Kāfi*, pp. 202f.) is built on analogy (وذلك قياس على قوله), on verses like *Num.* x, 33; *Ex.* iii, 18, *ibid.* v, 3 etc. (cf. Abdel-al, *op. cit.* pp. 586f., 786f.). Similarly the extension of putting on שעטנז (*Deut.* xxii, 11) other forbidden garments (*Kāfi* pp. 189f. = SLTh.A, pp. 21f.) is built on logical comparisons with *Lev.* xix, 19; *Deut.* xxii, 5f. etc. The same applies also about the prohibition of partaking in food prior to prayer (cf. *sup.* n. 662) and others.

long list of comparisons of the Nazirite with the High Priest.[703] While
the acceptance of the Naziriteship is entirely voluntary, from the moment
one embarks upon this way one is in duty bound to follow a well-organised and uniformly strict legal code far more than any arbitrary ascetical
exercises built on a self-imposed regime of physical deprivation. Similarly,
the attainment of 'holiness' is firmly assured to the devotee of this legal
code, and the candidate is not thereby required to embark upon the
untrodden paths of ascetical exercises, supposed in themselves to ensure
for him the eventual attainment of his ideals.

Even those rigoristic precepts of the Nazirite which appear to have
no biblical basis are in fact traditions based on biblical exegesis. Thus,
for example, the prohibition of work [704] is not only a preventive measure
so that the Nazirite shall be shielded from worldly desires, but it is based
on analogy with the High Priest, who himself is not supposed to forsake
his holiness.[705] Such analogies and similar exegetical devices are the
source of the law, although only the more philosophical and moral
justifications are given explicitly. The same applies to the prohibition
of sexual intercourse during the Naziriteship.[706] This is in line with the
general Samaritan (and sectarian) philosphy that marital relations
(which cause levitical pollution according to Scripture, *Lev.* xv, 18)
stand in diametrical opposition to 'holiness'. For the same reason,
cohabitation is prohibited on the Sabbath,[707] and hence the same applies
to the Nazirite, for during "all the days of his Naziriteship ... he shall
be holy ..." (*Num.* vi, 4-5 and 9). It is also not impossible that comparison
with the High Priest in the respect that "he shall not make himself
unclean", even in the case of the death of his nearest relatives (*ibid.*
6-7), opens the way to further analogies, and demands abstention even
from minor 'pollutions'.[708]

---

[703] *Kāfi*, pp. 229f. (= SLTh.A, p. 47).

[704] *ibid.* p. 238 (= SLTh.A, p. 53).

[705] A midrash on *Lev.* xxi, 23, which was understood also by the Rabbis "in order
that he should not leave his sanctity". cf. *Sanhedrin*, 18a.

[706] *Kāfi*, pp. 239f. (SLTh.A, p. 54). cf. also n. 703 *sup.*

[707] cf. my article in *ALUOS* VI (1969), pp. 112f., 147 (nn. 118-120).

[708] The reasons given in the *Kāfi* (*op. cit.*) for the celibacy of the Nazirite, as if
taken from Noah who during the flood was not allowed to cohabit (a midrash on the
orders of the words in *Gen.* vi, 18 as compared to *Gen.* viii, 16) is a secondary only.
The same applies concerning the period of Naziriteship fixed for a full solar year. Here
also the mere fact that besides the reason given — as if this period was taken from
the full year of Noah in the Ark — there are other explanations (some even very

It seems that Samaritan tradition 'elevated' even the naturally rigoristic tendencies which formed one essential part of their conservatism, and specifically embodied in the institution of Naziriteship is the status of an auxiliary to the priestly and legalistic hierarchy. The same diehrad opposition to any changes which characterized this stubborn priestly legalism was also clearly at work in limiting the naturally rigoristic psychology inherent in Naziriteship in order to prevent its becoming a disruptive power, even if this were expressed only in a search for new paths in asceticism and mysticism.

A similar attitude, furthermore, is clearly to be discerned if we look into their polemical outbursts. All differing traditions and practices are immediately branded by them as distortions and aberrations. In this respect they can use the polemical experiences of other sects, whether from the period of Antiquity or from the Middle Ages, whose systems are often very similar. The Dead Sea Scroll Sect, as well as the later Karaites, never tire of reproaching and denouncing their opponents in almost identical terms.[709] The recurrent war between the Muslim sects, each claiming to be the only true believers while all the others are infidels or godless heathens who profess Islam only outwardly,[710] only adds fuel to the flames. Nevertheless, Samaritan polemics finds its greatest 'ally' in Karaite writers, who from the earliest times have repeatedly prepared lists of "shameful things" by which the Rabbanites have 'violated' the Law.[711] The fact that a large amount of this type of litera-ture is written in Arabic (and often in Arabic characters) makes it easily accessible to the Samaritans, whose vernacular by that time is also Arabic. Naturally, this does not mean that prior to the availability of the Karaite material the Samaritans are not engaged in polemics. The Talmudic literature already reproduces discussions on various subjects which claim attention during this period. The most heated arguments center

---

artificial, depending on Gemaṭria) which show that the practice did not depend on the Midrash. It seems rather that all these midrashim are secondary in order to explain the legal tradition.

[709] The opponents' religion is likened to idolatry (Weider, *Judean Scrolls etc.*, p. 151), demands for social and territorial segregation (*ibid.* pp. 153f.). Both groups employed almost the same biblical verses as e.g. *Gen.* xix, 14; *Ex.* xxiii, 1; *Num.* xvi, 26 etc. (*ibid.* p. 156).

[710] D.B. Macdonald, *Development of Muslim Theology etc.*, p. 123.

[711] Poznanski, *The Karaite etc.*, p. 37. Qirqisāni's introduction to his *Kitāb a-Anwar etc.* (I, 3, 1-50, ed. Nemoy, I, pp. 15-31 = *idem. HUCA* vii (1930), pp. 330-350) could also serve the same purpose.

around the Jewish denial of the Israelite descent of the Samaritans, and around the centre of worship, namely Jerusalem versus Hargerizim.[712]

Despite the long history of anti-Jewish polemics, *Memar Marqah* lacks any *explicit* polemical features, although it abounds in apologetic items, employed mainly for internal Samaritan purposes. It is extremely difficult to find any satisfactory explanation for this total absence of polemics in Marqah, since his rigorism is in no way less than that of his successors in the later Samaritan literature. Maybe it is due to the character of the *Memar* itself which is intended to be an epic and pan-egyric in honour of Moses,[713] and such controversial details are felt to be inappropriate to the solemn tone of this work. As for the general attitude of Marqah we may be fairly certain [714] that he is guided by the same traditional legalistic approach which prevails throughout the entire Samaritan literature.

Apart from Marqah, polemics is a natural ingredient of all Samaritan literature. The *Asaṭir* [715] and the other chronicles simply cannot refrain from retaliation in the age-old controversy of Hargerizim versus Jerusalem.[716] Amongst the legal literature, the *Kāfi* is the most sober and topical, and seldom deviates from its matter-of-fact presentation of the laws and customs. Nevertheless, when it comes to points of difference with the Jewish practices, it never misses the opportunity of pointing out the superiority of the Samaritan religion. In particular, as regards the Priesthood, the focal point and the pride of their religion. even the *Kāfi*, despite its usually moderate and pragmatic discourses, feels bound to add the derogatory note that the Jews lack this institution.[717]

The *Ṭabbākh* is much more polemically inclined, and therefore it

---

[712] Halkin, "Sam. Polemics etc.", *PAAJR* viii (1935-6), pp. 26f. (n. 66) and 31-35 respectively; cf. also S. Kohn, *De Pentateucho Sam. etc.*, pp. 57f.; Appel, *Quaestiones de rebus Sam. etc.*, pp. 27ff.

[713] cf. my article *op. cit.* pp. 107, 141 (nn. 76f.).

[714] *ibid.* pp. 109f., 143 (nn. 93-101).

[715] On the polemics against Jerusalem cf. Ben Hayyim, "Sepher Asaṭir", *Tarbiz* XIV-XV (1943/4), pp. 13f. (= 20f.); 21 (= 51) etc. This is in diametrical opposition to the opinion of Gaster (*Asaṭir*, p. 110): "The *Asaṭir* serves no tendency, propagates no special doctrine, and serves no direct purpose".

[716] cf. n. 712 *sup.*

[717] cf. *sup.* n. 658. In another place (*Kāfi*, pp. 18f.), in discussing the role of the High Priest in the calendar calculations it states that the Jews lack the institution of High Priesthood (دون طائفة اليهود). (cf. also Abdel-Al, *op. cit.* p. 667).

is not surprising that it was described even by the most prominent bibliographer of the previous century as "a work of polemics against the Jews" (both Rabbanites and Karaites).[718] Although such a description amounts to a grave injustice to the wealth of material included in the *Ṭabbākh*, it does nevertheless contain a grain of truth since the *Ṭabbākh* is undoubtedly motivated by a strong polemical bias. As compared with the pragmatic expositions of the Law in the *Kāfi*, the *Ṭabbākh* lacks any systematic presentation even of the most fundamental precepts. Thus, for example, of the specific demands of the prohibitions of the Sabbath, where one might reasonably expect an extended treatment, Abū-l Ḥasan mentions only those concerning works of carpentry and building and similar things "which would take too long to explain in this discourse".[719] We have already seen [720] that the *Ṭabbākh*'s chapters are often widely different from those of the *Kāfi*; the former concentrates chiefly on differences between Samaritanism and other religions, while the latter gives a straightforward elucidation of the demands of the Law. Although both works are protagonists of a substantially identical rigoristic legalism, as is plainly indicated by their congruity and harmony in all fields, they are directed to different types of reader. The *Kāfi* is intended to meet the demand for a code of conduct, and is aimed at the *naive* follower of tradition who is in need of enlightenment concerning its detailed applications. The *Ṭabbākh* on the other hand has the sophisticated reader in mind who is perturbed by the prevalent foreign attacks on tradition. For such a type of reader it is necessary to counteract any incipient 'heresies' which may perplex him by a sturdy apologetic approach, often passing into active polemics.

This method is also adopted by the Samaritan legal writers of late times. The *Masā'il al-Khilāf* is even more polemical than the *Ṭabbākh*;[721] and even in the *Hillukh*, which is mainly designed to show the 'way', the element of polemics is at least as prominent as in the *Ṭabbākh*.[722]

Despite all these polemical features which permeate the entire legal section of Samaritan literature, there is no attempt to promulgate

---

[718] Steinschneider, *Die arabische Literatur der Juden*, p. 323. cf. Gaster, *The Samaritans*, pp. 151f.; Halkin, *op. cit.* p. 16.

[719] *Ṭabbākh*, f. 28b (SLTh.A, p. 84).

[720] cf. Abdel-Al, *op. cit.* pp. 102ff., 241ff.

[721] Wreschner, *Samaritanische Traditionen*, p. xxi.

[722] *idem. ibid.* p. 19. On the extent of Samaritan polemics, cf. Halkin, *op. cit.* and for further literature, *ibid.* p. 14.

additional restrictions in opposition to the opinions of opposing groups with a view to 'strengthening' their own views. Unlike the Talmudic legislators, [723] the Samaritans must have felt that their central priestly authority could adequately cope with counteracting 'heretical' practices and doctrines without resorting to such measures. It is also possible that their strong aversion to 'adding' to the Torah, (cf. *Deut.* iv, 2; *ibid.* xii, 32)[724] prevented them from embarking on this course. Nonetheless, it may be confidently affirmed that the rigorism of the Samaritans was in no way less stringent than that of the Rabbis.

L. SAMARITAN SECTARIANISM

This short paragraph on the vexed problem of Samaritan sects in general and the Dositehans in particular lays no claim whatever to an exhaustive treatment. Recent attempts to re-examine the problem, by utilizing evidence accruing during the half-century since the major works on this subject appeared in print, although commonly promising to offer a "new evaluation",[725] have added very little to our previous knowledge. As a matter of fact, as compared with the sober approach of works now almost a century old,[726] and whose authors bravely attempted to evaluate sources in themselves never fully reconciled, all that we can discover in contemporary writings is little else than unfounded hypothesis, more often than not without any documentary support.

The reason for this situation is the total absence of any writings whatsoever originating from within the circles of these sects themselves. All our knowledge is thus shrouded in darkness, and only a few dim rays of light penetrate the gloom here and there, most of them coming from external sources. All that it has been possible to do is to follow the lead of those external sources regarding these sects, and to try to faithfully assess what they describe. Whatever, then, may be the truth in regard to the extravagances of Samaritan sectarianism, insofar as it rests on sources not compiled by those sects themselves, it is conveyed, almost all of it, by hostile witnesses. These sources, applying as they do

---

[723] cf. my article in *JJS* IX (1958), pp. 131 (n. 111), 136 (n. 151), 137 (n. 157) and (n. 165); cf. also Wieder, *Judean Scrolls etc.*, pp. 65f.

[724] cf. *sup.* nn. 48f.

[725] Crown, "Dosietheans, Resurrections etc.", *Antichthon*, I (1967), p. 70. cf. also recently H.C. Kippenberg, *Garizim und Synagoge* (Berlin, N.Y.,1971), pp. 122-137; 314-327.

[726] Appel, *Questiones de rebus Sam. etc.*, pp. 91ff.

to the doctrines and practices of these sects standards widely different from their own, are seldom able, or apparently even inclined, to make any effort to be objective, much less sympathetic. As a result, most writers on the subject have uncritically followed this tendentious approach reflected in their sources. However, much that still is relevant to this problem has already been quite exhaustively recorded at the beginning of our century.[727]

It is, moreover, a fact known to every student of Samaritanism that, whatever the reason, its sects are only very scantily represented in Samaritan literature itself. Apart from the confused and bewildering reports of the Samaritan chronicles, in which there is never any real certainty as to which part is original and hence derived from earlier Samaritan sources and which is an adaptation of external historical wirtings, all other extant Samaritan sources are totally silent on the sects. There were indeed ample opportunities for at least introducing them into the exegetical and religious literature at relevant points which constantly formed bones of contention among the variant sects, if there had been any desire to do so. Although one may speculate on the reason underlying this silence on the sects and formulate theories necessarily at variance with one another, one thing is beyond doubt, namely that there must have been some cogent reason for thus totally ignoring the very existence of the sects. Particularly significant is the total silence on the sects in the otherwise highly polemical and even "coloured" literature, in which no opportunity is missed to attack any possible opponent.[728]

Despite the tempting hypotheses at present so often expressed and reiterated, and even at the hazard of having our views branded as banal, we must try to avoid the uncritical acceptance of any of the unprovable new 'solutions'. It seems to us much more rewarding to employ the reverse method, that of utilizing mainly Samaritan material, sorting out the significant points of contact from the underlying background, and examining their eventual relevance to the sects, starting from this standpoint, we may later scrutinize the older hypotheses according to their merits, as far as this is possible from the available evidence presented by the sources. We cannot, of course, avoid referring to such of these earlier hypotheses as may serve as guidelines in our own inquiry.

---

[727] Montgomery, *The Samaritans*, pp. 252ff. For further literature cf. *ibid.* p. 252, n. 1, to which we may add Kohler, "Dositheus, The Sam. Heresiarch etc.", *AJTh* XV XV (1911), pp. 404-435.

[728] cf. *sup.* nn. 709ff.

Obviously the conjectural origins of Samaritan sectarianism in early antiquity cannot be put to the test, since we have no literary sources for comparisons. It must be emphatically asserted that the vast number of opinions expressed on this matter bears no relation to the scantiness of the available sources. Moreover, often enough, what is propounded by certain scholars with great trepidity, and only as a probability, is taken up by others without any supporting evidence as a matter of certainty. Thus, for example, we are all aware of the early Samaritan claim to be the descendents of the tribe of Joseph, or, more precisely, "the sons of Ephraim and Manasseh". All their Chronicles and the whole of their literature are permeated by this claim to their ancestry, on which already the Talmudic literature records some hot debates.[729] We may be justified to a certian degree in taking such reports into account in framing the hypothesis that the Samaritans may have included amongst themselves descendants of the ancient Northern Kingdom, or even that they may have preserved traditions of Northern Israelite origins.[730] However, this is still a far cry from asserting that "the origin of Samaritanism in general and the Samaritan sectarianism in particular is *undoubtedly* to be traced ultimately to the division of the Kingdom... etc."[731] This and similar opinions, as, for instance , the acceptance of the Karaite polemical allegations that the calendation system of the Samaritans goes back to the reforms of Jeroboam,[732] must be treated with great caution. At their best, such claims are nothing more than ingenious possibilities still awaiting substantiation by far more reliable evidence.

Even less reliable and less concrete are the supposed connections with the Jewish colony of Elephantine. The superficial similarities adduced to show that these colonists were Samaritans [733] are not at all

---

[729] cf. *sup*. n. 712. Josephus (*Antiq*. XI, viii, 6) also reports their claim of being the descendents of Joseph.

[730] J. Macdonald, *The Theology of the Sam*., pp. 14f., 16ff.

[731] cf. Black, *The Scrolls etc.*, p. 65.

[732] Qirqisāni, *Kitāb al-Anwār etc.*, I, 5 (ed. Nemoy, I, p. 40); *ibid*. III, 1, 8-9 (ed. Nemoy II, pp. 185-6). cf. Black, *ibid*. Such allegations of Qirqisani are as reliable as those against the Rabbanites which maintain that their Oral Law originates from the reforms of Jeroboam (*Kitāb al-Anwār etc.*, I, 2, 6 and I, 3, 1 = ed. Nemoy, I, pp. 11 and 15f. = *HUCA* VII, pp. 325f. and 330f.). The Karaites themselves did not take such allegations seriously. cf. Pinsker, *Lickute Kadmoniot*, II, p. 101.

[733] Hoonacker, *Une Communauté Judéo-Araméenne* (London 1915, Schwich Lectures 1914) *passim*.

convincing. Upon similar 'evidence' almost any argument for affinity may be held to be valid. The claims for the identity of these groups, or even for contact between them, have been successfully challenged [734] and it seems that they must be totally abandoned. Despite the persistent allegations that the Samaritans worshipped a divinity called Ashima, which elicited the tempting identification with the Elephantine *ISHUMBETHEL*, there is no tangible proof for any such connections. In the case of the Elephantine colony we cannot of course exclude numerous syncretistic elements, all indicating a variety of foreign influences,[735] while the allegations concerning the Samaritans worshipping Ashima may have been revived by a simple misunderstanding, owing to their Samaritan pronunciation of the Tetragrammaton as Shemah.[736] It is an even more remote possibility that Samaritan sectarianism should have any connections with the Egyptian colony, although we do find in the Samaritan chronicles,[737] amongst the accusations hurled at the heresiarch Dosis, that he originated from Egypt. However, the context of this reference, by its stating that Dosis was of the "mixed multitude who came out of Egypt with the children of Israel and settled in Schechem (Nablus)", shows that it is devoid of any historical significance. This is rather an apologetic utilization of midrashim on *Ex.* xii, 38, in which the "mixed multitude" was to be blamed for all the evils befalling Israel.

It is often taken for granted, owing to the prevalent ignorance of Samaritan exegetical and legal literature, that gnosticism is in great measure identical with the ideas of the Samaritans. It is true that Samaria is regarded by the Church Fathers as the peculiar seed-bed of the gnostic heresy. There is no evidence, however, that what are termed "Gnostic elements" originate from Samaritan sources, since in general the regions

---

[734] A. Cowley, *Aramaic Papyri of the Fifth Century B.C.* (Oxford 1923), p. xv.

[735] A. Vincent, *La Religion des judéo-araméennes d'Éléphantine* (Paris 1937), pp. 19f.

[736] A. Cowley, *op. cit.* p. XIX. Relying on the biblical account of Ashima (2 *Kings,* xvii, 30ff.) and its confusion with true usage of 'Shemah', such allegations are often repeated by authors of the Middle Ages. Thus, for instance, the 12th century Ibn-Ezra in the introduction to his commentary on Esther כאשר עשו הכותים שכתבו תחת בראשית ברא אלקים, ברא אשימה cf. also Montgomery, *The Samaritans*, pp. 213 (n. 28) and 321.

[737] Vilmar, *Abulfathi annales Sam. etc.*, pp. 151f.; واصل دوسيس من العربرب الذين خرجوا مع بني اسرائيل من ارض مصر الى نابلس

around Samaria may be regarded as the gathering-ground of syncretistic cultures which have assimilated a more or less Christian character.[738] It is therefore highly doubtful whether this syncretism, with its strong gnostic elements, has any connection with the genuine Samaritan heritage, or whether it is only an aspect of a later development totally divorced from the true Samaritan religion. Even before the advent of Christianity, Samaria, or as it was renamed by Herod, Sebaste, had become a haven of a Hellenistic type of paganism,[739] in itself the fruitful source and cradle of all kinds of syncretistic ideologies.

The dissemination of Gnostic teaching specifically attributed to the Samaritan pseudo-Messiahs [740] does not in any way prove that their ideas arise out of their Samaritan background. Just as their Messianism is, by and large, a product of their contact with Christianity, so may their whole teaching come from a similar syncretistic environment. As compared with the figure of the Samaritan Taheb, these frenzied pseudo-Messiahs are seen to be of an entirely different background. Assuming that the concept of Taheb was already familiar in antiquity, his task must have been, as in later Samaritan literature, that of 'Restorer'. Such a description of the Taheb, then, agrees with the ancient Samaritan pretender executed by Pontius Pilate,[741] whose only object was the 'restoration' of the vessels of the Sanctuary, the reinstating of which would bring back the period of Rahutah (Divine Favour). The Gnostic pretenders on the other hand, represent the later type of personal Messiah modelled on details borrowed from the apocalyptic literature.[742] Such apocalyptic fantasies concerning a cataclysmic end of the present evil

---

[738] J. Weiss, *The History of Primitive Christianity* (English translation, F.C. Grant, London 1937), II, pp. 756f.

[739] Josephus, *Antiq.* XV, viii, 5.

[740] On Simon Magus, cf. *Acts*, viii, 9f. and Waitz, "Simon der Magier", in Herzog's *Realenzyklopadia* (3rd ed.), xviii, pp. 351ff. On Dositheus, Origen, *Contra Celsum*, I, 57; on Menander, Irenaeus, *Adversus haereses*, I, 23, 5.

[741] Josephus, *Antiq.* XVIII, iv, 1. cf. also K. Klausner, *The Messianic Idea in Israel* (English translation by W.F. Stinespring, N.Y. 1955), pp. 483f. (and for further literature, *ibid.* n. 4). Klausner (*ibid.*), was also quite right in accepting the majority opinion of scholars that the Jewish concept of "Messiah the Son of Joseph" or "Messiah the Son of Ephraim" could not have originated from the Samaritans. For further bibliography, *ibid.* nn. 6f. and recently, D.S. Russel, *The Method and Message of Jewish Apocalyptic* (Philadelphia 1964), pp. 430-436.

[742] *Enoch*, xlviii, 10; lii, 4; *Psalms of Solomon* xvii, 36; xviii, 8 etc. cf. M.S. Enslin, *Christian Beginnings* (Philadelphia 1938), pp. 138-143 and 351-372.

age, with a supernatural figure descending from heaven to administer a final judgment, have no place in Samaritan thought.

Simon Magus [743] is the most frequently mentioned 'Samaritan' heresiarch with Messianic pretentions. In his case it is certain that he had formally received baptism (*Acts*. viii, 13), and his major activities were only later, when he sought a certain collaboration with Christian heretics. His half-monotheistic, half-syncretistic viewpoint, upon which his emergence and activities depend, bear no trace of any Samaritan affinity.[744] On the other hand his mutually inconsistent claims, appearing under differing titles to differing groups (to some as "Father", to others as "Son", to others as the "Holy Spirit"), though grotesque and thoroughly deranged, are decisively of Christian origin.[745] We may well save ourselves the trouble of examining his exegesis, for we have the testimony of Hippolytus that he "interpreted in whatever way he wished both the writings of Moses and also those of the (Greek) poets". For this very reason, it is quite beside the point to quote some Gnostic or Simonean expressions and, on finding their Samaritan-Aramaic paraphrases, to suggest that these are synonymous. Even if the words are really synonymous, their meanings may be diametrically opposed, depending on the exegetical background of their respective origins. One may find in Samaritan literature a parallel to the Simonean ἡ μεγάλη ἀπόφασις but this is hardly a proof that the sect possesses "a clear Samaritan background".[746] This term may rather exemplify in the above-mentioned way the distorted employment of Christian terms and a deeply syncretistic tendency which, although freely borrowing its terminology from various sources, twists and misuses them in an entirely novel and quite inexcusable manner.

For this reason all alleged connections between Simon Magus or Dositheus and the Samaritan religion, and the conservability of their

---

[743] cf. Appel, *Quaestiones de rebus Sam. etc.*, pp. 49ff., n. 4 and *sup.* n. 740. In passing, it could be mentioned that the prophecy in the *Testament of Simeon*, VI (Charles, *Apocrypha and Pseudepigrapha etc.*, II, p. 303), about the resurrection of this Patriarch, may have some remote connection with the ostentatious claims of Simon Magus.

[744] cf. G. Widengren, *The Ascension of the Apostle and the Heavenly Book* (Uppsala 1950), pp. 40-58. The mere fact that these sects "founded their preaching and propaganda on a revealed holy writing, sometimes conceived of as brought down from heaven" precludes already any "Samaritan background".

[745] J. Weiss, *op. cit.*, pp. 759f.

[746] cf. Widengren, *op. cit.*, pp. 50f.

claiming to be 'the Taheb' in the orthodox Samaritan sense,[747] must be ruled out. Both of these pretenders have assimilated into their doctrines some Christian elements [748] which make their Messianic claims entirely different from those of the 'Restorer' figure of the Samaritans. Dositheus' claim to be "Prophet-Messiah" foretold by *Deut.* xviii, 15-18,[749] although often described as 'Samaritan Gnosticism', has far more to do with the latter than with the former. The whole concept of 'Messiah', although by its upholders associated with 'prophet' and based on Scripture, is alien to Samaritan thought.

It seems that, broadly speaking, the alleged Samaritan affinities with gnostic groups have been grossly exaggerated, often because of a Samaritan descent, as in the case of Simon Magus, or Dositheus; it has been too easily assumed that all that they represent is part and parcel of their Samaritan heritage. We may take the case of Justin Martyr to show how misleading such conclusions may be. He indeed speaks of his own nation, people, or race, the Samaritans,[750] when we know that he has absolutely no spiritual affinity with them whatsoever. If we take this expression ($\gamma\acute{\epsilon}\nu o\upsilon\varsigma$) loosely, the same standard should be applied to the 'Samaritanism' of Simon, Dositheus and all the 'Samaritan' gnostics. This is surely how we have to understand Justin's testimony concerning Simon Magus,[751] that "nearly all the Samaritans, and also a few in other *nations*, confess him and honour him as the supreme God". It is certain that the term 'Samaritans' is used by Justin in the loosest possible sense,[752] and it must refer to ethnical affinity only, and very possible to such 'Samaritans' as do not belong at all to the Samaritan religious community. It is also not impossible that these are no Samaritans, even ethnically, but belong to the Greco-pagan people of Sabaste

---

[747] cf. Schoeps, *Theologie und Geschichte etc.*, pp. 394f.

[748] Hilgenfeld, *Ketzergeschichte des Urchristentums*, pp. 155-161.

[749] Origen, *Contra Celsum*, I, 57. cf. Weiss, *op. cit.*, pp. 758-766.

[750] *Dialogue cum Tryphone Judeo*, CXX, 6 (οὐδὲ γὰρ ἀπὸ τοῦ γένους τοῦ εμοῦ, λέγω δὲ τῶν Σαμαρέων). He also calls Simon "a magician of their race". [cf. of recent date, Kippenberg, *op. cit.* (sup. n. 725), pp. 127f.]

[751] *Apology*, I, 26 and *ibid.*, II, 15, where he says: "the Samaritans... were in error in believing in Simon". Simmachus, the second century Bible translator, was also described as a Samaritan by Epiphanius, only because he was born in Samaria. However, all other Church Fathers affirm that he was an Ebionite. cf. Schoeps, *op. cit.*, p. 33 (and nn. 1-3 *ibid.*).

[752] Justin abounds with other similar vague definitions. All those who live according to the laws of Logos (or, reason), he refers to as Christians (*Apology*, I, 46). In another place (*ibid.* II, 13) he almost identifies Platonic philosophy with Christianity.

and its district. Another possibility which cannot be ruled out either is
that all these testimonies of Justin and others about 'Samaritans' refer
to those who are 'heretics', those who one way or other have already
embraced a certain deviant type of Christianity. The great anxiety
expressed in Christian literature regarding this movement and regarding
gnosticism is so greatly intensified only because they are considered as
Christian (and not Samaritan) heresies. Probably this is one of the
reason why Justin takes such great pains to dissociate Simon from the
cause which he himself is pleading.[753]

In general the figure of Simon Magus is conspicuously absent from
Samaritan religious literature;[754] and when he is mentioned by the
Chronicles his name is often misspelt,[755] which would indicate that even
his name is known from reports coming from outside sources. The further
consideration that in the pseudo-Clementine literature the figure of
Simon Magus is identified with Paulus [756] would likewise indicate that
the proper place of this character is more in the realm of Christian heretical sectarianism than in any form of Samaritan sectarianism.

As for the claim for a Samaritan origin of gnosticism, so far not a
single sources has borne it out. For the most part such claims are based
on supposed similarities gained from first impressions, usually depending
upon a few 'parallel' phrases which, at least in their Samaritan context,
are mostly ambiguous.[757] The constant hunt for Gnostic elements in
Samaritan literature, although yielding so far very meagre tangible results,
has nevertheless supplied, thanks to the assistance of a vivid imagination,
a great variety of theories and hypotheses. One is reminded of the similar
wild claims made when the Dead Sea Scrolls were first discovered, some
even going to the length of claiming that the find was the library of a
Gnostic sect.[758] Although, to be sure, many elements of later gnosticism

---

[753] *Apology*, I, 26.

[754] cf. may article in *ALUOS* VI (1969), pp. 99f., 133 (nn. 17-18).

[755] הסימונים J. Macdonald & A.J.B. Higgins, "The Beginnings of Christianity
according to the Samaritans", *NTS* XVIII (1971), p. 68 and p. 78 (cf. note on the
25th Gospel). Cf. however, Montgomery, *The Sam.*, p. 266, n. 39. In another place
(p. 256, n. 16) Montgomery remarks: "Abu'l Fath's narrative (on Dūsis) follows
immediately upon that concerning Simon Magus, a connection reminding us of some
Patristic arguments".

[756] Schoeps, *op. cit.* pp. 132f. cf. however, Kippenberg, *op. cit.* (*sup.* n. 725), pp. 129f.
(nn. 149-150 for further literature). All speculation about Samaritans in Rome, and
their pronunciation of the Tetragrammaton as Ιαβε are based on conjecture.

[757] cf. n. 746 *sup.* and n. 775 *inf.*

[758] R. McL. Wilson, *The Gnostic Problem* (London 1958), pp. 73f.

are already discernibly present in the Scrolls,[759] they fall short of 'real Gnosticism', and all the extravagant speculations have had to be abandoned.

The research into Samaritanism has a far longer history than that into the Scrolls. Since the hunt for probable Gnosticisms in Samaritan garb is constantly renewed with each new turn in the methods of the pursuit of the origins of Gnosticism, so the discovery of the Scrolls has resuscitated many of the old hypotheses propounded in this field. The advocates of a 'pre-Christian Jewish gnosticism', here again draw attention to the Samaritans.[760] Employing the most ingenious perversions of fragmentary 'evidence' culled from the New Testament,[761] and other early Christian sources centered upon Simon Magus and his influence in Samaria, such advocates have inevitably singled out Samaritanism as the chief culprit. Although there is a growing concensus of opinions which holds Gnosticism to be a pre-Christian oriental mysticism, motivated by syncretistic tendencies, the oriental features in this movement are not necessarily of Israelite origin. Despite the rich finds contained in the recent Coptic codices of Nag Hammadi, no further evidence has come to light which might cogently indicate the existence of additional and previously unknown Jewish or Samaritan features.[762] The claim for a "clear and unmistakable" affinity between Gnosticism and Samaritanism can be justified only if we accept the thesis of a pre-Christian Jewish Gnosis,[763] which was rightly rejected by scholars upon its appearance at the end of the previous century.

The so often overemphasized "evidence of Gnostic terminology", is on any showing most misleading. As stated above, such expressions may mean entirely different things to different groups. We know that even the word $\gamma\nu\hat{\omega}\sigma\iota\varsigma$, deliberately chosen for perpetrating a certain well-defined mystical teaching, may equally well be employed by non-

---

[759] R.M. Grant, *Gnosticism and Early Christianity* (N.Y. 1959), p. 39.

[760] M. Black, *The Scrolls and Christian Origins*, pp. 64f.

[761] The argument is based on the following lines: $o\tilde{v}\tau\acute{o}\varsigma\ \acute{\epsilon}\sigma\tau\iota\nu\ \acute{\eta}\ \delta\acute{v}\nu\alpha\mu\iota\varsigma\ \tau o\hat{v}\ \theta\epsilon o\hat{v}\ \acute{\eta}\ \kappa\alpha\lambda o\nu\mu\acute{\epsilon}\nu\eta\ \mu\epsilon\gamma\acute{\alpha}\lambda\eta$ (*Acts*, viii, 10) a mere editorial comment denoting $\acute{\eta}\ \mu\epsilon\gamma\acute{\alpha}\lambda\eta\ \delta\acute{v}\nu\alpha\mu\iota\varsigma$. In turn it "seems historically probable" that this was an appellation of Simon Magus. (cf. previous verse: $\lambda\acute{\epsilon}\gamma\omega\nu\ \epsilon\acute{\iota}\nu\alpha\acute{\iota}\ \tau\iota\nu\alpha\ \acute{\epsilon}\alpha\upsilon\tau\grave{o}\nu\ \mu\acute{\epsilon}\gamma\alpha\nu$; is this also an editorial comment?) Further $\delta\acute{v}\nu\alpha\mu\iota\varsigma$ = חיל which in turn "stands for God in Samaritanism". cf. also *sup.* n. 746.

[762] Driver, *The Judean Scrolls*, p. 562.

[763] M. Friedländer, *Der Vorchristliche jüdische Gnosticismus* (Göttingen 1898). cf. Black, *op. cit.* ibid.

Gnostics, deprived of all Gnostical meaning, and having no affinity with their way of thought.[764] Paraphrases or alleged 'translations' of Gnostical technical-terms are even more suspect as being devoid of any real Gnostical connotation. Individual expressions like "things concealed and revealed",[765] or "illumination"[766] and many others, even supposing that they conceal mystical theories, a supposition which in itself finds no evidence in the whole of Samaritan literature,[767] in their present context are innocent of any Gnosticism properly so-called.

The best example for the great flexibility of such expressions, though with enormous semantic differences, is the term 'Paradise',[768] which is mentioned also by Marqah.[769] But in the case of Marqah, notwithstanding the very strongly 'Gnostically' coloured vocabulary, it has no

---

[764] cf. my articles in *JJS* XI (1960), pp. 10f., 30f. (and especially p. 11, n. 72); and in *ALUOS* VI (1969), pp. 109f. (and especially p. 142, n. 90).

[765] cf. Trotter, *Gnosticism and Memar Marqah*, p. 10. Such expressions are rather free renderings of *Deut.* xxix, 28. cf. also *ibid.* p. 5. As for other 'gnostical' expressions from Marqah, however, in p. 6 it is shown that these are 'gnostical' only by language but without any real gnostical meaning. cf. also *ibid.* n. 8 where the discussion is based on misunderstanding and mistranslation of Marqah (*Memar* I, p. 18 = II, pp. 26-27).

[766] cf. Trotter, *A Critical Study etc.*, pp. 336ff. The Talmudical literature records also (*Lamentation Rabba* on I, 1; Ch. I, para 15, s.v. כותאי חד; cf. *Jer. Ma'aser-Sheni*, IV, 19, 55b) many anecdotes which show how significant was the terminology of 'light' for the Samaritans. These sources of the early 3rd century prove that this was an ancient Samaritan peculiarity. However, none of these anecdotes — although reproduced in a polemical and pejorative manner — show any sign of Gnosticism. It would be futile to discuss in detail all other cases in which Gnosticism is attributed to Marqah by Trotter (e.g. *ibid.* p. 341, wrongly identifying the midrashic *motif* of "seven things which existed before Creation" with emanations from the Pleroma, or *ibid.* pp. 310f., 324f. etc.) where the simple meaning of the context excludes any such connections. It is most unfortunate that a recent publication [cf. Kippenberg, *op. cit.* (*sup.* n. 725), pp. 125ff. (cf. also *ibid.* p. 317, n. 60)] follows such an indiscriminate system. cf. *inf.* n. 775.

[767] cf. my article in *ALUOS* (quoted *sup.* n. 764), *ibid.*

[768] פרדס appears already in the late books of the Hebrew Bible (cf. also for its ancient oriental origin *BDB*, p. 825). The LXX renders mainly גן (but also עדן in *Isaiah* li, 3), by παράδεισος (used by Xenophon to describe the parks of Persian Kings and nobles). In the N.T. the same term is used for the abode of the blessed dead (*Luke* xxiii, 43; *2 Corinthians* xii, 4; *Revelation* ii, 7. cf. Strack-Billerbeck, *Kommentar etc.*, II, pp. 264-269). The Samaritan Targum renders גן in the story of Creation as פרדס and similarly the Hebrew אשל in *Gen.* xxi, 33.

[769] *Memar Marqah* (ed. Macdonald), I, p. 37 = II, p. 56; I, p. 87 = II, p. 140; I, p. 89 = II, p. 143.

Gnostical undertones whatsoever. It is rather a *naive* midrash, utilizing plays on words and analogies.[770] The mere fact that this 'Paradise' appears in the Pseudepigrapha, in an Aramaic version from Qumran, in the New Testament (and other Christian writings), in the Merkabha-mysticism of the Rabbis,[771] and finally in Marqah, indicates that it is not so much the vocabulary as rather the content which is the deter-mining factor in these specialized shades of meaning. All Gnostic (or pre-Gnostic) characterisation read into Marqah must be rejected, unless indeed we find additional evidence that all the various circles which employed the term 'paradise' for their own purposes shared a common esoteric tradition, or unless we discover genuinely Gnostic thoughts in Samaritan literature. At least as regards to פרדיס, Marqah bears no responsibility for any esoteric speculation; he is not even inter-ested in the 'Heavenly Paradise'; but in line with his persuasive exposi-tion, he employs the symbolism of Paradise with a view to preaching observance, devotion and love of God, in which the "Garden planted by the (Law of the) Lord", is the major theme.

We have now to turn to other exaggerated claims about the Gnosticism of the Samaritans, in this case supported by parallels from Jewish mys-ticism.[772] According to these claims, Samaritanism, Gnosticism and Kabbalism do in fact ostensibly support each other by close "paral-lelism", showing ideological affinity, if not identity. Since these notions have been based upon expressions taken from the Samaritan liturgy, it would be unfair to pass judgement upon them from conclusions derived solely from sources dealing mainly with exegesis. It should, however, be borne in mind that the greatest authority on Samaritan Liturgy

---

[770] Although the expression ט׳ עבידה פרדיס גדיל׳ קשטה אמרה ואברהם חדדה (M.M. I, p. 37) is reminiscent of the פרדס קושטא a favourite term of the apocalyptics and other esoteric writings (cf. next note), it has no such meaning. The midrash of Marqah is based on the analogy of פרדיס as it was rendered by the Samaritan Targum (cf. *sup.* n. 768). 'Garden' and 'tree' are commonly used as a metaphor for the 'Law'. There is a further verbal analogy in Scripture by the expression ויטע. Thus it is said of God (*Gen.* ii, 8, who planted it by His 'word') and of Abraham (*ibid.* xxi, 33, who renewed, by his obedience the Divine plantations). The midrash is further extended to *Ex.* xv, 1 by playing on the word אז rendered in the Samaritan Targum as טטע (= טטה = τότε). By employing such primitive methods Marqah endeavoured to extend the Divine plantation (טטע = ויטע) to Moses and to his followers throughout the Torah.

[771] Scholem, *Jewish Gnosticism etc.*, pp. 14ff. (especially p. 16, n. 5 and p. 17, n. 10).

[772] Heidenheim, *Bibliotheca Samaritana*, II, pp. xxxv-xl.

strongly disapproved of any such allegations attributing Gnostical-mystical elements to the liturgy.[773]

Unfortunately, his warning was not taken at all seriously, otherwise it is hard to understand how such theories could have recently been revived with such great vigour, despite the fact that no new evidence has been unearthed in the field of Samaritan studies which could outweigh the sound judgment regarding the spuriousness of the claims for Samaritan Gnosticism. It is indeed strange that one of the very weakest links in this theory has hit the limelight. It was the identification of the expression קעם, so common in Samaritan liturgy with the gnostic ἑστώς [774] which gained so much favour, although the grounds of the additional new 'evidence' for it were deduced from Mandaic (not Samaritan) sources.[775] Furthermore, were this theory genuinely substantiated, it would indicate that the so-called 'Samaritan Gnosticism' is of a philosophical type presumably imbued with a Philonic type of theories.[776] It goes without saying that this theory diametrically opposes the equally categorical claim that Samaritanism is the source of the mythological type of Gnosticism.[777] The now established historical background, with its colourful intellectual variety, may well have given rise to both types of gnostical development. Eventually groups of Samaritan origin (or, more likely, Samaritan renegades, or people who were inhabitants of Samaria) may conceivably have been actively engaged in the formation of such groups. However, it would tax Samaritan tradition too heavily if we held its tenets to be 'per se' responsible for these mutually exclusive ideologies.

Instead of trying to sum up the bewildering and mutually contradictory reports and studies on Samaritan gnosticism, for which anyhow there is no shred of evidence in the Samaritan sources themselves, it would be

---

[773] Cowley, "Some remarks on Samaritan Literature and Religion", *JQR* VIII (1896), p. 571.

[774] Heidenheim, *op. cit.* pp. xxxvi f. (cf. *ibid.* vol. III, p. xviii).

[775] cf. *sup.* nn. 746 and 757. Recently, these arguments have been slightly modified, but nevertheless accepted by Kippenberg, *op. cit.* (*sup.* n. 725), pp. 125ff., 316f. (cf. especially p. 319, n. 72), 328ff. (cf. p. 347 "Dass aber die aram. Texte der Sam. uns den Mutterboden dieser Gnosis zeigen, erscheint mir sicher" etc.).

[776] cf. Heidenheim, *op. cit.* II, p. xxxix, n. 6 and recently Kippenberg, *op. cit.* pp. 347f., n. 136.

[777] E. Haenchen, "Gab es eine vorchristliche Gnosis?", *ZThK* XLIX (1959), pp. 326-349.

more appropriate and rewarding to quote an earlier authority,[778] whose sound evaluation is still unimpeachable:

> So far as we have been able to sound the obscure ages of Samaritan religion, even according to the hostile Jewish evidence, we can find no syncretistic features therein, no native tendency to Gnosticism. Simon Magus appears not as a type of Samaritanism, but only as an incident; doubtless there is exaggeration concerning the universality of his influence upon the Samaritans, as recorded in Acts and by Justin. From what we learn of his doctrine in these two sources, he probably found his following rather among the Hellenistic population of Samaria, than in the Samaritan sect. His claim to be the Great Power of God represents nothing we find in Samaritan doctrine, whose Messianism was of a very primitive type. Further, he left behind no influence, either upon Samaritan religion or upon its historical traditions.

Much that is pertinent to Samaritan sects is by its very nature built upon speculations, since the original writings of the sects were seldom preserved. As becomes evident from the history of sectarianism in general, despite the great upheavals, shismatic movements, by detaching themselves from the main body and owing to the consequent lack of unity in the main group, have recorded very little of these events in literature. The ruling party preserved only its own records,[779] so allowing the records of the dissident groups to fall into oblivion.

Furthermore, we have to take into account the possibility that the broad masses of the Samaritans, although following in principle the lead of their priestly leaders, remained by and large ignorant of the Law, and out of sheer ignorance violated a great part of its precepts. One is here justified in drawing an analogy from the Pharisaic circles, in which likewise there existed a certain degree of tension between the 'teachers' and the 'Am-ha-areṣ.[780] Such ignorant masses, who out of negligence failed to keep the burdensome details of the Law, were very likely treated with contempt by the priestly leadership. Such contempt may well have caused these lower classes to sink deeper and deeper into a despairing attitude of indifference and even animosity towards the spiritually *elite*, and thus towards the Torah they stand for. Being despised and considered as outcasts, they would easily become a hot-bed for all possible external influences, and supporters of schismatic

---

[778] Montgomery, *The Samaritans*, p. 268. cf. Introduction in new reprint (1968) by A.S. Halkin, p. xxiii: "Continued study of the history and culture of the Samaritans has not produced any startling revisions since the first publication of this volume".

[779] S.H. Blank, "The Dissdent Laity etc.". *HUCA* XIX (1954/6), pp. 1-42.

[780] cf. Montefiore, *Some elements of the Religious etc.*, p. 28.

movements. Just as in Rabbinic Judaism the zeal of the spiritual leaders, which of course fiercely combated paganism, was only partially successful and the uneducated masses on the outer fringes of the theocratic nation were prone to amalgamate pagan elements with their Judaism,[781] so surely would a similar situation exist among the Samaritan masses. We know from a later period that the Church Fathers often branded heretics with the label "Judaizers", although these were in actuality gnostics of non-Jewish origin, but propagating a secret wisdom commonly regarded as Jewish.[782] In some such manner it is possible that "Samaritan Gnosticism" owes much more to syncretistic cultures absorbed by the Samaritan masses living on the outer fringes of their people, than to Samaritan religion proper.

It is an equally impossible task to determine precisely how much 'authentic' Samaritanism is embodied in the dogmas and practices of the Samaritan sects. The available evidence of the Patristic literature is singularly confusing in this respect. Often one finds contradictory details about the Samaritans in general, and even more so about their sects, particularly about the Dositheans. Even the simplest allegedly historical settings are full of confusion, hopelessly irreconcilable with established historical events.[783] To take, for example, the problem of the numerical relationship between the main body and the Dosithean splinter group, we are treated to diametrically opposite opinions. While there is a testimony originating from the third century that the Dositheans are by this time almost extinct and that less than thirty of them have survived,[784] centuries later under Islamic rule they are still described as a thriving group.

One of the problems which still looms large in recent scholarly discussions is that of the Essene connections with the Samaritans. It is the testimony of Epiphanius, in which he enumerates four Samaritan sects, one of them called Essenes,[785] which forms the principal source of these speculations. The weakness of this testimony is immediately apparent

---

[781] Goodenough, *Jewish Symbols etc.*, II, p. 295.

[782] Joh. Weiss, *The History of Primitive Christianity*, II, p. 765 (cf. also *ibid.* p. 763 about the antinomian attitude of Simon).

[783] For an extreme example of these confusions, cf. *Clementine Recognitions*, I, 54. cf. also following notes.

[784] Origen, *Contra Celsum*, VI, 11. It has to be borne in mind that the author lived and taught in Caesarea, and must have had first-hand knowledge about the Samaritans. (On Samaritans in Caesarea, cf. Liebermann, *Tarbiz*, II, p. 107).

[785] cf. the whole discussion of Montgomery, *The Samaritans*, pp. 252ff.

upon comparison with other sources, since such a division into four sects is not mentioned in any other source.[786] On general historical considerations, too, one may be rightly suspicious of such late fourth-century 'evidence' about the Essenes, when all other sources are totally silent about them from the second century onward. There are moreover other good reasons for casting doubt on the accuracy of Epiphanius's report on the sects.[787] Obviously there are points of resemblance between Essene and Samaritan observance;[788] however, this in itself does not necessarily mean that the Essenes should or could be identified as one of the sects of the Samaritans. As we have seen on other occasions, all types of sectarian rigorism had much in common, especially in the matter of extending the scope of the 'Law' by their rigid expositions. The theme of ritual purity was, in particular, a fruitful field for such rigoristic exaggerations, in which most sects had a broadly common background.[789]

Although it might seem superfluous to re-emphasize so often this well-known fact (i.e. that external similarity does not prove identity), in view of the recent rehabilitation of claims for the existence of Samaritan Essenes, a warning here is by no means out of place. It was only natural that the discoveries of the Dead Sea Scrolls should increase such interest in the possible inter-connection between the sects. Ever since the Zadokite Fragments were found, scholars have sought to identify the sect which produced these documents with various groups, including the Dositheans.[790] While it has already been demonstrated beyond cavil that the Zadokite Fragments are coloured by very many features far closer to the Pharisaic or main-stream Jewish type of ideas than to anything resembling Samaritanism, attempts at trying to establish contacts between the Scrolls and the Samaritans have persisted.[791]

---

[786] With the exception of those who follow Epiphanius, cf. Montgomery, *op. cit.* p. 253, n. 3.

[787] M. Black, "The Patristic Accounts etc.", *BJRL* XLI, pp. 298f. (cf. *ibid.* n. 3); Alon, *Studies*, II, pp. 6f.

[788] Montgomery, *op. cit.*, p. 263; Even Montgomery's careful conclusion ("Some elements making the Essenes a Samaritan sect.") has to be modified. The *only* element of truth is the common sectarian mentality with all its extreme practices. cf. my article in *ALUOS* VI (1969), *passim.*

[789] cf. my article, *op. cit.* pp. 112f.; 147f. (nn. 118f.); 149f. (nn. 127f.).

[790] cf. Rowley, *The Zadokite Fragments etc.*, p. 79, n. 4.

[791] cf. Bowman, "Contact etc.", *VT* vii (1957), pp. 184ff.; Massingberd-Ford, "Can we exclude Sam. influence from Qumran?", *Revue de Qumran*, VI (1967), pp. 109ff.

Such arguments brush aside the wide and surely obvious ideological gulf which existed between the two groups, the Scrolls representing, as they do, the extreme glorification of the prophets. They find in the prophetic words the very key to their *raison d'être*, and their energies are devoted to the task of 'uncovering' these from any prophetic 'hints'. The Samaritan radically opose this trend of thought, denying the Prophets altogether. The superficial parallelisms of laws and practices tend also to exaggerate the apparent value of these similarities, without taking into account that such 'heterodox' tenets were common also amongst other sects.[792] It may be said in conclusion that, notwithstanding certain undeniable similarities in practice, it is quite inconceivable that any real mutual relationship existed between the Samaritans and the Essenes. If indeed there ever existed a Samaritan or Dosithean sect possessing real Essene characteristics, this must have been the outcome of a synchrenistic amalgamation equally remote from both sources of influence. The authenticity of Epiphanius's testimony is not borne out by any other source; and the assertion that it tallies with "particularly Samaritan sources"[793] is patently fantastic. The anyhow shaky evidence of this writer [794] is further seriously undermined by his polemical outbursts; in brief, "the insane practices" of these groups (as he calls them) blinded his innate lack of objectivity to such a degree as to lead to a general confusion of the sects. In the anti-heretical literature Epiphanius does not stand alone in committing such blunders. This confusion of the sects, and in particular of the Dositheans with similar sectarian groups, is a facile error of judgment, of which others are also guilty.[795]

If we may trust the majority of sources, which seems to be the most logical method, we may so subdivide the Samaritan Schismatic movement into two major groups. It looks as if the 'orthodox' Samaritans were constantly challenged by a Dosithean 'heresy' which in fact polarized the people into opposing factions, although the Dosithean faction

---

[792] The most important of these similarities are: prohibition of niece marriages (*Zad. Fragm.*, V, 8); quantity of pool for immersion (*ibid.*, X, 11); prohibition to spend the Sabbath amongst heathens (*ibid.* XI, 14); offerings on the Sabbath (*ibid.* XI, 18); ritual killing of fish and locust (*ibid.* XII, 13f.) etc. cf. my article, *op. cit. passim.*

[793] cf. Crown, "Dositheans, Resurrection etc.", *Antichthon*, I (1967), p. 74. A detailed discussion of the Samaritan sources will follow anon.

[794] cf. *sup.* n. 787.

[795] Schoeps, *Theologie und Geschichte etc.*, pp. 393f. (cf. also *ibid.* pp. 13, 247ff. on connections between Essenes and Ebionites).

may have occasionally further split into smaller splinter groups. The picture of this twofold division is most clearly discernible in the reports of early Mediaeval sources, where the two groups are normally termed Kūshān and Dūstān.[796]

From hints in the Talmudic literature it appears that this subsequently permanent division into two principal groups goes back to antiquity. The two archetypes symbolizing these groups are called סבאי (= Sabbei of Sabbuaei) and דוסתאי (= Dositheans).[797] Upon careful examination of the Talmudic sources it has been inferred [798] that the Sabbuaeans were in many respects closer to the Rabbinic opinions. It is therefore reasonable to suggest that this group must have been the 'orthodox' or the conservative element of the Samaritans, and that they thus retained more elements of the common Israelite heritage than did the schismatic and subversive Dositheans.[799]

While it is reasonable to assume that the main stream of Samaritans (whether the Sabbuai of Antiquity of the Kūshāniyya of our Mediaeval sources) adhered rigidly to their ancient traditions without any significant deviations, the position of the so-called Dosithean group is unclear. Although we may indeed be justified in calling this fraction by a single name, such as Dositheans, it is very doubtful whether the name connotes one continuous movement. There exists a bewildering and exasperating confusion in the literature concerning the Dositheans.[800] Many theories have been put forward by scholars on the exact number of heresiarchs named 'Dositheus', which in itself indicates how difficult it is to reconcile the details of our various sources, referring most probably to different groups of 'Dositheans'. The now almost century-old endeavour to synthesize all the heresiarchs called Dosis or Dositheus into one historical person [801] cannot be rationally maintained in face of the contradictory

---

[796] Hamburger, *Real-Encyclopädie etc.*, II, pp. 1068ff. For the etymological explanation of these terms, cf. Montgomery, *The Samaritans*, p. 253, nn. 5-6; p. 254, n. 10 and p. 259.

[797] Kirchheim, *Karme Shomron*, p. 1, n. 2 and p. 25. Josephus (*Antiq.* xiii, III, 4) mentions also these two legendary figures under the names of Sabbaeus and Theodosius. cf. Montgomery *op. cit.* pp. 254f. and p. 262, n. 32.

[798] Leiberman, *Shkiin*, pp. 25f. (and cf. *ibid.* for further bibliographical details).

[799] cf. *inf.* nn. 820ff.

[800] Montgomery, *op. cit.*, pp. 252ff. Driver, *The Judean Scrolls*, pp. 78ff.

[801] cf. *sup.* n. 726. The weakest point in Appel's thesis is the identification of the 'orthodox' groups with those who follow Sadducean practices and the Dositheans

data. It has been latterly suggested that we must reckon with at least two entirely different sects, going back very likely to different heresiarchs called by the same name.[802] This solution is on any showing the most reasonable, since Abu'l Fath records quite distinctly two manifestly different types of sects of Dositheans;[803] but even this theory by no means solves the many intricate problems created by contradictory reports concerning the 'Dositheans'.

Anything one might postulate about the Dositheans of Antiquity would thus necessarily belong to the realm of guesswork and hypothesis, since the sources do not enable us to form any clear-cut description of their real historical character.[804] On the later mediaeval sects there are more and more trustworthy reports; and we do know that, at least from the late Byzantine period, they maintained an energetic and forceful opposition to the 'normative' group. Abu'l Fath dates their origin from the time of Baba Rabba in the fourth century; however, scholars now incline to believe that Abu'l Fath post-dated their origin by several centuries.[805] At any rate, it is reasonable to assume that, even if we accept the fact that the Dosithean sects were founded by two separate heresiarchs living centuries apart, there may well have been contact between the earlier and the later sect, and even real resemblances (if not identity) in their schismatic approach and general disposition. This is all we are at present justified in regarding as credible on the available evidence.

From the Islamic conquest onwards, the sources speak invariably of these two factions of the Samaritans. Even in the histories of the Conquest, when administration, taxation and the various amounts of poll-tax are mentioned, any comment on the poll-tax imposed on the Samaritans draws into the report the contending groups.[806] The grim Supplement to Abu-l Fath's chronicle, outlining the Islamic period, likewise

---

with those who follow Jewish ones. The Rabbinic sources would indicate the opposite. However, the evidence from these sources (including that Josephus) is not conclusive and they should not be forced. cf. van Goudever, *Biblical Calendars*, p. 21; Crown, *op. cit.* p. 77. "It is *probable* that these names merely symbolise the sects." cf. *ibid.* p. 81 "Josephus *distinguishes* two sects".

[802] Montgomery, *The Samaritans*, p. 261.
[803] Vilmar, *Abulfathi annales Sam.*, pp. 82 and 151 respectively.
[804] Montgomery, *op. cit.* pp. 252-256.
[805] *ibid.* pp. 263f.
[806] Ben-Zevi, *Sepher ha-Shomronim*, p. 32; cf. *sup.* n. 796.

mentions the struggles of this sect against the 'normative' group down to the middle of the ninth century.[807]

As mentioned above, we are faced with the serious problem as to why the exegetical literature is silent about the Dositheans, in contrast to the Chronicles which devote much space to them. The easy answer, that Dosithean references may have been censored or excised, does not in itself eliminate the difficulty, since by the same token the Chronicles could have suffered the same fate. Equally untenable, surely, is the hypothesis that, from the time of Baba Rabba, the great writers, liturgists and commentators were all 'Dositheans' until the fourteenth century, when "the priestly party absorbed the Dositheans".[808]

This whole notion of Baba Rabba's heretical and schismatic inclination is pure imagination and demonstrably in diametrical opposition to the obvious meaning of all the Chronicles, all of which hail him as the great hero and the pious restorer of their ancient traditions. This mistaken notion is grounded on the false premise that, for the 'orthodox' or 'priestly' group, "the essence of worship had been sacrifices" on Hargerizim, to which Baba supposedly objected. Hence, his activities in building synagogues on this view are for the express purpose of replacing sacrifices (and of opposing the centralization of worship upon Hargerizim) by newly devised liturgical compositions (which could be recited in all places).[809] It is obvious enough that, according to this opinion, the praises of Baba, in response to his efforts in initiating a religious revival amongst the Samaritans, must somehow be explained away. The expression גלה אימנות קשטה however indicates that the synagogues he built were unquestionably dedicated for the sake of the *true* belief and the *true* God.[810] Similarly, ואלף מקרת ארהותה shows that his teaching and reading of *the Law* was the authentic one, without any Dosithean tinge or adulteration. Both expressions are the unequivocal and whole-hearted exaltations of a genuine 'Sage', and not in any sense vague references to an adversary, or said by one with his tongue in his cheek, merely to cover up his subject's true but 'scandalous' identity.

---

[807] Vilmar, *op. cit.* pp. LXXX-LXXXIV (a summary of the Supplement in the Paris Ms., Ms. C.); Montgomery, *op. cit.* p. 258.

[808] Bowman, "The Importance of Sam. Researches", *ALUOS* I (1958/9) pp. 48f.

[809] Bowman, "Pilgrimage to Mount Gerizim", *ERETZ-ISRAEL*, vii (1963), pp. 21f.

[810] Neubauer, "Chronique Sam. etc.", *JA* XV (1869), p. 404 (= Extract, 1873, p. 19). Bowman's explanation about Baba turning Dosithean ("This was embarrassing for later Sam. priestly historians... The Priestly Genealogy, the Tolidah, admits he was a priest, but covers up his anti-priestly and laicising practices...") has absolutely no support in the sources.

Furthermore, (and this is fairly conclusive), in none of our reliable sources is there any evidence whatever that the 'orthodox" or "Priestly" group practised any sacrificial cult (save for the Passover Offering),[811] or that the opposition of the Dositheans was in fact directed against any such cult. The whole of this fantastic theory of Baba's alleged 'revolution' is based on exaggerated and overstrained developments of an in any case legendary and inflated picture of Baba's activities, for which the narrator, Abu'l Fatḥ, disclaims any responsibility.[812] The significance of the building of synagogues by Baba has been also grossly distorted. Although it has to be admitted that from the Chronicles one may well get the (erroneous) impression that Baba's activity represents the earliest form of Synagogue worship,[813] there is nowhere any hint that this was an activity directed *against* the centralization of worship on Hargerizim. All in all, we have no knowledge of any Dosithean opposition to the worship on Hargerizim; the Chronicles mention only in connection with the splinter groups that they renounced the Holy Centre. On the contrary, from the end of the Supplement to the Chronicle of Abu'l Fatḥ [814] it may be deduced that, as late as the ninth century, the Dositheans were still actively interested in having access to the place of their Sanctuary. When the ruler of Palestine (Yūsuf ibn-Dasi) gave permission to the Samaritans to re-establish their worship on Hargerizim, this privilege was in point of fact denied to the Dositheans. This would indicate that the Dositheans were at that time desirous to have access to the Holy Mount and to participate in the worship. It is not entirely inconceivable that, owing to this very decree (which may have snapped their last link with Samaritanism) and to other troubles which ensued when Samaritanism experienced a mass and enforced conversion to Islam, the Dositheans may have thus become (and very understandably) the main participants in this apos-

---

[811] cf. *inf.* nn. 909ff.

[812] cf. *sup.* nn. 325f., 663ff. and text there.

[813] Adler & Seligson, "Une nouvelle chronique Sam.", *REJ*, Repr. 1903, p. 55; just as building synagogues does not automatically prove Dositheanism, similarly building (or digging) pools for immersion does not serve as an evidence for Essene-Dosithean practices. (cf. Crown, "Dositheans, Resurrection etc.", *Antichthon*, I (1967), p. 84). The strict rules of ritual purity amongst the Samaritans made such provisions essential. It seems only natural that as soon as Baba gained some concessions from the oppressive policies of the Byzantine rule, he hastened to provide all religious and ritual facilities for his persecuted people.

[814] cf. n. 807 *sup.*

tatizing. Perhaps in thus unavoidably dwindling, towards the end of the ninth century, to a negligible few, they lost any significance they had ever had.

If this theory is correct, we may gain a readier understanding as to why sources written in Arabic, and with the exception of those Chronicles which had necessarily to report history, are silent on the Dositheans. These authors, who wrote from the eleventh century onwards, were acquainted with the Dositheans from historical sources only. Having had them described as a wicked 'heretical' sect, which in the meanwhile had lost all significance, these authors did not feel at all inclined to enter into barren arguments with this type of 'apostates'. Even assuming that much of the material of these authors reflects the ancient traditions, i.e. the unpleasant and embarrassing details of the Dosithean controversy, all of course condemned it out of hand as outright 'infidelity', which could be conveniently deleted from their memory. This phenomenon is not unlike the almost total silence of the Rabbinic sources about the Essenes.[815]

Our problem is still not satisfactorily solved, since we have yet to deal with that most authoritative of Samaritan writers, namely with Marqah. Even accepting the hypothesis that Marqah himself was a Dosithean,[816] this again would not solve our problem, since in this case we could turn the tables and rightly ask: why then does he not mention the opposite "priestly party"? We have shown elsewhere,[817] that all the fanciful allegations attributing anti-priestly and antinomian tendencies to Marqah are based on a grave misunderstanding. Moreover, from a general survey of Marqah's writing it may be asserted without any shadow of doubt that there are absolutely no 'unorthodox' elements in his teaching; or, in other words, to quote an authority who, as a result of his ongoing work on Marqah, came to this same conclusion: (Marqah's) "general teaching was accepted by all later writers".[818]

That Marqah does not attack the Dositheans is not so very surprising in the light of our earlier findings,[819] namely, that even the most controversial points in the dispute with the Jews are not mentioned by him.

---

[815] Hamburger, *Real-Encyclopädie etc.*, II, pp. 172f.

[816] Bowman, "Pilgrimage etc.", *ERETZ-ISRAEL* VII (1963), p. 22.

[817] *ALUOS* VI (1969), pp. 110 and 156, n. 180; cf. *sup.* n. 667.

[818] J. Macdonald, *The Theology of the Sam.*, p. 35.

[819] cf. *sup.* n. 713-714 and text there. Recently H.G. Kippenberg argued that Markah's writings contain anti-Dosithean polemics (*Garizim und Synagogue*, Berlin 1971, pp. 313ff.).However, his arguments are not convincing. None of the sources

It seems that the deliberately solemn style of the Memar prevented him from incorporating any polemical material, or even hints of or subtle allusions to any of the adversaries of his people.

The total silence of the entire Samaritan literature (except the Chronicles) about the Dositheans, may also be validly attributed to the fact that this sect may have become entirely separate from the old fold. Consequently, they were no longer considered by the "orthodox" Samaritans as co-religionists, but rather as apostates who had corrupted the entire old tradition to the extent of creating a novel, false and wicked religion, which did not merit any mention when dealing with sacred subjects.

We may notice here that inconsistent reports concerning the Dositheans make it virtually impossible to state about them any certain and unequivocal characteristics. It is even uncertain whether they should be described as one continuous sect, with further schismatic vacillations, or as a series of successive and recrudescent heresiarchs, instigators of a number of sects of the same name. One point, however, may be regarded as certain, namely, that the Dositheans were treated by the opposing Samaritan 'orthodoxy' as infidels who should be totally divorced from their own religion.

Abu'l Fatḥ, when speaking on the ancient Dustān sect, supposedly going back to the time of Alexander the Great,[820] he hints that even the etymology of the name 'Dustān' indicates seduction and corruption.[821] According to this report: "a group separate itself from amongst the Samaritans and created for itself a *separate faith*; they were called 'Dustān' because they annulled the festivals of God and *all the traditions* of their fathers and ancestors, and they controverted the Samaritans on countless matters (of law)." Without here entering into the details of these 'un-Samaritan' usages, some of them enumerated by Abu'l Fatḥ,[822] for our purpose it is sufficient to note the general tenor of the controversy, which was in fact a matter of whether the Dositheans should be rejected

---

quoted by him are explicitly polemical. Even if we assume that these expressions are implicit polemics, these may be rather directed against the Hebrew Prophets (cf. *ibid.* p. 321, n. 84) or against Christianity.

[820] Vilmar, *Abulfathi annales Sam.*, p. 82. وفى ذلك الوقت انفصل من جماعة السامرة فرقة وعملوا لهم مذهبا بمفردهم وسميوا الدستان لاجل ابطالهم اعياد الحق وجميع ما نقلوه عن ابائهم واجدادهم وخالفوا السامرة فى اشياء

[821] As if دستان would be derived from the Arabic دس cf. *inf.* n. 828.

[822] Montgomery, *The Sam.*, pp. 254f.

as not being true Samaritans. Even more instructive is Abu'l Fatḥ's conclusion, in consequence of which the infidelity of the sect of Dustān is even more emphatically pointed out:[823] "They became antagonistic (owing to their apostasy) to the Samaritans in many matters of doctrine and religious precepts. Consequently, they became separated from them (i.e. the Samaritans), creating for themselves separate synagogues and a separate priesthood". From this last remark it at once becomes obvious, too, that one cannot generalize in an irresponsible way, by labelling the Dositheans an antipriestly sect.[824]

We know from the Zadokite fragments (iv, 3f.) that, despite their peculiar practice of utilizing for midrash priestly references to 'the sons of Zadok", as if these referred indisputably to the "elect of Israel", i.e. the Sect as a whole, this fact in itself does not imply that they did not recognize the priestly prerogatives. On the contrary, the priests "who had kept the charge" were by then highly regarded.[825] As a matter of fact, the whole hierarchy of the Sect is built on a priestly leadership. The same may very well also apply in the case of the Dositheans. Although, in matters of calendaric calculations, levitical purity and other 'priestly' precepts, they may have strongly opposed the 'orthodox' priesthood and even initiated heretical practices, the Sect may nevertheless have centred around its *own* priesthood. It is even possible that their reverence for their own concept of priesthood (as is instanced by Zadokite Fragments) exceeded that of the other Samaritans. One of the strange ordinances of the Dositheans, of which so far little notice has been taken, is their extension for the provisions for the immunity of the priest to defilement. Here we find a good Samaritan (or, in general, sectarian) hermeneutical principle, albeit employed in an 'unorthodox' manner, and designed solely for the purpose of elevating the status of the priests. According to Abu'l Fatḥ [826] the Dositheans allowed their

---

[823] Vilmar, *op. cit.* p. 83. وكانوا يخالفوا السامرة فى اشياء كثيرة من سـوى اعتقادات واحكام ولذلك افتردوا منهم وجعلوا لهم كنائس بذاتهم وكـهـنة بذاتهم

[824] cf. Goudoever, *Biblical Calendars*, p. 21 (and cf. *ibid.* n. 42 for his sources).

[825] Rabin, *Zad. Frag., ad loc.* n. 3.

[826] Vilmar, *ibid.* ما واباحوا لكهنتهم ان يدخلوا الى البيت الناطر ونظروا فيه ولا يتكلموا واذا خرجوا الى برّا يكونوا طاهرين والبيت ناطر قياسا على البيت الوضح

priests to enter an unclean house in order to decide on the degree of defilement of its contents, provided he remained silent about the matter until his coming out. Then the house might be proclaimed unclean while the priest himself remained in his state of levitical purity. This practice was in fact established by employing an anlogy from the case of the "plagued house" (*Lev.* xiv, 36-38).[827] Admittedly, analogy was one of the most frequently employed hermeneutical principles among all sectarians in general; however, this Dosithean usage is unique, because it stretches the legitimate scope of analogy too widely by far. This furthermore shows that, notwithstanding the extravagant and largely arbitrary expositions of the Dositheans, it is precisely the priestly aspect of their heretical schism which dominates their minds.

The importance of a really deep insight into exegesis can thus hardly be overestimated; this is demonstrated by the above mentioned case. Precisely because no notice was hitherto taken of the Dositheans' exegetical background, they were branded erroneously as an anti-priestly sect. However, the midrash shows their real character, as is evident also from other descriptions by Abu'l Fath. Much of their rigoristic legislation is also bound up with their notions of levitical purity, which would only add force to the above contentions.

But the most significant aspect of these exegetical points is that they aid us in determining the status of the Dositheans vis-a-vis the 'orthodox' group. It may be asserted that these points substantiate beyond cavil that the schism was not initiated because of anti-priestly feelings, but grew out of the tension between the ancient rigid traditionalism and certain Messianic pretensions, with all the reformistic features invariably attending them. Our whole argument thus stands or falls by these priestly elements which are clearly discernible in Dositheanism, since through them we may the better realize that our sources do not contrast priestly elements with anti-priestly ones, but 'orthodox' traditionalism with heretical sectarian innovations. While one may indeed not take very seriously Abu'l Fath's etymological derivation of Dustän, we have no reason to doubt the validity of the essential characteristics suggested by him, which are amply supported by our evidence from exegesis, all

---

[827] cf. *Sifra, ad loc.* (ed. Weiss, 73a); *Nega'im* XII, 5; *Ḥullin*, 10b; *Nedarim*, 56b. The Rabbis used also anaology for comparing defilement "by reason of a dead body" to that of a "plagued house" in some cases of impurity of vessels (*Nega'im* XIII, 12), but not for extending the immunity of the priest from impurity beyond the case mentioned in Scripture (*Lev.* xiv).

serving to show that the sect was not anti-priestly but rather revolutionary, nonconformist and anti-traditional. In any case, it is quite
unjustifiable to introduce a new etymology by assuming that Dustān
originated from דוש, and through such an exercise to reach the conclusion that the Dositheans were so called because they "tread well-known
paths."[828] Such a gratuitous hypothesis would certainly contradict the
plain sense of a great number of sources.

Briefly, any exaggerated claim for Dosithean elements in any of
the known Samaritan literature must be flatly rejected. To take one
instance only, the alleged Dosithean allusions in the "Book of Joshua"[829]
are patently fantastic. No single doctrine of the Book shows Dosithean
features, and its details and general outlook cannot at any point be
identified with Dosithean teachings.[830]

The problem of the belief in the resurrection of the dead is one of the
most intricate in Samaritan studies in general, and it becomes even more
complicated in the circles of their sectarians. The evidence gathered
from various sources is often self-contradictory. The extant Samaritan
literature in its entirety witnesses to a fully developed belief in the hereafter, contrary to the testimony of the Church Fathers and the Rabbis,
who denied this belief amongst the Samaritans. Nevertheless, we may

---

[828] Crown, "Dosietheans etc.", *Antichthon*, I (1967), p. 77. One could easily find
other explanations as e.g. دستان (Persian) scoffer or magician (cf. *Aruch Completum*,
III, p. 168b). It goes without saying that the explanation offered at the beginning of
the 18th century (de Sacy, *Chrestomathie arabe*, I, p. 335) are still superior to the
very modern ones. Similarly, we may answer negatively the following rhetorical
question: "Were the Dositheans those who in contrast to the Sabbeans with their
reversal of the festivals, continued to follow the familiar patterns whilst using a solar
calendar?" (Crown, *ibid.*). Apart from the fantastic setting of the sources on their
heads, making out of the Dositheans a conservatist movement, if we are permitted
to learn anything from Jewish sources (cf. *sup.* n. 798), then the Sabbeans were the
sect closer to Judaism, and consequently the more unchanged in their practices.

[829] cf. Bowman, "The Importance, etc.", *ALUOS* I (1958/9), p. 50; Trotter,
A Critical Study etc., p. 482; Crown, *op. cit.* p. 80. The latter in particular multiplies
all sorts of hypotheses without any support. The weakest link, however, is the alleged
Dositheanism "influenced by patristic typology" in connection with the circum-
cision ceremony of the Israelites in Gilgal, by Joshua. However, this incident was
omitted from all Samaritan versions of the Book of Joshua, cf. J. Macdonald, *The
Sam. Chronicle No. II*, pp. 17, 81f. and Hebrew text p. 12. cf. also A. Loewenstamm,
"A Karaite Commentary, etc.", *Sefunoth* viii (1965), p. 178.

[830] The copious notes and excurses of the Arabic version (*Chronicon Sam.*) edited
by Juynboll, show clearly the identity of ideas of this book with the whole of Samaritan
literature. cf. also J. Macdonald, *op. cit.* pp. 10ff., 38ff.

safely assume that at least from the 4th century the Samaritans held to a firm confession of this belief.[831] On the other hand, the Dositheans are reported by some external sources as believing in the resurrection of the dead and by others as rejecting this belief.[832] Disregarding, however, these conflicting reports, and even taking it for granted that all Dositheans strongly adhered to the belief in resurrection, it still by no means follows that their rejection of the formula "Blessed by our God for ever",[833] is in any way connected with this belief.

One is perfectly justified in pondering whether there exists any connection between this latter Dosithean rejection and the Rabbinic enactment (*Berakoth* IX, 5) to change "the conclusion of every benediction in the Temple" from "For everlasting" to "From everlasting to everlasting".[834] In the case of the Rabbis, it is certain that this change was devised as an anti-heretical enactment, most probably aimed against the Sadducees,[835] who of course proclaimed that "there is but one world". In their eagerness to reaffirm the belief in "the world to come", the Rabbis changed the original formula of the benediction. There is, however, no justification for arbitrarily transferring this practice to the Dositheans, since none of the sources mentions or even hints at any such, or similar, formula amongst the latter.

A variety of tentative explanations on entirely different grounds may be found for the rejection of the formula "Blessed be our God for ever" by the Dositheans, without unwarrantably connecting it with its 'Rabbinic parallel'. It is possible that the motivation was their belief in the externity of the material world, which would plausibly render the expression לעולם meaningless. Islamic sources, at least, provide us with

---

[831] Montgomery, *op. cit.* pp. 250f.

[832] *ibid.* pp. 257f.

[833] Vilmar, *op. cit.* p. 82. ברוך אלהינו לעולם وحرمـوا

[834] cf. Appel, *Questiones de rebus Sam. etc.*, pp. 92 (n. 4) and 96f.

[835] The common printed texts read צדוקים while Mss. מינים (cf. Rabbinovicz, *Varia lectiones... Talmud Babylonicum*, I, p. 289). Nevertheless it must refer to Sadducees. cf. *JQR* N.S. VI (1915), p. 314. It is most unlikely that such a change in the Jewish liturgy would be directed against the Samaritans. (cf. Jost, *Geschichte etc.*, I, p. 65, n. 5). The liturgies in the Temple in Jerusalem would not be altered to counteract Samaritan heresies. The Sadducees, on the other hand, were at times quite influential amongst the priestly aristocracy and their denial of "the world to come" is well known (*Sanhedrin* 90a & b). A number of enactments (e.g. *Menaḥoth*, x, 3; *Parah* III, 7; *Yadayim* IV, 8-6 etc.) were directed against them. cf. recently E.E. Urbach, *The Sages — their Concepts and Beliefs* (Hebrew, Jerusalem 1969), p. 109, nn. 37-38.

some evidence to show that such a belief served as an important demarcation-line between the sects of Dustān and Kūshān.[836]

Another possibility, which looks even more plausible, is that of
associating the rejection of this formula with some kind of opposition
to the employment of the Name of God or the Tetragrammaton. While
the exact debating points of this controversy are not crystal-clear, the
principle contentions are broadly discernible upon a through investigation. We are told by Abu'l Fath, with regard to the splinter-groups of
Dūsīs,[837] that Shaliyah altered the reading of the Great Name, and
enjoined that one should not say anything else but "Blessed be He".
Later, however, while describing another splinter-group (the sons of
Josadak), he asserts that they agreed with Shaliyah in abolishing the
formula "And blessed be His Name for ever".[838] Such a rejection by
Shaliyah is not mentioned at all by Abu'l Fath, so how could they be
said to agree on this particular point? It seems, therefore, that (at least
in the mind of Abu'l Fath) Shaliya and the Sons of Josadak commonly
opposed an 'orthodox' Samaritan formula which must be assumed to
have read: "Blessed be the Lord (or our God) for ever and blessed by
His Name for ever". At any rate, there must have been a controversy
about such or a similar liturgical refrain, which is still popular in the
Samaritan liturgy.[839] Hints dropped by Abu'l Fath indicate that the same
type of changes was common both to the ancient sect called Dustān [840]
and the later group of Dūsīs,[841] all centering around the enunciation
of the Name of God.

The horror of enunciating the Tetragrammaton was almost universal.

---

[836] De Sacy, *Chrestomatie arabe*, I, pp. 103, 342. احد الصنفين (الدوستان؟)

يقول بقدم العالم

[837] Vilmar, *op. cit.*, p. 162. [= negative?] وغير قراءة الاسم الاعظم وقال ما

يقرا' الا (إلّا) בריך הוא

[838] Vilmar, *op. cit.*, p. 163. וברוך שמו לעולם على ابطال (شليه =) واتفقوا معه على

[839] Cowley, *The Sam. Liturgy*, I, pp. 4, 5, 7, 9, 12, 38, 80f., 85, 100 etc. The Books
of *Memar Marqah* are also concluded by this refrain, Abu'l Fath reports (*ibid.*) that
the Sons of Josadak abolished another liturgical refrain (*Deut.* xxxiii, 4, used mainly
in Qeṭafim) which is still in use amongst the 'orthodox' Samaritans (Cowley, *op. cit.*
I, p. 115; II, p. 468 etc.).

[840] cf. *inf.* n. 842.

[841] cf. *inf.* n. 891. It seems that Abu'l Fath tended to identify the earlier and later
sects. In relating the schism of the splinter groups of Dūsīs he refers to them as Dustān

In most circles it was even considered that such an act of "blasphemy" should be punished by the death sentence. Philo, following the LXX on *Lev.* xxiv, 16, understood Scripture to be consistent with that vein.[842] Similarly, Josephus [843] must have relied on this verse when describing the miracles of Moses and the Holy Name whose meaning he was taught by God; and he hastens to add that it is forbidden to say anything further on this Name. This opinion was not confined to or exclusive to Hellenistic Judaism,[844] for it seems that even some Rabbinic circles too were in favour of it.[845] In general, moreover, the Rabbis considered this source of horror a cardinal offence, to be punished by denying the offender the "share in the world to come".[846] The only exception was made for the High Priest, who had perforce to enunciate the Tetragrammaton in public on the Day of Atonement during his ministration in the Temple of Jerusalem.[847] There was also a certain way of enunciating the Name allowed to priests administering the benediction in the Temple; but this was not done audibly, but rather in a secretive way, i.e. caught up in the melodies and in the dragged-out intonation of the words of the Blessing.[848]

Not only was the Tetragrammaton held in such sanctity, but even any of its substitutes or any other divine name was forbidden to be "taken in vain".[849] There were a host of substitutes for the Tetragrammaton, all most probably originating from this awe of enunciating the

---

وقال عن نفسه انه اب لكل من سمع منه وكانوا الدستان (*ibid.* p. 162) ينادوه يا ابونا وتلاميذه يقولوا فتح الله ابينا شليه cf. also Vilmar in his introduction, p. lxxiii. Appel (*Questiones de rebus Sam. etc.*, p. 95) relies too heavily on this evidence, thus unifies all groups into one continuous Dosithean sect. cf. Montgomery, *The Sam.*, pp. 261f.

[842] *De Vita Mosis*, III, para 25.

[834] *Antiq.*, II, xii, 3-4.

[844] B. Jacob, *Im Namen Gottes* (Berlin 1903), pp. 103f.

[845] Onqelos renders it (like the LXX) ודי פריש שמא די״י יתקטלא but it is not at all certain that it meant that the mere pronunciation is punished by death, but rather that one who blasphemes is liable to capital punishment only if he pronounced the Name (cf. *Sanhedrin*, 56a). However, the translation is ambiguous and one would expect Onqelos to add וארגם as in verse 11.

[846] *Sanhedrin*, X, 1 (= 90a; 101b) and parallels (cf. Tosafoth, *Abhoda-Zarah*, 18a, s.v. הוגה השם).

[847] *Yoma*, 39b; 69b. cf. Alon, *Studies etc.*, I, pp. 194ff.

[848] *Qiddushin*, 71a; cf. also *Sotah*, 36b, *Tamid*, 33b, and Alon (previous note) *ibid.* p. 199.

[849] *Nedarim*, 7b, 10a etc. cf. Jer. *Berakhoth*, VI, 1; 10a etc.

'real' Name.[850] Possibly the widespread employment of Divine Names for magical incantations, in which the *nomina sacra* were considered as the major 'powers' by which the charm was effected, intensified the objection to such enunciations, since there existed the constant danger that they might recall the syncretistic and pagan connotations attached to them.[851] However, although the attitude which equated the 'Name' with the 'Power' which might act unaccountably and hence supernaturally was almost taken for granted, and although all kinds of magical formulae were freely interchanged between Greco-pagan and Judahic circles,[852] this in itself could not have been the only reason for banning the enunciation of the Tetragrammaton. Admittedly, the derivatives of the Tetragrammaton, such as 'Ιαώ, 'Ιεου etc. were the most popular in this type of magical papyri; but other Names, including the substitutes for the Tetragrammaton (e.g. 'Αδωναιε), were also used by the same sources.[853] It looks very much as if the main reason for the awe felt in enunciating the Tetragrammaton must in fact have been connected with the prohibition in the Ten Commandments : "Thou shall not take the name of the Lord in vain".[854]

The question now arises, what was the attitude of Samaritans and their sectarians, the Dositheans, to this problem? The 'Orthodox' Samaritans are notorious for their replacement of the Tetragrammaton by שמה, just as the Jews universally use the substitute אדני; in either case, there is absolutely no precedent for any individual of these groups enun-

---

[850] Jacob, *op. cit.* (n. 844), pp. 1ff., L.Z. Lauterbach, "Substitutes for the Tetragrammaton", *PAAJR* II (1930/31), pp. 39ff.

[851] cf. Alon, *op. cit.* (n. 847), pp. 202f.

[852] Onqelos translates *Ex.* ix, 16, ובדיל דיהון משתען גבורת שמי בכל ארעא It is true that the context in *Sanhedrin* (*sup.* n. 846) suggest also magical connection, but the usage of the Name for miraculous actions is commonplace in the Talmud (*Giṭṭin*, 68a, *Babha-Bathra*, 73a etc.). None of those who were engaged in mystical and pneumatical uses of the Name would ever dream of pronouncing the Tetragrammaton. Despite the free interchange of magical formulae with their non-Jewish neighbours, they belonged to the main ('Orthodox') stream of Judaism. Scholem, *Major Trends etc.*, pp. 40ff. (and especially p. 358, n. 17); *idem. Gnosticism etc.*, pp. 41ff. cf. now Urbach, *The Sages etc.* (*sup.* n. 825), pp. 103-114.

[853] Alon, *Studies etc.*, I, pp. 196ff. In the Merkabha mysticism in common with the Pseudepigrapha 'names' like Jahoel etc. were popular. cf. Scholem, *Gnosticism, ibid.*

[854] Naturally its primary meaning was to prevent false testimonies but it was also extended to include such cases. cf. *Berakoth*, 33a כל המברך ברכה שאינה צריכה עובר משום לא תשא (cf. *sup.* n. 849 and *Temurah*, 3b, 4a. In this case, however, the Biblical source is *Deut.* vi, 13).

ciating the Name in the form in which it is spelt.[855] In remote antiquity, however, it seems clear that the Samaritans did not act with such scrupulosity. In the Talmudic literature they are singled out as an example of those who behave with slackness in this respect.[856] From such reports it has been deduced that the ancient Samaritans were in the habit of enunciating the Tetragrammaton as it is spelt, and that the Dositheans therefore must have objected to this practice. This argument has been carried to extremes by suggesting that, even amongst the ancient Pharisees, the 'old halakhah' enjoined this explicit enunciation, and that the Rabbinical prohibition was therefore a novel enactment to counteract the Dosithean heresy.[857] The flimsy structure of this hypothesis becomes obvious at first glance; and it has now been rightly rejected on the firm ground that the Talmudic sources themselves do not bear out the existence of such an imaginary 'old halakha', drastically replaced by novel enactments. As in all other such cases, here too the Talmudic sources reveal that, if indeed any change took place, this happened by way of a gradual development.[858]

We may now go a step further, and query whether this whole picture, depicting the Samaritans as freely enunciating the Tetragrammaton and the Dositheans as fiercely opposing this practice, is really supported by the sources. The context of the Talmudic sources is by no means free from ambiguity. The Mishnah indeed deals specifically with sinners who are excluded from having "a share in the world to come", and in accordance with whose teaching Abba Saul adds "also he that pronounces the Name with its proper letters". In illustration of this case the Palestinian Talmud speaks in the name of R. Mannah of those "like those Kutheans who swear (by the Name)".[859] The original and literal meaning

---

[855] Ben-Ḥayyim, "On the Pronunciation of the Tetragrammaton etc.", *Eretz Israel*, III (1954), pp. 147ff. *idem.*, *The Literary and Oral Traditions*, IIIa, pp. 35 (v. 18), 37 (vv. 1, 3), 38 (vv. 11, 16) and *passim*.

[856] Jer. *Sanhedrin*, X, 1; 28b. cf. also Ben Ḥayyim, "On the Pronunciation etc." (previous note), p. 150, n. 48.

[857] Geiger, *Urschrift etc.*, pp. 262f., 274f.; *idem. Nachgelassene Schriften*, IV, pp. 324f.; *ibid.* V (Hebrew vol.), pp. 97ff.

[858] Tos. *Soṭah*, XIII, 8 (Zuckermandel, p. 319) & parallels; Alon, *Studies etc.*, I, p. 199. It seems also quite impossible that the Rabbis should change their cherished "ancient halakhah" because of the Dositheans, cf. *sup.* n. 835. Furthermore, Geiger seems to contradict his own theory elsewhere. cf. next note.

[859] Jer. *Sanhed.* (*Sup.* n. 856). (מת׳: אבא שאול אומר אף ההוגה את השם באותיותיו) רבי מנה אמר כגון אילין כותאי דמשתבעין· ר׳ יעקב אחא אמר נכתב ביו״ד ה״א ונקרא באל״ף דל״ת (cf. the commentary of Pne-Mosheh). Geiger's interpretation

of this expression is undoubtably to take an oath in the presence of a Court of Justice. This meaning, even if correct, as it very likely is, does not necessarily indicate a lax employment of the Tetragrammaton by the Samaritans. It rather indicates, surely, that on certain solemn occasions and to a restricted extent, it was in fact allowed, just as, in extreme cases, the Rabbis were compelled themselves to allow it also (*Sanhedrin* vii, 5). Naturally, even the limited concessions allowed by the Samaritans were much more widely and more frequently exercised than those allowed by the Rabbis. However, if we keep firmly in mind that earlier on, before the gradual development in the Rabbinic halakhah took place, the Tetragrammaton was still enunciated in the Temple in Jerusalem during the priestly benediction,[860] the fundamental difference in practice is slight, and in truth merely quantitative. Generally, the Samaritans must have enforced, like the Rabbis, the banning of the enunciation of the Tetragrammaton; but exceptionally, they sanctioned it for the priestly benediction upon Hargerizim on the festive occasions of the Pilgrimages,[861] and likewise on the solemn occasion of taking on oath before a Court. They may well have deduced this practice from the Biblical expression "and by His name shall thou swear".[862]

An alternative explanation of this Samaritan "Swearing"[863] takes this expression in a magical sense, namely, as denoting the practice of conjuration by means of Sacred Names. The employment of Sacred Names for such purposes in antiquity was in truth widespread and almost universal. Were this interpretation correct, it must be emphasized, however, it would cause grave difficulties in interpreting other Samaritans traditions.

The biblical source (*Lev.* xxiv, 16), used by the Hellenists to justify the imposition of the death-penalty for the literal recitation of the Tetra-

---

(*Nachgelassene Schriften*, III, p. 261) that the Kutheans serve as an example to R. Mannah on how to pronounce the Name when taking an oath (שמה) as opposed to the normal Jewish way of pronouncing («אדני» =: ר' יעקב בר אחא) does not make sense.

[860] cf. *sup.* nn. 847, 848 and 858.

[861] cf. n. 878 *inf.*

[862] *Deut.* vi, 13; *ibid.* x, 20. There was also an opinion amongst the Rabbis that these verses should be regarded as a positive commandment, though they did not necessitate the employment of the Tetragrammaton. cf. *Temurah*, 3b. cf. also Maimonides, *Sepher ha-Miṣwoth*, Positive comm. para 7 (cf., however, Nachmanides, *ad. loc.*).

[863] cf. n. 859 *sup.*

grammaton, was actually translated by the Samaritan Targum as being a prohibition against divination by the Name.[864] Now it is most unlikely that the Samaritans should be singled out as an example of a practice which, by their own standards and by the precepts of their own tradition, was considered a cardinal offence deserving capital punishment. We have so often already seen that the Talmudic literature broadly testifies to the strict adherence of the Samaritans to their own traditons. Had the Talmud had the intention to throw in the face of the Samaritans the accusation of conjuring by the employment of the Divine Name, this accusation would have been equally repugnant to the Samaritans themselves; and it could assuredly not have referred to all the Samaritans, and not at all to the main Normative group. By some device of casuistry, it is not too difficult to explain away this difficulty by transferring the burden of the accusation onto the shoulders of certain antinomistic (or Gnostic) Samaritans, a group whose views may have been generalized by the Rabbis to cover "the Kutheans" in general.

The truth, however, almost certainly lies closer to the first inter-pretation. The tenor of this testimony which serves to illustrate a loose practice in connection with the enunciation of the Tetragrammaton must apply to a case which, although by Rabbinic standards outrageous, by the Samaritans is considered to be in line with the Law (according to their own interpretation). In most cases when the Talmudical sources level accusations against the Samaritans for breaking the Law, these are clear instances in which their own exegetical tradition considers them nevertheless permitted.[865]

On a closer examination, to return to the Samaritans' Targum on *Lev.* xxiv, 16, the sense here too is ambiguous. It is just possible that this Targum is identical with the other versions,[866] and that the reference

---

[864] בקסומה השם ;ומקסם for the Hebrew נקב cf. S. Kohn, *Sam. Studien*, pp. 75f. cf. however, *inf.* n. 866.

[865] Montgomery, *The Sam.*, pp. 166, n. 2; 170, nn. 8-12 etc. and pp. 196-203.

[866] cf. *sup.* nn. 842 and 845. As opposed to the rendering of נקב by the Aramaic קסם in *Lev.* xxiv, 16, נקב is rendered by ואגה (= והגה) in verse 11. This may indicate that קסם also means "pronouncing". cf. Geiger, *Nachgelassene Schriften*, V (Hebrew vol.), pp. 100ff. The same impression is gained when נקב in *Gen.* xxx, 28 and *Num.* i, 17 are rendered by the S.T. as כרד again meaning "to indicate", "to specify" = نص cf. Ben Ḥayyim, *Literary and Oral Trad. etc.*, II, p. 525, ll. 191-192; cf. also, *ibid.* p. 588, l. 291-292 where there is a mixed translation (including وقسم which is taken as a verb in past = A.T. وسب = to swear, to blaspheme, but still nothing to do with نقسيم).

is not to 'divination' but simply to 'enunciation' of the Name. Hence, we are not far from the mark if we conclude that, apart from the above considerations which in themselves tend to tilt the balance in favour of the opinion that the Samaritans themselves prohibited the enunciation of the Tetragrammaton, there must have been additional biblical warrants for intensifying this trend. As in the case of the Rabbis, the "taking the Name of the Lord in vain" of the Ten Commandments could readily have served as a source for such an exegesis.[867] This verse was indeed interpreted in a very wide sense, to cover an extensive range of details; and, by the very fact of its implying that the major was comprised in the minor, it would certainly be construed as including the more severe offence of enunciating the Name itself, "in vain". The Ṭabbākh extends this prohibition even to listening to or hearing blasphemous expressions or vain oaths on the Sabbath.[868] If listening to a vain oath, in which a substitute only is used, is included in this prohibition, it follows that enunciating the Name in strict accordance with its spelling, is so even more.

It might be thought that the reports originating from the anti-heretical Patristic literature, on the Samaritans' enunciating the Tetragrammaton as ʼΙαβε or ʼΙαβαι,[869] must conclusively prove that this represents the real testimony of eye-witnesses. However, these reports are nothing more than faulty transcriptions of incantatory formulae, derived from Samaritan magical texts.[870] Such transcriptions, of course, of the 'Names' in a magical context were not confined solely to the Samaritans. As we have seen earlier, such formulae were freely and reciprocally interchanged by various groups using magical inscriptions, quite irrespective of any barriers of nationality, religion or language.[871] Magical 'Names' in Greek form, representing words of Hebrew origin,

---

[867] cf. *sup.* n. 859. From the Sam. Targum of the Ten commandments (לא תסבל ית שם ה׳ אלהיך למגן) we cannot draw any conclusion concerning its exegesis because it is a literal translation of the Hebrew.

[868] f. 32a (SLTh.A, p. 87).

[869] Montgomery, *The Sam.*, p. 213, n. 31. Recently Kippenberg [*Garizim etc.* (cf. *sup.* n. 756), p. 223, nn. 136-137] tried to connect such 'evidence' with the Priestly Benediction through which this tradition of pronunciation of the Name allegedly survived. cf. *inf.* n. 878.

[870] G.A. Deissmann, *Bibelstudien* (Marburg 1895), pp. 18ff. (= English translation by A. Grieve, *Bible Studies*, 1901, pp. 15ff.). The various types of Greek transcription were widespread (*ibid.* pp. 3ff.). However, Deissmann (*ibid.* p. 20) greatly exaggerated the Samaritan origins of the ʼΙαβε type of transcriptions.

[871] cf. *sup.* n. 853.

were re-admitted into Jewish sources without their origins being detected, and vice-versa. It is not at all impossible also that such formulae were introduced into 'orthodox' prayers when the devotees of such super-stitions endeavoured to smuggle into the liturgical texts substitutes for the 'Name', resembling in intonation and enunciation the Tetragram-maton. We know of similar practices recorded in the Talmud, and from this fact it is obvious that "when such impudent people (who carelessly multiplied in their verbosity such intonations resembling the Tetra-grammaton) became numerous", the Rabbis restricted even more the already restricted employment of the "Ineffable Name".[872] Very similar to the Samaritan types of transcription are the Jewish forms of 'Ιωφη, 'Ιωπη or יופי [873] which, if ceremonially intonated could not have been far removed from the Samaritan forms of 'Ιαβε, 'Ιαβαι. There is good reason for believing that the names of the "Prince of the Torah" (יופיאל, 'Ιφιαφ, יפיפיה), found in early Jewish mystical texts,[874] originate likewise from such plays on the transcription of the Tetragrammaton. From all these sources it becomes increasingly evident that, far from finding any evidence for the Samaritans enunciating the Tetragram-maton frequently, we find here rather esoteric intonations of substitutes, admittedly resembling the enunciations of the 'Name', which could easily have been smuggled on certain rare occasions into the chanting of the melodious recitation of the Priestly Benediction.

The evidence often adduced from a 'living tradition of Priestly Bene-diction', in which supposedly the Tetragrammaton was literally enun-ciated, does not stand the scrutiny of criticism any better. Relying on liturgical pieces which do maintain that "the priest lifts up his hands and pronounces the mysterious Name", some scholars have taken it for granted that the statement applies to an everday factual situation.[875] From the mere expression "mysterious Name", it may be already

---

[872] Jer. *Yoma*, III, 7; 40d and parallels; *Sukkah*, IV, 5. cf. Alon, *Studies etc.*, I, pp. 199f.

[873] L. Blau, *Az ozsido büveszet* (= *Das Altjüdische Zuberwesen*) (Jahresbericht der Laudesrabbinerschule im Budapest, Strassburg 1898), p. 131. The expression יופי in *Sukkah*, IV, 5, may be explained differently (cf. e.g. Liberman, *Hellenism etc.*, p. 11, nn. 45-47), however, taking it together with אני והו (Blau, *ibid*. p. 134, n. 2) there is no reason to doubt this exegesis. cf. Alon, *op. cit.* p. 200 and recently Urbach, *The Sages etc.* (cf. *sup.* n. 835), p. 108.

[874] Scholem, *Gnosticism etc.*, p. 12 (nn. 6-7). It is analogous to מטטרון being called אדני קטן or ידוד קטן (*ibid.* p. 41).

[875] Montgomery (*The Sam.*, p. 213, n. 20) follows Heidenheim, *Sam. Liturgie* (Bibliotheca Sam. II), p. 117, v. 26 ויפרש ידיו הכהן וידבר בהשם הנסתר.

deduced that the text is dealing with an esoteric doctrine restricted to the
elite of the priesthood. This consideration excludes the interpretation
that in such sources the reference was meant to represent a common
enunciation in public, which would render the sounds of the Tetragrammaton clearly audible to the masses. Furthermore, from an earlier
section of the same liturgical pieces, it becomes obvious that this liturgist does not intend to report the situation of his own epoch, but gives
a romantic description of the remote past, that of the period of "the
Divine favour".[876] The whole passage deals with the utopian situation
(past or even future) in which the Tabernacle (hidden at the period of
the Judges) is restored, and serves as the only place of worship and to
which sacrifices are brought and offered. In this idyllic situation the
priests (who thus would possess a special mystical knowledge) are
commanded to pronounce the Benediction embellished by the enunciation of the Ineffable Name.

Not only is there no evidence from these liturgical compositions that
such a practice continued in the time of 'Disfavour', with the cessation
of the Sacrificial Cult on Hargerizim, but, from the very rhythms of
this composition, it is abundantly evident that the Tetragrammaton
was pronounced, in accordance with the traditional practice, as *Shemah*.[877]

Detailed description of the ceremony of the Priestly benediction
shows likewise that the employment of the 'Name' was not a straightforward and audible recital of the four letters as they are spelt, but
shrouds a solemn act, the details of which were designedly wrapped
in a shroud of mystery, and kept within the strict confidence of a limited
esoteric coterie of the High Priestly clan. The Chronicles [878] describe

---

[876] *ibid.* p. 114, ll. 1-3; פניך נפרט פתרון סדרי קרבנים דהוו לבני ישראל ביומי
הרצונים ויעשו באהל מועד בידי הכהנים

[877] *ibid.* pp. 111-112 (ל), ll. 1-29. In line 29 the tetragrammaton is spelled out and
it is the last word in the line which rhymes נמה׳ קאמה ראמה ורומה ויומה (מה) etc.).
For many other examples of this kind, cf. Ben Ḥayyim, "On the Pronunciation etc.",
op. cit. (*sup.* n. 855).

[878] J. Macdonald, *The Samaritan Chronicle No. II* (BZAW 107, Berlin 1969), pp. 36f.
וילמדו [אבישע בן פינחס את שישי בנו] את סוד השם ... וזה השם לו סוד גדול והיו
הכהנים הגדולים בני פינחס בימי המועדים יעמר (צ״ל יעמד?) אשר לו מתובית
הכהונה הגדולה מהם יקרא את זה השם לעת יברך את העם במקום המבחר הרגריזים
... ובעבור כן היו בני פינחס בימי הרצון ישכנו בזה ההר ובסביבו Recently Kippenberg [*Garizim etc.* (cf. *sup.* n. 756), p. 223, nn. 136-137] tried to use this source to
prove that the Tetragrammaton was pronounced in the Priestly blessing during the

how this mystery originated, namely by God's revelation to Moses (*Ex.* vi, 3), who then taught it to Aaron (*Num.* vi, 22f.) and from whom it was transmitted to his successors. The succession of High Priests, explicitly mentioned in this context, extends only to Sheshai (I, 5th generation from Aaron); but the Chronicler tacitly assumes that this succession continued at least to the end of the period of the 'Divine Favour'.[879] Be this as it may, there is assuredly no claim in this source that the practice of enunciation of the Ineffable Name continued into the epoch of 'Divine Disfavour'. Naturally, every kind of mystical speculations in connection with the Tetragrammaton and into the permutations of its letters has continued amongst the Samaritans until modern times. By far the greater part of such writings,[880] however, bear no real relevance to the problem of enunciation. The situation here is thus very similar to its parallel in Jewish mystical literature, wherein this type of Name-mysticism is even more widespread, although there was in the latter a total ban on enunciating the Ineffable Name. This type of book of the Lurianic School and later ones adopted by the Ḥassidim are merely contemplative manuals for guiding the pneumatic follower aright in the path of theosophical meditation (Kawwanoth).[881]

---

three yearly pilgrimages. As we have seen from the *whole* context, this refers to the period of the "Divine Favour" (cf. next n.). Kippenberg himself unwittingly contradicts his own theory, by quoting a remark of Theodoret to the effect that the Samaritans do not know the δύναμις of the Tetragrammaton. Theodoret, being a native of Syria, may have had personal aquaintance with Samaritans. His remark is a further evidence that in his time (5th century) the mystical tradition of the "Sons of Phinehas" fell into oblivion amongst the Samaritans. Kippenberg's work in general is full of such spurious arguments based on grave misrepresentation. To mention just one example: this Priestly Benediction is confused with the blessings and curses of Gerizim and Ebal (pp. 224ff.), the latter has absolutely no relation with the former. The Priestly blessing is a three times a year ceremony, while the other is unique historical act (cf. Macdonald, *Chronicle II etc.*, p. 18; Vilmar, *Abulfathi annales*, p. 27 etc.). The employment of Memar Marqah in this case shows that our author did not know what to make of Marqah's midrashic expositions.

[879] Until the day of 'Uzzi (7th generation from Aaron), altogether 260 years. cf. Macdonald, *Chronicle II*, pp. 43f. and Appendix IVa, p. 216; cf. also Vilmar, *Abulfathi annales*, p. 37. From this period onward the glory of the Divine Favour departed from them as well as from Hargerizim وعن — عنهم الرضوان وازال

الجبل الشريف

[880] J. Macdonald, "The Tetragrammaton etc.", *TGUOS* XVII (1958/9), pp. 37f.; *idem. Chronicle II*, p. 103, para Df. ; *idem. Theology etc.*, p. 95.

[881] Scholem, *Major Trends*, pp. 275ff. (and notes pp. 373f.).

The large number of Manuscripts and printed books, embracing liturgies with explicit instruction about the combination of various 'Names', among which the Tetragrammaton of course figures most prominently, do not in any way prove that there ever in fact existed a practice of actually enunciating these letters. All these works originate from and are directed by the most pious and orthodox elements in Jewry, who would not in their wildest dreams have transgressed the acknowledged prohibition of the enunciation of the Tetragrammaton.

From the whole of the Samaritan literature known to us the same picture emerges, and there is no sign whatsoever that there ever existed any doubt amongst the 'orthodox' group on the question of enunciating the 'Name' otherwise than by the substitute *Shemah*. It is therefore quite legitimate to regard this practice as universal amongst the Samaritans, at least from the fourth century onward. There is absolutely no truth in the commonly propounded allegation that they also used the Jewish substitute (Adonay). Such theories have been based upon a wrong inter-pretation of a Midrash in *Memar Marqah*.[882] In the Midrashic discussion between the letters of the alphabet and Moses, the letter *Aleph* boasts of its supremacy, of being in the leading position in the alphabet and "the first (letter) of the *Great Name* by which our Lord brought the world into being".[883] There can hardly be any doubt that the 'Great Name' referred to here is not the Tetragrammaton, but is a reference to אלהים, the only Divine Name mentioned in the first account in Genesis. Although "the Great Name" is indeed normally a technical term for the Tetragrammaton, here it is undoubtedly employed in a freer sense.[884] The wellnigh universal practice of treating all Divine names with great discrimination established itself also among the Samaritans; so, by them too, many of these names were treated with the utmost reverence, and often replaced by other expressions.[885]

---

[882] Heidenheim, *Commentar Marqah's* (Bibliotheca, Sam. III), p. xi.

[883] *Memar Marqah* (ed. Macdonald, I, p. 147) (= II, p. 243). cf. editor's n. 119
אנא אתעבדת שרוי כתביה ושרוי לשמה רבה דבה מרן אמצא עלמה

[884] Marqah, when he is not quoting Scripture but speaking about God freely, employs the Aramaic expression "Our Lord" מרן (cf. previous n.). Similar usages appear also in Talmudic literature (cf. *Aruch completum*, V, 234). The Sam. Targum renders אדון as רב (cf. *Gen.* xviii, 3; xix, 11; *Ex.* iv, 10 and 13; *Deut.* x, 17). cf. the Rabbinic רבש"ע, רבונא, רבן. (*Aruch*, VII, p. 224); Strack-Billerbeck, *Kommentar* etc., II, p. 25. cf. Arabic رب

[885] cf. Geiger, *Nachgelassene Schriften*, V (Hebrew part), pp. 97ff. cf. also *sup.* n. 746.

This explains also the frequent usage of חילה or חיולה as a translation or substitute of the name of God. Besides the main reason for this change, namely the regular confusion by the Samaritans of the gutturals, a habit which made the change from אלה to חילה relatively easy, the conscious wish to limit the usage of אלהים must also have played its part. There must, moreover, have been an urge to eliminate even the usage of אלהים. Such a tendency is also discernible amongst the sectarians of the Dead Sea Scrolls, wherein the widespread usage of אל, and the avoidance of other Names, are most conspicuous — often these instances are mere biblical quotations which originally contained the Tetragrammaton, here replaced by אל.[886] Even if we understand the Samaritan חילה and חיולה as "the Power", there is no reason why this expression should unwarrantably be assocaited with gnosticism. It may be that, by analogy with the Rabbinic usage of גבורה as a substitute for the Divine Name,[887] the Samaritans similarly selected for themselves a fitting substitute.

It has to be emphasized that all that has so far been said about the Samaritans' horror of enunciating the Divine Name by no means applies to the act of writing down the same Names. Not only in copying biblical texts, but even in ordinary writings such as letters,[888] they have no trepidation in spelling out even the Tetragrammaton, both in Hebrew characters and in various forms of transcription into Arabic script. In this respect, none of the scrupulosity known to us from ancient Manuscripts [889] and from modern Jewish printed books (using ה' or יי etc.), has found any echo in Samaritan writings; but, needless to say, this fact has no bearing at all on their practice of enunciation.

To carry our investigation a step further, we have yet to put to ourselves the question, despite the deficiency of information in our Samaritan sources : what then was the attitude of the Dositheans? If the 'Orthodox' Samaritan did indeed substitute *Shemah* for the Tetragrammaton,

---

[886] *Zadokite Fragments, passim.* cf. Rabin's note (p. 28) on VII, line 11 (n. 2).

[887] cf. מפי הגבורה e.g. *Shabbath*, 87a, 88b etc. cf. Ben Ḥayyim, *The Literary and Oral Trad.*, IIIb, p. 26. See now Urbach, *The Sages* (*sup.* n. 835), pp. 103f. Kippenberg's lengthy discussion (*Garizim und Synagogue*, pp. 328-349) has little new to offer (cf. *sup.* n. 878).

[888] J. Rosenberg, *Argarizim, Lehrbuch*, pp. 144-153. The facsimile (but not its transcription) is the only exception, but this is already influenced by Jewish epistolary style. In amulets the spelling out of the Tetragrammaton is even more frequent. cf. Montgomery, *The Sam.*, p. 276 and plate 5 facing p. 273.

[889] E. Würtwein, *The Text of the O.T.*, Oxford 1957, pp. 5, 24, 104 and 132.

what exactly were the changes that the Dosithean campaigned to introduce? Abu'l Fatḥ, who wrote his chronicle in the 14th century as part of a religious revival initiated at the instigation of the energetic High Priest, must therefore have expressed the official dogmatic line. No doubt by the 14th century the Samaritan traditions regarding the replacement of the "Name" by *Shemah* had been static and unalterable for many centuries. What exactly did he mean by reporting "changes" in this respect, as introduced by the Dositheans? Logically, we are not entitled to understand his remarks that the Dositheans "changed the reading of the Great Name",[890] as they have been commonly understood, namely, as an attack on the 'orthodox' group for their enunciation of the Tetragrammaton according to the letters of its spelling. This would imply that Abu'l Fatḥ testified to a recent change in Samaritan traditions; since, according to his own testimony, the earlier Samaritans enunciated the Tetragrammaton differently from the usage of the 'orthodoxy' of his own time. A further implication would surely be that the contemporary practice had been adopted from the 'infidel' Dositheans. Such a conclusion manifestly stands in diametrical opposition to all the ideological tenets of Abu'l Fatḥ, he who above all so staunchly supported the banner of tradition and the ideology of its perpetual unalterability. It is totally impossible that the implications of any such "change", several times repeated with minor differences by the chronicler, could have escaped the perceptiveness of this critically minded author. He would have thus impugned his own preconceived tradition, and thus defeated the very purpose for which his Chronicle was written.

When Abu'l Fatḥ describes the latter-day Dūsīs followers, he dramatizes the martyrdom of Levi; and one of the accusations which Levi hurls at the 'orthodox' majority is: "You have replaced the Great Name Y H W H".[891] This report surely reads, taken even in its plain and literal wording, and if Abu'l Fatḥ is speaking, as he invariably does, from the 'orthodox' Samaritan point of view, as a virulent attack on the more recent Samaritan tradition, which has replaced Y H W H by the reading *Shemah*.

Returning now to the ancient Dustān sect, although the report of Abu'l Fatḥ is not here so unmistakably clear, it may still be understood

---

[890] cf. n. 837 *sup.*

[891] Vilmar, *Abulfathi annales*, p. 156. יהוה وتبدلوا الاسم الاعظم

in the sense we have proposed in connection with his other reports. He says: "They banned the saying of 'Blessed by our God for ever; and prohibited (the reading of) Y.H.W.H. according to the reading (or, as in Mss. A and B: 'tradition') of the People, and they (insisted upon) reading it E L O H I M."[892] It is certain that in the mind of the Chronicler the ancient Dustān sect had broken away from a practice which for him, as well as for the whole 'orthodox' Samaritan group, was considered to be an oral tradition going back to Moses and the seventy elders, and thereafter preserved by an unbroken succession of trustworthy transmitters. It would constitute an anchronism to credit Abu'l Fath with the critical-historical approach, in which he would presumably have left implicit clues to his "objective and enlightened" opinion. Taking therefore his words at their face value, it seems reasonable to suppose that he intended to assert that from the earliest days of antiquity the Samaritans had used the very same substitute in enunciating the Tetragrammaton by *Shemah*; and this was the bone of contention, which the Dositheans attempted to dispute and actually alter.

Summing up all his reports of all the various Dosithean heresies and their vicissitudes,[893] they all boil down to the same issue. What Abu'l Fath intends to convey is his conviction that all these groups objected to the time-hallowed reading of *Shemah*. How precisely they intended to replace this reading is by no means clear. There is not enough evidence to justify us in turning the tables and suggesting that the Dositheans wanted to "return" to the literal enunciation of the Tetragrammaton.[894]

---

[892] *ibid.* p. 82. وحرّموا قول برוך אלהינו לעולם وحرّموا יהוה كَا يقولها

(Mss. A & B) نقلوها) الطائفة وكانوا يقولوها אלהים

[893] cf. *sup.* nn. 837, 838, 891, 892.

[894] Dositheanism was most probably a messianic movement. We know especially about the later splinter groups of Dūsīs that they believed in the prophecy of their leader. This belief is based on *Ex.* xiv, 31, combined with the belief in "the prophet like Moses" (*Deut.* xviii, 18). cf. Vilmar, *op. cit.*, pp. 155f. אימנותי בך ה' ובדוסיס

or עבדך ובנבותו אימנותי בך ה' ובדוסיס עבדך Similarly, Levi before his martyrdom chastizes the 'orthodox' Samaritans that they denied the prophecy of Dūsīs

(تنكروا نبوة دوسيس). This in itself does not prove that they pronounced in their proclamation the Tetragrammaton according to its spelling on this account. In Judaism there was certainly a case in which the messianic pretender pronounced the Name in public as a demonstration of his Messianic mission (cf. G. Scholem, *Shabbethai Ṣebhi*, Tel Aviv 1955, I, p. 144). This practice was probably based on the Talmudical saying (*Pesaḥim*, 50a): "In the world to come the Tetragrammaton will be pronounced according to its spelling". There is no evidence, however, that such traditions ever existed amongst the Samaritans.

It seems rather that, for some to us as yet unknown reason,[895] the Dositheans objected to the enunciation of *Shemah*. The earliest Dustân group is even reported to have read E L O H I M instead. Preoccupied as they were with such reforms as opposing the substitute שמה, they would certainly have objected to a similar substitute in the form of שמו (His Name); and on this ground alone they banned the ancient and cherished liturgical refrain: "Blessed be our God for ever and blessed be *His Name* for ever".

There is nothing to show which could justify the rash conclusion reached by some scholars in equating these Dosithean changes with those of the Rabbis. All artificial connections of these changes of the Dositheans with the controversy surrounding the belief in the resurrection of the dead are frankly figments of the imagination.[896] The real reason why these theories have been so readily accepted lies in the seeming plausibility and logicality of such rationalizations, especially in a field in which so many reports are ambiguous. These theories have succeeded in misleading not a few great scholars, even to the point of accepting them without further investigation; since, after all, there are some explicit testimonies indicating that the Dositheans (or at least some of them) believed in the resurrection of the dead.[897] Even archaeologists, on discovering an inscription with a similar formula, have been only too easily taken in by this false exegesis, and have unwarrantably read into the text some echo of this unsound reasoning, thus impairing and corrupting the reading of an otherwise perfectly sound text.[898]

---

[895] Even to the modern ear it sounds very harsh when the Samaritans speak about "The Name", or "The Great Name" as a reference to God. Abu'l Fath uses it also as an attribute as opposed to the idols. In the lamentation on the "disappearance of the Tabernacle" and the end of the Divine Favour it is said (Vilmar, *op. cit.* p.41) "And you have forsaken His Great name and worshipped those who have no ability". فتركت اسمه العظيم وعبدت من ليس له حيله cf. also *ibid.* p. xxxiv.

[896] cf. Appel, *Quaestiones de rebus Sam. etc.*, p. 92; Heidenheim, *Sam. Liturgie* [Bibliotheca Sam. II.], pp. xviif.; xxx, followed by many others.

[897] cf. *sup.* n. 832.

[898] cf. Montgomery, *The Sam.*, p. 275 (and literature *ibid.* n. 13). The Emmaus inscription was read ברוך שם ולעולם. From this it was assumed that :
"and forever" is reminiscent of the Pharisaic formula of benediction, "forever and ever". Apart from the impossible sense of ולעולם it 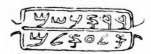 appears quite obvious that the letters were distributed evenly only for artistic reasons and the correct reading is ברוך שמו לעולם a perfectly normal, 'orthodox' Samaritan doxology.

Be this as it may, and even assuming that the formula "Blessed
be our God for ever and blessed be His Name for ever", together with
the horror of enunciating the Tetragrammaton, had in point of fact
something to do with the belief in the resurrection of the dead,[899] this
consideration does not in itself prove that the change was directed
against the "orthodox" group, or that the latter necessarily denied the
resurrection. We have in our possession after all, conflicting statements
even on the Dositheans in this respect. It seems therefore feasible to
suggest that at least some Dositheans at some time or other rejected
the belief in the resurrection. One should therefore always reckon with
the possibility that the Talmudic and the Patristic reports on the Samaritans regarding their denial of the belief in the resurrection may well
have referred to some such unbelieving Dosithean sect as may have
outnumbered the other Samaritans at certain periods and places in
antiquity.[900]

All the Samaritan sources known to us express one single line of
thought, which may properly be regarded with certainty as the 'orthodox' one. None of these sources have any qualms in expressing their
unqualified belief in the resurrection. There is no good ground for accepting the supposed results of the illusory hunt for Dosithean elements in
the Samaritan writings. Marqah's own belief in the resurrection [901]
cannot rest on Dosithean or gnostic sources. It is clear enough that,
broadly in common with the Jews, the Samaritans of this period (from
the 4th century onward) are likewise totally committed to the doctrine
of the resurrection.

Turning once more to the Rabbinic sources and their references to
Sabbai and Dustai as representing the two Samaritan factions, one
realizes that Sabbai (the orthodox) were more akin to Judaism than
were the Dositheans.[902] Was this affinity of the Sabbai faction with
Judaism tantamount to a dogma, like the resurrection? Qirqisāni

---

[899] In the Mishnah (*Berakhoth*, IX, 5) the enactment to say "from everlasting to
to everlasting" is followed by another decree that people shall salute each other
with the Name (of God). But this was not the Tetragrammaton, and if there is any
connection it is that they were both directed against the Sadducees; the former enactment against their denial of the resurrection, and the latter against their denial of
Divine providence. cf. *Mishnah*, ed. Albeck, I, pp. 33 and 339f.; III, p. 387.

[900] cf. J. Macdonald, *The Theology of the Sam.*, pp. 375-376 (cf. n. 1).

[901] cf. Bowman, "Early Sam. Eschatology", *JJS* VI (1955), p. 68; Trotter, *A
Critical Study etc.*, pp. 421ff. (cf. *ibid.* p. 424).

[902] Liebermann, *Shkiin*, pp. 25f. cf. *sup.* n. 798.

(like the Muslim writers) calls the two factions Kūshān and Dūstān, and adds that "one of the factions denied the resurrection", but unhappily he does not specify which faction it was.[903] Another Karaite writer, Yehuda Haddassi, however, makes it clear which one of the groups believed and which one did not believe in the resurrection. According to him, these were the Dositheans who denied it.[904] As a matter of fact, this source flatly contradicts the report of Abu'l Fath, who explicitly states that at least the splinter-groups of Dūsis (and maybe the whole body of the later Dositheans') expressed their belief in the resurrection in the most emphatic and indeed fundamentalist way.

For the time being, at least, we can offer no satisfactory or final reconciliation of these conflicting reports. The easy and very tempting solution, namely, that the ancient Sect (called Dustān by Abu'l Fath) in fact denied the belief in resurrection, while the later Sect (Dūsis) held the opposite view,[905] leaves, furthermore, many questions unanswered; and, besides, it does not at all cohere with all our other sources.

One point, however, is quite certain, that the 'orthodox' Samaritans did not engage in any controversy with the Dositheans, but rather treated them with contemps as 'infidels'. Secondly, no valid reason can be given, from our reading of the sources, why the Samaritans should be accused of denying the resurrection. Granted that the Dositheans advocated an extremely fundamentalist conception of the resurrection, there is absolutely no evidence that the 'orthodox' group held any drastically opposed view. The extant Samaritan literature amply proves that this very question had been settled centuries earlier in favour of a general belief in the afterlife.

Thus far, we have, to be sure, been only partially successful in verifying any exaggerated claims in connection with the Dositheans. Very little tangible new evidence has so far come to light which might have modified the accepted course of research in this field. These claims have been, nevertheless, useful exercises, challenging not a few of the accepted assumptions about this Sect and its alleged contact with the main stream of Samaritanism.

It is indeed a strange mixture of hair-splitting casuistry and inconsistency when scholars can speak in one breath of the "fossilized' and

---

[903] *Kitāb al-Anwār etc.*, I, 5 (ed. Nemoy, I, p. 40f.) واحدى الفرقتين لا تقر بالمعاد

[904] Hadassi, *Eshkol ha-Kofer*, p. 41b (alphabet 97) והם שתי כיתות האחת קוראים כושא״ן והשנית דוסת״אן האחת מודה בתחית המתים ··· דת שניה אינה מודה·

[905] cf. Montgomery, *The Samaritans*, pp. 261ff.

practically 'changeless' character of the Samaritan religion, even to the extent of deeming it valid to draw comparisons with the Dead Sea Scrolls Sect,[906] while at the same time they indulge in the wildest speculations on alleged revolutionary changes. Irrespective of conflicting opinions as to whether these changes were or were not piloted by the bulk of the Samaritan people, or whether they were only the innovations of the Dositheans, the issue revolves essentially around one of the most cherished doctrines of the Samaritans, namely the sanctity of Hargerizim.[907]

The examination of most of these perplexing questions regarding the genesis of Samaritanism and its Temple on Hargerizim with a clan of Zadokite priesthood, lies outside the framework of this investigation.[908] Biblical criticism has indeed attempted to confront, alas, mainly hypothetically, some of these problems. Although no school of criticism has as yet been able to solve these many problems satisfactorily, despite valiant efforts, and it is doubtful whether any truly final solution is in the end possible, yet the critics have at least been able to suggest genuinely constructive hypotheses, and to offer reasons, which, although not, of course, always convincing, nevertheless make their attempts more acceptable.

Without feeling obliged to take any stand on these problems — which would in any case be presumptuous in a work dealing exclusively with exegetical literature of a much later period — we are, nevertheless, in duty bound to examine some of the claims made for such subjects, if these are basing their 'evidence' upon late medieval Samaritan sources.

---

[906] Massingberd-Ford, "Can we exclude Sam. influence etc.", *Revue de Qumran*, VI (1967), p. 112 (cf. nn. 20-22).

[907] *ibid.* p. 110, relying on Bowman, "The Importance of Sam. etc.", *ALUOS* I (1959), p. 46. "This sect denied the sanctity of Mt Gerizim, stressed praying in water and believed in the ressurection of the dead..." It is strange how these confused remarks gained credence, and were accepted without further investigation. These characteristics have absolutely nothing to do with the Dositheans of antiquity (Abu'l Fath's دستان cf. ed. Vilmar, pp. 82ff.) but with later ones (دوسيس assigned by Abu'l Fath, *ibid.* pp. 151f. to the period of Baba Rabba). There is also other evidence (Philaster, *De haeres*, 4) that the ancient Dositheans denied the resurrection. cf. Montgomery, *The Sam.*, pp. 252-269 and n. 778 *sup.*

[908] We are unable to find in Samaritan literature any relevant comments on the real nature of early Dositheanism. Nevertheless from all that we know about them, the most far-fetched opinion would be that "these Dositheans could be proto--Pharisees or Ḥasidim...". Bowmann, *ibid.*

Of recent years, the 'crisis' caused by the destruction of the Temple on Hargerizim in the second century B.C.E. has been singled out as the crucial turning-pont in Samaritanism. In this connection Yūsuf b. Salāmah has been quoted as saying: "When the Temple was destroyed, some people did not see the need to make a pilgrimage to the mountain, or to worship there; they said that to worship in a synagogue was enough".[909] The attempt to connect these (quote) "some people" with the Dositheans and their allegedly anti-priestly attitude, as manifested in their preference for the synagogues as against Hargerizim, could be made to serve as very impressive evidence. Unfortunately for this theory, no such quotation can anywhere be found in the Kāfi; and hence, proportionately less credence may be attached to any conclusions drawn from it.

Now what is the real standpoint of the Kāfi? Is there any evidence of a polemical intention directed against the Dositheans? From the actual words of Yūsuf b. Salāmah,[910] and from the habitual placidity of his disposition, it is certain that he is not directing his words against heretical sectarians. Instead, he is giving a factual report of certain people from the villages around Hargerizim (in all likelihood ignorant of the precepts), who were reluctant to fulfil their duties in the matter of "pilgrimages" during the festivals. Instead, they thought that attending the local synagogues was sufficient for the purpose of fulfilling their religious obligations. He reprimands them in a temperate way, saying in sum that, although the local synagogues, possessing the "Holy Book" and served by priests, are in fact hallowed places, nevertheless, during the days of the pilgrimages, nothing may rightly replace Hargerizim.

More instructive, however, is the continuation of Yūsuf b. Salāmah's discussion. He asks the hypothetical question:[911] May it justly be claimed that pilgrimage is obligatory only when the Tabernacle and the Divine

---

[909] Bowman, *ibid.*

[910] *Kāfi*, pp. 213f. (SLTh.A, pp. 36f.).

[911] *ibid.* p. 214 (SLTh.A, p. 37). Such an artificial diatribe form فان قال قايلا is very common in Sammaritan exegetical literature: most probably taken either from Islamic or Karaite legal and religious literature where such expressions (فان ;

قال قائل، لو قال قائل، فان سالنا سائل، فان سال سائل منهم etc.)
are commonly employed both for polemics and to elucidate problems in which apparently there seems to be a valid claim. (The problem of the probable connection with the Greek diatribe or the Rabbinic expressions יכול, ואם תאמר etc., cannot be discussed here).

favour are present upon the Mount? The evidence in his view, and surely rightly, against such an erroneous opinion, lies in the practice of the Patriarchs, who (according to the Kâfi, and in line with the whole of Samaritan literature) honoured the Place and worshipped there,[912] despite the fact that the *Shekhinah* (Divine presence) was not as yet established there.

Not only is there no mention of any sacrificial cult involved in these pilgrimages, but there is even positive evidence from Yūsuf b. Salāmah that the only duty in the days of the period of 'divine Disfavour' consists solely in the ceremonial processions circling the Holy Mount in various forms (prescribed by tradition but without any sacrifices whatever). He goes on to describe these rites in reliance on Scripture;[913] some days of the Pilgrimage Festival are observed in the presence of "the Ark"; whereas others are observed without it. That these ceremonies were indeed devoid of any sacrificial cultus is evident from his subsequent conclusion: "whoever observes the Passover (offering) at the 'holy meadow' opposite the Holy Mountain can combine the two obligations: that of the Passover and that of the Pilgrimage". And finally, he concludes his discussion [914] of this pilgrimage, which falls "on the morrow after the Passover" (*Num.* xxxiii, 3), by invoking another verse (*Ex.* xii, 14), to prove that the pilgrimage is obligatory "throughout your generations" and is in fact "an ordinance for ever". Even apart from this explicit exposition of the duties of the pilgrimages, one might deduce from our last argument that only the Passover Sacrifice and the pilgrimage processions are perpetual duties; whereas the whole cultus of Sacrifices depends upon the existence of the Sanctuary and the Divine Favour, and is obligatory only when these are present.

"Burnt offerings" mentioned in literature, are similarly no proof of their having been practised, since they are in no sense evidence that reference is made to an actual sacrifice upon the altar. One very outstanding indication of this is the Kâfi's discussion of "observing (לעשות) the Sabbath" (*Ex.* xxxi, 16), which is here explained as "the burntoffering of the Sabbath" (*Num.* xxviii, 10). But he immediately adds that this embraces not only actual sacrifices (which cannot at this time be practised) but also the "potential sacrifice", which is the main concern

---

[912] cf. the beginning of Chapter 17 in the *Kâfi*, pp. 204ff. (SLTh.A, p. 30).

[913] In *Ex.* xxiii, 17 and *ibid.* xxxiv, 23, the Ark is mentioned (S.P. ארון M.T. האדן) while *ibid.* 24 only states "before the Lord thy God".

[914] *Kâfi*, pp. 215f. (SLTh.A, p. 38).

of the forgatherings in Schools, Synagogues for study and prayer.[915]
Similarly, the expression 'altar' can here mean the ark, which is in itself
a 'potential altar' towards which prayers are directed.

Marqah's mention of sacrifices indicates also that he speaks in a
symbolical way, intending to recall a hypothetical situation, whether
past or future. He takes it for granted that a "votive offering or a freewill
offering etc. can only be brought to the *Sanctuary*,[916] that is, only when
there is an actual Sanctuary in existence. The liturgies, likewise, in
describing the sacrificial injunctions of the priest, hasten to qualify
them by stating that they refer [917] to "the period of Divine Favour"
and to the existence of "the Tent of Meeting".

The Kāfi makes it abundantly clear that even an expression which
would normally mean "guilt offerings", is in practice taken to mean
(in the present epoch of Disfavour) redeeming sins by money, which in
turn is to be given to the priest. He explains that if it should happen to
anyone to transgress the Law by error or inadvertence, he is to bring
a guilt-offering. The case under discussion [918] refers to a traveller who
miscalculates the dates of the festivals, so causing a desecration by not
observing them at their proper dates. Relying on *Lev.* v, 15f., from which
he deduces: "that one should bring a ram worth two Israelite Darics
(or Drachmae) or its equivalent value to the priest, as it is written:
'in silver two (Samaritan reading: שְׁקָלִים) shekels after the shekel of the
Sanctuary', he leads up to the dictum: 'and he shall give unto the priest,
and the priest shall make atonement for him'; thus money may be
used".[919] Later, he goes on to generalize, and says: "And every sin of
inadvertence in desecration of the festivals or similar errors makes one
liable to make a guilt-offering: for (intentional?) defilement, however,
one is to bring a "sin-offering". Although the Kāfi does not state it

---

[915] *ibid.* pp. 84f. (SLTh.A, pp. 14f.). cf. also my article in *ALUOS* VI (1969),
pp. 116, 151 (nn. 141-142). cf. also Cowley, *Sam. Liturgy*, I, p. 103. עַל מזבח הצלות
נעמד

[916] *Memar Marqah* (ed. Macdonald), I, p. 58 (= II, p. 91). אנש ינדי אל משכנה
בהמה נדר etc.

[917] Cowley, *Sam. Liturgy*, II, pp. 519ff. (especially letter פ), cf. *sup.* n. 876.

[918] *Kāfi*, pp. 338f. (SLTh.A, pp. 76f.).

[919] According to the plain sense of II *Kings*, xii, 17, such was the practice in ancient
times. However, the Rabbis interpreted this verse as referring only to the *surplus*
which remained in the hands of the priests after spending the major part of the money
brought for guilt or sin-offerings on the victim. cf. *Siphra*, Lev. para 21 (ed. Weiss,
f. 27c) and parallels.

in so many words, it seems clear that what is here implied is quite plain: for minor 'errors' there is the possibility of the priest's making atonement (by acceptance of payment), but for major offences, which would be liable to a 'sin-offering', this is not possible in the days of Disfavour, since such an offering is equivalent to the burnt-offering (*Lev.* vi, 17-23), requiring actual Altar and Sanctuary.

Often we come across, in the field of Samaritan research, statements claiming to represent the results of a critical investigation of historical developments. One of such passages is quoted here, in order that it may speak for itself:[920]

> "This (synagogue, built by Baba Rabba), we know from Abu'l Fath, was built on the very site of the Temple which had once stood on Mount Gerizim, indeed over the altar place where, since the Temple's destruction, sacrifices had still been offered by priests... Baba, who established the synagogue on Mount Gerizim, engaged Amram Darah and Marqah to supply a synagogue liturgy... But after Baba's fall the old orthodox priestly party regained power; they had kept aloof from Baba and the Dositheans and were ready to restore sacrifices...'

By the acceptance of such hypotheses, one may find some explanation of why Marqah does not even condescend to mention sacrifices. However, the so-called 'orthodox priestly party' was the very same party to which all known Samaritan writers from the eleventh century onwards belonged; why then do they not at least hint at the existence of such a cult? All of them had a golden opportunity, while elaborating on the passover-sacrifice, to drop at least a hint about the other blood-sacrifices. It is surely inconceivable that, if the Ṭabbākh could devote such a large space to the allocation of the Passover sacrifice, actually drawing out the subject to include sixty separate precepts,[921] it would be totally silent on any other form of sacrifice, were such a thing still in force. Naturally the Kāfi [922] and all later legal and exegetical treatises show these same characteristics.

Another circumstance which has caused great confusion in this field is certain inaccurate reports from outside sources about a Samaritan sacrificial cult. Unfortunately, many Jewish sources (both Rabbanite

---

[920] Bowman, "The importance etc.", *op. cit.* pp. 48f.

[921] *Ṭabbākh*, ff. 58a-92b (SLTh.A, pp. 100-132).

[922] People were often misled by N. Cohn (*Die Zaraâth-Gesetze etc.*, p. 10) in his outline of the Chapters of the *Kāfi*, Chapter 30 (وشروطه فى الذبيح) was translated by him: "Über die *Opfer* etc.". Needless to say, this translation is misleading. The chapter deals simply with ritual slaughter.

and Karaite)[923] are unreliable in this respect. The preconceived theological reasoning of Jewish scholars has taken it for granted (drawing
this conclusion from their own accepted rulings concerning the abolish-
ment of *all* sacrifices following the destruction of the Temple) that these
same rulings have held good also in the case of the Samaritans. Hence,
when they learnt, to their dismay, that the Samaritans practise the cult
of Paschal offerings, they jumped to the (at least for them) logical conclusion that in *general* blood-sacrifices are still in usage amongst the
Samaritans.

The search for Dosithean elements was applied to almost every branch
of Samaritan literature; even the composition and the historical development of the Samaritan liturgy were 'examined' and forcibly drawn into
this inter-sectarian discussion.[924] Some modern scholars have found
it strange that the Sabbath service of the fourteenth century consisted
mainly of compositions of the fourth century; "whereas from the 14th
century to the 19th century, a mere 500 years as against 1000 years,
there have been vast additions to the Liturgy".[925] Obviously, those of
us who are not obsessed by literary heresy-hunting and do not tie down
every detail to a non-existent Dosithean type of ideology, should not
be at all impressed by such 'striking discoveries'. Apart from the inaccuracies of such generalizations, and disregarding liturgists like Abu-l
Ḥasan,[926] Ab Gelugah [927] and the later pre-14th century writers, there
is a perfectly logical explanation for the above-mentioned disproportion.
This phenomenon may result both from historical and linguistic reasons.
From the 9th century onwards, the Aramaic language became gradually
replaced by the Samaritans' newly acquired vernacular, i.e. Arabic.
Aramaic thus became more and more unintelligible to the Samaritan
community. Naturally enough, the learned intelligentsia was still able
to use it, though with ever more frequent Hebraisms. Hence, except
for the hallowed ancient liturgical compositions which were recited by
all and so acquired a sentimental aura causing them to be retained,

---

[923] cf. A.N. Adler, *The Itinerary of Benjamin of Tudelah*, Hebrew text, p. 22,
translation p. 20; Hadassi, *Eshkol ha-Kofer*, f. 41b & c. (Alphabet 15). However,
more than a century ago, Jost (*Geschichte des Jud. u. seiner Sekten*, I, pp. 54f., n. 3),
realized that such reports are mere generalizations built on the fact that the Samaritans
practised the Passover offering.

[924] cf. *sup.* n. 920 and text there.

[925] Bowman, *op. cit.* p. 49.

[926] Cowley, *Sam. Liturgy*, I, p. 70; II, 875.

[927] *ibid.* I, pp. 75, 77.

others were gradually replaced by modern compositions in Hebrew, much more easily comprehensible to the bulk of the worshippers. An analogy to this process may be drawn from the constantly reduced number of Biblical passages recited from the Targum.[928] There is no need to fabricate a stupendous 'reformation' in the 14th century, which in some miraculous way abolished all the dogmatic differences in the many complicated problems which had so bitterly divided the Dositheans from the 'Orthodox' Samaritans. Such long-standing feuds could not just have disappeared overnight to enable two enemy factions to be reconciled. No reformation could have brought about a union between the two groups, or created a situation in which "rather the priestly party absorbed the Dositheans".[929]

It goes without saying that, insofar as the sources support such changes in the 14th century, all scholars would agree that some religious movement indeed took place. The acceptance of the fact of a religious revival during this period has valid support from the best authorities.[930] However, such a religious revival is still a very far cry from a Reformation in which antinomian forces are supposed to be involved. It has to be strongly emphasized that, despite the frequent repetition of allegations of such an amalgamation of the sects, or of a great Reformation,[931] there is no evidence to support any such event, beyond (as we have said) some modest religious revival, involving literary activities both in Arabic and in Hebrew.

As has already been suggested, the Dositheans had lost all their significance by approximately the 10th century, and this is the true reason why, apart from the Chronicles, they are henceforth totally ignored. Even the references in the Chronicles to the Dositheans are sometimes confused; often one wonders whether the writers themselves had any clear idea or whether they were blindly copying from earlier sources, without properly grasping their significance.

The best evidence of the total disappearance of the Dositheans rests

---

[928] Ben-Ḥayyim, *Literary and Oral Trad. etc.*, I, pp. ס״ח and ע״ב; cf. *ibid.* n. 223.

[929] Bowman, *op. cit., ibid.*

[930] Abu'l Fath (ed. Vilmar, pp. 4f.) testifies about his contemporary the High Priest Phinehas b. Joseph, who was instrumental in the writing of his book. It seems that the revival under this High Priest engulfed other literary activities. cf. Cowley, *Sam. Liturgy*, II, pp. xxvii, xcviii.

[931] Following Bowman, Abdel-Al, *A Comparative Study etc.*, p. 18; Trotter, *A Critical Study etc. passim.* The latter, however, is still searching for Dosithean opinion in the writing of Ben Mannir, *ibid.* pp. 428f.

on the fact that travellers of the 12th century no longer know anything whatever, even about their existence. Thus, for example, the detailed reports of the Jewish traveller Benjamin of Tudela, who otherwise shows a keen interest both in the Karaite and in the Samaritan communities, which he vividly describes in his itinerary, does not mention any division amongst the Samaritan communities. It is true, admittedly, that not all his information is very accurate,[932] but he draws a very realistic picture of the environment of the Samaritan communities, including reasonably trustworthy figures about their sizes; and in general he may be regarded as quite a reliable eye-witness.[933] Had there been any intersectarian strifes or any separate existence of Dosithean communities, it would surely not have escaped the eagle eye of R. Benjamin. From the countless legends which he reproduces from hearsay, there is no hint of Samaritan strifes or peculiarities; which may indicate that, by the middle of the 12th century, the living memory (as distinct from the literary memory) of the Dositheans had long been forgotten.

Despite the general scarcity of information about the Dositheans in the Samaritan exegetical and religious literature, there nevertheless emerged occasionally, certain views attributing features of some legal peculiarities in Samaritan tradition to Dosithean influences. Such reports, although greatly suspect, must nonetheless be throughly investigated, since it is surely only by such matters of everyday practice as halakhah that we may verify whether or not there is any truth in such allegations. Only the established practice of the people, carried out consistently over long periods and reported without prejudice or polemical preconceptions, can really reveal whether in fact there remained any undetected relics of the Dosithean heresy within the Samaritan fold.

Let us examine, first of all, an allegation that the laws regarding the ritual impurity of women (menstruation and flux) of the Samaritan halakhah were modified and influenced by Dositheanism.[934] Obviously it would be impossible to deal here with all the intricacies of this problem, which served as one of the major lines of division in antiquity between the Pharisees and the Samaritans.[935] Suffice it to say, that it has been

---

[932] cf. *sup.* n. 923.

[933] A.N. Adler, *The Itinerary of Benjamin*; description of Shechem pp. כא–כ״ב (translation p. 20); Ashkelon, p. כ״ט (tr. p. 28); Damascus, p. ל״א (tr. p. 30).

[934] cf. Wreschner, *Sam. Traditionen*, pp. 30-38, cf. *inf.* n. 944.

[935] *Niddah*, IV, 1; cf. D. Daube, "Jesus and the Samaritan Woman: the meaning of συγχράομαι", *JBL* LXIX (1950), pp. 137-147.

understood by all exegetes that there are two distinct types of impurity already involved in Scripture: viz. *Lev.* xv, 19f. refers to menstrual impurity (נדה), while *ibid.* 25f. to that of fluxion (זבה). But the criteria and the laws to be observed in each of these distinct cases differed in these groups in accordance with the exegetical tradition of each group. Originally, Scripture was understood by all groups to mean that the impurity resulting from menstruation lasted for seven days, irrespective of the actual duration of the issue. Later, the Rabbis enacted a stricter ruling, equating this case with the originally more serious case of fluxion, where only after the woman was cleansed from the issue was she to number to herself seven days, and after that she would be "clean".[936] The Samaritan, naturally, did not have any such ruling, and probably based the details of their exegesis on the grounds of their own textual variants.[937]

The argument for the alleged Dosithean influence runs on the following lines: the Talmud adduces an additional reason [938] for considering Samaritan women unclean as menstruants, because "the day she ceases (to see blood), she counts it along with (the requisite) number of seven days". As opposed to this, the Dositheans are reported to have introduced a reform that the reckoning should begin only from the following day, namely, counting from sunset to sunset, as in the case of the festivals.[939] The very same requirement is put forward by Munajja in his Masā'il al-Khilāf, a fact which indicates that the Samaritans accepted the Dosithean reform.[940] Grave doubts, however, become apparent as soon as these "conclusions", or rather conjectures, are critically examined. The whole argument is based on false premises, owing to a

---

[936] *Niddah*, 66a.

[937] Wreschner (*op. cit.* pp. 33f.), has already pointed out the variant reading in *Lev.* xv, 24 instead of the M.T. וטמא, the S.P. has יטמא. The midrash derived from this reading is most probably responsible for the distinction made between "the first blood" causing defilement for seven days while the later ones cause only a single day's uncleanliness. Curiously, however, Wreschner sees Karaite influences here also, and causes total confusion by these imaginary mutual influences. In one respect he was certainly right, although he failed to grasp its reasons. He says: "Die Karäer haben hier, wie in zahlreichen anderen Fällen, die sam. Deutung mit Beibehaltung des massor. Textes angenommen und musten so jener andere Gründe unterschieben." For the reasons for this phenomen cf. my article in *ALUOS* VI (1959), pp. 112, 123f., 147 (nn. 118-119), 160f. (nn. 213ff.).

[938] A Baraitha in *Niddah*, 33a.

[939] cf. *inf.* nn. 941-942.

[940] cf. Wreschner, *op. cit.* p. 37, n. a; cf. however n. 943 *inf.*

radical misunderstanding of the sources. Whatever the Talmudic testimony means, it may fairly be judged only from the point of view of the Rabbinic halakhah, and is in any case entirely irrelevant to our discussion; since, according to this ruling, "the daughters of the Kutheans are (anyhow) deemed as 'menstruous' *from their cradle*".

The Dositean reform, as reported by Abu'l Fatḥ,[941] shows immediately that this was one of their puritanical devices, with a view to making the *menstruant* woman likewise *count* full days (not from the beginning, but) from the *cessation* of the issue. This reform is almost the same as the later Rabbinic ruling, and stands in diametrical opposition to the 'orthodox' Samaritan practice (as also to that of the Karaites), which counts in such cases *seven* days only from the inception of the issue.[942] Understandably, all Munajja's rulings are in strict line with the accepted Samaritan traditions. However, in the case mentioned, he is dealing with an entirely different law; he is dealing with the case of flux (זבה), in respect of which the counting is explicitly referred to in scripture (*Lev.* xv, 28). It is true that Munajja demands that this counting should be "from evening to evening according to the order of the Creation"; but he immediately inserts a suggestion that this case is "unlike other cases, when a part of a day may be reckoned as a day".[943] It seems, then, that Munajja refers in his suggestion to the *menstruant*, who is allowed to reckon her seven days from the beginning of the issue; even if it should occur just before sunset, it is *already* regarded as the first day.

This is not by any means the only instance in which the allegations against Munajja's 'unorthodox' views can easily be refuted. Reading impartially this whole Chapter about "the impurities concerning women", and in correlation with the treatment of the same subject by the earlier eleventh century codices, one becomes convinced that substantially they represent the very same tradition.[944]

---

[941] Vilmar, *Abulfathi annales*, p. 82. واذا حاضت الامة لا يحسبوا لها الا من

غد ذلك النهار شبه الاعياد من الغروب الى الغروب

[942] It is interesting to see how Wreschner twists the sources to suit his arguments: "Es stände demnach حاض bei זבה obwohl es sonst von der נדה gebraucht wird."

[943] لا يجوز فيها ما يجوز فى غيرها من خبر بعض اليوم بيوم Wreschner (*ibid.*) in his translation conveniently glossed over the crucial passage.

[944] A comparison of Wreschner's excerpts (Ms. Berlin used by him was not available to me) with our *Masā'il al-Khilāf*, II, shows that they cover the same ground, almost

The theory of the supposed Dosithean influence upon the halakhah of the *Masā'il al-Khilāf* would seem absurd in itself, even if we disregard the above-mentioned comparison. Such a theory can only be proposed on the ground that Abu'l Fath, who lived centuries after Munajja, must have copied his remarks concerning the 'Dosithean heresy', while at the time totally disregarding an identical practice, well established in the 'orthodox' tradition itself for centuries; or again he must have regarded Munajja (one of the most outstanding apologists of his nation) as unrepresentative of the established norm.[945] Neither of these assumptions can be rationally maintained; and the straightforward and unbiassed reading of the sources eliminates on any showing all such artificial fabrication and, in so doing, cuts out the possibility of any alleged 'Dositheanism' in this sphere.

---

the very same chapters. There are of course some differences, e.g. in our Ms. it is more obvious that it is the second half of the Work (Wreschner's Ch. IV is here entitled المقاله الخامسه and his Ch. VIII as المقاله السدسه etc. Otherwise the division into chapters is the same (فصل). In particular, this chapter about נדה etc. seems to be identical in both mss. (judging from quotations, pp. 31f. n. a; p. 33a, 35a, etc.). Comparing Munajja's treatment of the subject with those of the *Kāfi* (pp. 146f.) and the *Ṭabbākh* (f. 15a, ff.) it is clear that they all depend on the same traditions and, despite the different treatment, they may even go back to the same 'ancient' sources. cf. also Abdel-Al, *A Comparative Study etc.*, pp. 163ff.; cf. also *ibid.* texts pp. 631ff.; 681ff. and translations pp. 418ff., 508ff.

[945] cf. Wreschner, *op. cit.* p. 37, n. 5. Unfortunately we must postpone the discussion on all the other alleged 'inconsistencies' of Munajja, claimed by this author in his present chapter. We may, perhaps, be justified for a short digressional hint, in pointing out the two most significant distortions: A) There is no contraction between Munajja and the *Kāfi* concerning the colours of blood (cf. *ibid.* p. 33, n. 6). As opposed to the Rabbis (*Niddah*, II, 6) all Sam. exegetes agree that irrespective of the colour of the blood the woman is unclean, and there is no "clean blood". The only difference is that while Munajja treats mainly the cases of נדה (دم الحيض) and זבה (ذايبة), the *Kāfi* deals with a variety of cases including "blood of Doubtfulness" (دم الاشتباه).

However, even in these cases, despite the various colours, she is kept secluded (= impure), (فيحصل منه اشتباه ويجب اهمل الامراة مدة وجوده ...). B) "Wir haben *so viel* verschiedene Erklärungen über die Deutung von זבה..." is greatly exaggerated. The truth is that as opposed to the Rabbinic ruling, derived from the expression ימים רבים (*Lev.* xv, 25) that it means X *days* after menstruation (cf. *Siphra, ad. loc.*; *Niddah*, 72b-73c) all Samaritan exegetes, including Munajja, hold in common that זבה means X *weeks*. It is impossible to enter here into the problem of the differences in the number of days (= Rabbis) or weeks (= Samaritans). It is certain that all Samaritan writers agreed on the same principle. On Wreschner's general attitude, cf. my article in *ALUOS* VI (1969), pp. 137 (n. 41), 161 (n. 217).

Nor can any real Dosithean influence be found in the whole of Samaritan exegetical literature. Cases which outwardly resemble, or even at first appear identical with the reforms introduced by the Dositheans, are nothing other than concidences. We tend often to forget that, after all, Sectarians of all types, even if they are bent on the most radical reforms, are inevitably bound to retain certain elements of the original traditions, along with various degrees of similarity to the general framework of the practices which they themselves are trying to alter. Hence it is only natural that certain so-called 'Dosithean' practices remain, despite all, much closer to the 'orthodox' practices from which they broke away, than to any other traditions with which they have had a lesser degree of contact and affinity.

One of these similarities is found in the stringent ruling on matters of ritual impurity arising from a dead body.[946] We know, with regard to the ancient Dustān sect, that, although they changed and abolished many precepts in this very field of purity, they were in fact more rigorous than the 'orthodox' Samaritans. They considered even the shadow of a grave as a cause of 'defilement', and regarded a person whose mere shadow fell upon a grave as unclean for seven days.[947] A similar tradition is discussed in the Kāfi. Since, however, this problem has already been amply discussed,[948] we may be allowed simply to quote some of the conclusions already reached: "By the days of Jūsuf b. Salāmah, the controversy between the Dositheans and the orthodox Samaritans was not only over, but the rancour towards the former sect had been forgotten." There is, therefore, no need to regard the apparent similarity of practice in this case as an instance in which the 'orthodox' Samaritans reached a compromise with regard to Dosithean reforms. Rather does the matter stand the other way round: this process was part and parcel of the ancient and original austerity. Nevertheless, it never reached any such extreme position as was finally arrived at by the reforms of the sect of Dustān.[949] This and similar cases in the Kāfi, which are habit-

---

[946] cf. my article, *op. cit.* pp. 114, 149f. (nn. 130f.).

[947] Vilmar, *Abulfathi annales*, p. 82 وطموا ظل المقابر كل من وقع ظله على

المقابر يطا سبعة ايام

[948] Abdel-Al, *A Comparative Study etc.*, pp. 183f.

[949] It would be too complicated to demonstrate here all the differences between the "leniency" of 'orthodox Samaritanism' in laws of purity as opposed to the rigorism of the sect nf Dustān. cf. *sup.* nn. 827, 941 and 947. Abdel-Al (*op. cit.*) ignored the exegetical background of the rulings in the Kāfi, originating from the concept of אהל (*Num.* xix, 14) and therefore these distinctions between the groups were blurred.

ually introduced by hypothetical questions, were not necessarily meant "to refute some sectarian within the Samaritan community whom he (i.e. the Kāfi) left unmentioned";[950] but rather this is the common literary device of using the diatribe form, a feature borrowed in point of fact from the literature of the then current environment.[951]

To illustrate again one such case, we may take a rhetorical question from the Kāfi:[952] the problem in question is, whether one who carries out the rite of circumcision on a child, who, for hygienic reasons, was not "bathed" (and therefore was not purified from the uncleanliness of נדה), is himself contracting the 'uncleanliness' of the child and so liable to undergo a period of seven days' defilement, or not? Looked at superficially, this problem is actually very similar to that raised by one of the reforms of the later Dositheans (a splinger-group of the Dūsīs, headed by Shaliyah), equating the 'impurity' of the child with that of his mother.[953] Apart from the inherent weakness of such a comparison, in view of the very nature of these Sectarians who adhered to Shaliyah, and who are notorious for radically changing and even abolishing certain points of ritual purity in diametrical opposition to everything reflected in the 'orthodox' Samaritan literature, the text of the Kāfi itself shows that it has nothing whatsoever to do with this specific problem. The first answer given by the Kāfi categorically denies that there is any need for such a seven days' defilement; and, without the slightest polemical tinge, adduces as evidence "that which is established and practised in some of the (Samaritan) towns".[954] And even the second opinion, which requires that such a person be considered defiled, has absolutely no connection with the Dosithean 'reform', but is a direct outcome of genuine 'orthodox' exegesis.[955]

---

[950] cf. Abdel-Al, *op. cit.* pp. 171-172.

[951] cf. *sup.* n. 911.

[952] pp. 169f. (cf. Abdel-Al, *op. cit.* pp. 693ff. and translation, pp. 541f.).

[953] Vilmar, *Abulfathi annales*, p. 162 وقال ان المولود يلزمه ما يلزم والدته من الطاٴ وقال ليس قدس زمان الضلال ومنع من المواصلة والصبوغ فى يوم السبت As opposed to the last statement, cf. my article *op. cit.* pp. 113 and 148 (n. 123). It looks as if in this case these sectarians observed a strict ruling (which was even disputed amongst the 'orthodox' Samaritans) despite their general laxity in matters of ritual.

[954] p. 170 دليل ذلك ما يتعمد بعض البلاد

[955] *ibid.* p. 171. The baby is purified after seven days only by his being "bathed". This is in line with the other cases of impurities, in all of which the counting of the

A final assessment of the so-called 'Dosithean influences' on the Samaritan exegesis is thus hardly necessary in the light of the foregoing detailed discussions, all of which manifestly speak for themselves. We may perhaps briefly summarize, however, the reasons why such allegations cannot have been well-grounded, in view of the general characteristics of the Samaritan approach to their religion and of their Biblical exegesis resulting therefrom. The unyielding adherence of the group in general to the traditions so jealously guarded by their spiritual leadership, the priesthood headed by the High Priest, excluded of itself any unauthorized innovations. Exegeis was never left to the arbitrary tastes of the individual exponent, but closely and firmly 'guided' by this central authority. Time and again, we find in the entire exegetical literature, how even the slightest deviations were reprimanded,[956] and more serious infringements or objections ruled out of order.[957] No 'heretical' idea, no matter how piously disguised in theological verbiage, or how tempting it seemed to some 'enlightened' Samaritans, was ever admitted, or even considered as competent to rival in any way their cherished traditions.[958]

Especially as we know that the Dosithean reforms were actually founded on the changing of calendaric calculations,[959] it is altogether impossible that any fruitful connections between the rival actions could continue to exist. In this respect the Samaritan litterature is the most zealous of all, jealously outlawing any tampering, even by experts, with calculations and astronomical deductions based on their "hallowed calculations", which always remained the exclusive prerogative of the priesthood. The *Ṭabbākh*, while devoting a whole chapter to stressing "the significance of tradition",[960] adds that the purpose of this treatise is to warn each individual of the nation to be on guard against deviations in matters of calendaric calculations. Such an error is even equated with the apostasy involved in following the idolatry of the heathens, (*Deut.* xii, 30). The *Ṭabbākh* concludes this chapter by strongly asserting

---

days required for being purified are effective only if the ritual "washing" or sprinkling took place at the proper time: otherwise the days already counted are lost.

[956] A few examples will suffice: concerning tithes (*Kāfi*, pp. 30f.; SLTh.A, p. 2); Sabbath (*ibid.* p. 104; SLTh.A, p. 17); burning the remnants of the Passover offering (*Ṭabbākh*, f. 81b f; SLTh.A, p. 121) etc.

[957] cf. *sup.* nn. 347, 360, 358-359, 434, 465, 662 etc.

[958] cf. e.g. *sup.* nn. 96-107 and text there.

[959] Vilmar, *op.cit.* p. 82 (etc. حساب الزيج وبطلوا).

[960] ff.   151b-156a.

the correctness of the traditional reasoning of the priesthood, and by expressing abhorence at any "foreign" speculation.[961]

Nonetheless, in order to counteract any exaggerated claims for a total unanimity amongst the Samaritans, it should in fairness be mentioned that there *are* in fact some contradictions and opposing opinions. One of these significant divergencies of opinions is as a matter of fact, to be found in the *Kāfi* itself. This composition is earlier than most of the liturgical manuscripts which have survived, and therefore it is significant that it admits quite openly [962] that there existed conflicting customs respecting the order and nature of the liturgy. There are, further, a number of other instances in the *Kāfi* where more than one single ruling is given. It seems, moreover, that this applies mainly to rarely practised precepts, and that owing to their rare application, the oral tradition upon which the ruling may originally have been based has been forgotten. One cannot even exclude the possibility that such differences of opinion go back to antiquity, arising from various purely local practices faithfully reproduced in the *Kāfi*, side by side with others of different origin.[963] As far as it is possible to demonstrate from the earlier literature, there is only *one* case involving a common everyday matter, in respect of which conflicting opinions are reported. In dealing with birds which are permitted as food, the *Kāfi* openly states that there is a diversity of opinions. Some require that every fowl fit for consumption must have three marks [1, a crop, 2, a gizzard which can be excoriated, and 3, an extra toe on its foot], while others hold that two out of these three marks are sufficient.[964]

These few examples, however, have no visible or hidden connection with the inter-Samaritan heretical strife. These are rather exceptional

---

[961] f. 156a f. ... والغرض بكتب هذه المقاله ليقف كل احد من الامه على

מתל ذلك ... والتحذير من النظر فيها بيد المخالفين لقوله تعالى השמר לך

פן תנקש אחריהם ... وقد بان بجملة ذلك صحة الاستدلال على ما بيد الايمه

عليهم السلام وقبح الاستدلال على ما سواه cf. also *sup.* n. 439.

[962] pp. 69f. He nevertheless concludes (*ibid.* p. 74) that because of the residence of the High Priest in "the (Holy) Place", this local custom is preferable. Further investigation of this problem must be left to the expert on Samaritan Liturgy.

[963] cf. on the cutting of the hair of the leper (pp. 138f.; SLTh.A, p. 20); on the hair cut of the Nazirite (*ibid.* pp. 231f; SLTh.A, pp. 48f.); on the Hebrew slave girl (*ibid.* p. 250; SLTh.A, p. 56); Hebrew slave (*ibid.* p. 261; SLTh.A, p. 57); on the fine for seduction or rape (*ibid.* pp. 293f. SLTh.A, 67) etc.

[964] pp. 114f. (cf. Abdel-Al, *op. cit.* p. 139; text pp. 673f. translation p. 489f.).

cases in which (most probably) ancient disputes had not been finally and unanimously settled. It could fairly be asserted that these few exceptions rather prove the rule of the exceptionally close-knit cohesion amongst the Samaritans, who instinctively resisted any temptation to desert their intense loyalty to their tradition. It is therefore instructive to compare this situation with the Karaism of the same period,[965] with all its diversified rulings and practices. Compared with Rabbinic halakhah and its latitude in permitting and even defending the disagreements of opposing schools of thought, or in later times in upholding conflicting local customs, the Samaritans definitely stand out as by far the most unanimous in their traditions. As a matter of interest, the Karaites actually exploited the diversity of opinions amongst the Rabbanites, in particular by the juxtaposition of the opposing rulings of the Babylonians as opposed to the Palestinians, in order to cast doubt on the claim for the Divine origin of their Oral Law.[966] The Samaritans emphasized even more this belief in the uniqueness of the Word of God, which by its very Divine nature must necessarily have only one meaning, normally the one which was stamped on it by the authority of the upholders of their tradition. It goes without saying that such 'unanimity' limited the development of exegesis; and is in fact in no small measure responsible for the relatively unimaginative monotony of ideas and the poverty of exegetical and hermeneutical devices.

---

[965] Nemoy, "Al-Qirqisānī's Account etc.", *HUCA* VII (1930), p. 330.
[966] *ibid.* p. 378.

PART THREE

SAMARITAN HERMENEUTICS

A. SIMPLE EXEGESIS

In this section we deal only with the *simple* method of interpretation of the Samaritans, a term which connotes *primitive* devices, not dependent on complicated exegetical rules. The alternative interpretations interest us only insofar as they exhibit specific Samaritan characteristics. Much has been written about the lexicography, semantics and grammatical idiosyncrasies on the Samaritan,[1] all of which, of course, will be fairly rigidly excluded from our treatment. Such considerations must be severely limited here and will be treated only when they have a direct bearing on the problem of hermeneutics itself.

With those who believe tenaciously in the Divine origin of the Torah, in which every minutest detail is inspired,[2] it is only to be expected that there will be the closest inspection of all such details. However, this Samaritan study of minute detail is entirely different from that of the modern Bible critic. The latter may, for instance, occasionally trace in the text itself a process of re-interpretation, finding his grounds in the duplicate story, and with the set intention of discovering if possible the original documentary sources, and may thus arrive at certain critical conclusions.[3] But the Samaritans cannot even be suspected of the slightest awareness of any such critical approaches as, to them, the Torah is altogether perfect, and completely devoid of any discrepancy whatsoever. It is therefore impossible to expect from Samaritan exegesis any contributary factors to Higher Criticism.[4] Apart from this fact, both in

---

[1] Ben Hayyim's monumental work (Literary and Oral Tradition, etc.) deals mainly with these aspects and "contains almost the entire native philological literature of the Samaritans". However, the author admits that he did not include the material from the exegetical and halakhic literature (*ibid.* II, p. VI) hence our emphasis on these aspects. Nevertheless, we are greatly indebted to his findings, as is evident from the frequent references.

[2] cf. Heinemann, *Darkhei ha-Aggadah*, p. 96.

[3] Smart, *The Interpretation of Scripture*, pp. 168-9, cf. *ibid.* n. 8 for further bibliography.

[4] Lebram, "Nachbiblische Weisheitstraditionen", *VT.* XV (1965), pp. 222ff., 230f. (and previous literature quoted *ibid.*). Obviously oral traditions are less reliable

Judaism and Christianity there is a persistent literary continuity, leading directly from Scripture to its interpretation,[5] whereas the Samaritan, who accepts no Scripture of any kind other than the Pentateuch as authoritative, has a permanent and unbridgeable gap between the Written Word and its interpretation. Hence it follows that no far-reaching conclusions can be deduced by us from their oral tradition if, in it, certain elements are emphasised and others ignored; and any such conclusions would in any case have no bearing on the problem of the documentary hypothesis.[6] Despite the obvious fact that the Samaritan interpreter tackles the same problem as others and comes across the same difficulties, the results of his interpretations are and must be entirely different.[7] One of the principles observed by common consent in the interpretation of legal documents is that their precepts cannot be understood as superseding the narrowest meanings of the phraseology (i.e. there must be no generalizing except where there is another compelling reason in the text or another direction to do so).[8] But even this elementary rule is by no means universally accepted by the Samaritans. Just as in poetry we can often rightly expect some ambiguity, not only because of the presence of metre and verse, but also because it is sometimes necessary to diverge from everyday speech, thus maybe suggesting several meanings,[9] so in the same way we can expect ambiguities in the Samaritans' approach to their Holy Writ. In addition to the given Biblical style, with its (for them) unusual wording, there is the influence of their traditional intonation, which they were accustomed to chant, and whereby they could derive varieties of meaning and expression out of

---

than the S.P. itself, which is also not helpful in this respect. On the controversy on this line, cf. literature Montgomery (*The Sam.*, p. 289, n. 40). Since there was a slight reversion in positions (cf. Ewing, "The Sam. Pentateuch etc.", *Expositor*, 1919 pp. 451ff. (*idem. Bibliotheca Sacra*, LXXIX (1922), pp. 418ff. and the curious little book by Munro, *The Sam. Pentateuch, etc.*), see now Purvis, *The Sam. Pentateuch, etc.*, pp. 69ff. cf. also n. 6 *inf.*

[5] Weiss, *Dor Dor*, 11, pp. 179f.

[6] cf. my article *ALUOS* VI (1969), pp. 109, 143 (nn. 95f.).

[7] Smart, *op. cit.* p. 8. Further illustration may be taken from the comparison of details (plays on words, unusual expressions etc.) expounded both by Philo and the Rabbis, cf. Siegfried, *Philo von Alexandria als Ausleger des alten Testaments*, pp. 168ff. On the great differences of the results of such exegesis, and some examples of the same 'difficulties' expounded differently by the Samaritans and other sects, cf. my article in *ALUOS* VI (1969), *passim*.

[8] Rosenblatt, *The Interpretation etc.*, p. 3 (and for further details *ibid.* n. 25).

[9] Empson, *Seven types of Ambiguity*, p. 30.

the same text. It is not surprising, accordingly, that the Samaritans, far
more than most other interpreters of antiquity, hit upon the most
arbitrary type of division, which not only gave individuality to separate
words but even sometimes to separate letters.[10]

(1) *Literalism as a method*

It is well known that the Samaritans and the related sects have been
labelled as austere "literalists"; but this designation, especially in regard
to the Samaritans, needs further explanation here.[11] Clearly we are quite
unable to discuss the great majority of their interpretations on these
lines, which are only too obvious. These are rephrasings of Biblical
texts in accordance with the strictly natural construction of passages,
and following the plain, ordinary and apparent sense of the words.
Nor are we greatly interested in the often mechanical word-by-word
literalism which is carried out by the Samaritan Targum. It must, in
fairness, be stated from the outset that Samaritanism did not carry this
following of the literal sense to absurd extremes, as Anan, the founder
of Karaism, did.[12]

Nowadays, with the scientific development of linguistics and semantics, we know better than ever how to evaluate the sense of the written
word. We are, in fact, more aware than ever that "on the life and adven-
ture of a word" volumes may be written.[13] We cannot evidently expect
any such scientific awareness amongst the Samaritans, but they did have
their own approach to "the wisdom of the simple sense". It was confidently believed that trustworthy traditions, going back to the time of
Moses and the Elders, instructed them in the correct way of chanting
the Biblical verses, which in itself illuminated for them the true meaning
of the context. The divine precept regarding the teaching, studying
and constant revising of these ceremonial chantings was believed to be
formulated in *Deut.* xvii, 19.[14] It is very possible that, in consequence

---

[10] cf. *sup.* Part II, n. 305

[11] cf. *sup.* Part II, para (b).

[12] Qirqisāni, Kitāb al-Anwār, IV, 22, 2 (ed. Nemoy, II, p. 386).

[13] Ullmann, *Language and Style*, p. 29. We cannot enter into the intricate problems
of semantical changes due to the employment of so many languages (Hebrew, Greek,
Aramaic and Arabic) by the Samaritans. Recently the late Professor E.Y. Kutscher
has devoted a monograph dealing with some *Words and their History* (Jerusalem
1961). cf. however, some Samaritan examples *inf.* para (e).

[14] Ben-Hayyim, *Literary and Oral Tradition etc.*, II, pp. 380-381, cf. however,
Macuch, *Grammatic etc.*, pp. ix, 60, 235-239 and Ben Hayyim, *Biblica* 52 (1971),
pp. 229-252.

of these traditions, the tendency to understand the bulk of Scripture rather on the sentence-level than on the single-word-level, prevented their literalism from ever becoming too absurdly rigid. It may even have had some influence likewise on their Halakhic approach. Let us take, for example, the Rabbinic ruling that precepts were to be fulfilled precisely in the form stated, to the exclusion of any other (Deut. xi, 7 etc.)[15]; such a ruling was not at all popular amongst the Samaritans. The solemnity of their approach to Scripture also prevented them from juggling with the words. Unlike some Dead Sea Scroll commentators, who often adopted one reading in preference to another according to whim or seemingly arbitrary choice, and in order to suit their homiletical needs,[16] the Samaritans frowned upon such practises. Needless to say, the more daring homiletical plays on words as employed by the Rabbis, an extreme example of which is the midrash built up on the expression "do not read so" (אל תקרי)[17] were utterly unknown amongst the Samaritans.

It would surely be fruitless to speculate on whether this instinctive restriction and even condemnation of daring exegetical devices was in any way bound up with the fact that the Samaritans did not need rules to govern their interpretations. It is indeed often assumed that hermeneutical principles in general were laid down, not merely with a view to encouraging further exegesis, but also to obviating the real danger of overzealousness running into absurdities. Concerning these exegetical principles, it has been established that their development had something at least to do with the maxim "Make a fence around the Law" (Aboth, I, 1) directed mainly as a polemical device against heretical departure from traditional paths.[18] It is instructive to note that, during the Islamic period, when the Samaritans were greatly influenced by the literature of Muslims, Karsites and Jews written in Arabic, and although the bulk of the translation of the Pentateuch into Arabic was itself adopted by them from outside, their exegetical

---

[15] Rosenblatt, op. cit., p. 4. cf. for numerous examples in the Mishnah, ibid. nn. 28-29.

[16] Bruce, Biblical Exeg. etc., p. 11. On the Samaritan single-mindedness of stubbornly adhering to "the (single) tradition", cf. sup. n. 14.

[17] A good list of such midrashim is to be found in the article אל תקרי (by H. Torczyner), Eschkol (Hebrew Encyclopaedia), II, pp. 375-385. cf. also my article op. cit. p. 135, n. 22. cf. Heinemann, Darkhei ha-Aggadah, p. 127 (and ibid. n. 163).

[18] A. Schwarz, "Die Hauptergebnisse etc ", Scripta Universitates... Hierosolymitanarum etc., I, p. 5.

material on this literature is sufficiently divergent in method and treatment to indicate that they did not blindly accept it, but definitely made
an independent contribution, even to the point of producing an Arabic
version, and again needless to say, an interpretation of it.[19] As to exegetical principles very common in Islam and Karaism, we may see on
countless occasions that although the terminology is indeed ocasionally
adopted, its employment does not trespass away from the traditional
Samaritan paths. It seems, therefore, that, even in times when foreign
terminological and exegetical devices were current amongst the Samaritans, they seldom had to resort to restrictive formulations of hermeneutical principles. The only credible explanation for this must be
sought in the fact that their devotion to their traditionalism was in itself
sufficient to guard them against serious deviations.

Returning now to the question of literalism, what we ourselves see
as the literal meaning of a given text, and what the ancient and mediaeval
Samaritans saw as such a meaning, are two completely different things.
To even begin to understand their literalism, we must change our mode
of thinking and scale of values, and to try to comprehend the seemingly
'illogical' thinking of the Samaritans, we must enter into it from their
point of view, if we are ever to grasp what to them seemed simple and
straightforward.[20] We can hardly expect a scientific etymological
approach on the part of the Samaritans; and taking into account their
folkic or associative definitions, we can never guarantee that their understanding was the same as that of the modern reader, employing as he
does analytical definitions. Despite the justifiable criticism in modern
linguistics of what are generally called "operational definitions", in
order to understand the 'simple' sense as it was understood by the Samaritans, this term will probably serve us best.[21] Thus sometimes, from a
verb, one can create a noun or adjective with a variety of meanings
or shades of meanings, and whether the use of such a word is deliberate,
or merely a result of 'misunderstanding' of the grammatical point, the
result is of course 'ambiguity' for us, to resolve which we must "reconstruct" the popular thinking of the Samaritan.[22]

---

[19] Halkin, "The Relations of the Sam. etc.", *Saadia Anniversary Vol.*, p. 279
(cf. *ibid.* nn. 47-48).

[20] As in the case of the Qumran Sect, their own manner of reasoning must be
followed in order to comprehend their exegesis. cf. G.R. Driver, *The Judean Scrolls*,
p. 5.

[21] Ullmann, *Language and Style*, pp. 23ff. cf. however *ibid.* pp. 34f. and *idem.*,
Semantics, p. 101, n. 2.

[22] cf. e.g. *sup.* Part II, n. 447. For more details cf. *inf.* para (e).

(2) *Free (extra-Biblical) Homiletical Expansion*

It is wellnigh unavoidable, as is also the case with the Lore of the Rabbis,[23] that certain passages of homiletical expansion should be quite devoid of any discernible exegetical needs, and should be only interpolated into a Sermon or a Commentary from external sources. Samaritanism was not free from forms of eschatological speculation for which there was very meagre Scriptural warrant. However, even in Messianic speculations, where no explicit quotations but only vague allusions to the Pentateuch are to be found, the question arises: are homiletics in truth originally derived from Scripture or only later artificially linked with it?[24] There is a super-critical opinion that Aggadah was fabricated by political leaders of the community who had "an axe to grind" so as to further their polemical purpose. If so, it is to be suspected that extra-Biblical passages were in fact added to the Scriptures;[25] but, in the case of the Samaritans, there is little evidence for such a conclusion. Furthermore, even less is the degree of possibility that any contradiction between Scripture and any freely written homiletics should ever occur. A most suspect book, not so long ago, was the ASAṬIR, in which some scholars found irreconcilable items concerning Biblical personalities, chronology etc. However, it has been proved beyond doubt that most such allegations were based on the then faulty text of this composition; and it is therefore entirely wrong to suggest any independence from the Torah or any employment of conflicting sources on the part of the author of the Asaṭir. Obviously there are some legends taken from the Lore of the environment, but these must first have been "neutralised" and brought into conformity with Scripture.[26]

The Asaṭir is notorious for having long pieces of extraneous material; yet we have already seen that it does not take this material from external sources uncritically. In other literature, this process of adopting and adapting foreign elements is even more restricted in scope and operation. From this standpoint we shall have to criticise the previous generali-

---

[23] Weiss, *Dor Dor etc.*, II, pp. 179f.

[24] Merx (*Der Messias oder Ta'eb der Sam.*, p. 9), has already shown that to a great extent these speculations are based on the 'Samaritan interpolation' after *Ex.* xx, 18 (= *Deut.* v, 25-26; *ibid.* xviii, 18-22). This seems to be an ancient tradition polemicizing against all "false prophets" and at the same time an eschatological promise of a "Prophet like Moses".

[25] cf. A. Spiro, "Samaritans, Tobiads, etc.", *PAAJR* XX (1951), p. 317, n. 75.

[26] Ben-Hayyim, "Sepher Asaṭir", *Tarbiz* XIV-XV, pp. 3f.

sations of some scholars who held the opinion that legends were adopted in bulk from Jewish Midrashic literature.[27] Although it is no doubt hard to distinguish between material borrowed from external sources and that independently developed by the Samaritans, there are happily some means of comparison which may suggest to us, through the careful investigation of Samaritan exegetical forms, what might well be an original Samaritan development. Thus the Samaritan simple exegetical devices bear no comparison with the far more daring Rabbinical midrashim, which actually give a double meaning, not only to Scripture, but even to their own words and their own Midrash. Expressions counselling that, for instance, a person "profane the Shabbat" or "Sell himself to idol-worship" (both expressions are metaphorical), rather than become a burden on others,[28] would never occur to the Samaritan mind. We find indeed that the Samaritans, too, may give a double meaning to the text or employ it in a sense implying some strange interpretation, which we might ascribe to lack of exegetical talent; but even then, this fact is no guarantee that these features are taken from the outer world. The endeavour to find in Scripture the most sublime or the most suitable or the most educational and ethical was common to all believers in the Torah and the very endeavour to do so occasionally led them to what seem to us to be the strangest ways of exegesis.[29] It could still be said, by way of comparison, that neither ingenuity nor casuistry, so typical of some Rabbinic Midrashim, has much reflection in Samaritan literature.[30]

Even as compared with the Karaites, who "were exacting, penetrating (into the Scripture) and discovering (new) precepts", and thereby leaning heavily on Rabbinical sources, the Samaritans show a more literalist way of approach, which not only becomes a method, but also prevents the penetration of such alien material.[31] One can but conjecture here that the essential nature of the Samaritan Pentateuch, with its fuller text often bridging gaps which, for the expounders of other versions, created great difficulties contributed heavily towards this literalness of outlook, as

---

[27] Geiger, "Die gesetzlichen Differenzen", *ZDMG* XX (1866), p. 570.

[28] Shabbath 118a; *Babha Qamma*, 110a. No soubt these are further midrashim on "Howbeit there shall be no poor with thee" (*Deut.* xv, 4); cf. *Babha Meṣi'a*, 33a and *Sanhedrin*, 64b. For additional examples, cf. Jellinek (ed.), *Nophet Zufim*, p. 204.

[29] Heinemann, *Darkhei ha-Aggadah*, p. 3 (cf. *ibid.* nn. 36ff. for bibliographical details).

[30] cf. my article, *ALUOS* VI (1969), pp. 109f., 142f. (nn. 90ff.).

[31] cf. *sup.* Part I, n. 29.

they found their Holy Writ more or less self-explanatory and self-sufficient.[32] Naturally we shall often discover in Samaritan Midrashim artificial devices, which make one think that they were invented solely for the purpose of incorporating extraneous material into the text.[33] Nonetheless, the general impression is that these few exceptional cases actually demonstrate the rule and show how meagre in fact are the adoptions and adaptations from outside sources. In expounding the Samaritan exegetical devices, our constant interest will then also be devoted to trying to distinguish between the original and natural Samaritan developments on the one hand and the artificial ones, which usually simultaneously betray foreign influences on the other.

(3) *Allegory*

Although figurative expressions of all kinds, but especially allegory, must give us the impression of being opposed to any literalist exegesis and must necessarily be judged as artificial, bringing extraneous material into the expounded text,[34] this contrast is more apparent than real. Prophetic expressions in particular lend themselves easily to figurative and allegorical interpretation. If we may again use our comparison with poetry, it at once becomes obvious that, by the very intention of the poet, it would be quite absurd to take every detail in its literal sense. This rule was understood long ago by all expounders of the Aggadah. Often, to be sure, the most artificial devices (for example, the amplification of the particle את, so turning the whole context into an allegorised apology) originated simply because the literal sense was blasphemous or difficult to accept.[35] Philosophers, in particular, loved this device which made so much easier their task of 'rationalising' certain unpalatable legends.[36] In this field, the Samaritans of all generations did not differ from others in using allegory to avoid anthropomorphic expressions referring to God. In other fields, however, as we may see in connection with the more complex hermeneutical rules, the figurative interpretation, and especially the allegorical is used very sparingly. In

---

[32] cf. *sup.* Part II, para (b).

[33] cf. *sup.* Part II, para (g), (h) and (i).

[34] Farrar, *History of Interpretation*, pp. 127, 139f., 149.

[35] Jellinck, *op. cit.* p. 203 (cf. note). cf. my article *op. cit.* pp. 128f. (n. 6), 135f. (nn. 32f.).

[36] Maimonides, *Guide for the Perplexed*, I, ch. 71; *idem*, *Commentary on the Mishnah*, Irntoduction to Ch. Ḥeleq (*Sanhedrin* X).

the case of the harmonisation of various sources,[37] in which one would naturally expect a tendency towards the more abstract, the exact opposite is true; most Samaritan harmonisations are built on a sense very close to the literal.

As opposed to the wide ranging figurative interpretations in the aggadic method of the Rabbis, such devices in the matter of halakhah are extremely rare.[38] Contrary to all our expectations, in which we might think that the Samaritans would not use these devices of figurative interpretation at all in the matter of halakhah, it is very surprising that in fact they still appear. The most outstanding of these figurative and allegorical interpretations is in the שמע Deut. vi, 8. Here, as opposed to the literal interpretations of the Rabbis, who see in such expressions the justification of the use of phylacteries, the Samaritans always explain this term as an allegory or in a figurative way. "And thou shalt bind them for a sign upon thine hand" is taken by the Samaritans as a general exhortation to moderate the actions of the human person, and especially the actions of the hand; likewise "and they shall be for frontlets between thine eyes" is taken as referring generally to learning, or more particularly to "the duty of the study of the Hebrew language", on which the proper understanding of the Word of God, of course, depends.[39]

Such and similar considerations lead us to regard allegory in the Samaritan exegesis, not so much as an exegetical rule, but rather as a rare exegetical device depending on the tradition.[40]

B. From Spontaneous Interpretations to Exegetical Norms

As regards the Samaritans, it is, in any case, much too artificial to make a sharp distinction between spontaneous ways of interpretation, resulting from a naive and continuous reading of the text, and hermeneutical rules which are imposed on the text from outside. Insofar as we can speak at all of the Samaritan hermeneutics and the theory behind their exegesis, this can only be in general terms. Any awareness of the employment of hermeneutical rules seems rather subconscious amongst the Samaritans. Even the most frequently introduced devices usually

---

[37] cf. *inf.* para (g, 7).

[38] Heinemann, *op. cit.* p. 122 (cf. n. 145 for bibliography).

[39] *Tabbākh,* f. 138a (والزم تعليم الخط العبراني المدون به الفاظها) cf. also Abdel-Al, *A Comparative Study etc.,* pp. 653ff. (and translation pp. 468ff.).

[40] cf. *sup.* Part II, para (h) and *inf.* para (h, 3); cf. also my article *op. cit. passim.*

lack any explicit technical term or definition and to a lesser extent any rules as to how they should be utilised. At any rate, the average Samaritan interpreter himself is not fully aware of drawing any distinction as to when he is using the simple running commentary, derived from what we may call "operational definitions", and when he is using the more articulate and recondite "rules". Marqah, however, already shows a semi-awareness in his midrashim on his exegetical devices, and he uses them in such a way that they are interwoven with each other.[41]

As a rational approach only, shall we confine ourselves to such a classification in trying to describe the spontaneous interpretation first, and in dealing only later with what we define as "hermeneutical rules". Needless to say, we shall not be able to avoid entirely mentioning even the most complex rules which occasionally feature in the middle of a midrash that we would describe as simple or spontaneous exegesis. But systematic explanations of the more recondite 'rules' logically come later.

Here it is appropriate to mention that the contradiction in the minds of the Rabbis between the belief in the Sinaitic origin of the hermeneutical principles and the constant development of the Oral Law [42] which often occasioned real conflict between tradition and midrash,[43] apparently did not exist amongst the Samaritans. Their spontaneous approach in what we elsewhere term their "organic thinking", so typical of ancient oriental thought, and emphasising the sensuous and concrete aspects as opposed to methodical or systematic speculations, prevented them from garbing exegetical principles in schematic terminology;[44] but at the same time eliminated the 'logical' conflict between tradition and development. In other words, hermeneutical rules were not determined abstractly by the Samaritans in order to create traditions; but contrariwise a living tradition (or what they believed to be such) determined when, where and how to employ these 'rules'.

In cases, where according to the laws of grammar and linguistics, it would be possible to interpret the text in different ways, without a definitive tradition there would certainly be differences of opinion. It

---

[41] cf. *inf.* nn. 92-101. Examples for this 'method' may be multiplied *ad nauseam.*

[42] A. Schwarz, "Die Hauptergebnisse etc., *Scripta Universit. Hierosolym etc.*, I. pp. 2f.

[43] Weiss, *Dor Dor etc.*, I, p. 143.

[44] *sup.* Part II, n. 380 and text there.

often happened amongst the Rabbis that a number of traditions were multiplied, thus mutually excluding one another. The Samaritans, by leaning so heavily on their own well-marked traditions, reduced such possibilities to a minimum.[45] We still have with us, however, the problem which will occupy us later, i.e. the one of the possible ambiguous relationship of clauses in a sentence; for instance, in *Deut*. xix, 6, "whereas he was not worthy of death", it is not at all clear whether "he" refers to the murderer or the avenger of blood. There were, in this and similar cases, heated discussions amongst the Rabbis, but such and similar cases would have been, and were, eliminated by the Samaritans by relying on a single tradition as to the reading.[46] So it was not entirely impossible that precisely because of the Samaritans' emphasis on the proper reading in public and on the proper teaching of children, the range of the possible development of contradictions was limited.[47] Having regard to the overwhelming importance of tradition in Samaritan exegesis in general,

---

[45] M. Guttmann (*Die Anlehnung etc.*, pp. 8f.) brings a wealth of examples of cases in which the Rabbis did not have a firm traditional reading, causing controversies as to how to decide on the division of verses or clauses. Taking at random one of these examples will suffice to demonstrate the difference between Talmudical and Samaritan exegesis: from the verse "And thou shalt eat and be full and thou shalt bless the Lord etc." (*Deut*. viii, 10) the Talmud deduces various laws: One is obliged to recite 'grace' after meals. Furthermore, (*Berakhoth*, 48b) if three or more people dine together, they are obliged "to make an appointment for common grace" (= Mishnah, *ibid*. VII, I). The controversy, however, arose (*Pesahim*, 49b) on this point of definition of the terms "to eat" and "be full". As opposed to all this, Samaritan Tradition did not recognise the validity of such methods, namely, that such regulations of definitions should be "read into" the Scripture. When some Samaritans tried to introduce a novel midrash (relying on the simple order of the Biblical words) in order to sanction the partaking of food before the morning prayers, they were severely rebuked (*Kāfi*, p. 78 = SLTh. A, p. 14). In passing, we may remark that some of the cases upon which there was a unanimous tradition amongst the Rabbis (Guttmann, *ibid*. pp. 12f.) served as a bone of contention in the disputes with the sectarians, including the Samaritans. Again, one example may illustrate this gulf between the traditions: *Lev*. xxiii, 40, was explained by the Rabbis (*Sukkah* III, 1-VI, 7) in the sense that "the four plants" mentioned in Scripture must be carried during the Feast. The Sectarians, on the other hand, understood it generally as material to be used for building the "booth" (cf. Nehemiah, viii, 15). Detailed discussion of this and many other similar problems of halakhah cannot be undertaken here. Cf. however, Geiger, "Über die gesetzlichen Differenzen etc", *ZDMG* XX (1866), pp. 570f., Hanover, *Das Festgesetz etc.*, pp. 31f., 50f. and text on p. xvi. For Karaites, cf. P.R. Weis, "Ibn Ezra, the Karaites etc.", *MELILAH* II (1946), p. 133, n. 273.

[46] *Sifri, Deut.*, ad loc.; *Makkoth*, 10b.

[47] cf. *inf*. para (b, 2).

we may, by way of comparison, now give a further reason for the poverty of hermeneutical rules amongst them. If we compare the Samaritan with the Rabbinical exegesis, it becomes more and more evident that hermeneutical rules are not meant merely to promote interpretation or as a source of legislation, but rather to exclude a wild growth of uncontrolled and newfangled methods.[48] Thus, the Seven Rules of Hillel (the most ancient ones of the Rabbinic Oral Law) were assuredly not invented by him, but merely represent a compilation of the most customary methods.[49] Hillel himself used other rules, some of which, like the הקש (analogy),[50] may even be older than his own seven. With the development of the Oral Law, Rabbi Ismael, who expanded the Seven Laws of Hillel into thirteen, was motivated by the felt need for opposition to the free-ranging and manifold exegetical devices used by Rabbi Akiba. He propounded his own Thirteen Rules of hermeneutics to illustrate the maxim, "the Torah speaks in the language of man";[51] and therefore in disregard of the rules established, one was not allowed to force the language of Scripture beyond its literal meaning. For the Samaritans, with whom the "perfection of the Torah of God" was one of the major principles from earliest times, and with whom too, its "perfection" was interpreted in the sense of its being self-explanatory, such development of hermeneutical rules called for by the need to limit free exposition, was not necessary at all.[52]

(1) *Aggadah and Halakhah*

One can find examples by the score to show that Samaritan exegetes made no distinction in their practice between Halakhah and Aggadah. They applied the very same exegetical methods to both types, and, furthermore, they derived halakhic discussions from Biblical verses appearing in a narrative which has no legal connotation whatever. For example, *Gen*. i, 31 "and God saw everything that he had made and behold it was very good", was employed in the interpretation of Samaritan calendaric calculations. The argument runs broadly on these lines: — Since the world was created in perfect form, so calendaric calculations must also endeavour to place their zenith at the perfect

---

[48] cf. my article, *op. cit.* pp. 98, 128f. (nn. 6f.).

[49] Strack, *Introduction etc.*, pp. 93f.

[50] *ibid.* p. 94. For the use of analogy amongst the Sam. cf. *inf.* para (g, 1).

[51] Strack, *op. cit.* p. 95. cf. also, Weiss, *Dor Dor etc.*, II, pp. 102f.

[52] cf. *sup.* Part II, para (b).

point. From this it follows that since the "perfection" shewn by the constellation of the sun in relation to the moon on which relationship the calendar itself is based — occurs in Aries (the month of April) this must inevitably be the start of all calculations.[53]

Another example is the expression *Gen.* iii, 8. "the presence of the Lord". This was interpreted (relying on the philosophical principle that God is omnipresent) to mean that there was a certain defined direction, namely, towards Hargerizim, to which to turn in prayer.[54] The Halakhic principle, that speaking is equivalent to acting, was taken from *Gen.* iii, 12-14, "Thou hast done", in which, in the cases of both Eve and of the serpent, the only action was speech.[55] One might add countless examples from the rich Samaritan literature, of which throughout it is a common feature to derive halakhic decisions from innocent-looking narratives.[56]

Even the afore-mentioned few examples will indicate that, although no distinction was made between the legal portions of the Pentateuch and its narrative portions, nevertheless, the Samaritans did not force the simple meaning of these verses in order to read into them an 'Oral Law'. Unlike the Karaites, through their system of "Search" extracting the most unlikely senses from Scripture [57] the Samaritans, even assuming that some of their midrashim were later fabrications and only artificially attached to Scripture, never entirely removed them from the original sense by their novel legalist employment.

In this respect too, the Rabbinical practice can hardly be compared with that of the Samaritans. Although the Rabbis applied much freer hermeneutical rules to the aggadah (one could even call them principles of homiletics) traditionally ascribed to Rabbi Eliezer ben Jose Ha-Gelili,

---

[53] *Ṭabbākh*, f. 83a (SLTh.A, p. 123).

[54] *Kāfi*, p. 205 (SLTh.A, p. 30).

[55] *Kāfi*, pp. 106 and 330 (SLTh.A, pp. 18 and 70 respectively). cf. also *Ṭabbākh*, f. 28b (SLTh.A, p. 84).

[56] From the innocent description of Rebekah's action, "and she took her veil, and covered herself" (*Gen.* xxiv, 65), a whole series of instructions are derived concerning the chaste clothing of women, *Kāfi*, pp. 195f. (SLTh.A, pp. 24f.). In the narratives of the Book of *Genesis* alone, the present writer has found 167 instances which were utilized in the Samaritan literature (including later compilations) for halakhic allusions. Obviously, such and similar quantitative data has little value, since our knowledge of the Samaritan literature is far from being complete. Nevertheless, such and cognate problems deserve more advanced research, which have to be postponed.

[57] Harkavy, *Studien und Mitteilungen etc.*, pp. 133, 139, and notes there.

it has been shown that most of these rules were also employed for halakhic expositions.[58] Whether one agrees that the original meaning of the Rabbinic term "haggadah" was a penetrating search into the exposition of Scriptures, both for homiletical and legal purposes,[59] or not, the common ground, in not distinguishing between halakhic and aggadic interpretations still differs as between the Rabbis and the Samaritans. The Samaritans' legal system lacks all the logical principles which unify and rationalise a mass of particulars into a system which actually produces further applications to new cases, out of itself as it were. Naturally, the motive to discover the implications of newly discovered cases so as to apply them to new situations, also existed among the Samaritans. Samaritan law, however, was not structured after the manner of a syllogism, so as to create a logical system of jurisprudence. It is therefore only the truth to point out that their primitive system lacks all the casuistry necessary to a more developed and rationalized system, in order to eliminate the limitations necessitated by the uniformity of the law. The Rabbinic need to resort, in such manifest cases of hardship, to individualization or equity [60] was unheeded by Samaritan rigorism.

We may now profitably investigate a little further this inviting comparison between Samaritan exegesis and Rabbinic casuistry. It is often too easily assumed that 'legalism' must invariably be connected with such ingenious legal devices as we find in Rabbinic casuistry. However, this is rather a broad and questionable generalisation than a tangible fact. If we look at Samaritan exegesis in general and mark the all-pervasive legalistic approach, in which many purely narrative phrases and clauses are heavily loaded with a legalistic exegesis, even at a time when the influence of Rabbinic casuistry is almost non-existent, we may realise that these two concepts (legalism and casuistry) do not by any means necessarily go hand in hand. It is the especial weakness of all too easily accepted myths, often going along with partisan theological thinking, to create such an artificial picture.[61] It is true that, as a rule,

---

[58] cf. Bardowicz, *Die Abfassungszeit etc.*, p. 6, n. 1. For a bibliography on the "32 Middoth", cf. Strack, *Introduction etc.*, p. 95.

[59] Finkelstein, "Midrash, Halakhot etc.", *Bear Jubilee Vol.*, p. 32.

[60] Bokser, *Pharisaic Judaism in Transition*, p. 117 (and for further lit. cf. *ibid.* n. 1 and p. 120, n. 6).

[61] Such sweeping generalisations and the emphasis on the antithesis of 'legalism' as opposed to 'grace' caused some radical theologians to look upon the whole O.T. as having only negative value. Smart, *The Interpretation of Scripture*, p. 73. For Samaritan research all such dichotomy is irrelevant. cf. my article, *op. cit.* pp. 110, 143 (especially n. 96).

the Samaritans do not 'strain the letter of the law'. Nevertheless, their complete lack of some of the characteristic Rabbinic institutions, as for example Erubhin [62] is not due to their scorn of ratiocinative methods, which may perhaps be termed 'legal fictions',[63] but rather to their legalistic exegesis itself, based as it is, on entirely different traditions.

If we look from another point of view at this aspect of the Samaritan hermeneutic heritage, we may readily be led to compare it with the common attitude of the devout Biblical interpreter in general. To take, for example, the case of the Christian exponent for whom 'the centre of Scripture' (identified with the 'Salvation history') created for itself a circle, in which this cardinal point is the essence of the whole, we find that he subsequently superimposes — whether consciously or not — the results of his generalisation on the interpretation of as many as possible of the specific details.[64] In a somewhat similar fashion, the Samaritan's exegesis also runs in a circle from the centre to the whole and back again, utilising likewise his knowledge of the centre — which for him is the concept of the perfect Word of God — and pressing this generalisation into service for his elucidation of all the details. In earliest times, such was also the simple exposition of the Rabbis, in which too there was no strict division at all between the legal and the Aggadic hermeneutical rules.[65]

In a way, even in the later Rabbinic development when the hermeneutical rules were in full force, there are incidental remarks in the narrative portion of the Bible which are still regarded as "clues" to the definition of popular usages and the true nature of things.[66] One may even generalise here and fairly conclude that all commentators in fact have this in common. Since they cannot rewrite or alter Holy Writ,

---

[62] A whole tractate of the Talmud (108 folios) is devoted to this subject and this theme occupies some considerable part of other parts of the Talmud. These detailed regulations (based on Rabbinic Oral Law, often without any biblical support, or even contradicting the literal sense of some verses) were not accepted by the literalists. cf. *Zadekite Fragments*, X, *line* 21 (Rabin's notes, 4 and 5 and *ibid.* XI, 6 (ed.'s notes 1-2). cf. also Albeck, *Das Buch der Jubiläen etc.*, pp. 9f.

[63] cf. Robertson, "Law and Religion etc.", *Judaism and Christianity*, III, p. 77. The Samaritans, like other sectarians who believed in the strict literal sense of Scripture (cf. previous n.) could not accept the "lenient" rulings of the Rabbis. This was clearly realised by Montgomery, *The Sam.*, pp. 170 and 198. cf. Albeck, *Mishnah*, II, pp. 77ff., 434f.

[64] cf. Barr, *The Semantics of Biblical Language*, p. 259.

[65] Bacher, "The origins of the word Haggada", *JQR* IV (1892), pp. 406ff.

[66] Rosenblatt, *The Interpretation etc.*, p. 23 (cf. examples, nn. 41f.).

they are obliged, to a greater or lesser degree, to engage in harmonisations.[67] But whereas for others these harmonisations imply the awareness
of a certain differentiation between legalism and theological thought,
for the Samaritan there is never any real distinction between the various
aspects of the Word of God. Even amongst the Pharisees, there are
certain circles which teach that, not the legal parts of the Torah, but
rather its narrative chapters and their exposition reveal "the ways of God
to man", and these one should follow.[68] The literalism of the Samaritans
and their method of harmonisation of the various sections of the
Torah make of their exegesis one unit, because it does not occur to
them that in the Torah there may conceivably be distinctions between
the theological and the legal portions. In short, we can in truth say that
legalism is the quint essence of their theology.

(2) Masoretic Rules

It is well known that the 'Masoretic' text was most carefully guarded
by the Masoretes, who, during its long period of transmission, identified
themselves with certain peculiarities which have survived, and which
were intimately connected with Rabbinic exegesis. We have seen that
such features were wholly absent from the Samaritan Pentateuch.[69]
On the other hand, despite the fact that the orthography of the various
texts of the Samaritan Pentateuch exhibited a bewildering range of
variant readings, it has been amply proved that in face of this textual
confusion, the Oral Tradition in the light of which the text was read,
showed a remarkable unity.[70] There were even rules laid down for the
correct reading of the text, including directions for pronunciation,
grammatical, syntactical and like instructions, which prevented the
reader from deviating from the accepted tradition.[71] Obviously, the
minutiae and the techniques of this oral tradition, so admirably explored
only recently,[72] cannot be dealt with within the framework of our

---

[67] Weingreen, "The Rabbinic Approach etc.", *BJRL* XXXIV (1951/2), p. 187.
cf. *inf.* para (g, 7).

[68] Büchler, *Studies in Sin and Atonement*, p. 359 (cf. n. 1 for further bibliography).

[69] cf. *sup.* Part II, para (h), (i) and (j).

[70] Ben-Ḥayyim, *The Literary and Oral Tradition etc.*, IIIa, pp. 27f. (cf. *ibid.* n. 37)
(cf. however *sup.* n. 14).

[71] Ben-Ḥayyim, "The Hebrew of the Sam.", *Leshonenu* XII (1943/4), pp. 45ff.,
113ff.

[72] cf. *sup.* n. 1.

present investigations, although the findings must clearly guide us in looking for the principles of Samaritan hermeneutics.

The interdependence of the Written Word and the Living Tradition was naturally not confined to the reading alone; but, on the contrary, the reading was geared to the understanding, and the understanding to the practical application. The *Ṭabbākh* devoted a whole chapter to the importance of these aspects of the Living Tradition.[73] The most instructive element of this exposition is the fact that occasionally, but only occasionally, he actually gave more weight to the tradition than to Scripture itself. In Justification of this statement we may use the *Ṭabbākh*'s own explanation in asserting that the validity of the Written Word of God was enhanced by the fact of the unbroken Living Tradition. The most instructive examples (*ibid.* f. 152b-153a) are those of the Laws of Inheritance and Consanguinity which are and must be entirely dependent on the testimonies of the people of a single locality or family. The natural inference from this is that the tradition of the whole religious community had even more validity in this instance, since it established the interdependence of the Written Word of God and the tradition of the people.[74]

We now ask ourselves the rhetorical questions: how did the Samaritan exegesis take care of the deficiencies of what one may call, in Rabbinic terms, the Masorah? and what were the external guidelines which served as pegs for the Samaritan Midrash? The answer at one becomes obvious. The Samaritan 'Masorah', albeit oral rather than written, functioned in almost the same way as its counterpart in the Rabbinic Midrash. A great number of the difficulties which had perforce to be expounded in the Masoretic text, by the aid of the Masorah, were eliminated by the very nature of the Samaritan text itself. Thus, for instance, the question of Kethibh and Qeri did not exist at all in the Samaritan Pentateuch.[75]

---

[73] *Ṭabbākh*, ff. 151b-156a. It is regrettable that for reasons of space it was impossible to reproduce this whole chapter, which is crammed with information most relevant to our subject. cf. my article, *op. cit.* pp. 118f., 154 (nn. 167-171).

[74] One of the cornerstones of Abū'l Ḥasan's arguments is based on the fact that there exist 'Laws' entirely dependent on oral tradition without the scantiest scriptural source. Two of these examples, namely, the requirement of 'ritual' killing of fish and locust, have been challenged as being of Karaite influence. cf. Wreschner, *Sam. Traditionen*, pp. 51f. Needless to say, the similarities (although not identity!) in the Zadokite Fragments (xii, ll. 13-15) make such allegations obsolete. Unfortunately the detailed treatment of such problems cannot be carried out here.

[75] Obviously there could not have developed any conflicting opinions on such matters, unlike the Rabbinical controversy (יש אם למקרא; יש אם למסרת) *Sanhedrin*,

The same applies to rules about certain words written defectively and plene.[76] The remarkable stability and uniformity of pronunciation amongst the Samaritans in the reading of their Law, despite the bewildering diversity and multiformity of its orthography,[77] indicate that their Oral Tradition was a relatively secure defense against innovations and changes in the understanding of Scripture. Needless to say, Oral Tradition cannot be expected to be strictly infallible; and, as a matter of fact, semantic changes in the language and ignorance on the part of some readers occasionally engendered deviations from the traditional reading.[78] These, however, were infrequent cases, with which the authoritarian Samaritan leadership could easily cope.

Other 'artificial' types of Midrashim, built on capital and small letters, or on punctuated letters (*puncta extraordinaria*) in the Masoretic Text, or any similar Rabbinic devices [79] could not have originated from the

---

4a, *Sukkah*, 6b, etc.). To illustrate the way how the S.P. overcame the problems of Kethibh and Qeri we may take some examples from the Book of *Exodus*: vi, 2/S.P. = Qeri; xvi, 2 and 7/S.P. invariably without *waw* or *yodh*, if the sense is to "murmur" (cf. Ben-Ḥayyim, *The Literary and Oral etc.*, II, p. 501, ll. 122-127) while לין "to lodge" always with *yodh* (*ibid.* p. 498, ll. 44-46). There is no limit to such examples, but statistical data in any case no value in this field, since for the Samaritan not orthography but the oral traditional pronunciation was the determinative factor (*ibid.* IIIa, *passim*). cf. n. 78 *inf.*

[76] cf. *Qiddushin*, 30a. For the Rabbis such rules were very important since their midrash often depended on such 'peculiar' spellings. Of particular interest are the cases of לא/לו (cf. Krochmal, *More Neboche Ha-seman*, p. 169). The S.P. has, in these cases, the form which is closer to the literal sense (לא העדה) *Ex.* xxi, 8 and לו in both cases, *Lev.* xi, 21 and *ibid.* xxv, 30).

[77] Ben-Ḥayyim, *op. cit.* preface to IIIa and *passim*. We have also seen (*sup.* Part II, para (b) that the exegesis of various generations confirms the unanimity in transmission of the expounded text. The very few *doubtful* cases are mainly due to faulty texts (omissions, scribal errors etc.). cf. my article *op. cit.* pp. 107, 141 (n. 75) and *passim*. If statistics may offer some support, judging from the examination of commentaries on the greatest part of the Pentateuch (on more than 4000 verses) the present writer found only 12 cases which may suggest a different scriptural background. However, even these few cases may have resulted from scribal errors.

[78] The purpose of compositions 'on the correctness of reading', such as that of Abraham al-'Ayya (Ben-Ḥayyim, *Literary and Oral etc.*, II, pp. 377ff.) was to avoid any deviations from the traditional sense. This careful following of instructions was essential even in a case of a single word, since misreading it could contradict the traditional exegesis of the whole passage (e.g. המיתו in *Ex.* iv, 24, cf. Ben Hayyim, *op. cit.* 11, p. 453, l. 125; S. Kohn, *Sam. Studien*, pp. 76ff.), cf. *inf.* para (e, 2 and 3).

[79] Heinemann, *Darkhei ha-Aggadah*, pp. 100f.

Samaritan Pentateuch, as this did not have any such peculiarities in its text.

It looks as though, by refusing to countenance a written Masorah, the danger of marginal notes (stemming from hints on the Midrashic exposition of the text) eventually being inadvertently interpolated into the text itself, was minimised.[80] This does not mean that the Samaritans were utterly devoid of Midrashic creativity, or that their homiletical imagination was at all restricted by the absence of a written Masorah. Not at all; the pegs and hints which prompted Samaritan types of exposition were, in fact, embodied in the oral tradition itself. As we have seen in earlier cases, the instructions given to the reader, for example, "The Rules of Reading, by Ibn Dartha", although the major function of such instructions was to guide the reader in the proper intonated chantings of Scripture, were simultaneously themselves a source of Midrashic inspiration.[81]

Such inspiration was understandably not of the same wide range as that of the Rabbis, with their practically unlimited 'seventy faces (i.e. meanings) of the Torah'.[82] On the other hand the Samaritans' way of chanting their Torah in certain respects inspired them with a feeling similar to that experienced in reading poetry. Although there was only a semi-awareness of metre and rhythm, this was quite sufficient to give the Samaritans the feeling that even the really prose sections of the Pentateuch were written in poetry. We know from our modern literary critics that "a metrical scheme imposes a sort of intensity of interpretation upon the grammar, which makes it fruitful even if there is no 'song' ".[83] The many nuances evoked by the formal chanting of Scripture not only begot ambiguities, but also and at the same time begot answers to these probable and maifold meanings of the text.

We have moreover to bear in mind that, during the ensuing discussion of the types of what we shall call "simple exegeses", from contextual problems down to syntactical and etymological and even grammatical ones — all, as we shall see, conducive to the Midrashic development — the specific Samaritan way of thinking remains our major concern. In this connection, we have to remind ourselves continually that the very

---

[80] cf. Krochmal, *More Naboche etc.*, p. 174.

[81] Ben-Ḥayyim, *op. cit.* II, pp. 340ff. cf. *sup.* n. 78.

[82] cf. *Shabbath*, 88b (on *Jeremiah* xxiii, 29) and parallels, cf. Heinemann, *op. cit.* p. 12.

[83] Empson, *Seven types of Ambiguity*, p. 28.

limited vocabulary of the Hebrew Pentateuch and the entire lack of a direct progeny of similar literary creations (like the Prophets and the Hagiographa) necessarily make the Samaritan semantic development distinct from that of other types of classical Biblical semantics. Unlike our modern Biblical exegetes [84] with whom there is an awareness that words can only be intelligibly interpreted by the meaning they bore at the time of their employment and by the linguistic usage of the writer under consideration, the Samaritans have, of course, no such awareness. Furthermore, the historical gap between the writer and the interpreter increases the gulf of dissimilarity in the semantic sense, both in individual words and in the meaning of the broader thematic unit. By his inadvertent, and therefore blameless negligence in trying to accommodate himself to the lingual habits in accordance with which the text is written, the Samaritan interpreter takes, without fully realizing it, great liberties with his exegesis.

It goes without saying that this inadequacy on the part of the Samaritans, in the field of Pentateuchal semantics, is conducive both to errors and to novel reappraisals of the actual text. It is only the living tradition, or, as we shall call it, the 'Samaritan Masorah', which really prevents their exegetes from losing themselves in utter confusion of misinterpretation.

C. CONTEXTUAL PROBLEMS

(1) *The Broad Thematic Units*

The most natural and spontaneous methods of interpretation depend on a wide conceptual sense of the theme with which one deals. Whether it is a primitive or a sophisticated mind, each is more conscious in the first instance of the general outline of the context than of its separate components, i.e. the words themselves. It is thus evident that one cannot draw a sharp distinction between the exposition of a whole passage and of its separate details. But it is possible as a rule to discover how the interpreter first comes to a general understanding of the passage and how only later he elaborates it by more intricate devices. Some of these more detailed methods will be explained later when we shall be dealing with hermeneutical rules: but here our main concern is to notice how the Samaritan expositor follows the simplest method at his disposal.

---

[84] cf. Barr, *The Semantics etc.*, pp. 139-140.

Even in the principles of his broad contextual interpretatoin there arise
certain methods which we may fairly classify as rules. For example,
the drawing of inferences from the sequence of apparently unrelated
passages [85] is an obvious device which will engage even the primitive
mind: but which, for convenience sake, will be dealt with later.

The first of our examples showing such general contextual expositions
is taken from the Asaṭir.[86]

> Then Melchizedek pronounced a new blessing upon the Name that saved him
> (*Gen.* xiv, 19) and gave him a tenth of all (*ibid.* v, 20) and (Abraham) refused
> to accept it. Then he said to him, "*Give me the persons, and take the goods to
> thyself*" (*ibid.* v, 21), and Abraham answered the King of Sodom; "The goods
> of Sodom are as anathema to me" (*ibid.* v, 22). And in Nisan (the 1st month)
> the Lord revealed himself to Abraham, and (again) spoke to him His words in
> the fourth (month) and he told him in his dream, "*I am thy shield*" (*ibid.* xv, 1)
> and He brought him out and said "*Look now towards the heaven and count the
> stars*" (*ibid.* v, 5). Great is this saying and there is nothing like it. (These are) the
> sources (wellsprings) of faith, which are fear, righteousness and repentance.
> Now, all this (which follows) happened in one year, (i.e.) in the twentysecond
> (year). When God spoke with him he was 99 years old (*ibid.* xvii, 1). He received
> circumcission as a covenant in the seventh (*ibid.* v, 27) (month), and (at the same
> time) he welcomed the angels (*ibid.* xviii, 1). In the sixth (month) Sodom was
> burnt down (*ibid.* xix, 24) and in the seventh (month) Isaac was born (*ibid.*
> xx, 1).

No doubt we have here an attempt to interpret the chronology of
events without directly contradicting Scripture. Since Melchizedek is
spelt in the Samaritan Pentateuch and in the Targum as two words,
this name would easily be identified with a king of Sodom.[87] This led
in a further development, to the understanding that the "Priest of God
Most High" referred to Abraham, and naturally, therefore, that it was
the king of Sodom who gave Abraham a 'tenth of all'.

The second passage about God's revelation explains the difficulty
raised by what we may call a 'repetition'. There is one revelation in
Gen. xiii, 14-18, which, according to the Asaṭir, was in the first month
(before the war), and a second revelation in the fourth month, *Gen.*
xvi, 1f. However, the true revelation is certainly the latter.[88] These

---

[85] cf. *inf.* para (g, 3).

[86] Ben-Ḥayyim, "Sepher Asaṭir", *Tarbiz* xiv, xv (1943/4), p. 17 (and 39).

[87] This is the meaning of מלכי צדק ··· ויהב לה עסור מכלה ולא צבי מקבל ותמן
אמר לה הב לי נפשהתה וכו׳

[88] "and he *believed* in the Lord" (*Gen.* xv, 6) is both the essence of Religion and
the main purpose of Divine Revelation. The components of faith are (1) fear (*ibid.*

revelations must have been far remote from the birth of Isaac, for in between this revelation and the other, when Abraham accepted circumcision, the story of the birth of Ishmael is told in chapter xvi. Thus, the Asaṭir, basing itself on calculations,[89] reaches the conclusion that the previous revelations were 22 years before.

The remaining part of the Midrash is simple, as the opinion that all three events succeeded one another in one single year is almost explicit in the Bible.[90]

Obviously we cannot here allow ourselves the luxury of enumerating long midrashim of this kind, examples of which we could readily find in the whole of the Samaritan literature.[91] The method of the exposition of the broad thematic unit is so well defined and so well established that one may reasonably doubt whether, in fact, it can justifiably be included amongst the "simple rules" of exegesis. We emphasize this point mainly because it has been only too easily overlooked, since in most such cases attention is habitually focussed on the more sophisticated and recondite hermeneutical systems, inextricably intertwined as they are with what we here call the "thematic unit exposition", and so inevitably becoming oblivious of the latter.

In midrashim expounding the exhortations of the Pentateuch, it often happens that one does not see the wood for trees. This is especially so in the case of the midrashic exposition of Marqah. Thus, for example, the midrash that we shall have occasion to quote later (an exposition of *Deut.* xxxii, 22f.) can be rightly understood only if we look at its

---

v, 12), (2) righteousness (*ibid.* v, 6) and (3) repentance (most probably midrash on וישב *ibid.* v, 11).

[89] Gaster (cf. *Asatir.* vii, 1 and vii, 3) has already sensed that at the 12th year of the rule of Chedorlaomer, Abraham was 75 yars old and thus 77 at the Revelation (14th year of Chedorlaomer). The later events engulfing one year where the age of Abraham is given in Scripture (cf. next note), making this a difference of 22 years between the events.

[90] Circumcision was at his 99th year (*Gen.* xvii, 24) and the birth of Isaac, when Abraham was 100 years old (*ibid.* xxi, 5). In Rabbinic literature likewise the visit of the angels (אנושיה cf. S.P. and S.T. on *Gen.* xviii, 16, 22 and *ibid.* xix, 10. 16) is immediately following Abraham's circumcision (cf. *Soṭah*, 14a, *Babha Meṣia*, 86b etc.). The intricate problem of the 'exact' datings in the Asatir giving the exact month (which is often contradicted by other sources, cf. S. Kohn, *Zur Sprache Literature etc.*, pp. 53f., 59ff.) cannot be dealt with here.

[91] In *Memar Marqah* and the *Asatir* alone there are well over 50 such midrashim based on contextual problems arising from the broad thematic unit, however other 'hermeneutical rules' are likewise utilized in them.

entire setting as based on the standpoint of Marqah. In his view the thematic unit should be expounded on the assumption of its being self-explanatory, provided that one supplies it with guidelines and hints serving to explain some of its details.[92] It is quite easy to make valuable discoveries about the broad thematic exegesis of Marqah, if we look carefully at his actual words. The example which we adduce here has many advantages since it also clarifies some of the ambiguous variant readings of the Samaritans. Marqah builds this midrash on *Deut.* xxxii, 10-14 in his exposition of which he enumerates ten rewards for obedience,[93] followed by his exposition of the punishments for disobedience, based, of course, on *ibid.* 22-25. An understanding of this midrash grounded in the *motif* of using the fate of Sodom and Gomorrah as a striking instance of the punishment meted out to the sinners of both worlds,[94] depends on the realization that a little later, these same two cities figure prominently in the same scriptural context (v. 32). It is thus natural to expect that he will blend the immediate context of *Deut.* xxxii with examples taken from the "curses" (*Deut.* xxix, 13-28).[95]

> Let us hear words of admonition which Moses included with prophetic insight in his great Song — ten expressions that he uttered before the congregation with great effect.
>
> (*i*) *for a fire is kindled by my anger.* (*Deut.* xxxii, 22). Sodom and Gomorrah, an evil unclean place, like the defiled priest; thus the fire purified him. Thus He said *"consecrate yourselves"* (*Lev.* xi, 44); by this he warned of the fire.[96]
>
> (*ii*) *devours the earth and its increase* (*Deut. ibid.*); *Unsown and growing nothing* (*Deut.* xxix, 23). The land would be destroyed and all its inhabitants, in their evil-doing.
>
> (*iii*) *And setteth on fire the foundations of the mountains* (*Deut.* xxxii, 22). Then the sanctity of Mount Gerizim would be made known.[97]

---

[92] cf. my article *op. cit.* pp. 108, 110, 119f., 142f. (nn. 83ff.) and 156f. (nn. 174, 179-180).

[93] *Memar Marqah* (ed. Macdonald), I, p. 102f. (= II, p. 170f.).

[94] *Ibid.* I, p. 70 (= II, p. 111).

[95] *ibid.* I, p. 104 (= II, pp. 173f.).

[96] In an unidentified Microfilm of Memar Marqah this passage reads: סדם ועמרה אתר ביש טמא אכהן הטמא אשתה תדכינה ··· "S. and G. an evil and unclean place in accordance with its defilement the fire purified it". Either reading makes good sense, since Marqah uses here an analogy "Consecrate yourselves" otherwise the punishment is fire (cf. *Lev.* x, 3 (אקדש), *ibid.* 2 (אש ותצא). It is also possible that the analogy is derived from *Num.* xvi, 35 (אש), *ibid.* xvii, 2 (כי קדשו).

[97] It is taken for granted that Hargerizim will not be damaged, and thus its 'sanctity' established. This may be a veiled polemic against Jerusalem.

(iv) He said also, "*and I will heap evils upon them*" (*ibid.* 23). In the world they will be burnt, and in the Day of Vengeance they will be justly recompensed.[98]

(v) *And I will spend my arrows upon them* (*ibid.* S.P.). Pay attention, O World, to behold what will happen to them by way of recompense for the evils they have done.

(vi) *From this his bread shall be* (*wasted with hunger*) (*Deut.* xxxii, 24. S.P.). *And you shall eat and not be satisfied.* (*Lev.* xxvi, 26)[99].

(vii) That is their reward (for) *the fire* (= wrath, caused by) *the rebellious snatchers* (= instigators) (*Deut.* xxxii, 24, S.P.). This is a false prophet, poison and wormwood (cf. *Deut.* xxix, 18), a defiled apostate.[100]

(viii) *And I will send the teeth of beasts against them* (*Deut.* xxxii, 24); and the earth will swallow them up; vow unto them in this.

(ix) *With venom of crawling things of the dust* (*ibid.*); which will enter into their their houses and sting them.

(x) *In the open the sword shall bereave and in the chambers shall be terror* (*ibid.* 25). Not even one shall be left there.

Although at first sight this midrash reads very much like an arbitrary medley of unconnected verses, they are, in fact, carefully arranged; and likewise the supporting scriptures from elsewhere are carefully fitted in to enhance these ten expressions of admonition. These devices do not indeed disclose any novel or unexplored or deep layers in the Biblical text; but, by the mere juxtaposition of similarities from various parts of Scripture, they assuredly derive a new ethos from these familiar verses, while at the same time falling into line with the 'method' of favouring the number ten, so characteristic of Marqah.[101]

---

[98] אספה (T.S. אכנש Arab جمع‎) in the sense of double punishment in this world and in the future one.

[99] S.T. טעמה (‎כפן? =‎) גאה (מזה =‎) מדן. From *this* curse (the source of Marqah's analogy) food will not satisfy.

[100] S.T. רשוף חטיף עציאם. One wonders whether both Marqah and the Targum did not understand מררים as ממרים or מרדים? (The analogy with ראש ולענה may have followed the general pattern of comparing the verse here to *Deut.* xxix, 13-28). cf. Ben-Ḥayyim, *The Literary and Oral etc.*, II, p. 506, n. 149. cf. also *ibid.* p. 589, n. 300. Here again he polemicizes against Judaism (cf. n. 97 *sup.*), but it may be equally directed against Christianity. cf. however, for רשף *Berakhoth*, 5a. There is no point in comparing here Marqah's commentary with that of the *Ṭabbākh* (ff. 223a-224a). The few differences due to semantical changes will be mentioned *inf.* para (e, 1).

[101] cf. *sup.* Part II, para (g). Midrashim based on elaborate devices, but generally following the sense of the wider thematic principle, we will meet further in connection with 'hermeneutical rules' utilized in them. Thus on Hargerizim and the Creation of Adam (I, p. 46 = II, p. 73), or another of the calculation of the years of Egyptian enslavement (I, p. 31 = II, p. 47f.), cf. *inf.* para (g, 1) and (g, 3). cf. also *sup.* n. 91.

Nor are later writers unacquainted with such methods. To take an example from the *Ṭabbākh* we may at once see that the exposition of this eleventh-century writer in certain cases follows that of Marqah almost exactly. In the case at hand, the *Ṭabbākh* has a running commentary on the entire chapter xxxii of *Deut*. Admittedly, the *Ṭabbākh* contains more straightforward commentary and fewer midrashic and homiletic expositions. Nevertheless, apart from semantic divergencies (which will be later discussed) the basic understanding of Scripture is very similar. However, even the *Ṭabbākh* contains occasionally midrashic expressions, based on the exegesis of the wider thematic units. We now take another example; Abū'l Ḥasan explains *Deut*. xxxiii, 5, "And there was a king in Jeshurun when the heads of the people were gathered together, (S.P.) all the tribes of Israel were united". (S.P.).[102] This statement is compared with *Ex*. xxiv, 9-10, in which, according to the Samaritan reading, "and they feared the God of Israel" is a clear indication that Moses and Aaron and the Seventy Elders received an authority which caused the people of Israel to respect them, and, through them, God. Again, at first sight, the midrash looks like an arbitrary harmonisation of two passages. However, it is not a harmonisation only, but the outcome of the assimilation of the broad thematic units of Exodus to the shorter theme of Deuteronomy. According to the Samaritan division of Scripture the above-mentioned incident of the ascent of the Elders is a part of the section "In the third month". (*Ex*. xix, 1-24, xxiv, 18). From all this, the *Ṭabbākh* derives the midrash that a date was expressly given (the third month after the departure from Egypt), to serve as a warning against the denial of the Leadership of the Elders. The analogy with the verse in Deuteronomy is thus a deliberate insistence that the unity of the people entirely depends on the acceptance of the Authority of the Elders.

In the halakhic field, too, there is evidence to support the concept of whole portions being welded together to create a thematic unity out of the various regulations derived from individual verses, in order not to risk losing the contextual coherence of the deviously great number of details. In the Rabbinic literature of early times there was a noteworthy custom of dividing the Torah into fixed portions, in which the many detailed precepts might be conveniently counted and systematically arranged.[103] With the constant and ceaseless development of Rabbinic

---

[102] *Ṭabbākh*, f. 203a.

[103] M. Guttmann, *Eine Untersuchung der mosaischen Gebote*, pp. 22f.

laws, such ancient links, dependent on such a broad contextual interpretation, became rare, and indeed it now takes scholars no little time
and trouble to rediscover their faint clues.

Since Samaritan Halakhah never developed into such an involved and
comprehensive body as was the case with the Talmudic literature, it is
relatively easier for us to discover when such broad exegetical principles are being used. It will make our task much less complicated if
we follow the lines of the general trends in these cases which are but
seldom practised. In such cases our advantage lies in the fact that
here there was no constant and pressing need for application to everyday life, and therefore these precepts did not stand in need of elborate
amplifications and rearrangements into a new, more logical and more
practical order. In order not to be tedious, we may avoid any precise
follow-up and elaboration of details. All we are here interested in is to
demonstrate how this type of interpretation, which later branches
out into many varieties, depends entirely on the widest conception of the
textual unit, which can possibly be derived from the thematic colouring
of the even wider unit. In detail, it will suffice to adduce one specific
case, which is characteristic of the general trend of Samaritan
halakhic exegesis. It has again to be emphasized that, in this field,
as in the cases which have been seen earlier,[104] there is no basic difference
in the Samaritan mind between halakhah and aggadah. The afore-
mentioned examples from the aggadic field could actually suffice to
illustrate this. Because, however, of the intricate nature of the halakhic
exposition, we shall have to bring further examples in order to show
that, despite occasional deviation from the theme in the exposition of
minute details, the general principle of relying on the basic meaning
derived from the broad contextual unit still holds good.

We begin with the rare case of the rules regarding the "garment
plagued with leprosy" (Lev. xiii, 47-59) which include several ambiguous
items which may be interpreted in various ways. If we were to follow
in its literal sense the Hebrew text of verse 55, ("it is a fret, whether
it be bold in the head thereof or in the forehead thereof"), it would
make no kind of sense in a context speaking about garments. All the
versions, including our English translations, rephrase this passage to
mean "whether the bareness be within or without". The Samaritan

---

[104] cf. *sup.* para (b, 1).

Targum itself paraphrases this expression to suit the context, and renders it as "faulty or worn-out garments".[105]

However, this is not the major problem. There remain more serious, boradly contextual ambiguities which are much more perplexing than such minute textual details. There seems to be a real contradiction between the various rulings. We are given to understand that if a garment is plagued with leprosy it must be "shut up" for seven days (verse 50). and if the leprosy spreads it is unclean and should be burnt (verses 51-52). If the leprosy does not spread, the garment is washed and this process is followed by a second seven-day period of being "shut up" (verses 53-54). If there is no further change, "if the plague has not changed its colour", it is still unclean and should be burnt (verse 55). Now comes a difficulty since verse 56 demands "and if the priest look and, behold, the plague be dim after the washing thereof, then he shall rend it out of the garment" etc. It is not at all clear whether this is to be carried out immediately after the washing or after the second week's seclusion. Furthermore, there is an additional difficulty here, since we do not know for certain what the relationship of the foregoing verse is to verse 58, where it is stated "if the plague be departed from thence, it shall be washed the second time and shall be clean".

It is first of all necessary to establish the true relationship of "to be dim" in verse 56 to the last-mentioned verse: whether "to be dim" means something similar to "the plague has departed" or not. A further problem is the relationship between "has not changed its colour" (verse 55) and "to be dim" (verse 56). Do they oppose or complement each other? In our own expositions we cannot rightly relate this to Rabbinic interpretations, which themselves involve so many details and hair-splitting definitions that they have hardly any bearing on our problem.[106]

The *Kāfi* plausibly explains these difficulties by showing that there are two kinds of plague. "Any thing of skin" (veres 49) points to a general-isation, namely a garment which is entirely full of leprosy whereas the other details in the same verse such as "the warp and the woof" refer

---

[105] S.T. כתימה היא בצצעותה אי בנקיותה (cf. Ben-Ḥayyim, *op. cit.* II, p. 585, l. 218 and p. 442, l. 62). A similar interpretation was also that of the Rabbis — קרחתו חדשים — גבחתו ;שחוקים (Sifra, *Lev. ad loc.* Onqelos, Rashi etc.). Other medieval commentators (Ibn Ezra in the name of Saadya) resemble the English version. On the translation of this word in v. 42, there is less ambiguity, since it refers to the human body.

[106] cf. *Sifra*, *Tazri‘a*, para 13-15 (ed. Weiss, ff. 68a f.).

to cases in which the leprosy is only partially infecting the garment.[107] Only in cases where the leprosy infects olny a part of the garment, and after the first washing the infection fades (verse 56),[108] does the possibility lie that the rule of "tearing out" or "rending out" may save the garment. This interpretation, however, may be carried through only by translating (פחתת היא) (verse 55) (which is usually translated as "it is a fret") as "diminishing",[109] and it cuts verse 55 in the middle, connecting the end part of it with verse 56. This is plainly the sense of the *Kāfi's* conclusion. "The rule of the first one is to be burnt by fire, while in this case (i.e. when the leprosy is only in a part of the garment and it faded or diminished after laundering) He said פחתת היא". For this reason, the infected part is torn out, thus the garment becomes cleansed. By this device, he eliminates all possible contradictions, which certainly caused the Rabbis many difficulties.[110]

A much larger chapter about leprosy in general, which we can neither quote here nor even discuss adequately, shows the same approach. Fortunately for us this subject has been subjected to detailed analysis by previous scholars,[111] so here we may merely allude to the pattern of their expositions. These rules, covering Lev. xviii, 1-46, are arranged in a methodical order in Scripture.[112] The *Kāfi* does not follow the scriptural order, but uses an even more systematic presentation. Nonetheless, while this long chapter cannot thus easily be reconstructed to read like a running commentary, it can even now be seen that the broad thematic exegesis dominates every detail of it.[113]

---

[107] *Kāfi*, pp. 136f. (SLTh.A, p. 19).

[108] S.T. renders also (כמעה) in the same sense, to fade. cf. Ben-Ḥayyim, *op. cit.* II, p. 495, l. 271.

[109] S.T. כתימה (cf. *sup.* n. 105) is ambiguous. It may well mean "worn out" as well as "spot" or "spotty". cf. Ben-Ḥayyim, *ibid.* II, p. 566, l. 251.

[110] cf. *Sanhedrin*, 88a, there is a controversy whether if the whole garment is covered by leprosy (פרח בכולו) it is clean. Therefore פורחת (verse 57) is interpreted differently. Similarly פחתת (*ibid.* 56) is interpreted not as diminishing but as deepening. cf. Sifra, *ad loc.* and the commentaries of *RABaD, ibid.*

[111] N. Cohn, *Die Zarâath-Gesetze... nach dem Kitāb al-Kāfi etc.*; P.R. Weis, "Abū'l-Ḥasan Al-Ṣuri's discourse etc.", *BJRL* XXXIII (1950/51), pp. 131ff. cf. also Wreschner, *op. cit.* pp. xxiv, xxv.

[112] cf. Cohn, *op. cit.* p. 37.

[113] *ibid.* 39f. The Ms. used by Cohn agrees almost *verbatim* with the one used by us (pp. 120-146). Cohn has also pointed out that there are certain differences in exegesis between the *Kāfi* and Munajja, especially the definitions of שאת (*ibid.* p. 40f. cf. also text p. ix) and ספחת (*ibid.* p. 49f. text p. xiii f.). A comparison with the *Ṭabbakh*

In order not to enter into repetitive expositions, we cannot here amass examples; but, with a deeper and growing insight, it is not difficult to discover the thematic exegetical device which forms the background of all Samaritan halakhic development. Certain chapters, both in *Kāfi* and *Ṭabbākh*, dealing with matters which by the very nature of their theme closely follow a set pattern, often indeed remind us of a running commentary.[114]

By contrast with systems employing "Freer" hermeneutical rules, we may conclude that the Samaritan mentality seems to be much more restricted, although (as we shall see later) the Samaritan also occasionally allows some independence to the smaller textual units. Owing to his observance of the traditional rules, such breaking down of the text and giving of independence to smaller units, not only do not distort the general theme in his mind, but actually permit such minute expositions to be firmly integrated into the broad thematic unit.

(2) *The Verse*

It is hard to define what is meant by "a verse", and we have therefore no intention of strictly following the verse-order as it is known to us from the Masoretic text. Our major and primary interest must be concentrated on the relatively larger units which contribute to exegesis, prior to our involvement in syntactical problems and in the components of theese units. For convenience' sake we call these units "verse" (in the loosest sense of this word), since our sole aim now is to determine whether the awareness of such linguistic complexes as the sentence contributed in any way towards co-ordinating systematic interpretations, along these lines. Such an approach to the Biblical language has been perceived to be more appropriate by some others too, especially in following up the ideological background, since these larger linguistic complexes assuredly bring out the ideological statements in a sharper

---

(ff. 127a-135b) shows, however, that despite the slight differences in details, the exegetical principles in all three works are virtually the same. The detailed discussion of this subject must be postponed.

[114] The chapters on the Nazirite and Slaves in the *Kāfi* (pp. 227-239; SLTh.A, pp. 46-54; *ibid.* pp. 258-271; SLTh.A, pp. 55-64) and the Discourse on the Passover in the *Ṭabbākh* (ff. 50a-92a; SLTh.A, pp. 100-132) show such a pattern. Countless cases, seemingly based either on the exposition of etymological details or on more recondite hermeneutical devices, depend, nevertheless, on the interpretation of the broad thematic unit.

form than the minutely analytical approach, depending solely on the lexical unit, can possibly do.[115]

This approach is particularly pertinent to Samaritan exegesis, because their understanding of the Biblical idioms may well have been far removed from their original connotation, and may indeed have changed the meaning of a whole sentence. What to a person well-versed in Biblical Hebrew would seem crystal-clear, may have created ambiguity in the minds of the Samaritans, who, after all, had developed their own linguistic pecularities in directions influenced by their vernaculars, namely Aramaic and Arabic. Although the major differences in fact consist in lexical and syntactical peculiarities,[116] these can change the whole approach to the sentence.

If we once again look for a comparison with Rabbinic literature, we find that "a context which is disrupted"[117] forms a hermeneutical rule upon which midrashim are built. It seems likely that the development of such freedom of play on this hermeneutical rule develops out of genuine doubts about the exact division of the verse. Despite the fact that the Rabbis call their predecessors 'Soferim', a pun which can mean both "scribes" and "counters of letters of the Law", and that the Soferim do know exactly the numbers of verses and how they are to be divided, later generations have of necessity to admit that they themselves are no longer certain in this matter of the division of Scripture into verses.[118]

In view of the great significance among the Samaritans of the Oral Tradition, transmitted by their readers, it is not at all impossible that this living Masorah guards the individual units of the verses. It has always to be taken into account that the cantilations of the ceremonial reading not only have a musical value, but also give a coherent syntactical colouring — by serving as signs of inter-punctuation — to the portions read.[119]

---

[115] Barr, *The Semantics of Biblical Language*, p. 263.

[116] Cf. Empson, *Seven Types of Ambiguity*, p. 70. One could find many examples in Hebrew which are different in translation (e.g. use of the noun in construct and absolute cases, etc.), cf. *inf.* para (d).

[117] Strack, *Introduction etc.*, p. 96, n. 15; Bacher, *Aggada der Tannaiten*, IV, p. 73 (and *ibid.* p. 74, n. 13 for further literature); Heinemann, *Darkhei ha-Aggadah*, p. 110 (and nn. 13-16 *ibid.*) etc.

[118] Sperber, "The Targum in its Relation to the M.T.", *PAAJR* VI (1935), pp. 321ff.

[119] Ben-Ḥayyim, *The Literary and Oral Traditions etc.*, I, p. ג״י (cf. *ibid.* for further literature). It has to be emphasized that the terminology employed by us for

Obviously it is no easy task to discover from the midrash itself how the division of the expounded text into verses is carried out. However, in extreme cases, when a section (קצה) ends in the middle of a verse in the Masoretic text, it is considerably easier to discover such a division. One of the classical examples is the end of the section in the Samaritan Pentateuch in *Ex.* xiv, 10. This naturally results in the connection of part of the previous verse with this clause which ends the section. Thus it must have seemed to the Samaritans that the literal meaning of this verse is "in front of Baal-Zephon, Pharaoh made offerings". This has far-reaching consequences, since Marqah further expands this meaning by [120] drawing an analogy with the Ten Plagues in Egypt. He expounds the following verses in such a way as to closely parallel these events. In accordance with the laws of analogy and the midrashic motif of "a measure for a measure", Marqah discovers a new set of 'Ten Plagues' inflicted on the Egyptians on the shores of the Red Sea. This midrash could, of course, be worked out artistically from the standpoint that, as a punishment for their cleaving to the idol Baal-Zephon, Pharaoh and the Egyptians are shown the justice of God. Each contingent of the Egyptian host receives its well-deserved punishment for its rebellion against God, a punishment which at the same time also demonstrates the impotence of its own idol.

In modern writings we find that italics are commonly used for emphasis, but they are more often than not overdone, because the writer is not certain whether, without his italics, the proper stress will be evident from his sentence-construction.[121] With the development of Samaritan cantilations, a similar process may have happened, namely, that additional emphasis was added where originally it was not found necessary, and vice versa. An emphasis originally present in one clause may have been shifted to another, so creating new patterns in sentences. If we seek an example in the halakhic field, it is again convenient to choose a section in which the S.P. and the M.T. differ. *Ex.* xxii, 4, forms a section by itself in the M.T., while the S.P. verses 4 and 5 *together* create only

---

the Samaritans, stands in diametrical opposition to the usage of the Rabbis. For the Rabbis the *pronunciation* meant "scripture" מקרא while the spelling was termed by them "Tradition" מסורת, cf. Sperber, *op. cit.* p. 317.

[120] *Memar Marqah* (ed. Macdonald), I, p. 38 (= II, p. 59). On Marqah's exegesis built on the inner division of the verse in accordance with the Sam. tradition, cf. *Sup.* nn. 95-100.

[121] cf. Empson, *op. cit.* p. 28.

one section. Consequently, the Rabbis took verse 4 as referring to an ox devouring a field, and verse 5 only as referring to the burning of it. The Samaritans understood the *whole* passage as referring to one subject, namely the burning of fields.[122]

More important for the midrashim dependent on verses and sentences are those which are based, not so much on the syntactical order or determination of the sentence, as on comparisons with similar sentences elsewhere. Obviously this is not a peculiarly Samaritan device, and we know that in early medieval times there are whole compilations written on such devices. Take, for example, the question: why are certain sentences repeated in the Petateuch? "Thou shalt not seethe a kid on its mother's milk" actually recorded three times (*Ex.* xxiii, 19; *ibid.*, xxxiv, 26; *Deut.* xiv, 21) and "he that kills a beast shall make it good, and he that kills a man shall be put to death" (*Lev.* xxiv, 17-18; *ibid.* v. 21) is also reapeated; and one can find other examples.[123] In the Rabbinic literature such expositions are extremely important, and even in matters of aggadah such and similar repeated sentences from various parts of the Pentateuch are used for midrashim.[124]

In contrast to the Rabbinic method which relies on the principle that such repetition must necessarily introduce a new teaching, that of the Samaritans, with their fuller Pentateuch and its already repetitive amplifications, cannot be expected to be so consistent in this field. Nevertheless, one can find quite an impressive number of cases where a similar system is used.

The expression "and he built an altar" (*Gen.* xii, 8) may justly be queried, since this fact is already mentioned in the previous verse. As a natural outcome of this duplication arises the midrash which explains

---

[122] *Kāfi*, pp. 287f. (SLTh.A, p. 66). The translations (v. 5) influenced by Rabbinic exegesis (cf. *Mekhilta, ad. loc.*; *Babha Qama*, 2b) speak of "beast". (Only *ibid.* v. 6 refers to fire.) Naturally, not only the division of the section determined the Samaritan exegesis. There are very important additions in the S.P. of this section; similarly in the enumeration of precepts it is counted as one (Positive commands no. 23, cf. SLTh.A, p. 156). cf. Haran, "Shirath ha-Miṣwoth", *Israel Academy for Sciences*, IV, p. 258 (lines א״מר–מ״ר). On the semantical problem of בער cf. *inf.* para (e, 2).

[123] J. Rosenthal, "Ancient Questions etc.", *HUCA* XXI (1948), p. ע (question 38).

[124] For the midrash on "Thou shalt not seethe a kid in its mother's milk", cf. *Ḥullin*, 114a f. The S.P. has an addition to *Ex.* xxiii, 19 giving to this verse a different meaning, cf. *inf.* n. 200 and text there. For aggadic midrashim cf. Heinemann, *op. cit.* p. 140.

that his double expression serves to provide two witnesses for the location of the place of worship.[125]

"And the Children of Israel kept the Sabbath *to observe the Sabbath*" (*Num.* ix, 19) etc., may be questioned on the same grounds, since the previous verses elaborate this same fact. There are in the Samaritan literature, various interpretations of such repetitions.[126] One could amass many similar devices recurring in all Samaritan texts.[127] On the other hand, there are countless other cases, notably those where the Samaritan Pentateuch fills in some "gaps" of the Masoretic Text by taking verses from other parts of the Pentateuch. In all such cases they feel no need whatever to explain the purpose of the seeming repetition, as originally these verses were added to eliminate discrepancies. The strange phenomenon, however, may at times arise that expressions like "it is a Sabbath unto the Lord" are actually requoted five times from various verses without any significance being attached to this repetition.[128] Nonetheless, we cannot rightly accuse the Samaritan exegetes of inconsistency if and when they disregard such repetitions without creating new midrashim therefrom, they are restrained in the interpretation of such verses, by the larger thematic unit in which they occur. Had they used systems similar to those of the Rabbis in granting total independence to the smaller members of the unit, they would have destroyed the literal sense of the broader theme, and thereby introduced novel elements.[129]

Although one cannot lay down serviceable rules for determining on which particular occasion the Samaritans may or may not propound the reasons for duplication of verses, some guidelines may be gathered from the overall picture of the total extant literature. The tentative nature of

---

[125] *Kāfi*, p. 206 (SLTh.A, p. 31).

[126] *Kāfi*, pp. 84 (SLTh.A, p. 14), 106 (SLTh.A, p. 18), 329 (SLTh.A, p. 69). *Ṭabbākh*, ff. 32a (SLTh.A, p. 88), 33b (SLTh.A, p. 89) etc.

[127] On *Ex.* xxxiv, 24 — *Kāfi*, p. 214 (SLTh.A, p. 37); on *Lev.* xiv, 8-9 — *Kāfi*, pp. 138f. (SLTh.A, p. 20); on *Lev.* xviii, 16 — *Kāfi*, p. 272 (SLTh.A, p. 64); on *Num.* vi, 5, 6, 9, 11 — *Kāfi*, 231f. (SLTh.A, p. 49) etc.

[128] *Kāfi*, p. 327 (SLTh.A, pp. 68f.). The numerous similar cases do not follow any logical pattern. Therfore the relationship between couplets (or repetitions) expounded and those untreated (approximately one to nine!) is also irrelevant. Even the Rabbis who put forward hermeneutical principles about "two verses not teaching the same law" (*Sanhedrin*, 34a, cf. also *Qiddushin*, 24a and parallels) left some of these repetitions untreated.

[129] On the previously mentioned repetition (*Lev.* xxiv, 17-18; *ibid.* 21), cf. *Sifra*, *ad loc.* (ed. Weiss, p. 105a and commentary of *RABaD* לרפואה פטור etc.); *Sanhedrin*, 84b, cf. also n. 124 *sup.*

all such guidelines is obvious, since we have seen on many former occasions that the Samaritans are not, in general, fully aware of the existence of "hermeneutical rules"; but in most cases in which the repetition of verses serves as a source for a midrash, either there are differences between the two repeated sentences or such repetition is needed for apologetic reasons, say, to reinforce either the text itself or one or other of the cherished Samaritan beliefs.

A typical example of this is Marqah's exposition of Moses' constant and repeated refusal to accept responsibility for becoming the messenger of God (*Ex.* iii, 11, 13; *ibid.* iv, 1, 10). Marqah combines an apology for Moses' refusal to accept the messengership with a recondite midrash on *Ex.* iv, 10, which to his mind clarifies all four cases just mentioned. This verse is divided by Marqah into four parts; (1) "I am not a man of speech," (2) "neither heretofore", (3) "nor since Thou hast spoken unto Thy servant," (4) "for I am slow of speech and of a slow tongue". Only if we bear this division — and Marqah's purpose in apologising for the three previous pleas and for the above plain refusal — in mind, can we understand the substance of his midrash. Neither the parallel between this verse and the previous ones, nor his own apology is explicitly mentioned by him, but by the division of his words in his midrash he makes it all clear.[130]

> (1) When Moses heard these words he answered with mounting fear, "I am thy servant, Lord of the world. I will never disobey Thy words, but I wish to say before Thee, what experience I do possess?" (2) "I know within my own mind all that Thou sayest to me, but my experience is too small for it. My tongue is defective in speaking and I have no practice in this authority." (3) "It is easy for me both to speak and listen to Thee at once, but I cannot speak and listen to Pharaoh the king, although in my opinion he is not greater than Thou. I did not say, however, I cannot speak and listen to Thee". (4) "(The reason is that) a long time ago I left Egypt for Midian. Whatever secrets of theirs I possessed I have forgotten already. I was fostered and weaned in Pharaoh's house and went out a young man. I did not continually speak with an evil tongue nor had I any acquaintance with it, *for I am slow of speech and of a slow tongue*" (*Ex.* iv, 10).

Again, Marqah uses not one system of repetitions only but employs all exegetical devices as he goes on. Take, for example, the *third* paragraph; playing on the word "thy servant", Marqah employs a logical inference from major to minor.

---

[130] *Memar Marqah* (ed. Macdonald), I, p. 10 (= II, p. 12). Most of Marqah's midrashim are rather implicit than explicit. cf. my article *op. cit.* pp. 180f., 140f. (especially n. 76).

To mention now a case in halakhah where the midrash is based both on the discrepancies between repeated verses and on apologies for this, there is the example of the Passover Offering. While in *Ex.* xii, sheep only are required for the Offering, in *Deut.* xvi, 2, both sheep and cattle are mentioned. The Rabbis have difficulties in explaining this discrepancy.[131] In the Samaritan halakhah this is explained as referring to two different situations: the Exodus-passage (sheep only) applies to all times, places or situations, whereas the Deuteronomy-passage (sheep and cattle) is associated with the "Chosen Place", and refers to the special Passover Sacrifice in the Sanctuary, consisting of cattle.[132]

Often enough, a verse which is not repeated may still be considered as redundant and therefore expounded on the assumption that there are no unnecessary details in the Torah. The expression in *Numbers* ix, 10. "or be on a journey afar off", would be quite meaningless, according to Samaritan thinking, if it were allowable to sacrifice the Passover in *all* places. The *Kāfi* therefore argues that there is hardly a place in the country where there are no Israelite settlements, so one could reasonably go to the nearest settlement and sacrifice one's Passover Offering there. However, since it is impossible that the Torah should contain a redundant verse, this verse must prove that the Passover Sacrifice should be offered in the vicinity of Hargerizim.[133]

A very similar interpretation is given to *Exodus* xii, 18. where, in contrast to other Biblical passages defining the times of the festivals only in general terms, the exact beginning and end are here specifically indicated: "in the first month on the fourteenth day of the moth at even, ye shall eat unleavened bread until the one and twentieth day of the month at even". The *Ṭabbākh* explains that this verse is deliberately composed in such detail to mark the distinctiveness of the whole week by the eating of unleavened bread, which is its main feature. He connects it further with the philosophical thought that the knowledge of the true significance of the festival is a valuable aid to faith, by showing the exact sources of the doctrinal bases of this practise.[134]

A very similar query may be directed at *Exodus* vii, 8, the contents of which are repeated so often elsewhere in the Pentateuch. The *Ṭabbākh*

---

[131] *Sifri Deut., ad loc.* Pesaḥim, 70b; Menaḥoth, 82a f.

[132] *Ṭabbākh*, ff. 82a-85b (SLTh.A, pp. 122-125); *ibid.* f. 86a (SLTh.A, p. 126).

[133] *Kāfi*, pp. 221f. (SLTh.A, pp. 41f.).

[134] *Ṭabbākh*, f. 77b. (SLTh.A, p. 118). The Rabbis derived many halakhic details from this verse (*Mekhilta, ad loc.*; *Pesaḥim*, 5a, 35a, 120a; Jer. *Pes.* I, 1, 27a, etc.).

here uses the device of dividing the verse in two, and so by this very division indicates that there are two separate commands included in it. The meaning of "and they shall eat the flesh in that night roast with fire", which he regards as unconditional decree, is an absolute command concerning the offering. The other half is: "and unleavened bread with bitter herbs they shall eat", which directs that, even if these two requisites do not exist, or are unavailable, the Passover Offering still remains compulsory.[135]

With the repetition of redundant clauses we shall have to deal later, when we come to deal with syntactical and lexical problems. One instance, though, still belongs to our examples of the exegesis of the verse, properly so-called. The *Kāfi* questions in comparing the regulations as to the Nazirite (*Num.* vi, 7) with those as to the High Priest (*Lev.* xxii, 11), why there are more details in the case of the former? In both these cases we are dealing with a question of defilement arising from a dead body, and both the High Priest and the Nazirite are expressly forbidden to make themselves unclean even for their closest relatives. Why then should we find mentioned, in the case of the Nazirite, all these details regarding a brother or a sister? Surely the Nazirite is not higher in his state of sanctification than the High Priest?

The problem is actually a little more involved. According to Samaritan thinking, the narrative concerning the burial of the Patriarchs (*Gen.* xxv, 9; *ibid.* xxxv, 29; *ibid.* l, 13) are regarded as the actual source of the duty of the children to bury their deceased parents. Both the High Priest and the Nazirite are debarred from carrying out this duty because of their personal sanctity. Now, by inference from major to minor, one can justify the verse regarding the High Priest by inferring that, as he is absolved from the duty of honoring his father and mother (in this respect), how much more fitting it is that he should not be involved in the situation of a dead brother or sister. From this arises the conclusion that the phrase a "brother or a sister" when mentioned in connection with the Nazirites, is not meant literally, but figuratively, implying that even in a secluded place where there are only Nazirites, these are forbidden to bury even a member of their own Nazirite order.[136]

---

[135] *Ṭabbākh*, f. 65b (SLTh.A., p. 107). It is interesting to note that a similar explanation is given in the Mekhilta (*ad loc.* מניין שאם אין לו מצה ומרור יוצא חובתו בפסח לבד), but there are also many other Rabbinic expositions of this verse.

[136] *Kāfi*, p. 227 (SLTh.A, p. 46). Rabbinic literature (*Nazir*, 48b and parallels) derived from this passage that he is allowed to defile himself for a מת מצוה, but the details of these midrashim are most complicated (cf. Tosaphoth, *ibid.*).

As in the case of the larger contextual problems, so also in the case of the interpretation of the verse, while the ethos which is created by its reading and its division into parts is the essential factor in the understanding of its sense, the problems of the individual smaller unit still need further elucidations. These detailed comments are in all cases justified by the Samaritan principle of harmonisation. This point will become even clearer when we deal later with the so called "hermeneutical rules", which, in broad generalisation, are for the most part detailed devices designed to achieve such harmonisation.

D. SYNTACTICAL PROBLEMS

(1) *The Clause and its Place in the Verse*

It may occur to the mind of the reader that a certain phrase bears two or more meanings. If the syntax of the language is complicated, one may suspect that wherever there are irregularities there are also alternative meanings, even in the mind of the author. Such considerations do not entirely depend on differing emphasis on the parts of speech, for even in ordinary fluent reading, a certain phrase may seem ambiguous.[137]

Language does not essentially consist of words so much as of connected phrases; yet the understanding of these phrases largely depends on the subjective syntactical feeling of the reader, as the words of the phrases may of course be connected in various ways. The command of any language usually brings with it a simultaneous konwledge of its grammatical and syntactical rules, yet the less usual deviations from these established rules are still subconsciously present to the mind of the reader.[138]

In dealing with Samaritan exegesis it is important to remember that, on top of the above-mentioned obstacles, with which all interpreters are confronted, there are additional complications to be expected. We may justifiably be sceptical about the degree of awareness and knowledge of syntactical rules on the part of the Samaritan exegete.

Further problems arise from the fact that cognate languages, viz. Aramaic and Arabic, which after all served as their vernaculars, may well have played a part in their misconstruing of relatively simple phrases.

---

[137] Empson, *Seven Types of Ambiguity*, p. 48 (cf. Macuch, *Grammatik etc.*, p. 467).
[138] cf. *ibid.* p. 239.

We have seen on previous occasions, when we came across expositions which were similar to a running commentary on the scriptures, that very often the demarcation between phrases which came to be interpreted literally and those which came to be understood figuratively, depended largely on such syntactical considerations. To take for example, the exposition of the Shema, (*Deut.* vi, 40),[139] the doctrinal differences between the Samaritans and the Rabbis clearly originated in their respective attitudes to phrases contained in it. These largely depend on the received order of the words or other syntactical approaches held by the two groups.

In order to grasp the authentic Samaritan characteristics — and their understanding of these syntactical phenomena — although they themselves were only partially conscious of all this — we have to approach them gradually.

As our first task we therefore examine their reactions to the place of the clause in the verse. By shifting a word from one clause to another the whole sense of a sentence can admittedly be altered. Although the division into clauses depends, as we have seen, mainly on oral tradition it is nevertheless firmly established, passing unchanged from generation to generation. This is the reason for the fixity of the division into clauses which beyond doubt has fundamental consequences for Samaritan exegesis.

One of the classic examples of such rephrasing of clauses in the verse by differing divisions is *Exodus* xv, 17. According to Samaritan reading, it would run as follows, as a mere result of the rephrasing of the words : "The place, O Lord, which Thou hast made for Thee to dwell in, the sanctuary; O Lord, may Thy hands establish it".[140] On the basis of this rendering, and also by connecting verse 18 with the context, Marqah builds a whole midrash on the theme of the Chosen Place.[141] After admonishing those who have abandoned the Chosen Place, namely Hargerizim, he begins his sermon, based on these verses:

> It is good for us to walk in obedience to God and to give serious thought to the saying of the great prophet, Moses, *O Lord, may Thy hands establish it (Ex.*

---

[139] *Ṭabbākh*, ff. 138a-138b. cf. *sup.* n. 39; on the first verse alone Rabbinic midrashim are numerous and occupy a great part of *Berakhoth* (2-20b).

[140] T.S. כונה באדך and the verb was taken as a jussive. cf. Ben-Ḥayyim, *Literary and Oral etc.*, IIIa, p. 39.

[141] *Memar Marqah* (ed. Macdonald), I, p. 47 (= II, p. 76). The beginning of the sermon looks like an interpolation but the quoted passage (judging from the language) is genuine. Concerning the sanctity of sanctuary after it is destroyed, cf. *inf.* n. 174.

xv, 17) by the Holy Sanctuary — as He said, "*And I will dwell among the people of Israel*" (*Ex.* xxix, 45). There He will dwell and his wish will be fulfilled. He also repeated His saying to the Great Prophet Moses, "*and let them make a sanctuary that I may dwell in your midst*" (*Ex.* xv, 8, S.P.). What is the point of a sanctuary without an offering? What is the point of an offering without (divine) favour? Thus the Great Prophet Moses said, "*O Lord, may Thy hands establish it*" — a great prophecy, since (the meaning of) *may establish* (does not apply) until after its destruction.

The punch-line of this midrash is based on the fusion of verse 18 into the context, understood by the Samaritans as, "The Lord shall reign in the world and in the Hereafter".[142] Marqah's midrash is evidently directed at the situation of his own generation, when there is no possibility of building a sanctuary and likewise no possibility of offering, owing to the absence of Divine Favour. In such a situation, all commands regarding the building of a sanctuary are meaningless as, anyhow, they are quite beyond human control. The syntactical position of the words and clauses turns the meaning into a prayer or a prophecy for the future, and the whole exposition thus comes into proper focus.

It would not help our enquiry if we added further similar examples,[143] since they do not depend on rules but on oral tradition and on habits of reading which are arbitrary and unpredictable. In the majority of cases, the division of clauses in sentences is in any case the same as we should expect from the common understanding of the Hebrew idiom.

(2) *Order of Phrases*

More exacting than the division of the verse by splitting its words into different units is the exercise in which the reader is obliged to understand the verse by mentally rearranging its clauses. In European languages, wherein subordinate clauses are quite frequent, this mental exercise causes few difficulties, if the interpunctuation of the text is correctly supplied. In the Biblical text such guidelines are, of course, missing; but the nature of Biblical prose very largely compensates for this deficiency by co-ordinating the clauses in successive lines, as opposed to subordinating them to one other, as in other languages. Such com-

---

[142] S.P. ועוד S.T. מלאכה עלם ועורי ה׳. cf. also Ben-Ḥayyim, *op. cit.* II, p. 544, l. 104.

[143] cf. *sup.* nn. 95-100; cf. also my article, *op. cit.* pp. 106, 140 (nn. 65-66). By an unfortunate mistake the verse quoted there was almost identical with the R.V. It should be corrected as in n. 140 *sup.*

pound sentences, even if they are elaborate, do not normally require any rearrangement of clauses for them to make tolerable sense.

In general, Samaritan reading is geared to rendering the text self-explanatory;[144] this is the reason for the fact that, even in the foregoing cases, bound up with the division of the verse, there is always one reading which is firmly established in tradition, and upon which their midrash is built. Rabbinical midrashim are often built on the indecisive construction of the verse; the Rabbis apply different and sometimes even contradictory, syntactical rules to the same sentence, by reading a word or clause in conjunction either with the preceding or with the following word or clause.[145] The Samaritans are not fond of such nimble and artificial devices. In order to facilitate such devices, it is insufficient to exploit the external features of the text, as is the normal Samaritan way of exposition; it will be necessary to attach several mutually contradictory senses to the same text. In such a system, which really consists of juggling with the clauses in the sentence, one will have to presuppose that there are countless deeper implications between the lines of the text. In Rabbinic literature, where one of the principles is "the manifold faces (meanings) of the Torah", it is thus taken for granted that syntactical rules are not binding, even in those extreme cases where the absence of these rules will destroy the logic of the sentence.[146] The adherence of the Samaritans to the broad thematic unit restrains them ipso facto from such atomisation of the text, when such atomisation will render parts, or all, of it contradictory to the literal meaning. The exact opposite of this system may be seen in some of the *Pesher* types of exegesis of the Dead Sea Scrolls, where very often each phrase is made to fit into anew historical situation, regardless of its contextual meaning.[147] This method is much more nimble than that of the Rabbis themselves.

This does not mean that the Samaritans do not also occasionally break up the text into smaller units, relying on the possibility of an independent interpretation of these details. Such cases do however not depend on an awareness of some kind of syntactical rule which will dictate the order of the phrases in the verses. As opposed to the Dead

---

[144] cf. *sup.* para (b, 2).

[145] "Five verses in Torah where the sentences could be divided both ways" (as. e.g. *Deut.* xxxi, 16, etc.); *Mekhilta* on *Ex.* xvii, 9 (ed. Weiss, p. 61b); *Yoma*, 52a. cf. also Rosenblatt, *The interpretation etc.*, pp. 20f.; cf. n. 118 *sup.*

[146] cf. Rosenblatt, *op. cit.* p. 22; Heinemann, *op. cit.* pp. 100ff.

[147] Bruce, *Biblical Exegesis etc.*, pp. 11f.

Sea Scroll *Pesher* system, which often seriously distorts the sense of the
larger thematic unit, if such atomisation of the text is attempted at all
by Samaritan exegesis, it is certainly more logically carried out. It is
the peculiarities of the text itself, such as the seemingly unnecessary
repetition of phrases or the realization that details are missing, which
cause this splitting of the expounded text into smaller units. For the
sake of convenience and to avoid repetition, we shall now discuss a few
cases where the order of words may profitably be treated.[148] These
changes of the order by the Samaritans are not nearly as daring as those
of the Rabbis. The latter are fashioned, in principle at least, on the ways
of exposition known to their cultural environment, and which indeed
hardly differ from the Greek rhetorical practices of their time. It has
already been shown that there is a close resemblance between the simplest
forms of the Rabbinic Method known as "invert the order in which the
details are mentioned in that verse, and interpret it" and what the rhetorical exegetes would have called "dividing logically", "distinguishing"
and "precision of expression".[149] Not only are such extraordinary
devices employed by the Samaritans very sparingly, but also, in contrast
to the practice of the Rabbis, they are not at all consistently applied,
and are definitely not extended to numerous cases indiscriminately,
where such a fantastic system would plainly go against the grain of
the whole thematic unit. If a comparison of such a pressing of the Biblical
order of phrases into the service of Samaritan exegesis with its Rabbinical
counterpart is really possible, this comparison will apply only to questions of chronological order derived from Scripture, where otherwise
ambiguity would have arisen in this matter of order.[150]

Anyway, it is impossible to formulate any kind of rule employed by
the Samaritans in order to fix exegetical norms built on syntactical
peculiarities. Not only can we not find any formulation of such rules
in their literature in this respect, but it is doubtful whether, from our
study of extant exegetical material, we can trace even vague patterns
which would indicate their awareness of the nature of syntactical rules.

---

[148] cf. *inf.* para 3.

[149] Daube, "Rabbinic Methods etc.", *HUCA* XXII (1949), p. 261; cf. Liebermann,
Greek & Hellenism etc., pp. 199f.; Strack, *Introduction etc.*, p. 97, n. 38.

[150] cf. Rosenblatt, *op. cit.* p. 22 (nn. 21-22). In Samaritan exegesis as a rule the
order of the verse is strictly followed. In very rare exceptions (cf. *sup.* nn. 105-110)
there existed other problems, making the whole context if not self-contradictory at
least ambiguous. Hence there was no other way but to modify the simple order of
clauses.

This state of affairs is even more astonishing as regards their literature written in Arabic, in view of the fact that the Karaites, whose literary influence on the Samaritans is undeniable, had in fact a detailed formulation of such rules.[151]

(3) *Order of Words*

If there is no awareness of the rules of syntax, one might conclude that the word order is also unimportant, but this is not so, as we shall see from the subsequent examples. Even before bringing these examples, though, we have to re-emphasise that the midrash derived from the order of words never became an exegetical principle. There were no generalisations advocating the practice of the pedantic observation of the order of words, or of the use of the "irregular order" for the creation of midrashim when the context was still relatively easy of interpretation. Either in the tradition or in the expounded verse itself there must have existed a pointer which made the normal observation of the order of words a source of exposition.

The most logical type of observation of the order of words (or phrases) comes to light when the same, or a very similar phrase, is repeated in Scripture in various orders. To take as an example the command to Noah, his sons and their wives to enter the Ark (*Gen.* vi, 18; *ibid.* vii, 1); this differs markedly from the command to leave the Ark (*ibid.* viii, 16). While the former puts the males first and separately, and then the women, the latter mentions first Noah and his wife, then his sons and their wives. Here one might readily and naturally conclude that the order of words is deliberate and carefully constructed. The Samaritans noted this peculiarity. Their midrashic conclusion is, therefore, that the Divine Command implies that, during their stay in the Ark, they are prevented from cohabitation.[152] It is not at all surprising that in the Rabbinic literature the same conclusion is reached on the very same midrashic lines.[153]

The repetition of words or of phrases in the same context must have aroused the curiosity of the exegete even more. Such phenomena as

---

[151] H. Hirschfeld, *Qirqisāni Studies*, pp. 33-34 (para 10), cf. also Arabic tex, p. 51.

[152] *Kāfi*, p. 239 (SLTh.A, p. 54).

[153] Sanhedrin, 108b; *Tana debe Eliyahu*, ch. XXIX (ed. Friedmann, Jerusalem 1960), p. 162. cf. *ibid.* ed. note 43. On the rules concerning the order of words in Mishnah, cf. Rosenblatt, *op. cit.* p. 4 (nn. 30-31). For aggadic cases, cf. Heinemann, *op. cit.* p. 99.

"Abraham, Abraham", or "Moses, Moses", etc. are a constant and unfailing source of midrashic expositions.[154]

Questions which have great polemical significance, such as worship on Hargerizim, are seized upon as sources for midrashim and have far-reaching Halakhic consequences; so too does the repetition of words, especially the expression "the Place" (Deut. xii, 5, 11).

The Kāfi, on the strength of these peculiarities in connection with the proximity of the expression "tithes" (ibid. 6 and 11), concluded that all tithes are to be brought to "The Place". Such a generalisation then restricts all other reference to tithes (Num. xviii, 26) to "The Place".[155]

Despite the fact that there are, to be sure, other examples of such midrashim derived from the mere repetition of words, there is no wide-spread compulsion to carry these midrashim to extremes. Unlike the Rabbis, some of whom exploit for their midrash any repetition of a word,[156] the Samaritans are normally unimpressed by the mechanical extensioin of such devices, built on the mere repetition of words.

When the Samaritan tradition feels the need for certain repetitions for apologetic reasons, these are regularly exploited for midrashic exposition, even if these repetitions do not suggest any redundant word. In Ex. xiii, 10, it is stated "Thou shalt therefore keep this ordinance in its season *from year to year*" (מימים ימימה). Although the context here clearly demands the presence of both words, and, because the Samaritan apologists are preoccupied with defending their calendrical calculations, they look for the flimsiest Biblical support and make the very most of this double expression.

By the use of analogical comparisons with a source which forms their Biblical warrant for the calculations of their calendar, and in which the luminaries and their constellations are the determining factor, this expression becomes even more significant. In the story of Genesis, where the creation of the luminaries on the fourth day is mentioned, it is stated, "and let them be for signs and for seasons and for days (ולימים) and for years". (Gen. i, 14). Here the logical order of the words is surely (1) days, (2) seasons, (3) years. Now, by combining the midrash of both verses, the order in Genesis and its repetition in Exodus, they find a (for them) clear indication of the exact calendration of the year to the

---

[154] Farrar, *History of Interpretation*, p. 150. cf. *Memar Marqah* (ed. Macdonald), I, p. 5; II, p. 4 (cf. also *ibid.* I, p. 112; II, pp. 188f.).

[155] *Kāfi*, pp. 30f. (SLTh.A, p. 2).

[156] Weiss, *Dor Dor etc.*, p. 106.

very day. This apologetic exegesis is essential to the protection of their tradition in which the exact calculations of the yearly round depend on the constant intercalation of the solar and lunar years.[157]

All our examples point in one direction: even in those cases where the Samaritan exegetes question the order of words, their questions are intended, not to destroy the unity of the theme or to amputate its smaller units by giving them an independent sense, but rather to make the whole context more coherent in their own estimation. As opposed to the system of Rabbinic Aggadic interpretation, where stylistic peculiarities of Scriptures are often emphasised in order to achieve entirely subjective results by atomising the thematic unit, it may be said — though with some reservation — that the Samaritan exegete looks principally for the unity of his theme, in explaining it through what — at least to him — seems to be the only pragmatic and authentic meaning of Scripture.[158]

The same general system can also be seen when in some cases "missing details" of Scripture are supplied. In *Gen.* xii 4 it says "So Abraham went", which demands the relevant question: "where did he go"? Syntactically, strictly speaking, the sense is complete, but one can 'improve' the sense by filling it out with further details. It is possible that, despite the relevance of the question, the matter would not otherwise have been raised. However, in this case it serves the apologetic purpose of connecting with itself *ibid.* v, 6. "And Abram passed through the land unto the place of Shechem". By such a simple mental exercise the *Kāfi* introduces and strengthens the important Samaritan doctrine that the whole purpose of the wandering of the Patriarch was directed to the worship upon the Chosen Place (*ibid.* v, 8).[159]

Occasionally we may find that, in questioning the meaning of the sentence to find in it missing details, two different exegetes may apply this method to various verses and yet, by answering them, reach the same result. According to the strict ruling of *Ex.* xvi, 29. a person is forbidden to go out of his place on the Sabbath. The question arises — is one then allowed to go to places of worship on the Sabbath? According to the whole Samaritan tradition, this question is of course answered in the

---

[157] *Ṭabbākh*, f. 154a f. cf. P.R. Weiss, "Abū'l-Ḥasan etc."; *BJRL* XXX (1946), pp. 144ff.

[158] Heinemann, *op. cit.* pp. 100ff., 131, 184f, cf. also R. Loewe, "The 'Plain' *Meaning* etc.", *Papiers of the Institute of Jewish Studies*, I, pp. 167f. (nn. 128-130).

[159] *Kāfi*, p. 205, (SLTh.A p. 30).

affirmative. However, when looking for Biblical support, that *Kāfi* quotes *Ex.* xxxiii, 7; "And it came to pass that everyone which sought the Lord went out unto the Tent of Meeting which was without the camp". Since the seeking of the Lord is the major purpose of the Sabbath, and in this verse it is not expressly stated that there is any difference between weekday and Sabbath, and festival, the verse serves as evidence that going "outside the camp" for the sake of worship is in fact allowed.

The *Ṭabbākh* on the other hand, who deals with this matter in a different context, and who is interested in the wider question as to whether one is allowed to go out of one's place, not only for worship, but also for general purposes (which do not of themselves desecrate the laws of the Sabbath) finds his evidence in *Num.* xv, 32, "And while the Children of Israel were in the wilderness, they found a man gathering sticks on the Sabbath Day". The question arises: what happened to those who found him? Did they go out without permission? From the 'missing' detail that Moses did *not* reprimand them, it is assumed by the *Ṭabbākh* that their going out of the camp had been allowed by Moses.[160]

We may broadly sum up their approach to the details of the Scripture as one of extreme moderation. Owing to the powerful Samaritan tradition, with its emphasis on the literal sense of Scriptures, one can hardly find any overzealous search for irregularities in the structure of the verse or the clause. Even in some rare cases, where the clause is hard-pressed by the seemingly rhetorical question as to why a certain word is added, this midrashic device is not employed indiscriminately, but always and only when such a "redundant" word helps to clarify the general sense. One example may here suffice: In *Num.* vi, 18, it states: "And the Nazirite shall shave the head of his separation" etc. Why is it here *insufficient* to write only, "to shave his head"? The *Kāfi* deduces from the Biblical expression that only the hair which grows *during* his separation has to be shaved off. From this arises the implication that the Nazirite has to be clean-shaven *prior* to his Naziriteship.[161]

While the situation is certainly slightly different in purely aggadic expositions, especially in the case of *Marqah*, who is mainly interested in homiletical expansions of the Scriptures, even in this field the device of stressing 'superfluous' or 'missing' Scriptural details is not overdone.

---

[160] *Kāfi*, p. 105 (SLTh.A, p. 18). *Ṭabbākh*, f. 34b (SLTh.A, p. 90). On more cases of "missing or redundant passages", cf. *inf.* para (g, 4).

[161] *Kāfi*, pp. 231f. (SLTh.A, pp. 48f.). cf. *inf.* para (g, 4).

From *Deut.* xxxii, 19 "Because of the provocation of His sons and His daughters", one might gather that the last word is superfluous.[162] This implicit question is answered by the fact that, in the case of the Golden Calf, both men and women "were involved in the evil-doing" (*Ex.* xxxii, 25f.). A whole series of *Marqah's* other midrashim shows this self-same characteristic. Although in some external details they resemble tha aggadic expositions of the Rabbis, he seldom or never breaks up the thematic unit; and normally the syntactical, or other details expounded clearly support (although in a broader homiletic form) the general theme.[163]

By way of comparison, it may be noted that, while in Rabbinic literature the principle, "The Torah speaks in the language of man" had at all times to be heavily defended, because of the frequent employment of 'free' hermeneutical devices, by the Samaritan exegete, this very principle was taken for granted. Even further removed were the sectarian systems which employed much more daring methods interpreting each detail of Scripture as having within itself symbolical and allegorical meanings far removed form the literal sense.[164]

It is by no means easy to draw distinctions in the biblical languages between interrogative sentences or clauses and those which make simple statements. Even in cases where there is an explicit interrogative particle (e.g. the interrogative *He*, or אם׳ מי׳ מה׳ איך etc.), the exact length of the interrogative clause is not always certain, as one may easily either expand or contract the interrogative part of the sentence. This department of syntax depends largely on the taste of the reader or upon traditions of reading. For this reason, the LXX sometimes makes different sense of the Hebrew text as against the opinions of the Rabbis. Furthermore, the Rabbis often artificially turn a statement into a question, or *vice versa*, when this is convenient for their midrash. Such artificial exploita-

---

[162] *Memar Marqah* (ed. Macdonald), I, p. 100; II, p. 165.

[163] Cf. *ibid.* I, p. 6 (II, pp. 5f.) the long repetitions are a midrash on ראו ראיתי *Ex.* iii, 7, and on the repetitions of פדות *ibid.* 7-9, cf. also *sup.* n. 154 and Part II, n. 78. Similar midrashim on repeated words are quite common with Marqah, e.g. on *Ex.* xv, 2, "This is my God... My Father's God..." a whole list of the attributes of the "meritorious ones" is added (Memar Marqah, I, p. 40; II, p. 62). However, like the last example the source of the midrash is rather implicit than explicit. For the employment of this device in general, cf. Farrar, *op. cit.* pp. 22-23.

[164] cf. Heinemann, *op. cit.* pp. 97, 103, 108, 136. It has to be borne in mind that 'free' hermeneutical devices increased with the passage of time, cf. Weiss, *Dor Dor etc.*, I, p. 156ff. On the symbolical and allegorical sense, cf. *sup.* n. 7.

tions of syntax and alterations of the order of phrases or words are totally
absent from Samaritan literature. Obviously, certain clauses or words
which by them are understood as questions, whishes, prophecies, ect.,
would not be so understood by the modern Biblical student. However,
with the Samaritans, who take the syntactical peculiarities seriously
and not as mere plays on words, their reading depend almost always
on traditional considerations.[165]

E. Etymological and Lexical Interpretations

Although in fact we find a chapter in the *Ṭabbākh* on the definitions
of words, which is meant to guide us as to when words are to be taken
literally, figuratively in a general sense or even to be explained away,
in truth all these definitions are inadequate for our purpose. After a
philosophical discussion on a certain selected religious terminology,[166]
we are left just as bewildered as before our reading of this Chapter in
regard to the real methods of etymological and lexical interpretation.

With regard to expressions of which the Samaritan Pentateuch
has its own variant readings, there are not so many problems involved
here, since the original text genuinely lends itself to one or other particular way of understanding.[167] We are however confronted with some
difficulties by the fact that, despite semantic changes and developments,
the oral tradition remained almost completely static for many generations. Thus, it may happen that a word which is read in a certain way,
at a particular time, does not represent the meaning there attached to
it, but the residue of the semantic value it bore many generations before.
Such and similar considerations may engender contradictory interpretations of the same passage or word.[168] Nevertheless, we have always
to be beware of exaggeration in attaching too much midrashic significance to the exegesis of one single word.[169]

---

[165] Heinemann, *op. cit.* pp. 132f. cf. *sup.* nn. 140-142 and text there.

[166] Cf. *sup.* Part II, n. 129.

[167] Cf. *sup.* Part II, nn. 367, 436 and *inf.* nn. 188ff.

[168] Cf. *sup.* n. 13. On the contrast between semantical changes and static oral
traditions in reading, cf. Ben-Ḥayyim, *The Literary and Oral Tradition etc.*, IIIa,
pp. 27f. For examples of semantical changes, *idem. ibid.* I, pp. 218 (n. 3), 228 (n. 31),
280 (n. 7) etc.

[169] Cf. Gaster, *Asatir*, p. 16. It is true that the name Nimrod suggests 'rebellion'
(מרד). Like many other aetiological midrashim on names, this may have contributed
to the aggadic description of the character of Nimrod. However, this was not the
only "starting-point for the whole series of legends". There may well have been

(1) *The Word and its Place in Exegesis*

In a religious milieu where Halakhic definitions are of prime importance, the importance of faithful interpretation of the single word can hardly be over-estimated; but even in this field, while the weight even of a single word may be crucial, other considerations too are normally involved in the total sense. Thus, both etymological interpretations and general contextual principles are intimately interwoven. If there are additional polemical motives, for example, if the Samaritans want to defend their own text as opposed to the Jewish text, then the definition of the single word becomes even more important.

For example, in Genesis ii, 2. where, instead of the Masoretic reading "And of the seventh day", the Samaritan Pentateuch reads "On the sixth day", the definition of the word "day" clearly becomes crucial, not only for the purpose of defending the text, but also for the interpretation of the whole theme in accordance with their own tradition.[170]

Even if such polemical reasons do not exist, there remains the necessity to defend the traditional interpretation of the text. We know that questions were asked throughout medieval times; for example, in *Lev.* xxii, 27, "When a bullock or a sheep or a goat is born", why are not written "a calf, a lamb or a kid"? This was a question which greatly occupied medieval commentators.[171]

Although such questions, usually posed of course by heretics or by opponents of the Torah, may never have reached the ears of the Samaritans, it is interesting to note that they themselves are also occupied with similar questions. The verse in *Exodus* xii, 5. "Your lamb shall be without blemish... you shall take it from *the sheep or from the goats*", calls for elucidation. The *Ṭabbākh* interprets these words to imply the exclusion of the young of all the other permitted animals (*Deut.* xiv, 5).[172]

---

other factors: e.g. "he began (החל) to be a mighty hunter... before the Lord..." (*Gen.* x, 8-9) could have been understood as "he profaned (himself) etc.", cf. *inf.* para (e, 2).

[170] cf. *sup.* Part II, n. 144. cf. also Halkin, "*Sam.* Polemics etc.", *PAAJR* VIII (1935/6), pp. 52f. On the definition of "day" in the Mishnah, cf. Rosenblatt, *op. cit.* p. 8. It is interesting to note that the *Kāfi* in its discussion, *Lev.* xxv, 29 (p. 303f.) explains ימים תהיה גאולתו as a full year (solar) without reckoning of days.

[171] J. Rosenthal, "Ancient Questions etc.", *HUCA* XXI (1948), p. ס״ט (question 36); cf. Rosenblatt, *op. cit.* p. 8, n. 42.

[172] *Ṭabbākh*, ff. 60b-61a (SLTh.A, p. 102).

Another subject which may well have been connected with polemical matters is that of sacrifice. The *Kāfi* poses the question: was the Nazirite obliged to bring his sacrifice (*Num.* vi, 13f.) at a time when there was no sanctuary? The definition of the word "sacrifice" is crucial to this discussion. "Sacrifices" and "guilt-offerings" may evidently bear several interpretations, as e.g. blood-sacrifices or monetary expiations. By drawing an anlogy between all sacrifices and "guilt-offerings" which may be redeemed by paying their equivalent value to the priest (*Lev.* v, 15) it is deduced that all payments in lieu of such sacrifices are tantamount to redemption (from guilt, sin, defilement, etc.).[173]

Some of the exegetical points which we have mentioned earlier become even clearer when we consider the centrality of the accepted interpretation of some words in the midrash. Thus for example Marqah takes it for granted that "sanctuary" refers to "the Place", even after its destruction. If we bear in mind that the Rabbis hold the same view, i.e. that holy places even in ruins retain their sacred character, (relying on *Lev.* xxvi, 3), it becomes clear that the same centrality as is given to the exposition of this word is a widespread concept.[174] On the other hand, the accepted understanding of the "Place", interpreted as synonymous with Hargerizim, becomes almost axiomatic amongst the Samaritans. This interpretation is specifically Samaritan, resulting from the S.P. reading בחר instead of the M.T. יבחר (*Deut.* xii, 14, 18, etc.), and it is not shared by others. Thus, for example, the Rabbis and Philo often take the word "the Place" as a reference to God.[175]

There is no limit to the number of examples where definitions of words are the life and soul of the understanding of whole series of precepts. Missing details, essential to the execution of these precepts, are often supplied by the interpretation of words. This is the case when precepts, traditionally understood as being of Biblical origin, are not explicitly elaborated as regards the manner and mode of their execution. The best illustrations of this point are the various expressions in the Pentateuch concerning the slaughter of animals. These expressions are usually more closely defined by means of analogies and harmonisations, by which devices, although of course the words are all individually

---

[173] *Kāfi*, p. 234 (SLTh.A, p. 51). For a comparison of the Passover Offering to the 'Burnt Offering', cf. *inf.* para (g, 1).

[174] cf. *Sup.* nn. 141-142 and text there; cf. Rosenblatt, *op. cit.* p. 22, n. 27.

[175] Heinemann, *op. cit.* p. 116.

defined, they become inter-dependent and support the general assumption that all of them refer to the same ritual.[176]

If we look at the general picture of the single word in its context, despite the fact that in most cases the precise definition and exegesis of the word are indeed paramount, these are nevertheless not exaggerated so as to give the word more weight than it rightly deserves in its context. Unlike the practice in Rabbinic literature, there are no cases where a particle, for example "this" or the Hebrew את (אתי׳ אתך וכו׳ אותי וכו׳), is strenuously pressed into the service of reading novel details into the text.[177]

Although later we shall have to deal with semantic problems embracing various meanings of a word, the general rule is taking into account the position the word occupies, that word-interpretation does not distort the larger unit in which it appears. It is in fact very possible that this literalism is actually a development of the traditions already present in the S.P., which itself includes variant readings [178] to many idiomatic and figurative Hebrew expressions.

With their straigtforward approach to exegesis, one could hardly expect the developments one finds amongst the allegorists, where a certain word or name becomes the prototype of a symbolical notion, which, in most cases, has no apparent connection with the broader sense of the text.[179] Despite the fact that Scripture creates the whole ideological world of the Samaritans, in which each and every detail is imbued with pregnant allusions to the total aim — namely the salvation of mankind — for the Samaritans, unlike other seekers of Salvation, words remain words, not "concepts" expressing theological doctrines divorced from their contexts.[180]

Illustrative of the wider definition of a word is Marqah's attempt to expound the expression "lies with". He sums up, under that heading,

---

[176] *Ṭabbākh*, ff. 10b, f. cf. Abdel-Al, *A Comparative Study etc.*, pp. 620ff. (translation pp. 418ff.); *Kāfi*, pp. 319ff. cf. Abdel-Al, *op. cit.* pp. 671ff. (translation pp. 508ff.); Wreschner, *Sam. Traditionen*, pp. 46ff.

[177] Heinemann, *op. cit.* p. 188, cf. also my article *ALUOS* VI (1969), pp. 98, 128f. (n. 6). On such extreme midrashim of the Karaites, cf. Nemoy, *Karaite Anthology*, p. 11 (and p. 322 for notes).

[178] e.g. M.T. איש אל אחיו S.P. אחד אל אחד (*Ex.* xxv, 20). M.T. אשה אל אחותה S.P. אחת אל אחת (*ibid.* xxvi, 3) etc. cf. however, M.T. (*Ex.* xxxvi, 22. cf. Macuch, *Grammatik etc.*, pp. 495f.

[179] Heinemann, *op. cit.* p. 134.

[180] cf. Barr, *The Semantics*, pp. 208f.

the seven serious cases of consanguinity and even adds three more, in which his pointed, forthright style can scarcely be missed.[181]

> Let us turn again to the phrase "*Lies with*". It makes the deed in effect refer to: (1) *a virgin that is not betrothed and lie with her* (*Exod.* xxii, 16);[182] (2) *And whosoever lieth carnally with a woman* (*Lev.* xix, 20)[183]; (3) *and of him that lieth with her that is unclean* (*Lev.* xv, 33).[184] All these are illustrative of this expression. There is no need to examine this any further. All ten have been mentioned before you. Understand them and give praises to your Lord who warned you against being involved in evil doing...

Apart from Marqah's habitual love for the midrash on the number ten, this definition reached by the harmonisation of verses, is surely crystal-clear; the midrashic exposition and the clear definition of the word are equally important for Marqah. Although, in most cases, the sexual connotation of this word would certainly not be missed, owing to the very context in which it appears, Marqah, by quoting the last three verses, intends to exclude an excessively literalist interpretation. After all, there may well have been some exegetes, who, motivated by the current use of euphemisms, would have taken this expression in its simple semantic sense.

We can readily see, even prior to our forthcoming discussion of semantic problems, that etymological considerations are regularly governed by the unity of the context in which they appear; by way of comparison with other systems of exegesis, one could reasonably say that the use of words by the Samaritans is reasonably flexible, in that it avoids both unnecessary metaphorical deviations and the forcing of literalism to utter absurdities.[185]

Allegory is not, however, entirely absent from the Samaritan literature, as we know; and even simple narrative verses, for instance, certain details of the theophany on Mount Sinai, are used as a prophecy of the resurrection. In such cases each word is taken out of its real context to symbolise various eschatological points. However, such methods are

---

[181] Memar Marqah (ed. Macdonald), I, p. 74; II, pp. 119f. cf. my article *op. cit.* pp. 123, 162f. (n. 225). It has to be remembered that the S.P. in *Deut.* xxviii, 30 has no Kethibh an Qere but it reads ישכב עמה.

[182] cf. S.T. בתולה דלא ארוסה ושכב עמה בתולתה דלא ארסת ודמך עמה

[183] cf. S.T. וגבר אן ישכב עם א' שכבת זרע וגבר דידמך עם אתה אדמכת נוף

[184] cf. ולגבר דישכב עם מסבה (= מסאבה) cf. S.T. וגבר דידמך עם אתה דהבה

סביתה = סבאתה = דיאבה = דהבה (שכב = דמך) and *passim ibid.* 26

[185] cf. *sup.* n. 38.

usually late, and are in effect only extensions of the figurative interpretation of the genuine 'prophetic' passages of Scripture.[186]

(2) Semantic Problems

The very limited vocabulary of the Pentateuch and the relatively few semantic fields which it covers might, at first sight, look like a decided advantage for the correct appraisal fo the meanings of its text. But if we look more closely at Samaritan midrashic expositions, one of their greatest drawbacks arises from their unimaginative approach to Holy Writ, which really forces their semantic expositions into the straightjacket of literalism. Very often this is a by-product of the peculiarities of the S.P. We have previously dealt with one of the slight variants of *Deut.* xxvii, 26. "*all* the words of this law" which is explained by Marqah to mean that the curses mentioned in this context are directed against anybody who breaks even its smallest detail.[187] But Marqah does not stop in his midrash at the expansion of the meaning of the "Law". He brings evidence from many passages of the Pentateuch that the Torah can be defined as constituted by its very details.[188]

A similar variant reading of *Deut.* xxxiii, 11, likewise gives rise to a different semantic approach to this verse. It is understood as "Smite through the loins of them that rise up against him, and of them who hate him, whosoever will rise against him". Both Marqah and the *Ṭabbākh* alike follow this reading;[189] and the latter adds further midrashic elucidation of the first part of the sentence: he adds: "... because his (i.e. Levi's) prayer will penetrate them like an arrow".[190] On the second part of the sentence he adds the comment that this is a warning to the people not to object to the authority of the tribe of the Levi (i.e. the priesthood).[191]

---

[186] Gaster, *The Sam. Oral Law etc.*, I, p. 115 (on *Ex.* xix, 13). On allegorical interpretation on the Taheb (derived from biblical stories, as e.g. Noah etc.), cf. *sup.* nn. 34-40, *inf.* para (h, 3).

[187] cf. *sup.* Part II, n. 366.

[188] As opposed to Marqah's detailed treatment, other groups used the concept of 'Torah' mainly in general sense. cf. Heinemann, *op. cit.* p. 115 (and cf. *ibid.* nn. 85-90 for further literature).

[189] *Memar Marqah* (ed. Macdonald), I, p. 140; II, p. 229; *Ṭabbakh*, f. 205b.

[190] لان دغاه ينفذ كالسهم

[191] cf. sup. Part II, nn. 583, 585.

Similarly, the variant reading of the verse, *ibid.* v, 16, gives it an entirely
new semantic colouring. Although here the main difference is not so
much in the spelling as in the differing division of the phrases, this in
itself is sufficient to give it another sense. It is understood as: "And
from the good-will of Him who dwelleth in the bush, his fruits (be
blessed), for the head of Joseph and for the Crown of him that was
separated from his brethren".[192] The *Ṭabbākh* duly explains that this
whole passage speaks in advance of the blessing of the land in which
Joseph has an additional portion (namely שכם cf. *Gen.* xlviii, 22). On
this interpretation Joseph is in the vicinity of the Holy Place, and
Moses in his blessing fortifies the previous blessing of Jacob, thus making
it an everlasting prophecy. But the important semantic considerations
here are that Abū'l Ḥasan interprets the three words referring to Joseph
(i.e. head, crown and separation) as qualities by which Joseph surpasses
his brethren. Joseph's superiority over them thus manifests itself in three
ways: (1) leadership, (2) kingship, (3) devotion.[193] Semantic changes
could admittedly also have arisen from the attaching of certain theological connotations to words. Thus the word שכח appears in an addendum
to the S.P. (*Ex.* xxiii, 19) in a much stronger sense than the usual one
meaning "sinful negligence" rather than "forgetting". This new semantic
colouring is naturally enough transferred to other passages. For instance,
Deut. xxxii, 18 is understood as "and thou hast ignored God etc."
The *Ṭabbākh*, in reference to this word, speaks of the retribution with
which Israel will be confronted because of their "backsliding and negligence".[194]

From these examples, we may realize, moreover, that the semantic
value of phrases and words in "prophetic' passages is understood as
supporting the main purpose of forecasting the future. One hardly
finds any atomisation of these prophetic utterances leading to their
being taken out of context and used for midrashim derived from them.

---

[192] Ben-Ḥayyim, *Literary and Oral Trad. etc.*, IIIa, p. 163.

[193] *Ṭabbākh*, f. 208b. (ראש =) وبين مدح يوسف اخوته ثلثه اقسم الرياسه

والملك (= קדקד) والتنسك (= נזר)

[194] *Ṭabbākh*, f. 222b. وما قايلهم اسرائيل من الاسقاط والاطراح ... cf. Ben
Hayyim., *op. cit.*, II, p. 593, ll. 14-17; *ibid.* p. 600, l. 180. Very similar is Marqah's
midrash (*Memar*, I, p. 87; II, p. 140), comparing this "negligence" to the "stubborn
and rebellious son" (*Deut.* xxi, 18 צור ילדך תשא׳ בר ארדאי ומעזי׳ וילה ברה דיהי
כן).

Unlike the Rabbis, who often utilised individual phrases of *Deut.* xxxii to elaborate on the legends of the Patriarchs and other homiletical themes, the Samaritans followed the opposite course; even the explicit mention of the Patriarchs in such passages was generalised to refer to the whole people or the whole tribe.[195]

We have seen in many previous instances that it is uncommonly difficult, especially in the case of the Samaritan Targum, to distinguish between a slavishly literal and hence unintelligible translation and intentional paraphrase depending on the specifically Samaritan semantic understanding.[196] Unfortunately, we are still at a stage where a great number of words have not yet been satisfactorily identified, and where in many cases the semantic range of words and phrases cannot yet be exactly defined. This whole region awaits further research and is quite outside the framework of our present task. Nonetheless, occasionally we have to look more closely into some such cases in order to discover from available midrashim how far they are, in fact, based on a specifically Samaritan semantic approach. In one of the midrashic examples previously considered, based on the interpretation of *Ex.* xxii, 4, where this verse is connected with the following one and interpreted in the sense of "instigating a fire", there is a certain possibility that this midrash, too, has specifically Samaritan semantic foundations.[197]

Another rather doubtful case is the expression in *Deut.* xxxii, 14 which we have understood as "butter of kine". The S.P. spells this word differently (חמת, M.T. חמאת), which gave rise to the nonsensical translation "wrath of kine" (ארתע [= רתח] תורין). In this case the com-

---

[195] In the S.P. Jacob is mentioned twice in this chapter (i.e. vv. 9 and 15). The second verse is slightly amplified by Marqah (*Memar*, I, p. 96; II, p. 158); "All these words the great prophet Moses included in this Song; *Jacob shall eat and filled* through words of praise *Jeshurun shall wax fat and kick* through blessings". Another longer midrash is based on both of these verses (*ibid.* I, pp. 105f.; II, pp. 175f.), the theme of which is the "ten honours" by which Israel was honoured by God. Although Jeshurun is translated both by Marqah and the S.T. it is still a reference to Israel. There are two translations כשירה (from ישראל = ישר?) and משבח (cf. Ben-Ḥayyim, *op. cit.*, II, p. 485, l. 167). These translations are similar to that of the LXX: ἠγαπημένος (beloved). As opposed to this the Rabbis took verses from this chapter for various legends concerning the Patriarchs. cf. Heinemann, *op. cit.* 124, 125, etc.

[196] cf. *sup.* Part II, nn. 161ff.

[197] cf. *sup.* n. 122. The S.T. on this verse is not clear. יפעי is ambiguous and could have been understood as יפחי (kindle)? בעירנה is similarly unclear (cf. Ben-Ḥayyim, *op. cit.* II, p. 464, ll. 172-173; *ibid.* p. 470, l. 374). "Beast" is often not translated but the Heb. בהמה is left in the S.T. (cf. *Gen.* i, 24; vi, 7; vii, 23 etc.).

mentators did not follow the Targum. The *Ṭabbākh* explicitly understood this word as "butter" and attached to it a midrash explaining that all the affluence of the world was intended to lead them to bless God. (cf. *Deut.* xiii, 10).[198]

It is by no means easy to decide in many instances whether or not such discrepancies between the almost entirely unintelligible and literal translations of the Targum and the sense made of it by later commentators depend on semantic developments within the Samaritan fold. We have to reckon with the very real possibility that Arabic translations of the Pentateuch, in particular that of Saadia, reached them by the eleventh century, by which time their earliest exegetes were writing their expositions in Arabic. Understandably they would correct any translations which otherwise would not have made sense.[199] Obviously these Arabic translations would not be accepted without revision in any case. Hallowed traditions, appertaining both to practice and to doctrine, would resist new interpretations and therefore would hardly be affected by these translations. On the contrary, the translations would certainly be corrected to agree with the traditions. This conflict between tradition and external influences, lasting for many centuries, left its mark on such Samaritan midrashic development as depended on Samaritan semantic considerations. This may well be the reason why there is not always agreement between the Samaritan oral pronunciation and the sense attached to the words.[200]

For these reasons alone, etymological investigations, even when conducted on the soundest scholarly principles, are entirely irrelevant to our purpose.[201] We have rather to seek to reconstruct the proposed unscientific and primitive etymologies as well as the semantic range of clauses and words, in accordance with our knowledge of the Samaritan mentality.

If we want to understand Marqah's midrash, which often looks like a medley of words without any coherence, we find that it becomes tolerably clear once we know the semantic range of the words on which the midrash is based. Often, in expounding one verse, he utilises expres-

---

[198] *Ṭabbākh*, f. 211a, f. Although he quotes like S.P. חמת he explains الزبد It is possible that here we have the influence of Saadia's Arabic translation. cf. S Kohn, *Sam. Studien*, p. 39; cf. also Ben-Ḥayyim, *op. cit.* IIIa, p. 159, n. 14.

[199] cf. *sup.* Part II, para (j).

[200] cf. *sup.* Part II, nn. 82-85 and text there. Ben Ḥayyim, *op. cit.*, I, p. 134, *ibid.* II, p. 453, l. 125.

[201] cf. Barr, *Semantics of Bib. Language*, pp. 107f.

sions from another, which, by way of harmonisation, give the sense of the whole midrash. Thus, for example, in the interpretation of *Exodus* xv, 5, he actually employs six expressions from a neighbouring verse (*ibid.* 9), and each of them is duly exploited for his midrash. According to Marqah's understanding, the following six threats used by the Egyptians are condignly avenged, i.e. "measure for measure". They are: "(1) I will pursue; (2) I will overtake; (3) I will divide the spoil; (4) My lust shall be satisfied upon them; (5) I will draw my sword; (6) my hand shall destroy them". Marqah's midrash is built implicitly rather than explicitly, on these six points as follows:[202]

> The Seventh (punishment was) — what happened to the accursed foot-soldiers. The water which had dried up returned to its original state — as God said, "*The depths cover them*" (*Ex.* xv, 5). They had been journeying confidently. The kingdom of the deep engulfed them there with great affliction. (1) They had said "let us possess Israel", but judgments were saying "We will possess you, in truth". (2) They had said, "Let us kill Israel", but wrath said, "We will kill you, in truth". (3) They had said, "Let us take their possessions from them" The True One said, "Let them (i.e. Israel) take what rightfully belongs to *you*". (4) They had said "Let us take (our) possessions back from them". The True One said, "You will not even reach them". (5) They had said "Let us make war with them". The True One said, "Prepare now to war with me". (6) They had said, "Let us destroy their wall". The True One said, "I will shatter your walls".[203]

The emphasis on "judgment" and "wrath" carrying out their tasks "in truth" serves to illuminate the central teaching that every offence calls for retribution "measure for measure".

Many halakhic problems depend on the meaning and the semantic range of a single expression. Thus the problem whether it is meritorious for a married woman to adorn herself is answered by the *Kāfi*,[204] in the following way: If she does it for the sake of her husband with

---

[202] *Memar Marqah* (ed. Macdonald), I, p. 40; II, pp. 62f. (on the general character of Marqah's midrashim cf. *sup.* n. 130). For a very similar Rabbinic midrash, cf. Heinemann, *op. cit.* p. 130.

[203] שׁוּר here must mean either 'walls' or 'flanks' of the combating parties (cf. T.S., *Deut.* xxvii, 52). It is interesting to note that Pseudo-Jonathan renders תרעץ אויב (*ibid.* 6). מרעא ומרצצא שׁורי בעלי דבביהון The midrash is based upon the understanding of ירשׁ in Hiph'il as "destroy", T.S.: תערבנה (= תחרבנה) (cf. also T.S. *Ex.* xxxiv, 24; *Num.* xiv, 12; xxi, 32; xxxii, 21, 39; xxxiii, 42 etc.

[204] p. 199 (SLTh.A, p. 27); cf. also Ben-Hayyim, *op. cit.* II, p. 602, l. 17 (cf. also n. on. l. 15). The later interpretation is more similar to the Rabbinic one (cf. Onqelos and *Kethubboth*, 47b).

no ulterior motives, then it is enjoined by the Law. The proof-text used for this interpretation is *Ex.* xxi, 10, which is understood to mean "Her *make-up*, her raiment and her conjugal rights shall he not diminish". Just as the husband is obliged to take care of his wife's modest dress ("raiment") so is he obliged to supply her with cosmetics.

Similar discussion of the semantic range of words is also employed in polemics. The *Ṭabbākh* [205] disputing with the Jews their leniency towards the (fasting) of children on the Day of Atonement, supports his contention for the Samaritan practise of making children fast by a wide discussion on the meaning of the Hebrew word נפש (לא אשר הנפש תענה): "for whatsoever *soul* it be that shall not be afflicted in that day day, he shall be cut off from his people" (*Lev.* xxiii, 29) Abū'l Ḥasan offers four meanings for the word 'soul'; (1) literally, the soul; (2) the body; (3) people who are under obligation (to keep the laws); (4) people who have no such obligation. All these meanings are supported by Scriptural warrants. Since 'soul' is evidently an expression which depends on the interpretation deemed appropriate to any of the afore- said meanings, and none of thse meanings can claim any real preference over any other, it is therefore the duty of the person under religious obligation not to deviate therefrom by opting for a lenient interpreta- tion, which would lead to desecration. We see from this discussion that the strict enforcement of fasting upon children is not in any way decided by semantic considerations, but rather by relying entirely on traditional practice.

There is also full awareness among the Samaritans that certain words, although spelled and pronounced in the same manner, may have entirely different meanings. Accordingly they explain words like איש׳ אלהים etc., according to context. [206]

An interesting polemical employment of the semantic meaning of "shoulders" is most probably directed against the Jews. Basing them- selves on the textual variant in *Deut.* xxxiii, 12 in the S.P., [207] the Samari-

---

[205] ff. 190b-191a. The four definitions are supported by proof-texts: 1. النفس (*Deut.* iv, 9) ; 2. الجسم (مع عدم النفس) (*Num.* ix, 7); 3. المكلفين (*Num.* xv, 28); 4. المكلفين وغير المكلفين (*Num.* xix, 22).

[206] Ben-Ḥayyim, *op. cit.* I, p. 242 (cf. *ibid.* p. 240, n. 4). In the *Exodus Commentary* (attributed to Ghazal al-Duweik), p. 187ff., there is a lengthy discussion on the definition of אלהים in connection with *Ex.* vii, 2. For Rabbinic exposition, cf. Rosen- blatt, *op. cit.* p. 9.

[207] ולבנימים אמר יד יד ה׳ ישכן לבטח וחפף עליו כל היום ובין כתפותיו שכן

tans give a differing interpretation to the passage: "and he dwelleth
between his shoulders", making it mean, not that God would dwell
between the shoulders of Benjamin, but that Benjamin himself would
dwell inside his own *boundaries*. The *Ṭabbākh* [208] brings tangible evidence
for this reading of "shoulders" as "boundaries", and adds the following
comment: the adding of "boundaries" to the blessing of Benjamin
indicates his weakness when opposed by his enemies. He is unable to
gain anything from them except surreptitiously through deception.
Here the special semantic meaning of כתף serves as evidence against,
the Rabbinic understanding of this verse, for a reference to God's
dwelling in the allotment of Benjamin, namely Jerusalem.[209]

Another instance in which semantics are supposed to corroborate
the Samaritan point of view, as opposed to that of the Jews, is the
discussion on the expression (*Lev.* xxii, 24), "Neither shall you do thus
in jour land". The *Ṭabbākh* [210] has a special diatribe against the Jews'
allowing the slaughter of castrated or otherwise mutilated, animals.
The crucial point in his contention that the Jewish practise is erroneous
is his effort to prove that an Israelite is not even allowed to possess
such an animal, much less to slaughter one. The proof-text is the expression "do" (תעשו) which, by analogy with other verses (*Gen.* xii, 5) is
interpreted as 'possess'. It is interesting moreover to note that the same
root, in connection with the Sabbath (לעשות את השבת) is explained by
the *Kāfi* [211] as 'speech' thus indicating that the Sabbath must be honoured
by prayer and study. Although there are indeed other interpretations of
this expression,[212] the burden of the *Kāfi*'s exegesis is that this is the
cardinal meaning of this verb. He employs an analogy from the story

---

The LXX and Peshitta miss out also the word עליו in the first part of the verse. Cf.
Ben-Ḥayyim, *op. cit.* IIIa, p. 162 and *inf.* n. 292.

[208] ff. 206a and b. Abū'l Hasan connects this 'cunning' nature of Benjamin with
the expression "a wolf" in the Blessing of Jacob (*Gen.* xlix, 27).

[209] שכינה שורה בין כתפי בנימין *Siphri, Deut., ad loc.; Yoma,* 12a; *Soṭah,* 37a;
Zebhaḥim, 52b, 118b (Christian commentators saw likewise a hint to Jerusalem and
The Temple in this verse).

[210] ff. 24b. (cf. Abdel Al, *A Comparative Study etc.,* p. 629f., tr. 415f.). The same
argument is carried on in later Sam. literature, cf. Wreschner, *Sam. Traditionen,*
pp. 58ff. and notes there.

[211] p. 106 (SLTh.A p. 18).

[212] The opinion that it refers to circumcision was refuted because this rite only
rarely coincides with the Sabbath. Another opinion that it refers to the Sabbath
Offering was likewise rejected since mediaeval Samaritans did not practice blood
sacrifices.

of Eve and the Serpent (*Gen.* iii, 14), "Because thou hast done this", which involves not action, but speech.

Such contradictory analogical evidences from different Scriptures to substantiate various semantic values for the same word, strengthen our general picture of Samaritan exegesis as in fact depending more on tradition than on grammatical, or, even semantic considerations. Thus, what seems to us an arbitrary 'proof' with reference to the Nazirite, namely that the expression "all the days" (כל ימי) (*Num.* vi, 5) implies a whole solar year,[213] is likewise rather a tradition than a semantic proof. The 'evidence' brought from verses like *Gen.* ix, 29, and *Gen.* xi, 24, etc, is in reality merely secondary, to give further Scriptural support to this tradition.

Although one should not of course engage in sweeping generalisations, the examples of midrashim based on semantic considerations do not demonstrate that these are to be regarded as the true source of the teaching. Most of them strike us as of a secondary nature only, called in solely in order to strengthen a traditional approach by finding for it biblical pegs. The following examples are not intended to prove any such thesis, but rather to supply an outline of this general tendency to utilise semantic definitions for midrashic purposes.

Deut. xxxi, 20. "and they shall have eaten and filled themselves on waxen fat" is understood as if the last expresion does not mean "to wax fat", but "to scoff and to laugh at".[214] This reading in itself may have prompted the midrash by the *Kāfi* [215] that from this text one may deduce the prohibition of eating before prayers, since the partaking of food causes some demoralisation of the personality and impairs prayer. But it is also possible that the midrash is not built on this semantic range of דשן (S.T. דעץ = דיץ = בדח) but on the continuation of verse, "and they will turn to other Gods, etc.".

This same view is strengthened when we notice the comprehensive connotations which are conferred on certain nouns by the Samaritans thus broadening their application. The best example of this process is the word "brethren", which they interpret in the broader sense, in the context of levirate marriage (*Deut.* xxv, 5f.) as referring to *relatives* and not to blood-brothers.[216] If we bear in mind that the general sectarian

---

[213] cf. *sup.* n. 157 and Part II, nn. 634-636.

[214] Ben-Ḥayyim, *op. cit.* II, p. 449, l. 150.

[215] p. 78 (SLTh.A, p. 14).

[216] *Kāfi*, pp. 268f (SLTh.A, pp. 62f.); Munajja, *Masā'il al Khilāf*, Ib, p. 197. cf.

sentiment and practise are against the idea of marrying the deceased brother's wife, relying on *Lev.* xviii, 16. levirate marriage cannot have been construed as referring to the real brother but to the relative. We may safely assume that this represents an ancient tradition, not at all peculiar to the Samaritans, and independent of semantic considerations. The Karaites amongst themselves engaged in similar discussions. The same sort of picture emerges from the definition of "son" (*Deut.* xxii, 28) which in to sectarian understanding here includes the notion of "embryo". On the strength of this interpretation the Samaritan and other sectarians freely polemicise against the Jews on allowing the slaughter of a pregnant animal.[217] Again the same picture is confirmed by their strict definition of "labour" and "going out" on the Sabbath Day; while proofs of such definitions often indeed introduce semantic discussions, these latter are in fact secondary supports for the established practise.[218]

As opposed to the Jewish practise of explaining the expression "between the two evenings" (*Ex.* xii, 6), in connection with the Passover Offerings, as referring to the early afternoon, the Samaritans confidently insist that it means the time between twilight and total darkness. This view is supported to be sure by evidence drawn form the semantic values of "evening" and "two evenings", which prompt various definitions of each of the two expressions. However, the independent force of these semantic proofs will not in itself be sufficient to convince us that these midrashim are really unconnected with tradition.[219]

Obviously, there are many interpretations which must nevertheless depend on the exact definition of the semantic range of the word or clause. Such midrashim are frequently supplied to eliminate misunderstanding arising from the undue widening of the semantic range of a word which has only a limited sense. One example is the definition of the Hebrew word שאר meaning "leaven". Although in the same context (both in *Ex.* xii and *Deut.* xvi) the synonym חמץ is also mentioned, it has to be made clear that it is *leavened bread* — not some fermented substance such as vinegar or some other sour substance — which is here intended.

---

my article *ALUOS* VI (1969), p. 163, n. 230. On the Karaites, cf. Z. Cohen, *Karaite Halacha*, p. 86. On 'brethren' in the case of Nazirites, cf. *sup.* n. 136.

[217] *Ṭabbākh*, f. 24a, f.; cf. Abdel Al., *op. cit.* p. 628f. = tr. p. 412; Drabkin, *Fragmenta Commentarii etc.*, pp. 39ff., 56ff. Wreschner, *op. cit.* p. xxvii f (and lit. cited by them).

[218] *Kāfi*, p. 103f. (SLTh.A, p. 16f.); *Ṭabbākh*, ff. 26a f. (SLTh.A, p. 82f.).

[219] *Kāfi*, pp. 88f. (SLTh.A, pp. 13f.); *Ṭabbākh*, ff. 62a f. (SLTh.A, pp. 104f.), cf. Wreschner, *op. cit.* p. xxiii.

This clarification is a pressing Samaritan need, because, in their tradition, both these words are ambiguous, both meaning either "leavened bread" and "fermented substance". In the S.P. in *Num*. vi, 3 "vinegar of wine" (חמץ) and "liquor of grapes" (M.T. משרת — S.P. משארת) show a resemblance to the Hebrew expression "leaven". There is thus a pressing need to restrict its meaning, in connection with the Passover, to leavened *bread* only. "They shall be baken with leaven", (*Lev.* xxiii, 17) is adduced as evidence for the fact that reference is to this same material, i.e. bread.[220]

There is little need to multiply examples of the restrictions or expansion of the meaning of certain terms.[221] Undoubtedly the historical development of Samaritan midrashim cannot be entirely divorced from the environment in which it takes place. Thus, just as legendary, cultural and scientific items are adapted and later assimilated to the midrashic material, so likewise the constantly changing vernacular is not without its effect. By the adoption fo the Arabic language new semantic problems may very well be created as certain terms receive new meanings, in accordance with the new linguistic habits acquired from the use of Arabic. In the *Asaṭir* indeed we already find such influence,[222] and it is possible to find clues to such semantic changes if we compare Marqah's commentaries with those of the Islamic period. To take but one instance, if we compare Marqah's commentaries on *Deut.* xxxii, 23f.[223] with those of the *Ṭabbākh*,[224] we find of course that the latter's interpretation is broadly very similar, and built on the same views and the same divisions of the Biblical text. But we find too certain semantic differences. It seems that in verse 24, the word לחמו is understood by the *Ṭabbākh* as referring, not to food, but probably under Arabic influence — to flesh. So his interpretation runs along these lines:

> (God's punishment of the infidels) is likened to an arrow which penetrates into the body. This arrow is referred to in a general way in His saying, *"from this*

---

[220] *Ṭabbākh*, f. 86b (SLTh.A, p. 126). There are many other examples of this kind.
[221] cf. *Inf.*, para (g, 5).
[222] Ben Hayyim, "Sepher Asaṭir", *Tarbiz*, XV etc., pp. 7f.
[223] cf. *sup.* nn. 95-101.

[224] ff. 223b. ومثله بالسهام التي تغلغل فى الجسد وهي السهام الملقبة
من جملتها قوله مזה רעב לחמו لان الجوع وعدم الغذا ونقصان فى الاعظاء
وتسلط الحرارة ... وكذلك الحميات المحرقه المذيبه للنفوس وهو قوله
רשף קטף מרירי امن علامات الخلاف زوال الهيبه عن الحيوان ...

his flesh (לחמו) *shall become lean" (Deut.* xxxii, 23), because hunger and lack of nourishment cause damage to the organs, and fever will prevail over (the body) etc. Similarly, the fever which causes disintegration (i.e. melting of?) the (living) soul is referred to in *this* saying רשף קטף מררים (ibid.). One of the symptoms of apostasy is the disappearance of the respect of wild animals (towards human beings) etc.

It is just possible that this last reference to apostasy is in fact a pun on מררים, exactly as with Marqah's;[225] but since Abū'l Ḥasan does not translate this verse, there is also the possibility that here it is understood as a "fierce destroying heat", and the motive of apostasy thus comes into line with the general theme.

On the other hand, if we compare the commentaries of Marqah and the *Ṭabbākh* on verse 22, "and setteth on fire the foundations of the mountains", we find that both commentators have the same polemical approach.[226] The difference is due to the latter's further mental development, and this is dependent entirely on the changed environment.

Marqah's teaching about the distinctive position of Hargerizim following on this coming disaster — when all the foundations of the mountains will be set on fire, except Hargerizim — already contains a veiled reference to Jerusalem. Abū'l Ḥasan develops this fruitful idea a step further. He claims that:

> *And setteth on fire the foundation of the mountains,* refers to the two direcᵗions (of prayer) which the infidels rely upon, and turn towards.

Abū'l Ḥasan mentions Jerusalem, but the text is not very smooth, and it is possible that in other texts there are also specific references to Mecca. Probably for security reasons some scribe has omitted the specific mention; but the allusion to two directions of prayer (namely Jerusalem and Mecca) is quite evident. He later repeats the above-mentioned verse, adding the remark "this is a reference to the house built between the two mountains". This last allusion cannot have been directed towards Jerusalem, but surely towards Mecca.[227]

Here we see that, although this polemical tradition has not changed throughout all these centuries, the new Islamic cultural background

---

[225] cf. *sup.* n. 100.

[226] cf. *sup.* n. 97.

[227] *Ṭabbākh,* f. 223a: اشار الى الجهتين التين (اللتين) تعتمد عليها المخالفين يقصدوها ... اشارة الى البيت لانه منصوب بين جبلين ...

The reference must be to the two mountains Ḥirā' and Abu-Qubays on both sides of Mecca.

incontestably introduces an additional colouring. This new environment prompts Abū'l Ḥasan to limit the range of the expression "the mountains" to two specific places, in line with the polemical attitudes of the newly arisen situation.

This type of argument is central in all Samaritan writing, and Abū'l Ḥasan himself devotes a long discourse to proving the authenticity of the *Qiblah* (Hargerizim). The burden of this long discourse comprises harmonisation of verses from all parts of the Pentateuch. However, although the semantic range of "the place" is in itself of outstanding significance, we shall here deal with this exposition in terms of the hermeneutical 'rule' of analogy, which plays an even greater role in these harmonisations.[228]

Often it becomes necessary, because of the new Arabic meanings attached to a certain Biblical word, to explain away the difficulties created by these new meanings. Thus, for example, the verse *Ex.* xii, 11 "and ye shall eat it *in haste*, it is the Lord's Passover", created some misgivings in the minds of its readers. Abū'l Ḥasan, in explaining this passage in detail [229] asserts that all the conditions demanded during the eating of the Passover are demanded only to increase the awareness that God is hastening His people's redemption. However, this "haste" is quite the contrary of what one would now expect from the expression Passover, for, as we understood in the light of the new linguistic connotations suggested by Arabic, it would mean "comfort and rejoicing".[230] For this reason, the *Ṭabbākh* tacitly harmonises these contradictory meanings by saying that the word "haste" itself really means devotion and faithfulness. Thus he avoids the perplexing contradiction which may arise in the mind of the reader, by reassuring him that "haste", when serving as a symbol of this future redemption, is a source both of comfort and rejoicing.

In later commentaries, such interpretations are even more frequent. In the narrative of the birth of Moses it is stated that his mother Jochebed "hid him three months" ירחים (*Ex.* ii, 2). This elicits the question: why is it not written חדשים? The answer given is that she actually hid him for only two months. She gave birth in the seventh month of pregnancy, and pretended for another two months that she was still pregnant, thus confusing the officers of Pharaoh, who of course expected her to

---

[228] cf. *inf.* para (g, 1) (cf. also *sup.* Part II, n. 467).

[229] *Ṭabbākh*, f. 68a (SLTh.A, p. 109).

[230] الانفساح والفرحة

give birth after nine months. This apologetic midrash serves to prove in fact that the righteous woman does not lie, for in an Islamic environment, where the month is invariably reckoned according to the lunar calendar (ירחים) this proposed period of two solar months (i.e. 61 days or more) might clearly include three new moons, and thus correspond to a period of roughly three lunar months.[231]

Such novel midrashim, arising from the necessity of explaining matters with reference to the Islamic environment, are especially numerous in the later literature.

Moreover, the use of euphemisms also has its place in semantic development. Midrashim built on such a practice show two distinct trends: on the one hand, harsh words are often muted, when a midrash substitutes a euphemism so as to mollify the original harsh expression; and, on the other hand, once a term has come to be accepted as a euphemism for an original harsh expression, it may easily suggest the original expression even in contexts where it properly bears no such meaning.[232]

If we now look at the Samaritan Pentateuch and Targum (*Deut.* xxv, 11) we find that the expression "private parts" of the M.T. (במבושיו) is rendered as "flesh" (בבשרו). From such a euphemism we can readily understand Marqah's midrash when he speaks of the ten iniquitous actions associated with incest. The whole of this is built on the understanding that a verse like Genesis vi, 12 "for all flesh had corrupted etc." refers to carnal indulgence,[233]

> *Cursed be he who lies with his mother-in-law* (*Deut.* xvii, 23) — an iniquitous action. This evil deed contains ten shameful acts. He who does them dissociates himself from righteousness. Woe to the man who does this evil deed and involves himself in ten shameful, wholly wicked acts: (1) defiles the body of his mother-in-law and (2) uncovers her body and (3) pollutes her bed and (4) commits adultery with her. (5) He conjoins three fleshes, each one of them serious adulrety.[234] (6) He brings into being bad fruit and (7) begets sons of adultery and

---

[231] *Exodus Commentary, op. cit.* p. 46.

[232] cf. *sup.* Part II, nn. 171-172. cf. also following nn.

[233] *Memar Marqah* (ed. Macdonald), I, p. 75; II, pp. 121f. cf. *sup.* nn. 181-184 and text there. There is a similar Rabbinic midrash on *Gen.* vi, 12, cf. *Sanhedrin*, 57a; *ibid.* 108a.

[234] וירכב תלתה בסראן The proper meaning is "He catenates through intercourse three forbidden degrees of 'nakedness' ". It is reasonable to assume that the notorious Karaite catenary theory of forbidden degrees of marriage, the רכוב was a development of an ancient rigorous sectarian practice The terminology occurs only in Marqah and later amongst the Karaites. cf. my article, *op. cit.* pp. 123f., 162f. (nn. 224-225).

(8) evil blossoms in the world. (9) He profanes two seeds and (10) receives a curse with great distress ensuing... receiving the Curse in this world and affliction in the next... walking in the way of the people in (the days of) the Flood, of whom it was said *"For all flesh had corrupted their ways upon the earth"* (Gen. vi, 12).

Although such midrashim show that there is a marked tendency to play on certain words which, in their literal sense, are not euphemisms, and to associate them with their secondary or euphemistic meaning, in which they bear a pejorative sense, this practice is never overdone.[235] One hardly finds in Samaritan literature, any true equivalents of the daring Rabbinic midrashim. One of the latter, for example, is built on *Gen.* xxi, 9, where the "mocking" of Ishmael is explained as including the three cardinal sins; and another on *ibid.* xxv, 29f., where all the expressions there employed in regard to Esau are taken as euphemisms for various violations of the bounds of decency.[236] Another feature belonging partly to semantic considerations and partly to false etymology, is the frequent midrashic exposition of the origin of names. Aetiological interpretations are in very general use.[237] One of the aetiological midrashim of Marqah is typical in that it employs the Biblical name Succoth in multiple senses. Here not only are "tent" and "tent of meeting" (i.e. Tabernacle and House of GOD) associated with this name, but also the booths which the Israelites built on the Feast of Tabernacles to remind them of plants and gardens. But the most significant reference to Succoth is bound up with the idea that God's protecting wing serves as a tent enveloping the whole people of Israel. This midrash is built on *Ex.* xii, 37 "And the Children of Israel journeyed from Ramses to Succoth"; but subsequently this verse is harmonised with *ibid.* xiii, 20-21 "and the Lord went before them (i.e. the Holy Spirit) ... pillar of cloud... pillar of fire". Thus these three presences protect them as a tent on all sides.[238]

> Succoth was like the Garden of Eden and the Israelites were the trees in it. It was like the House of God, completely filled with the Ark (of testimony), and Sarah's offspring were there in communion.[239] The Ram [240] of Isaac per-

---

[235] cf. *sup.* nn. 181-184 and text there.

[236] *Tosephta*, Soṭah, vi, 6 (ed. Zuckermandel, p. 304); *Babha Bathra*, 16b etc. cf. also Heinemann, *Darkhei ha-Aggadah*, p. 123.

[237] Heinemann, *op. cit.* p. 111 and his notes 33-39 for further literature.

[238] *Memar Marqah* (ed. Macdonald), I, p. 25; II, p. 38.

[239] קנוניה from the Greek κοινωνία fellowship, communion. 'Baskets' does not make any sense here (cf. editor's n. 131).

[240] דכרה for the Heb. איל cf. S.T. on *Lev.* viii, 2, 18ff. etc.

meated it, goring with his horns all who would smite them. They were a crop which filled the House of the Lord, reaped, bound and pressed together by the arm of the Good One, assembled by the three glorious land-keepers [241] hedged in by three great fences; Cloud, Fire and the Holy Spirit; one leads, one illuminates and one protects.

In the *Asaṭir* there are even more aetiological midrashim as we have already seen, regarding Mount Ebal, whose name, it is explained, originates from the root אבל meaning mourning.[242] Another such interpretation is that of the name Hebron, as originating from the root חבר "joining together", or "assembling", as that was the place where the Patriarchs were gathered unto their people.[243] The most recurrent theme of these midrashim is naturally the central theme of all Samaritan theology — the sanctity of Hargerizim — with which expressions like "the place" are regularly identified.[244]

On the other hand, there are certainly some cases of proper names not being understood as names, and being therefore given novel interpretations.[245]

(3) *Hapaxlegomena*

Rare words in the Pentateuch are increased in number in Samaritan exegesis, owing to the simple fact that the Samaritans have no other Scripture with which to compare and harmonise it and its contents. Although we may indeed gain an insight, by etymological studies, into the nature and rationale and principles of Hebrew word-structure, this is not always in itself sufficient for a full understanding of the bases upon which Samaritan exegesis is built.[246] In many instances, a word which for us readily becomes transparent through comparison with a similar word in the Prophets, may remain a dark riddle to the Samaritans. And the contrary is also true; an occasional difficulty, or what

---

[241] אריסין יקירין tenants, or landkeepers, who guarded the 'trees', i.e. Israelites (a reference to the Patriarchs).

[242] cf. *sup.* Part II, n. 447.

[243] M. Gaster, *Asaṭir*, pp. 210, 212; Ben-Ḥayyim, "Sepher Asaṭir", *Tarbiz* XIV-XV (1943/4), pp. 13, 29.

[244] *Kāfi*, pp. 205f (SLTh.A, pp. 31f.); cf. *sup.* nn. 54, 131-134, 140-142, 155.

[245] cf. *inf.* nn. 248f. on מגוג cf. my article, *op. cit.* pp. 108, 142 (nn. 86-87). On other explanations of proper names, cf. Ben-Hayyim, *Literary and Oral Trad. etc.*, II, p. 446, l. 75; *ibid.* p. 568, l. 289 etc.

[246] cf. "Etymology and the Motivation of Words" in Ulman's *Language and Style*, pp. 40ff.

seems to us to be an opaque word, and is therefore normally regarded by exegesis as a legitimate subject for a conjectural interpretation, may find a simple explanation among the Samaritans. Such disparity in understanding does not depend on any lexical rule, or even on the relative frequency of certain words, but on a difference in mentality and background, the major factors in the undestranding of 'difficult' words.[247]

One of Marqah's midrashim is built on the interpretation of "Chemosh" (*Num.* xxi, 29). By the Samaritans in general, this is understood, not as a proper name, but as a combination of the inseparable preposition Khaf and something else. Thus a variety of commentaries originate from such interpretations as "Like Mosh".[248] Marqah himself actually understands the word to have originated from the Hebrew word אמש 'yesterday' and builds a complicated Midrash around Moses' song (*Ex.* xv) in the course of which the midrashic question arises: What reasons had the Moabites to fear the Israelites, when it was strictly forbidden to the latter to go to war against them?[249]

> The leaders of Moab trembling seized them (*Ex.* xv, 15). Where did Moses get this knowledge? If it had not been for his Prophethood, he could not have said it then. Thus the True One recorded what Balaam said about Israel: *It shall crush the corners of Moab* (*Num.* xiv, 17). Likewise the great prophet Moses (said) "*Woe to you O Moab*" (*Num.* xxi, 29). There was knowledge of the destruction underlying his saying: "*You are undone, O people, like yesterday*" (*ibid.*). Yesterday was Moses' saying, "*Woe to you*"; here (i.e. in the Song of Moses) it is the complete destruction.

The sequel of Marqah's homiletics is built on a comparison of past and future. If the Moabites, on seeing the affliction meted out to the Egyptians, trembled at the doom of the distant future, how much more should one repent for fear of the punishment awaiting apostates?

Midrashim built on *hapaxlegomena* are greatly to Marqah's liking, because he is particularly fond of building them on puns and harmonisations of like-sounding words. Very often such a play on words is unintelligible until we find the right key to open the lock of the midrash. The word תועבה appears only once in the Pentateuch, but since

---

[247] Ullmann, *op. cit.* pp. 66f. There are countless examples when one is confronted with most unexpected interpretation of words by the Sam. cf. Ben-Ḥayyim, *op. cit.* I, pp. מ״ה–ע״ג ibid. II, pp. 440ff.

[248] The Samaritans knew this expression only from *Num.* xxi, 29 (since they did not accept the prophets, e.g. I *Kings*, xi, 7, 23 etc.), cf. S. Kohn, *Sam. Studien*, pp. 57f.; Ben-Ḥayyim, *op. cit.* II, p. 496, l. 295 (and cross references *ibid.*).

[249] *Memar Marqah* (ed. Macdonald), I, p. 45; II, p. 72.

the S.P. contains the reading תנופת it is not a hapaxlegomenon for the Samaritans. Since, in connection with the priestly offerings, it is stated that the heave-offering in their gifts, even all the *wave-offerings* (תנופת) "belong to the priest" (*Num.* xviii, 11) this expression is harmonised so that it may bear a similar meaning elsewhere. With this in mind, we can now more fully understand Marqah's midrash.[250]

> He ate the choice (*increase?* תנופת) *of the field* (*Deut.* xxxii, 13). *And when the Lord your God brings you into the land which he swore to your fathers, to Abraham, to Isaac and to Jacob* (*Deut.* vi, 10) places filled with all glory and good, with which you will be satisfied, your mind shall not be astonished at what you find, and you shall not forget your Lord. *You shall fear the Lord your God: you shall serve Him* (*Deut.* vi, 13) on the Goodly Mount, Mount Gerizim, for on it all is blessing. When you arrive there, you will find all great glory. You will make an end of the nations and seize all their possessions.

This midrash, which comprises the Seventh Warning of Moses, according to Marqah, thus becomes intelligible when we once realise that what seems to be simply exaltation of Israel is understood by him to embody, at the same time, a warning. He bases this understanding on his comprehension of the word תנופת as implying a warning not to forget the wave-offering which is identical with the choice of the produce of the field.

Naturally, words which really are hapaxlegomena Marqah presses into the service of additional midrashim. For example, to the expression "keep silence" (הסכת *Deut.* xxvii, 9) he adds:[251]

> *Keep silence* to receive moral instruction and to hear what you will learn. "Keep silence" is commanded you here only that what will be teaching for you, and what will be moral instruction for you, may be revealed to you.

A long homily on total submission (הסכת) to God follows this, and is based entirely on the uniqueness of the expression "keep silence".

There was always the danger with such words that they would not be understood, and, although Samaritan script in common with other ancient scripts [252] had a dot to divide words from one other, when the particular word was not understood, there was the further danger of its being wrongly divided. One such case is the expression ידיד (beloved, *Deut.* xxxiii, 12), which was transmitted by Samaritan tradition as two words.

---

[250] *ibid.* I, p. 103; II, p. 172 (cf. *inf.* n. 493).

[251] *ibid.* I, p. 57; II, p. 89.

[252] G.R. Driver, *Semitic Writing etc.*, p. 186.

The *Ṭabbākh* [253] explains this whole verse on the assumption that it is dealing with the double expression יד יד in connection with the Lord, and hence he produces a list of definitions of the word יד — by adducing evidence from other verses. These are (1) omnipotence *Ex.* ix, 3f.; (2) rank or position *Ex.* xxix, 9; (3) Location — *Num.* xiii, 29; (4) a limb (passim). The *Ṭabbākh* goes on to explain that here two successive definitions are implied. The first יד denotes the third definition "location" and refers to the dwelling-place of Benjamin; the second יד denotes the first definition and refers to the omnipotence of God. Thus the whole verse, he says, means: " a place where he dwells by the power of God in tranquility and affluence".[254] It is not at all uncommon to find several interpretations of a strange word or phrase. For example, in *Deut.* xxxii, 31 "Even our enemies themselves being judges" (פלילים), the last phrase was by no means easy to understand.[255] The *Ṭabbākh* in fact gives three interpretations.[256] The first is rather in the nature of a paraphrase connecting it with verse 30, where it says, "except their rock had sold them and the Lord had delivered them up", which is interpreted to mean that the believers in idols have no success, whereas the Israelites realize this and believe in their own Rock and the promised redemption. He then connects the phrase with verse 31, and affirms that, nevertheless, their faith is weak and they deny His commandments. According to this, the meaning of verse 31 will be: "For their rock is not as our Rock and our enemies are (our disobedience of) the Laws". The second interpretation of the strange phrase is, "Our enemies (force us to obey their) laws." The third interpretation, again in harmony with previous verses, is that, despite the fact that Israel knows the futility of the laws of idol-worship, they nonetheless follow those laws and even take oaths in the idol-worshippers' courts of law. Accordingly, the meaning will be, "and they (Israel) appear in the courts of law of our enemies". The last interpretation is further connected with verse 32, in which the behaviour of Israel is likened to that of Sodom and Gomorrah.

---

[253] f. 206a. The S.T. renders it also אד אד cf. *sup.* nn. 207-208. cf. Macuch, *Grammatik etc.*, p. 57 and *inf.* n. 292.

[254] ومعنى هذا الفصل لבنيمים مكان يسكن فيه بقدرة الله تعالى مطان مغنى

[255] T.S. renders it ודבביון שדלין cf. Ben-Ḥayyim, *op. cit.* II, p. 565, ll. 214-215.

[256] f. 225b.

Such and similar interpretations of rare words and phrases, especially from the poetical parts of the Pentateuch, are very common. We have already seen how the *Ṭabbākh* interprets *Deut.* xxxii, 2. The word לקחי "my doctrine" does not appear elsewhere in the Pentateuch, and hence it is assumed to be derived from the root "to take", and to refer here to what Moses *took* from God, namely the Written Law. As a result of this interpretation, "my speech", which follows it, is paralleled to this expression so as to mean the "Oral Tradition".[257]

From the Samaritan Targum it appears that false etymologies are frequently called in to explain rare words by referring them to better understood words. Thus, for example, in *Ex.* i, 11 the word we understand as "taskmaster" creates a difficulty, since מסים is, in fact, a rare word, but by referring it to a similar word, they translate it "contemtible officers".[258] Although indeed one finds other similar cases in the Targum, this whole question needs further investigation, since very often what may seem an untenable etymology to us may be a perfectly genuine Aramaic translation of the Hebrew word.[259] Admittedly quite a number of targumic paraphrases are essentially midrashic rather than linguistic elaborations, though occasionally exhibiting a very fanciful etymological approach, whereas others are merely meaningless and unintelligent tautologies built on mechanical literal translations. For this reason, we cannot regard the midrashim found only in the Targum as trustworthy specimens of their kind.[260]

Interesting among such specimens is the verse *Lev.* xix, 19; "neither shall there come upon thee a garment of two types of stuff mingled together". This is understood by the Targum as "the garments of the mixed multitude". From such an interpretation it is easy to infer that here is a reference to the wearing of garments similar to those worn by people who disobey the laws of God. This is the real reason why the *Kāfi*, when speaking of forbidden garments in reliance on this verse, includes among them garments which are ornamented by the symbols of other religions or which are offensive to pious people in that they are immodest.[261]

---

[257] cf. *sup.* Part II, n. 506 (*Ṭabbākh*, f. 216b).

[258] S.T. מבאשין (= מאוסים?), cf. L. Goldberg, *Das Samaritanische Pentateuchtargum*, p. 52. cf. Ben-Ḥayyim, *op. cit.*, II, p. 516, l. 419. cf. also T.S. *Gen.* xlix, 15; לאריס

[259] S. Kohn, *Sam. Studien*, pp. 62ff.

[260] Ben-Hayyim, *op. cit.*, I, p. 238, n. 3; *ibid.* II, p. 453, n. 125; p. 472, n. 411.

[261] *Kāfi*, pp. 189ff. (SLTh.A, pp. 21f.). The Karaites often poked fun at the Rab-

Another Halakhic question to which an answer is found in a *hapax-legomenon* is seen in the rule that the eggs of unclean birds are just as much prohibited as the birds themselves. In the whole of Samaritan tradition the Biblical source quoted for this prohibition is the term בת היענה (*Lev.* xi, 16; *Deut.* xiv, 15), which we normally translate "the ostrich". Since the Samaritans do not have this term in their Scripture (cf. *Isiah*, xiii, 21; *Job.* xxx, 29, etc.) they regularly understand it as "the daughter of the ostrich". Thus it serves as the source of the prohibition of the eggs of unclean birds.[262]

The expression אביב, which we normally translate as 'spring' (*Deut.* xvi, 1), is understood by the Samaritans as "barley". They accordingly translate *Lev.* ii, 14 as follows: "And if thou offer a meal-offering of first-fruit unto the Lord, thou shalt offer for the meal-offering of the first-fruit *barley in the ear*, parched with fire, bruised barley, winnowed (barley)." The *Ṭabbākh* bases his polemics against the Jews both Karaites and Rabbinites — on this interpretation, and attacks them for looking on the ripening of the corn (for bread) as a sign of the month of Passover. The Samaritan in general opposes the postponement of Passover in deference to any such a sign, and depends entirely on calendaric calculations. He feels that his opponents' arguments are far less cogent, since in a year of famine such a sign may be entirely lacking. Even if a year of famine should occur, when external signs are quite lacking it is of no consequence because festivals are determined by calendaric traditions alone.[263]

We have seen in previous discussions [264] that the Samaritans understand the verb אצל to originate from the root "to exploit, save," etc. (in Hebrew נצל) (*Num.* xix, 17). Marqah in fact virtually builds on this understanding of the word a midrash in which the gift of the transmission of prophecy received through Moses and by him committed to the elders, forms the central theme of his interpretation. The midrash itself at least externally and as prompted by Marqah's rhetorical question,

---

binic interpretations of שעטנז cf. P.R. Weiss, "Ibn Ezra, The Karaites and the Halakhah", *Melilah*, II (1946), p. 128. cf. *ibid.* nn. 222-223 for further bibliography. cf. also Ben Ḥayyim, *op. cit.* II, p. 598, nn. 142, 143.

[262] *Kāfi*, p. 115. *Ṭabbākh*, f. 8b. (cf. Abdel-Al, *A Comparative Study*, pp. 674f., 622f., Translations, pp. 491f., 397f. respectively). cf. Wreschner, *Sam. Traditionen etc.*, p. 63, n. on p. VI. Obviously Wreschner's assumption that this was taken from Rabbinic literature cannot be maintained.

[263] *Ṭabbākh*, f. 91a (SLTh.A, p. 131).

[264] cf. *sup.* Part II, n. 33.

turns on the repetition of some expressions in *Deut.* xxxi 28 and *ibid.* 30. An additional colouring to the midrash is supplied by the expression, "assemble unto me all the elders of your tribes and your officers, that I may speak". This is understood by the Targum, it should be noted, as "The wise men of your tribes, and your scribes".[265]

> A problem arises here concerning the statement of the great Prophet Moses, *"That I may speak"* (*Deut.* xxxi, 28) to all the congregation. Observe what this statement means. When He proclaimed the Ten Words it was at the time of the meeting of God and Moses. Thus he said, *"That the people may hear when I speak with you"* (*Ex.* xix, 9) to witness your greatness among all the congregation. When He finished the proclamation He again said, *"And all the people heard"* (*Ex.* xx, 15, S.P.). Faithful are the men who have been chosen; they are the seventy from the elders of the people. Thus He said '*and I will take some of the spirit* [266] *which is upon you and put it upon them* (*Num.* xi, 17), because it was said to him *"And let them take their stand there with you"* (*Num.* xi, 16)[267] In the Tent of Meeting no man may speak except one like him (i.e. Moses). Since their status was high, they (i.e. the elders) were worthy to speak with them, (i.e. the congregation). The statement was made to them, and they would learn, and then speak to all the congregation who would listen.[268]

In general, we may say that rare expressions and *hapaxlegomena* are often correlated by folk-etymology with more familiar roots. This practice of attempting to elucidate rare words is of course familiar from Rabbinical midrashim.[269] One of these Rabbinic *hapaxlegomena* is the word דמע (*Ex.* xxii, 28) which puzzled both the Rabbis [270] and the Samaritans. However, in the Samaritan tradition it eventually became a familiar word with the acquired meaning "best thing". Marqah uses it in his midrashim and it becomes almost commonplace.[271]

If now we try to characterize the midrashic exploitation of the

---

[265] חכימי שבטיכון וספריכון *Memar Marqah* (ed. Macdonald), I, p. 84; II, p. 135.

[266] ואשוזב מן רוחה דעליך ואשוי עליון

[267] This expression apparently contradicts the following verse (17) where God's speech is exclusively directed towards Moses. Hence Marqah's explanation that no one is worthy of hearing the divine speech, unless, his status is raised to be equal with that of Moses.

[268] Actually the expression לית אנש ממלל אלאן דמותה וכד רמת דרגיון אשו ממלל עמון should be in the passive, with the meaning "In the tent of meeting no man is addressed etc., and when their status was high they were worthy of receiving the divine speech".

[269] Rosenblatt, *The Interpretation of the Bible etc.*, p. 7, n. 16.

[270] *ibid.* p. 8, n. 51.

[271] *Memar Marqah* (ed. Macdonald), I, p. 46; II, p. 73f. and *passim.* cf. also Ben-Ḥayyim, *op. cit.* II, p. 448, l. 135; p. 460, ll. 33, 34, 39.

semantic range of such rare words, we are again confronted by that deep-rooted principle of all Samaritan exegesis namely, its heavy dependence on tradition. Not only do the Samaritans themselves formulate no fixed rules, but it is difficult for the modern student even to find any coherent method of procedure which may fairly be termed an exegetical guide-line. We depend in the end on isolated fragments of this tradition which are hard to classify into patterns or groups. Nor are we at all helped by the fact that semantic habits have ceaselessly changed, and thus certain expressions may well have gained new meanings.[272]

One of these changes, and one which is interesting in itself, occurs in the expression נכרתה "to be cut off from his people" (Gen. xvii, 14), which is understood by Marqah, in his exposition of sexual offences, as "to be slain".[273] Hence the expression is confidently equated by Marqah with those which denote capital punishment as carried out by law courts; and thus the passing of judgement comes within human jurisdiction.

If we compare this view with that of the *Kāfi*, who also deals with the same subject and often repeats the very expression "cutting off", we find that it means something entirely different. He says:[274]

> Thus He made it obligatory that he should be excommunicated if he made himself defiled... he is excluded from the circle of Israel...

From this it seems evident that the *Kāfi*, relying on such pronouncements as "and thou shalt be holy" (קדישׁם) (e.g. in *Lev.* xix, 2) takes the view that, by defying the divine law, he who defiles himself ipso facto excommunicates and excludes himself from the Holy People. As opposed to Marqah's, the *Kāfi*'s interpretation is broadly similar to that of the Rabbis,[275] in not regarding "cutting off" as denoting a penalty to be inflicted by a court. It is still debatable whether we are entitled to detect

---

[272] While consciously there was no deviation from the accepted traditions (cf. *sup.* nn. 73-74 and text there), the change of vernacular from Aramaic to Arabic inevitably caused semantic changes (cf. *sup.* nn. 95-101, 229 etc.). cf. Ben-Ḥayyim, *op. cit.* I, p. ס״ט f.

[273] *Memar Marqah* (ed. Macdonald), I, p. 75; II, pp. 120f.

[274] pp. 169f. (cf. Abdel-Al), *op. cit.* p. 691; tr. pp. 539f.) فاجب عليه العدم اذا

... خرج عن الدايره الاسراييليه ...

[275] The resemblance is more apparent than real. According to the Rabbis all those who are liable to 'extirpation' (*Kerithoth*, I, 1-2), are treated differently (cf. *Makkoth*, III, 15).

here contradictions in the tradition itself. More probably, the *Kāfi* pays regard to the practical concrete situation, for he often admits that no legal power whatever is vested in the hands of the Samaritans such as would qualify them to inflict capital punishment. He therefore paraphrases the expression "cutting off" to make it mean something more practicable and more relevant to his own day.

Despite such minor aberrations and deviations, the general impression emerging from the Samaritans' treatment of *hapaxlegomena* and rare expressions for exegetical purposes, is one of steadfast self-assurance and self-consistency. Apart from minor semantic changes, the common ground shared by all the commentators, is amazingly wide. It is even possible that this uniformity of outlook is not an asset but a defect due to lack of imaginative powers. *Hapalegomena*, which claim so much of the attention of Bible commentators of all persuasions and ages, often lead to a fascinating and bewildering variety of interpretations of a single word. We can hardly claim that the Samaritans produce anything comparable to this sort of variety in their midrashim; and the unimportant contradictions which occur as between commentators living in different centuries are very rare. In general, the power of the traditional exegesis was strong enough to minimise any such discrepancies and to keep contraversial issues down to a bare minimum.

F. Grammar as a Factor of Exegesis

It is not our intention here to assess the Samaritans' ability to deal with grammatical problems. We know that a number of individual Samaritan works are devoted to this subject,[276] but even purely exegetical literature contains some such elements. The progress made by scholars during the past century in determining the precise morphology of the Samaritan tongue is truly astonishing and contemporary researchers in this field are constantly discovering hitherto unknown facts.[277]

---

[276] Ben-Hayyim, *op. cit.* I, pp. 6f. (on the noun); *ibid.* pp. 8f. (on the verb). Actually one can hardly find any proper order in these works which could appeal to the modern mind. We will have to follow the lingual habits as manifested in Samaritan literature dealing with exegesis.

[277] It is more than a century ago that Petermann's epoch making book (*Versuch einer hebraischen Formlehre etc.*), compelled experts in the field of Samaritan grammar to take notice of their pronunciation and oral traditions. Nevertheless, despite the constant developments in this field, there are still differences of opinions amongst contemporary scholars on these matters (cf. Ben-Ḥayyim, *op. cit.* IIIa, p. viii and *sup.* n. 14).

Moreover, just as in the case of semantics, the study of signification in language, one may distinguish between an inquiry which is a branch logic and one which is a branch of linguistics,[278] so also may we draw a like distinction in the field of grammar proper. We are here mainly interested in the utilisation of Samaritan grammar in exegesis so as to discover the logic and, if possible, the theory underlying the grammatical forms, and following the Samaritan exegete in his attempts to rationalize the concepts of his own language.

This being our central interest, the significance of the term "grammar" must inevitably include ungrammatical and linguistically false etymologies, if these may occasionally serve as the bases on which midrashim are built. We know for instance that the Samaritans are fond of transpositions of the radicals of the roots.[279] This fact, even when such metatheses do not follow grammatical principles, must clearly be taken into account. The same applies to arbitrary changes of the gutturals or the sibilants in particular,[280] which are so useful for homiletical expositions, since by such grammatically mistaken changes, difficulties may be conveniently explained away.

The criticisms appearing in such of the grammatical works of the Samaritans as are directed against their predecessors demonstrate that even amongst their earliest grammarians, there are already some who make needless mistakes, so leading the people into grave misunderstanding of fact and grave misuse of grammar.[281]

The greatest problem confronting us is that to the extent of grammatical awareness amongst the earliest Samaritan exegetes. Systematic grammatical treatises are found only from the twelfth century onwards.[282] These relatively late expositions may have been inspired by those Jewish grammarians — both Karaites and Rabbanites — who, under the profound influence of Arabic grammar, produced in Arabic a grammatical survey of the Hebrew language, which was accessible to the Samaritans.

For the Karaites it was very urgent to investigate Hebrew grammar

---

[278] Barr, *The Semantics etc.*, p. 1 (cf. n. 1, for further literature).

[279] Ben-Ḥayyim, *op. cit.* II, p. 454 (דפע); p. 601 (עשׁל) etc.

[280] *ibid.* II, p. 453, ll. 131-32; p. 597, l. 129. cf. also S. Kohn, *Sam. Studien*, pp. 93ff. (However, Kohn's views were not always accepted. cf. *sup.* n. 260.) cf. recently Macuch, *Grammatik etc.*, pp. 28ff., 132ff.

[281] Ben-Ḥayyim, *ibid.* I (introduction), pp. ל׳–ל״א; II, p. 318 (cf. nn. 7, 8).

[282] The only earlier work (cf. Ben-Hayyim, *op. cit.* I, p. ל״א) turned out to be of Karaite origin. cf. Loewenstamm, "A Karaite commentary etc.", *Sefunot* VIII (1963), pp. 167ff.

in its every detail since their rigid adherence to Biblical literalism, compelling them to reject any oral traditions not derived from Scripture, necessitated the substitution of grammar for the hermeneutical rules accepted elsewhere. They even developed this postulate further by insisting that the sole purpose of grammar was to be found in the analogical comparison of the various parts of Scripture, and by defending this tenet on the ground that the sages of all generations had based their interpretations on their observation of the grammatical structures and usages of the language. Thus, for the Karaites, such grammatical studies comprised a major part of their theological approach.[283] Obviously, we cannot expect of the Samaritans the truly scientific analysis of the Hebrew language that we find in the Karaites. It is indeed irrelevent to our purpose whether this awakening of the study of Hebrew grammar is due to the Karaites or not. One thing however is certain, that, since the Karaites were compelled by reason of their religious outlook to find means of achieving an accurate understanding of the Holy Text, this study was for them both a religious and a theological necessity. For the Rabbis, whose ritual and practice were regulated by the Oral Law mainly as embodied in the Talmud and its expositions), grammatical considerations were always only secondary and hence they were brought to full realization only through constant controversy with the Karaites.[284] In this respect at least, the Samaritans were closer to the Rabbis. Although they had, of course, no canonised Oral Law, they adhered tenaciously for their expositions to their ancient tradition which made their pursuit of purely academic grammatical investigations of very secondary importance.

Furthermore, the awakening of grammatical studies both among the Rabbis and the Karaites, was largely brought about by the cultural environment. The great centres of learning in Iraq in the ninth and tenth centuries, where the close study of the Arabic language flourished, had a direct effect on their own thinking, since by that time Arabic had become their vernacular. The books produced by Arab grammarians prompted them to pursue similar studies in Hebrew, and they, in their turn, learned to do this.[285] It is of interest to notice how some fragments of Qirqisāni's work immediately betray the inspiration derived from Arabic models. This is also the case with some early Rabbinic

---

[283] Pinsker, *Lickute Kadmoniot*, I, p. 106.
[284] H. Hirschfield, *Qirqisāni Studies*, pp. 31f.
[285] *ibid.* p. 32.

grammatical works.[286] In both groups, even stray grammatical notes, intended as keys for solving exegetical difficulties, are often demonstrably based on comparative studies of the grammatical parallels between Arabic and Hebrew.

In principle, for Samaritan exegesis, these very fine grammatical points are not of such great importance. When we consider their Pentateuch, with its numerous variant spellings, and, on the other hand, with its numerous harmonisations of similar expressions appearing in several separate places in the Pentateuch (e.g. the Ten Commandments etc.), we at once realize that many difficulties which would sorely puzzle the exegetes of the M.T. cannot and do not trouble them at all.[287] Another likely reason why the Samaritan awareness of any real need to pursue the scholarly approach to grammar may have been blunted is their total isolation. As opposed to the lively and virulent polemical and literary exchanges between Rabbinites and Karaites, lasting for long centuries and cross-fertilising the several linguistic outgrowths of Scripture, the Samaritans engage in no such disquisitions and their views are almost totally ignored. The Karaites, in particular, are fond of pointing out the orthographical and stylistic mistakes of the Rabbis, in order thus to disarm their opponents, ward off their attacks and prove their own superiority in the understanding of Scripture.[288] This powerful incentive to outdo one's opponents by displaying a more precise and methodical treatment of linguistic problems cannot have been present to the Samaritans. Their "Biblical Hebrew" includes so many "irregular elements" that certainly none of the defenders of the M.T. would bother to enter into the discussion of such "Barbaric anomalies". Even in later generations, when, from the eleventh century onwards, Samaritans writing in Arabic polemicise against the Jews, this material is intended far more for the Samaritans' internal consumption than for any external purpose.

Plainly we have to accept the Samaritan idiosyncrasies, both in their Scriptural tradition and in their grammatical understanding, quite apart from the many differences which divide their approach to Classical Hebrew from our own. We have had plenty of opportunities of evaluating

---

[286] On the similarities of the grammatical works all being modelled on their Arabic predecessors, there is a vast literature. cf. the comparisons of Hirschfeld, *passim* and the following note.

[287] cf. M. Friedlaender, *Ibn Ezra Literature*, Vol. IV (London 1877), pp. 110ff. (n. 2) and p. 145 (n. 1). cf. also Ibn Ezra's criticism of the Karaites (צדוקים דרך ,'השנית *ibid.* Hebrew Part, p. 2) and his approach to exegesis based on grammar (*ibid.* pp. 5-9).

[288] Pinsker, *Lickute Kadmoniot*, pp. 25, 27.

the main characteristics of the S.P. all of which are conducive to its right interpretation and to the realization of its hermeneutical practices.[289] At the same time, too, one should never treat their Oral Traditions lightly, as these preserve a very marked coherence in their understanding of Scripture, despite the enormous number of variant spellings. As opposed to the inconsistencies of the Written Word, i.e. the S.P., the Oral Traditions, which alone render the text intelligible to the Samaritans, serve to preserve the remarkable self-consistency of their exegesis.[290] The validity and comparative stability of these traditions are attested by certain ancient Palestinian evidences, preserved in their own literature. One of the best illustrations of this assertion is the agreement on place-names between the Samaritan Targum and other ancient sources.[291]

We cannot fairly be expected to determine the reasons underlying the idiosyncrasis occurring in the S.P., nor can we be expected to enter into the very intricate problem of precisely when such modifications took place. Even in instances where it would be comparatively easy to express opinions on these matters, our main endeavour must remain centred on the exegetical derivations from the text, while we have to be content to accept these modifications as they stand. To take the case of the division of words, although it is generally acknowledged that in ancient Hebrew script the point dividing words was indeed used regularly and that the Samaritans also used this dividing-point quite consistently, there is still no real certainty at all that, when an expressoin appears in the M.T. as one, and in the S.P. as two, this division actually goes back to antiquity.[292] In *Gen.* xxv, 34 the expression עֲדָשִׁים (lentils) is divided in some manuscripts of the S.P. into two words (עד שים). This division is also reflected in their Targum, and the commentaries understand this expression as "until satisfied". However, the main fact that it is also understood as "lentils", and in some manuscripts written as one word, makes the solution of this historical and philological problem almost impossible. For ourselves in all such and similar cases, we shall have to consider separately and on its merits each individual situation in which exegesis depends on the one form or the other.

---

[289] cf. *sup.* Part II, para (a), (b) and (c).

[290] cf. *sup.* Part II, nn. 110, 506.

[291] cf. *sup.* Part I, n. 171.

[292] S. Kohn, *Sam. Studien,* p. 36. cf. Ben-Ḥayyim, *op. cit.* I, p. נ״צ (n. 164), *ibid.* II, p. 543, ll. 77, 78. (On *Deut.* xxxiii, 12 יד יד, cf. *idem. ibid.* IIIa, p. 162), cf. *sup.* nn. 207, 253.

Purely grammatical knots are even more difficult to unravel; both the
categories and concepts on which exegesis may be based are often so
elusive that their precise connotations are very enigmatic. The question
whether, for instance, there was a real awareness of the distinction
between the verbal and the nominal forms of a particular word is
by no means clear. Thus in *Num*. vi, 5 the expression פרע "and he
shall let the locks of his hair *grow long*" is interpreted in various ways.
The *Kāfi* [293] in fact involves himself in a protracted discussion of the
meaning of this word, but his terminology is so vague that it is hard
to follow his reasoning from a strictly grammatical standpoint. The
discussion revolves round the question whether or not the Nazirite
is obliged to shave off his hair at the actual commencement of his Naziriteship. פרע is here treated as the operative word in solving the question.
The *Kāfi* accordingly speaks of the "essence" of the letters (radicals),
which may imply either that the stress falls on the first or second part
of the word, or that he perceives a distinction between the noun form
and the verb form. If it is the first part of the word which is regarded
as the "essence", it will mean that the Nazirite is not obliged to shave
his head, since the word may then be connected with the preceding phrase
"unto the Lord"; "grow long" thus becomes synonymous with letting
his locks grow from a religious motive. However, the *Kāfi* decides
to his own satisfaction that the "essence" must be found in the (פרע) ע
which will then give the sense of an increase in the (newly grown and
uncovered) hair, and thus indicate that it is the "increase" which com-
mences at he Nazirite initiation. This having been established as the
correct grammatical form, the ruling is undoubtedly that the Nazirite
is bound to shave his head *before* entering on his Naziriteship.[294]

To be sure, such recondite problems are very rare; and, although,
as a rule, no genuinely grammatical solution is forthcoming, we may
still trace in broad outlines the mental processes by which the Samaritan
exegetes employ such grammatical knowledge as they possess for the
purpose of interpretation. We may even generalise here by claiming
that the majority of the allied groups have this in common, that they

---

[293] p. 233 (SLTh.A, p. 50).

[294] Perhaps those who denied the initial haircut of the Nazarite explained the word
פרע as a verb and as referring to God (Essence here = stress on the syllable). This
seems to be the interpretation of the Sam. Targum (מרבי פרע). On the other hand,
the oral tradition of the S.P. reading would suggest גָּדֵל, a nominal form. cf. Ben-
Ḥayyim, *op. cit.* IIIa, p. 76.

are preoccupied with a type of exegesis which is entirely subordinate to a deeply ingrained tradition, for the support of which they attempt to find pegs in as many scriptural texts as possible, and by further claiming that these groups must by their very nature be mainly concerned with minute detail. They can readily discover meaningful indications even in grammatical points which in their own judgment seem irregular. Not uncommonly such "irregularities" and even discrepancies are artificially multiplied, so that, by the very process of reconciliation, further "indications" and pegs may be created.[295] The Samaritans, on the contrary firmly believe that their own exegesis is the direct outcome of rational and logical deductions from scripture, and hence pay comparatively less attention to such details.

In order to show how strikingly different such exploitations of grammatical particles are, one may compare typical Karaite interpretations, which of course also claim to be on a strictly literalist basis, with typical Samaritan ones. We have seen on previous occasions that personal, relative and interrogative pronouns are freely utilised by the Karaites in the interests of midrash. Often, very much as in Rabbinic interpretations even if such pronouns are in no way redundant, they may still serve as a source of midrash. This somewhat disconcerting device of the Karaites is, needless to say, hardly ever exploited by the Samaritans.

One of the classical examples of the Karaite type of discussion is to be found in Daniel Al-Qumisi's polemics against those of his predecessors who claimed that the signs indicative of the ritually clean bird (i.e. the one with a gizzard and crop) can be deduced from *Lev.* i, 16 "and he shall take away its gizzard and its crop".[296] Daniel disputes this claim by showing that these two expressions do not denote two parts of the bird's body, but only one, seeing that the next phrase is "and he shall cast *it*", and not "he shall cast *them*". This is one of the more extreme cases where the significance of a personal pronoun is very greatly stretched for the purpose of serving as a 'proof'. It is true that the Samaritans themselves interpret בנצתו as referring to the gizzard;[297] but, as

---

[295] Particles, adverbs, prepositions were forced into the service of fanciful interpretations such as allegory, etc. cf. Farrar, *History of Interpretation*, p. 151.

[296] Nemoy, *Karaite Anthology*, p. 32.

[297] It has to be admitted that the Sam. Targum also rendered נצתה as "gizzard". cf. Ben-Ḥayyim, *op. cit.* II, p. 528, ll. 268-270. Such a translation must have been universal. Onqelos renders it באוכלה (cf. *Zebhahim*, 65a). (cf. *B.D.B.*, p. 603). Both the *Kāfi* and the *Ṭabbākh* when dealing with the signs of the clean birds depend entirely on tradition and do not quote any verses.

we have seen from the *Kāfi*, not only do they not play on the personal pronoun, but this whole principle of requiring special signs for the ritually clean bird is dependent entirely on tradition and does not seek or lose itself on any fanciful or far-fetched scriptural warrants.

It is not surprising, therefore, that the precise grammatical rules govern-ing the use of such particles do not greatly impress the Samaritans. To take, for example, the rules of Qirqisāni,[298] extending as they do, not only to pronouns, but also to the inseparable interrogative particle ה (השמע), we find that he enters into such minute questions as: When are these inseparable particles not written, but nevertheless implied in the text? When is this particle vocalised in the same way as the definite article ה (החזק)? This kind of thing interests the Samaritan but little.

To a much lesser extent, one can find in Samaritan literature an echo of the Rabbinic midrashim based on demonstrative or relative pronouns, wherein even the difference between the expressions "these" and "*and* these", serves as a mine of new midrashic ideas;[299] but whereas to "redundant" pronouns a special significance is attached in Rabbinic literature,[300] they are in fact hardly utilised, or even 'searched out',in Samaritan exegesis.

Without entering into the notorious discussion whether the verb or the noun forms the more important component of the Hebrew lan-guage,[301] from the structure of form-patterns and paradigms we can readily appreciate that the verb can claim a certain priority, especially in exegesis. The tenses and their derivatives are certainly of primary importance, even to the rudimentary understanding of the text. Here again, if we consider the importance attached to the tenses amongst the Karaites, we immediately discern one reason for a real difference of approach.

Qirqisāni explores the tenses so throughly that he can point out scrip-tural instances where the verb appears in the past tense (perfect without Waw-Consecutive), and can claim that actually the future tense is meant.[302] Strangely enough, one of the instances quoted by Qirqisāni

---

[298] H. Hirschfeld, *op. cit.* p. 35.

[299] Heinemann, *Darkhei ha-Aggadah*, p. 142.

[300] Rosenblatt, *op. cit.* p. 4, nn. 34, 35. The discussion about the relative pronoun אשר should by right belong to this paragraph but it is more convenient to deal with it later. As far as Samaritan exegesis was concerned it was utilized mainly as a relative conjunction.

[301] cf. *sup.* Part II, n. 403 (and text there).

[302] Hirschfeld, *op. cit.* p. 36 (Arabic text, p. 56).

is *Deut.* xxxiv, 10 "and there hath no risen a prophet in Israel since, like unto Moses", a text which by the Samaritans too, is invariably understood as referring to the future. Nevertheless, although the Targum renders this expression as "there will not arise", and although indeed this exegesis permeates the whole of later Samaritan literature, any attempt at a grammatical justification of this understanding and any sort of correlation with similar instances elsewhere are altogether lacking.[303]

One encounters some extremely fanciful "grammatical" expositions in the *Book of Precepts* of 'Anan. A rule held in common by many sectarians, including the Samaritans, is "Ye shall kindle no fire... upon the Sabbath Day", (*Ex.* xxxv, 3), understood to mean that a fire lit before the commencement of Sabbath must be extinguished. 'Anan derives the reason for this prohibition from the premiss that, since this particular prohibition (תבערו) and the general prohibition of work on the Sabbath (תעשו) (*Ex.* xx, 10) both alike begin with a letter *taw*, they must be identical in purport; that is to say, just as any labour, even if begun on Friday, must cease on the Sabbath, so must a fire cease to burn on that day.[304]

The *Kāfi* too polemicises heavily against the Rabbanites for their "desecration" of the Sabbath, by their allowing fire to burn. No quasi-grammatical expositions however, are employed here: as we shall see later, the Samaritans prefer to rely far rather on 'logical' analogies.[305]

In their later literature, when the Samaritans are anxious to find Biblical support for their eschatological speculations they pay considerably more attention to tenses. The reason for this must be that certain Scriptures written in the future tense might easily be utilised as prophecies concerning the Hereafter and for which very little support may be found in the strictly literal sense of the Pentateuch's verses. Thus, for example, in *Gen.* iv, 23, 24; "Cain *shall be* avenged" is by some taken as a reference to reward and punishment in the next world. Such verses are by some even gathered together to serve as proof-texts and

---

[303] M.T. ולא קם נביא עוד; S.P. ולא קם עוד נביא; S.T. ולא יקום עורי cf. *Ṭabbākh*, f. 215a.

[304] Nemoy, *op. cit.* pp. 17f.

[305] *Kāfi*, p. 335 (SLTh.A, p. 74). The *Kāfi* uncharacteristically polemicises here against the Rabbanites. However, its arguments are more logical, quoting *Deut.* xxv, 4 "Thou shalt not muzzle an ox when it is treading (threshing)". Just as in the case of the ox muzzling is forbidden during the threshing even though it has been muzzled before the threshing similarly fire on the Sabbath is forbidden even if it has been kindled before.

testimonies of reward and punishment in the "Day of Revenge and Retribution".[306]

With regard to the art of deriving verbs from their radicals and that of distinguishing between similar verbs, Samaritan exegesis excels neither in displaying a penetrating knowledge of these radicals, nor in displaying the power to distinguish similar verbs from each other. Thus, for example, the words in *Deut.* xxi, 20, "a glutton and a drunkard" are taken by them in their proper sense i.e. as Hebrew participial forms. Moreover, while the first expression is again quite correctly translated as "light", "worthless" or "made light of", the second is understood as "despicable". This interpretation is most probably based on the Aramaic root meaning "being filthy" (סאב).[307] Clearly, one has to approach such an identification very cautiously, because, although some of the strange etymologies appearing in the Targum are undoubtedly based on non-Hebraic roots, so we have seen to be the case also with words which for the Samaritans are *hapaxlegomena*, such rare words are usually understood and interpreted from the context. Rare verbs or verbal forms by their very nature lend themselves very easily to midrashic exposition derived from an understanding of the broad thematic unit. In the particular case under consideration, where the son is "stubborn and rebellious" the mere context would cause the other rare verbal forms to be explained in a similar vein, as being so closely associated.

Occasionally the tense itself is the sole basis of the midrash, but here we have to take the correctness of the grammatical form for granted, and then try to find out for ourselves in each case how the midrash is built on it. It is of course easier to conjecture such methods and motives when the S.P. and M.T. show a different tense and the midrash is built on the variant. For example, in *Deut.* xv, 2 the M.T. reads "I will sing unto the Lord", (a cohortative), while the S.P. reads אשירו, which is understood as an imperative.[308] This understanding of the tense and mood of the verb serves as the basis of a midrash which then develops into an apologetic discourse.[309] There are in fact two problems to be

---

[306] Gaster, *The Sam. Oral Law etc.*, p. 151. Obviously such 'proof texts' are only of secondary nature, the central idea of "Day of Revenge and retribution" (*Deut.* xxxii, 35 S.P.), did not depend on them. cf. *Memar Marqab* (ed. Macdonald), I, pp. 108ff. (= II, pp. 181ff.).

[307] S.T. מזל ומתעב cf. Kohn, *Sam. Studien*, p. 60. They understood as originating from סאב. About transposition of letters, cf. *sup.* n. 279.

[308] Ben-Ḥayyim, *op. cit.* III a p. 230, n. 1.

[309] *Memar Marqah* (ed. Macdonald), I, pp. 37f.; II, pp. 57f.

settled in this exposition. How may the Song of Moses be reconciled with that of Miriam? And how may one say of God that He is "extremely boastful" (גֹה גָאָה)? Firstly, by construing the tense and mood as an imperative, the sense of the sentence becomes: "Sing unto the Lord, for (Pharoah) was extremely boastful, (and of whom, owing to his arrogance towards the Israelites) the horse and its rider Hath He thrown into the sea". Secondly in view of the imperative (as in the reference to Miriam, verse 21), the midrash explains that it seems as if, at the bidding of Moses, there was a definite agreement by which Moses should recite his song, and instruct the Elders to accompany it verse by verse. This was also done simultaneously by Miriam, who followed their example along with the women.

Here in this midrash, simply by taking the verbal form as an imperative, the mere consideration of the tense serves as a basis for the whole exegesis. The true distinction between the various tenses and even between the verb and the verbal noun is not always so clearly defined.[310] Frequently, expressions regularly understood by us as nominal forms are taken by Samaritan exegetes as verbs. For example, in *Num* xxviii, 14 "this is the burnt-offering of every month throughout the months of the year (חֹדֶשׁ בְּחָדְשׁוֹ)" is understood as "the month in its renewal".[311] This tradition of seeing the word בְּחָדְשׁוֹ as a verb is interestingly enough, also known to the Karaites. Munajjah polemicises against the Karaites on this point, but the polemics are directed to combating the Karaite view that the reference in this verse is to the "renewal" of the *moon*. According to Munajjah, the moon is not mentioned in this verse at all, for it actually refers, he insists, to the renewal of *time*. This means, then, that he accepts the traditional Samaritan exegesis in its understanding of the "renewal", but he disputes the Karaites', insistence that the visual sign of the renewal of the *moon* is here meant and urges, as usual, that the "renewal" depends on calculations.[312]

In this connection it is surely worth nothing that the matter of the calculations based on both luminaries is likewise explained by Munajjah

---

[310] Ben-Ḥayyim, *op. cit.* I, p. 230, n. 4.

[311] Ben-Ḥayyim, *op. cit.* II, p. 466, l. 232. Strangely enough, such interpretations of *Num.* xxviii, 14 also crept into Rabbinic literature; *Pirqe de R. Eliezer.* Ch. LI (cf. commentaries of R. David Luria, *ibid.* nn. 1, 2 and 25). In general, however, this expression was understood by the Rabbis as שַׁבַּת בְּשַׁבַּתּוֹ (*Num.* xxviii, 10) and all their halakhic midrashim are based on this understanding (cf. *Siphri, ad loc.*; *Rosh-Hashanah*, 7a; Jer. *Sheqalim*, I, 1; 45d).

[312] *Masā'il al-Khilāf*, Ia, pp. 19f.

through placing his reliance in a verb. As we have seen on previous occasions, "and *let them* be" (*Gen.* i, 14) referring as it does to the luminaries, is understood by the Samaritans as a Biblical warrant for their own calendar based on the intercalation of the solar and lunar movements.[313] Munajjah uses this verb (והיו) in illustration of his point that its plural form excludes the very possibility of placing reliance in the visual sign of the moon only. He further polemicises against the Karaites by declaring that, if the expression "and let them be for *signs*" refers to the visual appearance of the moon, additional evidence for so restrictive an interpretation would surely be supplied; but since there is no evidence at all for any so restrictive an interpretation, the plural in the verse must undoubtedly refer to "the two great lights" *ibid.* v, 16.[314]

The intricate interpretation supplied for double verbs (i.e. those in which the infinitive — absolute is followed by a finite verb) which we normally understand as strongly emphatic expressions (or asseverations), does not apparently cause the Samaritan exegete much difficulty. It seems that his strictly literalist approach prevents him from building midrashim on these double expressions. Nevertheless, it must here be pointed out that he understands the infinitive-absolute as being syn-onymous with the imperative.[315] This naturally could raise many prob-lems in the case of a double verb in particular, when the infinitive absolute at the head is invariably taken as an imperative. For example *Ex.* xxii, 22 "and they cry at all unto me", is especially hard to reconstruct. How can the first צעק really be explained as an imperative?[316] And of course the other double expression in the verse creates similar difficulties.

From the slavishly literal translation of the Samaritan Targum, no valid conclusion on this point can be drawn. It nevertheless seems likely that, in most cases where the finite verb is *not* itself an imperative, the infinitive absolute is understood, as by ourselves, as an emphatic form (e.g. *Gen.* xv, 13 חכים תחכם; *Ex.* xxii, 22 (צוח = צבע יצבע).

---

[313] cf. my article *ALUOS* VI (1969), pp. 110f., 143ff. (nn. 102-103).

[314] *Masā'il al-Khilāf*, Ia, p. 2.

[315] Ben-Ḥayyim, *op. cit.* I, p. 8f. (cf. *ibid.* n. 7). cf. recently Macuch, *Grammatik*, pp. 258, 514ff.

[316] Ben-Ḥayyim, *op. cit.* I, pp. 72f., nn. 7, 8. The Arabic translations normally render this double verb (infinitive absolute and the finite verb) as emphatic. Maybe this is a result of following Saadia's version, e.g. *Gen.* xv, 13 علم تعلم. cf. Saadia (ed. J. Derenbourg, Paris 1893, p. 23) אעלם עלמא. However, *Ex.* xxii, 22 is ren-dered by Saadia (*ibid.* p. 113) וצרך אלי.

We have mentioned this last use of the infinitive, not so much for its own sake, since anyhow no midrashic elaboration is attached to it, as rather to give a general picture which would also include certain cases inevitably puzzling to the exegetes. If we compare this situation with that prevalent in other groups, for instance, in Hellenistic Judaism or Rabbinic Judaism, where the slightest deviation from the expected tense serves as a source of intricate exposition,[317] we immediately see a world of difference.

A similar picture arises from the Samaritan approach to derived forms. One looks in vain for acute investigations into the difference between active and passive forms, or between simple, causative and reflexive forms, solely in the interests of midrashic expansion. Although, in general, their understanding of the Biblical text is what we might expect from a grammatical standpoint, this understanding does not of itself necessarily show that there is any penetrating grammatical awareness. After all, by mere reliance on the contextual sense, which may easily be derived from the broad thematic unit, and without any such grammatical awareness, the Samaritan would comprehend the derived form correctly.

In some cases, where doubt might arise as to whether a verb should be understood in its simple form (as intransitive) or in its intensive form (as transitive), the Samaritan tradition of reading guides the reader in the proper understanding of the text. Just as in the Rabbinic tradition the Masoretic vocalisation makes it clear in which derived from the verb is to be understood, so too the Samaritans rely on their Oral Tradition. For this reason, whenever the precise derived form of a verse is doubtful, each group falls back on its tradition for its understanding of it. One such case is *Deut.* xxvi, 5 which we normally translate as "a lost Aramean", basing ourselves on the reading of the Masoretic Text, which takes the word אבד as the active participle of the simple form. However, both the Rabbinic and the Samaritan traditions have here a midrash which understands this verb in a transitive sense i.e.: "(Laban) the Aramean (intended to) destroy my father".[318] Whether the verb

---

[317] Heinemann, *op. cit.* p. 116. cf. *sup.* Part II, n. 408.

[318] *Kāfi*, p. 29 (SLTh.A, p. 1). The S.T. follows the Hebrew (ארמי אבד אבי). It is possible that this case is also influenced by the translation of Saadia (אן לבן אלארמני כאד אן יביד אבי), *ibid.* p. 291, cf. n. 3. cf. Ben-Ḥayyim, *op. cit.* IIIa, p. 142. Even in *Deut.* xxxii, 28 (cf. *idem, ibid.* p. 160), one could find similarities to Saadia's translation (*op. cit.* p. 303, לאנהם קביל מציע אלחכמה)

is actually derived from the intensive or the causative does not alter the fact that both groups in this instance deviate from the literal sense by following an almost identical exegetical principle.

It still needs to be emphasized that such midrashim are extremely rare amongst the Samaritans, whereas amongst the Rabbis these devices are commonplace.[319] Furthermore, one must always reckon with the possibility that such interpretations may have been introduced to the Samaritans by the Arabic translation of the Pentateuch of Saadya. At any rate, in our present ignorance of the depth of the Samaritan exegetes' awareness of grammatical 'peculiarities' we can only state that with them such special cases are rather exceptional and most uncharacteristic.

If now we compare the employment of the derived forms by the Samaritans with their employment by the Rabbis, we see two conflicting tendencies. The Samaritans do not exploit the derivations of the verb at all for the purpose of creating midrashim, whereas amongst the Rabbis it is commonplace to do so. Even the Mishnah, which of course is not devoted to midrash but to abstract Halakhah, nevertheless contains an enormous number of instances dependent on the exploitation of the derivatives.[320] No such scholastic approach, which would allow the exegete unlimited scope for emphasising the significance of each and every detail of the derived forms of the verb ever existed amongst the Samaritans.

Again, if we consider the pronominal suffixes, these likewise are not pressed into the service of midrashim which would not otherwise be intelligible from the general sense of the passage in which they appear. Interesting, though, are those cases where there are differences between the M.T. and the S.P., since here the very close interdependence of Scripture and tradition is our only effective guarantee that we are following the genuine Samaritan mentality. An example which we have

---

[319] It is sufficient to mention for comparison the Rabbinic type of אל תקרי midrashim, of which one could adduce long lists (cf. *sup.* n. 17). Samaritan exegetes never indulged in such plays on words or alternative readings. On the contrary, even when accepting the strangest midrashic interpretations, they were under the impression that this is the *only* meaning of Scripture. Lack of grammatical awareness may have contributed to such a *naive* approach. The whole concept of a three radical stem was unknown to the early Samaritan exegetes. cf. Ben-Ḥayyim, *op. cit.* I, pp. ס״ו–ע״ז, nn. 210-212.

[320] Rosenblatt, *op. cit.* p. 10, n. 1; p. 11, nn. 5-24.

already seen in a different connection [321] is the mentoin of the animal
"which dieth of itself". Instead of the Masoretic Text "or thou mayest
sell it unto a foreigner" (*Deut.* xiv, 21), expressed in Hebrew by the
infinitive absolute (מכר לנכרי), the Samaritan Pentateuch has a finite
verb with a third person feminine pronominal suffix (מכרה לנכרי).
At first glance, the slight variation may be thought to be immaterial,
as both readings boil down to the same meaning. If, however, we look
at the Rabbinic midrash based on the Masoretic Text, we may see a
difference in meaning, since amongst the Rabbis there was a controversy
about the proper understanding of this verse. According to one opinion
(R. Judah), the verse should be understood literally i.e.: "to the stranger
in thy gate" one may *give* it, or may *sell* it to a foreigner. Another
opinion (R. Meir) leaves it optional whether one gives it or sells it to
the stranger or the foreigner.[322]

The *Kāfi*, relying on the Samaritan Pentateuch, concludes from this
form of the text that one is not allowed to sell it, since it is written "thou
shalt give it", and the next phrase, he explains, mean that the *stranger*
may eat it or sell it to the foreigner.[323]

Such and similar examples show that, if the pronominal suffix is
utilised at all, it is not merely as a pretext for widening or narrowing
the scope of the verb, but much more as a means of giving a 'perfect'
sense to the whole context. Another underlying motive for this type of
explanation, although not often explicitly avowed, is that of defending
the authenticity both of the text and of the traditional interpretation.
Such a widening of the scope of the pronominal suffixes, and such a
changing of their terms of reference from personal to impersonal, devices
which are very common in Rabbinic midrashim, both in halakhah and
in aggadah,[324] are hardly to be found amongst the Samaritans.

Great confusion, it will be realized, may arise from ignorance of the
exact root of a verb. This fact applies in particular to weak verbs, which
often appear in forms from which one or two radicals are missing. One
also has to bear in mind that the recognition of the Triliteral roots was
introduced to the Samaritans relatively late. From the available evidences
it is not at all easy to decide whether or not the elventh century writers

---

[321] cf. *sup.* Part II, n. 145.
[322] *Pesaḥim*, 22b, cf. *ibid.* Tosaphoth s.v. הלכה כר"י.
[323] pp. 315f. (p. 317).
[324] Rosenblatt, *op. cit.* p. 11, nn. 14-16; Heinemann, *op. cit.* p. 125.

knew of this principle.[325] Quite apart from the more involved semantic
treatment of homonyms and 'artificial homonyms', in which distinct
words are re-interpreted so as to be made to bear the same meaning,[326]
the mere misunderstanding of the grammatical roots or the substitution
of one weak verb for another are always adequate sources of strange
interpretations. We have had occasion to mention the classical example
of such aberrations and one which runs through the whole of Samaritan
literature, namely *Ex*. iv, 24, a text understood not as "and sought
to kill him" (from root המיתו – מות) but as "and sought to excite him"
(from root המה).[327] It is even very possible that, in this and similar cases,
we have a deliberately contrived semantic exposition with a view to
defending the honour of Moses. Similarly apologetic etymologies
may doubtless be found in connection with the same narrative. Thus
the verbs נמל, מול, כרת etc. are treated as if derived from different roots
to counter the otherwise possible objection that Moses committed an
error in apparently not circumcising his son. Nouns like בנה (her son)
and צור are transformed into verbs or verbal nouns for the self-same
purpose.[328]

But such perversely etymological approaches to the verb occur not
from apologetic motives only, but more often from sheer oversight in
discovering the true radicals of the root. Sometimes a pronominal suffix
is mistakenly understood as one of the radicals of the verb itself.
Normally in such cases a new semantic value is ascribed to the verb by
construing it as if from a better-known Aramaic root. For example
Deut. xxviii, 61, "bring upon thee" (יעלם) is traced back to the Aramaic
root עלם meaning "use of force, violence".[329]

It goes without saying that not all false etymologies in regard to the
weak verb again, are due to obstruse and sophisticated approaches.
Often sheer ignorance and lack of linguistic ability add to the already
present sources of confusion in the forms and meanings of the weak
verb.[330] Another source, naturally ingrained in the Samaritans but in

---

[325] Ben-Ḥayyim, *op. cit.* I, pp. ח''ס f. cf. also *sup.* n. 319. On the changes and
confusion of weak verbs cf. Macuch, *Grammatik*, pp. 256f.

[326] Ullmann, *Language and Style*, p. 32.

[327] Munajja, *Masā'il al-Khilāf*, Ib, pp. 26f. The same exegesis runs through the
whole of Samaritan literature (cf. *Ex Commentary* attributed to Ghazal al-Duweik,
pp. 152-155). cf. *sup.* n. 78 and Part II, nn. 82-85 and text there.

[328] Munajja, *op. cit.* pp. 23f. *Ex Commentary, op. cit.* pp. 159-161.

[329] Ben-Ḥayyim, *op. cit.* IIIa, p. 150.

[330] Ben-Ḥayyim, *ibid.* I, pp. 152f.; II, p. 563, ll. 171-172. cf. Kohn, *Sam. Studien*,
pp. 38f.

the etymological pursuits of the Rabbis a deliberate device,[331] is the constant interchange of gutturals. Despite the profusion of these rank 'etymological' outgrowths of the weak verb, there is hardly any intentional design to organize them into a system. Unlike the Rabbis with their midrashim based on a deliberate and constant interchange of such roots for midrashic expositions or even a desire to find a secondary sense for the perfectly natural meaning of the verb, the Samaritans do not adopt any such practices. In sporadic instances where midrashim are built on such foundations, they are in fact either apologetic devices for explaining away an embarrassing meaning or the spontaneous products of a confusion of the radicals of a weak verb. Although we may confidently assume that the earlier Samaritan grammarians were not aware of the three-letter root, they did not even follow the Rabbinic practice of building midrashim on a single letter of a weak verb when this was held to be the radical.[332]

We can nevertheless occasionally find in Samaritan exegesis the subconscious or even deliberate confusion of the verb with the verbal noun. Although the Samaritan Targum usually distinguishes between "a righteous man" (צדיק) and "righteousness' or "being just" or "being justified" (צדק),[333] this does not deter Marqah from playing on the assumed identity of these two forms.[334] Here is his midrash on *Deut.* xxxii, 4. "just and righteous is He":

> Observe the beginning of it and take note of the end of it. When it was said to Noah (*Gen.* vi, 9), it was complete with YUD, but when it was uttered from the mouth of the True One, there was no YUD in it. When Moses said it and magnified God with it, he put YUD in it, for it is the beginning of the Great Name and represents the foundation of Creation. He proclaimed ṢADDIQ and by it commanded Israel, *in righteousness shall you Judge* (*Lev.* xix, 15), *Justice and only justice you shall follow* (*Deut.* xvi, 20).

It is here again possible that Marqah deliberately dwells on this word צדיק for apologetic reasons. How could Moses use of God a word which, as used elsewhere in Scripture, refers to a righteous human being? It would be too much to expect Marqah to hold the purely philosophical

---

[331] H. Hirschfeld, "Pronunciation of the letter Ayn", *JQR* IV (1892), p. 500. As for the Sam. cf. Macuch, *Grammatik*, pp. 28ff., 132ff.

[332] Rosenblatt, *op. cit.* p. 71 (on the division of 'longer' words as if composed of several roots, cf. *ibid.* pp. 6f.); cf. also Jellinek (ed.), *Nophet Zufim*, p. 207.

[333] צדיק is usually rendered as זכאי, זכאה (*Gen.* vi, 9; vii, 1; xviii, 23 etc.) while the root צדק is translated by קשט (*Lev.* xix, 15; *Deut.* xxv, 15 etc.).

[334] *Memar Marqah* (ed. Macdonald), I, p. 91; II, pp. 147f.

notion that God, as a source of righteousness, should be characterised
as righteousness itself. It is more probable that, by equating the verb
with the noun and by adding the midrashic element about YUD (the
first letter of the Tetragrammaton) as the foundation of all existence,
he explains away such a difficulty to his own satisfaction and that of
his readers.

Obviously if the Samaritan Pentateuch by some special feature renders
a particular noun ambiguous, there is a further chance of its being
explained as a verb or vice versa. In *Ex.* xiv, 21 "and there was the cloud
and the darkness", the "and" is missing in the Samaritan Pentateuch,
and it is therefore understood as "that the cloud and darkness illuminated the night".[335] This in turn serves as a source for Marqah's
midrash, which increases the inflictions upon the Egyptians at the Red
Sea into ten (by analogy with the Ten Plagues in Egypt). The first of
these inflictions, according to Marqah, was:[336]

> The cloud caused illumination and darkening all that night, so that they were
> trembling at that wonder which was done first.

But Marqah does not depend only on such explicit Scriptural features;
often similarity of roots is the source of his midrash. One of these
midrashim which will occupy our attention later, in connection with
the hermeneutical device so common in Marqah (namely the play on
letters), is actually based on such a confusion of roots.[337] This is a
midrash on *Deut.* xxxii, 4, "*The Rock*, his work is perfect".[338] The
only portion of the Midrash which interests us here is his comparison
of צור (Rock) with the verb יצר to create. On the basis of this comparison,
Marqah interweaves his midrash on this verse with the doctrine of the
creation of man and man's perfect form (צורה).

Such midrashim as these for the most part characteristic of Marqah
himself are only very seldom followed up in later Samaritan literature.
Judging solely from the later attitude towards his more exotic midrashim,
it seems clear that this device is regarded, not so much as a hermeneutical
principle to be followed, as rather a momentary pun, thrown off in the
heat of a homiletical exposition. Marqah, as a preacher, believes himself
justified in allowing himself much more freedom in this respect, than

---

[335] S.P. ויאיר את הלילה (understood as Hiph'il) ויהי ענן החשך, S.T. והוה עננה
מחשך ומניר עם ליליה (M.T. והחשך הענן), cf. Macuch, *Grammatik*, p. 491.
[336] *Memar Marqah* (ed. Macdonald), I, p. 38; II, p. 59.
[337] cf. *inf.* para (g, 8).
[338] *Memar Marqah* (ed. Macdonald), I, pp. 87f.; II, pp. 140f.

would be justified in others, and it would not be unreasonable to liken his highly individualistic approach to poetic or artistic licence. If we take one extreme example, we may immediately recognise that, although analogy is in fact the main principle upon which it is built, Marqah adds a pun for additional effect, probably well aware himself of its far-fetched nature. Simply by playing on the similarity of a noun and a verb which are so obviously totally unconnected, he demonstrates that his pun cannot be due to linguistic ignorance on his part, but that it is a deliberate homiletical expedient, the real lesson of which could in any case be drawn from the context alone without any such extravagant methods.

> Let us contemplate with the inner eye, and see the great prophet Moses saying to the congregation, "*And there is none that can deliver out of my hand*" (*Deut.* xxxii, 39). *Is the Lord's hand shortened?* (*Num.* xi, 23). The Lord's hand began and it created. By it he restores everything to its original state through His greatness. Therefore he said "Hand" (יד) and "*will judge*" (ידין *Deut.* xxxii, 36).[339]

This connection between "hand" and "judgement" could easily have been established through many other methods of analogy. The essence of this midrash, that Creation and the Day of Judgement are both alike effected by the Hand of God, is, moreover, shared in common by many others. As a matter of fact, such expositions, based on similar analogies, are also found centuries later in the *Ṭabbākh*, and in the exposition of the same verses;[340] but it is worth noting that such plays on artificial equations between unrelated nouns and verbs are notably absent from the writings of Abū'l Ḥasan.

We should therefore not be unduly perturbed when extravagant midrashim reappear later, and of a character very similar to the plays of Marqah. These are usually constructed on themes well-established by long tradition, and for which the later commentators wish to find a Biblical warrant. Often we find speculations either directly or indirectly associated with eschatological subjects, a field not at all adequately documented by "proof-texts". Such "proof-texts" are therefore frocibly created by false etymologies connecting unrelated nouns to verbs.

---

[339] *Memar Marqah* (ed. Macdonald), I, p. 113; II, p. 189.

[340] ff. 227a, f. Abū'l Hasan correctly connects ידין with the reward (فى حصول الجزاء وقت واحد حسب قوله כי ידין). However, later the same idea about the equation of "the End of the Days" to Creation is still strongly emphasised. ... وبقا ذلك سببا

لثبات العالم ومتى عدم النكير ... فحينئذ يلحق الموجود من العالم بالمعدوم ... الى دار الجزا ...

The practise of turning towards Mt. Gerazim is so deeply rooted in Samaritan tradition that it is only too tempting to look out for Biblical evidences for the belief that a dying man especially should turn to Hargerizim. It is not at all impossible that such a belief is intensified by Islamic influence. However this may be, from the story of Jacob's death and from the verse "he gathered up his feet into the *bed*" (מטה Gen. xlix, 33), it is deduced by an artificial etymology, (or, in their terminology, by 'a secret meaning') that this noun מטה alludes to the verb נטה, "to turn", i.e. the sons of Jacob learnt from their father that a dying man is bound to turn towards the Qiblah.[341]

One can hardly fail to be reminded, by this forced exposition of מטה, of the similarly unnatural rendering in the LXX and some other versions of *Gen.* xlvii, 31 "and Israel bowed himself upon the bed's head", which is there understood and rendered not as "bed", but as "staff".[342] For us the important point is that, while in those other versions the variation from "bed" to "staff" originated from the mistaken vocalisation of two different Hebrew words having the same consonants, the later Samaritans' ebove-mentioned forced exposition was a wilful departure from the accepted practice of following the literal sense.[343]

In general, as we have already seen in most instances having a bearing on semantics, the definitions of nouns and verbs, although often slightly twisted for polemical reasons among the Samaritans, adhered strictly to the literal sense of these words. We may perhaps call to mind one such case, namely the heated discussion on the expression "between the two evenings" (*Ex.* xiv, 12). Despite the involved arguments adduced to

---

[341] Gaster, *The Sam. Oral Law etc.*, I, p. 110.

[342] Most versions of *Genesis* xlvii, 31 (Vulgate and Peshitta) read מַטֶּה instead of מטה (ῥάβδος). cf. *Hebrews* xi, 21. On the other hand the *Ex Commentary, op. cit.* p. 130, plays on the significance of the word מטה (*Ex.* iv, 3, as opposed to מקל, שבט, etc.) and explains that the former signifies that it was from the very best of the tree of knowledge. The following pages are full of legends in the name of earlier authorities, proving that the staff of Moses originates from the Garden of Eden and was transmitted by the Meritorious from one generation to another. Similar legends are also found in Rabbinic literature (cf. Heinemann, *op. cit.* p. 30).

[343] On the other hand the Rabbis employed the word אסף to connote "departing this life", even in places where this interpretation does not fit the context (as in the above quoted case, i.e. *Gen.* xlix, 33). cf. Rosenblatt, *op. cit.* p. 9, n. 75. The Samaritans, not unlike Philo (cf. Heinemann, *op. cit.* p. 125), tend to stress the other part of the expression "and was gathered *to his people*", e.g. *Gen.* xxv, 8.

substantiate the various definitions of "evening",[344] none of these definitions really deviate appreciably from the literal sense.

This does not necessarily mean that all nouns are understood in what we ourselves should term their 'literal' sense, since in countless cases where semantic 'deviations' are thought to be detected,[345] these are essentially the results of misunderstanding. Such misunderstanding is often a source of midrash, for example, "and by great terrors" (*Deut.* iv, 34) is spelt in all Samaritan texts in the defective form ובמראים which may also be understood as "great sights". Marqah evidently buils his midrash on this understanding when he expounds the word with the following comments:

> Containing everything marvellous to the sight of the eye, not to the hearing of the ear.[346]

Such instances of an unaccountable understanding of the noun or nominal form in combination with a preposition could be multiplied, and they regularly have a decisive influence on the exegesis resulting from them.[347] Occasionally, the midrash on such nouns is of a similar type to that of the Rabbis, but far more often it is entirely different.[348]

---

[344] cf. *sup.* para (e, 2) (SLTh.A, pp. 104f.). cf. also Wreschner, *Sam. Traditionen etc.*, pp. 25ff.

[345] Because of the countless semantical deviations among the Samaritans and the conflict with foreign influences, either through translations of or through infiltration of the Masoretic text, Samaritan readers were often reprimanded for their 'deviations' from the accepted Samaritan norm. cf. Ben-Ḥayyim, *op. cit.* I, p. 134; II, p. 453, l. 125, cf. *sup.* Part II, nn. 82-85.

[346] *Memar Marqah* (ed. Macdonald), I, p. 43; II, p. 68. The Samaritan Targum has already ובחזבים רברבים. Similarly in the Mishna we find such confusions of these two roots, cf. Rosenblatt, *op. cit.* p. 9.

[347] Thus e.g. the expression הגזרים in *Gen.* xv, 17 ("that passed between the *pieces*") is rendered by the S.T. דעברין בין קטריה האלן. No doubt the S.T. plays here on the motive גזרים = גריזים with the meaning "the mighty ones". cf. Ben-Ḥayyim, *op. cit.* II, p. 583, l. 151 (and *ibid.* p. 550, l. 294). The Arabic translation of Abu-Sa'id may be influenced by Saadia (although the latter uses the root שטר and the former the root بضع in the whole passage). Naturally the apparently 'simple' explanation that the S.T. reads הקשרים for הגזרים has no foundation. cf. S. Kohn, *Sam. Studien*, pp. 42f., and *ibid.* p. 52. As we have so often seen, the midrashim on the etymologies connected with Hargerizim were specially favoured.

[348] It is interesting to compare commentaries on verses as e.g. *Deut.* xxv, 5. cf. Montgomery, *The Samaritans*, p. 169, n. 7; cf. Ben-Ḥayyim, *op. cit.* II, p. 462, l. 112 and *ibid.* III, pp. 140f. cf. also my article in *ALUOS* VI (1969), p. 163, n. 230.

The pronoun and its relationship to the noun are not significantly exploited for midrashic exposition; we find hardly any forced extensions of the pronoun (or indeed as we shall see later, of the pronominal suffix) as is often the case amongst the exegetes of other groups.[349] We may perhaps here again speculate that the nature of the Samaritan Pentateuch itself and the received methods of literalist exposition do not readily allow much room for the strained or pedantic exploitation of the pronoun. We may further bear in mind that in expressions relating to controversial issues, such as those relating to Hargerizim, certain changes in the pronominal suffixes are already incorporated into the text of the S.P. For instance, *Deut.* xxxiii, 15 and *ibid.* 19, where the Samaritans read "my mountain" (הרי) as referring to God, serve as inexhaustible sources for doctrinal midrashim.

The pronominal suffixes attached to nouns are likewise not so extensively employed by the Samaritans for midrashic purposes as is the case with other groups; although, of course, relatively rare or ambiguous nouns naturally enough present a challenge to the exegete and so prompt midrashic expositions. Thus for example, "Thy Thummim and thy Urim" (*Deut.* xxxiii, 8) was already midrashically explained by the Samaritan Targum as "Thy perfections and thy lights".[350] The *Ṭabbākh* takes this expression as a reference to Moses.[351]

Undoubtedly, this understanding of the quality of perfection as pertaining to Moses (because of the pronominal suffixes attached to the nouns) forms an essential element of Marqah' expositions. Although in his midrash this particular verse is nowhere mentioned, his whole

---

[349] Rabbinic literature is filled with midrashim based on strained expositions of pronouns. Taking for example the demonstrative pronoun, one could amass cases (e.g. זה on *Gen.* l, 11, cf. Jer. *Soṭah,* I, 10; 17b. On *Ex.* xiii, 8. cf. *Mekhilta ad loc.* on *Ex.* xii, 3 and *ibid.* xxx, 3 etc. cf. *Menaḥoth,* 29a, *Sanhedrin,* 42a, *Ta'anith,* 31a *Soṭah,* 11b etc. One could find similar treatment of זאת; on *Num.* vi, 21, cf. *Nazir,* 46b on *Num,* xix, 2 cf. Yoma 42 b; on *Deut.* iv, 44, cf. *Makkoth,* 10a etc. R. Meir Leibush *Malbim,* in an introduction (called "Ayyeleth ha-Shahar") to his commentary on Leviticus (Wilna 1901), devotes several paragraphs to midrashim based on demonstrative pronouns (568-570), and many details on other pronouns are scattered throughout his other paragraphs (150-153; 179-188; 206-211; 232ff. etc.) The Hellenist although differed in exegesis from the Rabbis, nevertheless, in utilizing pronouns for 'deeper' meanings, they did not lag behind the latter. cf. Philo, *Legum Allegoria,* I, 97; 107, cf. also Heinemann, *op. cit.* pp. 96ff.; 138f.; 180f. etc.

[350] cf. *sup.* n. 323 and n. 38 in Part II.

[351] *Ṭabbākh,* f. 204a. cf. *sup.* Part II, n. 39, also text *ibid.*

exposition of *Deut.* xxxi, 30 (Tummam) takes this understanding for granted.[352]

Occasionally, we find that the pronominal suffix is translated in accordance with strict grammar as a singular or plural, as the case may be, although, as it appears in its context, it might well be taken more freely. Thus in the story of Rebecca, although only one brother is explicitly mentioned in Scripture, the expression "Our sister" (*Gen.* xxiv, 60) prompts Samaritan exegetes to suggest that she had in fact two brothers, both of whom blessed her.[353] Nevertheless, these and similar cases are not elaborated so as to form sources of further midrashim.

Although the rule that nouns with pronominal suffixes should be treated grammatically as specific objects, exactly as if they have the definite article, was certainly known to the Samaritan exegetes, it was not exploited so as to become an unlimited source of midrashim. The extant cases in which such a device is sporadically employed as an aid to exegesis are quite exceptional; it forms rather a buttress to the similar, but rarely used, device of basing expositions on the definite article or the construct case.[354]

Most probably because of the relative unimportance of the noun in general and its pronominal suffixes in particular in Samaritan exegesis, no meticulous or sustained observation of their grammatical features was pursued. We can therefore hardly expect any such formulations of exact rules as can be found among the Karaites. There we are con-

---

[352] *Memar Marqah* (ed. Macdonald), I, pp. 84f.; II, pp. 136f. cf. also *sup.* Part II, n. 593.

[353] Ben-Ḥayyim, *op. cit.* I, pp. 32f. cf. *ibid.* n. 9. It is possible that the reason why such midrashim were not further exploited is that the concept of 'brother' in Samaritan tradition was often interpreted in the widest possible sense (e.g. *Num.* iv, 7; *Deut.* xxv, 5. cf. *inf.*, para (g, 5).

[354] Munajja, in his *Masā'il al-Khilāf* (Ia, pp. 4f.), quotes Abu'l Ḥasan al-Ṣūri on the verse *Num.* xxviii, 11 ("And in the beginnings of *your* months"...) where the pronominal suffix is adduced as a proof that the date was known to them. This and other biblical proofs are brought in as evidence that the calendar depends on calculations (which make the dates known in advance) and not on observation of natural phenomena. Forms without the definite article, which according to the context have the definite article implied, were also recognised by the Samaritans. cf. Ben-Ḥayyim, *op. cit.* I, p. 158, n. 10. However, such cases were not pressed into the service of midrashic development. Even in the case of the Calendaric calculations, such "proof-texts" were only secondary to the texts (e.g. *Gen.* i, 14) which showed the same argument by (at least what seemed to the Samaritans) their literal sense.

fronted with whole lists of singular nouns treated as collective ones and vice versa.[355] It is true, however, that in some such cases the early editions of the text of the S.P. took care to simplify the matter by replacing an "illogical" singular with a plural.[356]

The main reason, let it be said, however, for not pressing such features into the service of midrashic expositions ultimately depends on the all-pervading attitude inherent in the Samaritan tradition. The general sense of the wider thematic unit is for the Samaritan exegete much more crucial than 'trifling corrections' of gender, number etc., if the text seems otherwise to be smooth enough for plain and matter-of-fact comprehension. Nothing could be further from the Samaritan mind than the kind of rulings found amongst the Rabbis, as for example: "unqualified plurals never exceed two".[357] Neither could one well expect the Samaritans to frame such a rule as that: "singulars and plurals should be taken in their narrowest meaning".[358] Of the very large number of Rabbinic 'hermeneutical principles', based on such nicities as the nominal form or its gender or its number or the pronominal suffixes [359] hardly an echo is found in Samaritan exegesis; not here does the Samaritans' interest lie. The few exceptions which we find are in Scriptural sources which served as basis for polemics as for example *Ex.* iv, 24-25. In such cases every detail was heavily exploited. In other fields, however, this did not become an established practice.

The definite article also provides, though sparingly, a basis for midrashim. Without here entering into these semantic problems of the

---

[355] H. Hirschfeld, *Qirqisāni Studies*, p. 34 (Arabic text, p. 52).

[356] e.g. *Num.* xiii, 22. S.P. ויבאו (M.T. ויבא).

[357] Rosenblatt, *op. cit.* p. 3, n. 26.

[358] *ibid.* p. 4, nn. 32 and 33. Again it is interesting to note that the Samaritan Pentateuch, itself corrects some of these singulars into plurals (e.g. *Lev.* xiv, 42, M.T. יקח וטח S.P. יקחו וטחו).

[359] We could single out hermeneutical rules as for example דרך קצרה and דבר המיוחד במקומו etc. cf. Strack, *Introduction etc.*, p. 96, nn. 13, 20. It is interesting to note that as regards the latter rule, where from *Num.* xv, 18 (in which the expression for Israel's coming to the land is different from other passages in Scripture dealing with the same subject) an important halakhic midrash about the 'heave offering' was derived from the divergent expression בבאכם. For the Samaritans such an expression could mean either "before" or "after". cf. my article in *ALUOS* VI, 1969, p. 148, n. 12. It must be emphasized that the Samaritans derived the perpetual value of the 'heave offering' from the literal sense of Scripture, which stresses "throughout your generations", *Num.* xv, 21. cf. *Kāfi*, pp. 30, 234 (SLTh.A, pp. 2, 51, respectively). cf. also my article *op. cit.* p. 155, n. 172. For aggadic expositions of the Rabbis on such lines, cf. Heinemann, *op. cit.* 118 (and *ibid.* nn. 118, 119).

definite article which have engaged the minds of modern scholars,[360] we have to remember that there are even so some salient differences between our understanding and the Samaritans'. Thus they understood that the Hebrew inseparable particle ה prefixed to words (for us the definite article) could also have other functions, for instance, as an interjection, or for strengthening or beautifying the noun.[361]

Our chief concern is however with such midrashim built on the article as gain a certain prominence in Samaritan tradition, and especially owing to the controversial expression "the place", which we find as one of the major doctrinal designations for Hargerizim. The article is, moreover, exploited for further midrashim on these lines in the story of the Binding of Isaac, where, according of the Hebrew text, there is a definite article in "the altar", (*Gen.* xxii, 9), this reading is understood in Samaritan tradition as a specific place, Hargerizim. According to this tradition, the predecessors of Abraham, including Adam and Noah, already knew of this place, and their altars were erected there too.[362]

> It is good that you should realise that Adam prostrated himself in its direction; that Enosh proclaimed the name of the Lord on it, and Enosh knew and hastened towards it. Noah built an altar in front of it and stood at it, and praised the Lord of the world. Thus it is said concerning him, just as with Abraham, "*Then Noah built an altar*" (*Gen.* vi, 20), "*And Abraham built the altar there*" (*Gen.* xxii, 9, S.P.); exactly as Noah did in truth, so Abraham did in truth. Ascribe greatness to our God who implanted secrets in the hearts of good men, that He might illumine them, and that they may in turn reveal them, for the hearts of good men are bound up with their Lord, and righteousness sustains them, and truth makes them abundent in goodness. Isaac saw it, Jacob knew it and Joseph possessed it, in great perfection he inherited it, from fathers to their sons. Happy are they that possess it and they that inherit it. There was no stubborn and rebellious son (cf. *Deut.* xxi, 18) [363] among them, but they were all good from beginning to end.

Obviously, the whole midrash originates from the definite articles in *Gen.* xxii, 9.

In the Samaritan Halakha on the subject of the reasoned calendaric calculations, especially, the definite article is adduced as proof that the

---

[360] Barr, *Semantics etc.*, pp. 31f.

[361] Ben-Ḥayyim, *op. cit.* I, p. 160 (cf. also n. 2, *ibid.*).

[362] *Memar Marqah* (ed. Macdonald), I, p. 47; II, p. 75. Just as in Sam. tradition המקום became a technical term for Hargerizim, so it became (for quite different reasons) amongst the Rabbis a technical term for God. cf. Rosenblatt, *op. cit.* p. 9 (nn. 72-73). cf. recently Urbach, *The Sages*, pp. 53ff.

[363] cf. S. Kohn, *Sam. Studien*, pp. 58f.

day of the New Moon may be accurately calculated in advance. As opposed to the Karaites' and the ancient Rabbis' method, which depends on the visual sign of the appearance of the New Moon, the Samaritans consistently rely on calculations. Munajjah begins by quoting Abū'l Ḥasan,[364] and then digresses into a long discourse entirely devoted to this subject. His major proof of the correctness of the Samaritan assumption that the New Moon may be calculated in advance is the fact that Scripture mentions New Moon either with a definite article or with a pronominal suffix, both of which prove that it is a fixed and therefore ascertainable day. His major proofs are in fact taken from *Num.* xxviii, 11 "and in the beginning of *your* months", and from *Num.* xxix, 1, "and in *the* seventh month of the first day". In the second case, the celebrations and sacrifice clearly must be on the first day on the month, and thus, according to Munajjah, may be duly carried out only if made dependent on calculations.

Again, in later literature, the midrashim based on the definite article are multiplied, extending even to cases which lead one, not without justification, to wonder whether or not there is some foreign influence at work. Thus in *Ex.* iv, 20, "and set them upon *the* ass", the article is pressed into service as the basis of a midrash. On this view, Moses did not use any insignificant ass, but actually used the very same ass he obtained before coming to Midian.[365]

This last case reminds us of certain Rabbinic Midrashim based on the article. As a matter of fact, this very case of "the ass", in common with many others, is fancifully elaborated in the Rabbinic midrash, as a rule in such a way as to refer to a familiar object previously mentioned in Scripture, or to a well-known doctrinal point which the Rabbis wish thus to introduce into their midrash through a definite article.[366] Even if we include the later Samaritan developments of this practice, such hard-pressed articles are comparatively rarely encountered in their literature and certainly their frequency bears no sort of relation to their frequency in the writings of the Rabbis.

The conjunction *Waw* may likewise become the source of a midrash. Thus for example, the missing Waw-conjunctive in *Gen.* viii, 22, "seed-time and harvest, cold and heat," (S.P.) causes "seedtime" in the

---

[364] *Masā'il al-Khilāf*, Ia, pp. 5f. (cf. *sup.*, n. 356).

[365] *Ex. Commentary*, *op. cit.* p. 150.

[366] Heinemann, *op. cit.* p. 117 (cf. nn. 113, 114). While in Rabbinic literature similar midrashim are commonplace, thise case is an exception in Sam. exegesis.

midrash to be equated with "cold", and "harvest" with "heat". This consideration carries a great weight as a vital part of the Biblical support for the Samaritan calendaric calculations.[367] There is no counterpart whatever to the Rabbinic employment of the conjunctive *Waw* as a rule in such a way as to oppose the same expression without a *Waw*;[368] nor is there any such precise exposition of the difference between Waw conjunctive and Waw-consecutive, as we know to have been prevalent among the Karaites.[369]

The difference, both in the Rabbinic and in the Karaite approach to the *Waw* is evident. Although the Samaritans would not reject out-of-hand a midrash built on the *Waw*, they have no tendency at all, as have other groups, to exploit it for unlimited midrashic expositions.

Syntactical laws are likewise not intelligently appreciated by the Samaritan exegetes. For this reason the particles are only seldom scrutinised closely. Such complex syntactical phrases as appear mainly in the poetical style are relatively rare in the Pentateuch, and hence it does not require any great skill on the part of the Samaritan exegete to comprehend the later, aven if there are no recognised rules for its exposition. To take, for example, the rule cited by Qirqisāni, in passages which begin with a negative, and are followed by an apparent affirmative, this latter in reality is also a negative, because the negative refers to the second part of the passage also,[370] it is at once clear that the Samaritans are woefully innocent of any understanding of such matters. On the other hand, of the many examples given here by Qirqisāni, only one actually comes from the Pentateuch. This particular example, however, could easily be interpreted by the Samaritans from the context alone. "God is not man that he should lie; (neither) the son of man etc." (*Num.* xxiii, 19).

One cannot, however, justly maintain that the particles are entirely ignored by the Samaritan exegetes, The particle אך (nevertheless, but, etc.) is quite often the source of a midrash, for example; *Lev.* xi, 36, "Nevertheless, a fountain or a pit wherein is a great gathering of water",

---

[367] *Ṭabbākh*, f. 8b (SLTh.A, p. 129).

[368] One of the classic examples is the sharp distinction between אלה and ואלה. On *Ex.* xxi, 1, cf. Mekhilta, *ad loc.* and Rashi, *ad loc.* On זאת and וזאת, cf. *sup.* n. 349. For further details cf. Weiss, *Dor Dor etc.*, I, p. 182.

[369] H. Hirschfeld, *op. cit.* pp. 35f. (Arabic text, p. 55). cf. Ben-Ḥayyim, *op. cit.* I, p. 166, n. 2.

[370] Hirschfeld, *op. cit.* pp. 34f. (Arabic text, p. 53).

is explained by the *Kāfi* [371] as implying that the word "nevertheless" might be repeated. The sense would then be: just as "the fountain" is clean, so is "the pit" clean, if the cause of defilement is removed. There is also the further employment of this particle for midrashic exposition mainly for the purpose of 'exclusion',[372] of which we shall see examples further on.

The particle 'also' (גם) is occasionally employed for midrash. Indeed, Marqah bases a whole midrash on this particle, although it is essentially clearly implicit. The midrash revolves around Moses' prayer to God for atonement, after the incident of the 'golden calf'. The text "And I prayed for Aaron *also*" (*Deut.* ix, 20) is not explicitly referred to by Marqah when he says;[373]

> See him pray for the healing of Miriam and *sparing* for the sake of Aaron, that there might be no blemish. He did not pray for him at first, but then he was afraid lest there should be an evil memory.

As we have seen elsewhere,[374] the particle 'also' here aids the harmonisation of this verse with the same story as told in *Ex.* xxxii, 10-11 (S.P. add.).

In the polemical argument directed against the Jews who deny the validity of the Samaritans' purification rites, the defence of the Samaritans' position leans heavily upon their own interpretation of a single particle. The Jews claim that, owing to the non-existence of the 'Sanctuary', there is now no justification for the ashes of the 'red heifer' or the 'water of separation' (מי נדה) prepared from these ashes. The *Ṭabbākh* [375] commenting on *Num.* xix, 4, "And sprinkle of her blood towards the front, Heb. פני i.e. 'face') of the tent of meeting", explains that this text does not in fact require the existence of the Sanctuary. It is only a command to sprinkle the blood of the 'red heifer' in the direction (פני) of the (place of the) Sanctuary. As evidence for this interpretation *Num.* iii, 38 is quoted, where this particle is likewise employed in the sense of direction only.[376]

---

[371] pp. 35f. (SLTh.A, pp. 5f.).

[372] cf. my article, *op. cit.* pp. 112, 146f. (nn. 115-117). For further examples, cf. *inf.* para (g, 5).

[373] *Memar Marqah* (ed. Macdonald), I, pp. 137f.; II, p. 225.

[374] cf. my article *op. cit.* pp. 107, 141 (nn. 79, 80). For further examples, cf. *inf.* para (g, 5).

[375] f. 51b (SLTh.A, p. 94).

[376] cf. my article, *op. cit.* pp. 114, 149f. (nn. 130, 132). As we have seen, *Gen.* iii, 9 was also explained in a similar way.

Some adverbs and adverbial particles are even explained on rare occasions in a way which is not in true accordance with their own exegetical habits. The majority of such cases, however, are without doubt merely feeble attempts to smooth out a relatively difficult text, for which some explanation of an uncommon adverb is attempted in a very forced manner.[377]

Such forced exegesis, moreover, does not rest so much on a 'rule' as on a felt necessity for the clarification of the text. Many such 'explanations', which to us seem quite fanciful, are in actual fact created by misunderstandings. Hence we should be careful not to draw hasty generalisations regarding the Samaritans' arbitrarily devising adverbial forms. Many attempts to account for such fanciful adverbial forms by positing a background of supposed midrashic expositions have been shown by later scholars to be built on false premises.[378]

The inseparable prepositions do not create any great problems for exegesis. The few grammatical works by the Samaritans on biblical Hebrew give us the same overall picture as regards their usages as one might fairly expect from any medieval grammar. Strangely enough, their list of preposition also include the שׁ (= אשׁר), which does not occur anywhere in the Pentateuch itself.[379]

They show withal an awareness, although their vocalisation is based on the traditional pronunciation, that the preposition ב (= בתוך) (in) may express both a definite and an indefinite concept. They have quite a clear understanding to discern in which cases the particle 'in' has assimilated the definite article and in which it has not.[380]

The exposition of this preposition in the contect of "the man with the issue" is of particular interest. In *Lev.* xv, 6, it is stated, "And he that sitteth on anything whereon he that hath the issue sat shall wash his clothes and bathe himself in water, and be unclean until the even". This

---

[377] The word מתים in *Deut.* ii, 34, was explained in a forced way (cf. Ben-Hayyim, *op. cit.* IIIa, p. 95). In the same way, the S.T. renders it משלם in *Deut.* iii, 6. On the other hand, the Hebrew word מתי in *Gen.* xxxiv, 30 is rendered by the S.T. (קליל (מניאן) (Similarly *Deut.* iv, 27; *ibid.* xxvi, 5; *ibid.* xxviii, 62). However, *Deut.* xxxiii, 6, is rendered ויהי מעמה מנין.

[378] S. Kohn, *op. cit.* p. 43 (on פתע *Num.* vi, 9 and *ibid.* xxxv, 22). cf. however, Ben-Hayyim, *op. cit.* II, p. 567, l. 266 (cf. *ibid.* p. 561, ll. 122-123).

[379] Ben-Hayyim, *op. cit.* I, p. ל"ב. The reason for this inclusion may have arisen from the midrashic expositions (e.g. שׁדי). cf. *ibid.* I, p. 216, n. 7; II, p. 595, l 36.

[380] *idem, ibid.* pp. 228f.

verse makes verse 8 *ibid.* almost superfluous. The *Kāfi* [381] explains away
this difficulth by his midrash on the preposition:

> The letter *Ba* in the word בטהור indicates any clean object, and any new clothes
> or garments which become moist thereby are defiled, and should be cleansed
> with water according to the manner ordained, which is practical and carried out
> according to tradition.

The inseparable preposition מ (= מן) (from) is also employed for
midrash, although such usages usually occur when there exists a parallel
expression without the preposition. Usually the comparison of the
two parallel forms clarifies difficulties. Thus, the prohibition on a priest
to marry a divorcee is stated in terms of one who is "put away from her
husband", but in the case of the High Priest it is simply stated in terms
of "one divorced". The *Kāfi* deals with the rpoblem of ordinary priests,
who are not forbidden to marry a virgin after she has been divorced
following on betrothal, (i.e. before the marriage is consummated).
Then he explains these verses as follows;[382]

> But she is prohibited after intercourse has taken place and after manifestation
> of 'indecency'. Because He (M.H. b.e.) said in their (i.e. priests') chapter: "a
> divorced woman" (*Lev.* xxi, 7), not (merely) a divorcee, but (added and) said
> "from her husband". That proves that divorce can take place without (her
> having) "her husband". He meant by (such a case, to wit:) "without her hus-
> band", when no copulation had taken place and she remained a virgin. But
> (as for) the High Priest, she is forbidden to him, whether (she is divorced from)
> "her husband" or (whether she is one of all those) who are called "divorced"
> (i.e. even if she was only betrothed); for He said regarding him "one divorced"
> (*Lev.* xxi, 14) without "her husband", to distinguish him from his family (the
> priests).

The preposition על with its pronominal suffixes is sometimes
expounded, just as are the pronominal suffixes of the verb *or* the noun.
Here again, it must constantly be remembered that the exposition of such
prepositions comes into the consideration of the Samaritan exegete
only in cases where, by using this device, the literal sense can be liberated
from possible distortion. "Thou shalt eat no leavened bread *with it*"

---

[381] والبا فى בטהור يفيد اعنى الطاهر من كل ويتلثق به اله pp. 147ff.
جديده من ملبوش او ملبوش تنجس ويجب ان يطهر بالماء على الوجع
المأمور به ... cf. Abdel Al, *op. cit.* p. 681 (the translation on p. 570, *ibid.* does not
make sense).

[382] *Kāfi* p. 253. cf. Abdel-Al, *op. cit.* p. 710 (translation p. 597). cf. also my article,
op. cit. p. 163, n. 230.

(עליו‎ Deut. xvi, 3) is thus understood to refer to the Passover Offering. The Ṭabbākh [383] takes this preposition as evidence that no-one is allowed to eat leavened bread at a time when the latter may eventually mix, inside one, with the flesh of the Offering. This then is the origin of the prohibition that no leavened bread be eaten after the morning of the the fourteenth day of the first month.

Only in very rare cases are these particles of prepositions with their pronominal suffixes given ididual treatment entirely out of context. Such treatment mainly occurs when they are employed for homiletical purposes as when the preacher is interested in exploiting Scriptural intricacies to point a moral lesson. In this respect then, and insofar as these few cases may be taken into account, at all, their treatment closely resembles the Rabbinic midrashim built on similar lines.[384]

The Ṭabbākh has an interesting interpretation of the particle מ‎ (= מן‎),[385] which is important in that it explains away a certain difficulty occurring in the story of the Garden of Eden. According to Gen. iii, 22, Adam was also prohibited from eating of "the tree of life", while in Gen. ii, 16 only "the tree of knowledge" was forbidden. The former verse clearly creates a theological difficulty, since, whether or not the three of life was included among the permitted ones, this verse indicates that there was an initiation into God' infinite knowledge. Two answers are given, the first being a philosophical one, namely that a condition (such as a command depending for its fulfilment on the freewill of man) does not constitute initiation into the mind of God; the second, quoted by the Ṭabbākh as an alternative opinion, being rather a grammatical one, depending on the preposition mem. According to this opinion, "the tree of life" was not included in the first permission, because it states: "of (מכל עץ הגן‎) every tree of the garden". This preposition is thus a limiting factor, meaning that originally Adam was not allowed to eat of every part, but only of some parts of the garden.

It is instructive to compare, on the other hand, the Karaites' treatment of the same problem. Qirqisāni states bluntly [386] that there are certain cases where a word in scripture is superfluous. One example he

---

[383] f. 75a (SLTh.A, p. 115).

[384] cf. e.g. ibid., f. 58b (SLTh.A, p. 101), on Ex. xii, 3 "Take unto you" and, sup. Part II, n. 479 and text there.

[385] ff. 100a f. (called here ميم التبعيض as opposed to the ميم المركبه which includes everything).

[386] cf. sup. Part II, n. 112.

gives of this is *Gen.* ii, 17, where the word ממנו is superfluous. Judging from this example, the philosophical difficulty remains where it was, since Adam was only prohibited from eating of "the tree of know-ledge".

In later Samaritan literature one finds some more fanciful treatments of the prepositions. In all such cases, however, one is never certain how original such midrashim are. In the majority of cases, they very closely resemble the lengends indigenous to the environment. Often, too, they give the imporession that they are in fact borrowed from outside sources and forcibly attached to Samaritan writings. One example will suffice to illustrate the artificiality of such a midrash. When God said to Moses, "And thou shalt take in thine hand this rod *wherewith* thou shalt do the signs. (בו)" (*Ex.* iv, 17), the particle בו is said to show that Moses had only one rod with which all the miracles were wrought.[387]

However, even in much later literature such forced midrashim derived from prepositions bear no comparison to those of the Rabbis, who made unlimited use of such devices. In comparison with the Samaritans' very sporadic employment of such particles for midrashic expressions, the Rabbis made free use of them both in the Halakhah and the Aggadah.[388]

Adjectives in general are mostly interpreted in conformity with the meaning of the nouns they qualify. In this field the broad contextual unit is even more significant than usual, since it is quite easy to guess the sense of even relatively rare and ambiguous adjectives by inquiring whether they can be explained by the wider thematic unit. There are cases, nevertheless, when an adjective is vitally essential to the definition of the whole context. So in such cases, if this adjective is at all ambiguous, one can expect the most startling results from the exegesis. One of the classic examples of such a 'clarification' is the case of the Hebrew slave. In the *Kāfi*,[389] the adjective 'Hebrew' is understood as being contrasted with Israelite'. Hence there must be three distinct categories of slaves: Gentile, Hebrew, meaning of the descendants of Abraham (e.g. Ishmael-ites, Edomites) and Israelite.[390]

---

[387] *Ex. Commentary, op. cit.* p. 149. It is interesting to note that Marqah in his *Memar* already uses this idea (*Memar,* I, p. 14; II, p. 18). However, his midrash is built on harmonisations and not by exploiting prepositions. cf. *inf.* para (g, 7).

[388] cf. Rosenblatt, *op. cit.* p. 8, n. 43; p. 27, nn. 34, 35; Heinemann, *op. cit.* pp.117, 120.

[389] pp. 258f. (SLTh.A, p. 55).

[390] Although we cannot enter here into the details of the Sam. halakhah, as it deserves a monograph of its own, one can point out that this example is typical of

The adjective 'meek' (עניו) is of course a commonplace in the Hebrew Bible; but for the Samaritan exegete, confined as he is to the Pentateuch for his Scripture, it can become ambiguous to such a degree that he can be led to interpret it as bearing the precisely opposite meaning, i.e. 'powerful', 'strong' 'violent' etc.[391] It seems likely that a midrash of Marqah's on the Seven Miraculous Distinctions with which Moses was glorified by the earth, is in its essence built upon such an understanding (or misunderstanding!).[392]

> The earth glorified him seven times: he wrote at the beginning of Genesis (1) The earth was without form and void (Gen. i, 2); (2) The earth trembled because of him on the third day, as he wrote in the Law, And the whole mountain quaked greatly (Ex. xix, 18); (3) he wrote of the natural state of the earth: And the land will yield its increase (Lev. xxvi, 4); (4) it swallowed up his enemies, as it is written, And the earth opened its mouth and swallowed them up, with their households (Num. xvi, 32); (5) he was elevated [393] above all the descendants of Adam, as he wrote, Now the man Moses was very powerful, more than all men that were on the face of the earth (Num. xii, 3); (6) Exalted is this great prophet Moses, to whom the Lord of the World said, "Go up to (this) mountain of the Abarim" (Num. xxvii, 12; Deut. xxxii, 49); and he ascended mount Nebo, and the Lord showed him all the land (Deut. xxxiv, 1). This was a great wonder, none like it.

The seventh wonder was that the earth listened to his speech (Deut. xxxii, 1). Our main interest here, however, is that Numbers xii, 3 can only be used as a 'glorification' if the adjective עניו is interpretated as bearing the opposite meaning to its true one.

However, the cases in which adjectives are used for the formation of patterns of exegesis are extremely rare in Samaritan literature. Although some of the results which emerge from the midrashim of other groups, when based upon the exploitation of adjectives, are indeed also to be found among the Samaritans, the latter obtain such results by literalist means [394] rather than by dependence on the minute features of adjectives.

Samaritan exegesis. The reason that they draw such distinctions lies in their rejection of the books of the prophets. If they had had Jeremiah xxxiv, or a similar passage, they could never have arrived at this distinction between the 'Hebrew' and the 'Israelite' slave.

[391] cf. Ben-Ḥayyim, op. cit. II, p. 554, ll. 389-390.

[392] Memar Marqah (ed. Macdonald), I, pp. 124f.; II, p. 204.

[393] אסתקף The S.T. renders קוממיות in Lev. xxvi, 13 as סקיפין. Again, no doubt if the Samaritans had made use of the book of Psalms such an interpretation would never have arisen. cf. sup. n. 390.

[394] Taking for example the Rabbinic deductions from the word תמיד (cf. Rosen-

The conjunctions, with the exception of *Waw*,[395] hardly make any new inroads into Samaritan exegesis; and even such cases as appear superficially to be based on conjunctions are in fact much more complicated, and really dependent on other exegetical methods. Marqah [396] presents a long midrash apparently based on the word (אשר), but in reality the determining factor here is the fundamental Samaritan conviction that Abraham knew in advance the exact location of 'one of the mountains'.[397] The postulate that Adam, Noah etc., being all of them righteous, themselves knew the 'place', indicates that Abraham had been previously directed towards a well-known location. So the word אשר in such a verbal clause is to be understood from Marqah's words as a relative conjunction, equivalent to כאשר;

> Hear now a question in connection with what was said to Abraham here. What is the purpose behind the True One's saying to him, when He requested Isaac to offer himself as a burnt offering *"upon one of the mountains of which you were told"* (*Gen.* xxii, 2).[398] When He made it known to him from the beginning of the speech? [399] Return your mind to the question and listen now. The answer: He does not need a second instruction concerning it (i.e. Hargerizim). When he came, supported in righteousness and truth, he sought the place God had chosen. When *he saw it at a distance* (cf. *ibid.* 4), he turned towards it and prayed. When he had finished praying, *he raised his eyes* (*ibid.*); he only raised his eyes from worship — for it was the morning-hour when he would stand and pray. And where was the direction of his prayer, unless towards Mount Gerizim? When

---

blatt, *op. cit.* p. 8, n. 45), one finds the Samaritan approach straightforward and literal (cf. *sup.* n. 359). If we go a step further and examine an extreme Rabbinic exposition of the expression "afar off" (*Num.* ix, 10), the contrast in approach is very obvious, for here even a Masoretic dot on the letter gave the Rabbis grounds for division of opinion in halakhah (cf. Rosenblatt, *ibid.* p. 22). The *Kāfi.* on the other hand, takes this word completely literally (p. 211, SLTh.A, pp. 41f.).

[395] cf. *sup.* nn. 367, 369.

[396] *Memar Marqah* (ed. Macdonald), I, pp. 46f.; II, pp. 74f.

[397] Marqah mentions previously that Enoch ran to this "place", like Abraham did when he was called upon. That the "place" was well known to all the Meritorious is taken for granted by Samaritan exegetes. cf. following notes.

[398] דאמיר which indicates that Marqah understood this passage as if it had been written אשר אמר. It has to be emphasized that the "*u* form" in passive is extremely rare in Samaritan usage, cf. Macuch, *Grammatik*, p. 269.

[399] From the beginning of the speech בזבן דאזדעק it was specified that he must go to "the land of Moriah" which was translated as ארעה מחזיה identifiable with Hargerizim. Furthermore, the expression "a land that I will shew thee" (*Gen.* xii, 1), followed by Abraham's building an altar (*ibid.* 6, 7), also goes to prove that Abraham knew "the place" previously.

he worshipped sincerely, he perceived it by the light (of morning). Do not say concerning *of which you were told*. (*Gen.* xxii, 2) that it refers to what is to come, but to what has been, as the word 'which' (AŠER) makes this clear and explains the matter.

Behold, I shall set out for you true evidence that the word AŠER may express the past. When God proclaimed the Words (*Ex.* xx), did He not say there AŠER HOṢETIKHA (verse 2)? If it referred to what is to come, Israel would not have gone forth from Egypt and would not have stopped to hear this.

The whole midrash is evidently an apologetic exercise to prove that 'the chosen place' was known to the ancestors.

Such occasional fanciful word-plays in the exposition of particles were never intended to become a permanent exegetical method for the Samaritans. If we compare their exegesis even with that of the literalistic Karaites, we are immediately struck by the great divergence, seeing that, for the latter, grammatical variations, alternative usages and sometimes even the presence or absence of a conjunction prompt a keen search for a 'deeper' meaning. This is especially the case with Anan, who finds in such 'deviations' justification for introducing new regulations. Similarly, Karaite Books of Precepts, usually adopting established sectarian customs as their framework, endeavour to find for them the maximum Biblical support by extending hermeneutical devices.[400]

Obviously Rabbinical interpretation, as we have so often observed, deviates even more widely from the literal sense of the Biblical text. Indeed, with the Rabbis it frequently happens that, in the course of their expositions, the Biblical words lose their original sense entirely. In particular, particles and prepositions are forcibly explained away in order to clear the way for midrashic expansions.[401]

To sum up, it may be said that the Samaritans, in contrast with other groups, whose deliberate aim is to find a peg in scripture upon which to hang all their traditions, and who thereafter cannot be satisfied with the simple meaning,[402] are perfectly content with their literalism; for, since they do not go out of their way to seek 'deeper' intimations in the Biblical text, they can always avoid stretching the grammatical forms

---

[400] cf. my article *ALUOS* VI (1969), pp. 112, 123, 147 (n. 118), 161 (nn. 215f.).

[401] Heinemann, *op. cit.* p. 118. For further literature, nn. 121, 123 (*ibid.* p. 246). It is not worth while to enter here into the problem of interjections which are totally ignored by the Samaritan exegetes. Even in Samaritan grammatical works no need is felt to explain their function. cf. Ben-Ḥayyim, *op. cit.* I, p. 262, n. 10.

[402] Rosenblatt, *op. cit.* p. 9, etc.; Heinemann, *op. cit.* pp. 99, 100, 126, 128 etc. Naturally we mentioned only those grammatical and semantical midrashim of the Rabbis which had at least some remote relevance for comparison.

beyond their regular and conventional sense. It would thus be quite inconceivable for a Samaritan exegete to adopt a hermeneutical device which would oppose the literal sense of the text by giving total independence to the individual particles. To his way of thinking, all these particles are merely aids to the comprehension of the whole theme. Atomization of the text can thus only on very rare occasions be permitted to him for homiletical purposes; and even then it must be pursued without actually destroying the simple meaning of the context from which his interpretations are taken.

With regard to Rabbinical exegesis, some scholars have suggested that a clear distinction should be made between their expositions of the words and that of the letters.[403] While in the former case any independence given to individual words must be intended to destroy the plain meaning of the context, in the latter case, namely, the midrashic exposition of letters, the intention must be simply to supplement the ethos of Scripture and not to disrupt the plain sense. Whether we accept such generalisations on Rabbinical exegesis or not, even Marqah's strange plays on the letters are far removed from the Rabbinical system. Not only does the plain meaning always remain unjeopardised by all his fanciful expositions of letters, but it can be stated that even without such fanciful devices Marqah could have achieved precisely the same results along the lines of simple straightforward exegesis. Although these plays on letters [404] do indeed add colour to the midrash, they are much more significant for homiletical purposes than for straightforward textual exegesis. Later expositors, who used such expositions of letters more reservedly would have considered the practice to be less a true constituent of the hermeneutical rules than would even Marqah.

On the other hand, if we compare the Samaritan approach to grammar with that of the Karaites, a far less favourable picture emerges; for, although the Karaites surpass the Samaritans in their strict literalism by placing their whole claim to authenticity on this system, they are nevertheless still bent on 'seeking' Biblical support for all their practices and doctrines. Grammar is thus substituted by the Karaites for the rejected hermeneutical principles of the Rabbis. Admittedly, even the earliest Karaite writers [405] are keen observers of the peculiarities of the

---

[403] cf. Heinemann, *op. cit.* p. 129.

[404] cf. *inf.* para (g, 8).

[405] Qirqisani, who antedates even the earliest Samaritan writers in Arabic, outdoes them in his wide awareness of the Hebrew language. cf. Hirschfeld, *op. cit.* p. 28.

Biblical style, which can hardly be said to be the case with the early Samaritan exegetes. Although this divergence certainly existed between the two groups, a persistent literary influence was exerted on the part of the Karaites. The grammatical observations made by the Karaites, on the other hand, left very little imprint on early Samaritan exegesis, most probably because the latter sensed that, although these grammatical observations were indeed sanctioned by their own creed, the Karaites overplayed the significance of Grammar in their eagerness to point out any slight 'deviations' with a view to utilising them as pegs upon which to hang their dogmas.[406] The Samaritans must have seen through this forcing of the rules; and insofar as they were aware of grammatical rules as such, they never turned them into hermeneutical principles.[407]

G. HERMENEUTICAL RULES

Our lengthy discussions of the grammar and the linguistic aspect of Samaritan exegesis has showh clearly that, in general, their methods of exposition are not governed by any fixed rule. The contrary is in fact the case; for the empirial method of traditional comprehension give rise only to very vague concepts of rule. In marked contrast to the Rabbinical mentality, with its firm belief in the Oral Law of Sinaitic origin, regarded by them as more important than even Scripture itself, the Samaritan exegete does not for a moment expect the Divine Lawgiver to omit anything from the 'perfect written Torah'. Unlike the Rabbis, who hold that the written statutes convey only the bare minimum and who rely for the rest on the Oral Law which can always be inferred from the traditional expositions,[408] the Samaritans hold no doctrine of a Sinaitic origin of the hermeneutical rules, conceived as so designed as to introduce novel matters, not already covered by the written Law. Although it is indeed a widespread and officially accepted beielf that the trained expos-

---

[406] cf. Gottlober, *Bikkoreth etc.*, pp. 92f.

[407] If one is permitted to make any distinction between rules and principles, one would say that the latter are fundamental laws used as a *conscious* basis for reasoning, whereas the former are simply customs or standards to which one should conform. We therefore talk of the Rabbis as having hermeneutical principles and the Samaritans as having hermeneutical rules (i.e. no real consciousness). cf. *inf.* nn. 408f.

[408] Daube, "Rabbinic Methods etc.", *HUCA* XXII (1949), pp. 248ff. As opposed to this, even the most frequently employed exegetical device of the Samaritans, the analogy, lacks defined limits which could guide the exegete concerning the extent of its employment. Even to a lesser degree do Samaritans hold to any 'principles' which may serve as guides for the further application of analogies (cf. *inf.* sub-para. 1).

itor can arrive by logical deductions at details not specifically covered
by the legal codes,[409] such a belief appears to have had but little influence
on the Samaritans. One cannot therefore fairly expect Samaritan exegesis
to operate in accordance with any fixed hermeneutical rules or to formulate any exact terminology for this purpose.

We may occasionally come across expositions which appear to be based
on hermeneutical principles identical with those of other groups. This in
itself however does not prove that the Samaritans are influenced by them,
or are even aware of the existence of such 'rules'. We have already seen
that the hermeneutical principles shared in common by Philo and the
Rabbis do not necessarily prove dependence on either side, since most
of these devices are in fact commonplace throughout the ancient mediter-
ranean world.[410]

Whether we accept that the Rabbis are influenced by Greek rhetoric
or not,[411] and even if they have developed their hermeneutical principles
independently of it, their technical terms still betray at least their familiarity with those of Greek and Latin; so that even if their own system has
been evolved separately and is not therefore really identical with those
other systems, there are at least quite a number of elements present
in it closely parallel to those found elsewhere.[412] If one looks for such
similarities, they are not to be found in the fields of Greek and Roman
dialectics or philosophy or logic, but rather in the jurist's terminology,
which was readily accessible and available in the courts all over the
Roman Empire.[413] Irrespective of some obvious differences, both the
rhetorical system and the syllogism of the Rabbis have this feature in
common with the style of the Roman jurists that they all like to depend
on a highly developed sophistication.

It is therefore of no practical advantage to compare the Rabbinical
hermeneutical rules with occasional empirical parallels of the Samaritans;
for not even the slightest resemblance can be detected between these
two groups. Although it remains true that the mature development of
these Rabbinical rules in their codified forms, the most systematic of
which is "The Thirty-two Middoth" ascribed to R. Eliezer b. Jose ha-

---

[409] *ibid.* nn. 33ff. cf. previous and following nn.

[410] cf. *sup.* Part I, para (e and f).

[411] cf. Liebermann, *Hellenism etc.* pp. 53f. (cf. *ibid.* nn. 54, 58 and 63-64).

[412] Daube, *op. cit.* p. 259 (cf. *ibid.* nn. 69-72).

[413] R. Loewe, "The 'Plain' Meaning etc.", *Papers of IJS London*, I, p. 413 (cf.
for further literature *ibid.* n. 38).

Gelili, is indeed quite late,[414] some Rabbis nontheless employed these rules in essence from the earliest time. Some of these devices, even in in their earliest forms, appear along with their technical terminology just as it is recorded in later sources. The Samaritans lack, not only the terminology, but even most of the devices themselves, which are almost totally unknown in their literature.

Early Karaite exegetes, although they vehemently reject the Rabbinical Oral Law, nevertheless make good use of the established hermeneutical principles.[415] The later Karaites, from Benjamin Nahāwandi onwards, try to find "the golden mean" between the two extremes of a rigid adherence to Scripture, on the one hand, and a pragmatic rationalism, on the other.[416] One may fairly maintain that the Karaites come very close to holding the principles advocated by the Islamic Shi'ah, in that they both alike reject the Oral Tradition. This affinity is plainly recognisable when we review the major tenets shared by these two groups in common namely; (1) Scripture (without oral explanation) (2) Community-consensus of opinion (3) Use of analogy.[417] Admittedly, analogy is an ancient device practised by almost all the groups, but in the case of the Karaites this device is carried to unlimited and even absurd lengths, The principle of community-consensus, not unsuitable for most Islamic groups, was bound to defeat itself amongst the Karaites since these were eternally doomed to be everywhere a tiny minority in the Jewish world. It became therefore progressively identified with tradition, so leading to the unchecked readmission of the very thing which theoretically had been rejected (namely tradition itself).[418] Hand in hand with the many face-saving disclaimers of the principle of tradition, tradition itself actually became a legitimate hermeneutical rule.

Among the Samaritan conversely there is no trace of any such vicissitudes in hermeneutics. Just as they are wholly unimpressed by the fixed hermeneutical rules, so they never totally reject tradition. Indeed, as we have seen already the opposite is rather the case: the stability of

---

[414] Strack, *Introduction etc.*, p. 95 (for further literature cf. *ibid.* nn. 1-3). The mere fact that in our subsequent treatment of Samaritan devices we could class them all under 7 sub-paragraphs shows that any occasional "parallel" to the "32 middoth" are purely coincidental.

[415] Gottlober, *op. cit.* pp. 81f.

[416] Nemoy, "Al-Qirqisāni's account etc.", *HUCA* VII (1930), p. 329.

[417] Gottlober, *op. cit.* p. 91.

[418] Gottlober, *op. cit.* p. 93; Ankori, *Karaites in Byzantium*, pp. 221 (n. 32), 223 (n. 38), 232 (especially nn. 44, 45).

Samaritan exegesis depends on a single-minded approach, in which Scripture and tradition are so thoroughly interpdependent as to form an indissoluble oneness. In contrast to its position among the Karaites, tradition, unsystematised as it is, and not subject to rules, constantly guards their exegesis from deviating from Scripture and from absorbing foreign influences. And not only this, tradition in fact serves as a substitute for fixed hermeneutical rules.

As between linguistics and hermeneutics there is also a parallel development among the Samaritans, which never allows rules to dominate over tradition. If their tradition demands literalism, this is never equated with rigid laws which have to be forcibly carried to illogical extremes. Their literalism again has just sufficient weight to prevent the disintegration of the wider thematic unit. In contrast to the Rabbinical system,[419] it is not the rule which in some cases causes a degree of independence to be granted to the parts of speech, but, on the contrary, the very absence of hermeneutical rules means that any such idea of atomising the *logos* of Scripture never occurs to the Samaritan. As we have seen in countless cases before, and even in those very exceptional ones where a word or a particle has been given a 'new' meaning, the individual word is always strictly related to the general sense of the Scriptural theme. Admittedly, we have occasionally come across almost wilful departure from the 'simple' meaning, but these can generally be attributed to reasons of polemics, or to an inherent textual difficulty, or to the need to explain a peculiarly Samaritan understanding of a certain text. Thus instead of elaborating a consistent 'system', they are preoccupied with details, which in their turn are governed by the sense given to them by traditional exegesis. The most interesting of such cases is the classic example of *Ex.* iv, 24-26. These verses, despite their relatively simple vocabulary, are explained in a specifically Samaritan way, owing of course to theological difficulties arising from them. Munajja is trying hard to create an exegetical rule. His arguments, however, are most unconvincing.[420] He claims that the word 'circumcise' (נמל) in the Pentateuch is always explicitly stated to denote this act. The text in question has in fact the expression 'cut off' (כרת) which therefore must indicate that something else is meant. Apart from the sheer weakness of the argument, by creating such a 'rule' Munajja is only creating further difficulties

---

419 Heinemann, *op. cit.* pp. 102f.
420 *Masā'il al-Khilāf*, Ib, pp. 52f.

for himself, as he now has to explain away למלות ("because of circumcism", *ibid.* 26).

It will not be at all out of place here to look more deeply into this question of the essence of hermeneutical rules. It must at once be said that any group who proudly confessed to possessing such rules, soon discovered that, by using the very same rules, its opponents arrived at entirely different results. To take the extreme cases of allegory and of 'number symbolism', both of which devices were employed by Philo and by the later Kabbalists, the results achieved by these two groups were completely at variance with each other; for while Philo used these devices for 'rationalizing" al antiquated or embarrassing Biblical texts, the symbolism of the Kabbalists led them in the opposite direction. They were interested rather in 'verifying' the supposed 'mythological' content of scripture.[421] There is, nevertheless, some measure of agreement between these two extreme approaches, in that they both rest upon the basic supposition that the Biblical language asserts something different from what, to the uninitiated, it appears to assert.

Moreover, it is not only in such extreme cases that hermeneutical rules, if taken far enough, achieve such extraordinary results. It may even be broadly asserted that all 'rules' present the exegete with the challenge to discover some acceptable means by which he can interpret the written word in a novel way which will thus make it more palatable to himself and his readers.

The Talmud will serve as the best of all illustrations of such a constant development, wherein not only do the hermeneutical rules perpetually create new interpretations, owing to their more and more frequent application, but even the number of such rules is itself constantly increasing.

Thus for instance, the 'Thirty-two Middoth' are certainly not mentioned by this name in the Talmud. We read there [422] however, "whenever thou hearest the words of R. Eliezer b. R. Jose ha-Gelili in the Haggada, incline thine ear, as unto a funnel". And indeed some of these rules at least are not only mentioned separately in the Talmud, but are in fact even older than R. Eliezer. Looking back on the development of the Rabbinical exegetical principles, we can clearly see that Hillel himself, the originator of the first Seven Rules, also employed

---

[421] J.L. Blau, "Tradition and Innovation", *Essays presented to S.W. Baron*, pp. 100f.
[422] cf. Strack, *Introduction etc.*, pp. 95f. (for further literature, cf. *ibid.* nn. 4-6).

the *Heqqesh*, which is not included in his own rules.[423] Hillel's opponents, the sons of Betherah, on the other hand, did not accept his methods of argumentation, based on his exegetical principles, until he had made it clear to them that these rules were firmly based on tradition. There must surely have been oppsition to the hermeneutical rules, and to the midrashim derived by their means, from some die-hard traditionalists.[424] Later, however, the hermeneutical rules were not only universally accepted, but even extended to many new avenues, despite the continuation of the controversy between the two groups. In the later development, when this same controversy was carried on by R. Ishmael and R. Akiba, the former, although indeed relying on tradition more than on the ever-growing influence of the midrash, not only accepted Hillel's rules but even extended them to thirteen. He postulated, however, that the "human" mode of expression found in Scripture should be faithfully followed in exegesis.[425]

R. Akiba, on the other hand, (following his teacher, Naḥum of Gimzo), confidently stated that even what appeared to be the most insignificant word in Scripture had a special meaning. Hence everything without exception contained in the text, must become the subject of a special or recondite interpretation.[426] R. Akiba's pupils carried this dogma to even further extremes. One of the results of this was Aquila's Greek version of the Bible, in which every word was translated literally in order to reproduce in detail the whole Hebrew text wich formed the basis of R. Akiba's hermeneutics.[427]

R. Akiba and his followers are not the only ones to multiply hermeneutical principles; and, despite the relatively 'simple' exegesis of the Tannaim, even the Mishnah demonstrates this same development.[428] The earlier Tannaim, to be sure, especially the conservative ones (like R. Eliezer b. Hyrcanus), employed the hermeneutical rules only to "confirm the words of the Sages". (*Negaim* ix, 3, *ibid.*, xi, 7). Most of them, however, employ midrash as a source of new halakhah, and this practice continues down to the very end of the Amoraic period.[429]

---

[423] *ibid.* p. 94 (cf. *sup.* n. 50). On the general principles of *analogy*, which was very much used by all groups of exegetes, especially the Samaritans, who regarded it as the most important method of exposition, cf. *inf.* sub-para. 1.

[424] Weiss, *Dor Dor etc.*, I, p. 150.

[425] *idem, ibid.*, II, p. 95.

[426] cf. *sup.* n. 51.

[427] cf. *sup.* Part II, n. 446. cf. also Weiss, *op. cit.* II, p. 108.

[428] Strack, *op. cit.*, p. 98 (cf. also nn. 4-9). Rosenblatt, *op. cit., passim.*

[429] cf. my article *op. cit.* pp. 125f. (n. 2).

Owing to this development, even the most novel expositions acquire a sanctity which in earlier times is reserved solely for the ancient traditions. No distinction therefore is made between novel or personal expositions and those "handed down from Sinai".[430] This situation clearly demonstrates that hermeneutical principles, although they certainly create a 'system', do not necessarily preserve the original interpretation for the sake of which such rules were instituted. The best testimony to this evident fact is the interminable controversy amongst Rabbinical scholars as to whether midrash preceded halakhah and is therefore the origin or the halakhic development, or wheter midrash serves only to confirm a halakhah already firmly established by the Oral Law.[431]

The Samaritans, lacking precise and binding hermeneutical principles, and hence obliged to fall back on the guidance of a traditional exegesis and while indeed committed to a fossilised type of interpretation, could at least cling wholeheartedly to their single and unmistakeable 'hermeneutical' assumption that the Biblical text is to be understood in its literal sense. In plain words, they could firmly adhere to the simple principle that the Torah does not assert something different from what it appears to assert.

We may now even go a step further, and state that by the Samaritans the Torah is looked upon as being not only self-explanatory but also as self-sufficient. To their mind it is intended and designed to cover all aspects of human life, being possessed of the perfect form which the Lawgiver explicitly established. Unlike the Rabbinic and the Roman law, both of which regard it as the task of the Lawgiver to lay down the *basic* principles only, from which the applications can then be inferred,[432] the Samaritan exegete relies on the Lawgiver for such matter of detail as, without any sophisticated principles whatsoever, be clearly gathered from Scripture.

Small wonder then that not even the awareness of a need for hermeneutical principles is felt among the Samaritans. Although undeniably they came into contact with alien cultures existing in their own environment, there is no evidence that the hermeneutical principles of any other groups attracted their attention. Obviously the *argumentum e*

---

[430] Jer. *Peah* II, 6; Lev. Rabba XXXII, b.

[431] Karl, "Maimonides etc.", *Tarbiz* VI (1935/6), pp. 398ff. cf. my article *op. cit.* pp. 98, 124f. (n. 1).

[432] Daube, *op. cit.* p. 250.

silentio is never very convincing, nor is the argument that, since some of the common norms arise solely out of man's reasoning faculties, the Samaritans may well have developed them independently and from an instinctive need. If however the more complicated forms show affinities or if they are expressed in almost the same technical manner, the likelihood of total independence is severely reduced.

The real touch-stone for establishing such a relationship is surely the proven awareness of using these hermeneutical principles, leading to their distinguishing them and tabulating them.[433] Amongst the Samaritans, not only is there no trace of any such methodical approach, but the modern scholar, in trying to elucidate their hermeneutics, finds it a most unrewarding task, often producing entirely negative results. Actually, it is by no means clear to what extent we can profitably analyse Samaritan hermeneutics into the components of a coherent system. At any rate, since the Samaritan exegete is not aware that he is following any system, or even that any system should be sought and conscientiously applied, all our analyses must remain tentative. It seems clear that, despite all foreign influences, Samaritan exegesis remains totally unaffected by the hermeneutical rules in use among outsiders.

If we take another look at Rabbinical hermeneutics, we find that, despite their sophisticated rules, no real awareness exists among their exegetes of any distinction between the literal sense of Scripture and the midrash derived from their own rules.[434] It is for this very reason that modern research into the aggadic midrash is not satisfied with following the customary tests for hermeneutical principles, since these in themselves do not reveal the whole basis of the midrashic exegesis.[435] We are confronted with the very same problem in another form when approaching Samaritan hermeneutics.

Our observations while investigating the etymological side of Samaritan exegesis also hold good substantially for our further search into their hermeneutical 'rules'. In both cases it is not the abstract rule which guides the Samaritan exegete, but rather the empirical heritage, which is in fact mostly confined to the understanding of details. Just as the modern orthodox Jew firmly believes in the Sinaitic origin of the hermeneutical principles upon which he bases his belief in the unity

---

[433] *ibid.* pp. 244f.

[434] Loewe, "The 'Plain' Meaning of Scripture", *Papers of the I.J.S.*, I, p. 183.

[435] cf. *sup.* Part II, n. 428.

of the Written and the Oral Law,[436] so likewise the Samaritan exegete mentally cements Scripture and Tradition into one organic unity. This single-minded approach makes him totally dependent on tradition, thus at all times leading him to subordinate any momentary awareness of hermeneutical 'rules' to this one principle.

(1) *Analogy*

If the Samaritans possessed a logically codified hermeneutical system, we could follow it according to the categories in which it was arranged, or alternatively we could rely on a comparison with the norms of one of the other groups. Once we have realized that no such systems exists, the most logical procedure will be to follow an artificial scheme by describing the hermeneutical norms in the order in which they most frequently present themselves to the Samaritan exegetes. For this reason again the question of the possible legal, logical or hermeneutical deductions arising out of such a pragmatic approach [437] is entirely irrelevent to our enquiry. A "logical" approach would probably begin with the most rational law of inferences, i.e. from major to minor, and proceed at a later stage to the method of the comparison of equals or of analogies based on this hermeneutical principle. Since, however, it is not logic but tradition which prompt Samaritan hermeneutics, we must realise that there is not in this tradition itself, any very marked distinction between the various types of comparison. Whether the points in question are really equals, or only what seem to them to be equals, or analogies of motive, based on associative thinking (some of them exhibiting the strangest thought-processes) they all figure equally prominently in Samaritan expositions.

In view of such considerations, then, we cannot be content with simply drawing up a list of such analogies, since very often there is no real awareness on the part of those employing them that they are here following a certain norm. Furthermore, a great number of these anlogies are actually implicit in the context, and only upon a very close scrutiny does the hermeneutical device, if any, make itself evident. As we shall see later, this attitude persists even into the Islamic period, when the *Qiyās* is wellknown and when its very terminology is regularly borrowed and adopted; but, even so there are even now very few clearly defined limits

---

[436] Strack, *op. cit.* p. 95 (for further literature cf. *ibid.* nn. 4-6).
[437] cf. Daube, *op. cit.* pp. 251f.

as to what may or may not rightly be included under the heading of "analogy". Moreover, even during these comparatively late periods, analogy is still occasionally employed without being comprehended under this specific term. It remains on the whole, a widely practiced device and one possessed of almost entirely unrestricted and unstylized possibilities. We shall, therefore, necessarily have to employ this term in its broadest possible sense.

Analogy is thus understood by the Samaritans as originating in, and even as prompted by, Scripture itself, since Scripture manifestly uses this device for equations.[438] The best example of analogy in the Torah appears perhaps in *Ex.* iv, 22-23. Israel is here called the "first-born" of God, and hereby Pharaoh is warned that, if he does not release the Israelites, God will kill his first-born. In the Samaritan Pentateuch this particular analogy with its warning, is repeated just as there are other similar additions in the S.P. containing similar warnings before each plague; and this fact serves as a source for Marqah's further exposition.[439]

> Moses repeated what was said to Pharaoh the king, warning him so that he might be just towards him; "*Thus said the Lord*, the God of the world, *Let the sons of my firstborn go, that they may serve me.* If you do not let them go, *He will kill your firstborn son* (*Ex.* xi, 4f., S.P.) and all the firstborn in your Land. *All these your servants shall come down to me* and ask me to leave, *myself and all the people who follow me, and after that I will go out* (*ibid.* 8).

Similar analogies are likewise based on Biblical precedents. Simply because the Israelites remained unharmed by some plagues, (*Ex.* viii, 18-19; ix, 4; *ibid.* 26; x, 23), it is assumed that such was the case with all the ten plagues. Marqah [440] uses this analogy in connection with the first plague (blood):

> The Egyptians remained in affliction, being also severely oppressed (*Ex.* vii, 19), while Moses and Aaron like two lights shone among the stars of Sarah and Abraham.

---

[438] It is a well known fact that the fuller text of the Samaritan Pentateuch explains 'missing details'. The ethical principle of the punishment fitting the crime is exhibited by the constant warnings to Paroah, which are missing in the M.T. (cf. S.P. *Ex.* vii, 18, 29; viii, 19; ix, 5, 19; x, 2; xi, 4 (= M.T. iv, 22-23). This could easily serve as a pattern for building further analogies on punishments meted out measure for measure. cf. also Heinemann, *op. cit.* p. 64 (and *ibid.* n. 68 for further literature).

[439] *Memar Marqah* (ed. Macdonald), I, p. 20; II, p. 30.

[440] *ibid.* I, p. 17; II, p. 24.

This is explained even more explicitly by Marqah in the course of a very complicated exposition.[441]

In this respect, Marqah is only following an ancient practice of almost universal prevalence. All exegetes endeavour to elucidate the more ambiguous details by means of the more explicit ones, by regarding them as equals and by drawing analogies. This device is considered on all sides as a legitimate method of exposition, and implicitly latent in Scripture itself.[442]

Thus analogy may be used to unravel many obscure problems or indeed any matter which may otherwise provoke great astonishment; here we often find that questions raised by heretics on paradoxical statements appearing in Scripture are explained away by analogies. One wonders for instance how the Israelites (600,000 men, excluding wives, children and a large mixed multitude) could possibly hear the blessings or curses pronounced by the priests, or how they could hear the blessing of Aaron (*Num.* vi, 23). Marqah [443] here uses an analogy from *Ex.* xix, 19 ("Moses spake and God answered him by a voice") and boldly extends this "miracle" to other cases. So, according to him, in all these cases a supreme power amplified the voice so that a vast multitude could hear it.

Such broad analogies mainly based on the comparison of themes or motives, are likewise a common feature, used by almost all Biblical commentators. We find it already in the New Testament, where such analogies are employed to explain even current events by means of Old Testament precedents.[444]

Rabbinical aggadists are also fond of such comparisons, as for instance between the lives of father and son (e.g. Jacob and Joseph or David and Solomon). They take great pains to multiply comparisons and similarities, employing all kinds of analogies in the process, to increase the dramatic effect of their midrash thereby.[445] As a matter of fact, our latter-day

---

[441] *ibid.* I, p. 33; II, p. 50. The first three of the fourteen miracles done through Moses by water is on the same subject (i.e. of the plague of blood). It has, however, to be pointed out that the language is suspect here and it may be a later interpolation.

[442] cf. my article *op. cit.* pp. 108, 142 (n. 84). cf. *inf.* n. 444.

[443] *Memar Marqah* (ed. Macdonald), I, p. 65; II, p. 103. The background of the midrash is not explicitly stated by Marqah but is rather taken for granted.

[444] cf. *Matthew*, xii, 5, where I *Sam.* xxi, 1f. (cf. also *Ex.* xxv, 30; *Lev.* xxiv, 5-9) is employed for analogy. cf. Farrar, *History of Interpretation*, p. 19. cf. also *sup.* n. 442.

[445] cf. Jellinek, *Nophet Zufim*, p. 206; Heinemann, *op. cit.* pp. 60 (nn. 52-54), 62 (nn. 55, 56), 63 (nn. 65f.), 64 (n. 68), etc. cf. also *sup.* n. 124.

commentators on Rabbinic hermeneutical principles find it quite difficult
to classify their analogies. In matters of halakhah especially, they are
hard put to it to clearly distinguish the fine shades of definition applied
to some of these devices, all coming under the heading of "analogy".[446]

We find quite a number of complicated forms of analogy used alike
by the Rabbis and the Rhetors. However, these complicated forms
are also employed on the assumption that one may expect the Lawgiver
to treat the most frequently occurring instances and leave the others to
be inferred by means of analogy.[447] Such an assumption is not shared
in any way by the Samaritans, since even their awareness of the existence
of 'rules' for the exegesis of Scripture is quite undeveloped. There is no
felt 'need' for the seeking and drawing of analogies on a certain fixed
pattern. Not experiencing any such compulsion to apply analogies
systematically, the Samaritans construct the very forms of their analogies in a relatively more primitive and much more naïve fashion.

Even as compared with the early Karaites, who certainly regarded
themselves as literalists, we may still regard the Samaritan analogists
as technically immature. The Karaites, in holding 'Searching' in Scripture
to be a religious obligation, were driven to extend analogy to quite
unconvincing lengths. The Samaritans, although always accepting
analogy as a legitimate hermeneutical norm, nevertheless did not press
this device into the service of deducing new precepts from Scripture.[448]
Another point which divides Karaite analogy from that of the Samaritans is that, whereas the former freely borrowed Rabbinic halakhic
principles, comprising a wide range of analogical rules, all of which were
utilised for the introduction of novel and sectarian halakhic deductions,[449]
the Samaritan employment of analogies was strictly limited to the simplest
forms. Although their analogy is then in itself simple, it unfortunately
often appears in most complicated midrash, where difficulty arises
from the analogy being obscured by a medley of other devices.

Most of Marqah's analogies, as we have seen [450] are of the kind

---

[446] cf. A. Schwarz, *Die Hermeneutische Analogie etc.*, p. 7 (n. 1).

[447] Daube, *op. cit.* p. 250.

[448] These relatively "simple" methods of analogy are evident on the first sight
if compared with those of the Karaites. cf. Wieder, *The Judean Scrolls and Karaism*,
p. 63.

[449] Z. Cohen, *The Halakhah of the Karaites*, pp. 43ff.

[450] cf. *sup.* nn. 120, 439, 440 etc. The best examples of later analogies appear in
the *Kāfi*, in the rules of washing etc. (cf. SLTh.A, pp. 7ff.). All the analogical extensions
of narratives into precepts may be termed very primitive when compared with those

which we may term primitive and naive. Even the most elaborate of his analogies lack any outward signs of closely reasoned thinking or of his even being aware that he is following a logical pattern. All that we can safely say about his analogies (which can also be said about those of early Samaritan literature in general) is that they may be classified into two groups, namely, those which are in the nature of generalized analogies and those which are built up on details.

If we examine the expositions of *Deut.* xxxii, where it is often possible for us to compare Marqah's commentaries with those of the *Ṭabbākh* we can easily verify for ourselves that, despite the historical gap and the environmental changes, the form of analogy has changed very little. Thus the *Ṭabbākh* [451] explains *Deut.* xxxii, 3 ("He set the bounds of the peoples according to the number of the children of Israel") by means of a generalized analogy. It employs for this purpose *Gen.* xv, 18-21 S.P., where eleven nations are mentioned. This number corresponds to the number of tribes "(the sons of Israel" with the exception of Levi, who did not receive an inheritance), and thus we have an analogy of eleven nations with eleven tribes. Later, this analogy is further connected with the promise of *Deut.* vi, 10-11.

However, many of these "wider-type" analogies, although unsystematic and not apparently following any hermeneutical rule, may, nevertheless, turn out to be the most complicated. Often their difficulty arises from the exegete's combination of several devices in the midrash. It is quite common for the first analogy to be built on a 'missing detail', and later to be expanded so as to suggest further analogies.[452] We may even claim that, although for convenience we include all these types under the heading of "analogy", they are in reality nothing else but the associative connections of vaguely similar motifs. Such connections so far from constituting a "system", are the natural results of 'organic thinking'.

One example of this is Marqah's midrash which follows,[453] based on the fact that, as opposed to *Deut.* xxvii, 9, in verse 11 *ibid.* no priests are mentioned. However, once this difficulty is resolved, the analogy proceeds to show that Moses' act was very similar to Jacob's.

---

of the Karaites or Rabbanites. The majority of such 'proof texts' are in one way or another built on analogies. cf. *sup.* Part II, n. 452.

[451] f. 218b. There is another opinion expressed there which is based on an analogy to the nations originating from the tower of Babel.

[452] cf. *sup.* n. 450.

[453] *Memar Marqah* (ed. Macdonald), I, p. 60; II, p. 94.

And Moses charged the people the same day. (*Deut.* xxvii, 11), the priests not being mentioned. Here he said something that his Lord taught him. It is not right for any man to be associated with him in this statement. *And Moses charged the people the same day* (*ibid.*) speaking of what would be manifested then. He showed them what God had said, and revealed to them by what they would be made great. When he began, he divided the tribes with great prophetic insight, those who deserved reproof from those who should not be reproved (*Deut.* xxvii, 12-13). Thus God said to Moses, at the time when He taught him, what was known to Jacob. He divided them, and appointed those for whom there would be a good deed (praise) and those for whom there would be reproof. Moses announced to them the crossing of the Jordan, and, concerning those who would receive the Blessing and who would receive the Curse. O people, be fully awake to what has been done for the tribes and learn perfection.

Moses alone, and not the priests, knew this divine teaching, which was also known to Jacob, who in a similar manner divided his people into "two companies", the concubines and their children first and the wives and their children last. (*Gen.* xxxiii, 2, cf. *ibid.* xxxii, 9, where it is clear that the "first " are more exposed.) From this we may understand the continuation of Marqah's midrash, based this time on another analogy taken from Abraham. This midrash is an answer to the rhetorical question; how could the children of the tribes who stood on Mount Ebal, thereby receiving the curses, come later to celebrate the pilgrimages on Hargerizim? The answer to this question also explains the previous analogy.[454]

You have done right, o questioner, in asking this. The great Powerful One desired to show the origins of their status. The four who were born of the handmaidens, he made them stand on Mount Ebal by his will. The True One purposed to show Israel that the sons of the handmaidens were not like the sons of the homeborn women. So from this it was decided that a firstborn son should not be born of a maidservant, for he could not enter into holiness; in order that this should serve as a lesson, both for the past and the future, that one should refrain from approaching a concubine. As for Ishmael — since Abraham had him by a maidservant, see what he meant to do with Isaac — if it had not been for what was made known to Sarah (*Gen.* xxi, 9), the deed of Cain would have been performed, enacted then.

The final analogy, which compares Isaac and Ishmael with Abel and Cain, is also of course a wellknown analogical motif, since Ishmael is charged by the Rabbis likewise with the three most heinous crimes.[455]

---

[454] *ibid.* I, p. 61; II, p. 95.

[455] cf. Rashi and Nachmanides on *Gen.* xxi, 9 s.v. מצחק and their sources in the Midrash (cf. Tosephta, *Sotah* VI, 6, ed. Zuckermandel, p. 304).

Such analogies on the lines of generalized motifs are the most common in Marqah's expositions. It would, needless to say, take a whole book to indicate all these implicit analogies fully, but fortunately the most self-explanatory ones, detectable by any reader at a glance, occur very frequently.[456] As may be surmised, Marqah is not the only expositor who employs such broad analogies, taking, for instance, a theme from another part of Scripture and by means of it elucidating the passage he is dealing with and which embodies a similar theme. This device is in fact often employed by the *Asaṭir* for the purpose of filling out 'missing details' in Scripture. Hence territories are already allotted to Cain and Abel by analogy with the case of the sons of Noah.[457] In the same context it is even inferred by analogy that each of them marries his brother's twin-sister (of *Gen.* xii, 13; *ibid.* xx, 12 etc.).

Similarly, many details taken from Moses' confrontations with Pharaoh, as for example the court, the magicians etc., are transferred to Abraham's confrontation with Pharaoh (*Gen.* xx).[458] In the same way again details from Abraham's confrontation with Abimelech are transferred to his confrontations with Paraoh. Such analogical devices are thus frequent in the *Asaṭir* legends about the birth of Moses even being transferred to the birth of Abraham, where Nimrod and his court

---

[456] The most obvious examples are in Marqah's comments on *Ex.* xv. Here he makes it quite clear that owing to the Egyptians' denial of the "Ten Miracles", similar plagues were meted out on them on the Red Sea (I, p. 27 = II, p. 43). Similarly the *motif* that all 'punishments' of the Egyptians were 'salvation' to Israel (*ibid.* I, p. 32 = II, p. 48) is based on analogies. Although the notion of "a measure for a measure" was universally known (cf. Heinemann, *op. cit.* p. 67; Rosenblatt, *op. cit.* p. 23, nn. 35-39; Ben-Ḥayyim, *op. cit.* II, p. 483, ll. 131-136; cf. also my article *op. cit.* p. 143, n. 100), Marqah uses it in the same way as other analogies (e.g. I, p. 40 = II, p. 63). Implicit midrashim based on analogies are even more numerous (e.g. comparisons between the coming of the Angels to Sodom in the evening to the Story of the Exodus : I, p. 12 = II, p. 15; I, p. 22 = II, p. 34 etc.). It is also a common feature of Marqah's midrashim that he fills out "missing" details by analogies, e.g. Moses's return to Egypt, *Ex.* iv, 19 filled out with details taken from Abraham, *Gen.* xii, 3 (*Memar*, I, p. 11 = II, p. 13); or Abraham planting trees, *Gen.* xxi, 33 harmonized with *ibid.* xviii, 4, 8 (*Memar*, I, p. 91 = II, p. 148). In order to demonstrate the enormous place which analogy occupies in Samaritan exegesis, it would be necessary to devote a monograph to "Samaritan Law and Lore", a task which still awaits realisation, cf. Epilogue.

[457] Ben-Ḥayyim, "Sepher Asaṭir", *Tarbiz* XIV-XV (1943/4), pp. 11 and 23.

[458] *ibid.* pp. 16 and 37. cf. Gaster, *Asaṭir*, p. 252, n. 1.

are pictured with many of the fanciful details to be found in the stories about Pharaoh.[459]

In ritual matters the employment of analogy is even more wide-spread. We have to emphasise however that analogy by itself is clearly not the sole source of a given precept. More often than not, several hermeneutical devices are conjoined and collated in order to substantiate the precept.

To take in the first instance, rituals connected with worship, analogy is here frequently employed, usually in conjunction with an explanation of the reasons underlying the precept. However, such explanations are often practical rather than theoretical, since they become the occasion of a detailed exposition of the regulations themselves. It must at this point be realised that the idea of a central authority on ritual matters is one of the very fundamentals of all Samaritan religion. This authority is by common consent attributed to the priests, since their prerogative is confidently derived from Scripture. Nevertheless, in those activities of public worship in which all participate, as in the observance of the Passover Offering, the priests could manifestly not supervise the execution by the general populace of all the meticulous details of the ceremony. The *Ṭabbākh* [460] therefore introduces a midrash on *Ex.* xii,3 (and also *ibid.* 47) wherein "all the congregation of Israel" is mentioned. Then follows an assertion (taken as implicit) that the keeping of the command was actually entrusted to the 'elders' (*ibid.* 21), because it was their special responsibility to supervise the detailed execution of the precepts. Since the populace (including children and other ignorant persons) could not be expected to be punctilious, there was an evident need for the lay spiritual-leaders to take this task upon themselves.

We are not concerned with this analogical midrash for its own sake, but rather with the method by which again one analogy is extended by associative thinking to many other fields. By this device the *Ṭabbākh* gives both a 'Biblical' and a logical explanation for this function of the elders, namely, that of lay-leadership.

In a similar midrash dealing with the reason behind the precept on on burning "that which remaineth" (*Ex.* xii, 10) the *Ṭabbākh* [461] draws several fruitful analogies. The expression "be much observed" (שמירים

---

[459] Gaster, *op. cit.* pp. 22ff., 66 (Ch. VII), 243f. One could multiply examples *ad libitum*, cf. however, n. 456 *sup.*

[460] f. 71b (SLTh.A, p. 112).

[461] f. 67a (SLTh.A, p. 108).

ibid. 42) is taken as the source of the other analogies indicating that special care is to be taken to observe every detail of the law.

This type of analogy, however, is also particularly interesting for us because it becomes a general principle. Although the midrashic background is chiefly implicit here, the *Ṭabbākh* is undoubtedly playing on the expression, "To be much observed of all the children of Israel *throughout their generation*" (cf. *Ex.* vii, 42). This and similar expressions become permanently attached to the Samaritan observances, always characterized by their rigorism. We may remind ourselves that שמרים, as the Samaritans think they should be named, are explained by them in this sense, namely, the 'real keepers' of the Law.

Many other matters of worship are explained with the help of analogies, as well as the Laws of holiness and ritual cleanliness, which all exhibit a similar pattern.[462] Most of such analogies we may broadly term "thematic", inasmuch as it is the principles involved rather than the details that are compared.

It is well-known to students of Semitic customs how socially hampered the Karaites were by the very wide scope of prohibited marriages resulting from their austere laws of consanguinity. These were based on

---

[462] Only a few explicit examples can be singled out here (cf. *sup.* n. 456). From an analogy of sequent verses (*Deut.* xii, 5 and *ibid.* 11), it was inferred that all 'tithes' must be brought up to the Chosen Place (*Kāfi*, p. 31; SLTh.A, p. 2). Likewise from an analogy in the case of sacrifices (*Lev.* v, 15 and *ibid.* 16) it was inferred that guilt offerings (with the exception of Burnt Offerings) may be substituted by a payment to the priest (*Kāfi*, p. 235; SLTh.A, p. 52). One could also mention the analogical deductions taken from the Passover Sacrifice (*Ex.* xii, 7) that there are two types of Altars (Sacrificial, and those for prayers, *Ṭabbākh*, f. 64b (SLTh.A, p. 107). cf. also my article in *ALUOS* VI (1969), p. 115f., 151, nn. 141-142. Thus, playing upon the analogy that a person in prayer is likened to a priest, ablutions before prayer were made to appear to be a biblical command (*Kāfi*, pp. 48f.; SLTh.A, p. 11). Similarly the Synagogue is compared to the Sanctuary (*ibid.* p. 102; SLTh.A, p. 16 etc.). Concerning the wide application of the concept of 'holiness' as a source of analogy to prohibit by it conjugal relations on the Sabbath, cf. my article *op. cit.* pp. 112f., 147 (nn. 119-120). Similar sentiments are expressed in the laws of ritual purity (*Kāfi*, pp. 39f.; SLTh.A, pp. 6ff. etc.). As opposed to this and on the strength of an analogy to certain vessels which can be cleansed from defilement only by fire, sins are described as defiling in a way that they cannot be purified by fire. It is also stated that this principle of analogy may be further extended. (*Kāfi*, p. 158. وهذه اصول ا وينقاس عليها ما هو مشابه لها cf. also Abdel Al, *A Comparative Study etc.*, p. 688 and translation p. 526).

analogies stretched to extreme lengths.[463] Although the Samaritans also of course employed analogy for guidance in the sphere of family life, prohibited degrees of kinship etc.,[464] these inferences were always kept within the framework allowed by the simple forms of analogy found throughout Samaritan exegesis. In following their traditionally moderate approach to analogy, in which the relevent context was not disrupted and never unduly stretched, they never reached such extremes as the Karaites did.[465]

In matters of civil law the use of analogy is actually prompted by the very text of the Samaritan Pentateuch. Thus, for example, in many instances when it is dealing with animals, their text itself will add "or

---

[463] The earlier Karaites (בעלי הרכוב) considered husband and wife as being "one flesh" (cf. *Gen.* ii, 24) and therefore prohibited any marriages between their respective relatives. For example, if a woman married several times (after being divorced or widowed) the relatives of all her husbands became forbidden to each other, cf. Qirqisāni, *Kitāb al-Anwār etc.*, XI, 1-20 (ed. Nemoy, V, pp. 1115ff.); Hadassi, *Eshkol ha-Kofer*, alphabetha 315-325 (pp. 115d-128b). The reformation of these austere laws is accredited to Joseph Albaṣir (XIth century). He was opposed to the unlimited power of analogy which led to all these absurdities. cf. Aaron b. Elijah, *Gan 'Eden*, f. 130a f.; Aaron b. Joseph, *Sepher ha-Mivḥar* on Lev. xviii, 12-13; Bashyatchi, *Addereth Eliyahu*, f. 149c f.; cf. also Hadassi, *op. cit.* alphabetha 338ff.; pp. 124a ff.; Pinsker, *Lickute etc.*, II, pp. 65ff., p. 172 etc.

[464] Very typical is the *Kāfi* (p. 271; SLTh. A. p. 63). The discussion of Jūsuf Ibn Salāmah revolves on the exegesis of *Lev.* xviii, 4. All prohibitions concerning forbidden marriages are of an everlasting nature in which no change whatsoever may be introduced. They are termed "judgements" (משפט) and "statutes" (חוק). Both "judgements", i.e. the wisdom of the application of the Scriptural commands, and "statutes", i.e. the wisdom of analogical inferences, its proper understanding and perseverance (معرفة علم اصناف القياسس وادراكها حفظا) depend entirely upon *tradition.*

[465] To illustrate the naive mode of Samaritan analogies it is sufficient to follow the explanations given to the meaning of "uncovering the nakedness of one who is near of kin". *Kāfi*, pp. 271f. (SLTh.A, pp. 64f.). Various other laws of marriage are based on analogy for clarification of details. Thus for example, after establishing the laws of Marriage Contract and Dowry (based on *Ex.* xxii, 16) it is inferred by analogy that in the case of divorce, the Divorce Bill (*Deut.* xxiv, 1) is also accompanied by payment. *Kāfi*, pp. 256ff. Cf. also, concerning the dowry of a widow, *sup.* Part II, n. 537. However, we cannot enter here into more details, cf. *sup.* n. 456. A general comparison of the *Kāfi* and the *Ṭabbākh* indicates that in both works the employment of analogy is similar and based on the same traditions (cf. Abdel-Al, *op. cit.* pp. 160ff., pp. 253ff. etc.). At any rate the Samaritan type of exegesis and analogy has nothing in common with that of the Karaites (*idem, ibid.* pp. 255f.).

any other animal".[466] It is therefore always easy to employ analogy to extend a law referring to "an ass" or to "an ox" to other similar animals.[467]

In order to discover all the precepts which are elucidated by broad analogical themes, it is an essential prerequisite that all the midrashic details of the laws should be thoroughly investigated. Such a task, which would entail minute comparisons and evaluations of the sources of Samaritan law as reflected in the whole literature pertaining to legal matters, is one which is obviously outside the scope of our present research.[468]

Again, in the field of aggadic exposition, there are countless cases in the literature of the Arabic period where analogies of this wider type are employed. The exposition by the *Tabbākh* of aggadic sections like that of *Deut.* xxxii, etc., although it is less fanciful than Marqah's, nevertheless in its employment of analogy presents us with an almost complete identity of approach, in spite of the centuries which divide them. This is most noticeably the case in matters of eschatological exposition.[469] Even in non-eschatological expositions, however, Abū'l Ḥasan likes to indulge in analogies. Thus, for example, *Deut.* xxxii, 26f. is explained by an analogy taken from *Deut.* ix, 14, indicating that had it not been for the interception of Moses, God whould havce destroyed Israel.[470] One could find many other examples explicitly built on such analogies,[471] and even more of the kind in which the analogy is not so prominent but is rather implied.

---

[466] *Ex.* xxi, 28-36; *ibid.* xxii, 3; *ibid.* xxiii, 4, 12 etc.

[467] cf. my article *op. cit.* pp. 103f., 137f. (nn. 46-50). Again, to use one well known example : the expression חמור (*Ex.* xiii, 13; *ibid.* xxxiv, 20) was extended to include all 'unclean' animals (*Kāfi*, p. 310). Strangely enough this extension is also known to Philo (cf. Heinemann, *Philons... Bildung*, p. 35, n. 1), the *Peshitta*, and even to some Rabbinical sources (cf. Mekhilta, *ad. loc.*; *Bekhoroth*, 5b). We cannot enter into the vexed question of the interpretation of וערפתו cf. Ben-Ḥayyim, *op. cit.* pp. 551f., ll. 329-330.

[468] cf. *sup.* n. 456.

[469] cf. *sup.* nn. 100, 189-194, 227, 303 etc.

[470] *Tabbākh*, ff. 224a f. On parallel thought in Marqah's exegesis, cf. my article *op. cit.* pp. 107, 141 (nn. 79-80). cf. also *sup.* nn. 373-374 and text there.

[471] Abū'l Ḥasan (*ibid.*) in his explanation of *Deut.* xxxii, 28-30 (why "there is no understanding in them") gives as the main reason that they forgot God's miracles. Further, he draws an analogy from *Num.* xxxi, 5-8 to show that only 1200 Israelites were involved in the war against the Midianites. The number of the Midianite warriors is then calculated from the number of the captive young women (32,000, *ibid.* v. 35), explaining by it *Deut.* xxxii, 30.

In later literature, although the majority of such analogies are now hidden behind a facade of fanciful and intricate midrashim, they are still easily recognisable, and in substance very similar to the earlier ones.[472]

What we have already termed 'a limited analogy' may be further sub-divided into two classes, the first one consisting of analogies depending on details (as opposed to a wider thematic motif) and the second consisting of those built on single words or expressions. Whether the Samaritan exegete himself was aware of such distinctions is very doubtful; for our purpose, however, the distinction is significant. While the analogies of the first class do indeed, in the majority of cases, fall into the same category as the thematic analogies, being built on associations which do not distort the sense of the thematic unit, those of the second class are entirely different, for the latter may often cause a total atomisation of the text, as is in fact the case with the Rabbinic *Gezerah Shawah*.[473]

---

[472] To take a midrash based on a variant reading, we may quote again the *Exodus Commentary* (attributed to Ghazal al-Duweik), pp. 29f. on *Ex.* i, 12 (M.T. ירבה; S.P. יפרה; a harmonisation with *ibid.* v, 7?). Playing upon an implicit analogy that "the fruit of the womb" is meant (cf. *Gen.* xxx, 2; *Deut.* vii, 13; *ibid.* xxviii, 4 etc.), a long exposition follows to show that the Egyptian plot against the Israelites, namely, to reduce their fertility by separating the sexes, prohibiting married life, achieved the opposite results. (Obviously the same midrash could have been built on the M.T., since both of the variant words often appear together, as in *Gen.* i, 22, 28; *ibid.* ix, 1, 7; *ibid.* xxv, 11. In fact the Rabbis based the same midrash on *Deut.* xxvi, 7. cf. *Siphri*, *ad loc.*; *The Passover Haggadah*; *Yoma*, 74b; cf. however, *Soṭah*, 12b.) From this point the *Ex. Com.* continues with other analogies on יפרץ as referring to wealth (cf. *Gen.* xxx, 43) and on ויקצו where the comparison is extended to the Moabites (*Num.* xxii, 3 ויקץ), who are known for their cunning in trying to overcome the Israelites by deceit. Here the way is open to introduce more analogies concerning Balaam (*ibid.* p. 30) etc. Such digressions are characteristic to this *Commentary*. Thus the case of Moses who "was keeping the flock" (*Ex.* iii, 1) immediately calls for an analogy with Jacob (*ibid.* p. 85). It is not easy to determine the extent of genuine Samaritan traditions incorporated in these midrashim, despite the fact that the motif of "separating the sexes" is certainly an ancient tradition. This was already extended by the *Asaṭir* and transferred by analogy to Nimrod in the story of the Birth of Abraham. cf. Miller, *The Sam. Molad Mosheh*, pp. 90ff. (cf. *ibid.* n. 463). The most complicated problem is the excessive employment of analogies in eschatological speculations, which is evident from the *Hillukh's* discussion of the "Garden of Eden". Cf. Gaster, *The Sam. Oral Law etc.*, I, pp. 179ff. These problems, however, must await further study. cf. *sup.* nn. 456ff.

[473] Strack, *Introduction etc.*, pp. 94, 285f. (nn. 4-5); Heinemann, *op. cit.* pp. 122f. cf. also Liebermann, *Greek & Hellenism*, pp. 195f. We cannot enter here into the

We may begin by discussing the first type, since these are very similar to the broader analogies which we have just examined. We have seen, while dealing with the exposition of nouns, that the expression 'the place' becomes a synonym for Hargerizim. The reason for this identification lies in such expressions as are found in *Deut.* xii, 5, 11, 14, etc. where the Samaritan Pentateuch reads "God *has* chosen" (M.T. יבחר S.P. בחר). From this we can see that, despite the fact that the expression "the place" plays the dominant part in the analogy, it is rather a conceptual unit than a single word. This is the real reason why the analogy based on the expression 'the Place' is not extended indiscriminately.[474]

When analogies of this type occur they are still firmly connected with the thematic unit. While discussing the differences between a passover-offering made on Hargerizim (in the sanctuary) and sacrifices offered elsewhere, the *Ṭabbākh* [475] employs an analogy based on the expression 'the place'; it quotes *Gen.* xxviii, 17 to prove that Hargerizim is the most distinguished and hallowed place on earth. This however is not a merely mechanical play on the similarity of the words. The reverse is the case, namely, that, since Samaritan tradition connects Jacob's dream with Hargerizim, all expressions contained in the passage "How dreadful is this place; this is none other buth the house of God and this is the gate of heaven" are instinctively employed for further analogies.

Marqah's midrashim, which often appear to be dependent on analogies of single expressions, are likewise certainly not merely mechanical handlings of words to introduce novel elements into the text. Such analogies are designed far rather for increasing the emotive effect of the midrashim.

---

problem whether 'analogy' and the inference *a minor ad majus* belong together as one hermeneutical device as σύγκρισις (cf. *idem, ibid.* pp. 190ff.). Although, as we will see later, the boundaries of Samaritan devices cannot be strictly defined, since Samaritan exegesis lacks precise technical terminology, we have to follow a division which looks most natural from a Samaritan point of view. Admittedly, many details classified by us as 'harmonisations' etc. include, nevertheless, elements of analogy. Our classification follows the naive Samaritan approach in which there is no trace of Greek rhetorical influence.

[474] One could expect that verses like *Ex.* iii, 5 may have lent themselves to such analogies. The alleged identification of Sinai (or Mount Nebo) with Hargerizim cannot be traced in Samaritan exegesis. cf. recently H.G. Kippenberg, *Garizim und Synagoge*, p. 227, n. 159. Moses' vision of Hargerizim is a midrash on *Deut.* xxxiv, 2 (S.P.). Thre great miracle of "seeing the land" naturally included the "chosen place". cf. *Memar Marqah* (ed. Macdonald), I, p. 125 = II, p. 204. On further midrashim on מקום cf. *inf.* nn. 492-3 and text there.

[475] f. 86a (SLTh.A, p. 126); cf. *sup.* n. 132.

The employment of 'darkness' for analogizing the Ten Plagues of Egypt with similar ones at the Red Sea, *Ex.* xiv, 19, 20 [476] is not nearly as artificial as it looks. The analogy itself is in fact built on the theme, well-known from the Biblical text itself, that the stubborness of the Egyptians after the Ten Plagues did not at all diminish. A natural deduction from this would be that they deserved the very same punishment for their second offence at the Red Sea. Not only then does this analogy not destroy the sense of the whole context, but it actually strengthens the original contextual unit.[477]

Many other examples illustrating those of Marqah's analogies which are based on details exhibit the same trend. The feature that all these examples hold in common is that no analogy is ever employed which runs contrary to the wider thematic unit in which it occurs.[478]

Even in later literature, when such small Scriptural units are explained by analogy, the theme of each context is not seriously impaired by the comparison.[479]

One may conveniently sum up this type of "analogy of details" by describing it as a support to, or a slight amplification of the theme with which it is associated. No attempt is ever made to forcibly apply this device, or to utilise it to import a totally foreign or external idea into the 'literal' sense of the context. We may profitably relate this consideration to what we have observed earlier when dealing with problems of semantics.[480]

Just as the synonyms, so often employed in the Biblical style, do not

---

[476] cf. *sup.* nn. 335f. and text there.

[477] As for the plague of 'darkness' in Egypt, Marqah (*Memar*, I, p. 20 = II, p. 29) explains the reason for their three day's arrest ("fettered in iron") by employing the analogy which compares *Ex.* x, 23 to *Deut.* iv, 20.

[478] Often Marqah's analogies are motivated by the desire to elucidate "missing details" in the text. Thus, for instance, in the story of Aaron's rod turning into a serpent before Pharoah (*Ex.* vii, 8f.) there is no explicit "message". So Marqah adds it by analogy (*Memar*, I, p. 14 = II, p. 19) : "Thus has He spoken, Let Israel go! just as He said in the first occasion" (cf. *Ex.* v, 1f.). Similar warnings (more than the additional texts in S.P.) are repeatedly supplied by Marqah through analogies (cf. *ibid.* I, p. 16 = II, p. 22). cf. also *ibid.*, "When it swallowed up the rods... yet there was no increase in its size". cf. my article, *op. cit.* pp. 110, 143, nn. 99-100 etc. Even the more daring 'verbal' analogies of Marqah (cf. *sup.* n. 96) are of this kind.

[479] Miller, *The Sam. Molad Mosheh*, pp. 190, *Deut.* xxxii, 36 analogized with *ibid.* viii, 16; or *ibid.* xxxii, 43 with *ibid.* viii, 16, 192 (*Ex.* xxxiii, 11 analogized with *Deut.* iv, 7) etc.

[480] cf. *sup.* para (e, 2).

provoke the imagination of the Samaritan exegete to invent plausible reasons for their presence, as is everywhere the case with other groups,[481] so too they remain quite unimpressed by the power which analogies can lend to exegesis. The use of spurious "analogies", based solely on an external similarity of expression, hardly ever feature in Samaritan literature. It is perhaps needless to say that analogies suggesting allegorical interpretations are again completely unknown here. Moreover, the strict form of the Rabbinic *Gezerah Shawah* is all but unknown among the Samaritans. As we shall see later, there are indeed cases of single words being employed for analogies, although they appear in different thematic contexts. However, these cases are in no way identical with *Gezerah Shawah*. The latter is in the true sense a *mechanical* analogy, because it employs identical words in a very arbitrary way. These identical words, though appearing in two separate Biblical passages, are nevertheless subjected to the same application, no matter how much the themes of the two contexts may, and do, differ.[482]

It may be true that originally even the Rabbinic *Gezerah Shawah* was based on strictly rational premises. The exposition of identical expressions analogically was also undoubtedly a legitimate device among the rhetors (δὶς λεγόμενον). However, in Rabbinic literature, at least from Hillel's time, the *Gezerah Shawah* came to be so intensively applied that its presumably logical prototype retreated into the background. In view of this situation the Rabbis felt the need to restrict this hermeneutical device severely and to allow its application only after certain stipulations limiting its use had been laid down.[483] How far these regulations were in fact adhered to is still a matter of dispute. In general, however, singularly little concern was expressed when this hermeneutical device commonly led to the 'simple' meaning of the context being distorted.[484].

Both the Rabbis and the Samaritans unreservedly acknowledged the *unity* of the Torah. It was therefore only the logical outcome of such a belief that expressions from one context should be freely utilised in

---

[481] cf. *sup.* para (d, 3). As compared with other groups, cf. Rosenblatt, *op. cit.* p. 4 (nn. 37-38); Farrar, *op. cit.* p. 151.

[482] cf. *sup.* n. 473.

[483] A. Schwarz, "Die Hauptergebniss etc.", *Scripta Univers... Hierosolymitanarum etc.*, I, pp. 3f.

[484] The rule laid down, that a *Gezerah Shawah* is valid only if it does not contradict the literal sense of Scripture (cf. *Kethubboth*, 38b), was not strictly enforced. cf. *Yebhamoth*, 24a (on *Deut.* xxv, 6).

order to illuminate those of another. But, while sharing this common ground, their approaches differed very radically. The Rabbis totally ignored the *logos* of the context in favour of their expositions [485] whereas the Samaritans, on the other hand, always held fast to the unity of the context. In their view, no 'explanation' could claim the right to destroy the natural meaning of the context.

In this respect the Karaites resembled the Rabbinites much more closely. For despite their claim to literalism, one finds the most bizarre verbal analogies in their exegesis.[486]

It is a familiar fact that Marqah is very fond of employing verbal analogies which, upon a superficial view, resemble the Rabbinical *Gezerah Shawah*. To take an extreme example, in his sixth miracle et the Red Sea, he comments as follows:[487]

> *The Sixth*: The Red Sea was split when it saw the sea of prophethood at the Lord's command. There was a way prepared in the midst of it for the hosts of the Lord — such a wonder as never was and never will be.

This analogy of Marqah's appears at first sight banal, since it is not clear what the relationship between the sea and prophethood is. Besides, there is no Biblical allusion to the "sea of prophethood". The midrash is in fact based on the expression "strong east wind" (*Ex.* xiv, 21) which, according to the Hebrew may also mean 'ancient spirit' (רוח קדים). Once we realize this, the analogy is not so strange after all: When Moses "stretched forth his hand over the sea", God moved His 'ancient spirit', which was like a sea of prophethood. (cf. *Num.* xi, 5; *ibid.* xxiv, 2.). Evidently the Red Sea could not withstand this 'spirit'.

Despite the strangeness of the analogies in this midrash, they manifestly do not disrupt the context, neither do they import into it external ideas which were entirely lacking before such analogies were introduced.

Another strange midrash of Marqah's is the one on the letter ט representing 'good' (טוב), which is inherently rich in analogies, all

---

[485] Rosenblatt, *op. cit.* p. 2, n. 8; Heinemann, *op. cit.* pp. 66, 67, 122f. (cf. also *ibid.* n. 148).

[486] 'Anan the founder of Karaism is notorious for his strange analogies : Gottlober, *Bikkoreth etc.*, p. 80; Z. Cohen, *The Halakhah of the Kar.*, p. 43; Nemoy, *Karaite Anthology*, pp. 17, 18 etc. cf. also my article, *op. cit.* pp. 112, 147 (n. 118).

[487] *Memar Marqah* (ed. Macdonald), I, p. 33; II, p. 51. Admittedly the language of this passage is suspect of being a later interpolation. However, this does not detract from the value of this evidence, since in later generations the analogy was employed in an even more limited scale.

dependent on this single word.[488] If however one probes it more closely, one finds these analogies are in no way indiscriminate. It is not any arbitrary connotation of 'good' which serves as the source of the midrash, but rather, on the contrary, the fact that such a word is deliberately sought out and utilized according to a preconceived plan. According to the Samaritan mentality, it is in every way natural that the Creation, Adam, Moses and the Law who are frequently associated in such analogies should represent 'perfection'. It is not so much, then, the word 'good' in itself which suggests this interpretation but rather the whole corpus of Samaritan theology. in that it is built on the concept of the perfect Creation, of the perfection of humanity and of the perfection of Moses' revelation.

The more daring of Marqah's verbal analogies are to be discovered only between the lines of his expositions. Some of these analogies come very close, be it said, to the ones in Rabbinic aggadic expositions.[489] There is, however, one fundamental difference which cannot be overlooked. Quite apart from the fact that Marqah never extends his temporary plays on words into a universal and all-embracing hermeneutical rule, it is certain that, when a far-fetched analogy is embodied in his midrash, even this does not contradict the context. It may be further affirmed that the ideas behind his analogies are not entirely foreign to new context in which they appear. There is thus no attempt on his part to rob the context of its plain meaning by replacing it by an entirely new dimension from outside. Although this is of course a generalization which may well have some rare exceptions, analogy in general is only of secondary significance in his exposition. The same or similar morals could

---

[488] *Memar Marqah* (ed. Macdonald), I, p. 138; II, pp. 225f. cf. also P.R. Weis, "Abū'l-Hasan... on the Calendar etc.", *BJRL* XXX (1946), p. 150 (*ibid*. n. 1)

[489] It would be quite impossible to quote here at length even a part of such midrashim, all awaiting further study (cf. *sup*. nn. 456f.) All one could do is to hint to some *analogies* without entering into the complicated details of these midrashim: Moses "saw it (i.e. his hand) that it was dead without any flesh" (I, p. 10 = II, p. 11), cf *Num*. xii, 12; for the analogies on את (I, p. 37 = II, p. 56), cf. *sup*. Part II, n. 283 the strenuous midrash on "bogging down" the Egyptians in the Red Sea (I, p. 39 = II p. 60) is based on the analogy of אסר (*Ex*. xiv, 6; *ibid*. 25, S.P. ויאסר) (cf. Macuch, *Grammatik*, pp. 38f.); the midrash on *Ex*. xv, 14 (I, p. 45 = II, p. 71) is based on the analogy חיל = איל, the ram of Isaac, *Gen*. xxii, 13; and that on *Ex*. xv, 15 (*ibid*.) on אלופי (cf. *Gen*. xxxvi, 15f.); the eschatological homily on the Taheb (I, p. 110f. = II, p. 184) is in itself a complex of analogies, the centre of which is עמו *Deut*. xxxii, 36 and *ibid*. 9 (S.P.) and ראו *Deut*. xxxii, 39 and *ibid*. iv, 5; there are also further analogies of this type (I, p. 112 = II, p. 189 etc.).

have been secured simply by homiletical edification and entirely without resorting to 'hermeneutical norms'.

In many cases analogy is introduced in the interests of harmonization and of explaining away difficulties. Here too one example may suffice to illustrate how in such cases analogy has still only a secondary role. We have already mentioned the midrashic elements associated with Moses' rod. The simple explanation, that Moses gave his rod to Aaron for carrying out their joint mission with its aid, would read quite naturally. However, both Marqah and the *Asaṭir* here prefer to use an analogy.[490] Both rely on *Ex*. iii, 12: "This shall be the token (הָאוֹת) unto thee". This verse and others, especially *Ex*. iv, 17 (אוֹתֹת), create the analogy that all 'signs' (miracles) are wrought by the selfsame rod. The same general picture emerges from later aggadic literature, where analogies or simple expansions are employed in a very similar manner.[491]

In halakhic problems also, in those cases where analogy is based on a single word, it still follows the same pattern as the wider-type analogy. The most fruitful example is the command concerning the Sabbath, "Abide ye, every man in his place". (*Ex*. xvi, 29). Here the nature of the prohibition against going out on the Sabbath depends on the analogical elucidation of the word 'place'. The *Kāfi* [492] offers three possible analogies: (1) a wider one referring to w whole country (*Ex*. iii, 8), (2) a narrower one referring to a city (*Deut*. xxi, 19), (3) a restricted one referring to a part of the body (*Lev*. xiii, 19). As the analogy is not being drawn arbitrarily but with regard to the context, the second possibility is chosen. Here again, as in many other cases,[493] it is not the formal verbal similarity which determines the true form of the analogy. Unlike the procedure in *Gezerah Shawah*, the suitability of the analogy to the context ultimately determines whether it should be applied or not.

In the example just quoted, the drawing of the analogy is done in conformity with principles that have been laid down previously, namely

---

[490] *Memar Marqah* (ed. Macdonald), I, p. 7 (= II, p. 7); Ben-Ḥayyim, "Sepher Asaṭir", *Tarbiz* xiv-xv (1943/4), pp. 19 and 44. cf. *sup*. n. 387.

[491] On analogies for eschatological speculation (*Gen*. xv, 8f.), cf. Merx, *Der Messias oder Ta'eb etc.*, p. 53. cf. also *sup*. nn. 472, 479.

[492] p. 103 (SLTh.A, p. 16). cf. however *sup*. n. 474.

[493] The best example is the discussion of לַעֲשׂוֹת in the *Kāfi* (pp. 84f.; SLTh.A, pp. 14f.) where the final analogy is determined by the context and *tradition*. For further examples cf. *sup*. Part II, n. 630. The *Ṭabbākh* employs likewise such analogies. One of these midrashim (f. 221a) on *Deut*. xxxii, 13 (S.P. תְּנוּפַת) is based on analogy with *Lev*. vii, 34 (and *ibid*. x, 14-15) (cf. Macuch, *Grammatik*, p. 110). This is very close to the exegesis of Marqah (cf. *sup*. n. 250).

that 'going out' from one's place for prayer, study and the like is allowed
on the Sabbath on other grounds. The analogy is thus here only a support
or a harmonizing device to aid the main theme.

To realize the real gulf between the Samaritans' simple analogies and
those of the *Gezerah Shawah* type, we must examine the limits imposed
on analogy by the Samaritans themselves. The Rabbinical *Gezerah
Shawah*, not unlike its parallels in rhetoric,[494] extended inferences by
analogy, even if they are based only on a single expression. Although
indeed there existed among the Rabbis some restrictions to prevent the
abuse of this device, their whole purpose was virtually nullified, inasmuch as it was still considered a general 'rule'. All rules of this type, like
the 'rule of equivalence ' so prevalent in scholastic systems even despite
the restrictions imposed on it, lead to the isolation of phrases, neglect
of the context, distortion of the original sense etc.[495]

As opposed to all these free usages of analogy in other groups, the
Samaritans, since they do not regard analogy as a recognised hermeneutical rule, do not extend ist employment beyond its natural traditional bounds. It seldom happens that novel extensions of the given
meaning of the context are formulated on the basis of a free analogy.

The best way to illustrate this severely limited usage of analogy will
be to reconsider the practice in its bearing on the laws of forbidden
marriages, The *Kāfi* [496] states that these laws depend on the principles:
i.e. "as understood from the (Biblical) text and as deduced by analogy

---

[494] Daube, "Rabbinic Methods etc.", *HUCA* XXII (1949), pp. 251f. (cf. nn. 44ff.).
It is not our concern here to inquire into the vexed questions whether such parallels
point to dependence, or whether one could precisely distinguish between the various
types of Rabbinic analogies (cf. *sup.* nn. 446, 473 etc.). The long list of analogies
based on single words in the Mishnah alone (cf. Rosenblatt, *op. cit.* pp. 28f.) shows
sufficiently the extent of this practice in the earliest Rabbinical sources. As for later
controversies in the Talmud and the distortion of the literal sense of the text by
verbal analogies, cf. R. Loewe, "The 'Plain' Meaning etc.", *Papers of the Institute
of Jewish Studies*, I, pp. 164f. (cf. *ibid.* nn. 110-122). There were also cases of double
application of analogies to the same context, cf. Strack, *Introduction etc.*, pp. 97
(rule 21) and 293f. (n. 25).

[495] Farrar, *History of Interpretation*, pp. 22, 271. Even some contemporary exegetes
accept the validity of analogy. They are, however, more selective in its application
and are confronted with the task of distinguishing between various types of analogies.
Smart, *The Interpretation of Scripture*, p. 125.

[496] cf. also على الاوام الشرعيه نصوصها وعكوسها وقياساتها : 241 .p
sup. n. 464 and Abdel Al, *op. cit.* p. 702 (transl. p. 573).

from it". The same opinion is also expressed in the *Ṭabbākh*;[497] and in order to gain a more precise picture of the limitations imposed on analogy, it is more profitable to follow the argument outlined in the latter as it is more systematic in this respect. Abū'l Ḥasan does not stop at merely citing the relevant analogies and the forbidden relationships revealed by them; for, while compiling a long *responsum* on a complicated problem most probably reflecting Karaite practices, he deals at the same time with the established principles of analogy. The actual question itself, which concerns the eligibility for marriage of parties with no blood-relationship whatever (e.g. of a man wishing to marry his son-in-law's sister's daughter), he answers in the affirmative. From his answer it is also evident that there were some Samaritans who, on the grounds of a false analogical rule (most probably under Karaite influence), sought to invent restrictions which Samaritan tradition did not prescribe. It has incidentally already been pointed out that the practice of analogy, as found in the *Ṭabbākh*, is almost coextensive with his opinions as to which traditional practices should be followed.[498]

More important however for our purpose are Abū'l Ḥasan's prescriptions of the extent to which analogy may be applied. He does not, interestingly enough, formulate any positive rules for creating analogical inferences. He is in fact quite content with laying down purely *negative* conditions as to how to avoid the abuse of this device. His first limitation is that the source of the analogy must be firmly established in Scripture. It will be worthwhile to quote his own words here:[499]

---

[497] cf. *sup.* Part. II, n. 508. In the same context Abū'l Ḥasan repeats the assertion that these laws are derived from both scripture and analogy (e.g. من طريق نص وقياس f. 46a etc.), cf. following notes.

[498] This subject is discussed in great detail by Abdel Al (*op. cit.* pp. 638ff.; translation 434ff.). Recently it was also summarized by S. Noja, "Abū al-Ḥasan al Ṣūrī's Discourses on the forbidden Degrees of Consanguinity etc.", *Abr-Nahrain* XI (1971), pp. 110-115. Most valuable, however, is Abdel Als examination (*op. cit.* p. 258) of the whole problem in relation to the *Ṭabbākh*'s traditional approach (cf. following nn.).

[499] *Ṭabbākh*, f. 49a : واما القياس فهو عكس النص ولا قياس الا نص ليكون
النص دلاله في المقاس عليه لا يجوز ان يقاس قياس على قياس
Actually the same statement is mentioned previously in an abstract way, *ibid.* f. 45b.

فهذه هي طريقه القياس ولا قياس الا علي نص ليكون النص دليلا علي
صحه القياس ولا يجوز ان قياس على قياس
(cf. also Abdel Al, *op. cit.* pp. 642, 639 and translation *ibid.* pp. 447, 457; cf. also Noja, *op. cit.* p. 112).

> The analogy is unlike the (Biblical) ordinance, and there can be no analogy without (Biblical) text. So that the text is a proof of that which is deduced by analogy. There can be no analogy (based) on (another) analogy.

Abū'l Ḥasan is then very emphatic in forbidding any excuse in the free application of analogy. To sum up, we may yet again quote his words:[500]

> This is the way of analogy, and he who goes beyond the converse of what is expressed in the text has followed a course with regard to the prohibitions, which the Law does not require.

Although, amongst the Karaites, those opposed to the unreasonable extension of the law of incest by means of countless analogies, among whom was Jeshuah b. Yehudah,[501] undoubtedly advanced similar arguments, there was still a marked difference between the two positions. Even after a considerable curbing of this unreasonable extention of analogies pertaining to the meaning of incest, the actual principle of analogy was not challenged among the Karaites. It remained permanently as a major pillar of their doctrine, dominating their whole exegesis.[502] As opposed to this, from the words of Abū'l Ḥasan we may safely conclude that the free extension of analogy was essentially incompatible with Samaritan exegesis. The view advocated previously as to the limitation of all hermeneutical devices by tradition is heavily substantiated by the arguments found in the Ṭabbākh.

There is therefore no point in comparing the Karaite hermeneutical rule with the Samaritan method of applyings analogies. Not only can one not trace any influence of the former on the latter,[503] but the whole

---

[500] Ṭabbākh, f. 49b. : فهذه هي طريقه القياس ومن يعدى في القياس عن عكس
النص فقد سلك في التحريم ما لا يقتضى به شريعه ... (cf. also Abdel Al.,
op. cit. p. 642 and translation p. 448; and Noja, op. cit. p. 111).

[501] Nemoy, Karaite Anthology, p. 127.

[502] Gottlober, Bikkoreth etc., pp. 94, 211 etc.; Poznanski, The Karaite Literary Oponents etc., pp. 22f.; Ankori, Karaites in Byzantium, pp. 17, 108 etc.

[503] cf. sup. nn. 463f., 486. We cannot enter here into the slightly different terminology of the 12th century Munajja (cf. Wreschner, Sam. Traditionen etc., pp. xii f. and ibid. n. 13). Even Munajja, who considers the analogy an important principle "applicable wherever it does not conflict with scripture or with other matters (of tradition?)" does not depart from the 'normative' Samaritan path. He formulates the same principles expressed in the Ṭabbākh into a more generalized pattern. Nevertheless, Munajja's practical application of the qiyās does not exceed that of his predecessors. Wreschner's allegation (ibid. p. xii, "Ganz abhängig von Karäern zeigte er sich in der Methode der Schrifterklärung") is contradicted by his own bizarre system (cf.

concept of positive rules is absent from the Samaritan ideology; there
are no instructions whatever as to the lines on which one should develop
analogies. If Abū'l Ḥasan disowns in a rigoristic manner the drawing
of analogies when Scripture and Tradition do not warrant it, he objects
even more strongly to the invention of analogies to facilitate lenient
rulings. His fierce polemics [504] against co-religionists who, by means of
faulty analogies, seek to lighten the burden of the Sabbath-laws, are
squarely based on the argument that, if one is allowed to go out to places
of worship on the Sabbath-day, this permission cannot possibly serve
as a source for analogies drawn in the interests of secular purposes.
If the legitimate employment of analogy depended solely on 'logic',
Abū'l Ḥasan could certainly not raise this objection here.

One could cite numerous instances of such polemics prompted by the
other types of hermeneutical norms as well. The absence of 'rules'
is no matter of chance, but seems rather to be inherent in the character
of Samaritan exegesis. It is hard to believe that the Samaritans, especially
in the Islamic period, would have been incapable of drawing up such
rules. So if they forewent any such 'systematizations" this self-restraint
must have been practised consciously and in accordance with their
tradition, which by its very nature depended, not so much on abstract
rules, as rather on ancient precedents.

Abū'l Ḥasan's approach endorses this tendency when he is dealing
with analogy. The principle here is substantially the same as the one
formulated by him on tradition in general. In other words, the validity of
the tradition depends on Scripture, which is itself tightly bound up with
its living transmission; Tradition and Scripture are thus organically
and inextricably interdependent; they mould as well as control each
other.

(2) *Inference a fortiori*

Such inferences are already present in the Torah. The Rabbis go to
great trouble in pointing them out. They are, however, in general, too
eager to find such inferences even in places where they are not so

---

inf. n. 523). Later he has to admit that some of these analogies are of secondary
nature and in reality they are based upon "ancient tradition". The explanation given
(*ibid.* p. xiii), however, that these are results of the "arbitrary" nature of Samaritan
borrowings, and his whole concept concerning the "hybridism" of Samaritan religion,
have no basis in reality.

[504] *Ṭabbākh*, f. 34a (SLTh.A, p. 90). cf. also *sup.* Part II, n. 347.

obvious.[505] The explicit inference in the Pentateuch are not of the type
which we may term 'popular usage'. In *Gen.* xliv, 8. Joseph's brethren
thus argue: if they return the money found in their own sacks all the
more probably will they not be suspected of theft. Logically in this
argument the connecting link is missing, since, after the case of '*a
minori*', we have to supply a clause to the effect that they would naturally return something taken by them inadvertantly. Only after this link
has been tacitly supplied, is the inference *ad maium* valid. For such and
similar reasons, we are entitled to call such inferences "naive" or "popular". In the New Testament such arguments are relatively highly
developed, thus acquiring a technical form. The Old Testament 'proof-
texts', in particular, are technically expounded, almost in the style which
one would expect from a jurist.[506] The Rabbis, likewise, after collecting
and scrutinising the Biblical instances of inferences *a fortiori*, establish
and generalize rules which are then methodically applied. It is therefore
important to distinguish between this development in the practice of
the Rabbis' *qal wa-homer* [507] and its consistent application to legal and
doctrinal teaching, on the one hand, and its naive and popular counterpart on the other.

An ancient writer may have been entirely innocent of any such tech-
nique as a hermeneutical norm, and may nevertheless have drawn inferences which really represent the same sort of logic in a popular way.
Once such inferences are classified, on the other hand, and occupy their
places in a well-organised hermeneutical system, their correct usage is
no longer left to native instinct, but rather is governed by the strict
criteria of jurisprudence. To take the case of Hillel with his *qal wa-homer*
along with its parallels among the Hellenistic Rhetors:[508] when this
device is systematically applied, its homely logic can likewise easily be
channelled into the mill-race of a legalistic rigidity or even of legal
fictions.

---

[505] cf. Weiss, *Dor Dor etc.*, I, pp. 6f. A somewhat forced *qal wahomer* is to be
found in *Num.* xii, 14, but the Rabbis needed it for the limitation of such inferences
(*Babha Qama*, 25a דיו לבא מן הדין להיות כנידון.) Most instructive are the discussions of the Sages with R. Tarfon on these problems (*ibid.*). There are also further
limits on the qal wa-homer (*Sanhedrin*, 24a, אין עונשין מן הדין).

[506] Daube, "Rabbinic Methods etc.", *HUCA* XXII (1948), pp. 225f. cf. Tasker,
The O.T. in the N.T., pp. 23 and 82.

[507] Strack, *Introduction etc.*, pp. 94, 285 (nn. 2-3), cf. *sup.* n. 505.

[508] Daube, *op. cit.* p. 251 (cf. *ibid.* n. 42).

Both the terms *Qal wa-ḥomer* and *a minori ad maius* may clearly become relative terms, very much dependent on the definitions of the jurists. What is 'light' (less important) and what is 'heavy' (more important) may well depend on conventional habits, education, tradition and the acquired tastes of the expositor. In the popular and naive employment of logical inferences from major to minor (or vice-versa), such inferences cannot however be extended to cover intricate and subtle cases. The best example for illustrating these differences in usage is surely the famous occasion of Johanan b. Zakkai's dispute with the Sadducees. These latter maintained that a daughter should inherit with the daughter of the son (*Babha Bathra* 115 b). They put forward a simple and naive inference, but stood no chance against the involved hermeneutical principles of the Rabbis.[509]

Even without much reflection, one may soon reach the conclusion that insofar as the literalist sectarians employ such inferences, their usage of them will be infinitely less sophisticated than that of the Rabbis.

All the attempts that have hitherto been made to show that *qal wa-ḥomer* is similar to logical deduction or identical with the Hellenistic syllogism are far from convincing. Even the advocates of such a parallel are forced to admit that, in the development of the Rabbinical *qal wa-ḥomer*, there are several distinct stages, each becoming more complicated than the last.[510]

We may broadly claim that the point of departure begins when the advocate of one of these stages puts forward an argument not universally applicable, or open to the suspicion of not being the soundest possible inference and so of not being applicable in practice as well as in theory.[511]

---

[509] The Sadducean inference ran on the following lines : "If the daughter of his son, who succeeds to an inheritance by virtue of his son's right, is an heir to him, how much more so his daughter who derives her right from himself!" At the end R. Joḥanan b. Zakkai dismisses the Sadducee by saying : "Fool, shall not *our perfect Torah* be as (convincing) as *your idle talk!*", cf. Yadayim IV, 6f.; *Toseptha, ibid.* II, 9f. (ed. Zuckermandel, p. 684). On the controversies of R. Joḥanan with the Sadducees cf. G. Alon, *Toledoth ha-Yehudim etc.* (Tel Aviv 1954), I, pp. 55f. cf. also J. Neusner, *A Life of R. Yohanan b. Zakkai* (Leiden 1962), pp. 49ff. Whether the bone of contention was "economic efficiency" (*ibid.* p. 55, n. 1) or straightforward Scriptural exegesis and exegetical traditions, has still to be substantiated. This problem, however, is outside the scope of our present concern.

[510] A. Schwarz, "Die Hauptergebnisse etc.", *op. cit.* pp. 4-7. cf. *sup.* Part II, n. 426.

[511] Daube, *op. cit.* pp. 256f.

The Rabbis themselves would evidently have agreed with these general principles, for they criticised the naive logic of the inferences drawn by the Sadducees. However, at this point 'light' and 'heavy' did not depend any more on logic, but on preconceived legal opinions and premises, which, while binding according to Rabbinical standards and traditions, were entirely irrelevant to the standpoint of Sadducees.

The simple inference *a fortiori*, that if the law expressly forbids marriage with the daughter's daughter (*Lev.* xviii, 10), although there is no explicit mention of the daughter's own ineligibility, the prohibition in the latter's case must necessarily be even stronger, must have appeared sound by universal standards. As a matter of fact, Anan explicitly states that this is the *true* inference.[512] While the Rabbanites had, to be sure, their own legalistic and traditional reasons for opposing the *force* of this particular *qal wa-ḥomer*,[513] they could not easily deny the logicality of it. They themselves were forced to reach the very same conclusion if by other hermeneutical devices. As a test case, we may now take the first *qal wa-ḥomer* of Hillel concerning the Passover-Sacrifice which illustrate these fundamental differences admirably. Even if we accept the view that his inference is built on the strict syllogism,[514] the premises of such syllogism may still depend, we may hold, on individual tastes and traditions.

The discussion revolves around the problem of whether the Passover-Sacrifice takes precedence over the Sababth (i.e. causes a suspension of Sabbath-laws or not) Hillel decides in the affirmative, on the basis of a *qal wa-ḥomer*. The arguments can be set down under the following headings: 1. The daily sacrifice takes precedence over the Sabbath. 2. All precepts which are suspended by the daily-sacrifice are also suspended by the Passover-Offering. 3. Therefore it may be inferred that the Passover-Offerings also takes precedence over the Sabbath. The first premise must have been acknowledged universally, since it is explicitly stated in Scripture (*Num.* xxviii, 10). The second premise, however, is purely Rabbinic tradition which was neither shared by the sectarians nor could easily have been inferred by them from the literal meaning

---

[512] Gottlober, *Bikkoreth etc.*, p. 80.

[513] The reason for rejecting this argument is, that according to the Rabbis "the trespass of a law derived by conclusion ad majus is not punishable". cf. *sup.* n. 505.

[514] Tosephta, *Pesaḥim* IV, 2 (ed. Zuckermandel, p. 162) and parallels in Babhli, *ibid.* 66a; *Jer.* VI, 1; 33a. The notion of קל וחומר being on the lines of syllogism was advocated by Schwarz (n. 510 *sup.*).

of Scripture. Indeed, we know that the Dead Sea Scroll Sect and the early Karaites objected to any offerings on the Sabbath other than those specified in Scripture.[515] The Samaritans also held to the same principle; and we have already seen [516] that they did not in fact suspend the Sabbath-laws because of the Passover-Offering.

This case of the Passover-Offering is not merely an illustration of the different approaches to this particular *a fortiori* inference, but also fully demonstrates the general trend. It must certainly have been the common view among the literalist Sectarians that inferences can only be utilised in a simple form, and only when they do not conflict with the literal sense of Scripture.

One glance at the use of such inferences by the Samaritans immediately reveals that they are employed only in their naive form, and that they are never pressed into a hermeneutical rule. Inference is rather implied than explicitly mentioned, and it is certainly taken for granted that such a logical device does not call for any further explanation. Just as it is the case with simple analogy that the prima facie understanding of the text necessitates its 'natural' employment, so the inference *a fortiori* is regularly made in the same way. In this respect, no difference is made between whether the inference is taken from major to minor, or vice versa.

Marqah in one of his midrashim, previously examined by us [517] bases his exposition on one such naive inference. In explaining Moses' multiple refusal to accept God's commission, Marqah puts forward the argument, in apology for Moses, that this multiple refusal was not out of fear of Pharaoh. The inference suggested by Marqah is: since Moses says to God that he can speak to Him without being terrified, he must surely have far less reason to fear Pharaoh.

Such inferences occur most frequently in moralizing explanations of the precepts. The *Ṭabbākh* is very fond of using them, especially in explaining the laws of the Passover Offering.

The Hyssop, used for sprinkling the blood of the Passover Offering, is a recognized symbol of the humble and the poor, Hyssop being a low-growing plant. According to Abū'l Ḥasan, the sprinkling of the blood

---

[515] *Zadokite Fragments*, XI, l. 18 (quoting *Lev.* xxiii, 28); Revel, *The Karaite Halakhah etc.*, p. 41.

[516] Wreschner, *Sam. Traditionen*, pp. 25-29; cf. also my article *ALUOS* VI (1969), pp. 111f., 146f. (nn. 109f.).

[517] cf. *sup.* n. 130 and text there.

in this manner exemplifies the merits of the poor. He immediately adds the inference that it exemplifies even more the duty of those who are in a position to do so to perform other and more exacting precepts (e.g. the discharging of financial burdens).[518] A similar type of exposition is given of the reason underlying the command that the animal to be used for the offering must be free from blemish. The inference here is even more rudimentary, namely, that if God demands perfection of an animal, He must surely demand it even more of an intelligent human being.[519]

Not so very far removed from this type of thinking is the exposition of the reason why the sojourner is mentioned in connection with the Passover Sacrifice. The reason here given is that one is meant to infer from the fact of this gentile's being accepted by God into His worship, that, if he can be so accepted, most assuredly a renegade Israelite has an even better chance of acceptance.[520]

In halakhic matters, the drawing of such inferences is still performed on the same naive level and in the same primitive form. The *Kāfi*, in connection with the rules of ceremonial washing, mentions the case of Joseph washing his face (*Gen.* xliii, 13), apparently to remove his tears. From this it follows that, if more defiling acts had taken place, or if Joseph were about to pray, he would be even more likely to wash himself.[521] The technical form of this inference is likewise utilised by the *Kāfi* when he is dealing with the prohibition to the Nazirite against defiling himself by contact with diseased relatives. The *Kāfi* then raises the question as to why "brother and sister" are mentioned. We have already dealt with this midrash.[522] It suffices here to say that the answer

---

[518] *Ṭabbākh*, f. 64a (SLTh.A, p. 105). Abū'l Ḥasan is very fond of such simple inferences, e.g. on *Deut.* xxxiv, 10 (*ibid.* f. 215a). If in Israel "no prophet will arise like Moses", amongst the gentiles even less so (cf. also Abdel Al, *op. cit.* pp. 659f., 482f.). The Rabbis did not always agree to such inferences. cf. *Siphri* on *Deut.* xxxiv, 10.

[519] *Ṭabbākh*, f. 60a (SLTh.A, p. 102).

[520] *ibid.* ff. 71b f. (SLTh.A, p. 113). A similar inference is developed concerning the "censers which were beaten into plates for covering the altar" (*Num.* xvii, 1-5). This is a reminder that one should not intrude into the Sanctuary. Carrying the censers is the lesser of the 'services'. If intruders who usurped this task were severely punished, then those who may covet more important 'services' will be punished even more. *ibid.* ff. 105b-108a.

[521] *Kāfi*, p. 46 (SLTh.A, p. 9).

[522] *ibid.* p. 227 (SLTh.A, p. 46); cf. n. 136 *sup.* Naturally the employment of such halakhic inferences is also shared by the *Ṭabbākh*, e.g. on *Ex.* xvi, 23-25 (f. 35b; SLTh.A, p. 91) if the simple preparation of food is prohibited on the Sabbath, more elaborate 'works' even more so.

depends on the double employment of the proper inference in a negative
sense.

In conclusion, it may be safely asserted that, in Samaritan exegesis,
the inference *a fortiori* is employed on a very modest scale. It is held to
be a 'natural' process rather than a hermeneutical principle. There is no
valid reason to suppose that the employment of this device by the Samaritans was in any way influenced by the more sophisticated and systematized hermeneutical rules of other groups.[523]

---

[523] No useful purpose would be served by amassing further examples of simple
inferences of this type. Those mentioned in the previous notes prove the point quite
adequately. We have not mentioned any of the *a fortiori* inferences of Munajja, since
they are of a secondary nature, mainly employed for polemical reasons. At any rate
Wreschner's opinion, that these inferences betray a marked Jewish influence (*Sam.
Traditionen etc.*, p. 54, n. 12, "den talmudischen קל וחומר nachgebildet") has
absolutely no foundation. Therefore, it is not out of place, even at the risk of digres-
sion from our main subject, to dispel such misconceptions. Unfortunately such
sweeping generalisations are accepted even by contemporary scholars (cf. Halkin,
"The Relation etc.", *Saadia Anniversary Vol.*, pp. 296f.). The polemics of Munajja
are directed against Saadia (and the Rabbanites) for the limitation of the law in *Lev.*
xvii, 13 (ordering the covering of the blood of wild-beasts and fowls) to the two
classes explicitly mentioned in Scripture. The Samaritans, relying on their tradition
based on an *analogy*, demanded the covering of all blood including that of cattle
and sheep. Their ruling is further supported by *Lev.* xvii, 11, and the equation of
"blood" to "soul" was taken as a sign of reverence towards the blood, and the act
of covering it equivalent to burial. Both the *Kāfi* (p. 319f.) and the *Ṭabbākh* (f. 51 f.)
express similar opinions (cf. Abdel Al, *op. cit.* pp. 130ff.; cf. also *ibid.* texts pp. 620ff.,
671ff.; translations, pp. 393ff., 481ff.). All this was known to Wreschner, who in *this*
case had to admit the antiquity of the Samaritan tradition (and brings even parallels
from the Book of Jubilees). Strangely enough the quotation from the *Masā'il al
Khilāf* on which Wreschner bases his theory shows also that Munajja's main premise

is an *analogy*: ولقد غلط الفيوسى وطائفته فى القياس لما تمسكوا بمجرد
النص فى قوله אשר יצוד ציד חיה או עוף וכו׳ فاقتصروا الدم على هذه
الانواع المنصوص عليها ... Furthermore, Wreschner in his summary of
Munajja's ch. XVI-XVII (*ibid.* p. xxvi) rightly identifies their contents with the fragment published by Drabkin (*Fragmenta commentarii etc.*, pp. 47ff., frag. II; *ibid.*
pp. 44f., frag. I). This can leave no doubt (although in the Fragments *Lev.* xvii, 11
is not explicitly mentioned) that we are confronted with a midrash equating "blood"
with "soul". In the full text of Munajja, from which Wreschner took his excerpts
(cf. J.R. Sam. Ms. 150, which has a double pagination ff. 118b f. = pp. ٢٣٥

فصل فى بيان امر الروح والرواح) this becomes even clearer. Munajja's polemical employment of طريق الاحرى والاولى has very little to do with a real קל וחומר
(cf. *sup.* n. 515 and text there). Having only a vague knowledge of Rabbinic literature,

(3) *Inference from Sequence of Passages*

We have seen, in reference to previous cases, that the observation of the sequence of passages is not only instrumental in expanding exegesis but also serves for the Samaritans, as it did for earlier sects, to completely identify two concepts simply through the fact of their close proximity. Thus, for example, the people of truth are identified with the observers of the law (*Ex.* xviii, 21) and "living water", "light" and other metaphors are likewise employed for a similar purpose on the strength of such midrashim.[524]

As we have seen earlier,[525] while discussing the broad thematic unit, a common feature of naive exegesis is to exploit such supposed inner connections to the maximum. Hence this process of inference from sequence of passages, although it is never turned into a genuine 'hermeneutical rule', is constantly employed as a 'natural' method of elucidating details by means of the wider contextual theme.

It is therefore only natural to expect that such a sequence will often add a new ethos to the individual members of verses of the greater unit. The best way of illustrating this 'system' will be to take examples of its use based on the Blessing of Moses.

Deut. xxxiii, 6 is understood in Samaritan tradition as : "May Reuben live and not die; and may a number (of others) joint him".[526] The *Ṭabbākh*[527] expounds these words with a view to justifying the order of blessings by employing inferences from the sequence of the verses. It explains that Moses began with Reuben:

---

mostly depending on secondary sources, he may have even borrowed his technical term from the Karaites. The plain fact is that the inference from minor (wild beasts) to major (domestic animals) is invalidated since according to the Rabbis "covering the blood" does not apply to animals sanctified for sacrifice (כסוי הדם נוהג בחולין ולא במקודשים Ḥullin, 84a). The whole section of *Deut.* xii, 15-17 is explained as referring to animals *sanctified* but found to have some blemish (cf. *Siphri ad loc.*; *Bekhoroth*, 32a; *Temurah*, 31a). Only *ibid.* verse 20 is explained as dealing with ordinary non-sacrificial ritual slaughter (בשר תאוה). In the same way *Deut.* xv, 22 was understood as referring to a "first born" which was found to have a blemish. For all these reasons a קל וחומר from sacrifices would sound absurd to the Rabbis. Secondly; fowls (= doves) are fit for sacrifice, thus the whole inference is not logical. Most of Munajja's "*a fortiori* inferences" are of a similar nature.

[524] cf. *sup.* Part II, n. 776 and text there.

[525] cf. *sup.* para (c, 1).

[526] S.P. ויהי מעמה; S.T. ויהי מאתו מספר

[527] ff. 203b f.

... that, in order that he should ascend to the status of (being deserving of) rewards (in the world to come) by his repentance, (the Scripture) omitted the direct mention of Simeon, but alluded to him by (the expression) *and may a number join him* (*Deut.* xxxiii, 6, S.P.), for his tribe joined Reuben (cf. *Num.* ii, 12), since Simeon's numbers decreased through the events at Shittim (cf. *Num.* xxv, 1-9). Zimri being of the tribe of Simeon, all the twenty-four thousand who died in the plague were Simeonites.

Next in sequence comes the tribe of Judah (*ibid.* 9), a fact which is explained by the statement that these three tribes, or rather the patriarchs Reuben, Simeon and Judah, having sinned, repented, and are therefore rightly mentioned before Levi.[528]

Since the tribe of Levi is the most glorified above all tribes, incorporating in themselves prophecy, priesthood, sanctity and priority (in leadership), and since some of the tribes who committed crimes were mentioned previously, to teach us (about their action) and subsequently to obliterate (their guilt), as they have repented and turned to become obedient, (all this was done) in order that grace should be bestowed (even) upon those mentioned before. Thus after this information was supplied by Scripture... (*ibid.* 1-7), came the mention of the tribe of Levi beginning with the allusion to Moses...

In the same way, verse eight is explained as referring both to Moses and to the Levites who prevented the people from sinning (cf. *Ex.* xvii, 2).

A similar type of exposition explains the sequence of the verses in the Blessing of Benjamin (v. 12) and that of Joseph. Logically, as Joseph is supposed to be more significant than Benjamin, he should have won a position of priority over the latter in the blessings. The *Ṭabbākh* [529] offers two interpretations of the 'change' of order. The first is that the superior is recognised as such by being compared with the inferior. The second is that this particular order was deliberately chosen in order that Benjamin should appear as an adjutant to Joseph in accordance with the custom commonly observed in royal ceremonies. There is no

---

[528] *ibid.* 204a ولما كان سبط لاوى اجل الاسباط لما قد اجتمع فيه من النبوه والامامه والشرف والتقدم على جميع الاسباط وكان منهم من قد وقع منه فعل مقبحات قدم ذكرهم ليخبر عنهم ويرفع الذم بما حصل منهم من التوبه ومصيرهم الى جانب الطاعه لتكون الفضيله لمن يذكر بالتقدم فلما انتهى من الاخبار عنهم بمثل ذلك حسب قوله יחי ראובן ואל ימות الى قوله שמע ה' קול יהודה اتبع ذلك بذكر سبط لاوى فابتدى بالاشاره الى النبي موسى

[529] *ibid.* ff. 205b f.

doubt that the *Ṭabbākh* is here engaged in implicit polemics. The apologetic undertone concerns the age old controversy of Hargerizim (= Joseph) versus Jerusalem (= Benjamin).

In the case of eschatological expositions inference from sequence of passages occurs quite frequently. Again, this is considered a valid way of establishing the inner conhesion of the smaller members of the wider theme. Thus, for example, *Deut.* xxxii, 36 is understood by the *Ṭabbākh* [530] as meaning, "and there is none remaining, neither evil nor righteous". Hence the next verse (37) "and they will say, where are their Gods?" is employed as a proof of the resurrection:

> This (verse) refers both to the believers (in idols) and to those who are not. All wil equally pass away. This will be followed by the resurrection, which is the return of all creatures to life as they were before, in accordance with the divine decree. The (holy) Book indicates this by saying, *and they shall say, where are their Gods?* (*Deut.* xxxii, 37, S.P.). However, being alive is a precondition for speaking. Consequently, the speakers are idol-worshippers, all those believing in others (deities) besides God. At the time when their punishment is due, they will appeal to the object of their worship and their belief...

We have observed on previous occasions [531] that, in common with the Rabbis, the Samaritans held also to the principle that there is no strict chronological order in the various passages of the Torah. The Samaritans, however, utilized such "derangements" in a limited scale. For the *Ṭabbākh* the strange sequence of certain passages serves as a proof that Moses received a written book, and not merely a verbal inspiration. According to Abū'l Ḥasan, if Moses had been in possession of a verbal message alone, the reported incidents would have been arranged in the Torah in a strict chronological order. The fact that the story of the cessation of the Manna (*Ex.* xvi, 35) is not at the end of the Torah, together with many other similar instances of lack of chronol-

---

[530] *ibid.* f. 227b ואפס עצור ועזוב يريد به فنا اصحاب المذاهب ومن ليس له مذهب ويتساوى جميعا بالفنى يتبع ذلك بالبعث وهو اعادة الخلق احيآ على ما كانوا على ما تقتضيه الحكمة وقد دل الكتاب على مثل ذلك بقوله ואמרו איה אלהימו والحياة شرط فى القول والقايلين هم عباد الاوثان كل من كان يعتقد من دون الله عندما يحل بهم العقاب يستنجدون بمعابيدهم ومعتقداتهم

[531] cf. *sup.* Part II, n. 99. For the Rabbinic rule cf. Strack, *Introduction etc.*, pp. 98 (rule 32); 296 (n. 39).

ogy, goes to prove sufficiently that this Scripture was in fact given in written form.

It is therefore only natural that, in places where the sequence really is logical and deliberate, it should be further exploited for midrashic exposition. Of course, in such cases inference from the sequence is not the only method employed, but is normally used in conjunction with others. Once a midrash is initiated, analogies can be sought from other instances where a similar sequence of passages suggests a parallel idea. Thus we find a midrash on *Ex.* ii, 23 [532] which suggests that "the course of those many days" was known to the Israelites by calculations. Hence realizing that. despite the fact that this length of time had passed it had not brought them redemtion, "they cried out and God heard their groaning" (*ibid.* 24).

> Ever commemorate well the great prophet Moses, who opened for us the Garden of Eden of the Law, when for its sake he freed the tribes of Jacob, the son of Isaac, the stars of Abraham, who underwent misery during the Third part — *one hundred and forty years of four hundred years.* They had a calculation for four hundred years, and at the end of the period they were to go forth as kings, and when they realized that the years were over [533], they sighed and cried out seeking relief (*Ex.* ii, 23), *and God remembered his covenant with Abraham, with Isaac and with Jacob* (Ex. ii, 24). Similarly the son of Lamech cried out after the passing of one hundred and fifty days (cf. *Gen.* vii, 2) and God remembered him (cf. *ibid.* viii, 1).

It is upon the analogy of the appointed time with the remembrance of God that a similar midrash is devised by means of an inference suggested by the sequence of the two verses concerning Noah.

In halakhic matters too there are examples of inferences drawn from the sequence of passages. In this field, moreover, just as in the aggadic one, such inferences are not translated into a hermeneutical rule such as would prompt further investigations into possible new sources of inferences drawn from a sequence in the interests of halakhic expansions. On the rare occasions when such sources are exploited, other exegetical considerations are normally involved and it is these which have really

---

[532] *Memar Marqah* (ed. Macdonald), I, p. 31; II, pp. 47f. On linguistic grounds this midrash must be considered as a later interpolation (cf. כרז for prayer).

[533] The midrash expounds *Ex.* II, 23 (ויהי בימים הרבים ההם). The calculation of the Israelites was from Abraham, *Gen.* xv, 13. However, according to *Ex.* xii, 40-41, it was prolonged by 30 years. According to Samaritan tradition the 430 years were equally divided (215 "in the land of Canaan" and 215 in Egypt. cf. my article *ALUOS* VI (1969), pp. 108, 141f., nn. 82-84). Out of 215 years in Egypt 75 passed during the life of Joseph, thus the remaining 140 years were years of affliction.

given rise to the midrash, and then the midrash based on the sequence of Scripture is only of secondary importance.

The *Ṭabbākh* [534] questions the purpose of *Ex.* xxxiv, 25, since this verse does not add anything new, both of the questions with which it deals having been previously explained, namely the injunctions not to offer the Passover Sacrifice "upon leavened bread" referred to in *Ex.* xxiii, 18, and not to leave the offering till the morning, in *Ex.* xii, 10. The whole passage (*Ex.* xxxiv, 18-26), however, is clearly one unit, and the verse preceeding the one in question (*ibid.* 24) speaks of the promise to "enlarge thy borders". From this the *Ṭabbākh* draws halakhic conclusions regarding the crucial difference between the celebration of the Passover in its proper place (surroundings of Hargerizim) and one in the far and remote corners of the country. The sequence of Scripture serves here as an aid to explaining a seemingly 'redundant' verse as referring to the promised wide borders of the Israelites.

Formal inferences drawn in cases where no inherent connection exists between the contents of the sequence of passages are largely dependent on tradition. Often, although there is indeed no logical connection between the passages, such midrashim are built on the traditional division of the Bible into sections. Thus, in the S.P. *Deut.* xix, 14-21 is regarded as one section, whereas in the M.T. verse fourteen forms a section in its own right. We find that a midrash by Marqah on the curses laid on a person who "removes his neighbour's landmark" (*Deut.* xxvii, 17) is only intelligible if taken in reference to such a background. It is based on an inference resulting from reading that passage, i.e. *Deut.* xix, 14ff., as *one* section. His preaching is then directed towards the princes who are responsible for judgement.[535]

> *What was said to the princes:* Observe how it is and learn it, that you may be increased in wisdom. Let no one man (cf. *Deut.* xix, 15) rise to make a false statement which will cause his enemy to be killed (cf. *Num.* xxxv, 30), and your companion's place to be a desolation and to be given over to him who does not deserve it (cf. *Deut.* xix, 14).

To take another example, the passage in *Num.* xv, 17-26 forms one section in the S.P., while the M.T. divides it into two.[536] The *Kāfi* [537]

---

[534] ff. 81b f. (SLTh.A, pp. 121f.).

[535] *Memar Marqah* (ed. Macdonald), I, p. 70; II, p. 112.

[536] Following the division of the M.T. the Rabbis explained v. 22 as referring to the transgression of idol worship. cf. *Siphri ad loc.*; Tosephta, *Bekhoroth*, III, 12 (ed. Zuckermandel, p. 537); *Harayoth*, 8a; Jer. *Nedarim*, III, 9; 38b. With the previous passage (17-21, dealing with "leave offering") they did not attempt to find connections.

[537] pp. 11f. There are further harmonisations in the *Kāfi*, as e.g. comparisons of

naturally exploits this sequence, and explains that if there are any priests at hand and the people do not bring them their heave-offerings, the whole leadership (מעיני) and the congregation (העדה) are alike guilty and are in duty bound to bring a guilt-offering.[538]

When in other halakhic matters there is an attempt to employ such inferences from the sequence of passages, and when the sequence is mechanically followed and there is thus no real connection, the midrash only serves to explain the reasons behind the precepts. The *Kāfi*,[539] after giving several explanations for the prohibition against drinking wine on the Sabbath Day, which, as we know, essentially depends on the sanctity of the day and its desecration by intoxicating drinks,[540] also gives biblical proof-texts. One of these [541] is the story of Nadab and Abihu, (*Lev.* x, 1-7) which of course is followed by the prohibition against the drinking of wine by the priests (*ibid.* 8-11). The inference here drawn is that the cause of their death was their intoxication.

Another such mechanical inference from the sequence of passages constitutes one of the reasons given by the *Kāfi* [542] against eating meat together with milk. The Bible simply states: "Thou shalt not seethe a kid in his mother's milk".[543] However, one of such prohibitions occurs (*Deut.* xiv, 21) after the enumeration of the clean animals (*ibid.* 4-6) and the clean birds (*ibid.* 11). The *Kāfi* employs here a *gematria* on the Hebrew word גדי ($ג+ד+י$ = גד״י) $י$ (= 10) + גד (= 7) = 17. This is an allusion to the ten permitted animals and the seven permitted birds. Thus the kid is only a symbolic representative of any kind of meat

---

our passage (vv. 22-26) with *Lev.* iv, 13-21 and *ibid.* 22-26, and further *Num.* xv, 27f. with *Lev.* iv, 27f. Although the Rabbis utilized each scripture for a different type of "guilt offering" (cf. *Sifra ad loc.*; *Horayoth*, 3b f.; *ibid.* 10a; cf. previous note), there were also Rabbinic midrashim which attempted to connect these various subjects (cf. *Zebhahim*, 41a).

[538] It is also very possible that in Marqah's midrash on *Deut.* xxvii, 17 (cf. *sup.* n. 535) "the five referring to the priests" (warnings not to remove the neighbour's landmark) is a similar result of harmonisation. Since *Num.* xv, 17-26 is one קצה, the "leave offering" and "when ye shall err" are here interrelated.

[539] p. 107 (SLTh.A, p. 18).

[540] cf. my article *op. cit.* pp. 112f., 147f. (nn. 118-121). cf. *sup.* Part II, n. 577.

[541] Although there is a possibility here of Rabbinic influence (cf. *Lev. Rabba* xii, 1), the inference is so simple that there is no need to suggest dependence.

[542] p. 318. The *gematria* of the *Kāfi* was not favoured by later expositors and they derived this prohibition from the sequence of passages by analogy. cf. Drabkin, *Fragmenta Commentarii etc.*, pp. 19ff.

[543] cf. *sup.* n. 124 and text there.

belonging to this species and to those having the signs of the permitted animals. Needless to say, just as the whole midrash is artificial and forced, so is the inference from the sequence of passages. Such midrashim, however, are extremely rare, and are recognizably quite distinct from those inferences built on a sequence of passages wherein there is not even a remote logical connection. This latter type we shall deal with next.

The few artificial inferences, when the significance implied by the sequence of passages is forced, are drawn mainly to explain other difficulties. One instance of this is the problem as to why Moses' removal of Joseph's bones is not mentioned when the Hebrews leave Egypt (*Ex.* xii, 37). In order to explain this, the sequence of the passage dealing with Joseph's bones (*ibid.* xiii, 19) is forcibly explained by Marqah by means of an inference drawn from the fact that the removal is in fact mentioned at their departure from Succoth (*ibid.* 20):[544] "The pillar of cloud and the fire stopped and they could not leave Succoth". Then follows the involved story of how the oath made to Joseph was forgotten and only at the instance of Asher's daughter Seraḥ was it remembered, and so they were allowed to continue under the guidance of the cloud and the fire.

A similar device is used by Marqah [545] to explain the difficulty in the Song of Moses, where the following passage appears to have little connection with the dividing of the Red Sea; "All the inhabitants of Canaan shall melt away. Fear and dread shall fall upon them" (*Ex.* xv, 15). The difficulty is solved by the inference drawn from the sequence (*ibid.* 17): "Thou shalt bring them in and plant them in the mountain of thine inheritance..." The complicated midrash connects the destruction of the Canaanites with the establishment of Hargerizim. Now perhaps we can understand the forced logic of this whole midrash, i.e. that the rumour reaching the inhabitants of Canaan simultaneously foretold their doom.

It is again quite common for a sequence of verses to be explained by analogizing each phrase with verses from elsewhere. By this method, although the context is undoubtedly enriched, the inference from the sequence of verses nevertheless also implies a "chronological" order.

---

[544] *Memar Marqah* (ed. Macdonald), I, p. 25f.; II, p. 39f. cf. also S. Kohn, *Zur Sprache etc.*, pp. 26ff. For an entirely different Rabbinic inference from sequence of verses, cf. Heinemann, *op. cit.* p. 136 and on Serah, Ginzberg, *Legends*, II, p. 181.

[545] *Memar Marqah* (ed. Macdonald), I, p. 46; II, p. 73.

To take an example from the exposition of the last section of the Penta-teuch,[546] *Deut.* xxxiv, 10 is regarded as a theological principle governing the entire Samaritan tradition, namely that none like Moses will ever arise. Even their messianic expectations (*Deut.* xviii, 18) are regularly minimised in order to underline this doctrine. The future Prophet, accord-ing to the *Ṭabbākh*,[547] is compared with Moses only for the sake of the latter's honour. In other words, the Taheb may vaguely resemble Moses, but will certainly not be his equal. In this light the whole sequence of verses is explained: verse 11 is a reference to Moses' great deeds in Egypt, while verse 12 is added to draw attention to the miracles at the Red Sea (S.P. המראה) i.e. 'spectacular miracles' of *Ex.* xv.[548]

From our discussion of such cases of inference from the sequence of passages, the clear generalization emerges that, even in comparison with the 'literalist' Karaites,[549] the Samaritans regularly keep much closer to the literal sense, and their midrashim do not interpolate subversive or untraditional ideas.

Again, if we compare their practice with the employment of such a device in the Mishnah, the wide difference immediately strikes us. For there it is an established hermeneutical rule (*semukhim*), and there one also finds the postulate that the characteristics appertaining to one member of a series, or to one item among several, items mentioned side by side and sharing a certain affinity, belong equally to the other individuals.[550]

In Rabbinic agadah its employment is even more frequent and much more consistent.[551] As a rule, every Scripture may be expounded in relation to the passages immediately preceding it; but there is even

---

[546] Amongst the Rabbis one finds also a similar interpretation, *Siphri ad loc.* (cf. however R. Elazar, *ibid.*) : בלעם ... אבל באומות העולם « לא קם בישראל »

[547] ff. 215a f. cf. Abdel Al, *op. cit.* pp. 657f.; translation, pp. 482f.

[548] On the Rabbinic discussion of the miraculous power on the Red Sea, cf. Heinemann, *op. cit.* p. 87.

[549] One of the most peculiar expositions of sequences is that of Anan, by which he prohibited the consumption of all birds except doves. He based his argument on the sequence of "every clean bird" and "burnt offering" in *Gen.* viii, 20. According to *Lev.* i, 14 only turtle doves and pigeons are fit burnt offering, thus all other birds cannot be "clean". cf. Nemoy, *Karaite Anthology*, pp. 16f. Qirqisāni reports (*Kitāb al-Anwār etc.*, I, 19, 3; ed. Nemoy, p. 61) that even among his contemporary Karaites the opinions were divided whether or not chickens are permitted for food.

[550] Rosenblatt, *The Interpretation etc.*, p. 4 (cf. examples *ibid.* n. 41). cf. also *ibid.* p. 22, n. 20.

[551] Heinemann, *op. cit.* pp. 141f. (cf. nn. 27-29, 35, 36).

a widespread opinion that this practice may be extended to those verses and passages not immediately preceding (לפני פניו) the expounded one. The same kind of opinion is often extended to cover even the passages following the passage in question.[552] Many details are invented and 'missing" passages supplied, on the basis of the theory that a sequence of Scripture entitles and enables us to deduce, not only what is written, but also what "ought" to be written.[553]

It has already been shown that such features of exegesis are not only exhibited by the Rabbis but are also quite prominent among the Hellenistic Jews, and even medieval Biblical scholars do not fight shy of such devices.[554]

In any case, there is no awareness among the Samaritans of a norm to be followed, let alone extended. If we compare their employment of this device even with Hillel's earliest rule, we immediately recognise the difference in approach. The seventh rule of Hillel's, however, regarding 'something that is deduced from the context',[555] although it appears to be merely a simple and logical guide, if consistently enforced, is liable to lead to far-reaching consequences. Even before this rule of Hillel's was further developed by Rabbi Ishmael, it radically changed the understanding of many precepts. "Thou shalt not steal", in the Ten Commandments, was interpreted by means of this device as referring to the kidnapping of a person, and not to the stealing of objects. The reason for this lies in the sequence: since this commandment appears in association with the other capital crimes, murder and adultery,[556] it must therefore be of the same nature. One may fairly pinpoint the main differences between the Samaritans' simple procedure and the hermeneutical rule of *semukhim* by delving into the recesses of the Rabbinic mind as it operated such rules, for the Rabbis hermeneutical rules were divised with a view to exhausting the "deeper" meanings of the Law and even to reading "between the lines". All attempts to delineate the Rabbinical system in logical and rational terms, and so to prove that the device of *semukhim* is virtually synonymous with 'hermeneutical context'[557] have had to conclude in the end that, if

---

[552] *ibid.* p. 136.

[553] *ibid.* p. 141 (cf. n. 31).

[554] *ibid.* pp. 143f.

[555] Strack, *Introduction etc.*, p. 94 (n. 11).

[556] Daube, "Rabbinic Methods etc.", *HUCA* xxii (1949), pp. 257f. (cf. nn. 62-64).

[557] A. Schwarz, "Die Hauptergebnisse etc.", *Scripta Univ. Hierosolym.*, I, pp. 23ff. cf. Strack, *op. cit.* pp. 98, 296 (nn. 1-3).

such was indeed the case at the inception of the operation of the rule, in its later development it certainly became highly mechanical and forced.

(4) *Missing and Redundant Passages*

No Samaritan writer can admit that certain details are in actual fact missing in Scripture and thus have to be supplied by humans with the aid of outside information. This attitude makes the search for 'logical' or 'artificial' *lacunae* very limited in scope. A long midrash of Marqah's [558] is based on a logical 'omission' in Scripture. A close scrutiny of *Deut.* xxvii, 12f. reveals that only the curses are quoted while the actual spoken words of the blessings are conspicuously absent. Marqah's whole long midrash is based on the assumption that we must take it for granted that the blessings were likewise pronounced, but that we have therefore to search carefully to discover the blessings from the following section — (*ibid.* xxviii, 2-7). In support of his argument, he claims that there is a general rule, and by divine decree, that blessings normally precede curses (*Gen.* i, 22). Obviously the Scripture in *Deut.* does not follow a chronological order.

The *Ṭabbākh* [559] argues very much on the same lines. Abū'l Ḥasan takes it for granted that, if information is not supplied explicitly, there must be a reason for this, but it is quite out of the question that it should have been inadvertently omitted. When Paraoh suggested to Moses that the Israelites should worship in Egypt (*Ex.* viii, 21), Moses replied that this could not be done, becasue it would outrage the Egyptians, who would then stone the Israelites (*ibid.* 22). In Scripture there is no report of Pharaoh's answer, and this, according to Abū'l Ḥasan, is in itself evidence that Moses "refuted him, showing that he had ordered something which was impossible" and freedom is in sight. The command to keep the lambs inteded for the Passover Sacrifice for four days (*Ex.* xii, 3-6) was therefore intended to demonstrate that the Israelites no longer feared the Egyptians.

It seems likely that such supposed 'missing' details are the main sources of the strange midrashim in the *Asaṭir*. Most of these expositions,

---

[558] *Memar Marqah* (ed. Macdonald), I, p. 63; II, p. 99. Obviously the main evidence is *Deut.* xxvii itself, where the blessings (vv. 1f.) precede the curses (vv. 15f.). Marqah concludes : "From here it is evident that they began the blessing before the curse" (מכן אתמר דאינון משרין בברכה קמי קללתה).

[559] f. 61b (SLTh.A, p. 103).

designed to supply 'missing details' of Scripture, are nontheless in the majority of cases based on harmonizations of the contents of a text with other Scriptural details.[560] However, as the sources of the *Asaṭir* are still unknown to us and we cannot therefore intelligently compare it with other works of Samaritan literature, it is by no means certain whether in many cases some strange and alien influence is not in fact at work. This perplexing obscurity is a peculiar characteristic of the book.

If we compare even the most daring midrashim on 'missing details', such as those commonly found in the *Asaṭir*, with those of other systems, we find that the Samaritan employment of this device is entirely undeveloped. At any rate there is no awareness of any necessity to follow a hermeneutical rule or to discover missing details by means of it. In most cases, such a device, if and when employed, can be satisfactorily explained by the presence of other real problems existing either in the text or in their own tradition.

'Missing details' are therefore most plausible to the Samaritan mind if they suggest themselves in repetitions from which a detail is seemingly omitted. To take, for example, an instance from the Passover Sacrifice, *Ex.* xii, 3 reads "Accordging to the house of their fatheis". In the next verse (*ibid.* 4) a similar expression occurs without '*fathers*'. The *Ṭabbākh* [561] explains this 'missing detail' as an intentional omission. 'House' alone is mentioned, because if the clan (i.e. the house of theii fathers) is numerous, it should nevertheless not be allowed more than one lamb, despite its very great number. The solution offered is therefore that the clan be divided into several 'houses'. The main motive underlying this suggestion is without doubt to encourage the multiplying of places of prayer and praise to the glory of God.

One glance at the Rabbinic midrash is sufficient to show how much more sophisticated here was the drawing of inferences based upon missing details. The Rabbis often asked themselves the question: What was Scripture's intention in keeping silent about details which 'ought to be' mentioned? Obviously 'what ought to be mentioned', according to

---

[560] Taking at random *Asaṭir*, I, 2, the division of land may originate from harmonizations. "Cain was a tiller of the ground" and "Abel was a keeper of sheep", therefore there was a need to allot to each of them a suitable part. Or, the marriage with their twin-sisters (*ibid.* I, 3), may answer the question how could they multiply if no female birth is recorded. It is equally possible (like the invented names of the twin sisters) that external influences are here at work. cf. Gaster, *Asaṭir*, pp. 138, 184 etc.

[561] f. 59a (SLTh.A, p. 101).

the Rabbis, was often very far removed from that tenacious loyalty to the literal sense so highly honoured by the Samaritans.[562]

Not seldom the Rabbis employed as evidence that something was indeed missing an *argumentum e silentio* drawn solely from Scripture itself, even when such a 'silence' did not arouse any surprise or any problems. The Hellenistic exegetes of Alexandria used similar devices, only in their case the supposed 'missing details' were supplied by allegorizations.[563]

Such devices came to be absurdly extended to expoound in a pedantically literalistic fashion passages of Scripture clearly meant as metaphors. From the expression "Cain rose up" (*Gen.* v, 8) it was accordingly concluded that he had previously fallen etc.[564] There was even a tendency to speculate on the (unrecounted) motives and emotions of the biblical characters; and it was a common feature of all apologists, both Hellenistic and Rabbinic, to exploit such 'missing' human characteristics in their expositions.[565]

The very limited use of 'missing details' among the Samaritans, on the other hand, leads us to expect that this device will be employed naively and unsystematically. In other words, hermeneutical devices, in general, although sporadically employed by them are demonstrably not regarded as consciously applied rules.

Although the Samaritans share the common belief that there are no unessential or meaningless expressions in Scripture, they do not feel called upon to go out of their way to justify each single expression by showing that it is essential. It is possible that the frequent additions to the S.P. (most of them repetitions of verses found elsewhere) led the Samaritans to hold that it was right and proper that some passages should be repeated. Such being the very nature of Scripture, there was no need to seek elaborate explanations of 'redundant 'passages. A further consequence, also an outcome of the Samaritans' explicit type of text, was that the exegete was not expected to read 'between the lines' or press each single word into the service of his exposition. Furthermore, their traditional literalism was a contributary factor in the securing of the relative simplicity of Scriptural exegesis. We should not then be unduly surprised to discover that the Samaritan exegete himself would have

---

[562] Heinemann, *op. cit.* pp. 98, 237 (nn. 13-16).
[563] *ibid.* p. 98. cf. Daube "Rabbinic Methods etc.", *HUCA* XXII, pp. 242f.
[564] Heinemann, *op. cit.* p. 119.
[565] *ibid.* p. 143.

wholeheartedly admitted that there existed side by side shorter and
longer expressions meaning the same thing. Certainly there were times,
as we have seen, when such 'redundant' words or passages were actually
employed as 'occasions for' hermeneutical devices. Even so, since this
was not a matter of 'rule' the question as to when or whether to utilise
such devices was entirely dependent on tradition.

We have already come across the question of 'work' upon festival
days.[566] The Samaritans do not, in fact, make any distinction between
the observance of the Sabbath and that of the festivals. The same strict
prohibition against all work applies equally to the festivals and to the
Sabbath and exegetes rely for this extension on expressions like "Ye
shall do no *servile* work therein" (*Lev.* xxiii, 7, 8, 25 etc.). The *Ṭabbākh* [567]
expressly polemicises against those coreligionists who think that, because
in some verses Scripture merely states: "No work shall be done in them"
(*Ex.* xii, 16) certain types of labour are permitted at festivals. The *Ṭabbākh*
affirms explicitly that these two expressions mean exactly the same thing,
although one is longer than the other. Although it is not here stated in
so many words that Abū'l Ḥasan regards the word עבודה as redundant,
we may safely conclude that such is the case.

What we may term a verbal redundancy, such as the repetition of
words for the sake of emphasis, where one could reasonably claim that
the second expression might have been omitted, is occasionally exploited
by the Samaritans. Marqah offers us a long and wellnigh epic composition on the eschatological motif of the Day of Revenge and Recompense.[568] The midrash is based on the theme of the unity of God, and
emphasizes the point that, despite the fact that both reward (good) and
punishment (evil) will indeed be meted bout by Him, the two strikingly
unlike operations are alike proper aspects of the same just Deity. The
verbal 'peg' upon which the midrash is hung in the seemingly 'redundant' expression "I" in *Deut.* xxxii, 39, which is understood by Marqah

---

[566] cf. *sup.* nn. 460, 461, 504. cf. also my article *op. cit.* pp. 112, 146 (nn. 116-117);
cf. Hanover, *Das Festgesetz etc.*, pp. 6f., v, ix, x, xiv and pp. 59f. n. 58 (Hanover's
exposition *ibid.* pp. 20-21 is obviously mistaken).

[567] f. 39f. Only in passing we have to remark that in essence Abū'l Hasan expresses
the same opinion as was held by the 'orthodox' Samaritan traditionalists (cf. previous n.). Wreschner's denial of the authenticity of this tradition (*Sam. Traditionen*,
p. 24, "nichts davon in älteren Schriften erwähnt wird") and his polemics against
Geiger (*ibid.* n. 18) are based on misconceptions. A fuller discussion of this and
similar legal problems must be postponed.

[568] *Memar Marqah* (ed. Macdonald), I, p. 98; II, pp. 161f. cf. *sup.* Part II, n. 330.

as "I (who punish), even I (who reward), am He, and there is no
God with me". From the same midrash it seems very likely that the
expression "I am that I am" (*Ex*. iii, 14) is also interpreted in the same
sense.

Many other midrashim by Marqah are built on the phenomenon of
repeated expressions in Scripture, such 'redundant' expressions being
made the actual basis of the midrash.[569]

There is one interesting case in which Marqah [570] presents an elaborate
exposition of such a repetition. Here he seems to take it for granted that,
after God's explicit command to Moses to employ Aaron in his service
(*Ex*. iv, 14-17), it would be superfluous to repeat the information "And
Moses told Aaron all the wonders of the Lord who sent him, and all the
signs which he had commanded him". (*ibid*. 28). Hence he works out
a long midrash on the phrase "And the Lord said to Aaron" (*ibid*. 27)
to show that this was not in fact an independent prophecy or invitation
to mission, but that the revelation to Aaron served only to instruct him
to meet Moses and to inform him that the latter would then instruct
him on his exact share in the mission. Here then the 'repetition' is
exploited for an apologetic purpose in defence of Moses' major role in
prophecy; Aaron is thus merely his assistant. (*ibid*. 16; cf. *ibid*. vii, 1).

We have already seen on many other occasions that redundant phrases
may serve as sources for midrash.[571] Such usages are not, however,
systematized or classified in such a way that through their consistent
application new regulations may be derived. No such prupose is in mind.
After reviewing many such instances we may conclude that, in the great
amjority of them, the employment of this device has as its sole purpose
that of explaining the reasons underlying the precepts.[572] In other cases

---

[569] *Memar*, *op. cit.* I, p. 8; II, p. 8. The expressions like "and He said", "thus
shalt thou say" etc. in *Ex*. iii, 14-16, although not 'redundant', are repetitive. Similarly
ibid. I, p. 23; II, p. 35, the loquacious expositions of "Then the people of Israel went
and did so" (*Ex*. xii, 28) is a result of scriptural repetition (cf. *ibid*. v, 50) etc.

[570] *ibid*. I, p. 11; II, p. 13.

[571] cf. *sup.* para (d, 2), (e, 1), (f) etc.

[572] *Ṭabbākh*, f. 59b (SLTh.A, p. 100). The midrash on *Ex*. xii, 3 and *ibid*. 21,
explains why "the elders" are singled out in the latter verse. *ibid*. f. 73b (SLTh.A,
p. 114). A rational midrash (on the real purpose of the Passover Sacrifice) is based
on the seemingly 'redundant' expression "no uncircumcised person shall eat thereof",
Ex. xii, 48 (which is clear from the first part of the verse). cf. also *sup.* n. 134 and
Part II, nn. 88-89 etc.

the 'redundant' phrase is utilised to elaborate on the details of the same precept.[573]

In the midrashim dealing with eschatology we occasionally find a more artificial employment of a redundant phrase.[574] Here it is as a rule easy to find a reason for such an artificial use of this device, for the Samaritans are at all times anxious to find proof-texts for their belief in an 'after-life', for which, as we know, there is little or no explicit and unquestionable support in their Scripture.

We may conclude by saying that it is difficult to make any valid comparisons between the systematic employment of 'redundant' words by the Rabbis and the Samaritans' employment of them. Among the former, any repetition is regularly utilised to bring out a new and distinct point.[575] The Samaritan exegete, on the other hand, accepts a repetition as a natural feature of Scripture. No word therefore is by them considered redundant unless other questions have brought a particular phrase into prominence, and unless, in the course of discussing these questions, the 'redundant' expression may be utilised. This device however is never governed by rules, but is entirely subservient to Samaritan tradition.

(5) *Extensions and Restrictions*

We may usefully open our discussion of this subject by drawing certain comparisons. Although throughout the preceding discussion of hermeneutical devices we have been constantly emphasising that these are never regarded by the Samaritans as rules, our first comparison will show at the very outset a very wide difference in possible approach. The Rabbis treat even the least significant recurrence of an expression as a mark of emphasis, intedend either to restrict or to extend its appli-

---

[573] Again the *Ṭabbākh*'s "sixty rules of Passover" serve the best examples e.g. on *Ex.* xii, 4 (f. 60a; SLTH.A, p. 102); *ibid.* v. 6 (f. 62a; SLTh.A, p. 104); *ibid.* vv. 8-9 (f. 65a f.; SLTh.A, p. 107f.); *ibid.* v. 10, compared with *Ex.* xxxiii, 18 (f. 81b; SLTh.A, p. 121). cf. also *sup.* n. 534 and Part II, n. 515. In the *Kāfi* the best examples occur in the chapter on the Nazirite (pp. 231f.; SLTh.A, p. 49f.), cf. also *sup.* nn. 211, 293f., 381, 389, 522 and 539. Although the clarification of some of these midrashim are connected with grammatical or stylistic points the problems of legal details arise from duplication of Scripture.

[574] Gaster, *Sam. Oral Laws etc.*, I, pp. 155 (on *Num.* xix, 14), 156 (on *Ex.* xx, 6), 159 (on *Ex.* xxxii, 34) etc.

[575] Strack, *Introduction etc.*, pp. 96, 98, 291 (n. 14), 296f. (nn. 4-8); Heinemann, *op. cit.* p. 117. cf. also following notes.

cation.[576] There are also other similar rules and assumptions of which more will be said in our conclusion. At this point, however, we can single out a feature common to all the Rabbinic hermeneutical rules, namely that they embody artificial devices which are nevertheless consistently and assiduously applied. This fact stands in total contrast to the empirical employment of the notions of extension or restriction among the Samaritans.

Extension is a favourite device used by Marqah in particular, and later by other writers. The easiest method of moralising is surely to add further details to an extended homiletical midrash. It is no less easy to explain any paradoxical detail in Scripture by introducing an extended sense of the scriptural word.[577] The same comment applies to halakhic matters, where certain types of precept may thus easily be extended far beyond their literal sense. Ethical injunctions in particular may come to assume an ideological sense in order to serve as prototypes for all cases falling within the same ethical range. Such extensions, however, are not necessarily applicable only to ethical precepts. From Marqah onwards we find these extended meanings applied to the laws in other

---

[576] Rosenblatt, op. cit. p. 4, n. 36. We cannot enter into the problem of whether such devices originate from ambiguity.

[577] Unfortunately the midrashic devices are not often discernible in *Memar Marqah*. It will suffice here to hint to some more obvious and almost explicit examples : In I, p. 5 (= II, p. 3), there is an obvious expansion of the biblical story (*Ex.* iii, 2). The antecedent appearance of an angel (before the burning bush), his discourse with Moses, the latter's trembling etc. (cf. S.P. וירא אליו מלאך). Similarly *ibid.* I, p. 11 (= II, p. 13) details are given not mentioned in *Ex.* iv, 20. "The proclamation (to return to Egypt) came with the fall of the evening, during the night he prepared for the journey *and Moses took his wife and his sons* on the morning following the proclamation." Here, however, it becomes obvious from the following context that the expansion was deduced by analogy (cf. *Gen.* xxii, 3). In another place (*ibid.* I, p. 20 = II, p. 30) a biblical contradiction is explained away by the expansion. After Moses is threatened with execution if he attempts to see Pharaoh again, the formers answers : "*As you say*" (*Ex.* x, 29). Nevertheless, we find later (*ibid.* xi, 4, S.P.). Moses speaking to Pharaoh. This is harmonized by the tacit assumption that before Moses could be expelled from the palace "The pillar of cloud descended with great might and the Lord addressed him in his (i.e. Pharaoh's) hearing". On the same additions of the S.P. (*Ex.* xi, 3-4) there are built further midrashic expansions (*ibid.* I, p. 23 = II p. 36). In later literature such devices are even more frequent. In the *Exodus Commentary* (attributed to Ghazal al-Duweik), pp. 32ff it is stated that there were many Israelite midwifes and the two mentioned (*Ex.* I 15) were their leaders. Obviously this and other similar expansions are apologetic in nature, to mitigate the inconsistencies of scripture often pointed out by sceptics.

fields, such as ritual.[578] They all, moreover, share one feature in common, namely that they, whether occurring in halakhic or aggadic subjects, are never applied artificially. They remain, despite their wide scope embracing topics not explicitly mentioned in Scripture, germane to the subject-matter. Another feature displayed by the Samaritans in their application of extensions, once again, is that they never follow any set rules or construct any system, but extend each meaning in a simple and unsophisticated manner.

The rare exceptions to these generalizations occur in the field of eschatology, as we might expect. Here the extension of the literal meaning very often assumes allegorical proportions, and the literal sense itself is frequently all but ignored.[579] As we have seen in connection with the hermeneutical devices already discussed, the field of eschatology tends always to give rise to much more strained and artificial methods of interpretation.

Obviously extensions of some kind are common to all groups. Thus, for example, the Dead Sea Scroll Sect, although in their halakhah they mainly followed a literalist approach, nevertheless extended some of the

---

[578] In *Memar Marqah* (ed. Macdonald), I, p. 20f. = II, p. 30f., the expositions on *Ex.* xii, 1-2 are mainly of aggadic nature. However, the connection between "the beginning of the months" and "creation" לכן אתעבד שרוי לירחיה הך בראשית) עבידה שרוי לבריתה) has also halakhic implications. By this midrash we are to understand the command of preparing the lambs on the tenth of the first month (*Ex.* xii, 3) and their being "kept" until the fourteenth (*ibid.* v. 6). A few further hints of the *Memar*'s expansionist halakhic expositions will suffice : honouring parents (I, p. 68 = II, p. 107f.); removing neighbours landmark (I, p. 70 = II, pp. 112ff. cf. *sup.* n. 538); misleading a blind man (I, p. 71 = II, p. 114); sexual offences (I, p. 74 = II, p. 119, cf. *sup.* n. 233); slaying a neighbour in secret (I, p. 75 = II, p. 122) etc. The treatment of halakhic expansions in the Samaritan legal literature would justify a special work devoted to this complicated subject. Here we have to limit our evidence to a few selected allusions. The *Kāfi* expands the priestly washing of hand (*Ex.* xxx, 21) to a general rule to be practised by every person before prayer (p. 10f. = SLTh.A, p. 47f., cf. *sup.* Part II, n. 530). The laws of Sabbath are very widely expanded (*ibid.* pp. 330, 335 = SLTh.A, pp. 70, 74). For further cases cf. *sup.* Part II, nn. 269, 630 etc. Just to show that the *Ṭabbākh* follows the same way, cf. the "laws of purification in water" (f. 55a = SLTh.A, p. 97, although shorter than those of the *Kāfi* they cover the same type of expansionist regulations). Typical are the *Ṭabbākh*'s expansions of the laws of the Passover (cf. e.g. *sup.* Part II, n. 176). Needless to say, such expansions (no matter what other exegetical devices they involve) depend entirely upon tradition. cf. *inf.* n. 581.

[579] Gaster, *op. cit.* (*sup.* n. 574), pp. 149f., 152, 154, 240f. cf. also *sup.* Part II, nn. 193, 196 etc.

precepts far beyond their literal sense.[580] These extensions, which we also find among other ancient literalists, were never executed in a mechanical or even systematic way, and we cannot, moreover, find any evidence for their following any set rules whatever. Most of these extensions depended accordingly on the exegetical traditions of each group.[581]

In marked contrast to this all-pervading simplicity, the extensions employed in Rabbinic hermeneutics appear as part of a complicated and elaborate system, in which preconceived patterns and rules are strictly and consistently applied. We began our discussion with an example of one of these rules, but the classic example, which by the way has no exact counterpart elsewhere, is the *Ribbui*. This rule asserts that certain particles (e.g. אף, גם and even את) of themselves indicate an inclusion and an amplification.[582]

It is of course true that some of these extensions are widely used in connexion with precepts of an ethical nature, as for instance ... "nor put a stumblingblock before the blind" (*Lev.* xix, 14).[583] Indeed, such extensions, as we have seen, are also employed by Marqah and other Samaritan writers. The peculiarity of Rabbinic exegesis here is the carrying over of such extensions into the field of ritual even where they conflict with the literal sense. It would be, then, an over simplification to state that the Rabbis apply the exegetical rule of *Ribbui* to rational precepts only, and that they refrain from applying it in the field of pure ritual, which can have no fully rational justification but is simply accepted as being a matter of Divine decree.[584] The truth is and this is the major and salient difference between the two systems — that the hermeneutical rules applied by the Rabbis do not in any way discriminate between

---

[580] cf. my artycle *ALUOS* VI (1969), pp. 102, 136 (n. 34) and *passim*.

[581] cf. previous note. The best evidence that the Samaritans likewise depend on their own tradition is expressed by Jūsuf ibn Salamah in connection with the laws of levitical purity, which are greatly expanded. He polemicises against sceptics who deny expositions not mentioned explicitly in Scripture (*Kāfi*, p. 177). His answer is that regulations satisfying the requirements of reason and established by the tradition of the nation do not even require additional proof. فان قال قايلا ان الشرع لا يذكرها الجواب ان كل ما نهط به (ينهض اليه .Ms. B) العقل (والامه متناقله فلا يحتاج الي دليل غير ذلك cf. also my article *op. cit.* p. 118, 154 (n. 171).

[582] Strack, *Introduction etc.*, pp. 96 (rule 1), 290 (n. 7).

[583] M. Gutmann, "Mashmaut ha-Katuv etc.", *Hazofeh*, V (1921), p. 115.

[584] cf. *idem. Eine Untersuchung über den Geltungsumfang etc.*, pp. 25f. cf. *sup.* Part II, n. 444.

the various subject-matters; and what makes the Rabbinic system quite distinct from others is that the Rabbis entirely ignore the simple meaning whenever the practice of *Ribbui* operates.

One of the most interesting of their examples of extension is that connected with the yearly half-shekel, which is only stipulated at times when the people are counted (*Lev.* xxi, 11f.). On this matter the Pharisees waged a fierce battle against the ancient literalists, the traces of which are to be found in the Talmud.[585] Even Rabbi Ishmael, who as a rule advocated the strict confinement of Biblical expressions to their narrowest application, had to admit that in certain cases tradition over-ruled Scripture. Although Rabbi Ishmael strongly objected to the practice of *Ribbui* once an extension had been sanctioned by tradition, he found himself obliged to accept it, despite its apparent discrepancy with Scripture.[586]

The most interesting halakhic rule is perhaps that known as the 'double extension' which in its effect is not unlike the mathematical rule that two negatives make a positive. According to this rule then, one extension on top of another to the Rabbis amounted to an exclusion and a limitation.[587]

Obviously one could multiply examples.[588] The general pattern, however, serves to throw into relief the great divergence between the Rabbis and the Samaritans in this respect.

When dealing with the Samaritan exegesis of grammatical points, we have already noted that certain words are hereby restricted in their meaning. If we take the definition of Abib [589] and other similar examples, we find that the restriction in their meaning is largely dependent on tradition. In the particular case of Abib there is an additional reason for polemics, namely, that of proving that calendaric calculations, and not the observance of natural phenomena, determine the proper times of the festivals. The protracted controversy with the Karaites on this point may well have lent support to this restricted meaning. We find already in Marqah that, owing to his apologetic attitude with regard to Moses, he restricts the meaning of *Ex.* iv, 14 to "Were it not for my favour

---

585 Jer. *Šeqalim*, I, 1; 45d.

586 Gutmann, *op. cit.* (*sup.* n. 584), p. 26.

587 Strack, *op. cit.* pp. 96 (rule 3), 290 (n. 9). This hermeneutical rule worked in two directions; one limitation on top of another amounted to an inclusion or amplification; cf. *inf.* nn. 592 and 597.

588 In purely aggadic matters, cf. Heinemann, *op. cit.* pp. 149f.

589 cf. *sup.* n. 132 and text there.

towards you from the beginning, my anger *would have* reached you".[590]
Such slight restrictions in meaning are found elsewhere in Marqah.
We have also observed [591] that "the Judge" (*Deut.* xvii, 12) is limited
in its meaning to the High Priest alone. In this case, however, although
there are certainly apologetic motives involved, the main reason for
assigning this limited meaning really arises out of the peculiarities of
the Samaritan Pentateuch, closely followed by the whole of Samaritan
tradition.

A strange situation, which we have discussed elsewhere, is created by
the particle אך which, according to Rabbinic tradition, invariably denotes
a very strict limitation or diminuation of the subject which it qualifies.[592]
In Samaritan usage, however, this particle has no such severely restrictive
function.[593] They do not of course dispute or modify the true meaning
of this particle, but they do not, on the other hand, seek any artificial
rule by means of which they may introduce limitations or diminutions
not explicitly mentioned in Scripture. To take one example only, and
a typical one, the expression אך in *Ex.* xii, 16, is interpreted as implying
that, despite the general prohibition against preparing food on a festival,
the limited amount of work necessary for the preparation of the Passover
Sacrifice is nevertheless permitted. Although the particle here is granted
a certain restrictive sense, it contributes nothing new whatever to the
Scriptural words.

There are very few instances of restriction in halakhic subjects which
are wholly dependent on single words. These few exceptions are built
up on the other exegetical factors involved.[594] At any rate, no rule is

---

[590] *Memar Marqah* (ed. Macdonald), I, p. 10; II, p. 12.

[591] cf. *sup.* Part II, para (j).

[592] Strack, *ibid.* (rules 2 and 4; nn. 8 and 10).

[593] cf. my article, *op. cit.* pp. 111f., 146f. (nn. 113-117).

[594] Because of the intricate nature of such halakhic restrictions we have to limit
our notes to one representative example. There is a general prohibition concerning
the Passover Offering, "ye shall let nothing of it remain until the morning" (*Ex.*
xii, 10, cf. also *Deut.* xvi, 4). The question arises, why is "fat" singled out in *Ex.*
xxiii, 18? This is explained by the *Ṭabbākh* (f. 81a; SLTh.A, p. 121) that the "fat" is
further restricted than "that what remaineth". When Passover falls on a Sabbath,
the Sacrifice is advanced to Friday afternoon (the 14th). Although "that what remaineth" can not be burnt before the termination of the Sabbath (the 16th), the "fat"
is burnt before the commencement of the Sabbath (on the 14th). There are more
complicated limitations in the *Kāfi* (e.g. on *Lev.* xv, 11, pp. 149f. and on *Deut.* xxiii, 11,
pp. 182f.) but these must await further discussion. The common feature of all such
restrictive devices is, that they do not depend on "exegetical principles" or rules, but
rather on tradition.

here applied which can be generally applied to other cases. It is also instructive to note that the artificial restriction either of the meanings of words or of halakhic or aggadic subjects is hardly ever found in Samaritan literature, except in the rare case where it is crucial for polemics.

To highlight this distinctiveness of the Samaritan method of exegesis, we may again compare it with the Rabbinical hermeneutical rules. In the Mishna already we find that injunctions having reference to certain specified objects or persons are not to be extended to any others.[595] Although this principle sounds reasonable enough, if it is applied mechanically, these restrictions may be carried to absurd lengths.[596] Even more complicated is the principle embodied in מעוט, which often not only excludes the object but even bestows an additional diminution. One exclusion on top of another amounted to an amplification.[597] No true equivalent of any of these rules can, we may safely say, ever be found amongst the Samaritans.

In addition to these extensions and restrictions in the narrower sense of the words, devices employing hermeneutical rules also create wider applications on similar lines. Rules for formulating broad generalizations or deducing far-reaching restrictive definitions are quite frequent amongst the Rabbinical hermeneutical principles.

Although we may perhaps call some of the analogies employed by the Samaritans 'broad generalizations', these are limited to particular types of case, and are never formulated as general rules. We have dealt, for instance, with the difference between the analogizing practices of the Karaites and those of the Samaritans. The most outstanding example may be found by a comparison of their respective approaches to forbidden marriages. It can in general be stated that, while the Karaite method of analogy known as the rule of רכוב developed into a system of broad generalizations having the effect of forbidding intermarriage between persons within various degrees of relationship, including those merely related by marriage,[598] the Samaritans limited their method of analogy to conform to traditional custom, closely linked to Scripture itself.

---

[595] Rosenblatt, *op. cit.* pp. 3f. (n. 27), p. 22 (nn. 24-26).

[596] Scholars often point to the exposition of זולל וסובא (*Deut.* xxi, 20) in *Sanhedrin* vii, 2 or to כאשר זמם (*Deut.* xix, 19) in *Makkoth*, I, 6. In the latter case the Sadducees disputed the Rabbis' restriction, however from Josephus (*Antiq.* iv, viii, 15) and *Susanna* (v. 62) it seems that the Pharissean ruling was prevalent.

[597] cf. *sup.* n. 592 and Part II, n. 598.

[598] cf. *sup.* nn. 448f., 463f., 496ff.

The Samaritans, then, did not create by their method any abstract rules or codified legislative principles. For this reason, their method of analogy could not develop or be further extended to embrace new situations not already covered by their existing tradition.

There are in Samaritan exegesis, no counterparts whatever to those Rabbinical rules which engender broad generalisations. A moment's thought upon hermeneutical rules like the *Binyan Abh* בנין אב,[599] or the *Perat ukhelal* כלל ופרט [600] is sufficient to make one realise how significant for Rabbinical literature are the generalizations they give rise to. If we do sometimes find a distinction drawn between the general and the particular in Samaritan exegesis, this is normally to be attributed to exegetical difficulties, which are as a rule solved by carefully distinguishing between the larger and smaller units. One of the instances which we have previously considered is the question of leprosy present in garments, as reviewed by the *Kāfi*. Here there is a somewhat vague attempt to introduce such a distinction.[601] We find in the *Ṭabbākh* too, in his explanation of the Passover Offering (*Ex.* xii, 8-9) that Abū'l Ḥasan points out the difference between these two verses. He asserts that the detailed enumeration of the victim's limbs (v. 9), as opposed to the general mention of the roast meat, is for a special purpose, namely, since the feet and the head may not be designated as 'meat', to point out the need here for generalization, so that the people will not be picking and choosing, and furthermore to ensure that the lamb will be roasted as a whole.[602]

Naturally, one could multiply examples of such cases where distinctions are drawn between the detailed and the general description. However, no general rule of any kind is in operation for drawing further inference from such cases. Any supposed resemblances, therefore, to Rabbinical hermeneutical principles that one may possibly come across will be purely coincidental, and to that extent meaningless.

We have already seen how limited in number are the restrictions in Samaritan exegesis: and clearly one cannot expect to find therein any counterparts to far-reaching restrictive definitions. As for such Rabbinical methods as *Kelal u-pherat* and other similar devices,[603] there is not even a formal resemblance to them in Samaritan exegesis.

---

[599] Strack, *op. cit.* pp. 99 (rules 3-4), 286 (nn. 6-7).
[600] *ibid.* (rule 5) (nn. 9).
[601] cf. *sup.* n. 107f.
[602] *Ṭabbākh*, ff. 66b f. (SLTh.A, p. 108).
[603] This rule was subdivided by R. Ishmael into eight principles (4-11). Needless

(6) *Harmonizations*

Strictly speaking, harmonization cannot be distinguished from other hermeneutical devices, since it does not show any specific external features, which would help towards its definition. All 'hermeneutical rules' are more or less intended to explain away moot points in Scripture. So if they themselves cannot be truly described as 'harmonizations', they do at least serve as accessories to the harmonization of obscure and conflicting details.

The Rabbis themselves, as we have remarked before, devised forced interpretations of apparent discrepancies.[604] Medieval heretics or sceptics were understandably very apt at pointing out such discrepancies as existed, for example in the varying number of Canaanite nations whose countries were allotted to the Israelites. Although the Rabbis dealt effectively with most of these problems by harmonization, by merely listing them these sceptics brought them to general attention so that medieval commentators were forced to tackle them ever anew.[605]

This need for harmonization was no less acute even in ancient times, when writers, embarrassed by the contrast between the strict demands of the Torah and the lax practices of later heroes, such as David and others, were forced to devise excuses in order to harmonise the two extremes of conduct.[606] The Rabbis with their naive approach, not unnaturally simply attempted to whitewash their Biblical heroes by aggadic inventions which transformed them into paragons of virtue and piety.[607]

It has been sufficiently shown that to find contradictions one does not need to be a logician or a trained biblical critic. Even a simpleton may ascertain with regard to one of his acquaintances that his present practices stand in striking contrast to his former behaviour. His acquaintance must, therefore, have changed and become a seemingly different person, and yet he is the same person. From a similar primitive standpoint, if any discrepancies are found between the various parts of Scripture and the expositor firmly believes in its divine origin and in its

---

to say, more sophisticated methods have even less relevance to Samaritan exegesis. cf. Strack, *op. cit.* pp. 97 (rules 19-20), 293 (nn. 23-24).

[604] cf. *sup.* nn. 550f.

[605] J. Rosenthal, "Ancient Questions etc.", *HUCA* XXI (1948), pp. ט״נ f.

[606] Spiro, "Samaritans, Tobiads, etc.", *PAAJR* XX (1951), p. 283, n. 14a.

[607] *Shabbath*, 55b, 56a-b; *Abhodah Zarah*, 4b etc.

perfect unity, he will try, nay he must try, to explain away the discrepancies by means of harmonization.[608]

Some of the earliest Rabbinical hermeneutical principles, already reviewed,[609] originate from this need to reconcile contradictory passages of Scripture. Hillel's main motive, according to the Talmud, "for coming up from Babylonia" was precisely to solve such difficulties by these methods.[610] There is no need to repeat here our previous discussion of such principles as found in the Mishna.[611]

When we come to compare this whole approach with that of the Samaritans', we find that the underlying motives are exactly the same. It has to be emphasised that the Samaritans' approach to Scripture, this comprising the Pentateuch only, is much more rigid in all respects, and they can never admit even the possibility of real discrepancies here. Their usual attitude is that there are two types of Scripture, the one, by far the larger, consisting of explicit and self-explanatory passages, the other, very much the smaller, of opaque ones. This less common type stands in need of further 'elucidation', which is to be carried out by harmonizing it with the commoner explicit type.[612]

The most prominent of Samaritan harmonizers is Marqah and his attitude is adopted in substance by all later exegetes. In his harmonizations in explanation of his points Marqah takes it for granted that all his readers are well acquainted with the intricacies of Scripture. Thus, in order to explain the Elders' function, he harmonizes their role with that of the Elders of the Levites who, after their retirement, "minister to their brethren in the Sanctuary". Their ministration evidently cannot mean actual service in the Sanctuary, since this is confined to the Aaronites. Here, then, it must mean teaching. By such an interpretation all three mutually contradictory expressions in *Num.* viii, 25 are satisfactorily harmonized.[613]

> *And honour the face of an old man* (*Lev.* xix, 32),[614] who makes himself honourable in knowledge. He who makes himself of little esteem, who could honour him? An Elder should be wise, for every Elder sits to teach; as He said, *And from the age of fifty years they shall withdraw* (*Num.* viii, 25), and sit to teach

---

608 Schwarz, *op. cit.* (*sup.* n. 557), pp. 11ff.
609 cf. *sup.* Part II, nn. 42-45.
610 Jer. *Pesaḥim*, VI, 2; 33a.
611 cf. *sup.* Part II, n. 43.
612 cf. *sup.* Part II, n. 132.
613 *Memar Marqah* (ed. Macdonald), I, p. 79; II, p. 128.
614 ותוקר אפי סהב .S.T cf. ותוקר אפי חכים.

in the Tent of Meeting as He said, *But minister to their brethren in the Tent of Meeting* (*Num.* viii, 26).[615]

Apply your mind. Do not say that it refers here to service, for the service of the Sanctuary is not for Israel (in the same manner) as it is meant for the Levites; and within (the Sanctuary) it is the prerogative of Aaron and his sons. Consider the former words and praise Him who said them. He commanded *To keep the charge* (*ibid.*), and again said "*And they shall do no service* (*ibid.*). Therefore Moses commanded these Elders teaching that would bring them honour.

There are many other examples of involved harmonisation in Marqah. There are, however, some luminous ones as well, which can be comprehended with no deep thought.[616]

We may now single out the *Ṭabbākh*, as best representing the early exegesis of the Islamic period, and as dealing both with halakhic and aggadic expositions. In the eyes of *Abū'l Ḥasan*, Marqah remains the greatest authority, and he faithfully and devotedly follows his master's methods of harmonization. Let us then take a verse containing especially difficult expressions and which the *Ṭabbākh* successfully interprets by harmonising it with more comprehensible verses. The Samaritan Pentateuch reads in *Deut.* xxxii, 10; "He encouraged him in a desert land and with praises He set him up".[617] The *Ṭabbākh* explains the first part as referring to Jacob when he was afraid to go down to Egypt, (*Gen.* xlvi, 3-4), or, in an alternative interpretation, as referring to the Israelites before their crossing of the Red Sea (*Ex.* xiv, 10f.). The second part is taken as referring to the praises of Pharaoh (inspired by God) when Jacob and his sons came to Egypt (*Gen.* xlvii, 5-6).[618] This is, of course, only one out of many other such harmonizations of verses in this book and the same is true of all the later literature.[619]

So far we have treated discrepancies between minor details in single verses. It is now necessary to examine the employment of har-

---

[615] S.T. ‏וילף עם אחיו‎. There is no need here to compare it with Rabbinic harmonizations. cf. C. Heller, *The Sam. Pentateuch etc.*, p. 200, n. 9.

[616] Most of the other exegetical devices used by Marqah are meant to serve as handmaids for harmonizing contradictory passages. cf. *sup.* nn. 93f., 130, 202f., 238, 250, 264f., 362. cf. especially the paragraph on 'analogy' e.g. 439f., 453 etc.

[617] S.P. ‏חיצה בארע מדברה‎ S.T. ‏יאמצהו בארץ המדבר ובתהללות ישימנהו‎
‏ובתשבחתה שבינה‎

[618] *Ṭabbākh*, f. 209b.

[619] In his exegesis on *Deut.* xxxii-xxxiii this is his common way, e.g. *Deut.* xxxiii, 9 (*ibid.* f. 204b) by harmonizing it with *Ex.* xxxii, 26-27. cf. also *sup.* Part II, nn. 96-99, and *Ṭabbākh*, ff. 50a f. (SLTh.A, pp. 92f.), *ibid.* f. 86b (SLTh.A, p. 126) etc.

monization on wider themes. The previously mentioned example from Marqah will serve well enough to illustrate this feature too. As we have said, there are many more complicated ones, too lengthy by far to deal with here.[620]

Again, the *Ṭabbākh* is very typical of the Samaritan approach here, and more than usually explicit whenever it employs harmonization on broad themes. *Abū'l Ḥasan* introduces a responsum on the question of the High Priest's fasting on the Day of Atonement.[621] According to *Lev.* x, 18, "sin offerings", if their blood is "not brought into the Sanctuary within", must be consumed by the priests. Now the "he-goat" prescribed for the Day of Atonement (*Num.* xxix, 11) is described as one such offering which is to be eaten by the High Priest, and evidence is brought from Marqah, whom our author regards as the equal of a prophet in authority, that he describes in one of his hymns how Aaron actually ate on this day to atone for the congregation. Obviously, to this a plausible objection might be raised on the basis of *Lev.* xxiii, 29, where it states that one who breaks the fast "shall be cut off from among his people". *Abū'l Ḥasan* ably disposes of this objection by comparing this special consumption of the sin-offering by the High Priest with all his other *cultic work*. From this standpoint, the same biblical injunction which dispenses the High Priest from the obligation to rest on the Sabbath also makes it obligatory for him to consume this offering, as an essential part of this cultic work. There are many other even wider contextual harmonizations in the *Ṭabbākh* and in the *Kāfi*. Some of them we have examined on previous occasions.[622]

There are in addition some instances of harmonization which are offered for the purpose of comparison, in order to show the similarities and differences between two sets of rules. Thus, for example, the *Kāfi* [623] compares the ceremony of the sprinkling of the "water of separation" (*Num.* xxx, 9) with that of the purification of the leper, in which

---

[620] cf. *sup.* n. 616 and Part II, nn. 70-71, 77, 345, 474 etc.

[621] *Ṭabbākh*, ff. 194b-195b.

[622] The most commonly mentioned harmonization in the *Ṭabbākh* is the attempt to reconcile the discrepancies of the Passover laws in *Deut.* and *Ex.* (cf. *sup.* n. 132). The most difficult problem, however, is the contrast between *Ex.* which limits the sacrifice to sheep and goats while *Deut.* xvi, 2 mentions also cattle (cf. f. 82a-85b; SLTh.A, pp. 122-125, and f. 86a; SLTh.A, p. 126). There is further, a fierce attack on the Jews on this point (ff. 192b-193b). We have also seen the general harmonization of Abū'l Hasan concerning the 'pilgrimages' (*sup.* Part II, n. 174) etc. As for the *Kāfi* cf. *sup.* nn. 382, 492f., 522, 536ff. etc.

[623] pp. 137f. (SLTh.A, pp. 19f.).

sprinkling also occurs, but, in this instance, using the blood of the bird brought as a sacrifice (*Lev.* xiv, 2f.).

If we take a comprehensive view of the Samaritan methods of harmonization, it becomes apparent that there are in truth no fixed rules as to when and in what way they may or must be utilized. Even themes which quite naturally and easily lend themselves to harmonization are not always treated as one might expect. A classic example of this fact is the requirement of 'fringes' (ציצית). The Rabbis, realizing the ambiguity in *Num.* xv, 38 & 39, here employ harmonization. Since the expression 'Ṣiṣith' may mean either locks of hair or fringes, and furthermore since the number of "borders" is not specified, they harmonise this passage with *Deut.* xxii, 12. ("Thou shalt make thee fringes upon the four quarters of thy vesture"), the details thereby becoming clear.[624] The Samaritans, on the other hand, cannot use this particular harmonization because the word 'ṣiṣith' does not occur in that place. The *Ṭabbākh*[625] instead harmonises 'ṣiṣith' with "the ribband of blue" worn by the High Priest (*Ex.* xxviii, 28), and then further proceeds to harmonize it with the breastplate in which the "jewels of twelve colours" are set. By means of this harmonization he arrives at the conclusion that there are intended to be silk fringes, thirty-two in number, comprising the twelve colours belonging to the jewels. Since there is here no harmonization with the verse in *Deut*, there are intended to be, not four fringes, but only two, worn on the sleeves.

There is no modus operandi whatever on the part of the Samaritan,

---

[624] Weiss, *Dor Dor etc.*, I, p. 7.

[625] ff. 108a-110a. اثنين وثلاثون زهرة حرير مجموع اثنا عشر لونا ... جعلها

... تعالى على العضوين يقع بها التصرف وهما الجناحين These fringes (= flower or blossoms) "confined by God to the *two* limbs causing the actions" have nothing in common with the Rabbinic ordinances of Ṣiṣith (*Menaḥoth*, 41b, cf. *ibid.* Tosaphoth, s.v. ש אומרים ארבע (ב״). The 32 'blossoms' of the Samaritans are certainly *not* divided (4 × 8) into four corners. cf. P.R. Weis, "Some Samaritanism etc.", *JThS* XLV (1944), pp. 202f. It was rightly pointed out that Justin Martyr's testimony shows the antiquity of Samaritan traditions. The exegetical background, however, was grossly misrepresented in the article (cf. *ibid.* p. 204, nn. 5-6). From Abū'l Ḥasan's own words it is obvions that the midrash does not depend entirely on תכלת = כלך = حرير The twelve colours are dependent on a play of = ציץ ציצית in the sense of "flower" زهرة This is stated quite explicitly (*Ṭabbākh*, f. 109a, cf. Weis, *ibid.* p. 204, n. 4). مثل البياض فى صحة الزهر والالوان فيه

unlike the Rabbis, for dealing with those cases where precepts apparently conflict with each other. In the Samaritans' unsophisticated and naive view, it would be quite impossible for the Divine Legislator to allow of such conflicts in His precepts.[626] A whole series of Samaritan polemics against the Jews is based on such cases as these, where Samaritan rigorism demands the literal execution of Scriptural precepts. To mention but a few examples, there is, first of all, the dilemma posed by the duty of circumcising a child whose life may be endangered thereby. The Rabbis always regard the preservation of life as an overriding Biblical precept which absolves any person from any other precepts, if these entail possible loss of life.[627] The Samaritans, on the other hand, insist that the child must be circumcised on the eigth day regardless of the consequence.[628] The same rigid principle is being applied when they force babies to fast on the Day of Atonement.[629]

The Passover Offering, which, like many other positive commands, is held by the Rabbis to be of superior force to any negative commands, such as, in this case, those pertaining to the desecration of the Sabbath, invariably takes place under their jurisdiction, even if its first day coincides with the Sabbath. The Samaritans, on the other hand, lacking any guidelines of this nature, either postpone the Passover till the Sabbath is just over (if the 14th Nissan falls on a Sunday), or advance it to the early afternoon of the Friday before the commencement of Sabbath (if the 14th Nissan is a Sabbath).[630] The Samaritans even have to find a justification for carrying out circumcision on the Sabbath, if this coincides with the eight day of the child's life.[631] By the Rabbis such a practice is taken for granted; and we find already in the New Testament (*John* vii, 14) that this particular abrogation of the Sabbath laws is used as a basis for further inferences in Christian preaching.[632]

We cannot enter here into further details of such controversies between the Samaritans and the Jews. It is, however, instructive to note that

---

[626] cf. my article *ALUOS* VI (1969), pp. 111, 145 (nn. 105-106).

[627] *Yoma* VII, 4-7 and parallels, cf. previous n.

[628] The *Kāfi* (pp. 162ff.) has a long polemics against the Jews on this problem. cf. also Abdel Al, *op. cit.* pp. 690f. (translation, pp. 531f.).

[629] Halkin, "Sam. Polemics etc.", *PAAJR* viii (1935/6), pp. 47f.

[630] cf. *Ṭabbākh*, ff. 67b f., 80a f., 81a, 85b (SLTh.A, pp. 109, 120, 121 and 125 respectively). The whole argument for this practice is clearly set out by Munajja (*Masa'il al-Khilāf*, Ib, pp. 10-12). cf. also *sup.* nn. 514-516.

[631] cf. my article, *op. cit.* pp. 111f., 146 (nn. 111-112).

[632] cf. E.C. Hoskyns, *The Fourth Gospel* (ed. F.N. Davey, London 1947), pp. 315f.

similar controversies existed amongst the Karaites themselves, who, as a general rule, rejected the Rabbinical harmonizations. Heated discussions on these matters took place amongst them as a result of later developments, when they keenly felt the need for the systematization of their own rules.[633]

To sum up, the basic differences between the Samaritans and the Rabbis have by now become quite evident to us. Whereas the latter admit possible conflicts between rules and make provision to resolve them by means of harmonizations,[634] the former will not even consider it such a possibility. As we have seen, they lack any kind of rule or system, and the question exactly when to harmonize is entirely dependent on their living tradition. For this reason, we hardly ever find among them the practice favoured by some Rabbis, namely that or artificially multiplying conflicts between Biblical passages for the purpose of deriving new midrashim from them by means of subsequent harmonization.[635]

(7) *Play on Letters*

There is no doubt at all that play on letters normally operates in such a way as to destroy fairly completely the simple and literal understanding of Scripture. It is therefore a matter for surprise that, despite the Samaritan principle of strict literalism, we find so many instances of this device throughout the whole range of Samaritan literature. We can well understand such a device being frequently employed by the Rabbis, since the general tendency among them is to atomise Scripture and to grant total independence to its smallest units. It seems, however, that even they are not unaware that such play on letters need not necessarily militate against the simple sense of Scripture,[636] but that it may merely add new colouring to its "hidden layers" if used with discretion.

The notion that there exist these "hidden layers" in Scripture is not favoured very greatly by the Samaritans. Nevertheless, always provided that 'deeper meanings' do not militate against the simple sense of Scripture, but merely supply additional 'hints' which may be of moral and religious value, they are eagerly sought by the Samaritans themselves. After all, the Divine Book is never to be treated like profane literature,

---

[633] Ankori, *Karaites in Byzantium*, pp. 404f., 407 etc. cf. *sup.* Part II, n. 46.

[634] Strack, *Introduction etc.*, pp. 95 (rule 13), 228 (n. 7); cf. also Daube, "Rabbinic Methods etc.", *HUCA* XXII (1949), pp. 259f. (cf. also nn. 73-76 *ibid.*).

[635] Heinemann, *Darkhei ha-Aggadah*, pp. 28f. (cf. specially nn. 27-31).

[636] *idem, ibid.* pp. 103ff.

and may well have been enriched by its Author with aids to the further enlightenment of the 'wise' who value the 'mysteries' of spiritual knowledge. One is certainly entitled to point out that, amongst all the peoples of the Bible, such a belief is greatly intensified by the Biblical accounts of God adding letters to the names of Abraham, Sarah and Joshua. We are, therefore, not entirely without justification in considering this belief a genuinely Samaritan one,[637] and not necessarily a later development mechanically adopted by the Samaritans from other groups.

Having regard to the fact that *Gemaṭria* was a very generally known device, it may certainly have belonged to the cultural stock of many nations. The Babylonian bricks from the eigth century B. C. E. exhibit even at this early date, some of these plays on words.[638] In Judaism it was much further developed and most probably under Greek influence.[639]

It may, moreover, be said that, in general, not unlike the Greeks, the other peoples of the ancient Near East saw in letters certain mystical 'elements of knowledge'.[640] Once such beliefs had become popular, all kinds of permutations and combinations were soon to be found everywhere; and although one should adopt a very cautious and critical approach to all claims made by the Biblical scholars to have discovered acrostics intended to convey an author's name, yet some truth may nevertheless at all times lie behind this idea.[641]

It seems that the Dead Sea Scroll Sect also made some use of such devices besides other ciphers and cryptograms, all of which were most probably intended to hint at secret doctrines.[642] Although as suggested above, the Rabbinical symbolisms based on letters are in some respects similar to their Greek counterparts, there are many developments within them which must be quite independent.[643] And in Christian literature too we find almost the same devices as those employed by the Rabbis.[644]

---

[637] Gaster, *The Samaritans*, p. 70.

[638] F. Dornseiff, *Das Alphabet in Mystic und Magie* (2nd ed., Leipzig-Berlin 1925), p. 91.

[639] *ibid.* p. 95.

[640] στοιχεῖον cf. *ibid.* pp. 14-17.

[641] Driver, *Semitic Writing etc.*, pp. 206f. (Appendix III).

[642] Brownlee, "Biblical Interpretation etc.", *BA* xiv (1951), pp. 66, 70f.; cf. Driver, *The Judean Scrolls etc.*, pp. 335ff.; 396ff.

[643] cf. *sup.* n. 636.

[644] cf. my article in *JJS* XI (1960), p. 18 (nn. 124-125). cf. Farrar, *History of Interpretation*, pp. 102f. Although Farrar ridicules Reuchlin for using erroneous Hebrew orthography for his *Gemaṭria* (n. 4), his own is also wrong. The most curious employment of such systems occurs in polemics by missionaries trying to gain converts by

It is a well-known fact that the Samaritans, even those with a certain degree of philosophical training (e.g. Abū'l Ḥasan), believe wholeheartedly that the Law was literally given to Moses as a written work from the hand of God. We shall now understand the following midrash of Marqah's which will serve admirably as a key to the whole Samaritan understanding of the deep significance of the letters.[645]

> Where is there the like of Moses and who can compare with Moses, a prophet to whom there is no like among all mankind? When God appeared to him in the Bush, he found twenty-two letters written before him with devouring fire; by means of these Moses expounded the Law. They are the elements of the words of Hebrew speech.

"The elements of the words of Hebrew speech" mean much more to Marqah than their merely phonetic and etymological values, and sound very much like the 'elements of knowledge' known to other groups.

The *gemaṭria*, which is so familiar a feature of Rabbinical literature,[646] is mainly employed in the computation of the numerical value of letters. Although the Rabbis have indeed more complicated systems like the א"ת ב"ש their use is rare in comparison with that of the *gemaṭria*, which they employ even in halakhic matters.[647] It is worthwhile noting that Philo, although he follows the Rabbinical systems as a rule, in common with other Hellenistic writers is completely unaffected by the *gemaṭria*.[648]

Since the *gemaṭria*-type of calculations in Marqah has already been fully discussed,[649] it will suffice here if we adduce one example of his more intricate use of *gemaṭria*:[650]

> Thus the beginning of the months is made like the Beginning (*BERESHITH*), which was made the start of Creation... (Then follows a description of what was created on each day)... On the seventh day I perfected holiness. I rested *in* it in my own glory. I made it my special portion. I was glorious in it. I established your name, then also my name and yours therein as one, for I established it, and you are crowned with it.

---

erratic methods. cf. J.L. Blau, "Tradition etc.", *Essays... in honour of S.W. Baron*, p. 101.

[645] *Memar Marqah* (ed. Macdonald), I, p. 135 (= II, p. 221).

[646] Strack, *Introduction etc.*, pp. 97, 295 (nn. 33-35).

[647] *Yoma*, 20a (and parallels); *Sukkah*, 45b; *Taanith*, 17a (and parallels); *Moed Qaṭan*, 17a, 28a; *Makkoth*, 23b; *Horayoth*, 11b (and parallels), *Niddah*, 38b.

[648] Heinemann, *op. cit.* p. 106; *idem*, Phillons ... Bulding, p. 490; "The Method of Josephus etc.", *Zion* V (1940), p. 201, n. 69.

[649] Rettig, *Memar Marqah*, pp. 23ff. cf. also my article, *op. cit.* pp. 110, 119, 143 (n. 100), 155 (n. 174).

[650] *Memar Marqah* (ed. Macdonald), I, p. 21 (= II, p. 31).

All these secret establishments of names are based on *gemaṭria*.[651] One could readily compile long lists of Marqah's applications of *gemaṭria*. Not all of them are discernible as such at first sight, and this particular group is quite numerous.[652] Some of Marqah's *gemaṭrias* are also repeated in later literature.[653]

Although it is true that at certain periods, when philosophical attitudes do not favour the use of *gemaṭria*, there is a marked reduction in its employment, all Samaritan exegetes use this device to a greater or lesser degree. Even the *Ṭabbākh*, the most philosophical in outlook and in many respects the most faithful follower of the Mu'tazilite school, employs the *gemaṭria* occasionally for explaining certain precepts.[654] Abū'l Ḥasan's contempory, the *Kāfi*,[655] uses this device more frequently.

In later literature the employment of the *gemaṭria* assumes a more

---

[651] ואשכנת שמך חורי תמן שמי (= שמי שמן תמן) (345 = שמה =) ושמך (= משה = 345) לגוה
(= שבת 702) כחדה; שבת = שמה (= 345) + משה (= 345) + חד (= 12) = 702
These are followed by more complicated gemaṭrias.

[652] It has to be admitted that even the relatively easy and almost explicit play on letters and gemaṭrias would occasionally need lengthy explanations. More conducive, however, for our purpose here is to hint to a few examples which may be discovered easily : Marqah plays on the word אך (1 + 7 = 8) symbolizing creation, (1) Sabbath, *ibid.* I, p. 37 = II, p. 56, cf. ed. note 40 and also circumcision (8). For the gemaṭria ישר (*ibid.* cf. ed. n. 50), cf. my article *op. cit.* pp. 108, 141f. (nn. 82-85). The play on וידבר is almost explicit (I, p. 83 = II, p. 134, cf. ed. nn. 5-7). More complicated is the midrash on עד (I, p. 84 = II, p. 136), but it is obviously based on the word's numerical value (74), i.e. 70 Elders, Eldad, Modad, Eleazar and Phinehas (= ע״ד = 74). cf. also השירה הזאת (I, p. 84 = II, pp. 135f.); והבו (I, pp. 86f. = II, pp. 139f.); אמונה (I, p. 90 = II, p. 146); צדק (I, p. 91 = II, p. 148); הלא (I, p. 97 = II, p. 159; אלהים (I, p. 117 = II, p. 194) etc. The substance of Book VI (I, pp. 131ff. = II, pp. 213ff.) is wholly built on such plays on letters. cf. also Baneth, *Des Sam. Marqah etc.*, pp. 8ff.

[653] Abraham Qabaṣi is particularly fond of gemaṭria, often connecting them with those of Marqah and the words of the early Liturgists (*Sir al-qalb*, pp. 22-24). cf. also Miller, *Molad Moseh*, pp. 162f. etc.

[654] f. 108b f. The purpose of the number 32 for the fringes (cf. *sup.* n. 625) is to remind about observing the Law (*Num.* xv, 39), in which the first (בראשית) and the last letter (ישראל) have the numerical value of 32 (ל״ב). It seems, however, that Abū'l Ḥasan was not happy with this type of exegesis, and he hastens to bring a more 'logical' alternative. According to this second interpretation the number 32 is a symbol of the 22 fiery letters of the alphabet and the Ten Commandments, both radiating in various colours at Sinai, serving the same (Biblical) purpose of keeping the Torah constantly in mind.

[655] cf. *sup.* n. 543. Abdel Al (*A Comparative Study etc.*, p. 76), brings a list of Gematrias. cf. now, Noja, *Il Kitāb al-Kāfi etc.*, pp. 13f. (and notes), 156. cf. *inf.* n. 665.

prominent role. Although it is not used as frequently in halakhic as in aggadic matters, it nevertheless becomes by and by one of the most popular devices, especially in the field of eschatology.[656] Indeed, it comes to be employed so frequently by late Samaritan teachers and preachers that it is found advantageous to compile a compendium of ready-made combinations for the special assistance of those engaged in exposition. Just as in later times it is found expedient to prepare catalogues of ready-made formulae for use in documents (marriage-contracts, etc.) business letters, amulets, popular medicines and other practical requirements, so this small catalogue is prepared to supply models for the numerical calculation of letters, so that the expositor may have ready-made examples to hand.[657]

It is, therefore, totally unfounded to speak here of Jewish influence or of the Samaritans accepting a Jewish lead in hermeneutics, merely on the ground that the Jews also happen to use *gemaṭria*.[658] Manifestly by the Jews *gemaṭria* is cherished as a favourite hermeneutical device, and is almost universally employed by them. It is interesting to note Tanḥum Yerushalmi's entry on this device, for he defines it as follows "*Gemaṭria* is a Greek word meaning calculation (الحساب = אלחסאב), seeing that we always count (the numerical value) of the letters of the word". He also brings examples of its use from the earlier Jewish tradition.[659]

Strange as it may at first seem, even the medieval philosophers do not wholly refrain from using such a device in their philosophical treaties. Maimonides, the great rationalist, although sceptical of the value of certain aggadic hermeneutical principles, nevertheless on occasions

---

[656] Miller, *Molad Moshe*, pp. 246f. (בשגם = 345 = משה); 248f. (סוד רעו = 346 שמו a further play on משה = שמה); Merx, *Der Messias etc.*, pp. 9, 17, 81f. In the *Exodus Commentary* (attributed to Ghazal al-Duwaik) there are even more gematrias : pp. 27f. (רעמסס = 430 as the years of exile, *Ex.* xii, 40, cf. my article *op. cit.* pp. 108, 141f. (nn. 82-84); p. 28 (quoting Marqah); p. 82 (אמלא = 72, *Ex.* xxxiii, 26, from here it is derived that prophecy does not occur before the age of 72); pp. 109f. (on *Ex.* iii, 14 on the first seven words having 26 letters as the number of the Meritorious ones from Adam to Moses, and 26 is also the numerical value of the Tetragrammaton) etc.

[657] *Mss J.R.* 311 includes a manual for gemaṭria, most probably to be used as material for exposition. cf. pp. 273ff. Quite a number of these gemaṭrias (pp. 293f.) are the same as those to be found in later commentaries (cf. previous n.).

[658] Robertson, "Law and Religion etc.", *Judaism and Christianity*, Vol. III, p. 87; Abdel Al, *op. cit.* p. 76.

[659] Bacher, *Aus dem Wörterbuche etc.*, p. 95.

employs *gemaṭria* in his *Guide for the Perplexed*. He considers that some 'mysteries of the Torah' can best be explained by this means, and he even considers this device to have been already employed in Scripture itself.[660]

Gemaṭria is thus a universal feature, and the Samaritan practiced it at all periods and entirely independently of the Jews. We can offer almost no attestation of any real similarity between the two groups in the actual employment of *gemaṭria*, for, although the system itself is the same, its application is totally different. The few resemblances referred to above are therefore to be ascribed rather to chance than to any interdependence.

The reason for the sparing use of *gemaṭria* by some Samaritan writers under Mu'tazilite influence can easily be found. The arguments for and against the 'uncreatedness of the Qūran', in the course of which the Mu'tazilites took up their stand to oppose this dogma, tended to appreciably diminish the ancient belief in the significance of letters and so in the virtue of their employment for calculations.[661] This tendency may well account for Abū'l Ḥasan's very modest use of this device. Just as he broadly accepts certain other Mu'tazilite tenets, so he accepts this one and it has its due influence. The power of tradition is, however, strong enough to keep him from repudiating *gemaṭria* altogether. Later generations, as we know, no longer pay any attention to such rationalistic demands and *gemaṭria* is again used as fully as it was in the time of Marqah.

Noṭriqon, (from *notorius* = νοταρικόν) a term which means the breaking-up of a word by the exposition of its separate letters, each of which is then made to stand for a new word beginning with the same letter as itself,[662] is not employed as consistently among the Samaritans as it is among the Rabbis. Among the former it frequently happens that, after a particular word has been broken up into its separate letters, each of these, instead of being invariably made to stand for a word with the same opening letter is made to merely characterize the word, and may for instance appear at the end.

Marqah employs *noṭriqon* in this free form, and his lengthy exposition

---

[660] II, Ch. XLIII. Followers of Maimonides used also such devices if it suited their rationalistic expositions. cf. *inf.* n. 662.

[661] Goldziher, "Mélanges judéo-arabes", *REJ.* L (1905), pp. 188f.

[662] Strack, *Introduction*, pp. 97, 295 (nn. 36-37). It is interesting to note that Maimonides (*Guide for the Perplexed*, III, Ch. VII) accepts the noṭriqon חש מל of the Midrash (*Ḥagigah*, 13b), because it suits his rationalistic system.

of the letters [663] are rather full of illustrations of it. One of the most interesting examples is his interpretation of the word אמן which he employs as a subject of *noṭriqon*. Each letter in this exposition represents a concept : Aleph stands for divinity, Mem for Moses and therefore prophethood, and Nun for Aaron (from the last letter of his name) and therefore priesthood.[664] In the *Kāfi* too we find similar devices, often mingled with the *gemaṭria*;[665] but elsewhere and also in later times these are not used as frequently as the *gemaṭria*.

In some rare cases a single word is understood by the Samaritan Targum as two, as in the case of the Rabbinical midrash on שדי understood as שׁ (= אשר) די and meaning something like 'the Omnipotent', a phrase which occurs thus in the Samaritan Targum.[666]

In contrast to the frequent use of the *gemaṭria*, the *noṭriqon*-type of combinations is relatively rare and again in contrast to the importance of this device for Rabbinical midrashim,[667] the Samaritan employment of them is really insignificant. It seems that after the Roman period the Samaritans employed such devices only on very rare occasions.

H. Comparison of Hermeneutical Principles in Aggadah and in Halakhah

Throughout our enquiry into the hermeneutical devices employed by the Samaritans, both in the field of lingual and semantic usages and in the field of what we have termed hermeneutical rules, we have been able to find hardly any distinction between the treatment of aggadic and that of halakhic subjects. For this reason, it is more profitable to us to investigate the reasons for their exegesis as given by the Samaritans themselves as well as the reasons for their several attitudes, for together these will serve to explain to us their fairly identical treatment of both fields.

---

[663] cf. *sup.* n. 652.

[664] *Memar Marqah* (ed. Macdonald), I, p. 67; II, p. 106. cf. ed. n. 66. As opposed to this cf. the Rabbinic *noṭriqon* on אמן (נאמן מלך אל) *Shabbath*, 119b.

[665] N. Cohn, *Die Zarâth-Gesetze etc.*, pp. 12f. (cf. n. 2 on pp. 13f.). In the late gemaṭria manual Ms. (cf. *sup.* n. 657), pp. 249f. we find also noṭriqon עוף בהמה רמש (ערב =) etc.

[666] Ben-Ḥayyim, *The Literary and Oral Trad. etc.*, II, p. 594, n. 36. cf. *sup.* n. 379.

[667] Heinemann, *op. cit.* pp. 104f., 239 (nn. 18-26).

(1) *Reasons behind Aggadic Interpretations*

The Pentateuch itself is by no means informative either as to the reasons for its precepts or as to the reason for certain outstanding events. Only in very rare cases are such reasons given, and these are mainly rather in the nature of formal explanations than of real reasons which the exegete might turn to imaginative use. The manifold explanations of a certain biblical expression thus originate for the most part from philosophical thought or from logical deductions from a certain action. The punishment of the wicked or the reward of the righteous may easily serve as a starting-point for an investigation of the motives and intentions behind this action. Indeed an investigation of this kind may have had its beginning in very early antiquity. It is of course also very possible that apologetic needs have prompted this search for rational explanations and for the motives behind the words of Scripture. It is thus no easy task to determine the course of such a philosophical development. Was it due to contact with other culture or was it mainly an internal and independent growth?.

If we now look into Marqah's midrashim, many of them are already based on an implicit question which demands reasons for the Scriptural matters which make them up. To revert to an exemple which we have seen recently, there is his treatment of *Ex.* viii, 25, where he answers the implicit question why was it impossible for the Israelites to sacrifice in Egypt, as Pharaoh had suggested?[668] The various reasons which Marqah adduces through analogy all possess an unmistakable tinge. They come to account for various moot points in Scripture by providing them with 'logical' explanations; and this is the real reason why it seems that, despite the fact that not all his aggadah is based on 'proof-texts' from Scripture, it came to be regarded by the Samaritans as regulative. We hardly find any explicit dissensions between Marqah and the later commentators. On the contrary, we even find cases where aggadic or liturgical expressions from Marqah are adduced as authoritative proofs of halakhic matters by writers of a much later generation.[669]

There are, notwithstanding, a few exceptions to this general conformity of approach to be found mainly in the strange legends of the *Asaṭir*, which are indeed often disputed in later literature.[670] At all events,

---

[668] cf. *sup.* Part II, n. 442.

[669] *Ṭabbākh* (f. 195a) calls Marqah "like the prohet of the Panutha" and quotes him as evidence for the practice of the High Priest (cf. *sup.* n. 621 and text there).

[670] Ben Ḥayyim, "Sepher Asaṭir", *Tarbiz* xiv-xv, pp. 4ff.

it seems either that the *Asaṭir* is not received by the eleventh- century writers, or that it is simply not known to them. Even if one does not find in the *Kāfi* or the *Ṭabbākh* explicit refutation of these legends, but these book are in fact notably silent about these legends.

It is usual to single out the *Ṭabbākh* for its relatively philosophical and rational approach, on which more will be said later in reference to the enquiry into the reason behind the precepts. However, even in aggadic matters the *Ṭabbākh's* 'rational exegesis' is in truth quite primitive. The author analogizes from one miracle to another. Thus *Lev.* ix, 24 ("and there came forth fire from before the Lord and consumed upon the altar the burnt-offering and the fat etc.") is explained by the fact that Aaron lifted up his hands (*ibid.* 22), and that this action had a special supernatural force, as in Egypt, (cf. *Ex.* vii, 19). Moreover, this miracle is granted further scope by extending Aaron's supernatural power to account for the reasons underlying other verses. Hence, according to Abū'l Ḥasan, whenever Aaron lifts up his hands in blessing, such a supernatural power reaches alike those who stand near-by and those far-away; and this same power is also possessed by Eleazar and Phinehas.[671] In the interests of economy of space, we may here simply add that, in the whole of the Samaritan aggadic literature the reasons given for scriptural matters are throughout very closely akin, in spite of their being scattered through the whole length of history. In contrast to this, if we look at the Rabbinical literature, even in its earliest form, we find a marked difference in the evaluation of the two types of writing, binding force being unfailingly granted to the halakhah, but the aggadah being regarded as quite unauthoritative and purely personal.[672] It may truthfully be said that, while halakhah is strictly bound by tradition and may only be quoted under the name of some widely acknowledged authority, aggadah may be freely produced or quoted without naming any authority in one's support.[673] In medieval commentaries the approach to the aggadah becomes ever more negative. Whereas in Talmudic times it is considered the most efficient way of learning of God's way and

---

[671] *Ṭabbākh*, ff. 3b f. (SLTh.A, p. 81); cf. *sup.* Part II, n. 583.

[672] cf. my article, *op. cit.* pp. 101, 134 (n. 27).

[673] Bacher, "The origin etc.", *JQR* IV (1892), pp. 407ff. On the other hand, this relatively lesser authoritative nature of the aggadah did in no way diminish its influence, even in halakhic matters. The Rabbis of earlier generation did not spare their efforts in reconciling conflicting aggadah. cf. Weiss, *Dor Dor*, p. 188; Jellinek (ed.) *Nopheth Zufim*, p. 206; R. Loewe, "The 'Plain' Meaning etc.", *Paper of the Institute of Jewish Studies*, I, p. 150.

doings, later, and very probably owing to its misuse at the hands of the sectarians, it falls into general disrepute. The reasons and explanations offered by the sectarians are of course often combated and hence new interpretations have to take the place of the old ones, which have now become highly controversial.[674] It is precisely due to his lack of sophistication that the Samaritan exegete on the other hand, with his relatively primitive reasons and justifications, does not need to disregard, much less disown, those offered by earlier generations, and so the homogeneity so characteristic of his aggadic literature is the natural outcome.

There is nevertheless a fairly close affinity between the reasons given by the Samaritan exegetes and those given by the Rabbis, as opposed to those given by the Hellenistic writers, especially Josephus, who is constantly exploring the causes of certain types of event. The reasons offered by the Samaritans and the Rabbis alike are of a character entirely different from his, for Josephus' favourite questions, persistently occurring in all his writings, are mainly concerned with the motives underlying his heroes' actions, as for example: Why did Isaac tolerate the Canaanite wives of Esau? Why did Jacob keep silent when he heard Shechem's proposal? Why did Joseph try only Benjamin? Such questions plainly show that Josephus, like a Greek, attributes certain actions to purely human decisions whereas the simple meaning of Scripture embodies the teaching that history is overruled by God.[675] Both the Rabbis and the Samaritans continue to give reasons which in their belief are consonant with those inherent in Scripture. Although we shall have to speak again later about the reasons offered in explanation of the precepts, even in this short comparison the general attitude in the service of which hermeneutical devices are employed has been amply highlighted. The ascription of equal worth to halakhah and aggadah and the formulation of reasons for various Scriptures in the light of this total harmony characterize almost the whole of Samaritan literature.

(2) *Reasons underlying the Precepts*

In general, we may say that this section too is quite disappointing in that, if we examine the reasons offered in explanation of the precepts, they display no characteristics other than those already found in the aggadah.

---

[674] Various reasons were given for this changed attitude to the aggadah. Strack, *Introduction etc.*, pp. 90, 284 (nn. 1-5); cf. Heinemann, *op. cit.* p. 187.

[675] *idem*, "The Method of Josephus etc.", *Zion* V (1940), p. 185.

We may begin once more with Marqah, who builds one midrash on what he understands as the reason behind the command to prepare a lamb for the Passover Sacrifice on the tenth day of the first month (*Ex.* xii, 3). Marqah paraphrases the relevant verses and says:[676] "It should be prepared during four days until the fourteenth" (cf. *ibid*, 6). But instead of giving an unequivocal reason for this precept, he proceeds to "explain' the whole matter in a quite different way, by giving his reasons for the significance of the first ten days. They stand for the *Ten Meritorious ones* from Adam to Moses, one day standing for the particular merit of each of these. The list ends: "The tenth day for the perfectness of your (Moses') prophethood". On the same lines the midrash is continued in respect of the following three days (when the Passover Offering was already prepared), each of these three days representing one of the three generations of the High Priests.[677]

> The tenth day is for you and what follows is for Aaron. I have vested you with my name and I have vested him with yours.[678] The tenth day is for you and what follows is for Aaron. You will start and he will finish.[679]
>
> Eleazar is appointed to the succession and his day is glorious; like him Phinehas is exalted and his day, which is like his father's, (is) enwrapped in blessedness. Behold, ten and three together crowned with perfection; behold, ten and three crowned with might.

The continuation is also quite simple: the fourteenth day is the Day of Redemption, symbolising the Taheb.[680]

Another type of Marqah's midrashim on the reasons underlying the precepts is the one in which wickedness is exhibited by the multiplication of its manifestations, thus showing how many evils are included under one prohibition. On *Deut.* xxvii, 21 ("Cursed is he who lieth with

---

[676] *Memar Marqah* (ed. Macdonald), I, p. 21 (= II, p. 32). cf. however, *sup.* n. 559 and text there.

[677] *Memar, ibid.* I, p. 22 (= II, p. 33).

[678] "I have vested you with My name" משה = שמה "and I have vested him with yours" is a reference to *Ex.* vii, i נתתיך אלהים (= שמה) ... יהיה נביאך (= משה)

[679] Moses was the first priest and only then came the inauguration of Aaron, cf. *Lev.* ix, 1f. The whole passage makes sense only if Marqah had this in mind : אתה משרי והוא מחסל' אלעזר לתינותה ויומה (יום י"ב) יקיר' כותה פינחס ירום וימה דילה (יום י"ג) ואבוה (= כאבוה?) הוה בטובה כחדה; הא עסרה (עד משה) ותלתה (ג' כהנים) הכללו בשלמו ...

[680] "The day which He made the fourteenth is the end of one affair and the beginning of another", *ibid.*, is taken here symbolically. The 14th day is not only the 'beginning' of the redemption in Egypt but, as the whole poem on the Taheb which follows indicates, a symbol of the 'final redemption'.

any kind of beast") Marqah says : "This is an exceedingly wicked thing to do. It consists of defiling evils, twelve shameful acts in number. Everyone of them incurs the death-penalty". He enumerates all twelve, concluding with an additional reason of his own, and affirming that all the curses will fall on this person, "because he wanted something that He did not establish for you".[681]

If we now pass on to the eleventh century Arabic writers, we again find a substantial difference created by their more pronouncedly philosophical approach. The one who displays this quality most vividly is the *Ṭabbākh*. However, even Abū'l Ḥasan, despite all his philosophical leanings, cannot altogether dissociate himself from the Samaritan tradition and sees in the Law first and foremost the duty of following unquestioningly the Will of God. This almost blind acceptance of divine authority is, after all, held to be the highest virtue to which one can ever attain. For this very reason, Abū'l Ḥasan emphasises the Law of Passover, for this is the first traditional *statute* set out by Moses in the Torah, and it is without doubt the strongest evidence of God's grace to Israel. The whole people is raised by the fulfilment of this precept and by participating in the sacrificial cult to the status of a 'Nation of Priests'.[682] The Passover Law is thus boldly elaborated in the *Ṭabbākh* into sixty precepts (by harmonising verses from *Ex.* and *Deut.*) which are all of them meant as "ordinances for ever" (*Ex.* xii, 14; *ibid.* 17, etc.). The main reason for keeping these ordinances is that Israel should visualize the rewards to be had through keeping them. They are termed 'statutes and judgements,' but we do not find any method of distinguishing

---

[681] *Memar Marqah* (ed. Macdonald), I, p. 75 (= II, p. 120). cf. also *sup.* nn. 233-234 and text there.

[682] *Ṭabbākh*, ff. 58a (= SLTh.A, p. 100), 75b (SLTh.A, p. 116). It is interesting to note that although the passover is considered the first of the "traditional' precepts (اول الفاريض السمعيه), Abū'l Ḥasan attempts to give 'rational' expositions to all its details. Apparently, there was no such dichotomy as the one in the philosophy of Saadia between "Rational' and "Traditional" commandments (الشرائع العقلية والسمعية). cf. *Kitāb al-Amānāt wa'l I'tiqadāt* (ed. Landauer, Leiden 1880), pp. 114ff. Most probably Sam. traditional doctrine did not allow for such sharp distinctions. The same picture emerges from the expositions of the Sabbath-laws. In this case the 'rational' explanation upon which all the preaching depends is holiness (*Ṭabbākh*, ff. 34a f. = SLTh.A, p. 89f.). Holiness is the opposite of defilement and degradation, and therefore all the calamities befalling the Samaritans are direct results of the desecration of the Sabbath. However, this element of 'holiness' as the background of the Sabbath goes back to early antiquity. cf. my article, *op. cit.* pp. 112f., 147f. (nn. 118-123); cf. also *sup.* n. 504.

in their treatment by the *Ṭabbākh* between what is to be considered a 'statute' and what a 'judgement'. Rational explanations, in the sense that the weak human mind may partially undrstand them, are freely given for most of these judgements. One can only conclude that the *Ṭabbākh* regards even the 'statutes' as having rational explanations which can be imparted to humans, in addition to their 'real' reasons, which are known to the Divine Legislator alone. If one looks through the list of the reasons given by the *Ṭabbākh* for these precepts, the impression gained is that the general tendency is to follow the Mu'tazilite school of thought.[683]

The *Ṭabbākh* gives additional explanations even for calendaric details. Although this subject is elsewheie regarded as a priestly mystery, in respect of which the layman is to accept the priests' rulings and is not to employ his rational faculties or offer views of his own, explanations of the reasons behind these calculations yet considered valid and valuable. The logicality of the seasons while dependent on Scripture, as following the order of the luminaries *Gen.* i, 4, is elucidated by the fact that the year begins with spring, when it is not too hot and not too cold. As opposed to this, the Sabbatical years and the Jubilees, when agriculture is forbidden, begins only after the harvest. From here Abū'l Ḥasan proceeds to give a logical interpretation of the four names of this 'new year' (based on *Lev.* xxiii, 24; 1. i.e. Solemn Rest, 2. Memorial, 3. Shouting = תרועה, 4. Holy Convocation), the first expression signyfying prohibiton of work, the second forgiveness, the third a loud outcry in order to arouse both young an old, and the fourth holiness.[684]

This tendency to rationalize is sometimes so strong that even reasons explicitly stated in Scripture itself are further rationalized. Thus to "Therefore the children of Israel eat not the sinew of the hip, because he touched the hollow of Jacob's thigh in the sinew of the hip" (*Gen.* xxxii, 32), the *Ṭabbākh* adds a long interpretation on the lines that it is meant to recall the favours of God towards Jacob, and to recall how God saved him from the evil intentions of Esau, when God changed the

---

[683] To single out only a few of these reasons it is quite sufficient to prove the point. Rule 2 (f. 59a = SLTh.A, p. 101) on *Ex.* xii, 3, the reason is given "to remember the *grace* of God; Rule 3, cf. *sup.* n. 561. In Rule 4 (*ibid.*) on *Ex.* xii, 4, the term employed for the Israelites is the Mu'tazilite terminology used as to characterize themselves : "the people of justice and monotheism", etc. cf. also *sup.* n. 172.

[684] *Ṭabbākh*, ff. 37a f.

latter's intentions and how, although Jacob was injured, Esau could not harm him.[685]

It has to be admitted that the last theme is given a similar explanation in the *Kāfi*.[686]. It is possible, however, that, since these details belong to the regulations for ritual slaughter, both the *Kāfi* and the *Ṭabbākh* have utilised the same sources. Indeed, these regulations as given in both works show a remarkable similarity.

In general, however, the *Kāfi* is the less rational of the two. The majority of the interpretations of the precepts given there are symbolical and the underlying reasons those of piety. Often more than one reason is offered, not all being of equal value. Some of his 'reasons' for the precepts are in fact strained and often fanciful and even fantastic.[687] It must, nevertheless, be pointed out that often too, purely ethical explanations are to be found in this book. Thus the author explains how it happens that an Israelite is forced to sell himself as a slave and to depend upon charity. This and similar facts are explained as punishments brought on the man now in distress by his previous uncharitable acts.[688]

It is noteworthy that, while the giving of plausible reasons for the precepts is a common feature of Samaritan literature, there are still great differences in approach between one writer and another. As we have seen, while the *Kāfi* cannot dissociate himself from this general interpretative tendency, there is no marked leaning towards Mu'tazilite thinking in his book as there is in the *Ṭabbākh*. It may be stated that in general, from Marqah onwards 'logical' explanations for the precepts can be found in almost every work dealing with the interpretation of precepts. In the twelfth century Munajja is even more insistent on multiplying rational interpretations of the Law than is the *Ṭabbākh*. One

---

[685] *ibid.* f. 14a f. cf. Abdel Al, *op. cit.* pp. 625ff. (Translation, pp. 405ff.) For other similar 'rational' explanations cf. sup. nn. 519-520.

[686] pp. 321ff. cf. Abdel Al, *op. cit.* pp. 50f. (Translation, pp. 678ff.) cf. *sup.* n. 325.

[687] e.g. the explanation of *tithe*, pp. 28f. (SLTh.A, p. 1f.); or the reasons why uncleanness in birth of a girl is double that of a birth of a boy, pp. 152f. (cf. Abdel Al, *op. cit.* pp. 689f.; translation, pp. 517f.); or the reasons for the prohibition of eating meat together with milk, pp. 317f. etc. cf. also *sup*. Part II, nn. 138 and 483.

[688] *Kāfi*, p. 266 (SLTh.A, p. 60). In an earlier passage (*ibid.* p. 265) a similar ethical reason is given to encourage the buying of the Israelite slave (despite that owner is not allowed to treat him as a slave). Ethical explanations are also given as the cause for leprosy, and here there is even a gradual description (first in house, then in garment and only when the warning is not accepted, in the body, *ibid.* pp. 143ff.). (cf. now *Noja, Il Kitāb Al Kāfi etc.*, pp. 63f.)

example may suffice. Munajja gives an ethical explanation for the precept of circumcision. He elborates greatly, not only on the sexual and ethical aspects of the rite and not only from the point of view of the circumcised male, but also on the responsibility of adults for the infant's future moral character.[689]

Later writers, as a rule, merely harmonise opinions already expressed by their predecessors, without adding much of their own, Moral and casuistic reasons are particularly prominent in the *Sir al-Qalb* of Abraham Qabaşi; This work shows, however, very little originality in its endeavour to give reasons for the precepts.

If we compare the Rabbinical literature with all this, we find that there is no great difference in the general approach. Allegorical explanations are rather rare, and are mostly confined to some special groups of preachers.[690] As we have seen earlier, the Pentateuch itself is not very communicative in offering reasons for its precepts. Only on rare occasions do we find explicit reasons given, as, for instance, for the command to love the stranger, (*Ex.* xxii, 20 and xxiii, 9 and *Lev.* xix, 34 etc.), here explained as serving to call to mind the people's own servitude in Egypt. So too, there are a few precepts which are justified as providing opportunities for mercy, as reflections and illustrations of the constant mercy of God. Naturally these scriptural reasons are elaborated by the Rabbis.[691] We nevertheless find that some deductions from the reasons given in the Pentateuch, as, for example, from *Deut.* xvii, with reference to the King, are actually resented by the Rabbis; for instance the deduction that Solomon, simply because he knew the reasons for such precepts and thought himself wise enough to know them, believed himself to be an exception and thus fell. Because of the obvious spiritual dangers involved, the Rabbis object to such and similar deductions.[692] There is no such misgiving amongst the Samaritans, and hence they freely expound the reasons behind the precepts.

Some other reasons for the precepts as given by the Rabbis such as those derived from familiarity with popular maxims, e.g. 'measure for measure', are also very commonly given by the Samaritans.[693]

---

[689] *Masā'il al-Khilāf*, Ib, pp. 17-21. Probably this is an apologetical explanation for the Samaritan practice to carry out the rite even if it involves a danger of life to the infant.

[690] M. Guttmann, *Die Anlehnung etc.*, p. 29.

[691] *idem, Eine Untersuchung... Geltungsumfang etc.*, pp. 28f.

[692] *ibid.* p. 30.

[693] *ibid.* p. 31.

Usually, when scripture offers a reason for a precept, its main intention is nontheless to emphasise its absolute authority (regardless of the explanation given), and to lead the reader towards a proper observance and an unreserved submission. Such reasons are seldom truly logical but are rather reasons with a view to inducing obedience to the Law and to God. Obviously they must be logical to the mind of the Lawgiver. However, their claim on man is not directed primarily to his rational faculties, but rather to his sense of duty and moral obligation.

While both the Rabbis and the Samaritans as a rule follow the course found in Scripture, the Hellenists are concerned not so much with the divine origin of the law, as rather with its utility from the human point of view.[694] It is therefore to be expected that, whenever ethical reasons are given, both the Rabbis and the Samaritans should expound them in such a way as to strengthen or to define the Biblical precepts. We know from very many examples how great and how persistent a stress is laid by the Rabbis on the need for avoiding and desisting from vice and evil habits and there are the famous questions like; why is the punishment of a thief greater than that of a bandit? or, why should the "stubborn and rebellious son" (*Deut.* xxi, 18) be executed? etc.[695]

We have seen in previous cases that amongst the Samaritans also, the reasons underlying the precept are further exploited for expanding the details of the actual precept.[696] Marqah always stresses the rigorous observance of the Law; but he affirms that, not only is the general and collective obligation of high importance, but not less the details and the particular precept concerning the individual are of the same paramount significance. He amasses biblical evidence in proof of his convictions that the very details of the Law are themselves called Torah.He who breaks even one of these details termed Torah is under the 'curse'.[697] Very similar sentiments are likewise expressed by the *Kāfi*, although based on different midrashic expositions;[698] but in his penetrating expositions of the 'Curses', Marqah undoubtedly gives his readers the benefit of a much deeper insight.[699] His reasons   for

---

[694] Heinemann, *Darkhei ha-Aggadah*, p. 146 (and *ibid.* p. 253), n. 60f. for further literature).

[695] Guttmann, *op. cit.* (*sup.* n. 691), p. 33.

[696] cf. *sup.* nn. 464ff.

[697] cf. *sup.* n. 187.

[698] pp. 157f. cf. Abdel Al, *op. cit.* pp. 525f. (Translation, pp. 687f.).

[699] This must be the reason that in all such cases he opens his exposition with the formula נתן אפרש. cf. *Memar*, I, p. 71 (= II, p. 114) on *Deut.* xxvii, 18. The same

these Curses and for the precepts the infringement of which calls down
these Curses are often in the nature of broad generalizations. These
generalizations, however, afford in fact, a practical means of extension
to the prohibitions. One example will serve to illustrate this approach.[700]

> Cursed be he who takes a bribe to slay an (innocent) person (Deut. xxvii, 25),
> making himself lower than one who kills with his own hand; [701] doing this deed
> (he is) worse than Cain when he treacherously slew his brother. He seeks his
> own advancement and does not realize the recompense for murder. He does
> evil and he does not receive nor is given what he demands. He hides himself
> from the will of his Lord and is left rejected and forsaken.

It is interesting to note that the *Kāfi* expresses exactly the same sentiments, but bases his midrash on *Ex.* xxi, 14, "To slay him with *guile*".[702]

In the *Ṭabbākh* such extensions of the reasons underlying the Law
are closer to our expectations. Its rationalistic approach becomes apparent when it gives the reasons underlying the Ten Days of Penitence.[703]
The first day of the seventh month, it points out, is the beginning of the
Sabbatical year, and the beginning of the Days of Penitence also, which
are concluded by the Day of Atonement. The interval of eight days is
decreed by divine wisdom for the specific purpose of repentance and to
afford ample time and equal opportunity to people of varying standards
of knowledge and spiritual attainment.

The Biblical proof-text is; "Ye stand *this day all of you*... that thou
shouldest enter into the *Covenant* of the Lord" (*Deut.* xxix, 9-11).
Abū'l Ḥasan then gives two explanations of the fact that there is an inter-

---

opening exclamation follows in the verses having similar significance. On the previous
Curses where there was no such intention he opens the exposition with single words.
Thus *ibid.* v. 16 (I, p. 67 = II, p. 107) הא אנן מחסלין מלתה קמאה וממללין במלתה
תנינתה *ibid.* v. 17 (I, p. 70 = II, p. 112) אזהרותה תליתה. In order to visualize the
importance attached by Marqah to this expression, we have to bear in mind that he
employs it only in connection with the most important subjects, e.g the interrelation
of Divinity with the Prophecy of Moses (I, p. 6 = II, p. 5), and a second passage on
the same subject (I, p. 10 = II, p. 12). Relationship between Moses and Aaron (I,
p. 14 = II, p. 14), Death of Moses (I, p. 117 = II, p. 193).

[700] *Memar Marqah* (ed. Macdonald), I, p. 76 = II, p. 122, on *Deut.* xxvii.

[701] מקדם גרמה לקטלה באדה literally, "he puts himself (i.e. the person who
takes a bribe) in front (in evilness) of an (actual) murderer, who does it by his own
hand".

[702] *Kāfi*, p. 273f. The reference here in the *Kāfi* is not so much to bribe, but one
who causes death by cunning speech as in the case of the serpent who 'acted' only
by speech (*Gen.* iii, 1f.). cf. now Noja, *Il Kitāb Al-Kāfi etc.*, pp. 134f.

[703] *Ṭabbākh*, ff. 41b f.

val of exactly eight days, the first of these being based on a comparison
with circumcision, which, of course, takes place on the eighth day from
birth and whereby the child enters into "Covenant". In default of this,
the child is condemned, as is likewise the person who does not repent
in the course of the eight days in question. The second explanation is
that this very period coincides with the anniversary of Moses' second
descent with the tablets, when the sin of Israel was forgiven; and hence
it is an appropriate time for a general repentance and the receiving of
forgiveness. At this point Abū'l Ḥasan turns to the more rationalistic
justifications for "afflicting the soul" (*Lev.* xvi, 31) on the Day of Atonement.[704] All these rationalizations alike lend weight to the general
ethos of these days. They are not then merely the reasons underlying the
precepts, but are rather their practical application with a view to an
intensive repentance.

Some of the explanations of the Passover Laws in the *Ṭabbākh*
although mainly intended to provide logical reasons, have nevertheless
further halakhic implications, and some of them are intended to
strengthen certain other practices.[705] This same method is also applied
by Abū'l Ḥasan to other halakhic fields.[706] Thus, the tenth condition
regulating the laws of ritual slaughter, according to the *Ṭabbākh*,[707]
is that this ritual may be performed only when there is a need for meat
(cf. *Deut.* xii, 20). Otherwise it is forbidden. Abū'l Ḥasan regards *Lev.*
xvii, 7 as the source of this prohibition, and understands it to refer to
the senseless killing of an animal.[708] This tradition concerning the laws of
slaughter runs through the whole of Samaritan literature and the *Kāfi* [709]

---

[704] Although all Ms. read "five explanations" for "the afflicting the soul", in
reality there are only three. In order to avoid the impression that *all* expositions
of Abū'l Ḥasan are rationalizations we have to bear in mind also his employment
of more naive devices, cf. *sup.* n. 654.

[705] In the following hints we refer by *N.* to the number of the rule (out of the 60
rules of Passover) by *f.* to folio in the text of the *Ṭabbākh* and by *p* to the page number
in SLTh.A, N. 5 (f. 60a = p. 102); N. 7 (*ibid.*); N. 29 (f. 69a = p. 110); N. 30 (*ibid.*);
N. 31 (f. 70a = p. 111); N. 33 (f. 71a = p. 112); N. 43 (f. 76a = p. 116); N. 48 (f.
80a = p. 120). For N. 5 cf. *inf.* nn. 707-709) and for N. 7 cf. *Kāfi*, p. 246. cf. Abdel Al,
op. cit. pp. 709f. (translation, pp. 683f.).

[706] P.R. Weis, "Abū'l-Ḥasan... Leprosy etc.", *BJRL* XXXIII (1950-51), p. 132.
cf. also *sup.* n. 572.

[707] f. 15a. cf. Abdel Al, *op. cit.* pp. 625ff. (Translation, pp. 405f.).

[708] This tradition is common in Samaritan literature. S. Kohn, *Sam. Studien*,
p. 49.

[709] p. 326, and cf. previous notes.

explains it in the very same way. In this latter case, however, the similarity between the two authors is such that we can be certain that they have both used the same sources.

Although such extensions as a result of rationalization occur in the *Kāfi*, since the practice is part of the general Samaritan tradition, they are not a chief characteristic of this book. The overall tendency of the *Kāfi* is to discover the reasons underlying the precepts in Scripture itself, by the use of harmonizations. Clearly the results of such harmonizations may have far-reaching consequences for the halakhah; once Biblical evidence is brought in to support the traditional reasons behind the precepts, it must give an impetus to further halakhic deductions.

The *Kāfi* opposes such ascetic doctrines as forbid the wearing of expensive garments, and he gives several reasons for this opposition: 1. The people of Israel being the Chosen People, it is inconceivable that even the choicest of garments should be forbidden to them. 2. From the verses on the building of the tabernacle (*Ex.* xxv, 2-8) it is evident that both men and women then possessed valuable ornaments, jewelry etc. (cf. *ibid.* xxxv, 22). 3. The Israelites took from the Egyptians all kinds of jewelry, and God commanded that these should be worn by their sons and daughters (*Ex.* iii, 22). For all these reasons it is apparent that there can be no objection to the wearing of such things; but the *Kāfi* goes a step further and deduces from these reasons that, if one's abstention from wearing luxurious garments is motivated by some form of piety, such as a sympathetic attitude to the poor, etc. it is to be considered a merit, but if, on the other hand, such abstention is motivated by miserliness or meanness, it is to be condemned.[710]

By a similar method evidence is adduced from Scripture for the proper degree of modesty in a woman's attire. Moreover, these proof-texts invest the reasons adduced with a binding force which makes them at least equal to or even one with the Biblical precepts themselves.[711] In contrast to this attitude, woman wearing jewelry while worshipping or on pilgrimage are censured. The reason for this censure is the implied association of jewelry on these occasions with "alien Gods" (cf. *Gen.* xxxv, 2). Jacob in his prophetic capacity knew that the Israelites would

---

[710] *Kāfi*, p. 191 (SLTh.A, p. 22).
[711] *ibid.* pp. 193f. (SLTh.A, pp. 23f.).

sin by donating their ornaments on the occasion of the Golden Calf (cf. *Ex.* xxxii, 2-3).[712]

Often the reasons given for the precepts, even if they are not explicitly stated in Scripture, are considered by the *Kāfi* as having an overriding force. Thus from the fact that the 'Chosen Place' was known to the patriarchs and to Moses, a whole series of proof-texts is adduced. The reason behind the precepts relating to the bringing of sacrifices and tithes is precisely that they might be offered only in this 'Chosen Place'. This reason is so compelling in the mind of our Samaritan exponent that he uses it is a polemical device against the Jews. The argument is broadly on the following lines it is impossible that Moses and Aaron should have died without the knowledge of this Place and its purpose; and furthermore, the Jews clearly could not carry out all these precepts until the time of Solomon (according to the *Kāfi*, between Moses and the building of the Temple in Jerusalem only two hundred and sixty years had elapsed).[713] Although other writers deduce the same points by other means, the concept that the Place was known to the ancestors is common to the whole of Samaritan literature.

Many of the logical reasons given by the *Kāfi* for the precepts also have a very practical application. One of the major prerequisites to ritual ablution, according to the *Kāfi*, is 'humility' and submission to God. The problem therefore arises whether ablution carried out without this proof of true intention is valid. The *Kāfi* accordingly adduces arguments, based on the reason behind this precept for the principle that washings without this religious intention must be repeated.[714]

In a similar vein, his explanation of the laws concerning the Hebrew slave is of a practical nature. This slave receives his manumission after six years of service.[715] His wife, given to him by his master, and her children will renain the master's property. The *Kāfi* explains this harsh rule as arising in reality out of compassion. The children of this union have been circumcised and are now in effect Israelites, and therefore forbidden to revert to their heathen ways. Since the children will hardly

---

[712] *ibid.* p. 196 (SLTh.A, p. 25); cf. also *sup.* n. 578 and Part II, n. 630.

[713] *Kāfi*, pp. 204f. (SLTh.A, p. 30f.). On the other hand the *Ṭabbākh* in his second rule of the laws of ritual slaughtering (cf. *sup.* n. 707) demanding the turning towards the *Qiblah* quotes *Deut.* xii, 5 as evidence for the practice.

[714] *Kāfi*, p. 49 (SLTh.A, p. 11); cf. also *sup.* nn. 403, 578 and Part II, n. 530.

[715] *Kāfi*, pp. 258f. (SLTh.A, pp. 55f.). According to the Samaritan view, "Hebrew" here is not an Israelite but it includes all the descendants of Abraham (e.g. Ishmaelites, Edomites etc.).

be able to survive without their mother, Scripture prescribes that she remain with the master.[716]

If set in contrast with that of other groups, the Samaritan type of exposition of the reasons underlying the precepts will take on a clearer shape. Let us take, for instance, the ecletic system of Philo, where the reasons are at once rationalistic and traditional and we shall find that in his many-sided explanations of the precepts these two attitudes can even stand side by side. Thus Philo can combine a utilitarian or an ethical explanation with an allegorical one in dealing with the same precept, despite the tension between them.[717] Such multiple reasons are not to be found in Samaritan literature. Josephus., on the other hand, is not at all interested in rationalistic expositions, but prefers to moralise with a view to the edification of man; for this reason, he concentrates on civil laws, which, according to him, do not require any rationalization, and often in fact turns in blind eye on difficult ritual laws.[718] His method would be totally alien to the Samaritans.

Among the Rabbis there is a diversity of opinion as to how far one may rightly go in rationalizing the precepts and in explaining the reasons behind them.[719] Although indeed they often enter into discussion with Gentiles on the reasons for the precepts, such reasons as given to the latter are not regarded as applicable to their own standards and purposes. For them the real reasons always remain the worship of God with rejoicing and the subjection of the human will to His.[720]

It may be asserted that in general the Samaritan search for rational explanations is in many ways similar to that conducted by the Rabbis. Among neither group is there any suggestion that the search for the reasons underlying the precepts is an act of sacrilege or an impious attempt to probe into God's secrets, as one finds it regarded by some traditionalists of Islam.[721] Another feature common to Rabbis and Samaritans is that the Mu'tazilite influence is felt by them both. This influence does not, however, lead them to the extreme position adopted

---

[716] *ibid.* pp. 260f (SLTh.A, pp. 56f.).

[717] Heineman, *Philons... Bildung*, pp. 498f., 554f.; cf. my article, *op. cit.* pp. 117, 153 (nn. 154-160).

[718] Heinemann, "The Method of Josephus etc.", *Zion* V (1940), pp. 196f.

[719] Weiss, *Dor Dor etc.*, II, p. 141. cf. also *sup.* nn. 690-693. cf. Heinemann, *Darkhei ha-Aggadah*, p. 69.

[720] *idem, ibid.* p. 82; *idem, Zion* V, *ibid.* (cf. n. 718). cf. my article in *JJS* IX (1958), p. 28.

[721] D.B. Macdonald, *Development of Muslim etc.*, p. 107.

by the Karaites, that every precept can be completely rationalised within
the confines of human understanding.[722] Rather in these two groups,
if no comprehensible reason can be found for a precept, they gladly
accept the position that the reason can be known only to God. The
Samaritan approach is well summed up by one of their writers [723]
when he argues along these lines: Divine worship means the acceptance
of the heavenly yoke. Man's sense of obligation originates from his
rational understanding of the divine grace which has granted him his
intellect. Gratitude for this is a sufficient reason for worship.

One cannot then expect any explanations for the reasons behind any
supposed 'hermeneutical rules', since there is in fact among the Samaritans no awareness whatever that they are using any such 'rules'; whereas
the search for the underlying reasons for the precepts is at all times a
rational exercise, recognised as early as Marqah. Any other so-called
'hermeneutical devices' are employed empirically by them, without any
awareness of a stereotyped way of proceeding.

(3) The Figurative, the Theoretical and the Practical

Although this present section cannot strictly be regarded as falling
under the heading of 'hermeneutical devices', it will nevertheless serve
as a fitting conclusion to that subject; for hermeneutical devices in
general, and especially those employed by the Samaritans in their own
naive way, can easily be characterized if we inquire diligently into the
relationship in view of their exponents, between a strictly literalist type
of exegesis and a freer and more figurative one.

To begin with the figurative type of exegesis, we have already observed
that even in aggadic matters, it is relatively rare. Allegory, in the proper
sense of the word, is employed only when the biblical treatment demands
it. Parables too are extremely rare.

We undeniably find in Marqah this careful approach, when he speaks
of the plague of the frogs in Egypt.[724] The only 'parable' which he dare

---

[722] Qirqisani, *Kitāb al-Anwār etc.*, IV, 1 (ed. Nemoy II, pp. 348ff.); *ibid.* IV, 7, 1
(pp. 362f.).

[723] Halkin, "The 613 Commandments etc.", *Goldziher Memorial Vol.*, Part II,
p. 90 (cf. *ibid.* n. 25).

[724] *Memar Marqah* (ed. Macdonald), I, pp. 17f. (= II, p. 25). Even in such cases
there is a possibility that the "parable" is a result of a midrash on *Ex.* vii, 27 (cf.
S.P. *ibid.* 29f., S.T. = ‏בערד תחומך כל ית מכתש האנה‏). Just as *leprosy* needs a
physician, so does this *plague*. The metaphors on schoolhouses, teachers etc. (cf.
sup. n. 569) are likewise midrashim.

use in this connection is a comparison of the Egyptian magicians with physicians. Although this 'parable' does not add much to our general knowledge of exegesis here, Marqah is clearly using it to demonstrate that although the Egyptian magicians could add to the number of frogs by their magic, they nevertheless could not dispel them. They were therefore compelled to ask Moses and Aaron to rid them of them (cf. *Ex.* viii, 3-4).

We have already seen that the *Ṭabbākh* gives some directions as to when to use the literal, the figurative or the collective meanings of the various expressions.[725] He is, however, in fact, much more interested in the philosophical definition of technical terms than in the actual exegesis of the Biblical text. Abū'l Ḥasan himself uses figurative expressions, some of which have been cited earlier on;[726] and it is interesting to note here that real parables occur when Scripture itself demands that passages be so treated. They chiefly appear in his exegesis of *Deut.* xxxii-xxxiii.[727] Again, when we come to the later literature, especially in the sphere of eschatology, we often find that verses containing only the slightest allusion to this subject are allegorized in such a way as to extract from Scripture so-called proof-texts in substantiation of a theme which is in reality scarcely dealt with at all in the Pentateuch.[728]

If we compare this approach with that of the Rabbis, we discover in the case of the latter a completely different approach. Although basically they too are opposed to entirely free allegorizations, especially to those of the Philonic type or to the 'spiritual' interpretations found in Christianity, they nevertheless frequently engage in plays on words understood in a figurative sense. They do not in fact refrain from employing in their ethical instructions figurative expositions of halakhic matters. This practice is, however, somewhat tentatively followed and generally without the literal meaning of the halakhic expression thus played on being seriously impaired.[729] In the aggadah, on the other hand, they make free use of a much more figurative type of exegesis, with a rich use of parables, often employed in much the same way as Aesop's fables.[730] It is nevertheless doubtful whether one can really draw a very sharp

---

[725] cf. *sup.* Part II, n. 130.

[726] *ibid.* nn. 206-7 (cf. SLTh.A, pp. 132-134).

[727] *Ṭabbākh*, ff. 226a f. cf. also *sup.* Part II, n. 336.

[728] Merx, *Taheb etc.*, pp. 53 (on *Gen.* xv, 10), 57 (on. *Ex.* iv, 7) etc.

[729] Krochmal, *More Neboche Ha-seman*, pp. 207, 209.

[730] *ibid.* pp. 209ff.; Heinemann, *Altjüdische Allegoristik, passim, idem., Darkhei ha-Aggadah*, pp. 105f.

distinction between their approach to the Torah and their approach to the other books of Scripture. The only sure distinction one can justifiably draw is to be found in their extreme care not to permit any definite precept to be allegorized.[731]

One may broadly assert, perhaps, that the Rabbis believe that the true meaning of Scripture is already inherent in the actual text and in the interrelation of its details. It is, for instance, only natural that if Judah is called a 'lion-cub', the context must in this case be taken figuratively. Although the Rabbis do indeed look for allusions and metaphors, they nevertheless endeavour never entirely to forsake the simple meaning fo the text and always to have at least a firm 'peg' in the actual letters or words on which they hang their midrash.[732] The determination of what is the *central* meaning of a metaphor or a metaphorical expression and what is only a marginal, i.e. transferred meaning [733] does not depend here so much on definition as on individual discernment. The proper understanding of the context, which in this case relies more on a stylistic than on a semantic approach, lends very great weight to such a detremination. The Samaritans' approach of course is always a preconceived one, and always very much dependent on the traditional understanding of their Bible. This is the real reason why, despite a very similar approach on the part of the Samaritans and the Rabbis on many occasions, one finds very little actual Rabbinical influence at work among the Samaritans in the matter of their understanding of metaphors and similar forms. Nor, as a matter of fact, can one find any echo of the Sufic type of highly allegorical interpretation among the latter.[734]

We come now to what we may call the question of theoretical speculations. As we have noted on many occasions, the Samaritans do not show much inclination to theorising. Whereas other groups have theories and even theoretical justifications for their hermeneutical rules, they at all times manifest an empirical approach to exegesis. They explain

---

[731] Bacher, *Die exegetische Terminologie etc.*, I, p. 122; cf. also Heinemann, *Allegoristik*, p. 37. All this relative "freedom" to allegorize did not allow any infringement on the literal sense of the Law. cf. Wolfson, *Philo*, I, p. 133.

[732] M. Guttmann, *Eine Untersuchung... Geltungsumfang etc.*, pp. 55f. cf. also my article *ALUOS* VI (1969), *passim*.

[733] cf. L. Bloomfield, *Language* (London 1935), pp. 149f.

[734] Goldziher, *Die Richtungen etc.*, pp. 216ff. The so-called "mysteries" of the Samaritans known from pre-Islamic times are nothing more than "the secrets of the Law" i.e. a deeper understanding of its demands. cf. my article *op. cit.* pp. 109f., 142f. (nn. 90-101).

matters as they occur, and in an indiscriminate way. As early as Marqah, we find this essentially empirical approach. Although there are indeed countless details which he superimposes on the Biblical text, and which appear to have no warrant whatever in Scripture, these are mostly in the nature of further developed midrashim. There is, that is to say, always some connection, even if remote, with the text itself, and these details are never imaginary or taken from foreign sources.[735]

In general, if one wishes to define the expository material not explicitly mentioned in Scripture as belonging to a certain type of exegesis, it is necessary first of all to distinguish clearly between the padding-out of the details and the invention of unrelated topics. It is a characteristic common to aggadah and halakhah, whether Samaritan or Rabbinic, that as many words and details of a verse as possible are expounded. This practice stands in marked contrast to that of the Hellenistic exegetes, who although interested in these details, do not take them only in their plain sense, but tend mainly to allegorize them, thus adding much totally alien subject-matter to Scripture.[736]

Midrash, broadly speaking, is concerned rather with 'elucidations' of the details, and with giving the reason, the background and the interpretation of a given text. One cannot rightly describe midrash as exegesis, for even those specimens of it which really are closely bound up with the Scriptural text would hardly be regarded as 'exegesis' by the modern mind. One might very well compare midrashic exposition with the free expression found in some schools of painting as opposed to the strictly scientific approach of the scholar. The custom of attaching significance to numbers is not by any means peculiar to Samaritan literature, for the Rabbis act similarly here.[737] These two groups also share the tendency to invent names for anonymous places and persons in Scripture, a tendency not uncommon even in classical literature.[738]

In these pages we have often referred to the peculiarities of the *Asaṭir*, with its countless fanciful midrashic elaborations. Although it certainly includes folkloric elements taken from its environment, they are here amalgamated with the basic elements of Biblical thought, so that a strong

---

[735] cf. *sup.* para (a) (2 and 3). cf. also nn. 95f., 130, 141f. etc.

[736] Heinemann, *Darkhei ha-Aggadah*, pp. 21f., 23, 31.

[737] The Talmudic Literature abounds in expositions on numbers. The greatest part of *Abhoth*, Ch. V (more expounded in Abhoth de R. Nathan) consists of such examples. cf. Albeck (ed.) on *Mishnah*, IV, p. 348, n. 6.

[738] Heinemann, "The Method etc.", *Zion* V (1940), p. 188 (cf. *ibid.* n. 2 for further literature).

bridge is created between Scripture and the more fanciful thought-patterns.[739]

It is worthy of note that Abū'l Ḥasan, in spite of his strong philo-sophical bent inherited from the Mu'tazilites, falls back almost invariably, when he comes to the exposition of Scripture having a deep theological significance for the Samaritan religion, on the same thought-patterns as his predecessors. One example of this is his exposition of *Deut.* xxxiv, 1, where his midrash on the excellence of Moses and his super-natural gifts reveals the same line of approach as that known from earlier traditions.[740]

The practice of creating fanciful expositions of personal names, place-names and other similar items, a spontaneous affair entirely untram-melled by theoretical rules, has been a constant feature of Samaritan literature from the Targum down to the works of modern exegetes.[741]

The practical approach of the Samaritans is manifested firstly and most strikingly in their literalistic exposition of the laws. In this field no scope at all is afforded to the imagination; and secondly in their aggadah, which, although, as in Rabbinic exegesis, much more freely conceived, is still extremely restricted in its use of the figurative and speculative and may, like their exposition of the laws, be described as pragmatic.

Josephus represents the other end of this scale. His researches into the Bible reveal a historian and an apologist for Judaism to the Gentiles. He accordingly adopts Greek literary mannerisms, such as the putting of fictitious speeches into his hero's mouth or the employment of para-bles or the persistent explaining away of the supernatural.[742]

The employment of parables in Samaritan literature is in fact very rare, although we do indeed find some collections of parables; these

---

[739] "Thus from a few stray threads drawn from separate words and then woven together, we get a complete history of events for which there is otherwise no warrant in the Holy Writ", Gaster, *Asaṭir*, p. 19. As far as we had the opportunity to examine the midrashic background of the *Asaṭir*, *this* conclusion of Gaster seems to be con-firmed. cf. *sup.* nn. nn. 86f. and Part II, nn. 449, 476.

[740] *Ṭabbākh*, ff. 212b f. cf. Abdel Al, *op. cit.* pp. 655ff. (Translation pp. 474f.).

[741] S. Kohn, *Sam. Studien*, pp. 67 (on *Num.* xxii, 5); 70f. (on *Gen.* x, 9-11; *ibid.* xiii, 3 etc.), cf. *ibid.* for further literature); cf. also Vilmar, (ed.), *Abulfathi Annales Sam.*, pp. 24-25 and now J. Macdonald, *Sam. Chronicle No. 11*, pp. 194ff. *The Exodus Commentary* (attributed to Ghazal al-Duweik) is full of such details. cf. e.g. the stories about Zipporah, *pp.* 63f. etc.

[742] Farrar, *History of Interpretation*, pp. 452f. (note 11).

are, however, simply Samaritan adaptations of verses from *Proverbs*.[743]
Although there are some figurative explanations given for the occasional
precept, these are always in addition to the exhortation to the strict and
literal observance of it. If and when some figurative explanations are
given these are entirely dependent on the Samaritan tradition, which
explains certain verses as metaphors.[744]

---

[743] Ben-Ḥayyim, *The Literary and Oral Trad. etc.*, I, p. קי״ב cf. T.H. Gaster,
"Sam. Proverbs", *Studies... A.A. Newman*, pp. 228-242.

[744] cf. *sup.* Part II, nn. 286-7 and text there.

EPILOGUE

In these concluding remarks we shall inevitably have to recapitulate some of our previous statements. In our whole investigation of Samaritan exegesis, we have encountered on various occasions instances testifying to their sheer stubbornness. Despite all their cultural short-comings and probable exegetical distortions, in a few cases, they succeeded by their consistent perseverence in preserving the distinctive character of their tradition. Although the Samaritans themselves could not remain forever in their self-imposed spiritual isolation, their religion remained virtually static for many centuries. No doubt the outer world made its impact and had its due effect on the development of their ideologies; such external influences, however, were mainly superficial and only skin-deep, and hardly affected their religious outlook to any material extent. Sporadic or reformatory changes, in particular, were almost unknown amongst them. Neither external influences nor internal conflicts and schisms left any lasting impression upon their rich midrashic literature.

Undoubtedly, minor changes, due both to ignorance and to "learned" adaptations of some of the exegetical elements of other groups, crept occasionally into their time-hallowed spiritual stock. However, such almost negligible innovations were quickly assimilated into the general corpus of their Law and Lore without creating any major crises. Eventually this whole organic growth became so much a part and parcel of their spiritual heritage that such alien elements became almost undetectable. Only by a meticulous and painstaking investigation can one now separate the different strata in their tradition and thus occasionally reveal some novel motives. In most cases such novel exegetical elements became so inextricably interwoven into the matrix of the older traditional material that their more recent origin was rapidly forgotten. We cannot even justly accuse the Samaritan leadership with conscious falsification or with "turning a blind eye" upon these novel exegetical intrusions into their hallowed tradition, since such a procedure, whenever it took place, was always more accidental than deliberate. It may also be pointed out here that, although Samaritan exegetes freely availed themselves of the philosophies of their alien environment, these influences did not cause much real damage to the old traditional patterns; and further that with the wholesale adaptation of foreign terminology, the *content* of their own literature hardly changed. The new garb, in short, was acceptable only insofar as it did not disguise or obscure any of the accepted characteristics of their religion.

On reaching the vantage-ground of a final summary, it is with this picture in mind that we survey the field we have traversed. The detailed investigation into both the theories underlying their exegesis and the internal sources of Samaritan hermeneutics point in the same direction; and unless indeed one is sadly biased or preoccupied with preconceived hypotheses, one cannot fail to realize the overwhelming support which these inquiries lend to our conviction of the almost total independence of Samaritan traditions. All the possible minute re-examinations of the details of their hermeneutical methods do but reinforce this impression. This understatement "impression" is employed advisedly here, since it is no part of our intention to exchange old dogmatic approaches for new ones. Insofar as the present state of our knowledge allows us to offer some conclusions, these are meant only as guidelines for such further research into this field as may be developed on similarly cautious and (we trust) unbiased lines as our own.

We have endeavoured to acquaint ourselves with the hermeneutics of the Samaritan sources from their earliest appearance in a tangible written form upon the stage of history (about the fourth century C.E.) and throughout several centuries to follow. Often we have gone even further by drawing comparisons with the exegetical writings of centuries later and closer to our own. In the setting of their various socio-political circumstances and differing cultural environments we have tried to observe the earlier spiritual developments of this literature. Admittedly our enquiry has been limited to exegesis. This limitation however has not hindered us from achieving deep insights into the sum-total of the Samaritan ideological and practical life as a whole. On the contrary, this method has aided us in bringing into clear focus the otherwise blurred and often indistinguishable phenomena. We may judge only from the nature and contents of the surviving literary works; and since the Pentateuch stands at the heart of the entire Samaritan culture, each and every one of its details figures as a permanent factor in the shaping and moulding of the characteristics of the Samaritans' religion and of the cast of their mentality.

Irrespective of the purely academic question, which comes first, scripture or exegesis, we have to accept as a practical observation that these two factors in Samaritan culture are not independent; instead of becoming polarised and so pulling in opposite directions, they are rather complementary factors in the one culture, and they go hand in hand in fostering the distinctively Samaritan mentality. As long as their text was not "canonised" and was lightly treated by tampering hands, it had not achieved its final authority and significance. Only at a point when it became a hallowed treasure, did it also assume the function and dignity of Holy Writ, demanding absolute respect and reverence. We are in no position to determine how gradual or how rapid such a process of "canonisation" was, but it certainly preceded by many centuries the available Samaritan literary sources. The eventuality that even during the later period further changes may have taken place cannot of course be excluded; after all, the Samaritan priests and scribes were no less fallible and prone to errors and unwitting emendations than the guardians of scripture in any other groups. All that we may say as a result of comparison with other literatures which make mention of the Samaritans (and especially with the frequent references in Talmudic literature) is, that they all alike testify to the static and almost stagnant nature of their religion's characteristics. Despite the enmity, the malice and the accusations of falsifying their Torah and other polemical allegations, the sum-total of these hostile testimonies proves beyond any reasonable doubt that from the first centuries C.E. Samaritanism changed very little.

This picture, although greatly generalised, does not warrant us in speculating further at present. Unless new archaeological discoveries force us in the future to judge otherwise, our present discription seems to be the most objective one attainable. It is logical, therefore, from every standpoint, to connect the genesis of the specifically Samaritan exegesis with their acceptance of the Pentateuch as their sole Holy Writ.

Unlike the Talmudic literature, which reflects the opinions of the exegetes of many centuries, and thus reveals the various layers in a continuing structure, both of exegesis and of practice, the Samaritans have not left us any such monumental work as would enable us to trace the various kinds of development. Up to the fourth century C.E. we are left totally in the dark, since nothing from the formative period of the growth of their spiritual activities has survived in literary form. When Samaritan literature at last emerges, it is already fully mature and already depicts an authoritarian theology, just as if this theology had been formulated and organized by the mind of a single hide-bound literalist theologian. None of the opposing schools of thought (such as, for example, one finds in the Talmud or in contemporary Patristic literature), embodying various hermeneutical systems, can ever be conclusively detected in this Samaritan literature. If we are permitted to learn from our knowledge of later developments, we may perhaps even go one short step further, and suggest that such divisions and conflicts as those other bodies knew, hardly existed in the whole history of Samaritan exegesis.

Obviously, the formative centuries of the history of Samaritan exegesis could hardly fail to exhibit some discrepancies and occasional contradictions. Nevertheless, we can safely assert that all these disagreements together do not amount to any radical divisions of opinion amongst the Samaritan exegetes of all the ages. For this reason alone we are surely entitled to assume with reasonable certainty that the oral traditions of the pre-fourth-century teachers and priests (which are in all likelihood incorporated in the later literature) were of the same or similar homogeneous nature.

Probably too their sectarian mentality and their specific characteristics, deeply rooted in the centralisation of worship in Hargerizim and in its priesthood which early assumed an authoritarian role, served as determining factors from the very inception of their cult. From the moment that such a process of separatist inner development became fully operative, the resultant centripetal forces would resist and reject any influx of foreign ideas. The priests or the guardians of the Law must have eliminated any and every innovation which could have endangered this precious distinctiveness, which alone kept the Samaritans together and at one in their faithfulness to their scripture and tradition. Nor is it too far-fetched either to surmise that it was this very uniformity that was upheld by the spiritual leadership as a standing proof of the truth of their version and traditions. The faithful of the Samaritan fold were thus reassured by their leadership both as to the truth and the superiority of their own common and strongly held beliefs, in contradiction to the diversity and consequent strife which existed amongst the other groups in their own environment.

Occasionally indeed we are tempted to regard the similarities of the Samaritan religion to that of other groups as the result of inter-relations. These similarities should not, however, be overemphasised. Obviously the mere fact that all the groups believed in the same (or nearly the same) Torah, and relied on its guidance for their everyday life, inevitably meant that there was much common to all of them. Social intercourse may also have occasionally introduced foreign exegetical elements from non-Samaritan sources. Only a keen and critical investigation can determine the existence and the extent of such influences; our whole exercises in the previous chapters has been devoted to the solving of such problems.

There is little reason to doubt that those hermeneutical devices which arose from within scripture itself amongst the followers of the various types of texts promoted the crystallisation of each respective group with its textual and exegetical peculiarities. Just as Philo and Hellenistic Jewry faithfully followed their own scripture (LXX) and the Rabbis their own (M.T.), so did the Samaritans always rally to defend their own peculiar text (S.P.). It is now admitted on all hands that scripture does not and cannot exist in a vacuum, and, moreover, that its value is by no means confined to the 'dead letter'; a living tradition, pre-occupied with the transmission and interpretation of scripture, will develop further those hermeneutical devices which emerge from and give meaning to the changing features in its traditional *milieu*.

Historical, social and political factors undoubtedly contributed their share in each case towards the formation of the group spirit. Although some of these external influences may well have been largely similar for all these groups, the reaction of each group to external factors in general was not always the same as that of the others. While, for example, the Alexandrian exegetes, with their assimilationist outlook would assume a tolerant stand towards social intercouse with pagans, Palestinian Jewry (both Pharisees and Samaritans) would tighten its hermeneutical teaching by invoking scripture more and more in the cause of separatism. On the other hand, while the destruction of the Temple in Jerusalem was instrumental in the permanent transformation both of Hellenistic and Rabbinic Judaism equally, it left the Samaritans totally unaffected. The very reasons which were leading the Jewish exegetes to find hermeneutical devices, heavily dependent on scripture, which should obviate the dangers of disintegration and assimilation consequent on the tremendous calamity of the fall of Jerusalem were influencing the Samaritan exegetes to explain the calamity quite otherwise. Even quite similar external stimuli had different effects on each group and thus served to deepen the divisions between the hermeneutical traditions. And just here lies the danger when some modern scholars try to explain all religious phenomena by purely socio-political causes. Although such considerations cannot indeed be ignored, neither should they be exaggerated. The internal development is not seldom not less significant than all the external pressures put together.

If we steadily bear in mind the fact that religious leaders were regarded rather as the exegetes of existing traditions than as legislators, we realise that their freedom of manoeuvre was in fact very limited. This point is particularly weighty in reference to the Samaritans, for their whole mentality was aligned to the conviction of being guided by the Divine Legislator and His sole messenger. Any major innovation in hermeneutical legislation would thus amount in their view to sacrilege. Unlike the Rabbis, who attributed Sinaitic authority to an 'ORAL LAW' which allowed constant developments, the Samaritans maintained their tradition in a static condition. New exegetical details, not covered by precedent or established tradition, even if worked out by extending the existing "hermeneutical rules", would be unacceptable to the inflexible Samaritan mind. This is the true reason why Samaritan exegetes never experience, much less enjoy, the freedom to express private opinions, or found opposing schools. As opposed to the Rabbis, among whom two opinions contraverting each other could both at the same time be accepted a authoritative, the Samaritan expositors of the Law and doctrines were at all times limited to a single traditional trend.

This situation can perhaps be explained partially by external causes, but there are strong possibilities that it was rather the outcome of an internal development depending both on the transmission of the appropriate *textus receptus* and on its exposition. If our working hypothesis is tenable, we may find the origins of the Samaritans' rigorism and unanimity already inherent in their very texts. The belief that the Law is in itself "perfect", needing no human agency or "Oral Law" to support it, prevents the Samaritan from departing from the "perfect" and literal sense of his text. No "hermeneutical rule" is in truth required nor is any such rule ever regarded as capable of being legitimately extended to cover further details not already covered by tradition.

The all-powerful and all-embracing authority of tradition is apparent from the whole of the Samaritan literature. Nonetheless, there is no law without its exceptions, and it would be rash to carry such a generalisation to extremes. Despite all the rigour and unanimity of the Samaritan exegesis, personal whims could not be entirely eliminated. There are still appreciable differences between the various Samaritan writers and sometimes even when these are contemporaries. Throughout this present work we have never selected our examples with a view to attempting to label certain opinions as *"characteristic"*, nor have we eliminated passages which seem to be "unrepresentative", yet despite this intentionally impartial treatment, the differences of opinoin which can fairly be discovered do not amount to much. Obviously, if one looks for discords and discrepancies, some examples can always be found, but even such deviationary opinions may readily be explained away, if one so desires. Even so, it has not been our aim to enter into hairsplitting arguments or on the other hand to try to smooth out occasional discrepancies by artificial means. The general picture emerging from the course of our investigation amply supports our contention that those Samaritan hermeneutical devices and their elaborations which are responsible for the creation of the entire legal and doctrinal system are substantially homogeneous throughout this whole literature.

There remains an unfulfilled task which awaits further research, namely, that of proving or disproving the claims put forward above, and of substantiating our theory of the overall significance of Biblical exegesis for all fields of Samaritan research; for all this it would be necessary to evaluate anew each item of the heritage. Many items for which material is readily available, such as the minutiae of Halakhah or Aggadah, would be and should be included within the framework of such an investigation. The enormous perimeter of the Samaritan midrashic activity has forced us, however, to limit our discussion to the bare minimum. Even with this modest aim before our eyes, the present size of our work has already exceeded its limits; the task cannot be completed here. Until the whole of the Samaritan Halakhah and Aggadah is thoroughly combed through, and analysed by modern techniques and by close scrutiny, some major problems must await their solution. But it is hoped that this present work will shortly be followed by another on these lines, describing the whole field of "samaritan Law and Lore".

SELECT BIBLIOGRAPHY

(for detailed Sam. Bibl. cf. L. A. Mayer, and R. Weiss).

Abdel-Al, D., *A Comparative Study of the Unedited Work of Abu'l-Ḥasan al-Ṣūri and Jūsuf Ibn Salāmah*, Leeds (Ph.D. dissertation, University of Leeds, unpublished), 1957.

Abu'l Fatḥ, cf. Vimar.

Abu'l Ḥassan al-Ṣūri, cf. *List of MSS.*, *Ṭabbākh*.

Adler, E.N. and Seligsohn, N., "Une nouvelle chronique samaritaine", *REJ* XLIV (1902), pp. 188-122; XLV, pp. 70-98, 160, 223-254; XLVI (1903), pp. 123-146. Repr. : Paris, 1903.

Alon, G., *Studies in Jewish History in the times of the Second Temple, the Mishna and the Talmud.* (Hebrew), (2 vols.), Hakibuts Hameuchad, 1957-58.

Ankori, Zvi, *Karaites in Byzantium*, N.Y.-Jerusalem, 1959.

Appel, M., *Quaestiones de rebus Samaritanorum sub imperio Romanorum peractis*, Breslau, 1874.

Aptowitzer, V., *Das Schriftwort in der rabbin. Literatur.* (5 vols.), Vienna, 1906-1915.

Bacher, W., *Die exegetische Terminologie der jüdischen Traditionsliteratur*; vol. I : *Terminologie der Tannaiten*, Leoizpzig, 1899; vl. II : *Terminologie der Amoräer*, Leipzig, 1905.

——, *Die jüdische Bibelexegese vom Anfange des zehnten bis zum Ende des fünfzehnten Jahrhunderts.* Trier, 1892.

——, *Aus dem Wörterbuche Tanchum Jeruschalmi's*, Strassburg, 1903. (Sonderausgabe aus dem Jahresberichte der Landes-Rabbinerschule in Budapest, für Schuljahr 1902/3).

——, "The origin of the word Haggada (Agada)", *JQR* IV, 1892, pp. 406-429.

Baguley, E.C., *A critical edition, with translation of the Hebrew text of the Malef; and a comparison of its teachings with those in the Samaritan Liturgy.* (Ph.D. dissertation, unpublished). Univ. of Leeds, 1962.

Bamberger, B.J., "The Dating of Aggadic Materials", *JBL* LXVII (1949), pp. 115-123.

Baneth, E., *Der Ursprung der Sadducäer und Boethusäer*, Berlin, 1882.

——, *Des Samaritaners Marqah an die 22 Buchstaben den Grundstock der hebräischen Sprache anknüpfende Abhandlung.* Heft i. Berlin, 1888.

Bardowicz, L., *Die Abfassungszeit der Baraita der 32 Normen für die Auslegung der heiligen Schrift : eine Untersuchung.* Berlin, 1913.

Barr, J., *The Semantics of Biblical Language.* London, 1961.

Belkin, S., *The Alexandrian Halakah in Agologetic Literature of the First Century C.E.* Philadelphia, 1936.

——, *Philo and the Oral Law.* Cambridge (Mass.), 1940.

Ben-Hayyim, Z., *The Literary and Oral Tradition of Hebrew and Aramaic amongst the Samaritans.* (Hebrew). 4 vols. (vol. III in two parts), Jerusalem, 1957-1967.

Ben-Zevi, I., *Sepher ha-Shomronim*, (Hebrew), Tel Aviv, 1935. (Articles published earlier and reprinted in this book are not listed separately.)

Bergmann, J., *Jüdische Apologetik im neutestamentlichen Zeitalter.* Berlin, 1908.

Betz, O., *Offenbarung und Schriftforschung in der Qumransekte.* (Wissenschaftliche Untersuchungen zum N.T., herausgegrben von Joachim Jeremias und Otto Michel, Band 6). Tübingen, 1960.

Bin Gorion, M.J., *Sinai und Garizim.* (Forschungen zum Alten Testament auf Grund rabbinischer Quellen). Berlin, 1926. (Quoted from the Hebrew translation, Tel-Aviv, 1962-63.)

Black, M., *The Scrolls and Christian Origins.* London, Edinburgh, Paris, Melbourne, Toronto and N.Y., 1961.

Blau, J.L., "Tradition and Innovation", *Essays on Jewish Life and thought, Presented in honour of S.W. Baron.* New York, 1959, pp. 95-104.

Bokser, B.Z., *Pharisaic Judaism in Transition,* New York, 1935.

Bonsirven, J., *Le judaïsme palestinien au temps de Jésus-Christ,* 2 vols., Paris, 1935.

Bowman, J., *Samaritanische Probleme : Studien zum Verhältniss von Samaritanertum, Judentum und Urchristentum.* Stuttgart, 1967.

Brown, S., *A Critical Edition of the Translation of the Ancient Samaritan Defter (i.e. Liturgy) and a Comparison of it with early Jewish Liturgy.* (Ph.D. Dissertation, University of Leeds, unpublished, 1955.)

Bruce, F.F., *Biblical Exegesis in the Qumran Texts.* London, 1959.

——, *Tradition Old and New.* (Paternoster Press). Exeter, 1970.

Büchler, A., *Der galiläische Am ha-Ares des zweiten Jahrhunderts.* Vienna, 1906.

——, *Types of Jewish-Palestinian Piety from 70 B.C.E. to 70 C.E. The Ancient Pious Men.* London, 1922.

——, *Studies in Sin and Atonement in the Rabbinic Literature of the First Century.* London, 1928.

Burrows, M., *More Light on the Dead Sea Scrolls.* London, 1958.

Churgin, P., *Studies in the Times of the Second Temple* (Hebrew), New York, 1949.

Cohen, Zvi, *The Halakhah of the Karaites,* New York, 1936.

Cohn, N., *Die Zarâath-Gesetze der Bibel nach dem Kitâb al-Kâfi des Jûsuf Ibn Salâmah.* Frankfurt a.M., 1899.

Cowley, A.E. (ed.), *The Samaritan Liturgy,* 2 vols. Oxford, 1909.

Cross, F.M. Jr., *The Ancient Library of Qumran and Modern Biblical Studies.* London, 1958.

—— & Freedman, D.N., *Early Hebrew Orthography (A Study of the Epigraphic Evidence).* Baltimore, 1952.

Crown, A.D., "Dositheans, Ressurection and a Messianic Joshua", *Antichton* (Journal of the Australian Society for Classical Studies), I (1967), pp. 70-85.

Daube, D., "Rabbinic Methods of Interpretation and Hellenistic Rhetoric", *HUCA* XXII (1949), pp. 239-264.

——, "Alexandrian Methods of Interpretation and the Rabbis", *Festschrift Hans Lewald,* Basel, 1953, pp. 27f.

——, *The New Testament and Rabbinic Judaism,* London, 1956.

Davis, W.D., *Paul and Rabbinic Judaism.* (Some Rabbinic Elements in Pauline Theology), London, 1955.

Derenbourg, J., *Essai sur l'Histoire et la Géographie de la Palestine d'après les Thalmuds et les autres sources rabbiniques,* Paris, 1867.

Drabkin, A., *Fragmenta commentarii ad Pentateuchum Samaritano-Arabici sex.* Lipsiae, 1875.

Driver, G.R., *The Judean Scrolls : The Problem and a Solution.* Oxford, 1965.

——, *Semitic Writing from Pictograph to Alphabet*. (Schweich Lectures, 1944), London, 1948.

Emmerich, L., *Das Siegeslied, (Exodus, Cap. 15), eine Schrifterklärung des Samaritaners Marqah*. Berlin, 1897.

Empson, W., *Seven Types of Ambiguity*. Peregrine Books, 1961.

Farrar, F.W., *History of Interpretation*. London, 1886.

Finkelstein, L., *The Pharisees: The Sociological Background of their Faith*, (2 vols.). Philadelphia, 1938.

——, "The Transmission of Early Rabbinic Tradition", *HUCA* XVI (1941), pp. 115-135.

——, "Midrash, Halakhot and Aggadot", (Hebrew). *Yitzhak (F.) Baer Jubilee Volume*, Jerusalem, 1960, pp. 28-47.

Frankel, Z., *Über den Einfluss der Palästinensischen Exegese auf die Alexandrinische Hermeneutik*. Leipzig, 1851.

——, *Darkhe ha-Mishnah*. (Hodegetica in Mischnam librosque etc.). Leipzig, 1859.

Freedman, D.N. and Greenfield, J.C., *New Directions in Biblical Archaeology*. (Anchor Book). New York, 1971.

Fritsch, C.T., *The Anti-Anthropomorphisms of the Greek Pentateuch*. Princeton, 1943.

von-Gall, A., *Der Hebräische Pentateuch der Samaritaner*. Giessen, 1914-1918.

Gaster, M., "Popular Judaism at the time of the Second Temple in the light of Samaritan traditions", *Transactions of the Third Intern. Congress for the history of religions*. 1908, vol. I., pp. 298-302.

——, *The Samaritans, their History, Doctrines and Literature*. (The Schweich Lectures, 1923). London, 1925.

——, *Studies and texts in folklore, magic, medieval romance, Hebrew Apocrypha and Samaritan archaeology*. 3 vols. London, 1925-28.

——, *The Asatir, the Samaritan book of the 'Secrets of Moses' together with the Pitron or Samaritan Commentary and the Samaritan Story of the Death of Moses*. London, 1927.

——, *The Samaritan Oral Law and Ancient Traditions*. Vol. I, Eschatology. London, 1932.

Geiger, A., *Urschrift und Übersetzungen der Bibel*. Breslau, 1857.

——, "Zur Theologie und Schrifterklärung der Samaritaner", *ZDMG* XII (1858), pp. 132-142. (= *Nachgelassene Schriften* III (ed. L. Geiger, 1876), pp. 255-266).

——, "Neurere Mittheilungen über die Samaritaner", *ZDMG* XVI (1862), pp. 714-728; *ibid.* XVIII (1864), pp. 590-597, 813-824; *ibid.* XIX (1865), pp. 601-615; *ibid.* XX (1866), pp. 143-170; *ibid.*, XXI (1867), pp. 169-182; *ibid.* XXII (1868), pp. 528-538.

——, "Die gesetzlichen Differenzen zwischen Samaritanern und Juden". *ZDMG* XX (1866), pp. 527-573. (= *Nachgelassen Schriften* III, pp. 283-321.)

Gerhardsson, B., *Memory and Manuscript: Oral tradition and Written transmission in Rabbinic Judaism and early Christianity*. Trans. by E.J. Sharpe. (Acta Seminarii Neotestamentici Upsaliensis XXII). Copenhagen, 1961.

Gertner, M., "Terms of scriptural Interpretation: a Study in Hebrew Semantics", *BSOAS* XXV (1962), pp. 1-27.

Gesenius, W., *De Pentateuchi Samaritani origine, indole et auctoritate commentatio philologica-critica*. Halle, 1815.

——, *De Samaritanorum theologia ex fontibus ineditis commentatio*. Halle, 1823.

Ginzberg, L., *Legends of the Jews*. 7 vols. Philadelphia, 1909-1928.

Goldberg, L., *Das samaritanische Pentateuchtargum. Eine Untersuchung seiner hand-schriftlichen Quellen.* Stuttgart, 1935. (Bonner Orientalische Studien, Heft 11.)

Goodenough, E.R., *The Jurisprudence of the Jewish Courts in Egypt.* Legal Administration by the Jews under the Early Roman Empire as described by Philo Judaeus. New Haven, 1929.

——, *Jewish Symbols in the Graeco-Roman Period.* Vols. I-XII, New York, 1952-66.

Gottheil, R.J.H., "The Dating of their manuscripts by the Samaritans", *JBL* XXV (1906), pp. 29-48.

Gottlober, A.B., *Bikkoreth Letoldoth Hakkaraim* (oder, Kritische Untersuchungen über die Geschichte der Karaer, Hebrew). Vilno, 1965.

Grant, R.M., *The Letter and the Spirit.* London, 1957.

——, *A Short History of the Interpretation of the Bible.* London, 1965.

Green, L.C., *A Critical Edition and Translation of the Samaritan Feast of Hag Ha-Succoth, with special reference to the Historical Development involved.* Ph.D. Dissertation, University of Leeds (unpublished), 1958.

Güdemann, M., "Spirit and letter in Judaism and Christianity", *JQR* IV (1892), pp. 345-356.

——, *Jüdische Apologetik.* Glogau, 1906.

Guillaume, A., *The Traditions of Islam.* (An Introduction to the Study of the Hadith Literature). Oxford, 1924.

Guttmann, M., "Mashmaut ha-Katuv ve-Darkhe ha-Midrash", (Hebrew), *HAZOFEH* (Quartalis Hebraica), V (1921), pp. 17-34, 113-129.

——, *Die Anlehnung. Ein Kapitel aus der healachischn Exegese,* (Hebrew), (Bericht des jüdisch-theologischen Seminars Fraenckel'scher Stiftung für die Jahre 1922 und 1923). Breslau, 1924.

——, *Eine Untersuchung der mosaischen Gebote,* (Hebrew). (Bericht des jüdisch-theologischen Seminars, für das Jahr 1927). Breslau, 1928.

——, *Eine Untersuchung über den Geltungsumfang der mosaischen Gebote.* (Hebrew). (Bericht des jüdisch-theologischen Seminars, 1930). Breslau, 1931.

Hadassi, J., *Eshkol ha-Kofer.* Eupatoria, 1836.

Halkin, A.S., "Samaritan Polemics against the Jews", *PAAJR* VIII (1935-36), pp. 13-59.

——, "The Relation of the Samaritans to Saadia Gaon", *Saadia Anniversary Volume,* (American Academy for Jewish Research, Texts and Studies, vol. II). New York, 1943, pp. 271-325.

——, "The Scholia to Numbers and Deuteronomy in the Samaritan Arabic Pentateuch", *JQR,* N.S. XXXIV (1943/4), pp. 41-59.

Halper, B., *A Volume of the Book of Precepts, by Ḥefeṣ B. Yaṣliaḥ.* Philadelphia, 1915. (Reprint from *JQR* IV-V (1914/15)).

Hamburger, J., *Real-Encyclopadie für Bibel und Talmud.* 3 vols. Neustrelitz-Leipzig, 1870-1901.

Hammer, H., *Traktat vom Samaritanermessias.* Studien zur Frage der Existenz und Abstammung Jesu. Bonn, 1913.

Hanover, S., *Das Festgesetz der Samaritaner nach Ibrāhīm Ibn Yaʿḳūb.* (Edition und Übersetzung seines Kommentars zu Lev. 23.). Berlin, 1904.

Haran (= Diman), M., "Maimonides' Enumeration of Precepts in a Samaritan Liturgical Poem", (Hebrew). *Eretz Israel* IV (1956), pp. 160-169.

Harris, I., "The Rise and Development of the Massorah", *JQR* I (1889), pp. 128-142, 223-257.

Heidenheim, M., *Bibliotheca Samaritana*, vols. I-IV. Leipzig, 1884-1887.

Heinemann, I., *Philons griechische und jüdische Bildung*. Breslau, 1932 (reprint, Hildesheim, 1962).

——, *Altjüdische Allegoristik*, Breslau, 1936.

——, "The Method of Josephus in describing Jewish Antiquities (Hebrew), *ZION* V (1940), pp. 180-203.

——, *Darkhei ha-Aggadah*. (The Methods of the Aggadah, Hebrew). Jerusalem, 1949.

Heller, B., "Grundzüge der Aggada des Flavius Josephus", *MGWJ* LXXX (1936), pp. 237-276.

Heller, Ch., *The Samaritan Pentateuch, an Adaptation of the Massoretic Text*. Berlin, 1923.

Hildesheimer, M., *Marqah's Buch der Wunder nach einer Berliner Handschrift*. Berlin, 1898.

Hilukh, cf. List of Mss.

Hirschfeld, H., *Qirqisāni Studies*. (Jews' College Publication No. 6). London, 1918.

Jellicoe, S., *The Septuagint and Modern Study*, Oxford, 1968.

Jellinek, A. (ed.), *Nophet Zufim* (Hebrew). Vienna, 1863.

Jeremias, J., "Die Passahfeier der Samaritaner und ihre Bedeutung für das Verständnis der alttestamentlichen Passahüberlieferung". Giessen, 1932. (ZATW, Beiheft 59). Cf. also note in *ZATW*, N.F., XIII (1936), p. 137.

Joël, N., *Blicke in die Religionsgeschichte zu Anfang des zweiten christlichen Jahrhunderts*, 2 vols. Breslau, 1880-1883.

Jost, J.M., *Geschichte des Judenthums und seiner Sekten*. 3 vols. Leipzig, 1857-59.

Juynboll, T.G.J., *Commentarii in historiam gentis Samaritanae*. Leiden, 1846.

——, *Chronicon Samaritanum arabice conscriptum, cui titulus est Liber Josuae*. Leiden, 1848.

Kaatz, S., *Die mündliche Lehre und ihr Dogma*, 2 vols. Leipzig and Berlin, 1922-23.

Kabaṣi, A., cf. List of Mss.

Kadushin, M., *Organic Thinking*. (A study of Rabbinic Thought). New York, 1938.

——, *The Rabbinic Mind*. New York, 1952.

Kāfi (By Jūsuf ibn Salāmah), cf. List of Mss.

Kahle, P., *Textcritische und lexicalische Bemerkungen zum samaritanischen Pentateuch-targum*. Leipzig, 1898.

——, *The Cairo Geniza* (2nd edition). Oxford, 1959.

Karl, Z., "Ha-peshat veha-derash", (Hebrew), *Hashiloach* XXIV (1911), pp. 418-426.

——, "Biblical Exegesis in the Midrashic Literature" (Hebrew), *Kneset* II (1937), pp. 417-434.

Kaufman, E., *The History of the Israelite Religion* (Hebrew), 8 vols. Tel-Aviv, 1937-42.

Kippenberg, H.G., *Garizim und Synagoge*. Berlin (N.Y.), 1971. (Religionsgeschichtliche Versuche und Vorarbeiten Band XXX).

Kirchheim, R., *Karme Shomron*. (Introductio in librum Talmudicum "de Samaritanis"). Frankfurt, 1851.

Klumel, M., *Mischpāṭīm. Ein samaritanische-arabischer Commentar zu Ex. 21-22, von Ibrāhīm ibn Ya'qūb*. Berlin, 1902.

Kohn, S., *De Pentateucho Samaritano ejusque cum versionibus antiquis nexo* (dissertatio inauguralis). Leipzig, 1965.

——, "Samaritanische Studien", *MGWJ* XV (1866), pp. 15-32, 58-68, 109-119, 217-231, 268-272; *ibid.* XVI (1867), pp. 174-189, 216-222, 252-269. (Reprint, Breslau, 1868).

Krochmal, N., *More Neboche Ha-seman* (Hebrew), ed. L. Zunz. Leopoli (Lemberg), 1851.

Keunen, A., *Specimen theologicum continens Geneseos libri capita triginta quatuor priora ex Arabica Pentateuchi Samaritani versione nunc primum edita cum prolegomenis.* Leiden, 1851.

——, *Libri Exodi et Levitici secundum Arabicam Pentateuchi Samaritani versionem ab Abu Saido conscriptam.* Leiden, 1854.

Lauterbach, J.Z., *Rabbinic Essays.* Cincinnatti, 1951.

Leaney, A.R.C., *The Rule of Qumran and its Meaning.* London, 1966.

Lerner, I., *A Ctitical Investigation and Translation of the Special Liturgies of the Samaritans for their Passover and their Feast of Unleavened Bread.* Ph.D. dissertation, Univ. of Leeds, 1956. (Unpublished).

Leslau, W., *Falasha Anthology.* (Yale Judaica Series, vol. VI). Yale University Press, New Haven, 1951.

Liebermann, S., *Greek in Jewish Palestine.* Philadelphia, 1942.

——, *Hellenism in Jewish Palestine.* (Studies in the Literary Transmission, Beliefs and Manners of Palestine in the 1st Century B.C.E.-IVth Century C.E.). New York, 1950.

Loewe, R., "The 'Plain' Meaning of Scripture in Early Jewish Exegesis", *Papers of the Institute of Jewish Studies, London,* ed. J.G. Weiss, vol. I. Jerusalem, 1964, pp. 140-185.

Loewenstamm, A., "A Karaite Commentary on Genesis in a Samaritan Pseudo-morphosis", *Sefunot,* VIII (1963), (Ben Zevi Memorial Volume), pp. 167-204.

Lowy, S., "Some aspects of Normative and Sectarian Interpretation of Scriptures". (The contribution of the Judean Scrolls towards Systematisation). *ALUOS* VI (1966/68), pp. 98-163.

——, An investigation into the sources and Hermeneutic method of the Samaritan midrashic literature from the Roman period to the Fourteenth Century and comparison with other relevant near Eastern literature during this period. (Ph.D. Dissertation, University of Leeds), 1972.

Macdonald, D.B., *Development of Muslim Theology, Jurisprudence and Constitutional Theory.* London and New York, 1903. (Reprint, JLahor, 1964).

Macdonald, J. (ed.), *Memar Marqah* (6 books in 2 vols.), Beihefte zu *ZATW* 84). Berlin, 1963.

——, *The Theology of the Samaritans,* London, 1964.

—— (ed.), *The Samaritan Chronicle No. II* (or, Sepher Ha-Yamim), (Beihefte *ZATW* 107), Berlin, 1969.

Macdonald, J. & Higgins, A.J.B., "The Beginnings of Christianity According to the Samaritans", *NTS* XVIII (1972), pp. 54-80.

Macuch, R., *Grammatik des samaritanischen Hebräisch.* Berlin, 1969. (Studia Samaritana, Band I).

Malef, cf. Baguley.

Margoliouth, D.S., *The Early Development of Mohamedanism.* (The Hibbert Lectures, second series, 1913). London, 1914.

Marqah, cf. Baneth, Emmerich, Macdonald, Munk, Retting, and Szuster. (Cf. also Mss.).

Mayer, L.A., *Bibliography of the Samaritans,* edited by Broadribb D., Leiden, 1954. (Supplement No. 1 to Abr-Nahrain).

Merx, A., *Der Messias oder Ta'eb der Samaritaner.* (Beihefte zur *ZATW* 17), Giessen, 1909.

Miller, S.J., *The Samaritan Molad Mosheh.* (Samaritan and Arabic texts edited and translated with Introduction and Notes). New York, 1949.

Montgomery, J.A., *The Samaritans, the earliest Jewish sect, their History, Theology and Literature*. Philadelphia, 1907.

Moore, G.F., *Judaism in the First Centuries of the Christian Era, The Age of the Tannaim*. 3 vols. Cambridge (Mass.), 1927-30.

Munajja, b.S., cf. List of Mss. and Wreschner, L.

Munk, E., "Des Samaritaners Marqah Erzählung über den Tod Moses' ". Berlin, 1890.

Munro, J.I., *The Samaritan Pentateuch and modern criticism*. (With an Introduction by James Orr). London, 1911.

Murtonen, A., *Materials for non-Massoretic Grammar*. 3 vols. Helsinki, 1958-64.

Nemoy, L., *Karaite Anthology*. (Yale Judaica Series, vol. VII). Yale, 1942.

Neubauer, A., "Chronique samaritaine, suivie d'un Appendice contenant de courts notices sur quelques autres ouvrages samaritains", *JA*, 6e sér., t. 14 (1869), pp. 385-470.

Noja, S., *Il Kitāb al-Kāfī dei Samaritani*. (Publicazioni del Seminaro di Semitistica, Ricerche VIII). Napoli, 1970.

Nutt, J.W., *Fragments of a Samaritan Targum, edited from a Bodleian Ms*. With an introduction, containing a Sketch of Samaritan History, Dogma, and Literature. (With an Appendix by Harkavy on Mss. at St. Peterburg, pp. 153-167). London, 1874.

Oesterley, W.O.E. (ed.), *Judaism and Christianity*. 2 vols. New York, 1937.

Petermann, J.H. & Vollers, C., *Pentateuchus Samaritanus ad fidem librorum Mss. apud Nablusianos repertorum*. Berlin, 1872-1891.

Pinsker, S., *Lickute Kadmoniot*. (Zur Geschichte des Karaismus und der Karäischen Literatur, in Hebrew). 2 vols. Vienna, 1860.

Poznanski, S., *The Karaite Literary Opponents of Saajia Gaon*. London, 1908. (Reprinted from *JQR* XVIII-XX.)

Purvis, J.D., *The Samaritan Pentateuch and the Origin of the Samaritan Sect*. Cambridge (Massachusetts), 1968.

al Qirqisānī, Y., *Kitāb al-Anwār wal-Marāqib*, 5 vols. (ed. L. Nemoy). Publications of the Alexander Kohut Memorial Foundation. New York, 1930-43).

Rawidowicz, S., "On Interpretation", *PAAJR* XXVI (1957), pp. 83-126.

Rettig, D., *Memar Marqa*. (Bonner Otrienalistische Studien. Heft 8.). Stuttgart, 1934.

Revel, B., *The Karaite Halakah and Its Relation to Sadducean, Samaritan and Philonian Halakah*. Part I (all published), Philadelphia, 1913. (Reprint from *JQR*, N.S. II (1911-12), pp. 517-544; III (1912-13), pp. 337-396).

Robertson, E., *Catalogue of the Samaritan Mss. in the John Rylands Library at Manchester*. 2 vols. Manchester, 1938-62.

Rosenblatt, S., *The Interpretation of the Bible in the Mishnah*. Baltimore, 1935.

Rosenthal, I.J., *Judaism and Islam*, London, 1961.

Rosenthal, J., *Hivi al-Balkhi : A Comparative Study*. Philadelphia, 1949.

Rowley, H.H., *The Zadokite Fragments and the Dead Sea Scrolls*. Oxford, 1955.

——, *Men of God*. London, 1963.

de Sacy, S., *Chrestomathie arabe*. Paris, 1806.

Schoeps, H.J., *Theologie und Geschichte des Judenchristentums*. Tübingen, 1949.

Scholem, G.G., *Major trends in Jewish Mysticism*. New York, 1946.

——, *Jewish Gnosticism, Merkabah Mysticism, and Talmudic Tradition*. New York, 1960.

Schürer, E., *Geschichte des jüdischen Volkes im Zeitalter Jesu Christi*. (3rd ed.). 3 vols. + Register. Leipzig, 1901-1909, Register, 1911.

Schwarz, A., "Die Hauptergebnisse der wissenschaftlich Hermeneutischen Forschung", *Scripta Universitatis Atque Bibliothecae Hierosolymitanarum Orientalia et Judaica*. Vol. I, Jerusalem, 1923.

——, *Die Hermeneutische Analogie in der talmudischen Litterature*. (IV. Jahresbericht der Israelitisch-theologischen Lehranstalt in Wien, für das Schulhjar 1896-97). Wien, 1897.

——, *Die Hermeneutische Antinomie in der Talmudischen Literatur*. (XX. Jahresbericht der Israelitisch-theologischen Lehranstalt in Wien für das Schuljahr 1912-13). Wien, 1913.

Seeligmann, J.L., "Voraussetzungen der Midraschexegese", *Congress Volume, 1953*. Supplement *VT*, I, pp. 150-181.

Segal, M.H. (= M.Z.), *Parshanut ha-Mikra* (Hebrew). Jerusalem, 1944.

Siegfried, C., *Philo von Alexandria als Ausleger des Alten Testaments*. Jena, 1875.

Skehan, P.W., "Exodus in the Samaritan Recension from Qumran", *JBL* LXXIV (1955), pp. 182-187.

——, "The Qumran Manuscripts and Textual Criticism", *Suppl. VT* iv, 1957, pp. 148-160.

Smalley, B., *The Study of the Bible in the Middle Ages*. Oxford, 1952.

Smart, J.D., *The Interpretation of Scripture*. London and Philadelphia, 1961.

Snaith, N.H., *The Distinctive Ideas of the Old Testament*. London, 1944.

Spiro, A., "Samaritans, Tobiads and Judahites in Pseudo-Philo. Use and Abuse of the Bible by Polemecists and Doctrinaires". *PAAJR* XX (1951), pp. 279-355.

Stein, E., *Philo und der Midrasch*. (Beihefte zu *ZATW*, 57), Giessen, 1931.

Steinschneider, M., *Jewish Literature from the Eighth to the Eighteenth Century with an Introduction on Talmud and Midrash*. London, 1857.

——, *Polemische und apologetische Literatur in arabischer Sprache zwischen Muslimen, Christen und Juden*. Leipzig, 1877.

——, *Die hebräischen Übersetzungen des Mittelalters und die Juden als Dolmetscher*. Berlin, 1893.

——, *Die arabische Literatur der Juden*. Frankfurt a.M., 1902.

Stendahl, K. (ed.), *The Scrolls and the New Testament*, London, 1958.

Strack, H.L., *Introduction to the Talmud and Midrash*. New York, Philadelphia, 1959.

—— & Billerbeck, P., *Kommentar zum Neuen Testament aus Talmud und Midrasch*, 6 vols., Munich, 1922-1965.

Szuster, I., *Marqa-Hymnen aus der samaritanischen Liturgie übersetzt und bearbeitet*. Bonn, 1936.

Ṭabbākh, by Abū al-Ḥasan al-Ṣūri. Cf. List of Mss.

Targum (Samaritan), cf. Petermann-Vollers.

Tasker, R.V.G., *The Old Testament in the New Testament*. London, 1946.

Tcherikover, V., *Hellenistic Civilization and the Jews* (trans. S. Applebaum), Philadelphia, 1961.

Thomson, J.E.H., *The Samaritans* (*Their testimony to the religion of Israel*). (Alexander Robertson lectures, delivered before the University of Glasgow in 1919). Edinburg-London, 1919.

Trotter, R.J.F., *A Critical Study of the Ideological Background of 14th century Samaritanism, with special reference to the works of Abisha b. Pinehas, Abdallah b. Solomon and Ben Manir*. Ph.D. dissertation. Leeds University (unpublished), 1961.

——, *Did the Samaritans of the Fourth Century know the Epistle to the Hebrews?* Leeds University Oriental Society, Monograph series, No. i, Oct. 1961.

——, *Gnosticism and Memar Marqah.* (Leeds Monograph series, no. 4). Leeds, 1964.

Ullmann, S., *Semantics : an introduction to the science of meaning.* Oxford, 1962.

——, *Language and Style.* Oxford, 1964.

Urbach, E.E., *The Sages : Their Concepts and Beliefs* (Hebrew). Jerusalem, 1969.

Vilmar, E. (ed.), *Abulfathi annales Samaritani* (quos ad fidem codicum manuscriptorum Berolinensium, Bodlejani, Parsini edidit et prolegomenis instruxit). Gotha, 1865.

Vermes, G., *Scripture and Tradition in Judaism, Haggadic Studies.* (Studia Post-Biblica 4), Leiden, 1961.

Waard, J.D., *A Comparative Study of the Old Testament Text in the Dead Sea Scrolls and in the New Testament.* Leiden, 1965.

Weingreen, J., "Exposition in the Old Testament and in Rabbinical Literature", in *Promise and Fulfilment : Essays presented to S.H. Hooke on his Ninetieth Birthday.* Edinburg, 1963, pp. 187-201.

Weis, P.R., "The Anti-Karaite Tendency of R. Saadya Gaon's Arabic Version of the Pentateuch", *Saadya Studies*, (ed. Rosenthal, E.I.J.). Manchester, 1933, pp. 227-244.

——, "Ibn Ezra, The Karaites and the Halakah", *Melilah* I (1944), pp. 33-53; II (1946), pp. 121-134; III-IV (1950), pp. 188-203.

Weiss, J.H., *Dor Dor we-dorshaw.* (Zur Geschichte der Jüdischen Tradition, Hebrew, 5 vols.). Wilno, 1911.

Weiss, R., *Leqet Bibliographi 'al ha-Shomronim* (Hebrew). 2nd ed. Jerusalem, 1970.

Wernberg-Møller, P., *The Manual of Discipline.* (Translated and Annotated with an Introduction). (Studies on the Texts of the Desert of Judah, vol. I). Leiden, 1957.

Wieder, N., *The Judean Scrolls and Karaism.* London, 1962.

Wolfson, H.A., *Philo* (3 vols.). Cambridge, Mass. 1947.

Wood, J.D., *The Interpretation of the Bible : A Historical Introduction.* London, 1958.

Wreschner, L., *Samaritanische Traditionen mitgeteilt und nach ihrer geschichtlichen Entwickelung untersucht.* Berlin, 1888.

Zeitlin, S., *Megillat Taanit as a Source for Jewish Chronology and History.* Philadelphia, 1922.

Zucker, M., *Rav Saadya Gaon's Translation of the Torah* (Hebrew). New York, 1959.

Zunz, L., *Zur Geschichte und Literatur.* Berlin, 1845.

——, *Gesammelte Schriften*, 3 vols. Berlin, 1875-76.

——, *Die Gottesdienstlichen Vorträge der Juden Historisch Entwickelt.* (Hebrew translation, ed. H. Albeck). Jerusalem, 1954.

LIST OF MANUSCRIPTS

Only the most frequently used manuscripts are listed here. When more than one manuscript was used for one text, the pagination follows the manuscript marked by *A*.

Microfilm
Leeds University
Dept. of Semitics

Pentateuch
    Arabic translation,   A.3
    JRL, Sam. Ms. 2.

Memar Marqah
    Arabic translation,
    JRL, Gaster, 825.   C.1.3

Kāfi
    A. B.M., OR, 1159.   D.1.2
    B. No siglum.   D.1.7
    C. JRL, Gaster, 878.   D.1.3

Ṭabbākh
    A. JRL, Cod. XI A.   D.5.7
    B. Bodleian, Hunt, 24. (listed by mistake as commentary
       on Pentateuch).   C.5.1

Masā'il al-Khilāf (Munajja)
    Ia. JRL, Gaster, 1981.   I.
    Ib. JRL, Gaster, 1996   D.7.4
    II. JRL, 150 (Gaster, 1917)   D.7.3
       (Excerpts edited by Wreschner).

Pentateuch Commentaries

    1. *Genesis* (Meshalmah)
       JRL, 136-9 (Gaster, 1184-7)   { C.4.1
                                             { C.4.2

       JRL, Gaster, 1157.   C.7.1

    2. *Exodus* (Attributed to Ghazal al-Duweik)
       JRL, Gaster, 1871.   C.3.3

Hillukh
    A. JRL, 182 (Gaster, 1707b),   D.3.2
       (Hebrew translation).

Microfilm
Leeds University
Dept. of Semitics

Ms. of Prof. Jeremias, Göttingen.   D.3.7
JRL, 182 (Gaster, 872).   D.3.1

Sir al-qalb (Abraham Qabaṣi)
   A. JRL, 178 (Gaster, 886),
      Hebrew translation.
      B.M. Or. 881.   E.1.1
      B.M. Or. 1154   C.2.1

Qabaṣi on the Taheb
      JRL, 185 (Gaster, 1974).

                                                       C.6.4

Abisha's Commentary on Liturgy
      JRL, 137 (Gaster, 1817).   C.6.3

SCRIPTURE INDEX

(PENTATEUCH)

GENERAL INDEX